Understanding Programming and Problem Solving with C++

Kenneth A. Lambert
WASHINGTON & LEE UNIVERSITY

Douglas W. Nance
CENTRAL MICHIGAN UNIVERSITY

WEST PUBLISHING COMPANY
Minneapolis/St. Paul New York Los Angeles San Francisco

To Demaree Peck, the world's best teacher

To Warren and Dorothy
Happy 50th Anniversary

Copyeditor: Lorretta Palagi
Interior design: Johnston Design Office
Composition: Carlisle Communications
Cover image: Pamela J. Vermeer

WEST'S COMMITMENT TO THE ENVIRONMENT

In 1906, West Publishing Company began recycling materials left over from the production of books. This began a tradition of efficient and responsible use of resources. Today, 100% of our legal bound volumes are printed on acid-free, recycled paper consisting of 50% new paper pulp and 50% paper that has undergone a de-inking process. We also use vegetable-based inks to print all of our books. West recycles nearly 22,650,000 pounds of scrap paper annually—the equivalent of 187,500 trees. Since the 1960s, West has devised ways to capture and recycle waste inks, solvents, oils, and vapors created in the printing process. We also recycle plastics of all kinds, wood, glass, corrugated cardboard, and batteries, and have eliminated the use of polystyrene book packaging. We at West are proud of the longevity and the scope of our commitment to the environment.

West pocket parts and advance sheets are printed on recyclable paper and can be collected and recycled with newspapers. Staples do not have to be removed. Bound volumes can be recycled after removing the covers.

Production, Prepress, Printing and Binding by West Publishing Company.

TEXT IS PRINTED ON 10% POST CONSUMER RECYCLED PAPER

British Library Cataloguing-in-Publication Data. A catalogue record for this book is available from the British Library.

Printed in the United States of America
03 02 01 00 99 98 97 96 8 7 6 5 4 3 2 1 0

Library of Congress Cataloging-in-Publication Data

Lambert, Kenneth (Kenneth A.)
Understanding programming and problem solving with C++ / Kenneth A. Lambert, Douglas W. Nance.
p. cm.
Includes index.
ISBN 0–314–06743–4 (soft : alk. paper)
1. C++ (Computer program language) I. Nance, Douglas W. II. Title.
QA76.73.C153L344 1996
005.13'3—dc20 95–34794
CIP

Table of Contents

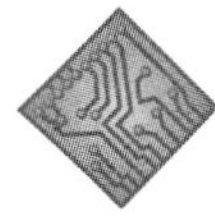

Preface

Those who teach entry-level courses in computer science are familiar with the problems encountered by beginning students. Initially, students can get so involved in learning the syntax and features of a programming language that they may fail to grasp the significance of using the language to solve problems. On the other hand, the solution of really interesting problems requires learning a great many features of a programming language. The intent of this text is to provide a happy medium between these two extremes. Besides providing a complete, one-semester course in the essential features of C++, the broader goals are for students to understand programming techniques and subsequently be able to use them to solve interesting problems.

Overview and Organization

The material in Chapters 1 through 6 covers the basics of problem solving and algorithm development, using the standard control structures of expression evaluation, sequencing, selection, iteration, and procedural abstraction. This material is presented at a deliberate pace. If students in the class have already had some programming experience, these chapters may be covered rapidly. However, students must be able to solve problems with top-down design and stepwise refinement. If this is overlooked, they will have difficulty designing solutions to more complex problems later.

Subprograms are presented fairly early in the text. User-defined functions with input and output parameters are presented in Chapter 4 before either selection statements (Chapter 5) or iteration statements (Chapter 6). This facilitates good problem-solving habits in that a completely modular approach can be emphasized early in the course.

We have made a large effort to acknowledge the increasing importance of object-oriented methods in the computer science community. In the first six chapters, this effort takes the form of allusions to and brief discussions of object-oriented design when appropriate. However, we have deliberately avoided presenting the object-oriented features of C++ in the first six chapters. We believe that students can best learn the fundamentals of algorithm development if they are provided with a simple model of computation and a small subset of C++ syntax. The object-oriented model of computation and the object-oriented features of C++ are neither simple nor small; they are best introduced only when needed, primarily to develop data structures in the second half of a first course in computer science.

The material in Chapters 7 through 11 covers the use of basic data structures such as strings, records, files, arrays, and pointers. Careful attention is paid to the specification and implementation of all data structures as abstract data types. The focus in this half of the text shifts from the procedural approach used in developing algorithms to an object-oriented approach used in developing abstract data types.

Chapter 7 provides a transition from a procedural approach to an object-oriented approach. We specify an abstract data type for strings, and then present the two different approaches as possible implementations. The first uses a C++ type definition and standard string library functions. The second develops a C++ class definition. We discuss the trade-offs in the use of the two approaches, and then use the string class to develop other data structures in the remainder of the text.

Chapter 8 explores object-oriented design in more depth, using examples from data processing (a bank account management system) and mathematics (rational numbers). Appropriate examples of some useful features of object-oriented design, such as operator overloading, inheritance, and software reuse, are discussed and developed in these examples. We introduce a standard method of discussing user requirements, specifying attributes and behavior, and declaring and implementing a class, and then we use this method in the remaining chapters.

Chapter 9 introduces file stream processing. The focus of this chapter is the use of file stream operations, primarily in conjunction with numeric, character, and string data. Because of its simple approach, this chapter could be used earlier or later in the course if desired.

Chapter 10 discusses array operations in detail. We develop three important classes using arrays—a safe array class with range checking, an ordered collection class, and a sorted collection class.

Chapter 11 introduces pointers and dynamic memory as a means of developing dynamic data structures. We first discuss the use of pointers in manipulating areas of dynamic memory, and then develop a linked list class using pointers. A linked implementation of the collection classes is contrasted with the array implementation presented in Chapter 10.

Chapter 12 gives a preview of topics normally presented in a second course in computer science—recursion and analysis of algorithms. We illustrate the use of recursion as a divide-and-conquer method of problem solving in implementing the quick sort and binary search algorithms. A brief comparison of the behavior of these algorithms with that of selection sort and linear search is provided.

Throughout the text, we have attempted to explain and develop concepts carefully. These are illustrated by frequent examples and diagrams. New concepts are then used in complete programs to show how they aid in solving problems. We place an early and consistent emphasis on good writing habits and neat, readable documentation. We frequently offer communication and style tips where appropriate.

There are at least three general scenarios for which this text would be appropriate:

1. A deliberately paced, thorough presentation of concepts would allow you to get through Chapter 10 in a one-semester course.
2. An accelerated pace with students who have had previous computing experience would allow you to get into Chapter 12 in a one-semester course.
3. A deliberate pace with a thorough presentation would allow you to present the material in Chapters 1 through 12 in a two-quarter course.

Features

This text has a number of noteworthy pedagogical features:

- *Chapter outlines:* Lists of the important topics covered are given at the beginning of each chapter.

- *Objectives:* Each section starts with a concise list of topics and learning objectives.
- *Communication and style tips:* These are suggestions for programming style that are intended to enhance readability. The ACM has recently encouraged the development of communication skills to enhance the portability of programs.
- *Exercises:* Short-answer questions appear at the end of each section that are intended to build analytical skills.
- *Programming problems and projects:* Starting with Chapter 2, lengthy lists of suggestions for complete programs and projects are given at the end of each chapter. These cover different problem areas in computer science, such as data processing and mathematics. Some problems and projects run from chapter to chapter, providing students with a sense of problem solving as a cumulative enterprise that often requires programming in the large. Several assignments focus explicitly on improving students' communication skills in refining designs and writing documentation.
- *Module specifications:* Specifications are given for many program modules.
- *Structure charts:* We provide charts that reflect modular development and include the use of data flow arrows to emphasize transmission of data to and/or from each module. These charts set the stage for understanding the use of value and reference parameters when functions are introduced.
- *Notes of interest:* These are tidbits of information intended to create awareness of and interest in various aspects of computer science, including its historical context. Special attention is paid to issuers of computer ethics and security.
- *Suggestions for test programs:* Ideas included in the exercises are intended to encourage students to use the computer to determine answers to questions and to see how to implement concepts in short programs.
- *Focus on program design:* With the exception of Chapters 1, 2, and 11, a complete program is listed at the end of the chapter that illustrates utilization of the concepts developed within the chapter. This section includes the complete development of a project, from user requirements to specifications to pseudocode design to implementation and testing.
- Running, testing, and debugging hints: These hints will be useful to students as they work on the programming problems at the end of each chapter.
- *Reading references:* When appropriate, pointers are given to excellent sources for further reading on topics introduced in the text.
- New terms are italicized when introduced.

In the back of the text there is a complete glossary, as well as appendixes on reserved words, useful library functions, syntax diagrams, and character sets. The final section of the book provides answers to selected exercises.

This book covers only that portion of C++ necessary for a first course in computer science. Students wanting to learn more about the language are referred to the excellent sources given in Appendix 1.

Ancillaries

It is our belief that a broad-based teaching support package is essential for an introductory course using C++. Thus, the following ancillary materials are available from West Publishing Company.

1. *Laboratory manual:* In keeping with our intent to provide a modern approach and to meet the growing need for laboratory experience as put forth by the new ACM curriculum guidelines, there is a laboratory manual closely tied to the text's pedagogy. The manual provides two kinds of exercises. Each lab experience begins with a few exercises relating to a small set of new concepts, such as the use of reference parameters with functions. The lab experience then uses these new concepts to extend several cumulative, semester-long programming projects. Students thus use the lab experience to build their competence incrementally, and to get a sense of how various concepts play a role in programming in the large. The example programs in the lab experiences are written in platform-independent C++.
2. *Program disk:* To give students direct access to programs from the text, a disk containing most of these programs is bundled with the book. The disk is in DOS format, but the programs are written in platform-independent C++, which can be run immediately on most implementations.
3. *Instructor's manual:* This manual contains the following for each chapter:
   a. Outline
   b. Teaching test questions
   c. Chapter test questions
   d. Answers to test questions.
4. *Transparency masters:* More than 75 transparency masters are available to adopters of the text. The set of masters includes figures, tables, and selected other material from the text.
5. *Computerized test bank:* Adopters of this edition will receive a computerized test-generation system. This provides a test bank system that allows adopters to edit, add, or delete test questions.

Each program segment in the text and in the lab manual has been compiled and run. Hence, original versions were all working. Unfortunately, the publication process does allow errors in code to occur after a program has been run. Every effort has been made to produce an error-free text, although this cannot be guaranteed with certainty. We assume full responsibility for all errors and omissions. If you detect any, please be tolerant and notify us or West Publishing Company so they can be corrected in subsequent printings and editions.

Acknowledgments

We would like to take this opportunity to thank those who in some way contributed to the completion of this text. Several reviewers contributed significant constructive comments during various phases of manuscript development. They include:

Vicki H. Allan
Utah State University

Clark B. Archer
Winthrop University

Kulbir S. Arora
SUNY–Buffalo

Bonnie Bailey
Morehead State University

David E. Boddy
Oakland University

Jeff Buckwalter
University of San Francisco

Debra Calliss
Arizona State University

Ernest Carey
Utah Valley State College

Tom Cheatham
Middle Tennessee State University

Henjin Chi
Indiana State University

John S. Conery
University of Oregon
Behrouz Forouzan
De Anza College
Roy Fuller
University of Arkansas
Peter J. Gingo
University of Akron
Jeff Guan
University of Louisville
R. James Guild
Cal Lutheran University
Jimmie R. Hattemer
Southern Illinois University
Jack Hodges
San Francisco State University
J. Andrew Holey
St. John's University
Mike Holland
North Virginia Community College
Randall L. Hyde
UC–Riverside
Peter Isaacson
University of Northern Colorado
Michael P. Johnson
Oregon State University
Gwen Kaye
University of Maryland—College Park
Joanne Koehler
University of North Carolina–Greensboro
Stephen P. Leach
Florida State University
Mary Lynch
University of Florida
Jerry Marsh
Oakland University
Eugene M. Norris
George Mason University
Mark Parker
Shoreline Community College
Jandelyn Plane
University of Maryland–College Park
Neelima Shrikhande
Central Michigan University
Michael Stinson
Central Michigan University
David Teague
Western Carolina University
Martha J. Tilmann
College of San Mateo
Ron Wallace
Blue Mountain Community College
Richard G. Weinand
Wayne State University

Pam Vermeer, of Washington and Lee University, has classroom tested the text for two terms and contributed much to the design and content of the laboratory manual. Tom Whaley, also of Washington and Lee University, offered many helpful suggestions on making the minefield of C++ safer for beginning students.

Five other people deserve special mention because, without their expertise, this book would not exist:

Lorretta Palagi, copyeditor. Lorretta has a wonderful sense of where to apply Occam's razor to a sentence or paragraph, and made many useful suggestions for improving not only style, but content as well.

Peter Krall, production editor. Peter has done a great job of coordinating work on several texts simultaneously. He keeps things running smoothly, and it is a pleasure working with him.

Ellen Stanton, promotion manager. Ellen worked hard to highlight the features of the text that will make it known to the computer science community, and has done a fine job.

Betsy Friedman, developmental editor. Betsy lined up great reviewers and provided them with all of the relevant questions. She then digested the reviews into analyses that focused our attention immediately on the improvements that needed to be made at each phase of the development process.

Jerry Westby, executive editor. Jerry initiated our collaboration on this project. His insight into what makes a book useful is uncanny. We are grateful for his high standards, and for pushing us to make needed changes one more time during the revision process. It is a privilege to work with an editor who is right at the top of his field.

Kenneth A. Lambert
August, 1995

CHAPTER 1

Computer Science, Computer Architecture, and Computer Languages

CHAPTER OUTLINE

A jet airplane crash-lands near a large American city. Though the plane catches fire on impact, all of the passengers and crew members miraculously survive. Investigators find no clues from the crew or the flight recorders that point to the cause of the crash. However, using reports of observers on the ground about the behavior of the plane, they construct a computer simulation of the plane's behavior in the air. From this simulation, they hypothesize that a flaw in the plane's rudder might have caused it to go into a tailspin. They examine the parts of the rudder found at the crash site, and confirm their hypothesis. The results of their investigation will be used to correct the flaw in the rudders of several hundred airplanes.

The investigators who constructed this simulation solved a problem by designing a program and running it on a computer. They may not have been trained as computer scientists, but they used techniques that have come to be associated with this exciting new field.

This chapter provides a quick introduction to computer science, computer architecture, and computer languages. Section 1.1 provides a preview of the study of computer science. Section 1.2 examines the structure and parts of a computer and introduces the idea of computer software. Section 1.3 analyzes how computer languages are used to make a computer run.

As you read this chapter, do not be overly concerned about the introduction and early use of technical terminology. All terms will be subsequently developed. A good approach to an introductory chapter like this is to reread it periodically. This will help you maintain a good perspective on how new concepts and techniques fit in the broader picture of using computers. Finally, remember that learning a language that will make a computer work can be exciting; being able to control such a machine can lead to quite a sense of accomplishment.

1.1 Computer Science: A Preview

Computer science is a very young discipline. Electronic computers were initially developed in the 1940s. Those who worked with computers in the 1940s and 1950s often did so by teaching themselves about computers; most schools did not offer any instruction in computer science at that time. However, as these early

OBJECTIVES

- to understand that computer science is
  a. mathematics and logic
  b. science
  c. engineering
  d. communication
  e. interdisciplinary

pioneers in computers learned more about the machines they were using, a collection of principles began to evolve into the discipline we now call computer science. Because it emerged from the efforts of people using computers in a variety of disciplines, the influence of these disciplines can often be seen in computer science. With that in mind, in the next sections we will briefly describe what computer science is.

Computer Science as Computer Literacy

In the 1990s, computer-literate people know how to use a variety of computer software to make their professional and domestic lives more productive and easier. This software includes, for instance, word processors for writing and data management systems for storing every conceivable form of information (from address lists to recipes).

The computer-literate person who wants to acquire an understanding of computer science is in much the same position as the driver of a car who wants to learn how to change its spark plugs. For the driver, this curiosity can lead to a study of how automobile engines function generally. For the literate user of computer software, this curiosity can lead from the software's instruction manual to designing and writing a program with that software, and then to a deep understanding of a computer as a general-purpose problem-solving tool. The computer-literate person will come to understand that the collection of problems that computer science encompasses and the techniques used to solve those problems are the real substance of this rapidly expanding discipline.

Computer Science as Mathematics and Logic

The problem-solving emphasis of computer science borrows heavily from the areas of mathematics and logic. Faced with a problem, computer scientists must first formulate a solution. This method of solution, or *algorithm* as it is often called in computer science, must be thoroughly understood before the computer scientists make any attempt to implement the solution on the computer. Thus, at the early stages of problem solution, computer scientists work solely with their minds and do not rely on the machine (except, perhaps, as a word processor for making notes).

Once the solution is understood, computer scientists must then state the solution to this problem in a formal language called a *programming language.* This parallels the fashion in which mathematicians or logicians must develop a proof or argument in the formal language of mathematics. This formal solution as stated in a programming language must then be evaluated in terms of its correctness, style, and efficiency. Part of this evaluation process involves entering the formally stated algorithm as a programmed series of steps for the computer to follow.

Another part of the evaluation process is distinctly separate from a consideration of whether or not the computer produces the "right answer" when the program is executed. Indeed, one of the main areas of emphasis throughout this book is in developing well-designed solutions to problems and in recognizing the difference between such solutions and ones that work, but are not elegant. True computer scientists seek not just solutions to problems, but the best possible solutions.

Computer Science as Science

Perhaps nothing is as intrinsic to the scientific method as the formulation of hypotheses to explain phenomena and the careful testing of these hypotheses to prove them right or wrong. This same process plays an integral role in the way computer scientists work.

When confronted with a problem, such as a long list of names that needs to be arranged in alphabetical order, computer scientists formulate a hypothesis in the form of an algorithm that they believe will effectively solve the problem. Using mathematical techniques, they can make predictions about how such a proposed algorithm will solve the problem. But because the problems facing computer scientists arise from the world of real applications, predictive techniques relying solely on mathematical theory are not sufficient to prove an algorithm correct. Ultimately, computer scientists must implement their solutions on computers and test them in the complex situations that originally gave rise to the problems. Only after such thorough testing can the hypothetical solutions be declared right or wrong.

Moreover, just as many scientific principles are not 100% right or wrong, the hypothetical solutions posed by computer scientists are often subject to limitations. An understanding of those limitations—of when the method is appropriate and when it is not—is a crucial part of the knowledge that computer scientists must have. This is analogous to the way in which any scientist must be aware of the particular limitations of a scientific theory in explaining a given set of phenomena.

Do not forget the experimental nature of computer science as you study this book. You must participate in computer science to truly learn it. Although a good book can help, *you* must solve the problems, implement those solutions on the computer, and then test the results. View each of the problems you are assigned as an experiment for which you are to propose a solution, and then verify the correctness of your solution by testing it on the computer. If the solution does not work exactly as you hypothesized, do not become discouraged. Instead, ask yourself why it did not work; by doing so you will acquire a deeper understanding of the problem and your solution. In this sense, the computer represents the experimental tool of the computer scientist. Do not be afraid to use it for exploration.

Computer Science as Engineering

Whatever the area of specialization, an engineer must neatly combine a firm grasp of scientific principles with implementation techniques. Without knowledge of the principles, the engineer's ability to design creative models for a problem's solution is severely limited. Such model-building is crucial to the engineering design process. The ultimate design of a bridge, for instance, is the result of an engineer considering many possible models of the bridge and then selecting the best one. The transformation of abstract ideas into models of a problem's solution is thus central to the engineering design process. The ability to generate a variety of models that can be explored is the hallmark of creative engineering.

Similarly, the computer scientist is a model-builder. Faced with a problem, the computer scientist must construct models for its solution. Such models take the form of an information structure to hold the data pertinent to the problem and the algorithmic method to manipulate that information structure to actually solve the problem. Just as an engineer must have an in-depth understanding of scientific principles to build a model, so must a computer scientist. With these principles, the computer scientist can conceive of models that are elegant, efficient, and appropriate to the problem at hand.

An understanding of principles alone is not sufficient for either the engineer or the computer scientist. Experience with the actual implementation of hypothetical

A NOTE OF INTEREST

Ethics and Computer Science

Ethical issues in computer science are rapidly gaining public attention. As evidence, consider the following article from the *Washington Post.*

> *Should law-enforcement agencies be allowed to use computers to help them determine whether a person ought to be jailed or allowed out on bond? Should the military let computers decide when and on whom nuclear weapons should be used?*

> While theft and computer viruses have not gone away as industry problems, a group of 30 computer engineers and ethicists who gathered in Washington recently agreed that questions about the proper use of computers is taking center stage. At issue is to what degree computers should be allowed to make significant decisions that human beings normally make.
>
> Already, judges are consulting computers, which have been programmed to predict how certain personality types will behave. Judges are basing their decisions more on what the computer tells them than on their own analysis of the arrested person's history. Computers are helping doctors decide treatments for patients. They played a major role in the July 1988 shooting of the Iranian jetliner by the USS *Vincennes,* and they are the backbone of this country's Strategic Defense Initiative ("Star Wars").
>
> Representatives from universities, IBM Corp., the Brookings Institution, and several Washington theological seminaries [recently discussed] what they could do to build a conscience in the computer field.

The computer industry has been marked by "creativity and drive for improvement and advancement," not by ethicalconcerns, said Robert Melford, chairman of the computing-ethics subcommittee of the Institute of Electrical and Electronics Engineers.

Computer professionals, Melford said, often spend much of their time in solitude, separated from the people affected by their programs who could provide valuable feedback.

Unlike hospitals, computer companies and most organized computer users have no staff ethicists or ethics committees to ponder the consequences of what they do. Few businesses have written policies about the proper way to govern computers. But there is evidence that technical schools, at least, are beginning to work an ethical component into their curricula. [For example, in recent years,] all computer engineering majors at Polytechnic University in Brooklyn [have been required to take a course in ethics.] The Massachusetts Institute of Technology is considering mandating five years of study instead of the current four to include work in ethics.

Affirmation that such questions should be addressed by computer scientists is contained in the 1991 curriculum guidelines of the Association for Computing Machinery, Inc. These guidelines state that "Undergraduates should also develop an understanding of the historical, social, and ethical context of the discipline and the profession."

You will see further Notes of Interest on this area of critical concern later in this book.

models is also necessary. Without such experience, you can have only very limited intuition about what is feasible and how a large-scale project should be organized to reach a successful conclusion. Ultimately, computers are used to solve problems in the real world. In the real world, you will need to design programs that come in on time, that are within (if not under) the budget, and that solve all aspects of the original problem. The experience you acquire in designing problem solutions and then implementing them is vital to your being a complete computer scientist. Hence, remember that you cannot actually study computer science without actively doing it. To merely read about computer science techniques will leave you with an unrealistic perspective of what is possible.

Computer Science as Communication

As the discipline of computer science continues to evolve, communication is assuming a more significant role in the undergraduate curriculum. The Association for Computing Machinery, Inc., curriculum guidelines for 1991 state, ". . . undergraduate programs should prepare students to . . . define a problem clearly;

. . . document that solution; . . . and to communicate that solution to colleagues, professionals in other fields, and the general public" (p. 7).

It is no longer sufficient to be content with a program that runs correctly. Extra attention should be devoted to the communication aspects associated with such a program. For instance, you might be asked to submit a written proposal prior to designing a solution, or to document a program carefully and completely as it is being designed, or to write a follow-up report after a program has been completed. These are some ways in which communication can be emphasized as an integral part of computer science. Several opportunities will be provided in the exercises and problem lists of this text for you to focus on the communication aspects associated with computer science.

Computer Science as an Interdisciplinary Field

The problems solved by computer scientists come from a variety of disciplines—mathematics, physics, chemistry, biology, geology, economics, business, engineering, linguistics, and psychology, to name but a few. As a computer scientist working on a problem in one of these areas, you must be a quasi-expert in that discipline as well as in computer science. For instance, you cannot write a program to manage the checking account system of a bank unless you thoroughly understand how banks work and how that bank runs its checking accounts. As a minimum, you must be literate enough in other disciplines to converse with the people for whom you are writing programs and to learn precisely what it is they want the computer to do for them. Because such people may be naive about the computer and its capabilities, you will have to possess considerable communication skills as well as a knowledge of that other discipline.

Are you beginning to think that a computer scientist must be knowledgeable about much more than just the computer? If so, you are correct. Too often, computer scientists are viewed as technicians, tucked away in their own little worlds and not thinking or caring about anything other than computers. Nothing could be further from the truth. The successful computer scientist must be able to communicate, to learn new ideas quickly, and to adapt to ever-changing conditions. Computer science is emerging from its early dark ages into a mature field, one that we hope you will find rewarding and exciting. In studying computer science, you will develop many talents; this text can get you started on the road to that development process.

1.2 Computer Architecture

OBJECTIVES

- to understand the historical development of computers
- to know what constitutes computer hardware
- to know what constitutes computer software

This section is intended to provide you with a brief overview of what computers are and how they are used. Although there are various sizes, makes, and models of computers, you will see that they all operate in basically the same straightforward manner. Whether you work on a personal computer that costs a few hundred dollars or on a mainframe that costs in the millions, the principles of making the machine work are essentially the same.

Modern Computers

The search for aids to perform calculations is almost as old as number systems. Early devices included the abacus, Napier's bones, the slide rule, and mechanical adding machines. More recently, calculators have changed the nature of personal computing as a result of their availability, low cost, and high speed. The development of computers over time is highlighted in Figure 1.1. For more

◆ **FIGURE 1.1**
Development of computers

Era	Early Computing Devices		Mechanical Computers	Electro-mechanical Computers
Year	1000 B.C.	A.D. 1614	1650 — 1900	1900 — 1945
Development	Abacus	Napier's bones	Adding machine Slide rule Difference engine Analytic engine	Cogged wheels Instruction register Operation code Address Plug board Harvard Mark I Tabulating machine

complete information, see *People and Computers, Partners in Problem Solving* by John F. Vinsonhaler, Christian C. Wagner, and Castelle G. Gentry, West Publishing Company, 1989.

The last few decades have seen the most significant change in computing machines in the world's history as a result of improvements that have led to modern computers. As recently as the 1960s, a computer required several rooms because of its size. However, the advent of silicon chips has reduced the size and increased the availability of computers so that parents are able to purchase personal computers as presents for their children. These smaller computers are also more powerful than the early behemoths.

What is a computer? According to *Webster's New World Dictionary of the American Language* (2nd College Edition), a computer is "an electronic machine which, by means of stored instructions and information, performs rapid, often complex calculations or compiles, correlates, and selects data." Basically, a computer can be thought of as a machine that manipulates information in the form of numbers and characters. This information is referred to as *data.* What makes computers remarkable is the extreme speed and precision with which they can store, retrieve, and manipulate data.

Several types of computers currently are available. An oversimplification is to categorize computers as mainframes, minicomputers, or microcomputers. In this grouping, *mainframe* computers are the large machines used by major companies, government agencies, and universities. They have the capability of being used by as many as 100 or more people at the same time and can cost millions of dollars. *Minicomputers,* in a sense, are smaller versions of large computers. They can be used by several people at once but have less storage capacity and cost far less. *Microcomputers* are frequently referred to as personal computers. They have limited storage capacity (in a relative sense), are generally used by one person at a time, and can be purchased for as little as a few hundred dollars.

◆ FIGURE 1.1
Continued

Noncommercial Electronic Computers	Batch Processing	Time-Sharing Systems	Personal Computers
1945 1950	1965	1975	Present
First-generation computers Vacuum tubes Machine language programming ENIAC	Second-generation computers Transistors Magnetic core memory Assemblers Compilers UNIVAC I IBM 704	Third-generation computers Integrated circuit technology Operating system software Teleprocessing	Fourth-generation computers Fifth-generation computers (supercomputers) Microprocessors Workstations

As you begin your work with computers, you will hear people talking about *hardware* and *software.* Hardware refers to the actual machine and its support devices. Software refers to programs that make the machine do something. Many software packages exist for today's computers. They include word processing, database programs, spreadsheets, games, operating systems, and compilers. You can (and will!) learn to create your own software. In fact, that is what this book is all about.

A *program* can be thought of as a set of instructions that tells the machine what to do. When you have written a program, the computer will behave exactly as you have instructed it. It will do no more or no less than what is contained in your specific instructions. For example, the following listing is a C++ program that allows three scores to be entered from a keyboard, computes their average, and then prints the result:

```
// Program file: average.cpp
// This program reads three scores and displays their average.

#include <iostream.h>
#include <iomanip.h>

int main ()

{

        int score1, score2, score3;
        float average;
        cout << ``Enter the first score and press <Enter>: '' ;
        cin >> score1;
        cout << ``Enter the second score and press <Enter>: '' ;
```

```
    cin >> score2;
    cout << ''Enter the third score and press <Enter>: '' ;
    cin >> score3;
    average = float(score1 + score2 + score3) / 3;
    cout << fixed << showpoint << setprecision(2);
    cout << ''The average score is '' << average << endl;
    return 0;
}
```

Do not be concerned about specific parts of this program. It is intended only to illustrate the idea of a set of instructions. Very soon, you will be able to write significantly more sophisticated programs.

Learning to write programs requires two skills.

1. You need to be able to use specific terminology and punctuation that can be understood by the machine; that is, you need to learn a programming language.
2. You need to be able to develop a plan for solving a particular problem. This plan—or algorithm—is a sequence of steps that, when followed, will lead to a solution of the problem.

Initially, you may think that learning a language is the more difficult task because your problems will have relatively easy solutions. Nothing could be further from the truth! **The single most important thing you can do as a student of computer science is to develop the skill to solve problems.** Once you have this skill, you can learn to write programs in several different languages.

Computer Hardware

Let's take another look at the question: What is a computer? Our previous answer indicated it is a machine. Although there are several forms, names, and brands of computers, each consists of a *main unit* that is subsequently connected to peripheral devices. The main unit of a computer consists of a *central processing unit (CPU)* and *main (primary) memory.* The CPU is the "brain" of the computer. It contains an *arithmetic/logic unit (ALU),* which is capable of performing arithmetic operations and evaluating expressions to see if they are true or false, and the *control unit,* which controls the action of the remaining components so your program can be followed step by step, or *executed.*

Main memory can be thought of as mailboxes in a post office. It is a sequence of locations where information representing instructions, numbers, characters, and so on can be stored. Main memory is usable while the computer is turned on. It is where the program being executed is stored along with data it is manipulating.

As you develop a greater appreciation of how the computer works, you might wonder: How are data stored in memory? Each memory location has an address and is capable of holding a sequence of *binary digits* (0 or 1), which are commonly referred to as *bits.* Instructions, symbols, letters, numbers, and so on are translated into an appropriate pattern of binary digits and then stored in various memory locations. These are retrieved, used, and changed according to instructions in your program. In fact, the program itself is similarly translated and stored in part of main memory. Main memory can be envisioned as in Figure 1.2, and the main unit can be envisioned as in Figure 1.3.

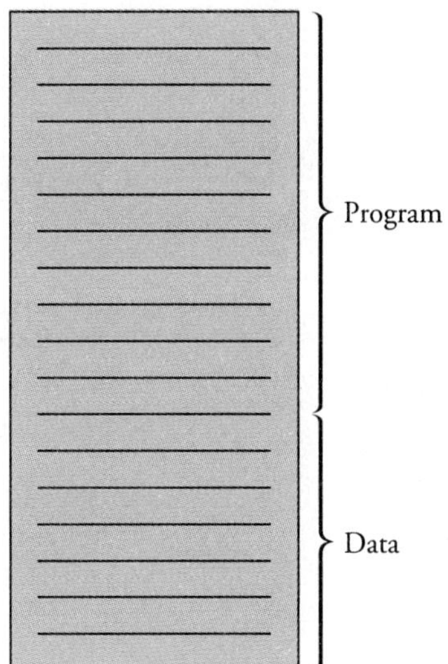

◆ **FIGURE 1.2**
Main memory

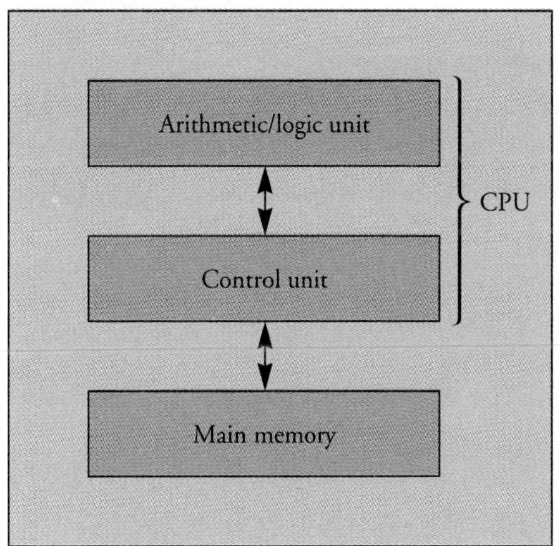

◆ **FIGURE 1.3**
Main unit

Peripherals can be divided into three categories: *input devices, output devices,* and *secondary (auxiliary) memory devices.* Input devices are necessary to give information to a computer. Programs are entered through an input device and then program statements are translated and stored as previously indicated. One input device (a typical keyboard) is shown in Figure 1.4.

Output devices are necessary to show the results of a program. These are normally in the form of a screen, line printer, impact printer, or laser printer (Figure 1.5). Input and output devices are frequently referred to as *I/O devices.*

Secondary (auxiliary) memory devices are used if additional memory is needed. On small computers, these secondary memory devices could be floppy disks or hard disks (Figure 1.6), CD-ROM disks, or magnetic tapes. Programs and data waiting to be executed are kept "waiting in the wings" in secondary memory.

Communication between components of a computer is frequently organized around a group of wires called a *bus.* The relationship between a bus and various computer components can be envisioned as in Figure 1.7. A photograph of a bus

◆ FIGURE 1.4
Keyboard

◆ FIGURE 1.5
(a) Screen, (b) line printer (mainframe), (c) impact printer (microcomputer), and (d) laser printer

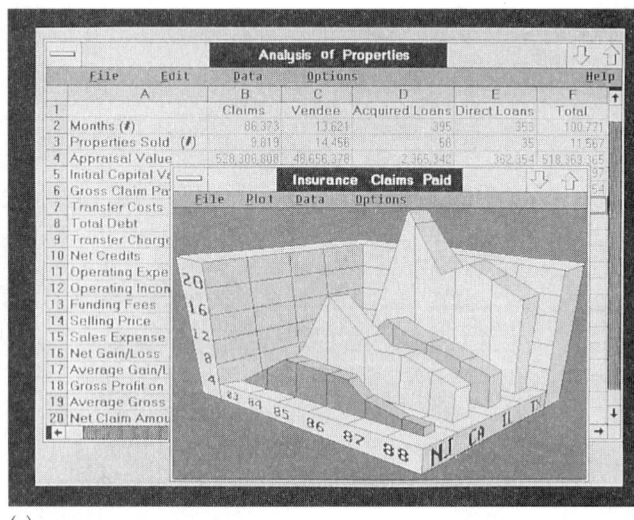

(a)

(b)

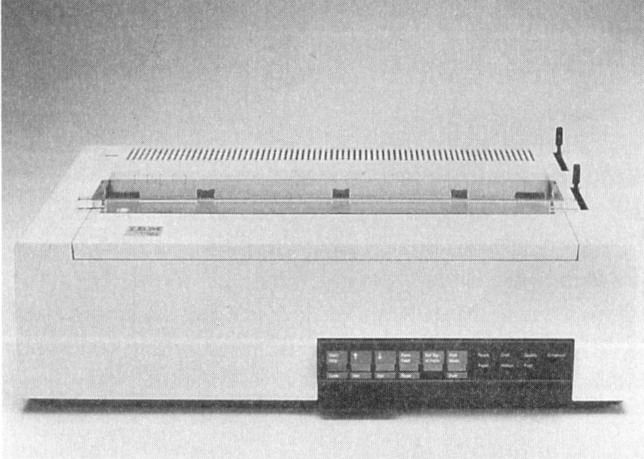

(c)

(d)

◆ FIGURE 1.6
(a) Disk drive and (b) microcomputer with hard disk

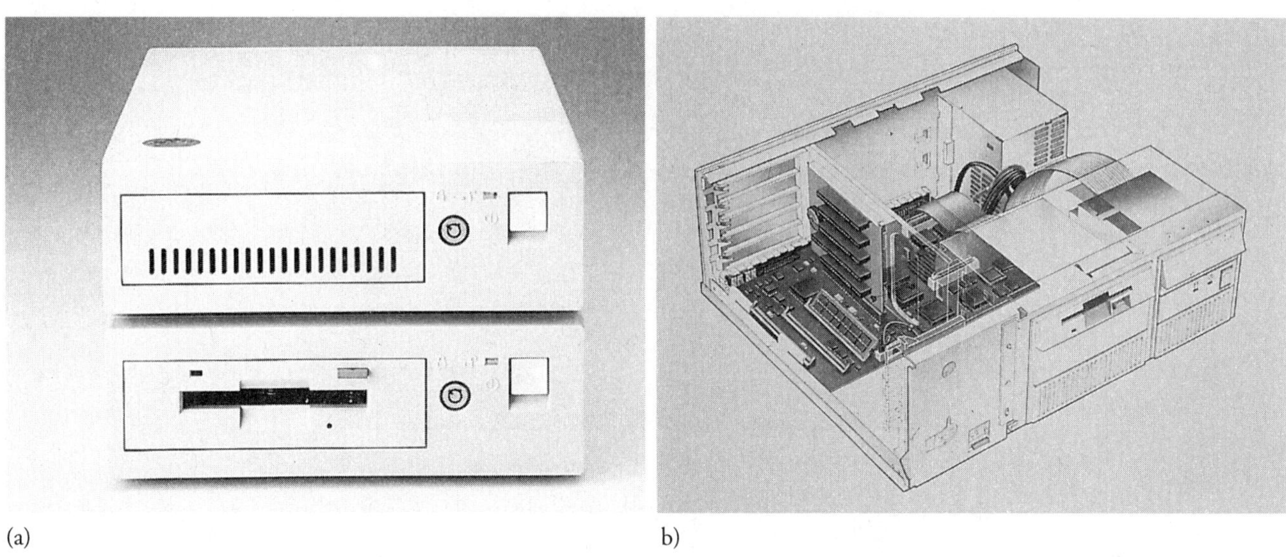

(a) b)

◆ FIGURE 1.7
Illustration of a bus

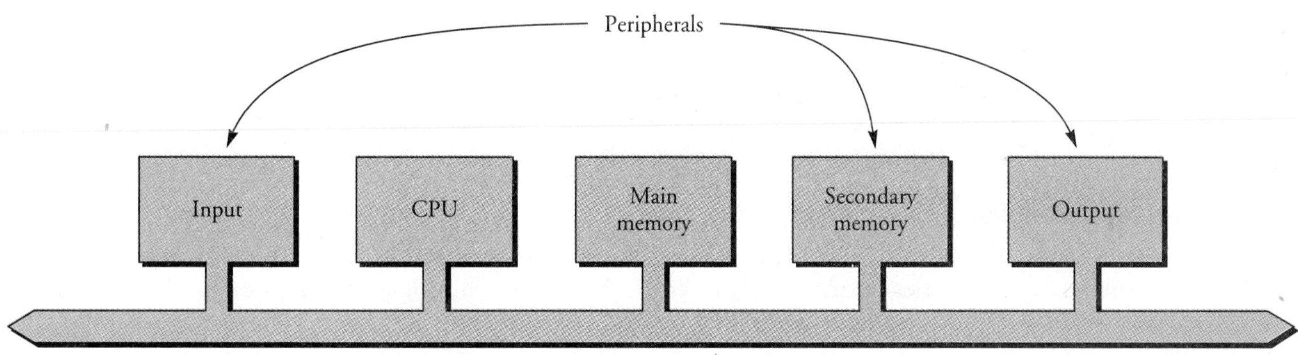

is shown in Figure 1.8. What appear to be lines between the slots are actually wires imprinted on the underlying board. Boards with wires connected to peripheral devices can be inserted into the slots.

Computer Software

As previously stated, software refers to programs that make the machine do something. Software consists of two kinds of programs: *system software* and *applications software.*

System software includes what is often called the *operating system.* (For instance, the ubiquitous DOS stands for Disk Operating System.) The operating system for a computer is a large program and is usually supplied with a computer. This program allows the user to communicate with the hardware. More specifically, an operating system might control computer access (via passwords), allocate peripheral resources (perhaps with a printer queue), schedule shared resources (for CPU use), or control execution of other programs.

◆ FIGURE 1.8
Bus

Applications software consists of programs designed for a specific use. Examples of applications software include programs for word processing, text editing, simulating spreadsheets, playing games, designing machinery, and figuring payrolls. Most computer users work with applications software and have little need to learn a computer language; the programs they require have already been written to accomplish their tasks.

1.3 Computer Languages

OBJECTIVES

- to understand what a computer language is
- to understand the difference between a low-level language and a high-level language
- to understand the difference between a source program and an object program

What is a computer language? All data transmission, manipulation, storage, and retrieval is actually done by the machine using electrical pulses representing sequences of binary digits. If eight-digit binary codes are used, there are 256 numbered instructions from 00000000 to 11111111. Instructions for adding two numbers would consist of a sequence of these eight-digit codes.

Instructions written in this form are referred to as *machine language.* It is possible to write an entire program in machine language. However, this is very time consuming and difficult to read and understand.

Therefore, the next level of computer language allows words and symbols to be used in an unsophisticated manner to accomplish simple tasks. For example, the machine code for adding two integers might be

```
010000110011101000111101010000010010101101000010
```

This is replaced by

```
LOAD A
ADD B
STORE C
```

This causes the number in **A** to be added to the number in **B** and the result to be stored for later use in **C**. This computer language is an *assembly language,* which is generally referred to as a *low-level language.* What actually happens is that words and symbols are translated into appropriate binary digits and the machine uses the translated form.

Although assembly language is an improvement on machine language for readability and program development, it is still a bit cumbersome. Consequently,

A NOTE OF INTEREST

Why Learn C++?

C++ is a superset of C, which is a programming language developed at AT&T Bell Laboratories by Dennis Ritchie in 1972. Ritchie originally intended C to be used to write the UNIX operating system and to write tools to be used with that system. Over the years, however, C has achieved widespread popularity for writing various systems' programs in industry, and is now the language of choice in most graduate schools of computer science. According to Richard P. Gabriel ("The end of history and the last programming language," *Journal of Object-Oriented Programming,* July–August 1993), C and C++ are among the few programming languages that are not either dead or moribund. There are several reasons for this. C is available on a wide range of computers and requires minimal computer resources to design, implement, and run programs. C represents a simple machine model, one that closely corresponds to the structure of actual computers. This property supports the development of very efficient programs. C is also similar to several different popular programming languages, like Pascal, FORTRAN, and assembly language. Finally, C requires almost no mathematical sophistication to learn.

Critics claim that C is a dangerous language in three respects. First, C encourages professional programmers to write large systems that lack structure and are difficult to read and maintain. Second, C encourages beginning programmers to learn bad habits, such as writing small programs that lack structure and are difficult to read and maintain. Third, C lacks many of the fail-safe features of modern programming languages, such as thorough compile-time type checking.

Responding to this challenge, Bjarne Stroustrup, also of AT&T Bell Laboratories, developed C++ in the 1980s. C++ incorporates all of the desirable and undesirable features of C enumerated above. However, some additional features, if used properly, make C++ a safer language and support the design and implementation of well-structured, easily maintained programs for both beginners and professionals. For example, C++ has strong support for data types and type checking, and also features that support the discipline of *object-oriented programming.* Object-oriented programming is a method of developing and maintaining large software systems that we will introduce and discuss in later chapters in this text.

Critics claim that C++ introduces its own costs: The language is enormous, the machine model that it represents is more complex than that of C, and programmers must have more mathematical sophistication to make use of its improved features. However, if Gabriel is right, students will do well to learn this language, because it will be used in industry for many years to come.

Our approach in this text will be to focus on those features of C++ that support the design and implementation of well-structured programs that are easy to read and maintain. C++ is a powerful tool that should be wielded carefully.

many *high-level languages* have been developed; these include Pascal, PL/I, FORTRAN, BASIC, COBOL, C, Ada, Modula-2, Logo, and others. These languages simplify even further the terminology and symbolism necessary for directing the machine to perform various manipulations of data. For example, in these languages, the task of adding two integers would be written as

```
C := A + B;             (Pascal, Modula-2, Ada)
C = A + B;              (PL/I, C++)
C = A + B               FORTRAN, BASIC
ADD A, B GIVING C       (COBOL)
MAKE ''C :A + :B        (Logo)
```

A high-level language makes it easier to read, write, and understand a program. This book develops the concepts, symbolism, and terminology necessary for using C++ as a programming language for solving problems. After you have become proficient in using C++, you should find it relatively easy to learn the nuances of other high-level languages.

For a moment, let's consider how an instruction such as

```
C = A + B;
```

gets translated into machine code. The actual bit pattern for this code varies according to the machine and software version, but it could be as previously indicated. In order for the translation to happen, a special program called a *compiler* "reads" the high-level instructions and translates them into machine code. This compiled version is then run using some appropriate data, and the results are presented through some form of output device. The special programs that activate the compiler, run the machine-code version, and cause output to be printed are examples of system programs (software). The written program is a *source program,* and the machine-code version generated by the compiler is an *object program* (also referred to as *object code*).

As you will soon see, the compiler does more than just translate instructions into machine code. It also detects certain errors in your source program and prints appropriate messages. For example, if you write the instruction

```
C = (A + B;
```

in which a parenthesis is missing, when the compiler attempts to translate this line into machine code, it will detect that ")" is needed to close the parenthetical expression. It will then give you an error message such as

```
Error: ')' expected
```

You will then need to correct the error (and any others) and recompile your source program before running it with the data.

You are now ready to begin a detailed study of C++. You will undoubtedly spend much time and encounter some frustration during the course of your work. We hope your efforts result in an exciting and rewarding learning experience. Good luck.

SUMMARY

Key Terms

algorithm
applications software
arithmetic/logic unit (ALU)
assembly language
binary digits
bits
bus
central processing unit (CPU)
comments
compiler
control unit
data executable statement
executed
hardware
high-level language
input device
I/O devices
low-level language
machine language
main (primary) memory
main unit
mainframe
microcomputer minicomputer
object code
object program
operating system
output device
program
programming language
secondary (auxiliary) memory devices
software
source program
syntax
system software

C H A P T E R

2 Problem Solving Fundamentals: Data Types and Output

CHAPTER OUTLINE

Chapter 1 presented an overview of computers and computer languages. We are now ready to examine problems that computers can solve. First we need to know how to solve a problem and then we need to learn how to use a programming language to implement our solution on the computer. Section 2.1 lays the foundation for what many consider to be the most important aspect of entry-level courses in computer science—program development. The problem-solving theme in this section is continued throughout the text.

Before looking at problem solving and writing programs for the computer, we should consider some psychological aspects of working in computer science. Studying computer science can cause a significant amount of frustration for these reasons:

1. Planning is a critical issue. First, you must plan to develop instructions to solve your problem and then you should plan to translate those instructions into code before you sit down at the keyboard. You should not attempt to type in code "off the top of your head."
2. Time is a major problem. You cannot expect to complete a programming assignment by staying up late the night before it is due. You must begin early and expect to make several revisions before your final version is ready.
3. Successful problem solving and programming require extreme precision. Generally, concepts in computer science are not difficult; however, implementation of these concepts allows no room for error. For example, one misplaced word in a 1000-line program could prevent the program from working.

In other words, you must be prepared to plan well, start early, be patient, handle frustration, and work hard to succeed in software development. If you cannot do this, you will probably not enjoy software development nor be successful at it.

2.1 Program Development—Top-Down Design

The key to writing a successful program is planning. Good programs do not just happen; they are the result of careful design and patience. Just as an artist commissioned to paint a portrait would not start out by shading in the lips and eyes, a good computer programmer would not attack a problem by immediately trying to write code for a program to solve the problem. Writing a program is like writing an essay: An overall theme is envisioned, an outline of major ideas is developed, each major idea is subdivided into several parts, and each part is developed using individual sentences.

Six Steps to Good Programming Habits

In developing a program to solve a problem, six steps should be followed: analyze the problem, develop an algorithm, document the program, write code for the

OBJECTIVES

- to understand what an algorithm is
- to understand what top-down design is
- to understand what step-wise refinement is
- to understand what modularity is
- to be able to develop algorithms

program, run the program, and test the results. These steps will help develop good problem-solving habits and, in turn, solve programming problems correctly. A brief discussion of each of these steps follows:

Step 1: Analyze the Problem. This is not a trivial task. Before you can do anything, you must know exactly what it is you are to do. You must be able to formulate a clear and precise statement of what is to be done. You should understand completely what data are available and what may be assumed. You should also know exactly what output is desired and the form it should take. When analyzing a complex problem, it helps to divide the problem into subproblems whose solutions can be developed and tested independently before they are combined into a complete solution.

Step 2: Develop an Algorithm. An algorithm is a finite sequence of effective statements that, when applied to the problem, will solve it. An *effective statement* is a clear, unambiguous instruction that can be carried out. Each algorithm you develop should have a specific beginning; by the completion of one step, the next step should be uniquely determined; and have an ending that is reached in a reasonable amount of time.

Step 3: Document the Program. It is very important to completely document a program. The writer knows how the program works; if others are to modify it, they must know the logic used. Moreover, users will need to know the details of how to use the program effectively. Documentation can come directly out of steps 1 and 2 before you write any code.

Step 4: Write Code for the Program. When the algorithm correctly solves the problem, you can think about translating your algorithm into a high-level language. An effective algorithm will significantly reduce the time you need to complete this step.

Step 5: Run the Program. After writing the code, you are ready to run the program. This means that, using an editor, you type the program code into the computer, compile the program, and run the program. At compile time, you may discover syntax errors, which are mistakes in the way you have formed sentences in the program. Once these errors have been corrected, you may discover other errors at run time. Some of these mistakes may be as simple as an attempt to divide by zero. Other errors, called logic errors, may be more subtle and cause the program to produce mysterious results. They may require a reevaluation of all or parts of your algorithm. The probability of having to make some corrections or changes is quite high.

Step 6: Test the Results. After your program has run, you need to be sure that the results are correct, that they are in a form you like, and that your program produces the correct solution in all cases. To be sure the results are correct, you must look at them and compare them with what you expect. In the case of a program that uses arithmetic operations, this means checking some results with pencil and paper. With complex programs, you will need to test the program thoroughly by running it many times using data that you have carefully selected. Often you will need to make revisions by returning to one of the previous steps.

You should bear in mind that programs of any significant size (more than 100 lines of code) are never constructed all at once. The six steps just described are used to build programs incrementally. That is, a program is created out of small pieces that are designed, coded, tested, and documented to solve small problems. These pieces are then glued together to solve the problem set for the overall program.

Developing Algorithms

Algorithms for solving a problem can be developed by stating the problem and then subdividing the problem into major subtasks. Each subtask can then be subdivided into smaller tasks. This process is repeated until each remaining task is one that is easily solved. This process is known as *top-down design,* and each successive subdivision is referred to as a *stepwise refinement.* Tasks identified at each stage of this process are called *modules.* The relationship between modules can be shown graphically in a *structure chart* (see Figure 2.1).

To illustrate developing an algorithm, we will use the problem of updating a checkbook after a transaction has been made. A first-level refinement is shown in Figure 2.2. An arrow pointing into a module means information is needed before the task can be performed. An arrow pointing out of a module means the module task has been completed and information required for subsequent work is available. Each of these modules could be further refined as shown in Figure 2.3. Finally, one of the last modules could be refined as shown in Figure 2.4. The complete top-down design could then be envisioned as illustrated in Figure 2.5. Notice that each remaining task can be accomplished in a very direct manner.

As a further aid to understanding how data are transmitted, we will list *module specifications* for each main (first-level) module. Each module specification includes a description of inputs or data received, outputs or information returned, and the task performed by the module. In cases where there are no inputs or outputs, none are specified.

For the checkbook-balancing problem, complete module specifications are as follows:

Module: Get information
Task: Have the user enter information from the keyboard.
Outputs: starting balance, transaction type, transaction amount

Module: Perform computations
Task: If transaction is a deposit, add it to the starting balance; otherwise, subtract it.
Inputs: starting balance, transaction type, transaction amount
Output: ending balance

Module: Display results

◆ FIGURE 2.1
Structure chart illustrating top-down design

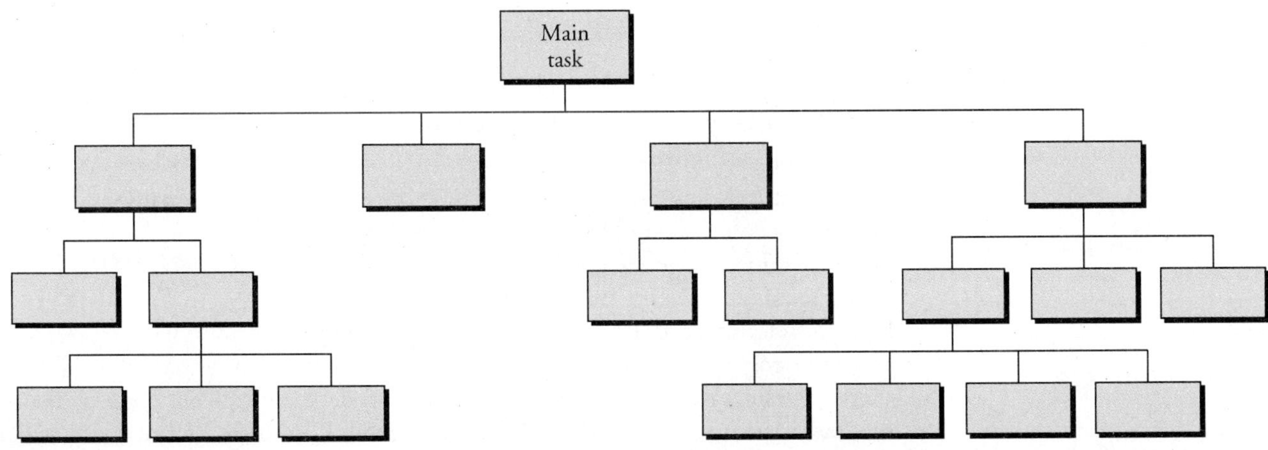

◆ **FIGURE 2.2**
First-level refinement

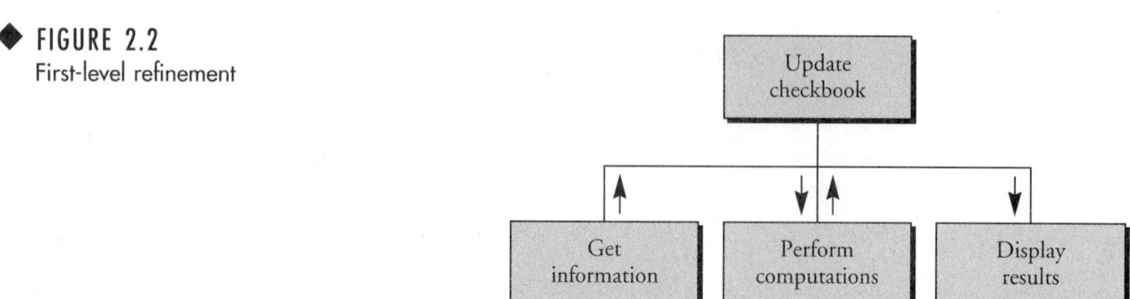

◆ **FIGURE 2.3**
Second-level refinement

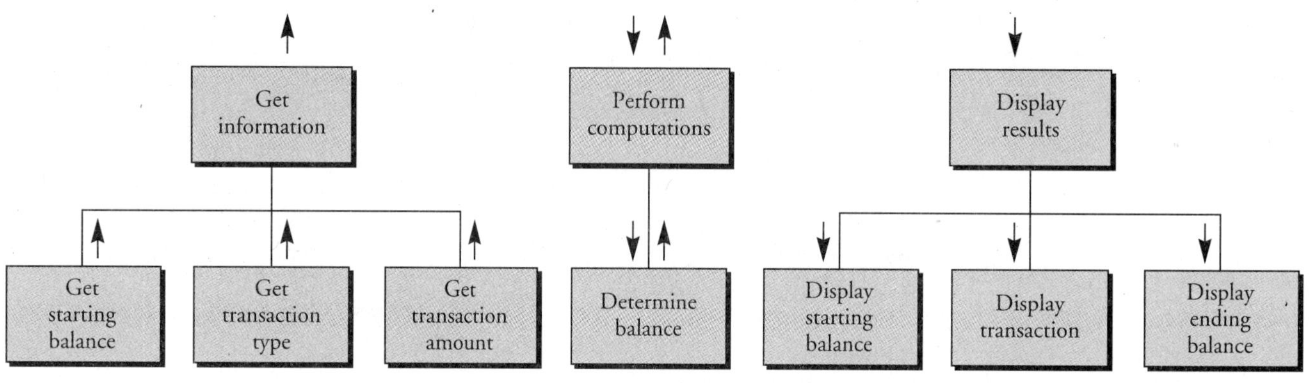

◆ **FIGURE 2.4**
Third-level refinement

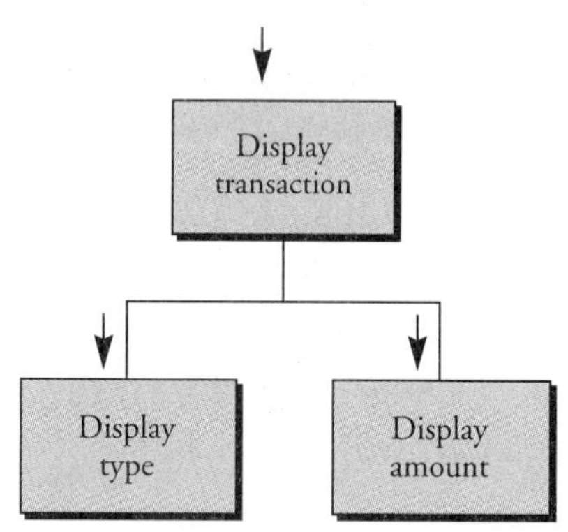

Task: Display results in a readable form.
Inputs: starting balance, transaction type, transaction amount, ending balance

At least two comments should be made about top-down design. First, different people can (and probably will) have different designs for the solution of a problem. However, each good design will have well-defined modules with functional subtasks. Second, the graphic method just used helps to formulate general logic for solving a problem but is somewhat awkward for translating to code. Thus, we will use a stylized, half-English, half-code method called *pseudocode* to illustrate stepwise refinement in such a design. Pseudocode is written in English, but the sentence structure and indentations will suggest C++ code. Major tasks will be

◆ **FIGURE 2.5**
Structure chart for top-down design

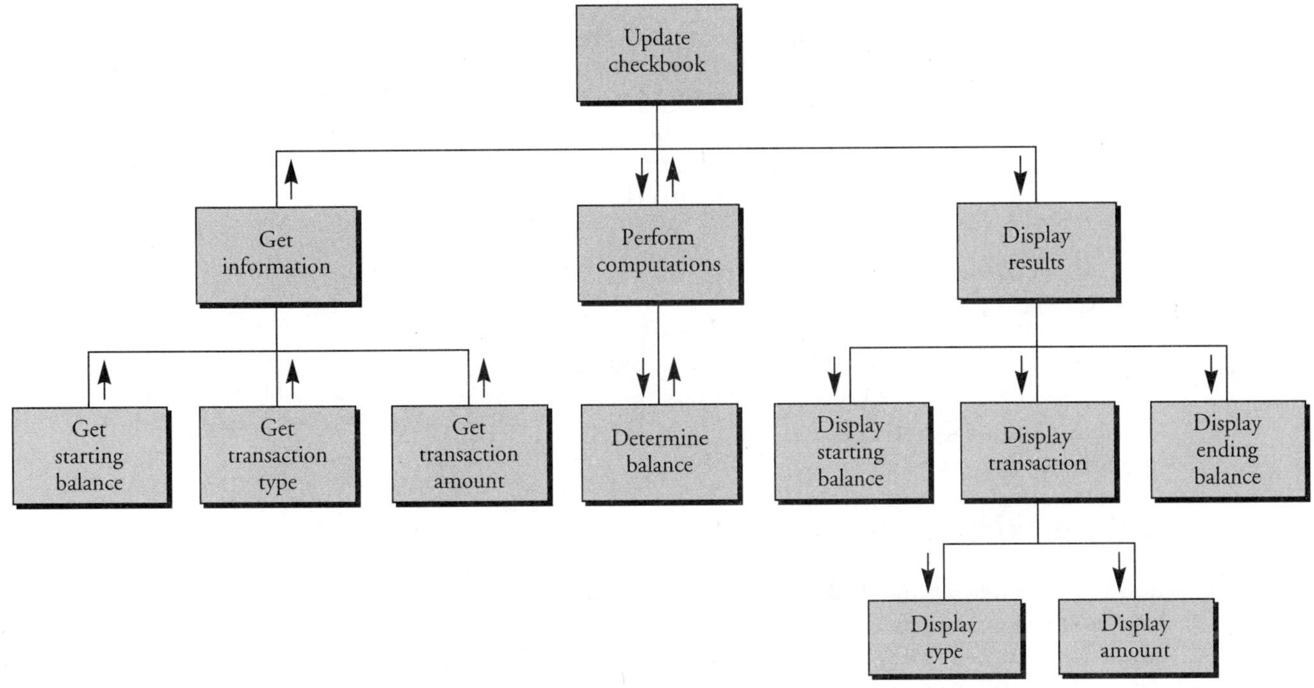

numbered with whole numbers and subtasks with decimal numbers. After you become used to the pseudocode notation, the numbering of lines will be omitted. First-level pseudocode for the checkbook-balancing problem is

```
1. Get information
2. Perform computations
3. Display results
```

A second-level pseudocode development produces

```
1. Get information
   1.1 get starting balance
   1.2 get transaction type
   1.3 get transaction amount
2. Perform computations
   2.1 if deposit then
              add to balance
       else
              subtract from balance
3. Display results
   3.1 display starting balance
   3.2 display transaction
   3.3 display ending balance
```

Finally, step 3.2 of the pseudocode is subdivided as previously indicated into

```
3.2 display transaction
    3.2.1 display transaction type
    3.2.2 display transaction amount
```

Two final comments are in order. First, each module developed should be tested with data for that module. Once you are sure each module does what you want, the whole program should work when the modules are used together. Second, the process of dividing a task into subtasks is especially suitable for writing programs in C++. As you will see, the language supports development of subprograms for specific subtasks.

A C++ program for the checkbook-balancing problem follows:

```
// Program file: chbook.cpp
// This program updates a checkbook.

#include <iostream.h>
#include <iomanip.h>

int main ()
{
        float starting_balance, ending_balance, trans_amount;
        char trans_type;

// Module for getting the data.

      cout << "Enter the starting balance and press <Enter>: " ;
      cin >> starting_balance;
      cout << "Enter the transaction type (D) deposit or (W) withdrawal " ;    1
      cout << "and press <Enter>: " ;
      cin >> trans_type;
      cout << "Enter the transaction amount and press <Enter>: " ;
      cin >> trans_amount;

// Module for performing computations.

      if (trans_type == 'D')
              ending_balance = starting_balance + trans_amount;    2
      else
              ending_balance = starting_balance - trans_amount;

// Module for displaying results.

      cout << fixed << showpoint << setprecision(2);
      cout << endl;
      cout << "Starting balance   $" << setw(8) << starting_balance << endl ;    3
      cout << "Transaction      $" << setw(8) << trans_amount << setw(2)
             << trans_type << endl ;
      cout << setw(33) << "---------" << endl ;
      cout << "Ending balance    $" << setw(8) << ending_balance << endl ;

      return 0;

}
```

Notice how sections of the program correspond to module specifications. Sample runs of the program produce this output:

```
Enter the starting balance and press <Enter>: 235.16
Enter the transaction type (D) deposit or (W) withdrawal and press <Enter>: D
Enter the transaction amount and press <Enter>: 75.00

Starting Balance              $  235.16

Transaction                   $   75.00 D

                                --------

Ending Balance                $  310.16

Enter the starting balance and press <Enter>: 310.16
Enter the transaction type (D) deposit or (W) withdrawal and press <Enter>: W
Enter the transaction amount and press <Enter>: 65.75

Starting Balance              $  310.16

Transaction                   $   65.75 W
                                --------

Ending Balance                $  244.41
```

You probably would not use the power of a computer for something as simple as this program. You could just press a few calculator keys instead. However, as you will see, the language supports development of subprograms for specific subtasks. You will, for example, soon be able to enhance this program to check for overdrafts, save the new balance for later use, and repeat the process for several transactions. Learning to think in terms of modular development now will aid you not just in creating algorithms to solve problems, but in writing programs to solve problems.

Software Engineering

The phrase *software engineering* is used roughly to refer to the process of developing and maintaining very large software systems. Before becoming engrossed in the specifics of solving problems and writing relatively small programs, it is instructive to consider the broader picture faced by those who develop software for "real-world" use.

It is not unusual for software systems to be programs that, if written in this size type, would require between 100 and 150 pages of text. These systems must be reliable, economical, and subject to use by a diverse audience. Because of these requirements, software developers must be aware of and practice certain techniques.

As you might imagine, such large programs are not the work of a single individual but are developed by teams of programmers. Issues such as communication, writing style, and technique become as important as the development of algorithms to solve particular parts of the problem. Management, coordination, and design are major considerations that need resolution very early in the process. Although you will not face these larger organizational issues in this course, you will see how some of what you learn has implications for larger design issues.

Software engineering has been so titled because techniques and principles from the more established engineering disciplines are used to guide the large-scale development required in major software. To illustrate, consider the problems faced

A NOTE OF INTEREST

Software Verification

Sitting 70 kilometers east of Toronto on the shore of Lake Ontario, the Darlington Nuclear Generating Station looks much like any other large nuclear power plant of the Canadian variety. But behind its ordinary exterior lies an unusual design feature.

Darlington is the first Canadian nuclear station to use computers to operate the two emergency shutdown systems that safeguard each of its four reactors. In both shutdown systems, a computer program replaces an array of electrically operated mechanical devices—switches and relays—designed to respond to sensors that are monitoring conditions critical to a reactor's safe operation, such as water levels in boilers.

Darlington's four reactors supply enough electricity to serve a city of 2 million people. Its Toronto-based builder, Ontario Hydro, opted for sophisticated software rather than old-fashioned hardware in the belief that a computer-operated shutdown system would be more economical, flexible, reliable, and safe than one under mechanical control.

This new approach, however, turned out to have unanticipated costs. To satisfy regulators that the shutdown software would function as advertised, Ontario Hydro engineers had to go through a frustrating but essential checking process that required nearly three years of extra effort. "There are lots of examples where software has gone wrong with serious consequences," says engineer Glenn H. Archinoff of Ontario Hydro. "If you want a shutdown system to work when you need it, you have to have a high level of assurance."

The Darlington experience demonstrates the tremendous effort involved in establishing the correctness of even relatively short and straightforward computer programs. The 10,000 "lines" of instructions, or code, required for each shutdown system pale in comparison with the 100,000 lines that constitute a typical word-processing program or the millions of lines needed to operate a long-distance telephone network or a space shuttle.

by an engineer who is to design and supervise construction of a bridge. This analysis was presented by Alfred Spector and David Gifford in an article entitled "A Computer Science Perspective on Bridge Design" published in *Communications of the ACM* (April 1986).

> *Engineers designing a bridge view it first as a hierarchy of substructures. This decomposition process continues on the substructures themselves until a level of very fundamental objects (such as beams and plates) ultimately is reached. This decomposition technique is similar to the stepwise refinement technique used by software designers, who break a complex problem down into a hierarchy of subproblems each of which ultimately can be solved by a relatively simple algorithm.*
>
> *Engineers build conceptual models before actually constructing a bridge. This model-building allows them to evaluate various design alternatives in a way which eventually leads to the best possible design for the application being considered. This process is analogous to the way in which a skilled software designer builds models of a software system using structure charts and first-level pseudocode descriptions of modules. The designer then studies these conceptual models and eventually chooses the most elegant and efficient model for the application.*
>
> *By the fashion in which engineers initially break down the bridge design, they insure that different aspects of the design can be addressed by different subordinate groups of design engineers working in a relatively independent fashion. This is similar to the goal of a software designer who oversees a program development team. The design of the software system must insure that individual components may be developed simultaneously by separate groups whose work will not have harmful side effects when the components are finally pulled together.*

This overview is presented to give you a better perspective on how developments in this text are part of a greater whole. As you progress through your study of C++, you will see specific illustrations of how concepts and techniques can be viewed as part of the software engineering process.

Software System Life Cycle

Software engineering is the process by which large software systems are produced. As you might imagine, these systems need to be maintained and modified; ultimately, they are replaced with other systems. This entire process parallels that of an organism. That is, there is a development, maintenance, and subsequent demise. Thus, this process is referred to as the *software system life cycle.* Specifically, a system life cycle can be viewed in the following phases:

1. Analysis
2. Design
3. Coding
4. Testing/verification
5. Maintenance
6. Obsolescence.

It probably comes as a surprise that computer scientists view this process as having a phase that precedes the design phase. However, it is extremely critical that a problem be completely understood before any attempt is made to design a solution. The analysis phase is complicated by the fact that potential users may not supply enough information when describing their intended use of a system. Analysis requires careful attention to items such as exact form of input, exact form of output, how data entry errors (there will be some) should be handled, how large the databases will become, how much training in the use of the system will be provided, and what possible modifications might be required as the intended audience increases/decreases. Clearly, the analysis phase requires an experienced communicator.

The design phase is what much of this book is about. This is where the solution is developed using a modular approach. Attention must be paid to techniques that include communication, algorithm development, writing style, teamwork, and so on. The key product of this phase is a detailed specification of the intended software product.

Coding closely follows design. Unfortunately, many beginning students want to write code too quickly. This can be a painful lesson if you have to scrap several days' worth of work because your original design was not sufficient. You are encouraged to make sure your designs are complete before writing any code. In the real world, teams of designers work long hours before programmers ever get a chance to start writing code.

The testing phase of a large system is a significant undertaking. Early testing is done on individual modules to get them running properly. Larger data sets must then be run on the entire program to make sure the modules interact properly with the main program. When the system appears ready to the designers, it is usually field tested by selected users. Each of these testing levels is likely to require changes in the design and coding of the system.

Finally, the system is released to the public and the maintenance phase begins. This phase lasts throughout the remainder of the program's useful life. During this phase, we are concerned with repairing problems that arise after the system has been put into use. These problems are not necessarily bugs introduced during the coding phases. More often they are the result of user needs that change over time. For instance, annual changes in the tax laws necessitate changes in even the best payroll programs. Or problems may arise as a result of misinterpretation of user needs during the early analysis phase. Whatever the reason, we must expect that a program will have to undergo numerous changes during its lifetime. During the maintenance phase, the time spent documenting the original program will be repaid many times over. One of the worst tasks imaginable in software development is to be asked to maintain an undocumented program. Undocumented code can quickly become virtually unintelligible, even to the program's original author. Indeed, one of the measures of a good program is how well it stands up to the maintenance phase.

Of course, no matter how good a program is it will eventually become obsolete. At that time, the system life cycle starts all over again with the development of a new system to replace the obsolete one. Hence, the system life cycle is never ending, being itself part of a larger repetitive pattern that continues to evolve with changing user needs and more powerful technology.

Object-Oriented Design

During the last few years, a methodology has emerged that promises to make the task of maintaining large software systems easier. According to this method, large software systems should be constructed from smaller software components called objects. Software objects are a bit like building blocks, in that they can be pulled out of a box and put together in different ways to construct different applications. Objects can also be customized, that is, they can be adapted if they do not quite fit the task at hand. It is claimed that the use of software objects results in several benefits:

1. Because software objects can represent the behavior of the "real" objects that a software system is created to model, the differences between the analysis, design, and coding phases of the software life cycle tend to collapse.
2. Instead of changing existing code or writing new code, software maintenance involves plugging objects into a system or unplugging them from a system.
3. Systems can be more easily developed in increments, starting with a rough prototype whose detailed functions are eventually filled in until they are complete.

Although object-oriented design holds much promise for the development of solutions to complex problems, it is not necessarily the easiest and most straightforward way to learn to solve problems with a computer. In particular, the need for objects will not become apparent until we begin to define and use our own data structures for solving problems in Chapters 7 and 8. After we have explored some other typical problem-solving techniques, we will introduce object-oriented problem solving and programming with C++ in Chapters 7 through 11.

EXERCISES 2.1

1. Which of the following can be considered effective statements; that is, considered to be clear, unambiguous instructions that can be carried out? For each statement, explain why it is effective or why it is not.
   a. Pay the cashier $9.15.
   b. Water the plants a day before they die.
   c. Determine all positive prime numbers less than 1,000,000.

   d. Choose X to be the smallest positive fraction.
   e. Invest your money in a stock that will increase in value.
2. What additional information must be obtained in order to understand each of the following problems?
   a. Find the largest number of a set of numbers.
   b. Alphabetize a list of names.
   c. Compute charges for a telephone bill.
3. Outline the main tasks for solving each of the following problems.
   a. Write a good term paper.
   b. Take a vacation.
   c. Choose a college.
   d. Get a summer job.
   e. Compute the semester average for a student in a computer science course and print all pertinent data.
4. Refine the main tasks in each part of Exercise 3 into a sufficient number of levels so that the problem can be solved in a well-defined manner.
5. Use pseudocode to write a solution for each of the following problems. Indicate each stage of your development.
   a. Compute the wages for two employees of a company. The input information will consist of the hourly wage and the number of hours worked in one week. The output should contain a list of all deductions, gross pay, and net pay. For this problem, assume deductions are made for federal withholding taxes, state withholding taxes, social security, and union dues.
   b. Compute the average test score for five students in a class. Input for this problem will consist of five scores. Output should include each score and the average of these scores.
6. Develop an algorithm to find the total, average, and largest number in a given list of 25 numbers.
7. Develop an algorithm to find the greatest common divisor (GCD) of two positive integers.
8. Develop an algorithm for solving the following system of equations:

   $ax + by = c$

   $dx + ey = f$
9. Draw a structure chart and write module specifications for each of the following exercises.
   a. Exercise 5a.
   b. Exercise 5b.
   c. Exercise 6.
10. Discuss how the top-down design principles of software engineering are similar to the design problems faced by a construction engineer for a building. Be sure to include anticipated work with all subcontractors.
11. Using the construction analogy of Exercise 10, give an example of some specific communication required between electricians and the masons who finish the interior walls. Discuss why this information flow should be coordinated by a construction engineer.
12. State the phases of the software system life cycle.
13. Contact some company or major user of a software system to see what kinds of modifications might be required in a system after it has been released to the public. (Your own computer center might be sufficient.)

2.2 Writing Programs

OBJECTIVES

- to be able to recognize reserved words and standard library identifiers
- to be able to recognize and declare valid identifiers
- to know the basic components of a program
- to understand the basic structure of a C++ program

Words in C++

Consider the following complete C++ program.

```
// Program file: reswords.cpp
// This program illustrates the use of reserved words.

#include <iostream.h>
#include <iomanip.h>

const int LOOP_LIMIT = 10;
const char SKIP = ' ';

int main ()
{

        int j, number, sum;
        float average;

        sum = 0;
        for (j = 1; j <= LOOP_LIMIT; ++j)
        {
                cout << "Enter a number and press <Enter>: ";
                cin >> number;
                sum = sum + number;
        }
        average = sum / LOOP_LIMIT;
        cout << fixed << showpoint << setprecision(2);
        cout << endl;
        cout << setw(10) << SKIP << "The average is"
              << setw(8) << average
              << endl ;
        cout << endl ;
        cout << setw(10) << SKIP << "The number of scores is"
              << setw(3)
              << LOOP_LIMIT << endl ;
        return 0;
}
```

This program—and most programming languages—requires the use of words when writing code. In C++, words that have a predefined meaning that cannot be changed are called *reserved words.* Some other predefined words (*library identifiers*) can have their meanings changed if the programmer has strong reasons for doing so. Other words (*programmer-supplied identifiers*) must be created according to a well-defined set of rules, but can have any meaning, subject to those rules.

C++ is case sensitive. This means that the word **while** will have a different meaning to the compiler than the word **While**, even though the two words might appear to mean the same thing to a human being. All reserved words and all library identifiers in C++ must be typed in lowercase letters only. Identifiers that you create for your own purposes may be typed in any case you like, as long as you remember that the same words written in different cases will mean different things.

Reserved Words

In C++, reserved words are predefined and cannot be used in a program for anything other than the purpose for which they are reserved. Some examples are **for**, **if**, **while**, **do**, **switch**, and **int**. As you continue in C++, you will learn where and how these words are used. The C++ reserved words are listed in Table 2.1.

Library Identifiers

A second set of predefined words, library identifiers, can have their meanings changed by the programmer. For example, if you could develop a better algorithm for the trigonometric function **sin**, you could then substitute it in the program. However, these words should not be used for anything other than their intended use. This list will vary somewhat from compiler to compiler, so you should obtain a list of library identifiers used in your local implementation of C++. Some library identifiers are listed in Table 2.2 and in Appendix 2. The term *keywords* is used to refer to both reserved words and library identifiers in subsequent discussions.

Syntax

Syntax refers to the rules governing construction of valid statements. This includes the order in which words and statements occur, together with appropriate punctuation. We use two methods of expressing syntax rules in this book. In the body of the text, the form of most new expressions in the language will be written using an angle bracket notation. In this notation, words that appear directly in the expression, such as **if** and **==**, will be written as is. Other components of the expression requiring further definition, such as type names or parameter lists, will be described by enclosing a term, like **type name** or **parameter list** within angle brackets (< and >). Thus, the rule for function call expressions looks like this:

```
<function name> (<actual parameter list>)
```

◇ **TABLE 2.1**
Reserved words

asm	continue	float	new	signed	try
auto	default	for	operator	sizeof	typedef
break	delete	friend	private	static	union
case	do	goto	protected	struct	unsigned
catch	double	if	public	switch	virtual
char	else	inline	register	template	void
class	enum	int	return	this	volatile
const	extern	long	short	throw	while

◇ **TABLE 2.2**
Some library identifiers

cin
cout
fixed
pow
setprecision
setw
showpoint
sin
sqrt

A NOTE OF INTEREST

Program Libraries

When the computer scientist John Backus developed the programming language FORTRAN in 1954, he decided to place the code for frequently used mathematical functions in compiled libraries. Programmers writing applications in FORTRAN had merely to link their own programs with the libraries to use these functions. Soon they began to construct and share libraries of their own functions. The practice of borrowing software tools "off the shelf" from libraries became a standard way of constructing large software systems quickly and safely. A library enhanced program safety, in that its tools were already debugged or shown to work correctly. A library enhanced system maintenance, in that changes to the importing application or to the exporting library could be made independently. Finally, a library enhanced the portability of a software system from one hardware installation to another, in that low-level, machine-dependent tasks could be packaged in the library and thereby insulated from the rest of the system.

One of the reasons C++ is so popular is that there are so many program libraries that enhance the safety, maintenance, and portability of systems written in the language.

◇ TABLE 2.3
Valid and invalid identifiers

Identifier	Valid	If Invalid, Reason
`Sum`	Yes	
`X+Y`	No	+ is not allowed
`Average`	Yes	
`Text1`	Yes	
`1stNum`	No	Must start with a letter or _
`X30`	Yes	
`K mart`	No	Spaces are not allowed
`ThisIsaLongOne`	Yes	

This rule means that a function call expression is a function name, followed by a left paren, followed by a list of actual parameters if the function expects any, followed by a right paren.

Another method of expressing a syntax rule uses a diagram. A list of syntax diagrams covering the portion of C++ used in this text appears in Appendix 3.

Identifiers

Reserved words and library identifiers are restricted in their use. Most C++ programs require programmer-supplied identifiers; the more complicated the program, the more identifiers are needed. **A valid identifier must start with a letter of the alphabet or an underscore (_) and must consist of only letters, digits, and underscores.** A syntax diagram for forming identifiers appears in Appendix 3.

Table 2.3 gives some valid and invalid identifiers along with the reasons for those that are invalid. A valid identifier can be of any length. However, some versions of C++ recognize only the first part of a long identifier, for example, the first 8 or the first 10 characters. Therefore, identifiers such as **`MathTestScore1`** and **`MathTestScore2`** might be the same identifier to a computer and could not be used as different identifiers in a program. Thus, you should learn what restrictions are imposed by your compiler.

The most common use of identifiers is to name the variables to be used in a program. Other uses for identifiers include symbolic constants, new data types, and subprogram names, all of which are discussed later. Even though single-letter identifiers are permitted, you should always use descriptive names for identifiers because, you'll see, descriptive names are easier to follow in a program.

Basic Program Components

A large, well-structured C++ program normally consists of many small *modules* whose text appears in different files. A small, simple program like many of those used in this text appears in a single file. For now, a simple program in C++ consists of five components: an optional set of *preprocessor directives,* an optional *constant and type definition section,* a *main program heading,* an optional *declaration section,* and a *statement section.* These five components are illustrated in the program shown in Figure 2.6.

Figure 2.7 illustrates the program components of the sample program that started this section; appropriate program parts are indicated.

The preprocessor directives are usually the first part of any C++ program. Preprocessor directives are preceded by the symbol **#**. One of them, **#include**, should be used if you wish to use certain library identifiers in your program. **#include** directs the preprocessor to include the contents of the designated library file with your source program for compilation. **#include** should be followed by the name of a library file. For now, the name of the library file should be enclosed in angle brackets. In later chapters of this text, we will see some library file names enclosed in double quotes.

The constant and type definition section contains the definitions of symbolic constants and names of data types used in the rest of the program.

Constants name values that cannot change in a program. The form for defining a constant is

```
const <type identifier> <identifier> = <value>;
```

An example of a constant definition is

```
const int LOOP_LIMIT = 10;
```

◆ **FIGURE 2.6**
Components of a simple C++ program

PREPROCESSOR DIRECTIVES	(Here we include any libraries required by the program.)
CONSTANT AND TYPE DEFINITION SECTION	(Here we define any constant or type names required by the program.)
MAIN PROGRAM HEADING	
DECLARATION SECTION	(Here we list any data variable declarations.)
STATEMENT SECTION	(Here is the source program version of the algorithm.)

◆ **FIGURE 2.7**
Components of example program

```
// Program file: reswords.cpp
// This program illustrates the use of reserved words.
```

Preprocessor directives →

```
#include <iostream.h>
#include <iomanip.h>
```

Constant definition section →

```
const int LOOP_LIMIT = 10;
const char SKIP = ' ';
```

Main program heading →

```
int main ()
{
```

Declaration section →

```
        int j, number, sum;
        float average;
```

Statement section →

```
        sum = 0;
        for (j = 1; j <= LOOP_LIMIT; ++j)
        {
                cout << "Enter a number and press <Enter>:";
                cin >> number;
                sum = sum ; pl number;
        }
        average = sum / LOOP_LIMIT;
        cout << fixed << showpoint << setprecision(2);
        cout << endl;
        cout << setw(10) << SKIP << "The average is"
             << setw(8)
             << average << endl;
        cout << endl;
        cout << setw(10) << SKIP << "The number of scores is"
             << setw(3)
             << LOOP_LIMIT << endl;
        return 0;
}
```

If a constant is used that has not been declared, an error will occur when the program is compiled. Values of constant identifiers cannot be changed during program execution.

If a value is of type **char**, it must be enclosed in single quotation marks (apostrophes).

Any number of constants can be defined in this section. A typical constant definition portion of the declaration section could be

```
const char SKIP = ' ';
const int CLASS_SIZE = 35;
const int SPEED_LIMIT = 65;
const float CM_TO_INCHES = 0.3937;
```

We will discuss the mechanism for defining new data types in Chapters 5 and 7.

The main program heading is required in any C++ program. It consists of the word **int**, followed by the word **main**, followed by a set of parentheses. The program heading indicates the starting point of execution at run time.

The remainder of the program is sometimes referred to as the *main block*. A main block must begin with a left curly brace ({) and end with a right curly brace (}). The major parts of a main block are a declaration section and a statement section. The declaration section is used to declare (name) variables that are necessary to the program. If a variable is used that has not been declared, an error will occur when the program is compiled. For now, we assume all data used in a C++ program must be one of three *simple types:* **int**, **float**, or **char**. Types **int**, **float**, and **char** are discussed in Section 2.3.

Variables name values that can change in a program. The form required for declaring variables is somewhat different from that used for defining constants. One form simply omits the reserved word **const**:

<type identifier> <identifier> = <value>;

```
int sum = 0;
char ch = 'a';
```

When you need to declare more than one variable of the same type, it is convenient to list the variable names after the type on one line.

```
int length, width, area;
```

In general, it is considered good, defensive programming practice to provide variables with initial values when they are declared. Failure to do so can be the cause of mysterious program errors at execution time.

The fifth basic component of a simple C++ program is the statement section. This section contains the statements that cause the computer to do something.

Writing Code in C++

We are now ready to examine the use of the statement section of a program. In C++, a basic unit of grammar is an *executable statement,* which consists of library identifiers, programmer-defined identifiers, reserved words, numbers, and/or characters together with appropriate punctuation.

One of the main rules for writing code in C++ is that a semicolon almost always terminates executable statements. For example, if the expression

```
cout << setw(20) << "The results are" << setw(8) << sum << "and" << setw(6)
     << aver
```

is to be used in a program, it will not be treated as a statement unless it is followed by a semicolon. Thus, it should be

```
cout << setw(20) << "The results are" << setw(8) << sum << "and" << setw(6)
     << aver;
```

There is one typical instance where a semicolon is not needed. Occasionally, you will wish to enclose a series of statements within curly braces, so that they can be treated as a statement unit (the main program block is a good example). In this case, a semicolon is not needed after the right curly brace. You can visualize the statement section as shown in Figure 2.8.

◆ FIGURE 2.8
Executable section

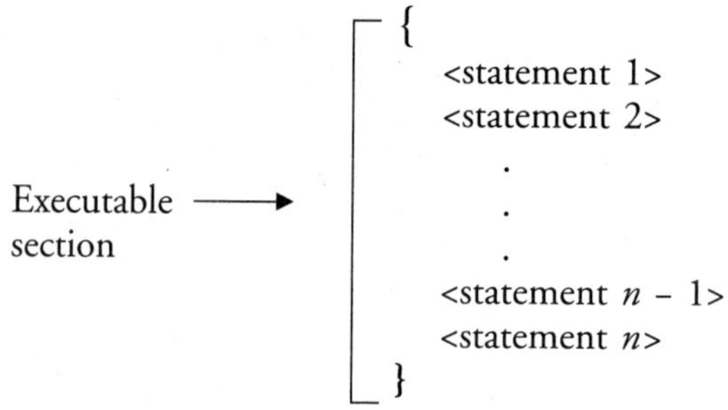

```
            {
              <statement 1>
              <statement 2>
                  .
Executable →      .
section           .
              <statement n – 1>
              <statement n>
            }
```

C++ does not require each statement to be on a separate line. Actually, you could write a program as one long line (which may wrap around to fit the screen) if you wish; however, it would be difficult to read. Compare, for example, the readability of the following two programs.

```
// program file: format.cpp
// This program illustrates the use of formatting.
#include <iostream.h> #include <iomanip.h> const int AGE = 26; void main () { int
j, sum; sum = 0; for (j = 1; j <= 10; ++j) {sum = sum + j;} cout << setw(28) << "My
name is George" << endl; cout << setw(27) << "My age is " << AGE << endl; cout <<
endl; cout << setw(28) << "The sum is " << sum << endl; return 0;}
```

```
// Program file: format.cpp
// This program illustrates the use of formatting.

#include <iostream.h>
#include <iomanip.h>

const int AGE = 26;

int main ()
{
        int j, sum;

        sum = 0;
        for (j = 1; j <= 10; ++j)
        {
               sum = sum + j;
        }
        cout << setw(28) << "My name is George" << endl;
        cout << setw(27) << "My age is " << AGE << endl;
        cout << endl;
        cout << setw(28) << "The sum is " << sum << endl;
        return 0;
}
```

You are not expected to know exactly what the statements mean at this point, but it should be obvious that the second program is much more readable than the first. In addition, it is easier to change if corrections are necessary. Note, however, that these programs would be executed similarly because C++ ignores extra spaces and line boundaries.

We will discuss many kinds of statements in the following chapters. The only statement that is required in a C++ program is the last one—the **`return`** statement. In every program in this text, you will see the statement

```
return 0;
```

at the end. When it occurs in the main program, this statement tells the computer that the program is finished running.

Formatting Conventions for Identifiers

You will have noticed by now that in our examples, constant identifiers have been written in uppercase letters, and all other identifiers, including variable and function names, have been written in lowercase letters. We believe that this convention helps the reader to pick out the constant names from the other names, when no other cues are available from the context. In addition, underscores are used to make multiword identifiers, like monthly_pay, more readable.

Program Comments

Programming languages typically include some provision for putting *comments* in a program. These comments are nonexecutable and are used to document and explain various parts of the program. In C++, progammers commonly use an *end-of-line comment.* An end-of-line comment begins with two slash characters (//) and runs for just one line. For multiline comments, we just place the slash characters at the beginning of each line.

EXERCISES 2.2

1. List the rules for forming valid identifiers.
2. Which of the following are valid identifiers? Give an explanation for those that are invalid.
   a. **`7Up`**
   b. **`Payroll`**
   c. **`Room222`**
   d. **`Name List`**
   e. **`A`**
   f. **`A1`**
   g. **`1A`**
   h. **`Time&Place`**
   i. **`const`**
   j. **`X*Y`**
   k. **`ListOfEmployees`**
   l. **`Lima,Ohio`**
3. Which of the following are valid program headings? Give an explanation for those that are invalid.
   a. **`int main()`**
   b. **`PROGRAM GettingBetter (output);`**
   c. **`main(input, output)`**
   d. **`MAIN();`**
4. Name the five main sections of a simple C++ program.
5. Write constant definition statements for the following.
   a. your gender
   b. your age
   c. pi

6. Find all errors in the following definitions and declarations.
   a. `const char ch 'a';`
      `float salary;`
   b. `int const;`
   c. `int 32;`
   d. `area int;`
   e. `char int;`
7. Discuss the significance of a semicolon in writing C++ statements. Include an explanation of when semicolons are not required in a program.

2.3 Data Types and Output

OBJECTIVES

- to understand and be able to use the data types **`int`**, **`float`**, and **`char`**
- to understand the difference between the floating-point form and the fixed-point form of decimal numbers
- to understand the syntax for and use of output statements
- to be able to format output

Type int

C++ requires that all variables used in a program be given a *data type.* Since numbers in some form will be used in computer programs, we will first look at numbers of type **`int`**. Values of this type are used to represent integers or whole numbers. Some rules that must be observed when using integers follow:

1. Plus (+) signs do not have to be written before a positive integer, though they may be.
2. Minus (–) signs must be written when using a negative number.
3. Decimal points cannot be used when writing integers. Although 14 and 14.0 have the same value, 14.0 is not of type **`int`**.
4. Commas cannot be used when writing integers; hence, 271,362 is not allowed; it must be written as 271362.
5. Leading zeros should be avoided. If you use leading zeros, the compiler will interpret the number as an octal (base 8) number.

There is a limit on the largest and the smallest integer constants. The way you determine this limit is discussed in Chapter 3. Different machines have different values for these constants; you should check your C++ implementation to see what they are. Operations with integers and integer variables are examined in Chapter 3.

C++ also supports the data types **`short int`** and **`long int`**, which represent, respectively, a smaller and a larger range of integer values than **`int`**. Adding the prefix **`unsigned`** to any of these types means that you wish to represent nonnegative integers only. For example, the declaration

```
unsigned short int x, y;
```

reserves memory for representing two relatively small nonnegative integers.

Type float

Values of type **`float`** are used to represent real numbers. Plus (+) and minus (–) signs for data of type **`float`** are treated exactly as with integers. When working with real numbers, however, trailing zeros are ignored. As with integers, leading zeros should be avoided. Thus, +23.45, 23.45, and 23.450 have the same value, but 023.45 may be interpreted by some C++ compilers as an octal number followed by a decimal point, which is a syntax error.

All real numbers seen thus far have been in *fixed-point* form. The computer will also accept real numbers in *floating-point* or exponential form. Floating-point form is an equivalent method for writing numbers in scientific notation to accommodate numbers that may have very large or very small values. The difference is that, instead of writing the base decimal times some power of 10, the base decimal is followed by E and the appropriate power of 10. For example, 231.6 in scientific notation would be 2.316×10^2 and in floating-point form would be 2.316E2. Table 2.4 sets forth several fixed-point decimal numbers with the equivalent scientific notation and floating-point form. Floating-point form for real numbers does not require exactly one digit on the left of the decimal point. In fact, it can be used with no decimal points written. To illustrate, 4.16E1, 41.6, 416.0E–1, and 416E–1 have the same value and all are permissible. However, it is not a good habit to use floating-point form for decimal numbers unless exactly one nonzero digit appears on the left of the decimal. In most other cases, fixed-point form is preferable.

In addition to **`float`**, C++ supports the types **`double`** and **`long double`**. The latter two data types support increasingly precise representation of real numbers, at the cost of more computer memory. Also, **`double`** is the data type of any numeric literal that is expressed in fixed-point notation in a program. However, to avoid confusion, we will use the term "real number" or **`float`** to characterize fixed-point numeric literals in this text.

When using real numbers in a program, you may use either fixed-point or floating-point form. But the computer prints out real numbers in floating-point form unless you specify otherwise. Formatting of output is discussed later in this section.

Type char

Another data type available in C++ is **`char`**, which is used to represent character data. In standard C++, data of type **`char`** can be only a single character (which could be a blank space). These characters come from an available character set that differs somewhat from computer to computer, but always includes the letters of the alphabet (uppercase and lowercase); the digits 0, 1 , 2, 3, 4, 5, 6, 7, 8, and 9; and special symbols such as #, &, !, +, –, *, /, and so on. A common character set is given in Appendix 4.

Character constants of type **`char`** must be enclosed in single quotation marks when used in a program. Otherwise, they are treated as variables and subsequent use may cause a compilation error. Thus, to use the letter A as a constant, you would type **`'A'`**. The use of digits and standard operation symbols as characters is also permitted; for example, **`'7'`** would be considered a character, but 7 is an integer.

Several nonprintable characters, such as the backspace, the horizontal tab, the newline, and the bell, are represented by using the backslash (\) in an escape sequence. For example, to use the backspace character, one would type '\b' in a C++ program.

Strings

Strings are used in programs to represent textual information, such as the names of people and companies.

◇ **TABLE 2.4**
Forms for equivalent numbers

Fixed-point	Scientific Notation	Floating-point
46.345	4.6345×10	4.6345E1
59214.3	5.92143×10^4	5.92143E4
0.00042	4.2×10^{-4}	4.2E–4
36000000000.0	3.6×10^{10}	3.6E10
0.000000005	5.0×10^{-9}	5.0E–9
-341000.0	-3.41×10^5	-3.41E5

In C++, a string constant must be enclosed in double quotation marks. The following are examples of strings:

1. **`"Hello world!"`**
2. **`"125"`**
3. **`""`**
4. **`"\n"`**
5. **`"\t"`**
6. **`"the word \"hello\""`**

Note the difference between the second string, "125", and the integer value 125. They are different data types in C++. The third string, " ", is the empty string, because it contains no characters.

The fourth string contains a backslash (\) or escape character. This character tells the compiler to treat the following character, **`'n'`**, not as a literal character, but as a special code that represents a special character, in this case, a newline character. Thus, the string **`"\n"`** really contains just one character, the newline character. The fifth string represents a horizontal tab character. The last string uses two backslash characters to wrap double quotes around the word "hello". Note that when you wish the double quotes to appear literally in a string, they must be escaped with the slash character. In general, to mention any special character in a string, including the backslash character itself, you prefix it with a backslash character. Consult your local implementation for a list of these special characters.

Students with experience in BASIC usually expect the equivalent of a string variable for storing names and other textual information. String variables are discussed in Chapter 7.

Output

The goal of most programs is to output something. What gets printed (either on paper, on a screen, or in a file) is referred to as output. The simplest way to produce screen output in C++ is to direct a value to the *standard output stream.* This stream is made available to a program by including the C++ library file **`iostream.h`**:

```
#include <iostream.h>
```

The name of this stream is **`cout`**, and the operator used to direct output to this stream is **`<<`**. Output values are usually character strings, numbers, numerical expressions, or variable names. The general form of an output statement is

```
cout << expression 1 << expression 2 << . . . << expression n;
```

You can think of **`cout`** as the name of an intelligent agent. This agent receives a message from you that you wish to display a value on the terminal screen and it then performs the desired action. The agent may also understand messages to format the output in a special way. We will discuss the methods for creating our own intelligent agents when we introduce object-oriented programming in Chapters 7 through 11.

Normally, the output statement causes subsequent output to be on the same line. If you wish subsequent output to begin on the next line, you must direct an end-of-line character to the standard output stream. When output is to a monitor, the following two lines each cause the cursor to move to the next line for the next I/O operation:

```
cout << '\n';

cout << endl;
```

The following are examples of single-line and multiline output:

```
cout << "This is a test. ";

cout << "How many lines are printed?" << endl;
```

causes the output

```
This is a test. How many lines are printed?
```

whereas,

```
cout << "This is a test." << endl;

cout << "How many lines are printed?" << endl;
```

causes the output

```
This is a test.
How many lines are printed?
```

Character strings can be printed by enclosing the string in double quotation marks. Numerical data can be printed by typing the desired number or numbers. Thus,

```
cout << 100;
```

produces

```
100
```

EXAMPLE 2.1

Let's write a complete C++ program to print the address

1403 South Drive
Apartment 3B
Pittsburgh, PA 15238

A complete program to print this is

```
// Program file: printaddr.cpp
// This program prints an address

#include <iostream.h>

int main()
{
        cout << "1403 South Drive" << endl;

        cout << "Apartment 3B" << '\n';

        cout << "Pittsburgh, PA 15238" << "\n";

        return 0;
}
```

Note the different ways of instructing the computer to output a newline to the terminal screen.

Formatting Integers

Output of integers can be controlled by *formatting.* First, you must include the library file **iomanip.h** to have access to the formatting functions:

```
#include <iomanip.h>
```

Second, you specify the field width for the next output directive by calling the **setw** function with the size of the number of columns to be filled. Then, on the next output directive, the value of an integer, identifier, or integer expression will be printed on the right side of the specified field. Thus,

```
cout << setw(10) << 100 << setw(10) << 50 << setw(10) << 25 ;
```

produces

```
-------100-------50--------25
```

where each "-" indicates a blank.

Some illustrations for formatting integer output are

Program Statement	Output
`cout << setw(6) << 123;`	`---123`
`cout <<15 << setw(5) << 10;`	`15---10`
`cout << setw(7) << -263 << setw(3) << 21`	`----263-21`
`cout << setw(6) << +5062;`	`--5062`
`cout << setw(3) << 65221;`	`65221`

The output of end of lines at the beginning and end of the executable section will separate desired output from other messages or directions. Thus, the previous program for printing an address could have been

```
int main()
{
        cout << endl << endl;

        cout << "1403 South Drive" << endl;

        cout << "Apartment 3B" << endl;

        cout << "Pittsburgh, PA, 15238" << endl;

        return 0;
}
```

Formatting Real Numbers

Output of real numbers can also be controlled by formatting. First, you must include the **iomanip.h** library to have access to the formatting functions. As with integers, you use **setw** to specify the total field width of each real number. However, if you wish real numbers to be displayed in decimal form, you must specify a fixed-point format with the number of positions to the right of the decimal. The following output statement does this for a desired precision of two places to the right of the decimal:

```
cout << fixed << showpoint << setprecision(2);
```

Then,

```
cout << setw(8) << 736.23;
```

produces

```
--736.23
```

The functions **fixed** and **showpoint** instruct the output stream to display real numbers in fixed-point format using a decimal point. The function **setprecision** specifies the number of digits to the right of the decimal point to be displayed. A precision of 2 will remain in effect for all subsequent outputs of real numbers, until the programmer specifies a change with another **setprecision** function.

Formatting real numbers causes the following to happen:

1. The decimal point uses one position in the specified field width.
2. Trailing zeros are printed to the specified number of positions to the right of the decimal.
3. Leading plus (+) signs are omitted.
4. Leading minus (–) signs are printed and use one position of the specified field.
5. Digits appearing to the right of the decimal have been rounded rather than truncated.

As with integers, if a field width is specified that is too small, most versions of C++ will default to the minimum width required to present all digits to the left of the decimal as well as the specified digits to the right of the decimal. Real numbers in floating-point form can also be used in a formatted output statement. The following table illustrates how output using data of type **float** can be formatted.

Program Statement	Output
`cout << setprecision(3) << setw(10) << 765.432;`	`---765.432`
`cout << setprecision(2) << setw(10) << 023.14;`	`-----23.14`
`cout << setprecision(2) << setw(10) << 65.50`	`-----65.50`
`cout << setprecision(2) << setw(10) << +341.2;`	`----341.20`
`cout << setprecision(2) << setw(10) << -341.2;`	`----341.20`
`cout << setprecision(2) << setw(10) << 16.458;`	`-----16.46`
`cout << setprecision(4) << setw(10) << 0.00456;`	`----0.0046`
`cout << setprecision(2) << setw(6) << 136.51;`	`136.51`

Formatting Strings

Strings and string constants can be formatted by using **setw** to specify field width. The string will be right justified in the field. Unlike real numbers, strings are truncated when necessary. Thus,

```
cout << "field" << setw(10) << "width" << setw(15) <<
"check" << endl;
```

would produce

```
field-----width----------check

setw(10)   setw(15)
```

and

```
cout << setw(4) << "check" << endl;
```

would produce

```
chec
```

Test Programs

Programmers should develop the habit of using *test programs* to improve their knowledge and programming skills. Test programs should be relatively short and written to provide an answer to a specific question. Test programs allow you to play with the computer. You can answer "What if . . . " questions by adopting a "try it and see" attitude. This is an excellent way to become comfortable with your computer and the programming language you are using.

EXERCISES 2.3

1. Which of the following are valid **int** constants? Explain why the others are invalid.

a. `521`
b. `-32.0`
c. `5,621`
d. `+00784`
e. `+65`
f. `6521492183`
g. `-0`

2. Which of the following are valid **float** constants? Explain why the others are invalid.

a. `26.3`
b. `+181.0`
c. `-.14`
d. `492.`
e. `+017.400`
f. `43E2`
g. `-0.2E-3`
h. `43,162.3E5`
i. `-176.52E+1`
j. `1.43000E+2`

3. Change the following fixed-point decimals to floating-point decimals with exactly one nonzero digit to the left of the decimal.

a. `173.0`
b. `743927000000.0`
c. `-0.000000023`
d. `+014.768`
e. `-5.2`

4. Change the following floating-point decimals to fixed-point decimals.
   a. `-1.0046E+3`
   b. `4.2E-8`
   c. `9.020E10`
   d. `-4.615230E3`
   e. `-8.02E-3`
5. Indicate the data type for each of the following:
   a. `-720`
   b. `-720.0`
   c. `150E3`
   d. `150`
   e. `"150"`
   f. `"23.4E2"`
   g. `23.4E-2`
6. Write and run test programs for each of the following:
   a. Examine the output for a decimal number without field width specified; for example,

```
cout << 2.31;
```

   b. Try to print a message without using quotation marks for a character string; for example,

```
cout << Hello;
```

7. For each of the following, write a program that would produce the indicated output.

```
a. Score                  b. Price

86                           $19.94
82                          $100.00
79                           $58.95
```

   where "S" is in column 10. where "P" is in column 50.

8. Assume the hourly wages of five students are 3.65, 4.10, 2.89, 5.00, and 4.50. Write a program that produces the following output, where the "E" of Employee is in column 20.

```
Employee     Hourly Wage

1              $  3.65
2              $  4.10
3              $  2.89
4              $  5.00
5              $  4.50
```

9. What is the output from the following segment of code on your printer or terminal?

```
cout << "My test average is" << 87.5;
cout << setw(20) << "My test average is"
     << setw(10) << 87.5;
cout << setw(25) << "My test average is"
     << setprecision(2) << setw(10) << 87.5;
cout << setw(25) << "My test average is"
     << setprecision(2) << setw(6) << 87.5;
```

10. Write a program that produces the following output. Start Student in column 20 and Test in column 40.

```
Student Name                   Test Score

Adams, Mike                      73

Conley, Theresa                  86

Samson, Ron                      92

O'Malley, Colleen                81
```

11. The Great Lakes Shipping Company is going to use a computer program to generate billing statements for their customers. The heading of each bill is to be

```
         GREAT LAKES SHIPPING COMPANY
         SAULT STE. MARIE, MICHIGAN

Thank you for doing business with our company. The information listed below
was used to determine your total cargo fee. We hope you were satisfied with
our service.

      CARGO       TONNAGE          RATE/TON          TOTAL DUE
```

Write a complete C++ program that produces this heading.

12. What output is produced by each of the following statements or sequence of statements when executed by the computer?

a.
```
cout << 1234 << setw(8) << 1234 << setw(6) << 1234;
```
b.
```
cout << setw(4) <<12 << setw(4) << -21 << setw(4)
     << 120;
```
c.
```
cout << "FIGURE AREA PERIMETER";
cout << "";
cout << endl;
cout << "SQUARE" << setw(5) << 16 << setw(12) <<16;
cout << endl;
cout << "RECT " << setw(5) << 24 << setw(12) << 20;
```

13. Write a complete program that produces the following table:

```
WIDTH        LENGTH        AREA
  4            2             8

 21            5           105
```

14. What output is produced when each of the following is executed?

a.
```
cout << setprecision(2) << setw(15) << 2.134;
```
b.
```
cout << setprecision(2) << setw(5) << 423.73;
```
c.
```
cout << setprecision(3) << setw(8) << -42.1;
```
d.
```
cout << setprecision(2) << setw(2) << -4.21E3;
```
e.
```
cout << 10.25;
```
f.
```
cout << 1.25 << setprecision(2) << setw(6)
     << 1.25 << setprecision(1)
     << setw(2) << 1.25;
```

15. Write a complete program that produces the following output:

Hourly Wage	Hours Worked	Total
5.0	20.0	100.00
7.50	15.25	114.375

16. What type of data would be used to print each of the following?
 a. your age
 b. your grade-point average
 c. your name
 d. a test score
 e. the average test score
 f. your grade

SUMMARY

Key Terms

comments	keyword	standard identifier
constant definition	module	standard simple type
data type	module specifications	statement section
declaration section	object-oriented design	stepwise refinement
executable statement	program heading	string
fixed point	pseudocode	string constant
floating point	reserved words	structure chart
formatting	software engineering	top-down design
identifier	software system life cycle	variable declaration

Keywords

int	**long**	**char**
float	**unsigned**	**const**
short	**double**	

Key Concepts

- Six steps in problem solving include the following: analyze the problem, develop an algorithm, document the program, write code for the program, run the program, and test the results against answers manually computed with paper and pencil.
- Top-down design is a process of dividing tasks into subtasks until each subtask can be readily accomplished.
- Stepwise refinement refers to refinements of tasks into subtasks.
- A structure chart is a graphic representation of the relationship between modules.
- Software engineering is the process of developing and maintaining large software systems.
- The software system life cycle consists of the following phases: analysis, design, coding, testing/verification, maintenance, and obsolescence.
- Valid identifiers must begin with a letter or underscore and they can contain only letters, digits, and underscores.
- The five components of a simple C++ program are preprocessor directives, constant and type definitions, program heading, declaration section, and executable statement section.
- Semicolons are used to terminate most executable statements.
- Extra spaces and blank lines are ignored in C++.
- Output is generated by using **cout** and **<<**.

- Strings are formatted using the function **`setw`** with a positive integer that specifies the total field width, for example,

```
cout << setw(30) << "This is a string";
```

- The following table summarizes the use of the data types **`int`**, **`float`**, and **`char`**.

Data Type	Permissible Data	Formatting
`int`	Numeric	**`setw`**(an integer); for example **`cout << setw(6) << 25;`**
`float`	Numeric	**`fixed`**, **`showpoint`**, **`setprecision`**(an integer), and **`setw`**(an integer); for example **`cout << showpoint`** **`<< setprecision(2)`** **`<< setw(8) << 1234.5;`**
`char`	Character	**`setw`**(an integer); for example **`cout << setw(6) << 'A';`**

PROGRAMMING PROBLEMS AND PROJECTS

1. Write and run a short program to print your initials in block letters. Your output could look like

```
 JJJJJ            A           CCC
   J             A A         C   C
   J            A   A       C
   J           AAAAAAA      C
J  J          A       A      C   C
 JJJ         A         A      CCC
```

2. Design a simple picture and print it using output statements. If you plan the picture using a sheet of graph paper, keeping track of spacing will be easier.
3. Write and run a program to print your mailing address.
4. Our lady of Mercy Hospital prints billing statements for patients when they are ready to leave the hospital. Write a program that prints a heading for each statement as follows:

```
////////////////////////////////////////////////
/                                              /
/                                              /
/             Our Lady of Mercy Hospital       /
/                                              /
/                                              /
/                                              /
/                                              /
/                1306 Central City             /
/                                              /
/                                              /
/                Phone (416) 333-5555          /
/
/                                              /
/
/                                              /
/
////////////////////////////////////////////////
```

5. Your computer science instructor wants course and program information included as part of every assignment. Write a program that can be used to print this information. Sample output should look like this:

```
****************************************
*                                      *
*      Author:           Mary Smith    *
*      Course:           CPS-150       *
*      Assignment:       Program #3    *
*                                      *
*      Due Date:         September 18  *
*      Instructor:       Mr. Samson    *
*                                      *
****************************************
```

6. As part of a programming project that will compute and print grades for each student in your class, you have been asked to write a program that produces a heading for each student report. The columns in which the various headings should be are as follows:
   the border for the class name starts in column 30
   Student Name starts in column 20
   Test Average starts in column 40
   Grade starts in column 55.

   Write a program to print the heading as follows:

```
*************************
*                       *
*   CPS 150      C++    *
*                       *
*************************

Student Name   Test Average   Grade
```

CHAPTER 3 More Problem Solving Fundamentals: Calculation and Input

CHAPTER OUTLINE

You have probably used a pocket calculator. Pocket calculators provide a set of built-in arithmetic functions. Many pocket calculators also provide built-in constants, such as PI, and users can program them to perform a series of functions that share data with variables. In this chapter we will discuss all of these concepts, including arithmetic operations, using data in a program, obtaining input, and using constants and variables. We will also discuss the use of functions to perform standard operations such as finding a square root or raising a number to a given power.

3.1 Arithmetic in C++

OBJECTIVES

- to understand what an expression is in C++
- to be able to evaluate arithmetic expressions using data of type **int**
- to be able to evaluate arithmetic expressions using data of type **float**
- to understand the order of operations for evaluating expressions
- to be able to identify mixed-mode expressions
- to be able to distinguish between valid and invalid mixed-mode expressions
- to be able to evaluate mixed-mode expressions

Basic Operations for Integers

Integer arithmetic in C++ allows the operations of addition, subtraction, multiplication, division, and modulus to be performed. The notation for these operations is shown on Table 3.1.

In a standard integer division problem, there is a quotient and a remainder. In C++, the slash (/) produces the quotient and **%** produces the remainder when the first operand is positive. For example, in the problem 17 divided by 3, **17 / 3** produces 5, and **17 % 3** produces 2. Avoid using / 0 (zero) and % 0 (zero). Division by zero will cause a run-time error. Several integer expressions and their values are shown in Table 3.2. Notice that when 3 is multiplied by –2, the expression is written as **3 * (-2)** rather than **3 * -2**. The parentheses make the expression more readable, but are not required.

Order of Operations for Integers

Expressions involving more than one operation are frequently used when writing programs. When this happens, it is important to know the order in which these operations are performed. The priorities for these are as follows:

1. All expressions within a set of parentheses are evaluated first. If there are parentheses within parentheses (the parentheses are nested), the innermost expressions are evaluated first.

◇ **TABLE 3.1**
Integer arithmetic operations

Symbol	Operation	Example	Value
+	Addition	`3 + 5`	8
-	Subtraction	`43 - 25`	18
*	Multiplication	`4 * 7`	28
/	Division	`9 / 2`	4
%	Modulus	`9 % 2`	1

◇ **TABLE 3.2**
Values of integer expressions

Expression	Value
`-3 + 2`	-1
`2 - 3`	-1
`-3 * 2`	-6
`3 * (-2)`	-6
`-3 * (-2)`	6
`17 / 3`	5
`17 % 3`	2
`17 / (-3)`	-5
`-17 / 3`	-5
`-17 % 7`	3
`-17 / (-3)`	5

◇ **TABLE 3.3**
Integer arithmetic priority

Expression or Operation	Priority
`( )`	1. Evaluate from inside out.
`*, %, /`	2. Evaluate from left to right.
`+, -`	3. Evaluate from left to right.

2. The operations *, %, and / are evaluated next in order from left to right.
3. The operations + and – are evaluated last from left to right.

These operations are the operations of algebra and are summarized in Table 3.3.

To illustrate how expressions are evaluated, consider the values of the expressions listed in Table 3.4. As expressions get more elaborate, it can be helpful to list partial evaluations in a manner similar to the order in which the computer performs the evaluations. For example, suppose the expression

(3 – 4) + 18 / 5 + 2

is to be evaluated. If we consider the order in which subexpressions are evaluated, we get

```
(3 - 4) + 18 / 5 + 2
   ↓
  -1    + 18 / 5 + 2
               ↓
  -1    +      3 + 2
        ↓
        2        + 2
               ↓
               4
```

◇ TABLE 3.4
Priority of operations

Expression	Value
`3 - 4 * 5`	-17
`3 - (4 * 5)`	-17
`(3 - 4) * 5`	-5
`3 * 4 - 5`	7
`3 * (4 - 5)`	-3
`17 - 10 - 3`	4
`17 - (10 - 3)`	10
`(17 - 10) - 3`	4
`-42 + 50 % 17`	-26

Using Modulus and Division

Modulus and division can be used when it is necessary to perform conversions within arithmetic operations. For example, consider the problem of adding two weights given in units of pounds and ounces. This problem can be solved by converting both weights to ounces, adding the ounces, and then converting the total ounces to pounds and ounces. The conversion from ounces to pounds can be accomplished by using modulus and division. If the total number of ounces is 243, then **243 / 16** yields the number of pounds (15), and **243 % 16** yields the number of ounces (3).

Representation of Integers

Computer representation of integers is different from what we see when we work with integers. Integers are stored in *binary notation,* and the operations performed on them are those of *binary arithmetic.* Thus, the integer 19, which can be written as

$$\begin{aligned} 19 &= 16 + 0 + 0 + 2 + 1 \\ &= 1 * 2^4 + 0 * 2^3 + 0 * 2^2 + 1 * 2^1 + 1 * 2^0 \end{aligned}$$

is stored as 1 0 0 1 1. This binary number is actually stored in a *word* in memory, which consists of several individual locations called bits, as mentioned in Chapter 1. The number of bits used to store an integer is machine dependent. If you use a 16-bit machine, then 19 is

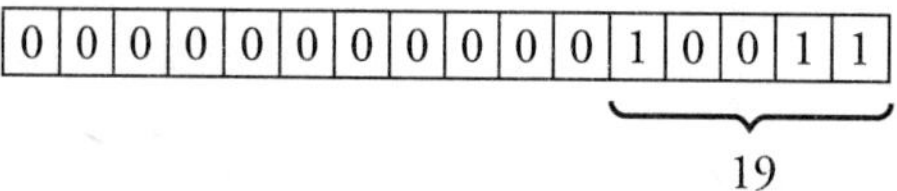

In this representation, the leftmost bit is reserved for the sign of the integer (1 meaning negative, 0 meaning positive).

We can make two observations regarding the storage and mechanics of the operations on integers. First, integers produce exact answers; numbers are stored exactly (up to the limits of the machine). Second, a maximum and a minimum number can be represented. In a 16-bit machine, these numbers are

0	1	1	1	1	1	1	1	1	1	1	1	1	1	1	1

where the leftmost 0 represents a positive number equaling 32,767, and

1	0	0	0	0	0	0	0	0	0	0	0	0	0	0	0

where the leftmost 1 represents a negative number equaling -32,768.

To find out what the minimum and maximum integer values for your particular system are, you can use the C++ library constants discussed in Section 3.4.

If a program contains an integer operation that produces a number outside of your machine's range, this is referred to as *integer overflow,* which means that the number is too large or too small to be stored. Ideally, an error message would be printed when such a situation arises. However, many systems merely store an unpredictable value and continue with the program. In Section 5.3, we will discuss how to protect a program against this problem.

Basic Operations for Real Numbers

The operations of addition, subtraction, and multiplication are the same for data of type **`float`** as for integers. Additionally, real division is now permitted. Modulus is restricted to data of type **`int`**. The symbol for division of data of type **`float`** is the slash (/). The *real arithmetic operations* are shown on Table 3.5.

◇ TABLE 3.5
Real arithmetic operations

Symbol	Operation	Example	Value
+	Addition	**`4.2 + 19.36`**	23.56
-	Subtraction	**`19.36 - 4.2`**	15.16
*	Multiplication	**`3.1 * 2.0`**	6.2
/	Division	**`54.6 / 2.0`**	27.3

Division is given the same priority as multiplication when arithmetic expressions are evaluated by the computer. The rules for order of operation are the same as those for evaluating integer arithmetic expressions. A summary of these operations is shown in Table 3.6. Some example calculations using data of type **`float`** are shown on Table 3.7.

◇ TABLE 3.6
Real arithmetic priority

Expression or Operation	Priority
( )	1. Evaluate from inside out.
*, /	2. Evaluate from left to right.
+, -	3. Evaluate from left to right.

◇ TABLE 3.7
Type float calculations

Expression	Value
`-1.0 + 3.5 + 2.0`	4.5
`-1.0 + 3.5 * 2.0`	6.0
`2.0 * (1.2 - 4.3)`	-6.2
`2.0 * 1.2 - 4.3`	-1.9
`-12.6 / 3.0 + 3.0`	-1.2
`-12.6 / (3.0 + 3.0)`	-2.1

As expressions get a bit more complicated, it is again helpful to write out the expression and evaluate it step by step. For example,

```
18.2 + (-4.3) * (10.1 + (72.3 / 3.0 - 4.5))
                                ↓
18.2 + (-4.3) * (10.1 +    (24.1     - 4.5))
                                      ↓
18.2 + (-4.3) * (10.1 +            19.6)
                            ↓
18.2 + (-4.3) *            29.7
                      ↓
18.2 +           -127.71
          ↓
     -109.51
```

Representation of Real Numbers

As with integers, real numbers are stored and operations are performed using binary notation. Unlike integers, however, the storage and representation of real numbers frequently produce answers that are not exact. For example, an operation such as

1 / 3.0

produces the repeating decimal .3333. . . . At some point, this decimal must be truncated or rounded so that it can be stored. Such conversions produce *round-off errors.*

Now let us consider some errors that occur when working with real numbers. A value very close to zero may be stored as 0. Thus, you may think you are working with

$1.23 * 10^{-20} = .0000000000000000000123$

but, in fact, this value may have been stored as a zero. This condition is referred to as *underflow.* Generally, this would not be a problem because replacing numbers very close to zero with 0 does not affect the accuracy of most answers. However, sometimes this replacement can make a difference; therefore, you should be aware of the limitations of the system on which you are working.

Because operations with real numbers are not stored exactly, errors referred to as *representational errors* can be introduced. To illustrate, suppose we are using a machine that only yields three digits of accuracy (most machines exhibit much greater accuracy) and we want to add the three numbers 45.6, –45.5, and .215. The order in which we add these numbers makes a difference in the result we obtain. For example, –45.5 + 45.6 yields .1. Then, .1 + .215 yields .315. Thus, we have

(–45.5 + 45.6) + .215 = .315

However, if we consider 45.6 + .215 first, then the arithmetic result is 45.815. Since our hypothetical computer only yields three digits of accuracy, this result will be stored as 45.8. Then, –45.5 + 45.8 yields .3. Thus, we have

–45.5 + (45.6 + .215) = .3

This operation produces a representational error.

Another form of representational error occurs when numbers of substantially different size are used in an operation. For example, consider the expression 2 + .0005. We would expect this value to be 2.0005, but stored to only three digits of accuracy, the result would be 2.00. In effect, the smaller of the two numbers disappears or is cancelled from the expression. This form of error is called a *cancellation error.*

Although representational and cancellation errors cannot be avoided, their effects can be minimized. Operations should be grouped in such a way that numbers of approximately the same magnitude are used together before the resulting operand is used with another number. For example, all very small numbers should be summed before adding them to a large number.

Attempting to store very large real numbers can result in *real overflow.* In principle, real numbers are stored with locations reserved for the exponents. An oversimplified illustration using base 10 digits is

1	2	3	+	0	8

for the number 123 * 10^8. Different computers place different limits on the size of the exponent that can be stored. An attempt to use numbers outside the defined range causes overflow in much the same way that integer overflow occurs, with results that depend on the particular run-time system.

Mixed-Mode Expressions

Arithmetic expressions using data of two or more types are called *mixed-mode expressions.* In a mixed-mode expression involving both **int** and **float** data types, the value will be of type **float**. When formatting output of mixed-mode expressions, always format for real numbers. *Note:* Avoid using % with mixed-mode expressions. The way in which C++ deals with mixed-mode expressions in general is fairly complex and is discussed in detail in Section 3.6. You may wish to avoid using mixed-mode expressions until you read that section.

EXERCISES 3.1

1. Find the value of each of the following expressions:
   a. `17 - 3 * 2`
   b. `-15 * 3 - 4`
   c. `123 % 5`
   d. `123 / 5`
   e. `5 * 123 / 5 - 123 % 5`
   f. `-21 * 3 * (-1)`
   g. `14 * (3 - 18 / 4) - 50`
   h. `100 - (4 * (3 - 2)) * (-2)`
   i. `-56 % 3`
   j. `14 * 8 % 5 - 23 / (-4)`
2. Find the value of each of the following expressions:
   a. `3.21 - - 5.02 - 6.1`
   b. `6.0 / 2.0 * 3.0`
   c. `6.0 / (2.0 + 3.0)`
   d. `-20.5 * (2.1 + 2.0)`
   e. `-2.0 * ((56.8 / 4.0 + 0.8) + 5.0)`
   f. `1.04E2 * 0.02E3`
   g. `800.0E-2 / 4.0 - 15.3`

3. Which of the following are valid expressions? For those that are valid, indicate whether they are of type **int** or **float**.
   a. `18 - (5 * 2)`
   b. `(18 - 5) * 2`
   c. `18 - 5 * 2.0`
   d. `25 * (14 % 7.0)`
   e. `1.4E3 * 5`
   f. `28 / 7`
   g. `28.0 / 4`
   h. `10.5 + 14 / 3`
   i. `24 / 6 / 3`
   j. `24 / (6 / 3)`
4. Evaluate each of the valid expressions in Exercise 3.
5. What is the output produced by the following program?

```
#include <iostream.h>
#include <iomanip.h>

int main()
{
        cout << showpoint << fixed << setprecision(3);
        cout << endl << "Expression Value" << endl;
        cout << "----------------" << endl << endl;
        cout << " 10 / 5" << setw(12) << 10/5 << endl;
        cout << " 2.0+7*(-1)" << 2.0 + 7 * (-1) << endl << endl;
        return 0;
}
```

3.2 Using Variables

OBJECTIVES

- to understand the utilization of memory for storing data
- to distinguish between the name of a memory location and the value stored in a memory location
- to be able to use variables in assignment statements, expressions, and output statements

Memory Locations

It is frequently necessary to store values for later use. This is done by putting the value into a *memory location* and using a symbolic name to refer to this location. If the contents of the location are to be changed during a program, the symbolic name is referred to as a *variable;* if the contents are not to be changed, it is referred to as a *constant.*

A graphic way to think about memory locations is to envision them as boxes; each box is named and a value is stored inside. For example, suppose a program is written to add a sequence of numbers. If we name the memory location to be used **sum**, initially we have

?

sum

which depicts a memory location that has been reserved and can be accessed by a reference to **sum**. If we then add the integers 10, 20 , and 30 and store them in **sum**, we have

60

sum

It is important to distinguish between the name of a memory location (**sum**) and the value or contents of a memory location (**60**). The name does not change during

A NOTE OF INTEREST

Herman Hollerith

Herman Hollerith (1860–1929) was hired by the U.S. Census Bureau in 1879 at the age of 19. Since the 1880 census was predicted to take a long time to complete (it actually took until 1887), Hollerith was assigned the task of developing a mechanical method of tabulating census data. He introduced his census machine in 1887. It consisted of four parts:

1. A punched paper card that represented data using a special code (Hollerith code)
2. A card punch apparatus
3. A tabulator that read the punched cards
4. A sorting machine with 24 compartments.

The punched cards used by Hollerith were the same size as cards still in use until recently.

Using Hollerith's techniques and equipment, the 1890 census tabulation was completed in one-third the time required for the previous census tabulation. This included working with data for 12 million additional people.

Hollerith proceeded to form the Tabulating Machine Company (1896), which supplied equipment to census bureaus in the United States, Canada, and western Europe. After a disagreement with the census director, Hollerith began marketing his equipment in other commercial areas. Hollerith sold his company in 1911. It was later combined with 12 others to form the Computing-Tabulating-Recording Company, a direct ancestor of International Business Machines Corporation.

In the meantime, Hollerith's successor at the census bureau, James Powers, redesigned the census machine. He then formed his own company, which subsequently became Remington Rand, then Sperry Univac, and finally Unisys.

a program, but the contents can be changed as often as necessary. (Contents of memory locations that are referred to by constants cannot be changed.) If **30** were added to the contents in the previous example, the new value stored in **sum** could be depicted as

90

sum

Those symbolic names representing memory locations whose values will be changing must be declared before they are used (as indicated in Section 2.4); for example,

```
int sum;
```

Those that represent memory locations whose values will not be changing must also be defined before they are used.

Assignment Statements

Now we will examine how the contents of variables are manipulated. When variables are declared in a C++ program, they contain values. However, a programmer does not know what these values are. Henceforth, we shall denote these system-supplied values with a question mark (?). The programmer may put a value into a memory location with an *assignment statement* in the form of

<variable name> = <value>;

or

<variable name> = <expression>;

where **<variable name>** is the name of the memory location. For example, if **sum** has an unknown value, then

```
sum = 30;
```

changes

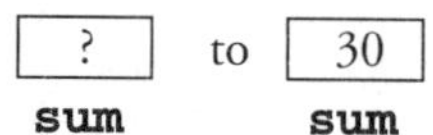

Some important rules follow concerning assignment statements:

1. The assignment is always made from right to left (←).
2. Constants cannot be on the left side of the assignment symbol.
3. The expression can be a constant, a constant expression, a variable that has previously been assigned a value, or a combination of variables and constants.
4. Normally, values on the right side of the assignment symbol are not changed by the assignment.
5. The variable and expression must be of compatible data types.
6. Only one value can be stored in a variable at a time, so the previous value of a variable is thrown away.

One common error that beginners make is trying to assign from left to right.

Repeated assignments can be made. For example, if **sum** is an integer variable, the statements

```
sum = 50;

sum = 70;

sum = 100;
```

produce first 50, then 70, and finally 100 as shown.

5ø 7ø 100

sum

In this sense, memory is destructible in that it retains only the last value assigned.

C++ variables are symbolic addresses that can hold values. When a variable is declared, the type of values it will store must be specified *(declared)*. Storing a value of the wrong type in a variable leads to a program error. This means that data types must be compatible when using assignment statements. For now, consider all of the basic data types—**char**, **int**, and **float**—as compatible with each other. This means that assignments of values to variables are allowed for any possible combination of these types on both sides of an assignment statement. Type compatibility and type conversion are discussed in Section 3.6.

Assignments of character constants to a character variable require that the constant be enclosed in single quotation marks. For example, if **letter** is of type **char** and you want to store the letter C in **letter**, use the assignment statement

```
letter = 'C';
```

This could be pictured as

C
letter

Furthermore, only one character can be assigned or stored in a character variable at a time.

Expressions

Actual use of variables in a program is usually more elaborate than what we have just seen. Variables may be used in any manner that does not violate their type declarations. This includes both arithmetic operations and assignment statements. For example, if **score1**, **score2**, **score3**, and **average** are **float** variables,

```
score1 = 72.3;

score2 = 89.4;

score3 = 95.6;

average = (score1 + score2 + score3) / 3.0;
```

is a valid fragment of code.

Now consider the problem of accumulating a total. Assuming **new_score** and **total** are integer variables, the following code is valid:

```
total = 0;
new_score = 5;
total = total + new_score;
new_score = 7;
total = total + new_score;
```

As this code is executed, the values of memory locations for **total** and **new_score** could be depicted as

	total	new_score
`total = 0;`	0	?
`new_score = 5;`	0	5
`total = total + new_score;`	5	5
`new_score = 7;`	5	7
`total = total + new_score;`	12	7

Output

Variables and variable expressions can be used when creating output. When used in an output statement, they perform the same function as a constant. For example, if the assignment statement

```
age = 5;
```

has been made, these two statements

```
cout << 5;
cout << age;
```

produce the same output. If **age1**, **age2**, **age3**, and **sum** are integer variables and the assignments

```
age1 = 21;
age2 = 30;
age3 = 12;
sum = age1 + age2 + age3;
```

are made, then

```
cout << "The sum is" << 21 + 30 + 12;
cout << "The sum is" << age1 + age2 + age3;
cout << "The sum is" << sum;
```

all produce the same output.

Formatting variables and variable expressions in output statements follows the same rules that were presented in Chapter 2 for formatting constants. The statements needed to write the sum of the problem we just saw in a field width of four are

```
cout << "The sum is" << setw(4) << 21 + 30 + 12;
cout << "The sum is" << setw(4) << age1 + age2 + age3;
cout << "The sum is" << setw(4) << sum;
```

EXAMPLE 3.1

Suppose you want a program to print data about the cost of three textbooks and the average price of the books. The variable declaration section could include:

```
float math_text, bio_text, comp_sci_text, total, average;
```

A portion of the program could be

```
math_text = 23.95;

bio_text = 27.50;

comp_sci_text = 19.95;

total = math_text + bio_text + comp_sci_text;

average = total / 3;
```

The output could be created by

```
cout << setprecision(2) << endl;
cout << "Text                    Price" << endl;
cout << "----                    -----" << endl;
cout << endl;
cout << "Math" << setw(18) << math_text << endl;
cout << "Biology" setw(15) << bio_text << endl;
cout << "CompSci" << setw(15) << comp_sci_text << endl;
cout << endl;
```

```
cout << "Total" << setw(17) << total << endl;
cout << endl;
cout << "The average price is" << setw(7) << average << endl;
```

The output would be

```
Text                 Price
----                 -----

Math                 23.95

Biology              27.50

CompSci              19.95

Total                71.40

The average price is   23.80
```

Software Engineering

The communication aspect of software engineering can be simplified by judicious choices of meaningful identifiers. Systems programmers must be aware that over time many others will need to read and analyze the code. Some extra time spent thinking about and using descriptive identifiers provides great timesavings during the testing and maintenance phases. Code that is written using descriptive identifiers is referred to as *self-documenting code.*

EXERCISES 3.2

1. Assume the variable declaration section of a program is

   ```
   int age, IQ;
   float income;
   ```

   Indicate which of the following are valid assignment statements. If a statement is invalid, give the reason why.

   a. `age = 21;`
   b. `IQ = age + 100;`
   c. `IQ = 120.5;`
   d. `age + IQ = 150;`
   e. `income = 22000;`
   f. `income = 100 * (age + IQ);`
   g. `age = IQ / 3;`
   h. `IQ = 3 * age;`

2. Write and run a test program to illustrate what happens when values of one data type are assigned to variables of another type.

3. Suppose **a**, **b**, and **temp** have been declared as integer variables. Indicate the contents of **a** and **b** at the end of each sequence of statements.

   a.
   ```
   a = 5;
   b = -2;
   a = a + b;
   b = b - a;
   ```

   b.
   ```
   a = 31;
   b = 26;
   temp = a;
   a = b;
   b = temp;
   ```

c.
```
a = 0;
b = 7;
a = a + b % 2 * (-3);
b = b + 4 * a;
```

d.
```
a = -8;
b = 3;
temp = a + b;
a = 3 * b;
b = a;
temp = temp + a + b;
```

4. Suppose **x** and **y** are real variables and the assignments

```
x = 121.3;
y = 98.6;
```

have been made. What output statements would cause the following output?

a.
```
The value of x is  121.3
```

b.
```
The sum of x and y is  219.9
```

c.
```
x =             121.3
y =              98.6
               -------
Total =         219.9
```

5. Assume the variable declaration section of a program is

```
int age, height;
float weight;
char gender;
```

What output would be created by the following program fragment?

```
age = 23;
height = 73;
weight = 186.5;
gender = 'M';
cout << setprecision(1);
cout << "Gender" << setw(10) << gender << endl;
cout << "Age" << setw(14) << age << endl;
cout << "Height" << setw(11) << height << " inches" << endl;
cout << "Weight" << setw(14) << weight << " lbs" << endl;
```

6. Write a complete program that allows you to add five integers and then print
   a. The integers.
   b. Their sum.
   c. Their average.
7. Assume **ch** and **age** have been appropriately declared. What output is produced by the following?

```
ch = 'M';
age = 21;
cout  << setw(40) <<  "******************************" << endl;
cout << setw(11) << "*" << setw(29) << "*" << endl;
cout << setw(11) << "*"<< setw(7) << "Name" << setw(9) << "Age";
cout << setw(6) << "Gender" << setw(4) << "*" << endl;
cout << setw(11) << "*" setw(7) << "____" << setw(9) << "___" << setw(9)
     << "____" << setw(4) << "*" << endl;
cout << endl;
cout << setw(11) << "*" << setw(8) << "Jones" << setw(8) << age << setw(9) << Ch
     << setw(4) << "*" << endl;
```

```
cout << endl;
cout << setw(11) << "*" << setw(29) << "*" << endl;
cout << setw(40)  << "******************************"  <<  endl;
```

8. Assume the variable declaration section of a program is

```
int weight1, weight2;
float average_weight;
```

and the following assignment statements have been made:

```
weight1 = 165;
weight2 = 174;
average_weight = (weight1 + weight2) / 2;
```

a. What output would be produced by the following section of code?

```
cout << "Weight" << endl;
cout << "______" endl;
cout << endl;
cout << weight1 << endl;
cout << weight2 << endl;
cout << endl;
cout << "The average weight is" << (weight1 + weight2) / 2 << endl;
```

b. Write a segment of code to produce the following output (use **average_weight**).

```
              weight
              ------
                165
                174
                ---
Total           339
```
The average weight is 169.5 pounds.

9. Assume the variable declaration section of a program is **char letter;** and the following assignment has been made: **letter = 'A';** . What output is produced from the following segment of code?

```
cout << setw(40) << "This reviews string formatting" << endl;
cout << "When a letter" << letter << "is used" << endl;
cout << setw(14) << "Oops!" << setw(20) << "I forgot to format." << endl;
cout << setw(22) << "When a letter" << setw(2) << letter << setw(9) << "is used"
     << endl;
cout << setw(38) << "it is a string of length one." << endl;
```

3.3 Input

OBJECTIVES

- to be able to use the standard input stream and its operator to get data for a program
- to be able to design a program that supports interactive input of data

Earlier, "running a program" was subdivided into the three general categories of getting the data, manipulating it appropriately, and printing the results. Our work thus far has centered on creating output and manipulating data. We are now going to focus on how to get data for a program.

Input Statements

Data for a program are usually obtained from an input device, which can be a keyboard or disk. When such data are obtained from the keyboard, the standard input stream, **cin**, normally is associated with one of these input devices.

The standard input stream, **cin**, is used in a similar way to the standard output stream, **cout**. **cin** behaves like an intelligent agent that knows how to take input from the keyboard and pass it back to a program. To make **cin** available to a program, you must include the C++ library file **iostream.h**:

```
#include <iostream.h>
```

To obtain input from the standard input stream, you direct it into a variable with the operator >> (note that the arrows point in the opposite direction from the output operator, <<). For example, assume that **length** is a variable of type **int**. Then the following statement takes input from the keyboard and stores it in **length**:

```
cin >> length;
```

When an input statement is used to get data, the value of the data item is stored in the indicated memory location. Data read into a program must match the type of variable specified. To illustrate, if a variable declaration section includes

```
int age;
float wage;
```

and the data items are

```
21          5.25
```

then

```
cin >> age >> wage;
```

results in

21	5.25
wage	**wage**

Interactive Input

Interactive input refers to entering values from the keyboard while the program is running. An input statement causes the program to halt and wait for data items to be typed. For example, if you want to enter three scores at some point in a program, you can use

```
cin >> score1 >> score2 >> score3;
```

as program statements. At this point, you must enter at least three integers, separated by at least one blank space, and press <Enter>. The remaining part of the program is then executed. To illustrate, the following program reads in three integers and prints the integers and their average as output.

```
// Program file: input.cpp
// This program illustrates the use of input statements.

#include <iostream.h>
#include <iomanip.h>

const char SKIP = ' ';

int main ()
{
```

```
    int score1, score2, score3;
    float average;

    cin >> score1 >> score2 >> score3;
    average = float(score1 + score2 + score3) / 3;
    cout << endl;
    cout << setw(10) << SKIP << "The numbers are" << setw(4)
         << score1 << setw(4) << score2 << setw(4) << score3
         << endl;
    cout << endl;
    cout << setprecision(2);
    cout << setw(10) << SKIP << "Their average is" << setw(8)
         << average << endl;
    return 0;
}
```

When the program runs, if you type in

```
89 90 91
```

and press <Enter>, output is

```
The numbers are  89  90  91

Their average is   90.00
```

Interactive programs should have a prompting message to the user so the user knows what to do when the program pauses for input. For example, the problem in the previous example can be modified by the line

```
cout >> "Please enter 3 scores separated by spaces, ";
cout >> "and then press <Enter>. ";
```

before the line

```
cin >> score1 >> score2 >> score3;
```

The screen will display the message

```
Please enter 3 scores separated by spaces and then press <Enter>.
```

when the program is run. Another method for getting the three inputs mentioned above is to prompt the user for each one on a separate line. Clearly stated screen messages to the person running a program are what make a program *user-friendly.*

EXAMPLE 3.2

Pythagorean triples are sets of three integers that satisfy the Pythagorean theorem. That is, integers *a, b,* and *c* such that $a^2 + b^2 = c^2$. The integers 3, 4, and 5 make up such a triple because $3^2 + 4^2 = 5^2$. Formulas for generating Pythagorean triples are $a = m^2 - n^2$, $b = 2mn$, and $c = m^2 + n^2$ where m and n are positive integers such that $m > n$. The following interactive program allows the user to enter values for m and n and then have the Pythagorean triple printed:

```
// Program file: triples.cpp
// This program illustrates Pythagorean triples.
```

```
#include <iostream.h>
#include <iomanip.h>

int main ()
{

      int m, n, a, b, c;

      cout << "Enter a positive integer and press <Enter>. ";
      cin >> n;
      cout << "Enter a positive integer greater than " << n << endl;
      cout << "and press <Enter>. ";
      cin >> m;
      a = (m * m) - (n * n);
      b = 2 * m * n;
      c = (m * m) + (n * n);
      cout << endl;
      cout << "For m = " << m << " and n = " << n << endl;
      cout << "the Pythagorean triple is ";
      cout << setw(5) << a << setw(5) << b << setw(5) << c << endl;
      return 0;

}
```

Sample runs of this program (using data 1,2 and 2,5) produce the following:

```
Enter a positive integer and press <Enter>. 1
Enter a positive integer greater than 1 and press <Enter>. 2

For M = 2 and N = 1 the Pythagorean triple is 3 4 5

Enter a positive integer and press <Enter>. 2
Enter a positive integer greater than 2 and press <Enter>. 5

For M = 5 and N = 2 the Pythagorean triple is 21 20 29
```

Reading Numeric Data

Reading numeric data into a program is reasonably straightforward. At least one character of whitespace must be used to separate numbers. Whitespace characters are typed by hitting the space bar, the Tab key, or the Enter key.

Character Sets

Before we look at reading character data, we need to examine the way in which character data are stored. In the **char** data type, each character is associated with an integer. Thus, the sequence of characters is associated with a sequence of integers. The particular sequence used by a machine for this purpose is referred to as the *collating sequence* for that *character set.* The principal sequence currently in use is the American Standard Code for Information Interchange (ASCII).

Each collating sequence contains an ordering of the characters in a character set and is listed in Appendix 4. For programs in this text, we use the ASCII code. As shown in Table 3.8, 52 of these characters are letters, 10 are digits, and the rest are special characters.

◇ **TABLE 3.8**
ASCII ordering of a character set

<table>
<tr><th>Ordinal</th><th>Character</th><th>Ordinal</th><th>Character</th><th>Ordinal</th><th>Character</th></tr>
<tr><td>32</td><td>b̸</td><td>64</td><td>@</td><td>96</td><td>'</td></tr>
<tr><td>33</td><td>!</td><td>65</td><td>A</td><td>97</td><td>a</td></tr>
<tr><td>34</td><td>"</td><td>66</td><td>B</td><td>98</td><td>b</td></tr>
<tr><td>35</td><td>#</td><td>67</td><td>C</td><td>99</td><td>c</td></tr>
<tr><td>36</td><td>$</td><td>68</td><td>D</td><td>100</td><td>d</td></tr>
<tr><td>37</td><td>%</td><td>69</td><td>E</td><td>101</td><td>e</td></tr>
<tr><td>38</td><td>&</td><td>70</td><td>F</td><td>102</td><td>f</td></tr>
<tr><td>39</td><td>'</td><td>71</td><td>G</td><td>103</td><td>g</td></tr>
<tr><td>40</td><td>(</td><td>72</td><td>H</td><td>104</td><td>h</td></tr>
<tr><td>41</td><td>)</td><td>73</td><td>I</td><td>105</td><td>i</td></tr>
<tr><td>42</td><td>*</td><td>74</td><td>J</td><td>106</td><td>j</td></tr>
<tr><td>43</td><td>+</td><td>75</td><td>K</td><td>107</td><td>k</td></tr>
<tr><td>44</td><td>,</td><td>76</td><td>L</td><td>108</td><td>l</td></tr>
<tr><td>45</td><td>-</td><td>77</td><td>M</td><td>109</td><td>m</td></tr>
<tr><td>46</td><td>.</td><td>78</td><td>N</td><td>110</td><td>n</td></tr>
<tr><td>47</td><td>/</td><td>79</td><td>O</td><td>111</td><td>o</td></tr>
<tr><td>48</td><td>0</td><td>80</td><td>P</td><td>112</td><td>p</td></tr>
<tr><td>49</td><td>1</td><td>81</td><td>Q</td><td>113</td><td>q</td></tr>
<tr><td>50</td><td>2</td><td>82</td><td>R</td><td>114</td><td>r</td></tr>
<tr><td>51</td><td>3</td><td>83</td><td>S</td><td>115</td><td>s</td></tr>
<tr><td>52</td><td>4</td><td>84</td><td>T</td><td>116</td><td>t</td></tr>
<tr><td>53</td><td>5</td><td>85</td><td>U</td><td>117</td><td>u</td></tr>
<tr><td>54</td><td>6</td><td>86</td><td>V</td><td>118</td><td>v</td></tr>
<tr><td>55</td><td>7</td><td>87</td><td>W</td><td>119</td><td>w</td></tr>
<tr><td>56</td><td>8</td><td>88</td><td>X</td><td>120</td><td>x</td></tr>
<tr><td>57</td><td>9</td><td>89</td><td>Y</td><td>121</td><td>y</td></tr>
<tr><td>58</td><td>:</td><td>90</td><td>Z</td><td>122</td><td>z</td></tr>
<tr><td>59</td><td>;</td><td>91</td><td>[</td><td>123</td><td>{</td></tr>
<tr><td>60</td><td><</td><td>92</td><td>\</td><td>124</td><td>|</td></tr>
<tr><td>61</td><td>=</td><td>93</td><td>]</td><td>125</td><td>}</td></tr>
<tr><td>62</td><td>></td><td>94</td><td>^</td><td>126</td><td>~</td></tr>
<tr><td>63</td><td>?</td><td>95</td><td>—</td><td></td><td></td></tr>
</table>

Note: Codes 00–31 and 127 are nonprintable control characters.

Reading Character Data

Reading characters from the standard input stream using >> is much the same as reading numeric data. If you want to read in a student's initials followed by three test scores, the following code will do that:

```
char first_initial, middle_initial, last_initial;
int score1, score2, score3;

cin >> first_initial >> middle_initial >> last_initial >> score1
    >> score2 >> score3;
```

When program execution is halted, you would type in something like

```
J D K 89 90 91
```

and press <Enter>.

A NOTE OF INTEREST

Communication Skills Needed

Emphasis on communication has been increasing in almost every area of higher education. Evidence of this is the current trend toward "writing across the curriculum" programs implemented in many colleges and universities in the 1980s. Indications that this emphasis is shared among computer scientists was given by Paul M. Jackowitz, Richard M. Plishka, and James R. Sidbury, University of Scranton, when they stated, "Make it possible to write programs in English, and you will discover that programmers cannot write in English."

All computer science educators are painfully aware of the truth of this old joke. We want our students to be literate. We want them to have well-developed writing skills and the capacity to read technical journals in our area. But too often we produce skilled programmers whose communication skills are poor and who have almost no research skills. We must alleviate this problem. Because the organizational techniques used to write software are the same ones that should be used to write papers, computer science students should have excellent writing skills. We should exploit this similarity in skills to develop better writers.

Further, Janet Hartman of Illinois State University and Curt M. White of Indiana-Purdue University at Fort Wayne noted: "Students need to practice written and oral communication skills, both in communications classes and computer classes. Students should write system specifications, project specifications, memos, users' guides or anything else which requires them to communicate on both a nontechnical and technical level. They should do presentations in class and learn to augment their presentations with audiovisual aids."

On a more general note, the need for effective communication skills in computer science has been acknowledged in the 1991 curriculum guidelines of the Association for Computing Machinery, Inc. These guidelines state that "undergraduate programs should prepare students to apply their knowledge to specific, constrained problems and produce solutions. This includes the ability to . . . communicate that solution to colleagues, professionals in other fields, and the general public."

Debugging Output Statements

A frequently used technique for debugging programs is to insert an output statement to print the values of variables. Once you have determined that the desired values are obtained, you can delete the output statements. For example, if your program segment is to read in three scores and three initials, you could write

```
cin >> score1 >> score2 >> score3;
cout << score1 << " " << score2 << " " << score3;
// for debugging
cin >> first_initial >> middle_initial >> last_initial;
cout << first_initial << " " << middle_initial << " " last_initial;
// for debugging
```

These debugging lines might be left in until the program has been sufficiently tested for input.

EXERCISES 3.3

1. Discuss the difference between **cin** and **cout**.
2. Assume a variable declaration section is

```
int num1, num2;

float num3;

char ch;
```

and you wish to enter the data

```
15   65.3   -20
```

Explain what results from each statement. Also indicate what values are assigned to appropriate variables.

a. `cin >> num1 >> num3 >> num2;`
b. `cin >> num1 >> num2 >> num3;`
c. `cin >> num1 >> num2 >> ch >> num3;`
d. `cin >> num2 >> num3 >> ch >> num2;`
e. `cin >> num2 >> num3 >> ch >> ch >> num2;`
f. `cin >> num3 >> num2;`
g. `cin >> num1 >> num3;`
h. `cin >> num1 >> ch >> num3;`

3. Write a program statement to be used to print a message to the screen directing the user to enter data in the form used for Exercise 2. Write an appropriate program statement (or statements) to produce a screen message and write an appropriate input statement for each of the following.
   a. Desired input is number of hours worked and hourly pay rate.
   b. Desired input is three positive integers followed by -999.
   c. Desired input is price of an automobile and the state sales tax rate.
   d. Desired input is the game statistics for one basketball player (check with a coach to see what must be entered).
   e. Desired input is a student's initials, age, height, weight, and gender.
4. Assume variables are declared as in Exercise 2. If an input statement is

```
cin >> num1 >> num2 >> ch >> num3;
```

indicate which lines of the following data do not result in an error message. For those that do not, indicate the values of the variables. For those that produce an error, explain what the error is.

a. `8395 100`
b. `8395.0 100`
c. `83-72 93.5`
d. `83-72 93.5`
e. `83.5`
f. `7073-80.5`
g. `919293 94`
h. `-76-81-16.5`

5. Why is it a good idea to print values of variables that have been read into a program?
6. Write a complete program that will read your initials and five test scores. Your program should then compute your test average and print all information in a reasonable form with suitable messages.

3.4 Using Constants

The word *constant* has several interpretations. In this section, we distinguish between a symbolic constant, like PI, and a literal constant, like 3.14. Symbolic constants are defined by giving them the values of literal constants. Recall that a C++ program consists of preprocessor directives, an optional constant and type definition section, a program heading, an optional variable declaration section, and an executable section. We will now examine uses for constants defined in the constant subsection.

OBJECTIVES

- to be aware of the appropriate use of constants
- to be able to use constants in programs
- to be able to format constants

Rationale for Uses

There are many reasons to use constants in a program. If a number is to be used frequently, the programmer may wish to give it a descriptive name in the constant definition subsection and then use the descriptive name in the executable section, thus making the program easier to read. For example, if a program included a segment that computed a person's state income tax, and the state tax rate was 6.25% of taxable income, the constant section might include:

```
const float STATE_TAX_RATE = 0.0625;
```

This defines both the value and type for **STATE_TAX_RATE**. In the executable portion of the program, the statement

```
state_tax = income * STATE_TAX_RATE;
```

computes the state tax owed. Or suppose you wanted a program to compute areas of circles. Depending on the accuracy you desire, you could define π as

```
const float PI = 3.14159;
```

You could then have a statement in the executable section such as

```
area = PI * radius * radius;
```

where **area** and **radius** are appropriately declared variables.

Perhaps the most important use of constants is for values that are currently fixed but subject to change for subsequent updates of the program. If these are defined in the constant section, they can be used throughout the program. If the value changes later, only one change need be made to keep the program current. This prevents the need to locate all uses of a constant in a program. Some examples might be

```
const float MINIMUM_WAGE = 4.25;
const int SPEED_LIMIT = 65;
const float PRICE = 0.75;
const float STATE_TAX_RATE = 0.0625;
```

Software Engineering

The appropriate use of constants is consistent with principles of software engineering. Communication between teams of programmers is enhanced when program constants have been agreed on. Each team should have a list of these constants for use as they work on their part of the system.

The maintenance phase of the software system life cycle is also aided by use of defined constants. Clearly, a large payroll system is dependent on being able to perform computations that include deductions for federal tax, state tax, FICA, Medicare, health insurance, retirement options, and so on. If appropriate constants are defined for these deductions, system changes are easily made as necessary. For example, the current salary limit for deducting FICA taxes is $53,400. Since this amount changes regularly, one could define

```
const float FICA_LIMIT = 53400.00;
```

Program maintenance is then simplified by changing the value of this constant as the law changes.

Library Constants

Some constants are provided in C++ libraries. For example, it is often necessary to determine the range of integer values allowed by a particular computer system, or

A NOTE OF INTEREST

Defined Constants and Space Shuttle Computing

An excellent illustration of the utilization of defined constants in a program was given by J. F. ("Jack") Clemons, former manager of avionics flight software development and verification for the space shuttle on-board computers. In an interview with David Gifford, editor for *Communications of the ACM,* Clemons was asked: "Have you tried to restructure the software so that it can be changed easily?"

His response was, "By changing certain data constants, we can change relatively large portions of the software on a mission-to-mission basis. For example, we've designed the software so that characteristics like atmospheric conditions on launch day or different lift-off weights can be loaded as initial constants into the code. This is important when there are postponements or last-minute payload changes that invalidate the original inputs."

◇ TABLE 3.9
Library constants for maximum numeric values

Library Constant	Meaning
INT_MAX	The maximum allowable positive integer value
INT_MIN	The maximum allowable negative integer value
FLT_MAX	The maximum allowable positive float value
FLT_MIN	The maximum allowable negative float value
FLT_DIG	The maximum number of digits of precision

the range of real number values, or the number of digits of precision supported by the system. The C++ library files **limits.h** and **float.h** define constants for each of these important values for your particular system. When you include this file at the beginning of your source program, each of the constants appearing in Table 3.9 will be available for use.

Formatting Constants

Formatting symbolic constants is identical to formatting real and integer values as discussed in Section 2.3.

3.5 Library Functions

OBJECTIVES

- to understand the reasons for having library functions
- to be able to use library functions in a program
- to be able to use appropriate data types for the arguments of library functions

Some standard operations required by programmers are squaring numbers and finding square roots of numbers. Because these operations are so basic, C++ provides *library functions* for them. Different versions of C++ and other programming languages have differing library functions available, so you should always check which functions can be used. Appendix 2 sets forth many of those available in most versions of C++.

A function can be used in a program if it appears in the following form:

```
<function name>(<argument list>)
```

where the *argument* is a value or variable with an assigned value. When a function appears in this manner, it is said to be *called* or *invoked.* A function is invoked by using it in a program statement. After the function performs its work, it may *return a value.* If, for example, you want to raise 3 to the fourth power, you include the **math.h** library and then

```
cout << pow(3, 4) << endl;
```

produces the desired result and returns it as a value to the caller.

Many functions operate on numbers, starting with a given number and returning some associated value. Table 3.10 shows five math library functions, each with its argument type, data type of return, and an explanation of the value returned. A more complete list of library functions can be found in Appendix 2.

Several examples of specific function expressions together with the value returned by each expression are depicted in Table 3.11.

◇ TABLE 3.10
Some math library functions

Function Declaration	Action of Function
`double fmod(double x);`	Returns floating-point remainder of **x / y**
`double log(double x);`	Returns natural logarithm of **x**
`double pow(double x, double y);`	Returns **x** raised to power of **y**
`double sqrt(double x);`	Returns square root of **x**
`double cos(double x);`	Returns cosine of **x**

◇ TABLE 3.11
Values of function expressions

Expression	Value
`pow(2, 4)`	16
`pow(2.0, 4)`	16.0
`pow(-3, 2)`	9
`sqrt(25.0)`	5.0
`sqrt(25)`	5
`sqrt(0.0)`	0.0
`sqrt(-2.0)`	Not permissible

Using Functions

When a function is invoked, it produces a value in much the same way that 3 + 3 produces 6. Thus, use of a function should be treated similarly to use of constants or values of an expression. Typical uses are in assignment statements,

```
x = sqrt(16.0);
```

output statements,

```
cout << setw(20) << pow(2, 5);
```

or arithmetic expressions

```
hypotenuse = sqrt(pow(base, 2) + pow(height, 2));
```

Arguments of functions can be expressions, variables, or constants.

3.6 Type Compatibility and Type Conversion

We mentioned in Section 3.2 that the operands of arithmetic expressions and assignment statements must be of compatible data types. For example, we saw that we could not only add an integer to an integer, but also add an integer to a real number. In the latter case, the run-time system performs an *implicit type conversion* of the integer operand before performing the addition, and then returns a real number as the sum. This kind of type conversion is also referred to as *type*

OBJECTIVES

- to be able to understand how different data types are related to each other
- to be able to understand how one data type can be converted to another

promotion, in that the value of a less inclusive type, **int**, is elevated to a value of a more inclusive type, **float**.

Implicit type conversion also occurs when an integer value is assigned to a variable of type **float**. In this case, a copy of the integer value is placed in the real number's storage location, and then promoted by adding to it a fractional part of zero. For example, assuming that **real_number** is of type **float**, the following two lines of code would produce an output of 3.00:

```
real_number = 3;
cout << fixed << setprecision(2) << showpoint
     << real_number << endl;
```

Conversely, when you assign a real number to a variable of type **int**, the system drops or truncates a copy of the real number's value before placing it in the integer's storage location. Thus, the following two lines of code would display the value 5, assuming that **whole_number** is an **int**:

```
whole_number = 5.76;
cout << whole_number << endl;
```

The Character Set Once Again

It turns out that characters and integers are also compatible types in C++. This means that character values can be assigned to integer variables, integer values can be assigned to character variables, and integers can be added to characters. Moreover, each of these operations involves an implicit type conversion. To make sense of this apparently strange phenomenon, we must consider the character set once more.

Ordering a character set requires association of an integer with each character. Data types ordered in some association with the integers are known as *ordinal data types.* Each integer is the ordinal of its associated value. Character sets are considered to be an ordinal data type, as shown in Table 3.8. In each case, the ordinal of the character appears to the left of the character. Using ASCII, as shown in Table 3.8, the ordinal of a capital a (A) is 65, the ordinal of the character representing the Arabic number one (1) is 49, the ordinal of a blank (b) is 32, and the ordinal of a lowercase a (a) is 97.

Once we realize that characters are really represented as integers in a computer, we can begin to see how we can perform mixed-mode operations on these two data types. When a character value is assigned to an integer variable, the run-time system copies the character's ordinal into the integer's storage location. Thus, assuming an ASCII representation and our **whole_number** variable of type **int**, the following two lines of code would display the number 65:

```
whole_number = 'A';
cout << whole_number << endl;
```

Conversely, assuming that letter is of type **char**, the following two lines of code would display the letter A:

```
letter = 65;
cout << letter << endl;
```

When arithmetic operations are performed on characters (either two character values or one character and one integer), each character value is first promoted to a more inclusive type, namely, an integer. Then the system performs the operation, and the result returned is an integer. For example, the following two lines of code would display the value 66:

```
whole_number = 'A' + 1;
cout << whole_number << endl;
```

It turns out that since the decimal digits are in the collating sequence from 0 to 9 in the character set, the integer value of a given digit can be computed quite easily with *character arithmetic.* For example, assuming that **digit** is of type **int**, the following two lines of code compute and display the integer value of the digit 5:

```
digit = '5' - '0';
cout << digit << endl;
```

In the next example, we show how to use character arithmetic to convert an uppercase letter to lowercase.

EXAMPLE 3.3

To show how character arithmetic can be used to convert an uppercase letter to lowercase, let us assume that our task is to convert the letter **'H'** into the letter **'h'**. We first subtract **'A'** from **'H'** to obtain

```
'H' - 'A'
```

which is

```
72 - 65 = 7
```

We now add **'a'** to get

```
'H' - 'A' + 'a'
```

which yields

```
72 - 65 + 97 = 104
```

This is the ordinal of **'h'**. It can be converted to the letter by assigning it to a variable of type **char**. Thus,

```
letter = 'H' - 'A' + 'a';
```

places the letter **'h'** in the variable **letter**, where **letter** is of type **char**.

In general, the following is sufficient for converting from uppercase to lowercase, where the two names are of type **char**:

```
lower_case = upper_case - 'A' + 'a';
```

Note that if you always use the same ASCII ordering,

```
-'A' + 'a'
```

could be replaced by the constant 32. If you choose to do this, 32 should be given a name. A typical definition is

```
const int UPPER_TO_LOWER_SHIFT = 32;
```

You would then write the lowercase conversion as

```
lower_case = upper_case + UPPER_TO_LOWER_SHIFT;
```

Type Casts

Occasionally, we would like to force the conversion of a value from one type to another without resorting to an assignment statement. For example, the expression **whole_number % real_number** will generate an error, because the modulus operator is not defined on real numbers. We would like to convert the real number to an integer within the expression, rather than complicate matters by declaring an extra integer variable, assigning the real number to it, and then using the integer variable.

C++ provides a set of operators called *type casts* for performing *explicit type conversions* of this sort. You can think of a type cast as a function, whose name is the name of the type to which you wish to convert a value. The argument of this function is the value to be converted, and the value returned by the function is the converted value. For example, the following line of code uses the type cast for integers to display the integer value 3:

```
cout << int(3.14) << endl;
```

Our method of converting an uppercase letter to lowercase can make good use of the type cast for characters:

```
cout << char(upper_case - UPPER_TO_LOWER_SHIFT) << endl;
```

The form of a type cast that we will use in this text is

<type name> (<expression>)

where **<type>** is the name of the target type and **<expression>** evaluates to a type of value that the cast is capable of converting. This form may not be recognized by some C++ compilers. In those cases, a more standard, but less readable form to use is

(<type name>) <expression>

EXERCISES 3.6

1. Find the value of each of the following expressions.
   a. `sqrt(15.51)`
   b. `pow(-14.2, 3)`
   c. `4 * 11 % sqrt(16)`
   d. `pow(17 / 5 * 2, 2)`
   e. `-5.0 + sqrt(5 * 5 - 4 * 6) / 2.0`
2. Write a test program that illustrates what happens when an inappropriate argument is used with a function. Be sure to include something like **sqrt(-1)**.
3. Two standard algebraic problems come from the Pythagorean theorem and the quadratic formula. Assume variables *a, b,* and *c* have been declared in a program. Write C++ expressions that allow you to evaluate the following.
   a. The length of the hypotenuse of a right triangle: $\sqrt{a^2+b^2}$
   b. both solutions to the quadratic formula:

$$\frac{-b \pm \sqrt{b^2-4ac}}{2a}$$

4. Indicate whether the following are valid or invalid expressions. Find the value of those that are valid; explain why the others are invalid.
   a. `-6 % (sqrt(16))`
   b. `8 / sqrt(65)`
   c. `sqrt(63 % (2))`
   d. `-sqrt(pow(3, 2) - 7)`
   e. `sqrt(16 / (-3))`
   f. `sqrt(pow(-4, 2))`
5. Using ASCII, find the values of each of the following expressions.
   a. `13 + 4 % 3`
   b. `'E'`
   c. `'E' + 1`
   d. `5`
   e. `'5'`
   f. `'+'`
   g. `40`
6. Assume the variable declaration section of a program is

   ```
   float x; int a; char ch;
   ```

   What output is produced by each of the following program fragments?

   a.
   ```
   x = -4.3;
   cout << setprecision(2) << setw(6) << x << int(x)
        << endl;
   ```
   b.
   ```
   x = -4.3;
   a = x;
   cout << a << int('a');
   ```
   c.
   ```
   ch = char(76);
   cout << setw(5) << ch << setw(5) << char(ch - 1);
   ```
7. Write a complete program to print each uppercase letter of the alphabet and its ordinal in the collating sequence used by your machine's version of C++.
8. Using ASCII, show how each of the following conversions can be made.
   a. A lowercase letter converted into its uppercase equivalent.
   b. A digit entered as a **char** value into its indicated numeric value.

Writing styles and suggestions are gathered for quick reference in the following style tip summary. These tips are intended to stimulate rather than terminate your imagination.

1. Use descriptive identifiers. Words—sum, score, average—are easier to understand than letters—a, b, c or x, y, z.
2. Use the constant definition section to define an appropriately named blank and use it to control line spacing for output. Thus, you could have

```
const char SKIP = ' ';
const char INDENT = ' ';
```

and then output statements could be

```
cout << setw(20) << SKIP << message
     << setw(10) << SKIP << message;
```

or

```
cout << setw(20) << INDENT << message
     << setw(10) << SKIP << message;
```

3. Output of a column of reals should have decimal points in a line.

```
 14.32
181.50
 93.63
```

4. Output can be made more attractive by using columns, left and right margins, underlining, and blank lines.
5. Extra output statements at the beginning and end of the executable section will separate desired output from other messages.

```
cout << endl;
     .
     .
     .
(program body here)
cout << endl;
```

FOCUS ON PROGRAM DESIGN

Complete programs are used to illustrate concepts developed throughout the text. In each case, a typical problem is stated. A solution is developed in pseudocode and illustrated with a structure chart. Module specifications are written for appropriate modules. Now, on to the problem for this chapter.

Write a complete program to find the unit price for a pizza. Input for the program consists of the price and size of the pizza. Size is the diameter of the pizza ordered. Output consists of the price per square inch. A first-level development is

1. Get the data
2. Perform the computations
3. Print the results

A structure chart for this problem is given in Figure 3.1. Module specifications for the main modules are

Module: Get data
Task: Gets cost and size of pizza from the user at the keyboard.
Outputs: cost and size

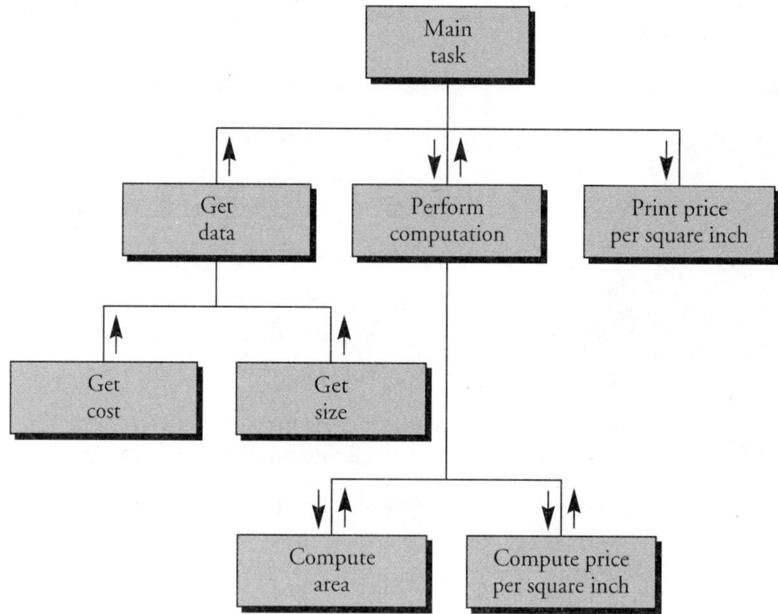

◆ FIGURE 3.1
Structure chart for the pizza problem

Module: Compute price per square inch
Task: Compute the price per square inch of pizza.
Input: cost and size of pizza
Output: price per square inch

Module: Print results
Task: Print the price per square inch.
Input: price per square inch

A further refinement of the pseudocode produces

1. Get the data
   1.1 get price
   1.2 get size
2. Perform the computations
   2.1 compute area
   2.2 calculate unit price

Step 3 of the pseudocode, "Print the results," only requires printing the price per square inch, so no further development is required. A complete program for this follows:

```
// Program file: pizza.cpp

#include <iostream.h>
#include <iomanip.h>
#include <math.h>

const float PI = 3.14;

int main ()
{

        float size, radius, cost, area, price_per_square_inch;

        // This module gets the data.
```

```
        cout << "Enter the pizza price and press <Enter>. ";
        cin >> cost;                                              1
        cout << "Enter the pizza size and press <Enter>. ";
        cin >> size;

        // This module computes the unit price.

        radius = size / 2;
        area = PI * pow(radius, 2);                               2
        price_per_square_inch = cost / area;

        // This module prints the results.

        cout << setprecision(2) << endl;
        cout << "The price per square inch is $" << setw(4)
             << price_per_square_inch << endl;                    3
        return 0;

}
```

A sample run of this program yields

```
Enter the pizza price and press <Enter>. 10.50
Enter the pizza size and press <Enter>. 16
The price per square inch is $0.05
```

SUMMARY

Key Terms

argument
assignment statement
batch input
binary arithmetic
binary notation
cancellation error
character set
collating sequence
constant
input
integer arithmetic operations: +, –, *, /, %
integer overflow
interactive input
invoke (call)
library (built-in) constant
library (built-in) function
memory location
mixed-mode expression
ordinal data type
overflow
prompt
real arithmetic operations: +, –, *, /
real overflow
representational error
self-documenting code
underflow
user-friendly
variable
word

Key Concepts

◆ Operations and priorities for data of type **int** and **float** are summarized as follows:

Data Type	Operations	Priority
int	***, %, /**	1. Evaluate in order from left to right.
	+, -	2. Evaluate in order from left to right.
float	***, /**	1. Evaluate in order from left to right.
	+, -	2. Evaluate in order from left to right.

◆ Mixed-mode expressions involving **int** and **float** values return values of type **float**.

- Priority for order of operations on mixed-mode expressions is
  1. *, /: in order from left to right.
  2. +, –: in order from left to right.
- Overflow is caused by a value too large for computing on a particular machine.
- Underflow is caused by a value too small (close to zero) for computing. These numbers are automatically replaced by zero.
- A memory location can have a name that can be used to refer to the contents of the location.
- The name of a memory location is different from the contents of the memory location.
- Self-documenting code is code that is written using descriptive identifiers.
- Assignment statements are used to assign values to memory locations, for example

```
sum = 30 + 60;
```

- Variables and variable expressions can be used in output statements.
- **cin** is used to get data; the correct form is

```
cin >> variable1 >> variable 2 . . . >> variable n;
```

- **cin >> <variable>**; causes a value to be transferred to the variable location.
- Interactive input expects data items to be entered from the keyboard at appropriate times during execution of the program.
- Data types for variables in an input statement should match data items read as input.
- Appropriate uses for constants in the declaration section include frequently used numbers; current values subject to change over time, for example, **(MINIMUM_WAGE = 4.25)**.
- Five math library functions available in C++ are **pow**, **sqrt**, **sin**, **cos**, and **tan**.
- Functions can be used in assignment statements, for example,

```
x = sqrt(16.0);
```

  in output statements

```
cout << pow(-8, 2);
```

  and in arithmetic expressions

```
x = sqrt(3.78) + pow(5, 5);
```

- Type casts can be used to convert one type of value to another type, for example **int(3.14)**.

PROGRAMMING PROBLEMS AND PROJECTS

Write a complete C++ program for each of the following problems. Each program should use one or more input statements to obtain the necessary values. Each input statement should be preceded by an appropriate prompting message.

1. Susan purchases a computer for $985. The sales tax on the purchase is 5.5%. Compute and print the total purchase price.

2. Find and print the area and perimeter of a rectangle that is 4.5 feet long and 2.3 feet wide. Print both rounded to the nearest tenth of a foot.
3. Compute and print the number of minutes in a year.
4. Light travels as $3 * 10^8$ meters per second. Compute and print the distance a light beam would travel in one year. (This is called a light year.)
5. The 1927 New York Yankees won 110 games and lost 44. Compute their winning percentage and print it rounded to three decimal places.
6. A 10-kilogram object is traveling at 12 meters per second. Compute and print its momentum (momentum is mass times velocity).
7. Convert 98.0 degrees Fahrenheit to degrees Celsius.
8. Given a positive number, print its square and square root.
9. The Golden Sales Company pays its salespeople $0.27 for each item they sell. Given the number of items sold by a salesperson, print the amount of pay due.
10. Given the length and width of a rectangle, print its area and perimeter.
11. The kinetic energy of a moving object is given by the formula $KE=(1/2)mv^2$. Given the mass (m) and the speed (v) of an object, find its kinetic energy.
12. Dr. Lisa Thompson wants a program to enable her to balance her checkbook. She wishes to enter a beginning balance, five letters for an abbreviation for the recipient of the check, and the amount of the check. Given this information, write a program that will find the new balance in her checkbook.
13. A supermarket wants to install a computerized weighing system in its produce department. Input to this system will consist of a single-letter identifier for the type of produce, the weight of the produce purchase (in pounds), and the cost per pound of the produce. A typical input screen would be

```
Enter each of the following:

Description <Enter> A
Weight <Enter> 2.0
Price/lb. <Enter> 1.98
```

Print a label showing the input information along with the total cost of the purchase. The label should appear as follows:

```
%%%%%%%%%%%%%%%%%%%%%%%%%%%%%%%%%%%%%%%%%%%%%%%

              Penny Spender Supermarket
                 Produce Department

  ITEM          WEIGHT         COST/1b        COST

  A             2.0 1b         $1.98          $3.96

                     Thank you!

%%%%%%%%%%%%%%%%%%%%%%%%%%%%%%%%%%%%%%%%%%%%%%%
```

14. The New Wave Computer Company sells its product, the NW-PC, for $675. In addition, they sell memory expansion cards for $69.95, disk drives for $198.50, and software for $34.98 each. Given the number of memory cards, disk drives, and software packages desired by a customer purchasing an NW-PC, print out a bill of sale that appears as follows:

```
****************************
      New Wave Computers

        ITEM                    COST
1 NW-PC                      $675.00
2 Memory card                 139.90
1 Disk drive                  198.50
4 Software                    139.92

                 TOTAL      $1153.32
```

15. Write a test program that allows you to see the characters contained within the character set of your computer. Given a positive integer, you can use the **char** type cast to determine the corresponding character. On most computers, only integers less than 256 are valid for this. Also, remember that most character sets contain some unprintable characters such as ASCII values less than 32. Print your output in the form:

```
Character number nnn is x.
```

16. Mr. Vigneault, a coach at Shepherd High School, is working on a program that can be used to assist cross-country runners in analyzing their times. As part of the program, a coach enters elapsed times for each runner given in units of minutes, seconds, and hundredths. In a 5000-meter (5K) race, elapsed times are entered at the one-mile and two-mile marks. These elapsed times are then used to compute "splits" for each part of the race; that is, how long did it take a runner to run each of the three race segments. Write a complete program that will accept as input three times given in units of minutes, seconds, and hundredths and then produce output that includes the split for each segment. Typical input would be

```
Runner number                234

Mile times:       1          5:34.22

                  2          11:21.67

Finish time:                 17:46.85
```

Typical output would be

```
Runner number                234

Split one                    5:34.22

Split two                    5:47.45

Split three                  6:25.18

Finish time                  17:46.85
```

17. Many (but not all) instructors in beginning computer science courses encourage their students to use meaningful identifiers in writing code. It is natural to wonder to what extent this practice is followed outside the educational world. Investigate this issue by contacting several programmers who work for nearby companies. Prepare a complete written report of your conversations for distribution to class members. Include charts that summarize your findings.

CHAPTER 4 Subprograms: Functions for Problem Solving

CHAPTER OUTLINE

Recall from Section 2.3 the process of solving a problem by stepwise refinement of tasks into subtasks. This top-down design method is especially suitable for writing C++ programs to solve problems using *subprograms.*

The concept of a subprogram is not difficult to understand. It is a program within a program and is provided by most programming languages. Each subprogram should complete some task, the nature of which can range from simple to complex. You could have a subprogram that prints only a line of data, or you could rewrite an entire program as a subprogram. To extend the metaphor of the programmable pocket calculator introduced in Chapter 3, we create a subprogram by giving a name to a sequence of program statements. We then specify the data that this sequence will take as inputs and return as outputs. Next, we store this name with the built-in functions in the calculator. Finally, we use the name as if it were a built-in function wherever it is appropriate in any program.

4.1 Program Design

OBJECTIVES

- to understand the concepts of modularity and bottom-up testing
- to be aware of the use of structured programming

Modularity

We have previously discussed and illustrated the process of solving a problem by top-down design. Using this method, we divide the main task into major subtasks, and then continue to divide the subtasks (stepwise refinement) into smaller subtasks until all subtasks can be easily performed. Once an algorithm for solving a problem has been developed using top-down design, the programmer then writes code to translate the general solution into a C++ program.

As you have seen, code written to perform one well-defined subtask can be referred to as a *module.* One should be able to design, code, and test each module in a program independently from the rest of the program. In this sense, a module is a subprogram containing all definitions and declarations needed to perform the indicated subtask. Everything required for the subtask (but not needed in other parts of the program) can be created in the subprogram. Consequently, the definitions and declarations have meaning only when the module is being used.

At the lowest level in a programming language like C++, a module is a single function. However, one can also think, at a higher level in a design, of a module as consisting of several functions and related data. One important kind of higher level module of this sort is known as an *abstract data type*. The design and construction of abstract data type modules are discussed in some detail in Chapters 7 through 11. You have already been using some standard abstract data type modules whenever you have used the operations on integers, real numbers, and characters in your C++ programs.

A program that has been created using modules to perform various tasks is said to possess *modularity*. In general, modular programs are easier to test, debug, and correct than programs that are not modular because each independent module can be tested by running it from a test driver. Then, once the modules are running correctly, they can become part of a longer program. This independent testing of modules is referred to as *bottom-up testing*. A modular program is also easier to maintain than a nonmodular program, because we can replace one module without modifying the other modules at all. For example, a new version of the C++ compiler might provide faster operations for floating-point arithmetic in the module that defines these operations. All you would have to do to maintain your system is to recompile your program.

Structured Programming and Design

Structured programming is the process of developing a program where emphasis is placed on the flow of control between independent modules. *Structured design* is the process of organizing communication between modules. Connections between these modules are specified in parameter lists and are usually controlled by the main program. Structured programming and design are especially suitable to large programs being worked on by teams. By carefully designing the modules and specifying what information is to be received by and returned from the module, a team of programmers can independently develop a module and then connect it to the complete program.

The remainder of this chapter is devoted to seeing how subprograms can be written to accomplish specific tasks. Subprograms in C++ are called *functions*. We discussed library functions in Section 3.5. We will now learn how to write our own functions.

4.2 User-Defined Functions

OBJECTIVES

- to understand the need for user-defined functions
- to be able to use correct syntax when declaring and implementing a function
- to be able to use stubs and drivers to test functions

User-defined functions resemble the library functions **sqrt** and **pow** that were introduced in Section 3.5. To review briefly, note the following concepts when using these functions:

1. An argument is required for each; thus, **sqrt(y)** and **pow(2, 5)** are appropriate.
2. Functions can be used in expressions; for example,

```
x = sqrt(y) + sqrt(z);
```

3. Functions can be used in output statements; for example,

```
cout << setw(8) << setprecision(2) << sqrt(3);
```

Need for User-Defined Functions

It is relatively easy to envision the need for functions that are not on the list of library functions available in C++. For example, if you must frequently cube numbers, it would be convenient to have a function named **cube** that would allow you to make an assignment such as

A NOTE OF INTEREST

Structured Programming

From 1950 to the early 1970s programs were designed and written on a linear basis. Programs written and designed on such a basis can be called unstructured programs. These programs consist of long linear sequences of statements. Control flows from each statement in the sequence to the next statement, unless it is transferred by means of a **GOTO** statement. Structured programming, on the other hand, organizes a program around separate semi-independent modules that are linked by a single sequence of simple commands, including structured control statements for selection and iteration (see Chapters 5 and 6).

In 1964, mathematicians Corrado Bohm and Guiseppe Jacopini proved that any program logic, regardless of complexity, can be expressed by using the control structures of sequencing, selection, and iteration. This result is termed the *structure theorem*. This theorem, combined with the efforts of Edger W. Dijkstra, led to a significant move toward structured programming and away from the use of **GOTO** statements.

In fact, in a letter to the editor of *Communications of the ACM* (Volume 11, March 1968), Dijkstra stated that the **GOTO** statement "should be abolished from all 'higher level' programming languages. . . . [The **GOTO** statement] is just too primitive; it is too much an invitation to make a mess of one's program."

Structured programming concepts were applied to a large-scale data processing application for the first time in IBM Corporation's "New York Times Project," which ran from 1969 to 1971. Using these techniques, programmers posted productivity figures from four to six times higher than those of the average programmer. In addition, the error rate was a phenomenally low 0.0004 per line of coding.

```
x = cube(y);
```

Other examples from mathematics include computing a factorial ($n!$), computing a discriminant ($b^2 - 4ac$), and finding roots of a quadratic equation:

$$\frac{-b \pm \sqrt{b^2 - 4ac}}{2a}$$

In business, a motel might like to have available a function to determine a customer's bill given the number in the party, the length of stay, and any telephone charges. Similarly, a hospital might need a function to compute the room charge for a patient given the type of room (private, ward, and so on) and various other options, including telephone (yes or no) and television (yes or no). Functions such as these are not library functions. However, in C++, we can create *user-defined functions* to perform these tasks. The following diagram illustrates the components of a simple C++ program that has one user-defined function:

```
#include <iostream.h>

// Function: cube
// Computes the cube of an integer
//
// Input: an integer value
// Output: an integer representing the cube of the input

int cube (int x);

int main()
{
```

```
        int number;

        cout << "enter a number followed by <Enter>."
        cin >> number;
        cout << "The cube of"<< number <<"is"<< cube(number) << endl;
        return 0;
}

int cube(int x);
{
        return x * x * x;
}
```

Function Declarations

In the previous two chapters of this text, you learned how to import library functions from library files with the **#include** directive, and then how to invoke or call these functions in your application program. An important point to remember is that you do not know anything about how these functions are written or *implemented.* All you know is the *declaration* of a function. A function's declaration consists of its name, the number and kind of arguments it expects when you invoke it, and the type of value, if any, that it returns when its job is done. A function's declaration gives you all the information you need to know in order to use the function, and no more. For example, the declaration of the library function **pow** might be written as follows:

```
double pow(double base, double exponent);
```

The first word in this expression, **double**, tells us the type of value returned by the function. The second word, **pow**, is the name of the function. The words enclosed in the parentheses and separated by commas denote the types of arguments expected when the function is invoked, that is, two arguments of type **double**. Note that the names used for these arguments, **base** and **exponent**, also serve to document the role that they play in the function.

The general form for a function declaration is

<return type> <function name> (<list of argument specifiers>);

to which the following comments apply:

1. **<function name>** is any valid identifier.
2. The function name should be descriptive.
3. **<return type>** declares the data type for the function name. This indicates what type of value, if any, will be returned to the caller.

It is good programming practice to supply with a declaration some comments that describe the inputs or data received by the function (its *arguments*) and the output or information returned (its *value* or *result*). In addition, we might specify any assumptions about the function's arguments that must be satisfied so that the function can perform its task correctly. For example, the function **sqrt** assumes that its argument is not just any double, but a nonnegative double. Therefore, we supply a comment about the function's arguments and value:

```
// Function: sqrt
// Compute the square root of a double-precision floating-point number
//
// Input: a nonnegative double-precision floating-point number
// Output: a nonnegative double-precision floating-point number
// representing the square root of the data received

double sqrt(double x);
```

Note that we have given the reader no information about *how* the function performs its task. Nonetheless, the reader has enough information to invoke or use the function. This is the kind of function declaration and comment that we will use in examples of user-defined functions throughout this text. Hereafter, when we say declaration, we mean a C++ function declaration and any supporting comments. Writing out all of your function declarations in this way will encourage you to think in terms of the uses of your functions before you become immersed in their implementation details.

Declaring Functions in a Program

Before you can use functions that you write yourself, you must provide declarations for them. All function declarations, if there are any, should appear in the region of your source program file between the global data declarations and the main program heading:

```
preprocessor directives

global data declarations

function declaration 1
.
.
.
function declaration n

int main()
{
        main program data declarations

        statements

}

function implementation 1
.
.
.
function implementation n
```

Implementing Functions in a Program

After you have decided how your functions will be used and what their declarations will be, and even after you have written a main program that will call them, you can then turn to the job of implementing or writing them. A function *implementation* describes in detail how the function performs its task. Simply put, a function implementation is a complete, brief program that produces some effects if certain assumptions about the arguments to the function are satisfied. For example, let's assume that the data value **x** is a number. Then the following expression produces the square of the number:

```
x * x
```

We can use this expression to implement a function **sqr(x)**, where **x** is any number, as follows:

```
double sqr(double x)
{
        return x * x;
}
```

You will note that the first line of the implementation, called the *function heading*, looks almost like a function declaration. The only difference is that the semicolon following the right parenthesis is omitted. The rest of the implementation after the heading is a little program block. Like the main program block, this block contains optional data declarations and at least one executable statement. The single statement in our example says that the block will return (as the value of the function) the result of multiplying **x** (the argument of the function) by itself. The form for a function implementation is

```
<function heading>
{
        <optional data declarations>
        <executable statements>
}
```

Function Headings

A function heading in a C++ program must match up with a corresponding function declaration. A return type and a function name must be the same in a heading as they are in a declaration, and the types of the arguments must match and be in the same positions. In addition, each type in the argument list of a function heading must be followed by an argument name, usually called a *formal parameter*. The formal parameter list must match the number of the arguments (usually called *actual parameters*) used when the function is called. Thus, if you are writing a function to compute the area of a rectangle and you want to call the function from the main program by

```
rect_area = area(width, length);
```

the function implementation might have

```
int area (int w, int l)
```

as a heading. The two formal parameters, **w** and **l**, correspond to the actual parameters, **width** and **length**. In general, you should make sure the formal parameter list and actual parameter list match up as indicated;

```
(int w, int l) (width, length)
```

A function to compute the cube of an integer could use the following as a heading:

```
int cube(int x)
```

The general form for a function heading is

<return type> <function name> (<list of formal parameters>)

Using this general form, we note the following:

1. **`<function name>`** is any valid identifier.
   a. The function name should be descriptive.
   b. If it is expected, some value should be returned in the executable section of the function.
2. **`<return type>`** declares the data type for the function name. This indicates what type of value will be returned to the caller, if expected.
3. The list of formal parameters consists of a series of pairs of names, where the first name in the pair is the name of a data type, and the second name in the pair is the name of a formal parameter. The pairs in the list must be separated by commas.

Hereafter in this chapter, when we say *heading,* we mean a C++ function heading.

The formal parameters in a function heading must also match the types of the arguments used when the function is called. The compiler uses the same type checking rules for matching the types of formal and actual parameters as it does for matching the operands of an assignment statement. When an actual parameter passed to a function is not exactly the same type as the formal parameter in its position, the compiler checks to see whether or not the actual parameter's type can be converted by an implicit type cast to the type of the formal parameter. For example, an integer value passed to a function that expects a **`float`** would be converted to a float before being processed in the function. Conversely, a **`float`** that is passed to a function expecting an **`int`** would be implicitly rounded to an **`int`**.

Data and Executable Statements in a Function Implementation

As in the main program, a function does not have to have a declaration section, but when there is one, only constants and variables needed in the function should be declared. Further, the section is usually not very elaborate because the purpose of a function is normally a small, single task.

The executable statement section of a function's implementation has the same form as the executable statement section of the main program. Remember that at least one statement, of the form **`return <expression>`**, should return the value of the function if a returned value is expected.

We will now illustrate user-defined functions with several examples.

EXAMPLE 4.1

Implement a function to compute the cube of an integer. First, consider what a typical call to this function from the main program will look like:

```
a = cube(5);
```

Then decide what the assumptions about the arguments are, what the effects of the function will be, and write down a function declaration:

```
// Function: cube
// Computes the cube of an integer
//
// Input: an integer value
// Output: an integer representing the cube of the input

int cube (int x);
```

Because the actual parameter from the caller will be of **int** type, we have as an implementation

```
int cube (int x)
{
        return x * x * x;
}
```

EXAMPLE 4.2

Let us write a function to perform the task of computing unit cost for pizza. Data sent to the function are size and cost. The function returns the unit cost. Formal parameters are cost and size. Using the function name **price_per_square_inch**, the function could be invoked in a main program as follows:

```
unit_cost = price_per_square_inch(cost, price);
```

Therefore, we write the declaration

```
// Function: price_per_square_inch
// Computes the price per square inch of pizza
//
// Input: two positive real numbers representing the cost in dollars and
// cents and the diameter in inches of a pizza
// Output: a real number representing the price, in dollars and cents, per
// square inch of pizza

float price_per_square_inch(float cost, float size);
```

The implementation then is

```
float price_per_square_inch(float cost, float size)
{
        float radius, area;

        radius = size / 2.0;
        area = PI * sqr(radius);
        return cost / area;
}
```

You should note that this function has some *locally declared data.* The variable **radius** is declared within the local block of the function, because it is needed only for computing the area of a pizza. In general, data that are not needed elsewhere in a program should be declared locally within functions. You should also note that there are two important, unstated assumptions made by this implementation: first, the constant **PI** must be defined; and second, the function **sqr** must be declared. These names can be defined or declared in the area above the main program. The function **sqr** must then also be implemented, along with the function **price_per_square_inch**, after the main program.

EXAMPLE 4.3

We want to implement a function that converts digits to integer values. Our version of the function, called **char_to_int**, has the following declaration:

```
// Function: char_to_int
// Computes the integer value of a digit
//
// Input: a digit
// Output: the integer value represented by the digit

int char_to_int(char ch);
```

The implementation uses the method we developed in Chapter 3:

```
int char_to_int(char ch)
{
        return ch - '0';
}
```

Use in a Program

Now that you have seen several examples of user-defined functions, let us consider their use in a program. Once they are written, they can be used in the same manner as library functions. This usually means in one of the following forms.

1. *Assignment statements:*

```
a = 5;

b = cube(a);
```

2. *Arithmetic expressions:*

```
a = 5;

a = 3 * cube(a) + 2;
```

3. *Output statements:*

```
a = 5;
cout << setw(17) << cube(a) << endl;
```

Using Stubs

As programs get longer and incorporate more subprograms, a technique frequently used to get the program running is *stub programming.* A stub program is a no-frills, simple version of what will be a final program. It does not contain details of output and full algorithm development. It does contain declarations and rough implementations of each subprogram. When the stub version runs, you know your logic is correct and values are appropriately being passed to and from subprograms. Then you can fill in the necessary details to get a complete program.

Using Drivers

The main program is sometimes referred to as the *main driver.* When subprograms are used in a program, this driver can be modified to check subprograms in a sequential fashion. For example, you can start with a main driver that gets some input data:

```
// Program file: driver.cpp

#include<iostream.h>

int main()
{
	int data;

	cout << "Enter an integer:";
	cin >> data;
	return 0;
}
```

You can think of this driver as a "function factory" for building and testing functions. First, you add a function declaration, and then add a rough implementation of the function that simply returns a value, usually, the value of one of the arguments of the function. You test this function stub by placing a call to the function, with an input value, inside of an output statement in the main driver. If you were building the **sqr** function, your next version of the program would look like this:

```
// Program file: driver.cpp

#include <iostream.h>

// Function: sqr
// Computes the square of a number
//
// Input: a double-precision floating-point number
// Output: a double-precision floating-point number representing the square
// of the input

double sqr(double x);

void main()
{
	int data;

	cout << "Enter an integer:";
	cin >> data1;
	cout << "The square is " << sqr(data) << endl;
}

double sqr(double x)

{
	return x;
}
```

Once you are sure that a subprogram is running and that data are being transmitted properly to it, you can proceed to fill in the rest of the details of its implementation. In the case of the **sqr** function, you merely substitute **x * x** for **x** in the **return** statement, and test the driver again. As you complete the implementation, you can be more confident that the function will return the values expected.

Functions Without Returned Values

Some functions require data to do their work, but return no values to their callers. For example, displaying several values with their labels to the terminal screen is such a task. This function might be called as follows:

```
display_results(result1, result2, result3);
```

The implementation of this function would probably send the parameter values and the appropriate string labels to the standard output stream. Note that the function call appears all by itself in a complete C++ statement. That is, a value is not assigned to a variable or passed on as intermediate value within a more complex expression. Functions of this sort are called *void functions,* in that they return no values. You have already seen an example of this kind of function: the main program of any C++ program. The example function is declared as follows:

```
void display_results(int result1, int result2,
     int result3);
```

The reserved word **void** indicates that the function is not meant to return a value. When a void function is implemented, it need not end with a return statement:

```
void display_results(int result1, int result2, int result3)
{
     cout << "The first result is " << result1 << endl;
     cout << "The second result is " << result2 << endl;
     cout << "The third result is " << result3 << endl;
}
```

The declarations of **void** functions have the following form:

void <function name> (<list of argument specifiers>);

Functions Without Parameters

Occasionally, a function is needed to do some work without receiving any data from the caller. It may or may not return a value as well. An example of such a function is one whose task is that of displaying a chunk of text as a header for a table of output data. One might invoke this function as follows:

```
display_header();
```

This function takes no data from parameters, and returns no value to the caller. Its sole purpose is to display some text on the terminal screen. Its declaration is

```
void display_header();
```

Its implementation might display a header for a table of names and grades:

```
void display_header()
{
     cout << "GRADES FOR COMPUTER SCIENCE 110" << endl;
     cout << endl;
     cout << "Student Name               Grade" << endl;
     cout << "------------               -----" << endl;
}
```

Another example of this kind of function would display a sign-on or greeting at the start of a program.

An example of a function that takes no parameters, but still returns a result to the caller, would be a function that controls interactive input. The function prompts the user for input, reads the input value, and then returns it to the caller. The function might be used as follows:

```
data = get_data();
```

Note that since this function returns a value, the value should be used by the caller. In this example, the value is stored in a variable with an assignment statement. A declaration for the function is

```
int get_data();
```

Its implementation would prompt the user for an integer value, read it in from the standard input stream, and then return it as the value of the function. Because a place is needed to store the value during input, we declare a local variable for this purpose within the function:

```
int get_data()
{
        int number;

        cout << "Enter an integer value, followed by "
             << "<Enter>.";
        cin >> number;
        return number;
}
```

EXERCISES 4.2

1. Indicate which of the following are valid function declarations. Explain what is wrong with those that are invalid.
   a. `round_tenth (double x);`
   b. `double make_change (X, Y);`
   c. `int max (int x, int y, int z);`
   d. `char sign (double x);`
2 Find all errors in each of the following functions.
   a.
   ```
   int average (int n1, int n2);
   {
      return N1 + N2 / 2;
   }
   ```
   b.
   ```
   int total (int n1, int n2)
   {
      int sum;
      return 0;
      sum = n1 + n2;
   }
   ```
3. Write a function for each of the following.
   a. Round a real number to the nearest tenth.
   b. Round a real number to the nearest hundredth.

   c. Convert degrees Fahrenheit to degrees Celsius.

   d. Compute the charge for cars at a parking lot; the rate is 75 cents per hour or fraction thereof.

4. Write a program that uses the function you wrote for Exercise 3d to print a ticket for a customer who parks in the parking lot. Assume the input is in minutes.

5. Use the functions **sqr** and **cube** to write a program to print a chart of the integers 1 to 5 together with their squares and cubes. Output from this program should be

```
Number          Number Squared          Number Cubed
------          --------------          ------------
  1                   1                      1
  2                   4                      8
  3                   9                     27
  4                  16                     64
  5                  25                    125
```

6. Write a program that contains a function that allows the user to enter a base (*a*) and exponent (*x*) and then have the program print the value of a^x.

4.3 Parameters

OBJECTIVES

- to be able to understand the need for and appropriate use of parameters in functions
- to be able to understand the difference between value and reference parameters

Value Parameters

We have seen that parameters are used so that data values can be transmitted, or passed, from the caller to a function. If values are to be passed *only* from the caller to a function, the parameters are called *value parameters.* The following program demonstrates the use of value parameters:

```
// Program file: area.cpp

#include <iostream.h>

// Function: area
// Computes the area of a rectangle
//
// Inputs: two integers representing the length and the
// width of the rectangle
// Outputs: an integer representing the area of the
// rectangle

int area(int length, int width);

int main()
{
       int this_length, this_width;

       cout << "Enter the length: ";
       cin >> this_length;
```

```
        cout << "Enter the width: ";
        cin >> this_width;
        cout << "The area is "
             << area(this_length, this_width) << endl;
        return 0;
}

int area(int length, int width)
{
        return length * width;
}
```

In this program, the formal parameters **length** and **width** are used for one-way transmission of values to the function **area.** When the function is called, the values of the actual parameters, **this_length** and **this_width**, are copied into separate memory locations for the formal parameters **length** and **width**. The fact that there are separate memory locations for the formal and actual parameters guarantees that any changes to the formal parameters will leave the actual parameters unchanged.

Suppose that the user enters 8 for **this_length** and 7 for **this_width**. The state of the machine is now

8
this_length

7
this_width

Note that the only memory locations visible to the program are those for the variables **this_length** and **this_width**. The function is then called to compute the area. The system *allocates* memory locations for the formal parameters **length** and **width**. These names and their memory locations now become visible to the block of statements within the function. The system then places copies of the values 8 and 7 into the memory locations for **length** and **width**. This is why value parameters are said to be *passed by value.* The state of the machine is now

8
this_length

7
this_width

8
length

7
width

When the function returns from its call, the system *deallocates* the memory locations for **length** and **width**. Also, because the function is no longer active, its formal parameters are no longer visible to the program. The values of **this_length** and **this_width**, which are still visible, have not changed. A value parameter always indicates a *local copy* of the value transmitted to the function.

Reference Parameters

You will frequently want a function to return more than one value to a caller. A good example of a task that calls for more than one value to be returned is the interaction with the user for two input values in the program that computes the area of a rectangle. The C++ code for this task reads integer values from the keyboard into two variables:

```
cout << "Enter the length: ";
cin >> this_length;
cout << "Enter the width: ";
cin >> this_width;
```

We could document this task as follows:

```
// Prompts the user for two input integers representing the length and
// width of a rectangle
```

We can represent information to be returned with *reference parameters* in the parameter list of a C++ function. In a function declaration, reference parameters are declared by using the symbol **&** before the appropriate formal parameters. The form of a reference parameter declaration in a function declaration is

<type name> &<formal parameter name>

The C++ declaration for a function **get_data** to perform this task can be added to the documentation:

```
// Function: get_data
// Prompts the user for two input integers representing the length and width
// of a rectangle
//
// Outputs: two integers representing the length and width of a rectangle

void get_data(int &length, int &width);
```

Note that the parameter and type names look the same as they would in declarations of functions that would use the parameters to receive data. However, in this function they will be used to return information to the caller, as is indicated by the **&** symbols.

The form of a reference parameter declaration in the heading of a function implementation is

<type name> &<formal parameter name>

Our **get_data** function can now be implemented as follows:

```
void get_data(int &length, int &width)
{
      cout << "Enter the length: ";
      cin >> length;
      cout << "Enter the width: ";
      cin >> width;
}
```

When reference parameters are declared, values appear to be sent from the function to the caller. Actually, when reference parameters are used, values are not transmitted at all. Reference parameters in the function heading are merely *aliases* for actual variables used by the caller. Thus, variables are said to be *passed by reference* rather than by value. When reference parameters are used, any change of values in the function produces a corresponding change of values in the caller's block.

The notion of aliasing can be seen during a run of the program where the user enters the values 8 and 7 as inputs. Just before the function **get_data** returns, the state of the machine is as follows:

8

this_length
length

7

this_width
width

Note that there are only two memory locations for data in the program thus far. However, each location has two different names associated with it, which means that an assignment to either of the two names, say, **this_width** or **width**, will change the value stored in the corresponding memory location.

Technically, **length** and **width** do not exist as variables. They contain pointers to the same memory locations as **this_length** and **this_width**, respectively. Thus, a statement in the function such as

```
length = 5;
```

causes the memory location reserved for **length** to receive the value 5. That is, it causes the net action

```
this_length = 5;
```

Thus, constants cannot be used when calling a function with reference parameters. For example,

```
get_data(8, 7);
```

produces an error because 8 and 7 are passed in the positions of reference parameters.

An error would also occur if we tried to pass the value of an expression in the position of a reference parameter. For example, the following call would generate an error for the second parameter:

```
get_data(this_length, this_width + 1);
```

In general, the only legitimate actual parameter to pass by reference is a variable or the name of another function's parameter. The reason for this is that only names of this sort can refer to memory locations capable of being aliased by a reference parameter.

The next example also shows a useful function that requires reference parameters.

EXAMPLE 4.4

Many problems call for a function that will exchange the values of data in two variables. For any two variables **a** and **b**, the effect of calling the function **swap(a, b)** will be to replace the value of **a** with the value of **b**, and to replace the value of **b** with the value of **a**. Clearly, a function that returns a single value cannot accomplish this task. We will assume that the values to be swapped are real numbers. Two parameters will be used both to receive data from the caller and to return information as well. Thus, the function's declaration can be written as follows:

```
// Function: swap
// Exchanges the values of the two input variables
//
// Inputs: two real numbers
// Outputs: the two real numbers in reversed order

void swap(float &a, float &b);
```

The function's implementation will use a temporary variable to save one of the input values during the exchange:

```
void swap(float &a, float &b)
{
     float temp;

     temp = a;
     a = b;
     b = temp;
}
```

Note that this function itself returns no value to the caller. This is not unusual for functions that have reference parameters.

COMMUNICATION AND STYLE TIPS

It is considered good programming practice to design a function to be as *general* as possible. General functions solve a *class* of problems rather than a particular problem. For example, functions to get the length and to get the width solve particular problems, whereas a function to get any integer value solves both of these particular problems, as well as others. You should strive to make your functions as general as those you find in the C++ libraries. Designing general functions from scratch is not an easy thing to do. Frequently, you will not spot the need for a general function until you have written several more specialized functions that reveal a common or redundant pattern of code. When that happens, you can take two steps to design a more general function. First, write a single function that contains the common pattern of code that you see in the more specialized functions. Second, add parameters that will allow the callers of the new function to use it for their more specialized purposes.

A NOTE OF INTEREST

The History of Parameter Passing

The use of parameters to communicate information among subprograms is almost as old as the use of subprograms. As soon as subprograms became available in high-level programming languages, programmers realized that subprograms would be virtually useless without parameters. The inclusion of parameters in programming languages allowed programmers to design better code in two respects. First, the use of parameters made code more readable. The parameters of a subprogram module gave it a manifest interface for receiving information from and sending it to other modules. Second, the use of parameters made subprograms more general. Before parameters became available, each subprogram's operations were restricted to a particular problem involving particular data. The addition of parameters allowed programmers to generalize their solutions to manipulate whole classes of data.

The design of different parameter passing mechanisms has been an important chapter in the history of programming languages. Each major step in this process has reflected both the vision of computer scientists about what they consider important in a programming context and the limitations of the available hardware and software technology.

When the use of parameters first appeared in the mid 1950s in the programming language FORTRAN, the focus of programmers was on efficiency. FORTRAN was used primarily to perform mathematical and scientific computations (the acronym stands for **FOR**mula **TRAN**slation language). This kind of application demanded a high processing speed and large amounts of memory. But early processors were slow, and memory was expensive. With these resources at a premium, John Backus, the designer of FORTRAN, decided that all parameters in the language would be passed by reference. Pass by reference is less expensive than pass by value, because no extra memory needs to be allocated for a local copy of the actual parameter, and no extra processing time is needed to copy it. Because FORTRAN subprograms always manipulated the actual arguments passed to them by reference, the subprograms ran very quickly even when large data structures were passed. The use of a single-parameter passing mode also made the language easy to learn and the compiler for it easy to write.

Needless to say, the early FORTRAN programs were not safe. Programmers discovered this to be true especially for large programs that passed many parameters among subprograms. Unintended side effects were numerous. Because of the way that constant symbols were represented, even constants could be changed if they were passed as parameters to FORTRAN subprograms!

After a few years of experience with FORTRAN, John McCarthy, a mathematician at the Massachusetts Institute of Technology, designed LISP. LISP, short for **LIS**t **P**rocessing Language, was intended for processing lists of symbols and was based on a theory of computation known as the recursive lambda calculus. According to this theory, programs should consist of functions that receive zero or more arguments and return a single value. In the process, these functions should not change the arguments themselves. To enforce this requirement, McCarthy designed a pass by value mechanism for parameters. In cases where an actual argument was a simple data type, like a number, functions worked on a local copy of the actual argument, so that no side effects were possible. Efficiency was not important, because LISP was a highly interactive and interpreted language. Thus, the time taken to allocate the extra memory for a formal parameter and copy the value of the actual parameter to it was insignificant when compared to the time taken to interpret LISP expressions generally. In cases where an actual argument was a structured data type, such as a string or a list of numbers, a copy of a pointer to the argument was passed for reasons of efficiency. The parameter passing mechanism of LISP thus reflected concerns of both safety and efficiency.

The primary teaching language in computer science for the last 20 years until recently has been Pascal. Named after the French mathematician, Pascal was designed by Niklaus Wirth. Pascal has two parameter passing modes. Pass by value worked like pass by value in LISP. However, Wirth extended pass by value to structured data values as well, making this mode expensive to use at run time. Pass by reference worked as in FORTRAN, except that constants and expressions were disallowed as actual reference parameters. Pascal also allows subprograms to be passed as parameters. This is an important development in our story, in that subprograms can be generalized still further by being parameterized for more specific subprograms. The following example of a general summation function in Pascal illustrates this point:

```
function sum(low, high : integer;
function f(x : integer) : integer) :
integer;
        var
           i, accum : integer;
        begin
        accum := 0;
        for i := low to high do
            accum := accum + f(i);
        sum := accum;
        end;

begin
writeln(sum(1, 10, square));
end.
```

continued

A NOTE OF INTEREST (continued)

The syntax of Pascal is fairly close to that of C++. Assuming that the function **square** had been defined elsewhere, the **sum** function would return the summation of the squares of all of the integers between 1 and 10 in this example. The name **square** substitutes for **f** inside of the function at run time. The summation function will work with any function parameter of one integer argument that returns an integer value. As you can see, passing functions as parameters is a powerful way to generalize functions and reduce the redundancy of code in programs. C++ allows functions to be passed as parameters, as discussed in Chapter 11.

EXERCISES 4.3

1. Find the errors in the following function headings.

   a.
   ```
   // Function: get_data
   // Prompts user for two integer input values
   //
   // Outputs: two integers

   void get_data(int length, int width);
   ```
   b.
   ```
   // Function: area
   // Computes the area of a rectangle
   //
   // Inputs: two integers representing the length and
   // the width of the rectangle
   // Outputs: an integer representing the area of the
   // rectangle

   int area(int length, int &width);
   ```
   c.
   ```
   // Function: circle_attributes
   // Computes the diameter and area of a circle
   //
   // Input: a real number representing the radius of the
   // circle
   // Outputs: two real numbers representing the diameter
   // and area of the circle

   void circle_attributes(float &radius,
         float &diameter, float &area);
   ```
2. Write and test a function **int_divide** that receives two integer values and two integer variables from the caller. When the function completes execution, the values in these variables should be the quotient and the remainder produced by dividing the second value by the first value. Be sure to name your parameters descriptively so as to aid the reader of the function.

4.4 Functions as Subprograms

Functions can be used as subprograms for a number of purposes. Two significant uses are to facilitate the top-down design philosophy of problem solving and to avoid having to write repeated segments of code.

Functions facilitate problem solving. Recall the Focus on Program Design problem in Chapter 3. In that problem, you were asked to compute the unit cost for a pizza. The main modules were

OBJECTIVES

- to understand how functions can be used to design programs
- to be able to use functions to get data for programs
- to be able to use functions to perform required tasks in programs
- to be able to use functions for output

1. Get the data
2. Perform the computations
3. Print the results

A function can be written for each of these tasks and the program can then call each function as needed. Thus, the statement portion of the program would have the form

```
data = get_data();
results = perform_computations(data);
print_results(results);
```

This makes it easy to see and understand the main tasks of the program.

Once you develop the ability to write and use subprograms, you will usually write programs by writing the main program first. Your main program should be written so it can be easily read by a nonprogrammer but still contain enough structure to enable a programmer to know what to do if asked to write code for the tasks. In this sense, it is not necessary for a person reading the main program to understand *how* a subprogram accomplishes its task; it need only be apparent *what* the subprogram does.

When you design subprograms, you should also consider the problem of data flow. The most difficult aspect of learning to use subprograms is handling transmission of data. Recall from the structure charts shown earlier that arrows were used to indicate whether data were received by and/or sent from a module. Also, each module specification indicated if data were received by that module and if information was sent from it. Since a subprogram will be written to accomplish the task of each module, we must be able to transmit data as indicated. Once you have developed this ability, using functions becomes routine.

Using Subprograms

Use of subprograms facilitates writing programs for problems whose solutions have been developed using top-down design. A function can be written for each main task.

How complex should a function be? In general, functions should be relatively short and perform a specific task. Some programmers prefer to limit functions to no more than one full screen of text. If longer than a page or screen, the task might need to be subdivided into smaller functions.

Cohesive Subprograms

The cohesion of a subprogram is the degree to which the subprogram performs a single task. A subprogram that is developed in such a way is called a *cohesive subprogram.* As you use subprograms to implement a design based on modular development, you should always try to write cohesive subprograms.

The property of cohesion is not well defined. Subtask complexity varies in the minds of different programmers. In general, if the task is unclear, the corresponding subprogram will not be cohesive. When this happens, you should subdivide the task until a subsequent development allows cohesive subprograms.

To illustrate briefly the concept of cohesion, consider the first-level design of a problem to compute grades for a class. Step 3 of this design could be

3. Process grades for each student

Clearly, this is not a well-defined task. Thus, if you were to write a subprogram for this task, the subprogram would not be cohesive. Consider the subsequent development:

3. Process grades for each student
   while not end of input
   3.1 get a line of data
   3.2 compute average
   3.3 compute letter grade
   3.4 print data
   3.5 compute totals

Here we see that functions to accomplish subtasks 3.1, 3.2, 3.3, and 3.4 would be cohesive because each subtask consists of a single task. The final subtask, compute totals, may or may not result in a cohesive subprogram. More information is needed before you can decide what is to be done at this step.

Functional Abstraction

The purpose of using functions is to simplify reasoning. During the design stage, as a problem is subdivided into tasks, the problem solver (you) should have to consider only what a function is to do and not be concerned about details of the function. Instead, the function name and comments at the beginning of the function should be sufficient to inform the user as to what the function does. Developing functions in this manner is referred to as *functional abstraction* (this notion is also called *procedural abstraction,* because some languages support subprograms known as *procedures* that are similar to functions).

Functional abstraction is the first step in designing and writing a function. The list of parameters and comments about the action of the function should precede development of the body of the function. This forces clarity of thought and aids design. Use of this method might cause you to discover that your design is not sufficient to solve the task and a redesign is necessary. Therefore, you could reduce design errors and save time when writing code.

Functional abstraction becomes especially important when teams work on a project. Each member of the writing team should be able to understand the purpose and use of functions written by other team members without having to analyze the body of each function. This is analogous to the situation in which you use a predefined function without really understanding how the function works.

Functional abstraction is perhaps best formalized in terms of preconditions and postconditions. A *precondition* is a comment that states precisely what is true before a certain action is taken. A *postcondition* states what is true after the action has been taken. Carefully written preconditions and postconditions used with functions enhance the concept of functional abstraction. (Additional uses of preconditions and postconditions are discussed in Sections 5.6 and 6.5.)

In summary, functional abstraction means that, when writing or using functions, you should think of them as single, clearly understood units, of which each accomplishes a specific task.

Information Hiding

Information hiding can be thought of as the process of hiding the implementation details of a subprogram. This is just what we do when we use a top-down design to solve a problem. We decide which tasks and subtasks are necessary to solve a problem without worrying about how the specific subtasks will be accomplished. In the sense of software engineering, information hiding is what allows teams to work on a large system: It is only necessary to know what another team is doing, not how they are doing it.

A NOTE OF INTEREST

Computer Ethics: Hacking and Other Intrusions

A famous sequence of computer intrusions has been detailed by Clifford Stoll. The prime intruder came to Stoll's attention in August 1986, when an intruder attempted to penetrate a computer at Lawrence Berkeley Laboratory (LBL). Instead of denying the intruder access, management at LBL went along with Stoll's recommendation that they attempt to unmask the intruder, even though the risk was substantial because the intruder had gained system-manager privileges.

The intruder, Markus H., a member of a small group of West Germans, was unusually persistent, but no computer wizard. He made use of known deficiencies in the half-dozen or so operating systems, including UNIX, VMS, VM-TSO, and EMBOS, with which he was familiar, but he did not invent any new modes of entry. He penetrated 30 of the 450 computers then on the network system at LBL.

After Markus H. was successfully traced, efforts were instituted to make LBL's computers less vulnerable. To ensure high security, it would have been necessary to change all passwords overnight and recertify each user. This and other demanding measures were deemed impractical. Instead, deletion of all expired passwords was instituted; shared accounts were eliminated; monitoring of incoming traffic was extended, with alarms set in key places; and education of users was attempted.

The episode was summed up by Stoll as a powerful learning experience for those involved in the detection process and for all those concerned about computer security. That the intruder was caught at all is testimony to the ability of a large number of concerned professionals to keep the tracing effort secret.

In a later incident, an intruder left the following embarrassing message in a computer file assigned to Clifford Stoll: "The cuckoo has egg on his face." The reference was to Stoll's book, *The Cuckoo's Egg,* which tracked the intrusions of the West German hacker just described. The embarrassment was heightened by the fact that the computer, owned by Harvard University with which astronomer Stoll is now associated, was on the Internet network. The intruder, or intruders, who goes by the name of Dave, also attempted to break into dozens of other computers on the same network—and succeeded.

The *nom de guerre* of "Dave" was used by one or more of three Australians recently arrested by the federal police down under. The three, who at the time of their arrest were respectively 18, 20, and 21 years of age, successfully penetrated computers in both Australia and the United States.

The three Australians went beyond browsing to damage data in computers in their own nation and the United States. At the time they began their intrusions in 1988 (when the youngest was only 16), there was no law in Australia under which they could be prosecuted. It was not until legislation making such intrusions prosecutable was passed that the police began to take action.

Interface and Documentation

Independent subprograms need to communicate with the main program and other subprograms. A formal statement of how such communication occurs is called the *interface* of the subprogram. This usually consists of comments at the beginning of a subprogram and includes all the documentation the reader will need to use the subprogram. We have seen examples of subprogram interfaces in the function declarations and headings that have appeared in this chapter.

Software Engineering

Perhaps the greatest difference between beginning students in computer science and "real-world" programmers is how they perceive the need for documentation. Typically, beginning students want to make a program run; they view anything that delays this process as an impediment. Thus, some students consider using descriptive identifiers, writing variable dictionaries, describing a problem as part of program documentation, and using appropriate comments throughout a program as a nuisance. In contrast, system designers and programmers who write code for a living often spend up to 50% of their time and effort on documentation. There are at least three reasons for this difference in perspective.

First, real programmers work on large, complex systems with highly developed logical paths. Without proper documentation, even the person who developed an algorithm will have difficulty following its logic six months later. Second, communication among teams is required as systems are developed. Complete, clear statements about what the problems are and how they are being solved are essential. Third, programmers know they can develop algorithms and write the necessary code. They are trained so that problems of searching, sorting, and file manipulation are routine. Knowing that they can solve a problem thus allows them to devote more time and energy to documenting how the solution has been achieved.

We close this section with a revision of the program from Chapter 3 that found the unit cost for a pizza. The original program was designed using module specifications, but implemented in C++ as a long sequence of statements in the main program section. The revision will implement each module of the design as a C++ function to be called from the main program section. The structure chart is shown in Figure 4.1. The module specifications are

Module: Get data
Task: Gets cost and size of pizza from the user at the keyboard.
Outputs: cost and size

Module: Compute price per square inch
Task: Compute the price per square inch of pizza.
Input: Cost and size of pizza
Output: price per square inch

Module: Print results
Task: Print the price per square inch.
Input: price per square inch

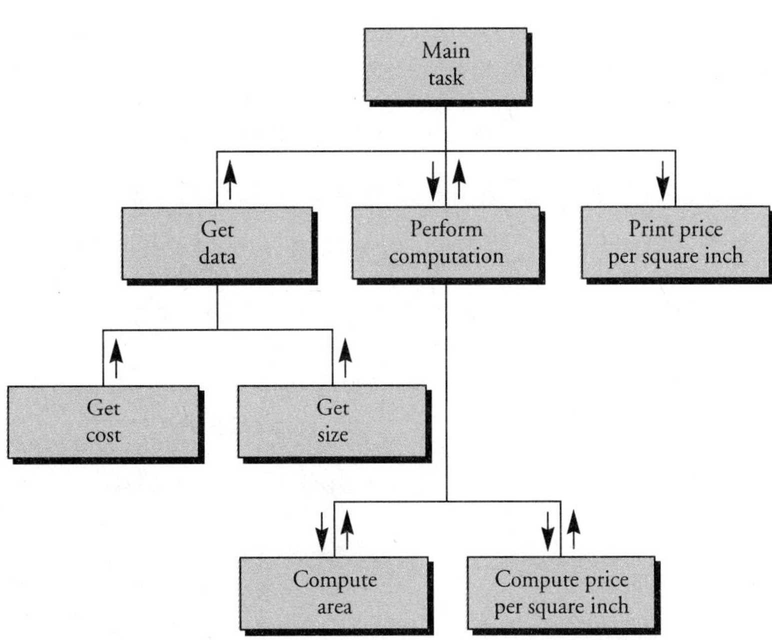

◆ FIGURE 4.1
Structure chart for the pizza problem

The module for getting the data receives no data, but returns two data values to the caller. The C++ function declaration specifies a function named **get_data** and two reference parameters, **cost** and **size**, in which the input data are returned to the caller:

```
// Function: get_data
// Gets cost and size of pizza from the user
// at the keyboard
//
// Outputs: The cost and size

void get_data(float &cost, int &size);
```

The C++ function implementation prompts the user for the cost and then for the size of the pizza, and returns the two input values in the reference parameters:

```
void get_data(float &cost, int &size)
{
        cout << "Enter the pizza price and press"
             << "<Enter>. ";
        cin >> cost;
        cout << "Enter the pizza size and press"
             <<"<Enter>. ";
        cin >> size;
}
```

We next write a function for performing the desired computations. This function receives the cost and size and then returns the price per square inch. Thus, cost and size are parameters and the price per square inch is the returned value of the function. If we name the function **price_per_square_inch**, we can write its declaration as follows:

```
// Function: compute price per square inch
// Compute the price per square inch of pizza
//
// Input: cost and size of pizza
// Output: price per square inch

float price_per_square_inch(float cost, int size);
```

The implementation of this function also requires variables **radius** and **area** to be declared in the data declaration section of the function. Assuming **PI** has been defined as a constant and **sqr** has been defined as a function, the function's implementation is

```
float price_per_square_inch(float pizza_cost,
     int pizza_size)
{
     float radius, area;
     radius = pizza_size / 2;
     area = PI * sqr(radius);
     return pizza_cost / area;
}
```

A function to print the results receives the unit cost. A declaration for the function is

```
// Function: print results
// Print the price per square inch
//
// Input: price per square inch

void print_results(float price_per_sq_inch);
```

The function's implementation is:

```
void print_results(float price_per_sq_inch)
{
      cout << fixed << showpoint << setprecision(2) << endl;
      cout << "The price per square inch is $";
      cout << setw(6) << price_per_sq_inch << endl;
}
```

The complete program for this problem is as follows:

```
// Program file: pizza.cpp

#include <iostream.h>
#include <iomanip.h>

const float PI = 3.14159;

// Function: get_data
// Gets cost and size of pizza from the user at the keyboard
//
// Outputs: The cost and size

void get_data(float &cost, int &size);

// Function: compute price per square inch
// Compute the price per square inch of pizza
//
// Input: cost and size of pizza
// Output: price per square inch

float price_per_square_inch(float cost, int size);

// Function: print results
// Print the price per square inch
//
// Input: price per square inch

void print_results(float price_per_sq_inch);

// Function: sqr
// Computes the square of a number
//
// Input: a real number
// Output: a real number representing the square of the input
```

```
float sqr(float x);

int main()
{
      int size;
      float cost, price;

      get_data(cost, size);
      price = price_per_square_inch(cost, size);
      print_results(price);
      return 0;
}

void get_data(float &cost, int &size)
{
     cout << "Enter the pizza price and press <Enter>. ";
     cin >> cost;                                                 1
     cout << "Enter the pizza size and press <Enter>. ";
     cin >> size;
}

float price_per_square_inch(float cost, int size)
{
      float radius, area;
      radius = size / 2;                                          2
      area = PI * sqr(radius);
      return cost / area;
}

void print_results(float price_per_sq_inch)
{
     cout << fixed << showpoint << setprecision(2)
          << endl;                                                3
     cout << "The price per square inch is $";
     cout << setw(6) << price_per_sq_inch << endl;
}

float sqr(float x)
{
     return x * x;
}
```

Note the way in which the use of subprograms has simplified the structure of the main program, as compared with the original version in Chapter 3.

```
get_data (cost, size);
```

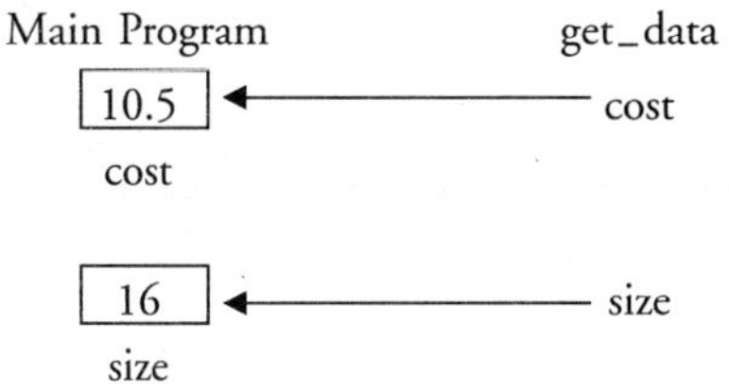

Main Program get_data

10.5 ← cost

cost

16 ← size

size

```
Price = Price_per_square_inch (cost, size);
```

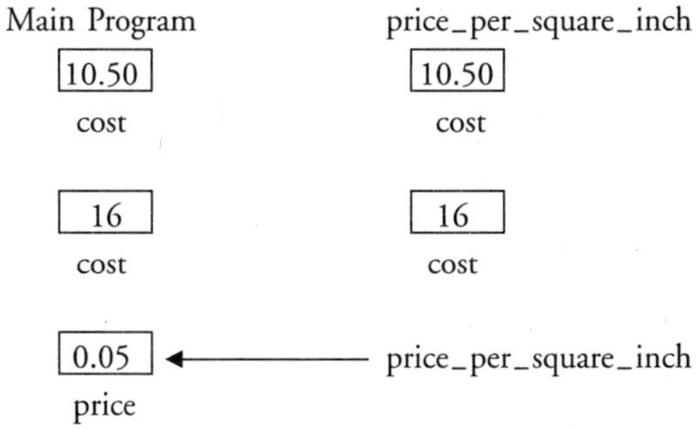

Main Program price_per_square_inch

10.50 10.50

cost cost

16 16

cost cost

0.05 ← price_per_square_inch

price

```
Print_results (Price);
```

Main Program print_results

0.05 0.05

price price

Sample runs of this program produce the following output:

```
Enter the pizza price and press <Enter>. 10.50
Enter the pizza size and press <Enter>. 16

The price per square inch is $ 0.05

Enter the pizza price and press <Enter>. 8.75
Enter the pizza size and press <Enter>. 14

The price per square inch is $ 0.06
```

EXERCISES 4.4

1. Draw a structure chart for a program that prompts the user for an integer, computes its square root, and displays this result with an informative label on the terminal screen. Your chart should contain three modules: one for getting the data, one for computing the result, and one for printing the result. Be sure to label the data flow between the modules with arrows.
2. Construct a main program module in C++, and add to it the declarations of three functions that will carry out the tasks of the modules from the previous exercise.
3. Implement and test each of the functions from Exercise 2. You will have to declare at least one integer variable to pass the data from module to module.

4.5 Scope of Identifiers

OBJECTIVES

- to understand what is meant by local identifiers
- to understand what is meant by global identifiers
- to understand the scope of an identifier
- to recognize the appropriate and inappropriate uses of global identifiers
- to be able to understand and control side effects in programs
- to be able to use appropriate names for identifiers

Global and Local Identifiers

Identifiers used to declare variables in the declaration section of a program can be used throughout the entire program. For purposes of this section, we will think of the global text of the program file as a *block* and the main program and each subprogram as a *subblock* for the main program or subprogram. Each subblock may contain a parameter list, a local declaration section, and the body of the block. A program file block can be envisioned as shown in Figure 4.2. Furthermore, if **X1** is a variable in the main program block, we will indicate this as shown in Figure 4.3, where an area in memory has been set aside for **X1**. When a program contains a subprogram, a separate memory area within the memory area for the program is set aside for the subprogram to use while it executes. Thus, if the program file contains a function named **subprog1**, we can envision this as shown in Figure 4.4. If **subprog1** contains the variable **X2**, we have the program shown in Figure 4.5. This could be indicated in the program by

```
const float PI = 3.14;

float subprog1 (float x2);

int main;
{
        float x1;

        subprog1(x1);
        .
        .
        .
```

◆ FIGURE 4.2
Program file block

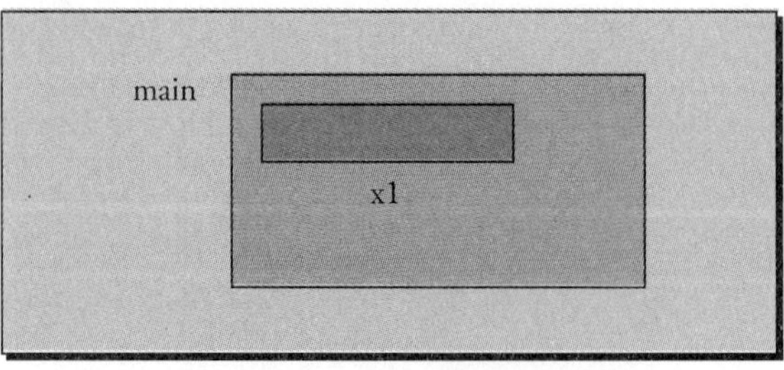

◆ FIGURE 4.3
Variable location in main block

The *scope of an identifier* refers to the area of the program text in which it can be used. When subprograms are used, each identifier is available to the block in which it is declared and any nested blocks. Identifiers are not available outside their blocks.

Identifiers that are declared before the main block are called *global identifiers;* identifiers that are restricted to use within the main block or a subblock are called *local identifiers.* Constant **`PI`** in Figure 4.5 can be used throughout the main program and in the function **`subprog1`**; therefore it is a global identifier. Variable **`X1`** can be used in the main program but not in the function **`subprog1`**; it is a local identifier. Variable **`X2`** can only be used within the function where it is declared; it is a local identifier. Any attempt to reference **`X2`** outside the function will result in an error. Lastly, function **`subprog1`** can be used either in the main program block, within another function's block, or within its own block. This last use is a recursive one, which we will discuss in Chapter 12.

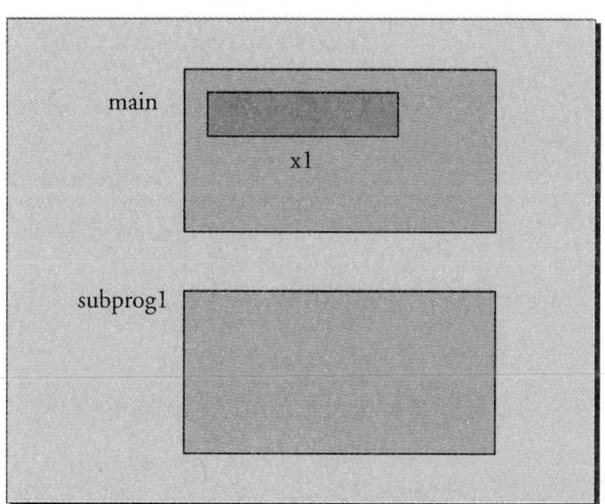

◆ FIGURE 4.4
Illustration of a subblock

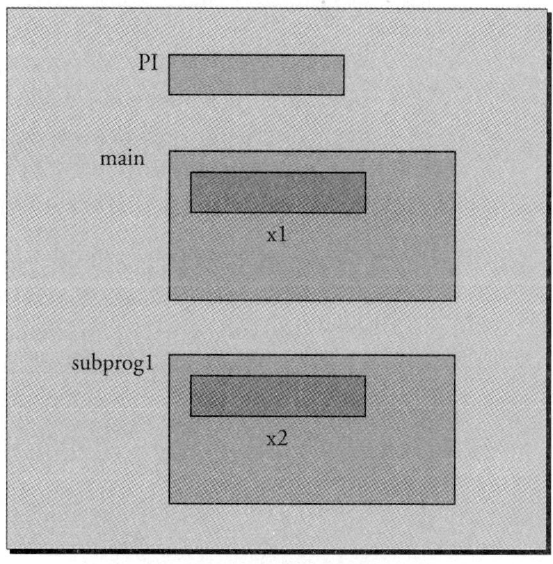

◆ FIGURE 4.5
Variable location within a subblock

As a matter of C++ syntax, function names must be declared as global identifiers. Constant, variable, and type names can be declared either globally or locally. However, as a matter of good programming style, constant and type names are usually declared globally, and variable names are declared locally.

Let us now examine an illustration of local and global identifiers. Consider the program and function declaration

```
const int A = 10;

subprog(int a1);

int main()
{
      int x, y;
      .
      .
}

int subprog (int a1)
{
      float x;
      .
      .
```

Blocks for this program can be envisioned as shown in Figure 4.6. Because **A** is global, the statement

```
cout << A << a1 << x << endl;
```

could be used in the function **subprog** although **A** has not been specifically declared there. However,

```
cout << A << a1 << x << endl;
```

could not be used in the main program because **a1** and **x** are local to the function **subprog**.

Using Global Identifiers

In general, it is not good practice to refer to global variables within functions. A *side effect* is a change in a nonlocal variable that is the result of some action taken in a program. The use of locally defined variables in functions and in the main program block helps to avoid unexpected side effects and protects your programs. In addition, locally defined variables facilitate debugging and top-down design and enhance the portability of functions. This is especially important if different people are working on different functions for a program.

The use of global constants is different. Because the values cannot be changed by a function, it is preferred that constants be defined in the data declaration section before the main program block and then be used whenever needed by any subprogram. This is especially important if the constant is subject to change over time, for example, **STATE_TAX_RATE**. When a change is necessary, one change in the main program is all that is needed to make all subprograms current. If a constant is used in only one function, some programmers prefer to have it defined near the point of use. Thus, they would define it in the subprogram in which it is used.

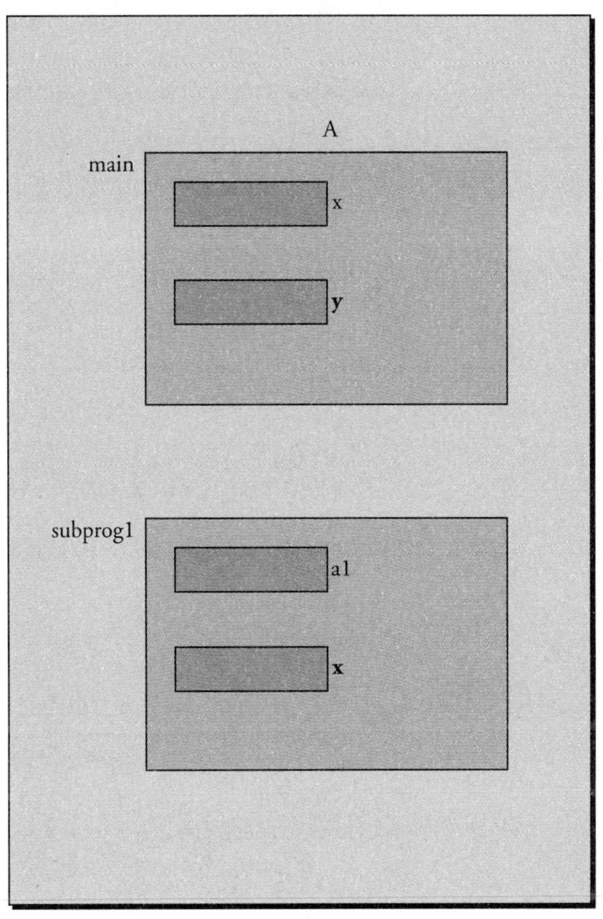

◆ FIGURE 4.6
Scope of identifiers

Side Effects and Parameters

Unintentional side effects are frequently caused by the misuse of reference parameters. Since any change in a reference parameter causes a change in the corresponding actual parameter in the calling program or function, you should use reference parameters only when your intent is to produce such changes. In all other cases, use value parameters. For example, the following program would produce a syntax error, because a function attempts to access a variable declared in the main block:

```
void bad_square();

int main()
{
      int main_data;

      bad_square();
      return 0;

}

void bad_square();
{
      main_data = main_data * main_data;
}
```

If we move the declaration of **main_data** outside of the main block, we can extend its scope into the local block of the function, unless the name is redeclared within the function as a parameter or local variable:

```
int main_data;

void bad_square();

int main()
{

        bad_square();
        return 0;
}

void bad_square();
{
        main_data = main_data * main_data;
}
```

We have named the function **bad_square** to indicate that the assignment that occurs in the function is bad programming practice, even though the result might be intended by the programmer. Not only does the use of this function result in a serious side effect, but there is no indication in the function's declaration or in the function's call that the function will modify the global variable. Keeping the declarations of these variables inside the main program block will help to guard against this problem.

A better version of this program moves the declaration of the global variable back into the main block and passes the variable as a reference parameter to the function:

```
void better_square(int &x);

int main()
{
        int main_data;

        better_square(main_data);
        return 0;
}

void better_square(int &x)
{
      x = x * x;
}
```

The function **better_square** improves on **bad_square** in two respects. First, the function now has a *manifest interface.* A function has a manifest interface if we can see, just from looking at the function's declaration and the function's call, exactly what data the function is manipulating, and that it will be subject to change within the function. In other words, we are given clear notice that a side effect will occur in the function, and a clear indication of what that side effect will be. Second, the function can be used to take the square of any variable passed to it as an actual parameter. We have indicated this by using **x** to name the formal parameter of the function. Thus, **better_square** is more general than **bad_square**, which could take the square of just one variable.

While **better_square** is an improvement on **bad_square**, we can write a still better version of this function:

```
int best_square(int x);

int main()
{
       int main_data;

       main_data = best_square(main_data);
       return 0;
}

int best_square(int x)
{
     return x * x;
}
```

This version of the function is the best one for two reasons. First, it has a manifest interface. The caller knows exactly what data will be used by the function. Second, the function produces no side effects. The caller passes the function a value to be squared, and the square of this value is returned to the caller. In particular, if the caller passes a variable to this function, the caller can be sure that the function will not change the variable. If the caller wants to set a variable to the value returned by the function, then this assignment must be explicitly done by the caller after the function returns its value.

All three versions of the function in this example are technically correct, in that they accomplish the task intended by the programmer. However, as the example demonstrates, whenever possible, it is best to write functions that have manifest interfaces and that produce no side effects.

1. Adopt a convention of listing all of the value parameters in a function declaration and heading before you list any of the reference parameters. This will aid in reading the function. For example, the following declaration has six parameters, three of which are value parameters and three of which are reference parameters:

```
void process_data(float a, float b, int x, float &c,
float &d, int &y);
```

2. In most cases where a function returns a single value to the caller, you should use value parameters only. You should use reference parameters only where you wish to return more than one value to the caller.
3. Most functions that use reference parameters should be **void** functions. This will avoid confusion about how many values are returned.
4. To help minimize side effects, declare all variables used by the main program within the main program block.

A NOTE OF INTEREST

John Backus

You have read about John Backus, the inventor of FORTRAN, in a note of interest on program libraries in Chapter 2 and we also mentioned him earlier in this chapter. Backus has had a long and distinguished career as a computer scientist with IBM. During the late 1950s, he sat on a committee that developed ALGOL, the first *block-structured* programming language. The block structure of ALGOL represented a significant advance over FORTRAN. A block in ALGOL is a set of related data declarations and executable statements. The data declared in a block are visible only within it. This greatly enhances program security, readability, and maintenance. Most modern programming languages developed after ALGOL, including C++, have been block structured.

In 1977, Backus was given the Turing Award for his contributions to computer science at the annual meeting of the Association for Computing machinery. Each recipient of this annual award presents a lecture. Backus discussed a new discipline in his talk called *function-oriented programming.* This style of programming was developed to address concerns about the reliability and maintainability of large software systems. One of the principal causes of errors in large programs is the presence of side effects and unintentional modifications of variables. These modifications can occur anywhere in a program with assignment statements whose targets are global variables. Backus proposed that function-oriented programming could eliminate side effects by eliminating the assignment statement and keeping global variables to a minimum. Function-oriented programs consist of sets of function declarations and *function applications.* A function application simply evaluates the arguments to a function, applies the function to these values, and returns a result to the caller. No assignment statements to global variables are allowed within a function. No side effects occur.

The philosophy of function-oriented programming has motivated the design of function-oriented languages. These languages do not allow the programmer to perform assignments to global variables within functions. Though C++ allows programmers to declare and use functions, the language does not forbid this kind of side effect. However, by exercising some discipline, C++ programmers can still emulate a function-oriented style to prevent side effects from occurring in their programs.

Names of Identifiers

Because separate areas in memory are set aside when subprograms are used, it is possible to have identifiers with the same name in both the main program and a subprogram. Thus

```
int main()
{
       int age;
       .
       .
}

int subprog (int age)
```

can be envisioned as shown in Figure 4.7. When the same name is used in this manner, any reference to this name results in action being taken as locally as possible. Thus, the assignment statement

```
age = 20;
```

made in the function **subprog** assigns 20 to **age** in the function but not in the main program (see Figure 4.8).

Now that you know you can use the same name for an identifier in a subprogram and the main program, the question is "Should you?" There are two schools of thought regarding this issue. If you use the same name in the functions, it facilitates matching parameter lists and independent development of functions.

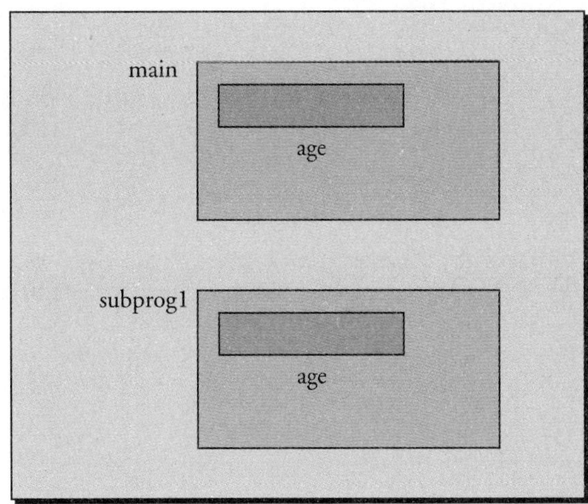

◆ FIGURE 4.7
Relation of identifiers

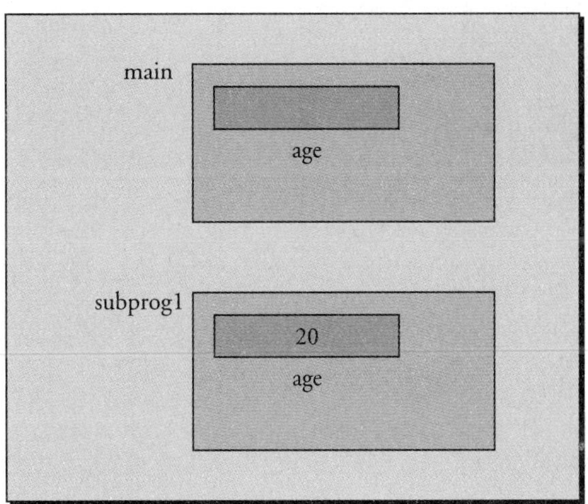

◆ FIGURE 4.8
Assigning values in subprograms

However, this practice can be confusing when you first start working with subprograms. Thus, some instructors prefer using different, but related, identifiers. For example,

```
display_data (score1, score2);
```

in the main program could have a function heading of

```
void display_data (int sc1, int sc2);
```

In this case, the use of **sc1** and **sc2** is obvious. Although this may facilitate better understanding in early work with subprograms, it is less conducive to portability and independent development of functions. Both styles are used in this text.

Multiple Functions

More than one function can be used in a program. When this occurs, all of the previous uses and restrictions of identifiers apply to each function. Blocks for

◆ **FIGURE 4.9**

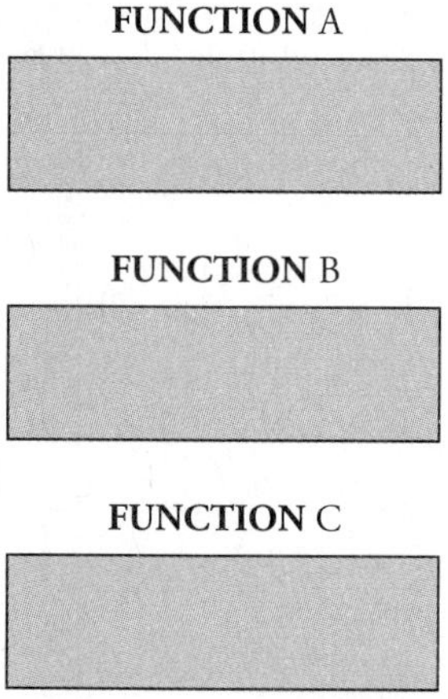

FUNCTION A

FUNCTION B

FUNCTION C

◆ **FIGURE 4.10**
Identifiers in multiple subprograms

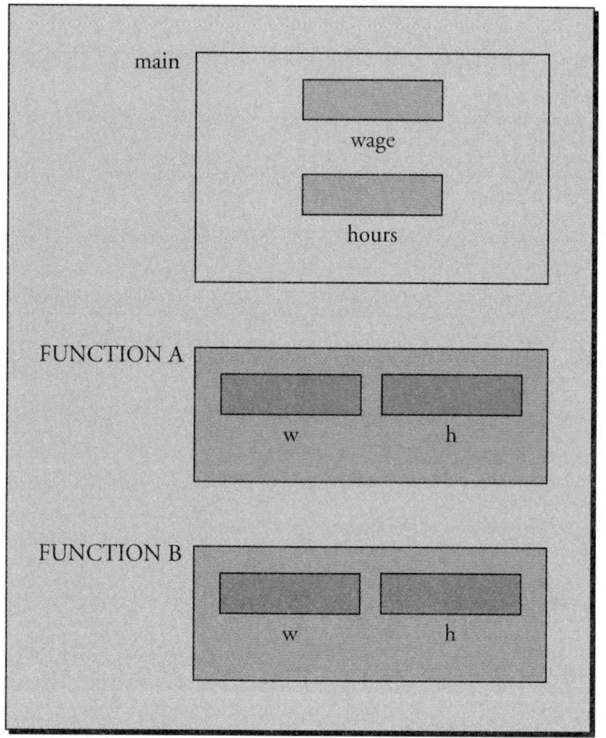

multiple functions can be depicted as shown in Figure 4.9. Identifiers in the main program can be accessed by each function. However, local identifiers in the functions cannot be accessed outside their blocks.

When a program contains several functions, they can be called from the main part of the program in any order.

The same names for identifiers can be used in different functions. Thus, if the main program uses variables **`wage`** and **`hours`**, and both of these are used as arguments in calls to different functions, you have the situation shown in Figure 4.10.

Using the same names for identifiers in different functions makes it easier to keep track of the relationship between variables in the main program and their associated parameters in each subprogram.

EXERCISES 4.5

1. Explain the difference between local and global identifiers.
2. State the advantages of using local identifiers.
3. Discuss some appropriate uses for global identifiers. List several constants that would be appropriate global definitions.
4. What is meant by the scope of an identifier?
5. Write a test program that will enable you to see
   a. what happens when an attempt is made to access an identifier outside of its scope; and
   b. how the values change as a result of assignments in the subprogram and the main program when the same identifier is used in the main program and a subprogram.
6. Review the following program:

```
int main;
{
        int a, b;
        float x;
        char ch;
        .
        .
}
int sub1(int a1)
{
        int b1;
        .
        .
        }

int sub2(int a1, int b1)
{
        float x1;
        char ch1;
        .
        .
}
```

   a. List all global variables.
   b. List all local variables.
   c. Indicate the scope of each identifier.
7. Provide a schematic representation of the program and all subprograms and variables in Exercise 6.
8. Using the program with variables and subprograms as depicted in Figure 4.11, state the scope of each identifier.

◆ FIGURE 4.11

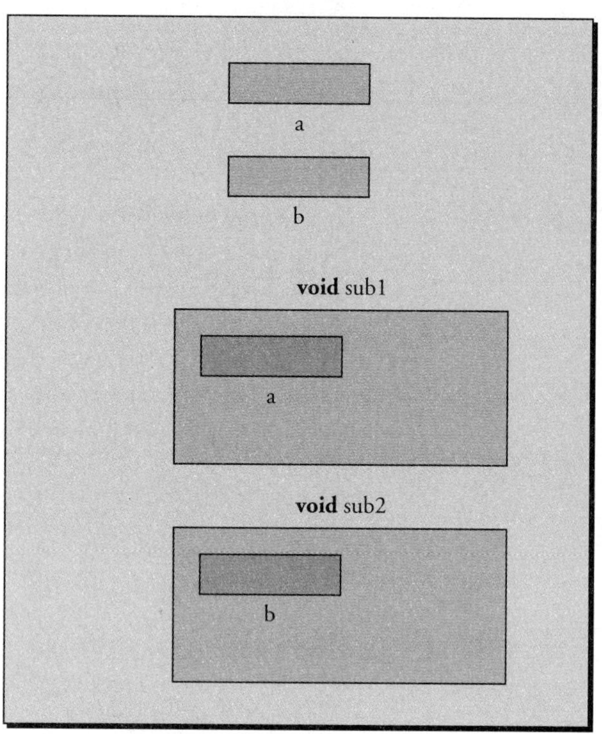

9. What is the output from the following program?

```
#include <iostream.h>

void sub1 (int a);

int main()
{
        int a;
        a = 10;

        cout << a << endl;
        sub1 (a);
        cout << a << endl;
        return 0;
}

void sub1 (int a)
{
        a = 20;
        cout << a << endl;
}
```

10. Write appropriate headings and declaration sections for the program and subprograms illustrated in Figure 4.12.

◆ FIGURE 4.12

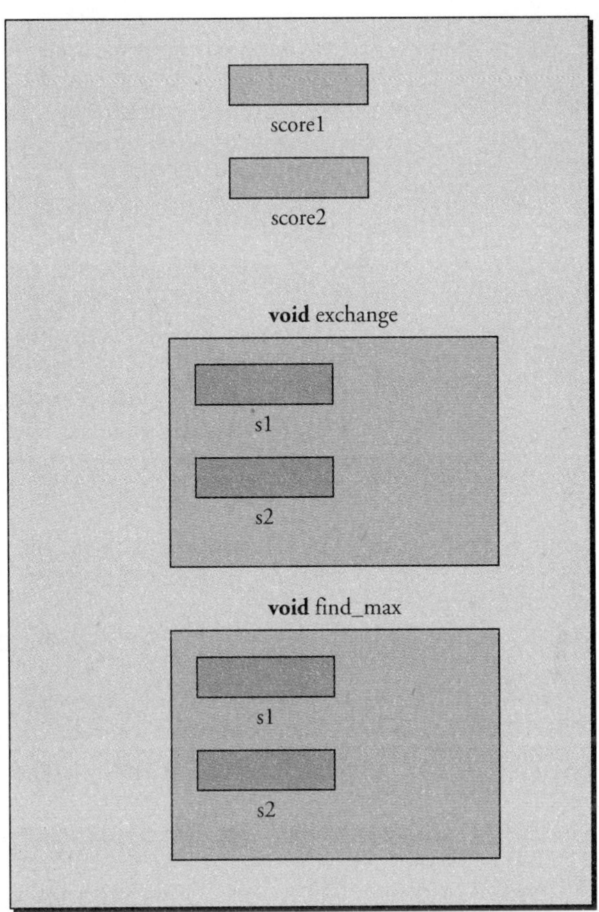

11. Find all errors in the following program.

```
int main()
{
        float x, y;
        x = 10;
        y = 2 * x;
        cout << x << y << endl;
        sub1(x);
        cout << x1 << x << y << endl;
        return 0;
}

void sub1 (int x1)
{
        cout << x1 << x << y << endl;
}
```

12. Discuss the advantages and disadvantages of using the same names for identifiers in a subprogram and the main program.

FOCUS ON PROGRAM DESIGN

To encourage people to shop downtown, the Downtown Businesses Association partially subsidizes parking. They have established the E-Z Parking parking lot where customers are charged \$0.75 for each full hour of parking. There is no charge for part of an hour. Thus, if someone has used the lot for less than an hour, there would be no charge.

The E-Z Parking parking lot is open from 9:00 A.M. until 11:00 P.M. When a vehicle enters, the driver is given a ticket with the entry time printed in military style. Thus, if a car entered the lot at 9:30 A.M., the ticket would read 930. If a vehicle entered at 1:20 P.M., the ticket would read 1320. When the vehicle leaves, the driver presents the ticket to the attendant and the amount due is computed.

Let us now develop a solution and write a program to assist the attendant. Input consists of a starting and ending time. Output should be a statement to the customer indicating the input information, the total amount due, a heading, and a closing message. Sample output for the data 1050 (10:50 A.M.) and 1500 (3:00 P.M.) is

```
Please enter the time in and press <Enter>. 1050
Please enter the time out and press <Enter>. 1500

              E - Z Parking

    Time in: 1050 Time out: 1500

    Amount due      $ 3.00

Thank you for using E - Z Parking

               BUCKLE UP
             and DRIVE SAFELY
```

A first-level development for this problem is

1. Get the data
2. Compute amount
3. Print results

A structure chart for this problem is given in Figure 4.13. (Recall, an arrow pointing into a module indicates data are being received, whereas an arrow pointing out indicates data are being sent from the module.) Module specifications for the three main modules are

Module: Get data
Task: Prompts user for and inputs entry time and exit time.
Outputs: integers representing entry time and exit time

Module: Compute amount
Task: Computes the amount due in dollars and cents.
Inputs: integers representing entry time and exit time
Output: a real number representing the amount due

Module: Print results
Task: prints heading, entry and exit times, amount due, and closing message.
Inputs: integers representing entry time and exit time and a real number representing the amount due

◆ FIGURE 4.13
Structure chart for the parking lot program

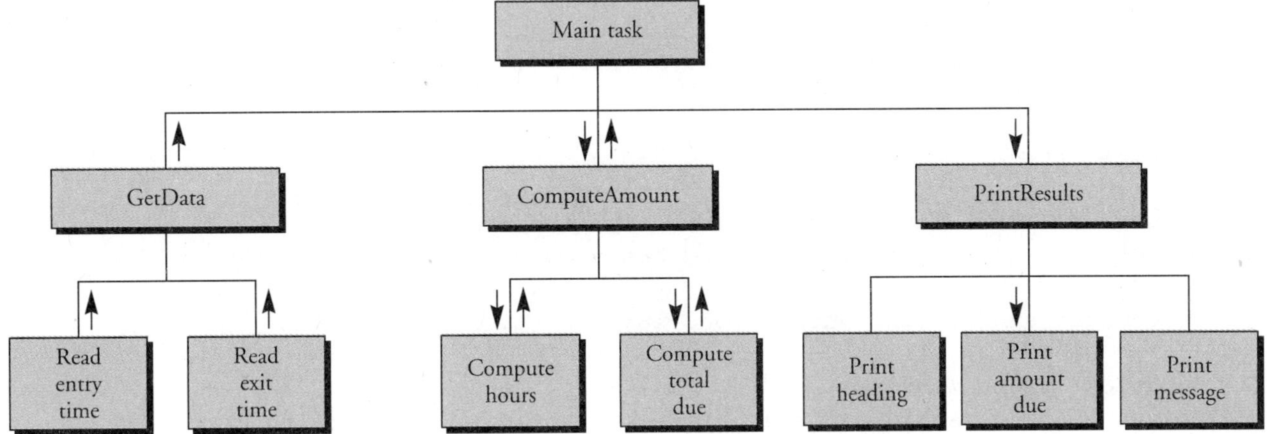

By examining the module specifications, we see that **get_data** needs two parameters, **compute_amount** needs two parameters, and **print_results** needs three parameters.

A second-level pseudocode development is

1. Get the data
   1.1 prompt user for time entered
   1.2 read time entered
   1.1 prompt user for time exited
   1.4 read time exited
2. Compute amount
   2.1 compute number of hours
   2.2 compute amount due
3. Print results
   3.1 print a heading
   3.2 print amount due
   3.3 print a closing message

A complete program for this is

```
// This program prints statements for customers of the E-Z
// Parking lot.  Interactive input consists of entry
// time and exit time from the lot. Output consists of a
// customer statement. Emphasis is placed on using
// functions to develop the program.

// Program file: parking.cpp

#include <iostream.h>
#include <iomanip.h>

const float HOURLY_RATE = 0.75;
const char INDENT =' ';
```

```
// Function: get_data
// Prompts user for and inputs entry time and exit time

// Outputs: integers representing entry time and exit time

void get_data (int 8entry_time, int 8exit_time);

// Function: compute_amount
// Computes the amount due in dollars and cents
//
// Inputs: integers representing entry time and exit time
// Output: a real number representing the amount due

float compute_amount (int entry_time, int exit_time);

// Function: print_results
// Prints heading, entry and exit times, amount due, and closing message
//
// Inputs: integers representing entry time and exit time and a real number
// representing the amount due

void print_results (int entry_time, int exit_time, float amount_due);

// Function: print_heading
// Print a heading for the ticket

void print_heading();

// Function: print_message
// Print a closing message for the ticket

void print_message();

int main()
{
      int entry_time;     // Time of entry into parking lot
      int exit_time;      // Time of exit from parking lot
      float amount_due;   // Cost of parking in lot

      amount_due = compute_amount(entry_time, exit_time);
      print_results (entry_time, exit_time, amount_due);
      return 0;
}

void get_data(int &entry_time int &exit_time)
{
      cout << "Please enter the time in 24 hour notation and press <Enter>. ";
      cin >> entry_time;                                                          1
      cout << "Please enter the time out and press <Enter>. ";
      cin >> exit_time;
}
```

```
float compute_amount (int entry_time, int exit_time)
{
      int number_of_hours;
                                                                  2
      number_of_hours = (exit_time - entry_time) / 100;
      return number_of_hours * HOURLY_RATE;
}

void print_heading()
{
      cout << endl;
      cout << setw(11) << INDENT << "E - Z Parking" << endl;
      cout << setw(11) << INDENT << "------------------" << endl;
      cout << endl;
}

void print_message()
{
      cout << endl;
      cout << setw(1) << INDENT << "Thank you for using E - Z Parking" << endl;
      cout << endl;
      cout << setw(13) << INDENT << "BUCKLE UP";
      cout << setw(16) << INDENT << "and";
      cout << setw(11) << INDENT << "DRIVE SAFELY";
      cout << endl;                                               3
}

void print_results (int entry_time, int exit_time, float amount_due)
{
      print_heading();
      cout << fixed << showpoint << setprecision(2);
      cout << setw(4) << INDENT << "Time in: " << setw(6) << entry_time
        << endl;
      cout << setw(4) << INDENT << "Time out:" << setw(6) << exit_time
        << endl;
      cout << endl;
      cout << setw(4) << INDENT << "Amount due $"
        << setw(6) << amount_due << endl;
      print_message();
}
```

A sample run using the data 930 as entry time and 1320 as exit time produces

```
Please enter the time in and press <Enter>. 930
Please enter the time out and press <Enter>. 1320

            E - Z Parking

    Time in: 0930 Time out: 1320

    Amount due     $  2.25

Thank you for using E - Z Parking

             BUCKLE UP
            and DRIVE SAFELY
```

RUNNING, DEBUGGING AND TESTING HINTS

1. Each subprogram can be tested separately to see if it is producing the desired result. This is accomplished by a main program that calls and tests only the subprogram in question.
2. You can use related or identical variable names in the parameter lists. For example,

```
float compute (int n1, int n2);
```

or

```
float compute (int number1, int number2);
```

could be called by

```
compute (number1, number2);
```

3. Be sure the type, order, and purpose of actual parameters and formal parameters agree. You can do this by listing them one below the other. For example,

```
void display_data (char init1, char init2, int sc);
```

could be called by

```
display_data ('a', 'b', 9);
```

4. Be sure that you really need to use a reference parameter in a function before you declare it. If a function returns only one value to the caller, use no reference parameters.
5. If a function does not seem to return a value to the caller as expected, perhaps a parameter has not been declared as a reference parameter. Check the function's heading and declaration to be sure that the symbol **&** is associated with the desired output parameter.

SUMMARY

Key Terms

actual parameter
address
alias
block
bottom-up testing
cohesive subprogram
formal parameter
functional abstraction
global identifier
information hiding
interface
local copy
local identifier
main driver
manifest interface
modularity
pass by reference
pass by value
postcondition
precondition
procedural abstraction
reference parameter
scope of an identifier
side effect
structured design
structured programming
stub programming
subblock
subprogram
user-defined function
value parameter

Keywords

return void

Key Concepts

- A subprogram is a program within a program; functions are subprograms.
- Subprograms can be utilized to perform specific tasks in a program. Functions are often used to initialize variables, get data, print headings (no parameters needed), perform computations, and print data.

- The general form for a function declaration is

<type identifier> <name> (<parameter list>);

- A typical parameter list is

```
void display_data (int n1, int n2, float x, float y);
```

- A formal parameter is one listed in the subprogram heading; it is like a blank waiting to receive a value from the calling program.

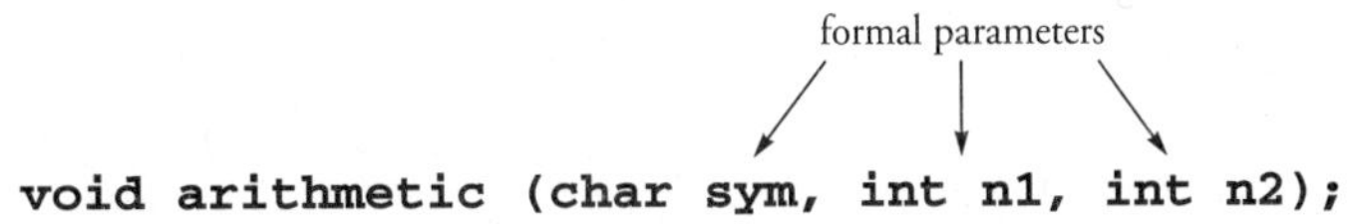
formal parameters
void arithmetic (char sym, int n1, int n2);

- An actual parameter is a variable listed in the subprogram call in the calling program.

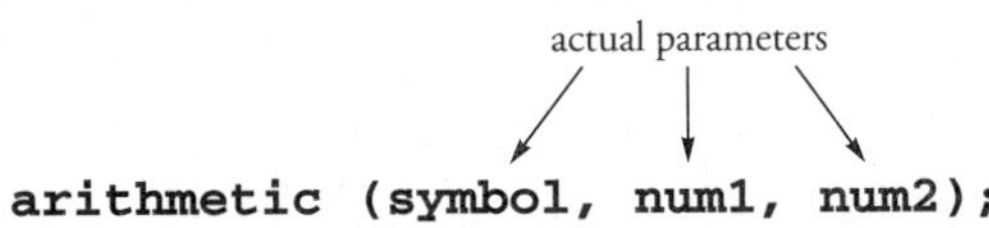
actual parameters
arithmetic (symbol, num1, num2);

- The formal parameter list in the subprogram heading must match the number and types of actual parameters used in the main program when the subprogram is called.

```
void arithmetic (char sym, int n1, int n2);
arithmetic (symbol, num1, num2);
```

- The type of an actual parameter being passed to a function must be compatible with the type of the formal parameter in its position in a function heading; implicit type conversions are made whenever possible.
- If the symbol `&` appears in a formal parameter declaration, then the formal parameter is a reference parameter; otherwise, the formal parameter is a value parameter.
- For value parameters, a copy of the actual parameter's value is passed to a function when it is called.
- Pass by value is safe; the value of the actual parameter does not change during the call of the function.
- For reference parameters, the address of the actual parameter is passed to the function when it is called.
- Pass by reference is not safe; it should be used with caution and only when side effects are intended.
- Global identifiers can be used by the main program and all subprograms.
- Local identifiers are available only to the main program block or the subprogram block in which they are declared.
- Each identifier is available to the block in which it is declared.
- Identifiers are not available outside their blocks.
- The scope of an identifier refers to the area of text in which the identifier is available.
- Understanding the scope of identifiers is aided by graphic illustration of blocks in a program; thus, the following program can be visualized as shown

◆ FIGURE 4.14

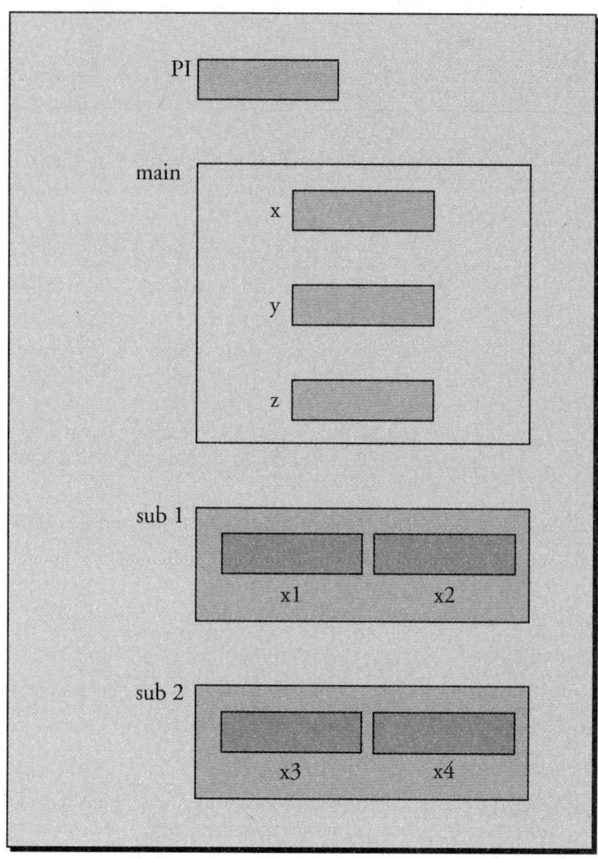

in Figure 4.14. A user-defined function is a subprogram that performs a specific task.

```
const float PI = 3.14;

float sub1(float);
float sub2(float);

int main()
{
    float x, y, z;

    .
    .
    .
}

float sub1(float x1)
{
    float x2;
    .
    .
    .
}
```

```
float sub2(float x1)
{
    float z2;
    .
    .
    .
}
```

- The form for a user-defined function is

```
<type identifier> <function name> (<parameter list>)
{
        <data declarations>
        <executable statements>
}
```

PROGRAMMING PROBLEMS AND PROJECTS

The following programming problems will be run on a very limited set of data. In later chapters, as you build your programming skills, you will run these problems with larger databases and subprograms for various parts. Problems marked with a box to the left of the number are referred to and used repeatedly; carefully choose the ones on which to work and then develop them completely. *Be sure to package coherent tasks in functions wherever possible.*

1. Write a program to get the coefficients of a quadratic equation

$ax^2 + bx + c = 0$

from the keyboard and then print the value of the discriminant $b^2 - 4ac$. A sample display for getting input is

```
Enter coefficients a, b, and c for the quadratic equation
```

$ax^2 + bx + c = 0$
a = ?
b = ?
c = ?

Run this program at least three times using test data that result in $b^2 - 4ac = 0$, $b^2 - 4ac > 0$, and $b^2 - 4ac < 0$.

2. Write a program to compute the cost for carpeting a room. Input should consist of the room length, room width, and carpet price per square yard. Use constants for the pad charge and installation charge. Include a heading as part of the output. A typical input screen would be:

```
What is the room length in feet? <Enter> ?
What is the room width in feet? <Enter> ?
What is the carpet price/square yard? <Enter> ?
```

Output for a sample run of this program (without a heading) could be

```
Dimensions of the room (in feet) are 17 x 22.
The area to be carpeted is 41.6 square yards.
The carpet price is $11.95 per yard.
```

```
Room dimensions            17 x 22
Carpet required            41.6 square yards
Carpet price/yard         $11.95
Pad price/yard             $2.95
Installation cost/yard     $ .95
Total cost/yard           $15.85
Total cost               $659.36
```

3. Williamson's Paint and Papering store wants a computer program to help them determine how much paint is needed to paint a room. Assuming a room is to have four walls and the ceiling painted, input for the program should be the length, width, and height of the room. Use a constant for the wall height (usually eight feet). One gallon of paint should cover 250 square feet. Cost of paint for the walls and ceiling should be entered by the user. Output should be the amount and cost for each kind of paint, and the total cost.

4. The Fairfield College faculty recently signed a three-year contract that included salary increments of 7, 6, and 5% respectively, for the next three years. Write a program that allows a user to enter the current salary and then prints the compounded salary for each of the next three years.

5. Several instructors use various weights (percentage of the final grade) for test scores. Write a program that allows the user to enter three test scores and the weight for each score. Output should consist of the input data, the weighted score for each test, and the total score (sum of the weighted scores).

6. The Roll-Em Lanes bowling team would like to have a computer program to print the team results for one series of games. The team consists of four members whose names are Weber, Fazio, Martin, and Patterson. Each person on the team bowls three games during the series; thus, the input will contain three lines, each with four integer scores. Your output should include all input data, individual series totals, game average for each member, team series, and team average. Sample output is

```
NAME        GAME 1     GAME 2     GAME 3     TOTAL     AVERAGE

Weber       212        220        190        622       207.3

Fazio       195        235        210        640       213.3

Martin      178        190        206        574       191.3

Patterson   195        215        210        620       206.7

     Team Total:   2456

     Team Average:   818.7
```

7. The Natural Pine Furniture Company has recently hired you to help them convert their antiquated payroll system to a computer-based model. They know you are still learning, so all they want right now is a program that will print a one-week payroll report for three employees. You should use the constant definition section for the following:

a. Federal withholding tax rate, 18%

b. State withholding tax rate, 4.5%

c. Hospitalization, $25.65

d. Union dues, $7.85

Each line of input will contain the employee's initials, the number of hours worked, and the employee's hourly rate. Your output should include a report for each employee and a summary report for the company files. A sample employee form follows:

```
Employee:                                  JIM
Hours Worked:                                40.00
Hourly Rate:                                  9.75
Total Wages:                                390.00

      Deductions:
      Federal Withholding                    70.20
      State Withholding                      17.55
      Hospitalization                        26.65
      Union Dues                              7.85
      Total Deductions                      122.25

      Net Pay                              $267.75
```

Output for a summary report could be

```
          Natural Pine Furniture Company

                    Weekly Summary

Gross Wages:

Deductions:
      Federal Withholding
      State Withholding
      Hospitalization
      Union Dues
            Total Deductions

Net Wages
```

8. The Child-Growth Encyclopedia Company wants a computer program that will print a monthly sales chart. Products produced by the company, prices, and sales commissions for each are

   a. Basic encyclopedia, $325.00; 22%

   b. Child educational supplement, $127.50; 15%

   c. Annual update book, $18.95; 20%

   Monthly sales data for one region consist of a two-letter region identifier (such as MI) and three integers, representing the number of units sold for each product listed above. A typical input screen would be:

```
What is your sales region? MI
How many Basic Encyclopedia were sold? 150
How many Child Supplements were sold? 120
How many Annual Updates were sold? 105
```

Write a program that will get the monthly sales data for two sales regions and produce the desired company chart. The prices may vary from month to month and should be defined in the constant definition section. The commissions are not subject to change. Typical output could be:

```
                        MONTHLY SALES CHART

                        Basic               Child         Annual
       Region           Encyclopedia        Supplement    Update

Units sold   MI             150             120           105
(by region)  TX             225             200           150

Total units sold:           375             320           255
Price/unit                  $325.00         $127.50       $18.95
Gross Sales:                $121,875.00     $40,800.00    $4,832.25

Commission rate               22%             15%             20%
Commissions paid:  $26,812.50   $6,120.00      $966.45
```

9. The Village Variety Store is having its annual Christmas sale. They would like you to write a program to produce a daily report for the store. Each item sold is identified by a code consisting of one letter followed by one digit. Your report should include data for three items. Each of the three lines of data will include item code, number of items sold, original item price, and reduction percentage. Your report should include a chart with the input data, sale price per item, and total amount of sales per item. You should also print a daily summary. Sample input is

```
A1 13  5.95 15
A2 24  7.95 20
A3 80  3.95 50
```

Typical output form could be:

```
Item Code  # Sold  Original Price  Reductions  Sale Price  Income

   A1        13          $5.95        15%        $5.06      $65.78

Daily Summary

   Gross Income:
```

10. The Holiday-Out Motel Company, Inc., wants a program that will print a statement for each overnight customer. Each line of input will contain room number (integer), number of nights (integer), room rate (real), telephone charges (real), and restaurant charges (real). You should use the constant definition section for the date and current tax rate. Each customer statement should include all input data, the date, tax rate and amount, total due, appropriate heading, and appropriate closing message. Test your program by running it for two customers. The tax rate applies only to the room cost. A typical input screen is

```
Room number? 135
Room rate? 39.95
Number of nights? 3
Telephone charges? 3.75
Meals? 57.50
```

A customer statement form is

```
          Holiday-Out Motel Company, Inc.

Date:                 XX-XX-XX
Room #                135
Room Rate:            $39.95
Number of Nights: 3
Room Cost:           $119.85
Tax: XXX%            4.79
     Subtotal:       $124.64

Telephone:           3.75
Meals:               57.50

     TOTAL DUE       $185.89

    Thank you for staying at Holiday-Out
                Drive safely
              Please come again
```

11. As a part-time job this semester, you are working for the Family Budget Assistance Center. Your boss has asked you to write and execute a program that will analyze data for a family. Input for each family will consist of

```
Family ID number (int)
Number in family (int)
Income (float)
Total debts (float)
```

Your program should output the following:

a. An appropriate header.

b. The family's identification number, number in family, income, and total debts.

c. Predicted family living expenses ($3000 times the number in family).

d. The monthly payment necessary to pay off the debt in one year.

e. The amount the family should save [the family size times 2% of the income minus debt—Fafam_Size * 0.02 * (income - debt)] .

f. Your service fee (0.5% of the income).

Run your program for the following two families:

Identification Number	Size Income	Debt
51	18,000.00	4800.00
4	26,000.00	3200.00

Output for the first family could be:

```
         Family Budget Assistance Center
            March 1989
         Telephone: (800)555-1234

   Identification number          51
   Family size                    4
   Annual income                  $ 18000.00
   Total debt                     $ 2000.00
   Expected living expenses       $ 12000.00
   Monthly payment                $ 166.67
   Savings                        $ 1280.00
   Service fee                    $ 90.00
```

12. The Caswell Catering and Convention Service has asked you to write a computer program to produce customers' bills. The program should read in the following data.

a. The number of adults to be served.
b. The number of children to be served.
c. The cost per adult meal.
d. The cost per child's meal (60% of the cost of the adult's meal).
e. The cost for dessert (same for adults and children).
f. The room fee (no room fee if catered at the person's home).
g. A percentage for tip and tax (not applied to the room fee).
h. Any deposit should be deducted from the bill.

Write a program and test it using data sets 2, 3, and 4 from the following table:

Set	Child Count	Adult Count	Dessert Cost Adult Cost	Room Cost	Tip/Tax Rate		Deposit
1	7	23	12.75	1.00	45.00	18%	50.00
2	3	54	13.50	1.25	65.00	19%	40.00
3	15	24	12.00	0.00	45.00	18%	75.00
4	2	71	11.15	1.50	0.00	6%	0.00

Note that data set 1 was used to produce the following sample output.

```
      Caswell Catering and Convention Service
                   Final Bill

Number of adults: 23
Number of children: 7
Cost per adult without dessert:        $     12.75
Cost per child without dessert:        $      7.65
Cost per dessert:                      $      1.00
Room fee:                              $     45.00
Tip and tax rate:                             0.18

Total cost for adult meals:            $    293.25
Total cost for child meals:            $     53.55
Total cost for dessert:                $     30.00
Total food cost:                       $    376.80
```

```
Plus tip and tax:                    $    67.82
Plus room fee:                       $    45.00
Less deposit:                        $    50.00

Balance due:                         $   439.62
```

13. The Maripot Carpet Store has asked you to write a computer program to calculate the amount a customer should be charged. The president of the company has given you the following information to help in writing the program.

a. The carpet charge is equal to the number of square yards purchased times the carpet cost per square yard.

b. The labor cost is equal to the number of square yards purchased times the labor cost per square yard. A fixed fee for floor preparation is added to some customers' bills.

c. Large-volume customers are given a percentage discount but the discount applies only to the carpet charge, not the labor costs.

d. All customers are charged 4% sales tax on the carpet; there is no sales tax on the labor cost.

Write the program and test it for customers 2, 3, and 4.

Customer	Sq. yds.	Cost per sq. yd.	Labor per sq. yd.	Prep. Cost	Discount
1	17	18.50	3.50	38.50	0.02
2	40	24.95	2.95	0.00	0.14
3	23	16.80	3.25	57.95	0.00
4	26	21.25	0.00	80.00	0.00

Note that the data for customer 1 were used to produce the following sample output.

```
Square yards purchased:                 17
    Cost per square yard:      $     18.50
   Labor per square yard:      $      3.50
   Floor preparation cost:     $     38.50
         Cost for carpet:      $    314.50
          Cost for labor:      $     98.00
     Discount on carpet:       $      6.29
          Tax on carpet:       $     12.33
     Charge to customer:       $    418.54
```

14. The manager of the Croswell Carpet Store has asked you to write a program to print customers' bill. The manager has given you the following information.

The store expresses the length and width of a room in terms of feet and tenths of a foot. For example, the length might be reported as 16.7 feet.

The amount of carpet purchased is expressed as square yards. It is found by dividing the area of the room (in square feet) by nine.

The store does not sell a fraction of a square yard. Thus, square yards must always be rounded up.

The carpet charge is equal to the number of square yards purchased times the carpet cost per square yard. Sales tax equal to 4% of the carpet cost must be added to the bill.

All customers are sold a carpet pad at $2.25 per square yard. Sales tax equal to 4% of the pad cost must be added to the bill.

The labor cost is equal to the number of square yards purchased times $2.40, which is the labor cost per square yard. No tax is charged on labor.

Large-volume customers may be given a discount. The discount may apply only to the carpet cost (before sales tax is added), only to the pad cost (before sales tax is added), only to the labor cost, or to any combination of the three charges.

Each customer is identified by a five-digit number and that number should appear on the bill. The sample output follows:

```
   Croswell Carpet Store
           Invoice

Customer number:                26817

           Carpet :            574.20
              Pad :             81.00
           Labor :              86.40

          Subtotal :           741.60
    Less discount :             65.52

        Subtotal :             676.08
         Plus tax :             23.59
           Total :             699.67
```

Write the program and test it for the following three customers.

a. Mr. Wilson (customer 81429) ordered carpet for his family room, which measures 25 feet long and 18 feet wide. The carpet sells for $12.95 per square yard and the manager agreed to give him a discount of 8% on the carpet and 6% on the labor.

b. Mr. and Mrs. Adams (customer 04246) ordered carpet for their bedroom, which measures 16.5 by 15.4 feet. The carpet sells for $18.90 per square yard and the manager granted a discount of 12% on everything.

c. Ms. Logan (customer 39050) ordered carpet that cost $8.95 per square yard for her daughter's bedroom. The room measures 13.1 by 12.5 feet. No discounts were given.

15. Each week Abduhl's Flying Carpets pays its salespeople a base salary plus a bonus for each carpet they sell. In addition, they pay a commission of 10% of the total sales made by each salesperson. Write a program to compute a salesperson's salary for the month by inputting Base, Bonus, Quantity, and Sales, and making the necessary calculations. Use the following test data:

Salesperson	Base	Bonus	Quantity	Commission	Sales
1	250.00	15.00	20	10%	1543.69
2	280.00	19.50	36	10%	2375.90

The commission figure is 10%. Be sure you can change this easily if necessary. Sample output follows:

```
    Salesperson  :        1
           Base  :        250.00
          Bonus  :         15.00
       Quantity  :         20
    Total Bonus  :        300.00
     Commission  :        10%
          Sales  :       1543.69
Total Commission  :        154.37
            Pay  :        704.37
```

16. "Think Metric" is the preferred way of having members of a nonmetric society become familiar with the metric system. Unfortunately, during the transition, many people are forced to rely on converting from their present system to the metric system. Develop a solution and write a program to help people convert their height and weight from inches and pounds to centimeters and kilograms. The program should take keyboard input of a person's height (in feet and inches) and weight (rounded to the nearest pound). Output should consist of the height and weight in metric units.

17. Discuss the issue of documenting subprograms with instructors of computer science, upper-level students majoring in computer science, and some of your classmates. Prepare a report for the class on this issue. Your report should contain information about different forms of documentation, the perceived need for documentation by various groups, the significance of documenting data transmission, and so forth. If possible, use specific examples to illustrate good documentation of subprograms versus poor documentation of subprograms.

18. Reread the material in Section 4.4 concerning functional abstraction. Then, from Problems 5, 7, 8, and 11, select one that you have not yet worked. Develop a structure chart and write module specifications for each module required for the problem you have chosen. Also, write a main driver for your program and write complete documentation for each subprogram including comments about all parameters.

CHAPTER

5 Selection Statements

CHAPTER OUTLINE

The previous chapters set the stage for using computers to solve problems. You have seen how programs in C++ can be used to get data, perform computations, and print results. You should be able to write complete, short programs, so it is now time to examine other aspects of problem solving.

Let us review the metaphor of the programmable pocket calculator that we have been using in the last two chapters. Our calculator allows us to solve some simple and complex problems by using built-in functions or by creating and using functions of our own. However, the calculator is limited in that it can only take input, calculate results, and display them as output. We would like the calculator to be more flexible, to be able to respond in different ways to different inputs or changes in its environment.

A major feature of a full-fledged computer, as opposed to our calculator, is the ability to make decisions. For example, a condition is examined and a decision is made as to which program statement is executed next. Statements that permit a computer to make decisions are called *selection statements.* Selection statements are examples of *control structures* because they allow the programmer to control the flow of execution of program statements.

5.1 Boolean Expressions

Before looking at decision making, we need to examine the logical constructs in C++, which include a new data type called *Boolean.* This data type allows you to represent something as true or false. Although this sounds relatively simple (and it is), this is a very significant feature of computers.

Defining Boolean Constants and a Boolean Data Type

Thus far we have used only the three data types **int**, **float**, and **char**. In any C++ program, the value 0 means *false,* and any other value means *true.* Instead of having to remember these associations, it would be convenient to use the names **TRUE** and **FALSE** to denote the boolean constants, as well as to use the name **boolean** when we wish to refer to the data type itself. For example, we might like to declare a variable **b** of type **boolean**, and assign it an initial value of **TRUE**:

```
boolean b = TRUE;
```

So that C++ programs can use these names properly, we define the constants **FALSE** and **TRUE** to have the values 0 and 1, respectively:

```
const int FALSE = 0;
const int TRUE = 1;
```

OBJECTIVES

- to understand the need for a Boolean data type
- to be able to use relational operators
- to understand the hierarchy for evaluating simple Boolean expressions
- to be able to use the logical operators that express and, or, and not
- to be able to use compound Boolean expressions
- to understand the short-circuit evaluation of compound Boolean expressions

To create a new type name for declaring variables, function parameters, and function returns of these values, we use a C++ *type definition:*

```
typedef int boolean;
```

typedef is a reserved word in C++. The general form of a type definition is

```
typedef <data type> <new type name>;
```

where data type is any C++ data type. All our **typedef** example does is to create a synonym, **boolean**, for a built-in type name, **int**.

Some systems may have already defined the words **TRUE** and **FALSE** for system use. In that case, you can override these definitions by using the preprocessor directive **#undef**, as follows:

```
#undef FALSE
#undef TRUE

const int FALSE = 0;
const int TRUE = 1;
```

If we define the new names above the main program, Boolean variables can be declared anywhere in the program and manipulated according to the scope rules:

```
#undef FALSE
#undef TRUE

const int FALSE = 0;
const int TRUE = 1;

typedef int boolean;

int main()
{
      boolean a, b;

      a = FALSE;
      b = TRUE;
      .
      .
      .
```

As with other data types, if two variables are of type **boolean**, the value of one variable can be assigned to another variable as

```
b = TRUE;
a = b;
```

and can be envisioned as

TRUE
a

TRUE
b

Saving a New Type Definition in a Library File

The Boolean values **TRUE** and **FALSE** and the type name **boolean** will be mentioned in many applications. Entering the same five lines of code by hand to define these names in every new source program will be an annoying task. Instead, we can place the definitions in a library file to be included at the top of every program that uses them. The file is named **boolean.h** and contains these definitions:

```
// Library file: boolean.h

// Defines Boolean constants and a type name for any application.

#undef FALSE
#undef TRUE

const int FALSE = 0;
const int TRUE = 1;

typedef int boolean;
```

This file can then be included in any source program by means of the following line of code:

```
#include "boolean.h"
```

Note the use of double quotes to enclose the file name rather than angle brackets. In general, names of programmer-defined libraries will appear this way when they are included in example programs in this text. Names of standard libraries will continue to appear in angle brackets.

Placing the definitions of a new type in a library file is another example of information hiding. Programmers who use the **boolean.h** library need not be concerned with the representation of Boolean values as integers, any more than they have already been concerned with the representation of integers as bit patterns. All that we need to know about Boolean values, aside from their names, is how they can be used to make decisions in programs.

Relational Operators and Simple Boolean Expressions

In arithmetic, integers and reals can be compared for the relationships of equality, inequality, less than, and greater than. C++ also provides for the comparison of numbers or values of variables. The operators used for comparison are called *relational operators* and there are six of them. Their arithmetic notation, C++ notation, and meaning are given in Table 5.1. Note that the equality operator in C++ is `==`, not `=`. As you know, `=` means assignment in C++. The equality operator

◇ TABLE 5.1
Relational operators

Arithmetic Operation	Relational Operator	Meaning
$=$	`==`	Is equal to
$<$	`<`	Is less than
$>$	`>`	Is greater than
$\leq$	`<=`	Is less than or equal to
$\geq$	`>=`	Is greater than or equal to
$\neq$	`!=`	Is not equal to

◇ TABLE 5.2
Values of simple Boolean expressions

Simple Boolean Expression	Boolean Value
`7 == 7`	**TRUE**
`-3.0 == 0.0`	**FALSE**
`4.2 > 3.7`	**TRUE**
`-18 < -15`	**TRUE**
`13 < 0.013`	**FALSE**
`-17.32 != -17.32`	**FALSE**
`a == b`	**TRUE**

does not change the values of its operands, whereas the assignment operator does. Be careful not to confuse them.

When two numbers or variable values are compared using a single relational operator, the expression is referred to as a *simple Boolean expression.* Each simple Boolean expression has the Boolean value **TRUE** or **FALSE** according to the arithmetic validity of the expression. In general, data of most of the built-in types can be compared. For example, when a character value is compared to an integer, the ASCII value of the character is used. When comparing reals, however, the computer representation of a real number might not be the exact real number intended.

Table 5.2 sets forth several Boolean expressions and their respective Boolean values, assuming the assignment statements **a = 3** and **b = 3** have been made.

Arithmetic expressions can also be used in simple Boolean expressions. Thus,

```
4 < (3 + 2)
```

has the value **TRUE**. When the computer evaluates this expression, the parentheses dictate that **(3 + 2)** is evaluated first and then the relational operator. Sequentially, this becomes

```
4 < (3 + 2)
4 < 5
TRUE
```

What if the parentheses had not been used? Could the expression be evaluated? This type of expression necessitates a priority level for the relational operators and the arithmetic operators. A summary for the priority of these operations follows:

Expression	Priority
`( )`	1
`*, /, %`	2
`+, -`	3
`==, <, >, <=, >=, !=`	4

Thus, we see that the relational operators are evaluated last. As with arithmetic operators, these are evaluated in order from left to right. Thus, the expression

```
4 < 3 + 2
```

could be evaluated without parentheses and would have the same Boolean value.

The following example illustrates the evaluation of a somewhat more complex Boolean expression.

EXAMPLE 5.1 Indicate the successive steps in the evaluation of the following Boolean expression:

```
10 % 4 * 3 - 8 <= 18 + 30 / 4 - 20
```

The steps in this evaluation are

```
10 % 4 * 3 - 8 <= 18 + 30 / 4 - 20
↓
2 * 3 - 8 <= 18 + 30 / 4 - 20
↓
6 - 8 <= 18 + 30 / 4 - 20
↓
- 2 <= 18 + 30 / 4 - 20
                 ↓
- 2 <= 18 + 7 - 20
-2 <= 25 - 20
        ↓
-2 <= 5
     ↓
TRUE
```

As shown here, even though parentheses are not required when using arithmetic expressions with relational operators, it is usually a good idea to use them to enhance the readability of the expression and to avoid using an incorrect expression.

Boolean Functions

Suppose we wish to have a function called **even** that takes an integer as an argument and returns the value **TRUE** if the integer is even and **FALSE** otherwise. We compare the remainder of dividing the argument by 2 to 0. We then return this result:

```
boolean even(int x)
{
        return x % 2 == 0;
}
```

Logical Operators and Compound Boolean Expressions

Boolean values can also be generated by using *logical operators* with simple Boolean expressions. The logical operators used by C++ are **&&** (meaning *and*), **||** (meaning *or*), and **!** (meaning *not*). Operators **&&** and **||** are used to connect two Boolean expressions, and **!** is used to negate the Boolean value of an expression; hence, it is sometimes referred to as *negation.* When one of these connectives or negation is used to generate Boolean values, the complete expression is referred to as a *compound Boolean expression.*

If **&&** is used to join two simple Boolean expressions, the resulting compound expression is true only when both simple expressions are true. If **||** is used, the result is true if either or both of the expressions are true. This is summarized as follows:

Expression 1 (E1)	Expression 2 (E2)	E1 && E2	E1 || E2
TRUE	TRUE	TRUE	TRUE
TRUE	FALSE	FALSE	TRUE
FALSE	TRUE	FALSE	TRUE
FALSE	FALSE	FALSE	FALSE

As previously indicated, ! merely produces the logical complement of an expression as follows:

Expression (E)	! E
TRUE	FALSE
FALSE	TRUE

Illustrations of the Boolean values generated using logical operators are given in Table 5.3.

Complex Boolean expressions can be generated by using several logical operators in an expression. The priority for evaluating these operators is

Operator	Priority
!	1
&&	2
||	3

When complex expressions are being evaluated, the logical operators, arithmetic expressions, and relational operators are evaluated during successive passes through the expression. The priority list is now as follows:

Expression or Operation	Priority
( )	Evaluate from inside out
!	Evaluate from left to right
*, /, %	Evaluate from left to right
+, -	Evaluate from left to right
<, <=, >, >=, ==, !=	Evaluate from left to right
&&	Evaluate from left to right
||	Evaluate from left to right

◇ TABLE 5.3
Values of compound Boolean expressions

Expression	Boolean Value
(4.2 >= 5.0) && (8 == (3 + 5))	TRUE
(4.2 >= 5.0) || (8 == (3 + 5))	TRUE
(-2 < 0) && (18 >= 10)	TRUE
(-2 < 0) || (18 >= 0)	FALSE
(3 > 5) && (14.1 == 0.0)	FALSE
(3 > 5) || (14.1 == 0.0)	FALSE
! (18 == (10 + 8))	FALSE
! (- 4 > 0)	TRUE

As a matter of style, it is useful to parenthesize any comparison that is used as an operand for a logical operator. The following examples illustrate evaluation of some complex Boolean expressions.

EXAMPLE 5.2

```
(3 < 5) || (21 < 18) && (-81 > 0)
TRUE || (21 < 18) && (-81 > 0)
(parentheses first) TRUE || TRUE && (-81 > 0)
TRUE || TRUE && FALSE
TRUE || FALSE
TRUE
```

EXAMPLE 5.3

```
! ((-5.0 == -6.2) || ((7 < 3) && (6 == (3 + 3))))
          ↓                 ↓                 ↓
! (      TRUE       || (  TRUE    &&    (6 == 6)))
! (      TRUE       || (  TRUE    &&    (TRUE))
! (      TRUE       ||          TRUE                  )
!                  TRUE
          ↓
        FALSE
```

Short-Circuit Evaluation of Boolean Expressions

Whenever two Boolean expressions are separated by a logical operator in C++, either **&&** or **||**, the run-time system uses *short-circuit evaluation.* The rules for this kind of evaluation are as follows:

1. In compound Boolean expressions connected by **||**, stop and return **TRUE** at the first Boolean expression that returns **TRUE**. Evaluate the next Boolean expression only if the current one returns **FALSE**. This rule captures the notion that a disjunction is **TRUE** only if at least one of the disjuncts is **TRUE**, and **FALSE** only if all of the disjuncts are **FALSE**.
2. In compound Boolean expressions connected by **&&**, stop and return **FALSE** at the first Boolean expression that returns **FALSE**. Evaluate the next Boolean expression only if the current one returns **TRUE**. This rule captures the notion that a conjunction is **FALSE** only if at least one of the conjuncts is **FALSE**, and **TRUE** only if all of the conjuncts are **TRUE**.

Short-circuit evaluation can enhance the efficiency of programs. For example, C++ actually evaluates the expression in Example 5.2 in three lines rather than six:

```
(3 < 5) || (21 < 18) && (-81 > 0)
 ↓
TRUE || (21 < 18) && (-81 > 0)
 ↓
TRUE
```

Short-circuit evaluation can also be used to make some simple decisions. For example, one might guard against division by zero as follows:

```
(y != 0) && (x / y == 2)
```

Note that if **y** equals zero, the second expression, which divides a number by **y**, will not be evaluated in C++.

EXERCISES 5.1

1. Assume the variable declaration section of a program is

```
boolean flag1, flag2;
```

What output is produced by the following segment of code?

```
flag1 = TRUE;
flag2 = FALSE;
cout << flag1 << " " << TRUE << << " " << flag2 << endl;
flag1 = flag2;
cout << flag2 << endl;
```

2. Assume the variable declaration section of a program is

```
char ch;
boolean flag;
```

For each of the following assignment statements indicate whether it is valid or invalid.

a. `flag = "true";`
b. `flag = T;`
c. `flag = TRUE;`
d. `ch = Flag;`
e. `ch = true;`
f. `ch = 'T';`

3. Evaluate each of the following expressions.

a. `(3 7) && (2 < 0) || (6 == 3 + 3)`
b. `((3 7) && (2 < 0)) || (6 == 3 + 3)`
c. `(3 7) && ((2 < 0) || (6 == 3 + 3))`
d. `! ((-4.2 < 3.0) && (10 < 20))`
e. `(! (-4.2 < 3.0)) || (! (10 < 20))`

4. For each of the following simple Boolean expressions, indicate whether it is **TRUE**, **FALSE**, or invalid.

a. `-3.01 <= -3.001`
b. `-3.0 == -3`
c. `25 - 10 < 3 * 5`
d. `42 % 5 < 42 / 5`
e. `-5 * (3 + 2) >= 2 * (-10)`
f. `10 / 5 < 1 + 1`
g. `3 + 8 % 5 == 6 - 12 % 2`

5. For each of the following expressions, indicate whether it is valid or invalid. Evaluate those that are valid.

a. `3 < 4 || 5 < 6`
b. `! 3.0 == 6 / 2`
c. `! (TRUE || FALSE)`
d. `! TRUE || FALSE`
e. `! TRUE || ! FALSE`
f. `! (18 < 25) && || (-3 < 0)`
g. `8 * 3 < 20 + 10`

A NOTE OF INTEREST

George Boole

George Boole was born in 1815 in Lincoln, England. Boole was the son of a small shopkeeper and his family belonged to the lowest social class. In an attempt to rise above his station, Boole spent his early years teaching himself Latin and Greek. During this period, he also received elementary instruction in mathematics from his father.

At the age of 16, Boole worked as a teacher in an elementary school. He used most of his wages to help support his parents. At the age of 20 (after a brief, unsuccessful attempt to study for the clergy), he opened his own school. As part of his preparation for running his school, he had to learn more mathematics. This activity led to the development of some of the most significant mathematics of the nineteenth century.

Boole's major contributions were in the field of logic. An indication of his genius is given by the fact that his early work included the discovery of invariants. The mathematical significance of this is perhaps best explained by noting that the theory of relativity developed by Albert Einstein would not have been possible without the previous work on invariants.

Boole's first published contribution was *The Mathematical Analysis of Logic,* which appeared in 1848 while he was still working as an elementary teacher and the sole support for his parents. In 1849, he was appointed professor of mathematics at Queen's College in Cork, Ireland. The relative freedom from financial worry and time constraints the college appointment provided allowed him to pursue his work in mathematics. His masterpiece, *An Investigation of the Laws of Thought, on which Are Founded the Mathematical Theories of Logic and Probabilities,* was published in 1854. Boole was then 39, relatively old for such original work. According to Bertrand Russell, pure mathematics was discovered by Boole in this work.

The brilliance of Boole's work laid the foundation for what is currently studied as formal logic. The data type Boolean is named in honor of Boole because of his contribution to the development of logic as part of mathematics. Boole died in 1864. His early death resulted from pneumonia contracted by keeping a lecture engagement when he was soaked to the skin.

6. Assume the variable declaration section of a program is

```
int int1, int2;
float fl1, fl2;
boolean flag1, flag2;
and the values of the variables are
```

0	8	-15.2	-20.0	FALSE	TRUE
int1	**int2**	**fl1**	**fl2**	**flag1**	**flag2**

Evaluate each of the following expressions:

a. `(int1 <= int2) || ! (fl2 == fl1)`
b. `! (flag1) || ! (flag2)`
c. `! (flag1 && flag2)`
d. `((fl1-fl2) < 100/int2) && ((int1 < 1) && ! (flag2))`
e. `! ((int2 - 16 / 2) == int1) && flag1`

7. DeMorgan's Laws state the following:

a. `! (A || B)` is equivalent to `(! A) && (! B)`
b. `! (A && B)` is equivalent to `(! A) || (! B)`

Write a test program that demonstrates the validity of each of these equivalent statements.

5.2 if Statements

OBJECTIVES

- to learn the syntax of the **if** statement
- to understand the flow of control when using an **if** statement
- to be able to use an **if** statement in a program
- to understand why compound statements are needed
- to be able to use correct syntax in writing a compound statement
- to be able to design programs using **if** statements

The first decision-making statement we will examine is the **if** statement. An **if** statement is used to make a program do something only when certain conditions are used. The form and syntax for an **if** statement are

```
if (<Boolean expression>)
        <statement>
```

where **<statement>** represents any C++ statement. Note that the parentheses enclosing the Boolean expression are required.

The Boolean expression can be any valid expression that is either true or false at the time of evaluation. If it is **TRUE**, the statement following the Boolean expression is executed. If it is **FALSE**, control is transferred to the first program statement following the complete **if** statement. In general, code would have the form

```
<statement 1>
if (<Boolean expression>)
        <statement 2>
<statement 3>
```

as illustrated in Figure 5.1.

As a further illustration of how an **if** statement works, consider the program fragment

```
sum = 0.0;
cin >> num;
if (num > 0.0)
     sum = sum + num;
cout << fixed << showpoint << setprecision(2) << setw(10) << sum << endl;
```

FIGURE 5.1
if flow diagram

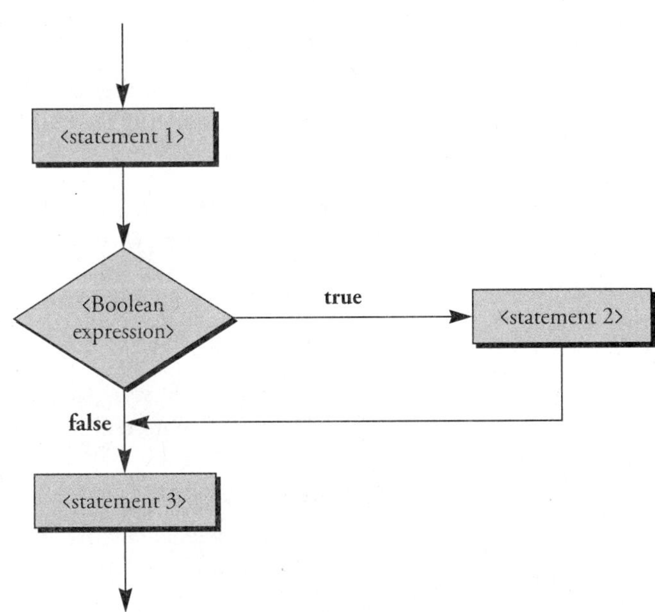

If the value read is 75.85, prior to execution of the **if** statement, the contents of **num** and **sum** are

75.85	0.0
num	**sum**

The Boolean expression **num > 0.0** is now evaluated and, since it is **TRUE**, the statement

```
sum = sum + num;
```

is executed and we have

75.85	75.85
num	**sum**

The next program statement is executed and produces the output

```
75.85
```

However, if the value read is -25.5, the variable values are

-25.5	0.0
num	**sum**

The Boolean expression **num > 0.0** is **FALSE** and control is transferred to the line

```
cout << fixed << showpoint << setprecision(2) << setw(10) << sum << endl;
```

Thus, the output is

```
0.00
```

Now, let's suppose you want a program in which one objective is to count the number of zeros in the input. Assuming suitable initialization and declaration, a program fragment for this task could be

```
cin >> num;
if (num == 0)
     zero_count = zero_count + 1;
```

One writing style for using an **if** statement calls for indenting the program statement to be executed if the Boolean expression is **TRUE**. This, of course, is not required. The following code

```
if (num == 0)
     zero_count = zero_count + 1;
```

could be written

```
if (num == 0) zero_count = zero_count + 1;
```

However, the indenting style for simple **if** statements is consistent with the style used with more elaborate conditional statements.

Compound Statements

The last concept needed before looking further at selection in C++ is that of a *compound statement.* In a C++ program, simple statements end with a semicolon. Thus,

```
cin >> a >> b;
a = 3 * b;
cout << b;
```

are three simple statements.

In some instances, it is necessary to perform several simple statements when some condition is true. For example, you may want the program to do certain things if a condition is true. In this situation, several simple statements that can be written as a single compound statement would be helpful. In general, there are several C++ constructs that require compound statements. A compound statement is created by using the symbols **{** and **}** at the beginning and end, respectively, of a sequence of simple statements. Correct syntax for a compound statement is

```
{
      <statement 1>
      <statement 2>
      .
      .
      .
      <statement n >
}
```

Simple statements within a compound statement end with semicolons. The end of the compound statement is not followed by a semicolon.

When a compound statement is executed within a program, the entire segment of code between **{** and **}** is treated as a single action. This is referred to as a *statement block*. It is important that you develop a consistent, acceptable writing style for writing compound statements. What you use will vary according to your instructor's wishes and your personal preferences. Examples in this text will align each statement within the compound statement with the enclosing symbols. Thus,

```
{
      cin >> a >> b;
      a = 3 * b;
      cout << b;
}
```

is a compound statement in a program; what it does is easily identified.

Using Compound Statements

As you might expect, compound statements can be (and frequently are) used as part of an **if** statement. The form and syntax for this are

```
if (<Boolean expression>)
{
      <statement 1>
      .
      .
      .
      <statement n>
}
```

Program control is exactly as before depending on the value of the Boolean expression. For example, suppose you are writing a function to keep track of and compute fees for vehicles in a parking lot where separate records are kept for senior citizens. A segment of code in the procedure could be

```
if (customer == 'S')
{
      senior_count = senior_count + 1;
      amount_due = senior_citizen_rate;
}
```

if Statements with Functions

The next example designs a program to solve a problem using an **if** statement with function.

EXAMPLE 5.4

Let us write a program that reads two integers and prints them in the order of larger first, smaller second. The first-level pseudocode solution is

1. Read numbers
2. Determine the larger
3. Print results

◆ FIGURE 5.2
Structure Chart for Ordering Two Numbers

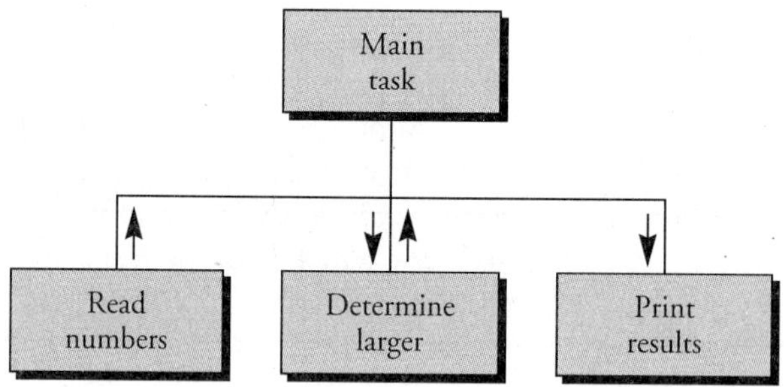

A structure chart for this is given in Figure 5.2. Reading the numbers and printing the results require no further discussion of their design or implementation. Our strategy for determining the larger of the two numbers will be to maintain three variables, **min**, **max,** and **temp**. Step 2 assumes that the numbers have been read in to variables **min** and **max**. We will compare the values, and if **min** is greater than **max**, we will use the variable **temp** to help swap the values of **min** and **max**. Thus, step 2 will have the effect of placing the larger value in **max** and the smaller value in **min**. The pseudocode for step 2 is

```
if min > max
      assign min to temp
      assign max to min
      assign min to max
```

This algorithm translates to the following C++ function:

```
// Function: determine_larger
// Enforces the ordering relation min <= max between two integer variables
//
// Inputs: two integer variables in random order
// Outputs: min will contain the smaller of the two inputs, and max the larger
```

```
void determine_larger(int &min, int &max)
{
      int temp;

      if (min > max)
      {
            temp = min;
            min = max;
            max = temp;
      }
}
```

A complete program for this follows:

```
// Program file: minmax.cpp

#include <iostream.h>
#include <iomanip.h>

const char SKIP = ' ';

// Function: get_data
// Prompts for and obtains two integers from user
//
// Outputs: two integers

void get_data(int &first, int &second);

// Function: determine_larger
// Enforces the ordering relation min <= max between two integer variables
//
// Inputs: two integer variables in random order
// Outputs: min will contain the smaller of the two inputs, and max the larger

void determine_larger(int &min, int &max);

// Function: print_results
// Displays results on screen
//
// Inputs: two integers, the smaller in min, the larger in max

void print_results(int min, int max);

int main()
{
      int min, max;

      get_data(min, max);
      determine_larger(min, max);
      print_results(min, max);
      return 0;
}
```

```
void get_data(int &first, int &second)
{
      cout << "Enter the first number and press <Enter>."
      cin >> min;                                                   1
      cout << "Enter the second number and press <Enter>."
      cin >> max;
}

void determine_larger(int &min, int &max)
{
      int temp;
      if (min > max)
      {
             temp = min;                                            2
             min = max;
             max = temp;
      }
}

void print_results(int min, int max)
{
       cout << setw(19) << SKIP << "Larger number" << setw(15)
            << "Smaller number" << endl;
       cout << setw(19) << SKIP << "-------------"                  3
            << setw(15) << "-------------" << endl;
       cout << endl;
       cout << set(26) << min << setw(15) << max << endl;
}
```

Sample runs of this program produce

```
Enter the first number and press <Enter>. 35
Enter the second number and press <Enter>. 115

                         Larger number           Smaller number
                         -------------           --------------

                              115                      35

Enter the first number and press <Enter>. 85
Enter the second number and press <Enter>. 26

                         Larger number           Smaller number
                         -------------           --------------

                               85                      26
```

Note that two runs of this program are required to test the logic of the **if** statement.

EXERCISES 5.2

1. What is the output from each of the following program fragments? Assume the following assignment statements precede each fragment:

```
a = 10;
b = 5;
```

a.
```
if (a <= b)
      b = a;
cout << a << endl << b << endl;
```

b.
```
if (a <= b)
{
      b = a;
      cout << a << endl << b << endl;
}
```

c.
```
if (a < b)
      temp = a;
a = b;
b = temp;
cout << a << endl << b endl;
```

d.
```
if (a < b)
{
      temp = a;
      a = b;
      b = temp;
}
cout << a << endl << b << endl;
```

e.
```
if ((a < b) || (b - a < 0))
{
      a = a + b;
      b = b - 1;
      cout << a << endl << b << endl;
}
cout << a << endl << b << endl;
```

f.
```
if ((a < b) && (b - a < 0))
{
      a = a + b;
      b = b - 1;
      cout << a << endl << b << endl;
}
cout << a << endl << b << endl;
```

2. Write a test program to illustrate what happens when a semicolon is inadvertently inserted after a Boolean expression in an **if** statement. For example,

```
if (a > 0);
      sum = sum + a;
```

3. Find and explain the errors in each of the following program fragments. Assume all variables have been suitably declared.

a.
```
if (a == 10)
      cout << a << endl;
```

b.
```
x = 7;
if (3 < x < 10)
{
      x = x + 1;
      cout << x << endl;
}
```

c.
```
count = 0;
sum = 0;
a = 50;
if (a > 0)
      count = count + 1;
sum = sum + a;
```

d.
```
cin >> ch;
if (ch = 'a' || 'b')
      cout << ch << endl;
```

4. What is the output from each of the following program fragments? Assume all variables have been suitably declared.

a.
```
j = 18;
if (j % 5 == 0)
      cout << j << endl;
```

b.
```
a = 5;
b = 90;
b = b / a - 5;
if (b > a)
      b = a * 30;
cout << a << endl << b << endl;
```

5. Can a simple statement be written using a **{ . . . }** block? Write a short program that allows you to verify your answer.

6. Discuss the differences in the following programs. Predict the output for each program using sample values for **num**.

a.
```
int main()
{
     int num;
     cout << "Enter an integer and press <Enter>.";
      cin >> num;
      if (num > 0)
            cout << endl;
      cout << setw(22) << "The number is" << setw(6)
            << num << endl;
      cout << endl;
      cout << setw(30) << "The number squared is"
            << setw(6) << num * num << endl;
      cout << setw(28) << "The number cubed is"
            << setw(6) << num * num * num << endl;
      cout << endl;
      return 0;
}
```

b.
```
int main()
{
     int num;
     cout << "Enter an integer and press <Enter>. ";
     cin >> num;
     if (num > 0)
     {
           cout << endl;
           cout << setw(22) << "The number is"
                 << setw(6) << num << endl;
           cout << endl;
```

```
            cout << setw(30) << "The number squared is"
                 << setw(6) << num * num << endl;
            cout << setw(28) << "The number cubed is"
                 << setw(6) << num * num * num << endl;
            cout << endl;
        }
        return 0;
    }
```

7. Discuss writing style and readability of compound statements.
8. Find all errors in the following compound statements.

   a.
   ```
   {
        cin >> a
        cout << a << endl
   }
   ```
   b.
   ```
   {
        sum = sum + num
   };
   ```
   c.
   ```
   {
        cin >> size1 >> size2;
        cout << setw(8) << size1 << setw(8) << size2
             << endl
   }
   ```
   d.
   ```
   {
        cin << age << weight;
        total_age = total_age + age;
        total_weight = total_weight + weight;
        cout << setw(8) << age << weight << endl;
   ```
9. Write a single compound statement that will do the following:
   a. Read three integers from the keyboard.
   b. Add them to a previous total.
   c. Print the numbers on one line.
   d. Skip a line (output).
   e. Print the new total.
10. Write a program fragment that reads three reals, counts the number of positive reals, and accumulates the sum of positive reals.
11. Write a program fragment that reads three characters and then prints them only if the letters have been read in alphabetical order (for example, print "boy" but do not print "dog").
12. Given two integers, **A** and **B**, **A** is a divisor of **B** if **B % A = 0**. Write a complete program that reads two positive integers **A** and **B** and then, if **A** is a divisor of **B**,
    a. Print **A**.
    b. Print **B**.
    c. Print the result of **B** divided by **A**.

    For example, the output could be

    ```
    A is 14

    B is 42

    B divided by A is 3
    ```

5.3 if . . . else Statements

OBJECTIVES

- to learn the syntax of **`if . . . else`** statements
- to understand the flow of control when using **`if . . . else`** statements
- to be able to use an **`if . . . else`** statement in a program
- to be able to design programs using **`if . . . else`** statements

Form and Syntax

The previous section discussed the one-way selection statement **`if`**. The second selection statement we will examine is the two-way selection statement **`if . . . else`**. Correct form and syntax for **`if . . . else`** are

```
if (<Boolean expression>)
        <statement>
else
        <statement>
```

Flow of control when using an **`if . . . else`** statement is as follows:

1. The Boolean expression is evaluated.
2. If the Boolean expression is **`TRUE`**, the statement following the expression is executed and control is transferred to the first program statement following the complete **`if . . . else`** statement.
3. If the Boolean expression is **`FALSE`**, the statement following **`else`** is executed and control is transferred to the first program statement following the **`if . . . else`** statement.

A flow diagram is given in Figure 5.3.

A few points follow that you should remember concerning **`if . . . else`** statements:

1. The Boolean expression can be any valid expression having a value of **`TRUE`** or **`FALSE`** at the time it is evaluated.
2. The complete **`if . . . else`** statement is one program statement and is separated from other complete statements by a semicolon whenever appropriate.
3. Writing style should include indenting within the **`else`** option in a manner consistent with indenting in the **`if`** option.

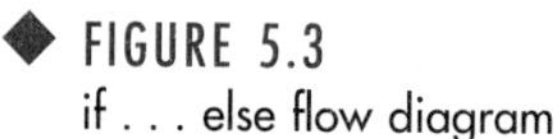

◆ FIGURE 5.3
if . . . else flow diagram

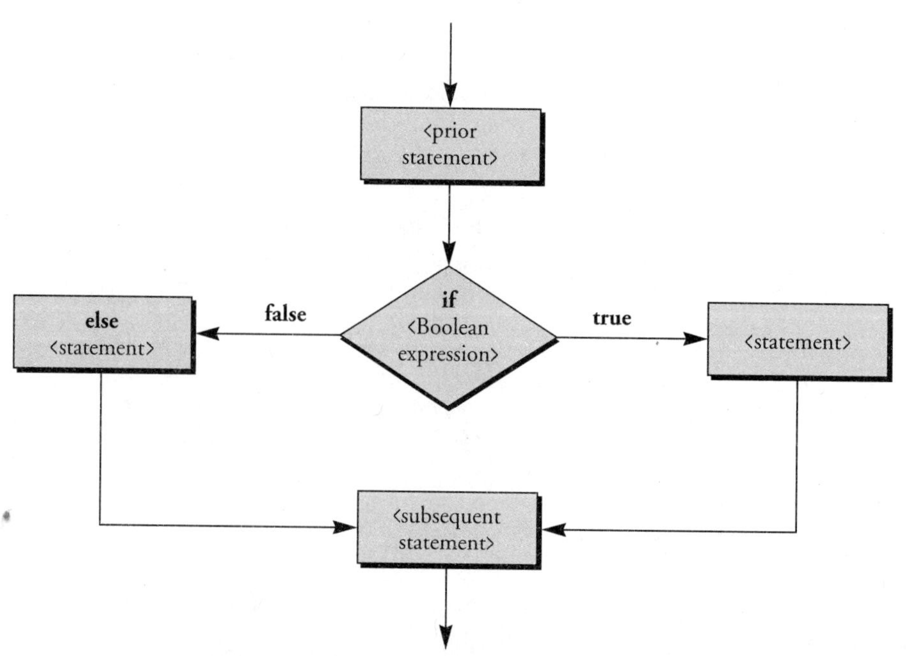

A NOTE OF INTEREST

Artificial Intelligence

Artificial intelligence (AI) research seeks to understand the principles of human intelligence and apply those principles to the creation of smarter computer programs. The original goal of AI research was to create programs with humanlike intelligence and capabilities, yet after many years of research, little progress has been made toward this goal.

In recent years, however, AI researchers have pursued much more modest goals with much greater success. Programs based on AI techniques are playing increasingly important roles in such down-to-earth areas as medicine, education, recreation, business, and industry. Such programs come nowhere near achieving human levels of intelligence, but they often have capabilities that are not easily achieved with non-AI programs.

The main principles of AI can be summarized as follows:

Search: A method whereby the computer solves a problem by searching through all logically possible solutions.

Rules: Knowledge about what actions to take in particular circumstances is stored as rules; each rule has the form **if** situation **then** action or conclusion.

Reasoning: Programs can use reasoning to draw conclusions from the facts and rules available to the program.

Planning: The control program plans the actions that must be taken to accomplish a particular goal, then modifies the plan if unexpected obstacles are encountered; this is most widely used in robot control.

Pattern recognition: Important for rule-based systems, the **if** part of a rule specifies a particular pattern of facts; the rule is to be applied when that pattern is recognized in the facts known to the program.

Knowledge bases: Storage of the facts and rules that govern the operation of an AI program.

EXAMPLE 5.5

Let us write a program fragment to keep separate counts of negative and nonnegative numbers entered as data. Assuming all variables have been suitably declared and initialized, an **if . . . else** statement could be used as follows:

```
cout << "Please enter a number and press <Enter>.";
cin >> num;
if (num < 0)
        neg_count = neg_count + 1;
else
        non_neg_count = non_neg_count + 1;
```

Using Compound Statements

Program statements in both the **if** option and the **else** option can be compound statements. When using compound statements in these options, you should use a consistent, readable indenting style; remember to use **{ . . . }** for each compound statement; and do not put a semicolon before **else**.

EXAMPLE 5.6

Suppose you want a program to read a number, count it as negative or nonnegative, and print it in either a column of nonnegative numbers or a column of negative numbers. Assuming all variables have been suitably declared and initialized, the fragment might be

```
cout << "Please enter a number and press <Enter>.";
cin >> num;
if (num < 0)
{
     neg_count = neg_count + 1;
     cout << setw(15) << num << endl;
}                                              // end of if option
else
{
     non_neg_count = non_neg_count + 1;
     count << setw(30) << num << endl;
}                                              // end of else option
```

We next consider an example of a program fragment that requires the use of compound statements within an **if . . . else** statement.

EXAMPLE 5.7

We want to write a function that computes gross wages for an employee of the Florida OJ Canning Company. Input includes hours worked and the hourly rate. Overtime (more than 40 hours) pay is computed as time-and-a-half. A function would be

```
const float WEEKLY_HOURS = 40.0;
const float TIME_AND_A_HALF = 1.5;

float compute_wages (float hours, float pay_rate)
{
      float overtime;
      if (hours <= WEEKLY_HOURS )
           return hours * pay_rate;
      else
      {
            overtime = TIME_AND_A_HALF *
                   (hours - WEEKLY_HOURS ) * pay_rate;
            return WEEKLY_HOURS * pay_rate + overtime;
      }
}
```

Robust Programs

If a program is completely protected against all possible crashes from bad data and unexpected values, it is said to be *robust.* The preceding examples have all assumed that desired data would be accurately entered from the keyboard. In actual practice, this is seldom the case. The **if . . . else** statements can be used to guard against bad data entries. For example, if a program is designed to use positive numbers, you could guard against negatives and zero by

```
cout << "Enter a positive number and press <Enter>. ";
cin >> number;
if (number <= 0)
    cout << "You entered a nonpositive number." << endl;
```

```
else

        .
        . (code for expected action here)
        .
```

This program protection can be used anywhere in a program. For example, if you are finding square roots of numbers, you could avoid a program crash by using this code:

```
if (num < 0)
        cout << "The number " << num << " is negative"
             << endl;
else
        .
        . (rest of action here)
        .
```

In actual practice, students need to balance robustness against amount of code and efficiency. An overemphasis on making a program robust can detract from time spent learning new programming concepts. You should discuss this with your instructor and decide what is best for your situation. Generally, there should be an agreement between the programmer and the customer regarding the level of robustness required. For most programs and examples in this text, it is assumed that valid data are entered when requested.

EXAMPLE 5.8

Callers of functions that take input would like to be signaled that it is within a given lower and upper bound. For example, a function that inputs the age of an employee might check to see that the integer value entered by the user is greater than 17 and less than 70 (assuming these are conventional age limits for employable persons). In this example, the function would return **TRUE** if the age is greater than 17 and also less than 70, or **FALSE** otherwise. The caller of the function takes care of prompting the user for information, and of error recovery, such as an error message and a loop for more input. The function, named **get_valid_data**, is passed the values of the lower and the upper bounds, and variables for the data and a Boolean flag indicating a valid input value. One might invoke the function as follows:

```
boolean age_ok;
int age;

cout << "Enter the employee's age: ";
get_valid_data(17, 70, age, age_ok);
if (! age_ok)
      cout << "Age must be greater than 17 and less than 100" << endl;
else
      <process the age, etc.>
```

A declaration of the function is therefore

```
// Function: get_valid_data
// Takes an input integer from the user and checks it for validity
```

```
//
// Inputs: two integers representing the lower and upper bounds of valid input
// Outputs: an integer representing the input and a Boolean value representing
// its validity

void get_valid_data(int low, int high, int &data, boolean &data_ok);
```

The function does not prompt the user, but simply reads data. The function then compares the data to the limits. If the data are within the limits, the flag is set to **TRUE**; if not, the flag is set to **FALSE**.

```
void get_valid_data(int low, int high, int &data, boolean &data_ok)
{
      cin >> data;
      if ((data > low) && (data < high))
            data_ok = TRUE;
      else
            data_ok = FALSE;
}
```

Guarding Against Overflow

As we discussed in Chapter 3, integer overflow occurs when the absolute value of an integer exceeds a maximum, and real overflow occurs when a value is obtained that is too large to be stored in a memory location. Both of these values vary according to the compiler being used. The maximum value of an integer is named by the constant **INT_MAX**, and the maximum value of a real number is named by the constant **FLT_MAX**. Both constants become available to a C++ program by including the library files **limits.h** and **float. h.**

One method that is used to guard against integer overflow is based on the principle of checking a number against some function of **INT_MAX**. Thus, if you want to multiply a number by 10, you would first compare it to **INT_MAX / 10.** A typical segment of code could be

```
if (num > INT_MAX / 10)
      (overflow message)
else
{
      num = num * 10;
      (rest of action)
}
```

We can now use this same idea with a Boolean-valued function. For example, consider the function

```
boolean near_overflow (int num)
{
       return num > INT_MAX / 10;
}
```

This could be used in the following manner:

```
if (num > near_overflow(num))
      (overflow message)
```

```
else
{
        num = num * 10;
        (rest of action)
}
```

EXERCISES 5.3

1. What output is produced from each of the following program fragments? Assume all variables have been suitably declared.

   a.
```
a = -14;
b = 0;
if (a < b)
       cout << a << endl;
else
       cout << a * b << endl;
```
   b.
```
a = 50;
b = 25;
count = 0;
sum = 0;
if (a == b)
       cout << a << b << endl;
else
{
       count = count + 1;
       sum = sum + a + b;
       cout << a << b << endl;
}
cout << count << sum << endl;
```
   c.
```
temp = 0;
a = 10;
b = 5;
f (a > b)
       cout << a << b << endl;
else
       temp = a;
a = b;
b = temp;
cout << a << b << endl;
```

2. Find all errors in the following program fragments.

   a.
```
if (ch < '.')
       char_count = char_count + 1;
cout << ch << endl;
else
       period_count = period_count + 1;
```
   b.
```
if (age < 20)
{
       young_count = young_count + 1;
       young_age = young_age + age;
};
else
{
```

```
            old_count = old_count + 1;
            old_age = old_age + age;
      };
   c. if (age < 20)
      {
            young_count = young_count + 1;
            young_age = young_age + age
      }
      else
            old_count = old_count + 1;
      old_age = old_age + age;
```

3. Write a program to balance your checkbook. Your program should get an entry from the keyboard, keep track of the number of deposits and checks, and keep a running balance. The data consist of a character, D (deposit) or C (check), followed by an amount.

5.4 Nested and Extended if Statements

OBJECTIVES

- to learn the syntax of nested **if** statements
- to know when to use nested **if** statements
- to be able to use extended **if** statements
- to be able to trace the logic of nested **if** statements
- to develop a consistent writing style when using nested **if** statements

Multiway Selection

Sections 5.2 and 5.3 examined one-way (**if**) and two-way (**if . . . else**) selection. Because each of these is a single C++ statement, either can be used as part of a selection statement to achieve multiple selection. In this case, the multiple selection statement is referred to as a *nested if statement.* These nested statements can be any combination of **if** or **if . . . else** statements.

To illustrate, let us write a program fragment to issue interim progress reports for students in a class. If a student's score is below 50, the student is failing. If the score is between 50 and 69 inclusive, the progress is unsatisfactory. If the score is 70 or above, the progress is satisfactory. The first decision to be made is based on whether the score is below 50 or not; the design is

```
if score >= 50
        .
        . (progress report here)
        .
else
     cout << setw(34)
          << "You are currently failing." << endl;
```

We now use a nested **if . . . else** statement for the progress report for students who are not failing. The complete fragment is

```
if score >= 50
     if score >= 69
          cout << setw(38) << "Your progress is satisfactory." << endl;
     else
          cout << setw(40) << "Your progress is unsatisfactory." << endl;
else
     cout << setw(34) << "You are currently failing." << endl;
```

One particular instance of nesting selection statements requires special development. When additional **if . . . else** statements are used in the **else** option, we call this an *extended if statement* and use the following form:

```
if (<condition 1>)
        .
        . (action 1 here)
        .
else if (<condition 2>)
        .
        . (action 2 here)
        .
else if (<condition 3>)
        .
        . (action 3 here)
        .
else
        .
        . (action 4 here)
        .
```

Using this form, we could redesign the previous fragment that printed progress reports as follows:

```
if (score > 69)
      cout << setw(38) << "Your progress is satisfactory." << endl;
else if (score > 50)
      cout << setw(40) << "Your progress is unsatisfactory." << endl;
else
      cout << setw(34) << "You are currently failing." << endl;
```

If you trace through both fragments with scores of 40, 60, and 80, you will see they produce identical output.

Another method of writing the nested fragment is to use sequential selection statements as follows:

```
if (score > 69)
      cout << setw(38) << "Your progress is "
           << "satisfactory." << endl;
if ((score <= 69) && (score >= 50))
      cout << setw(40) << "Your progress is "
           << "unsatisfactory." << endl;
if (score < 50)
      cout << setw(34) << "You are currently failing."
           << endl;
```

However, there are two reasons why this is not considered good programming practice. First, this is less efficient because the condition of each **if** statement is evaluated each time through the program. Second, only one of the three conditions can be true; they are said to be *mutually exclusive.* In general, mutually exclusive conditions are most accurately represented with nested **if . . . else** statements. You should generally avoid using sequential **if** statements if a nested statement can be used.

Tracing the flow of logic through nested or extended **if** statements can be tedious. However, it is essential that you develop this ability. For practice, let us trace through the following example.

EXAMPLE 5.9

Consider the nested statement

```
if (a > 0)
      if (a % 2 == 0)
               sum1 = sum1 + a;
      else
               sum2 = sum2 + a;
else if (a == 0)
      cout << setw(18) << "a is zero" << endl;
else
      neg_sum = neg_sum + a;
cout << setw(17) << "All done" << endl;
```

We will trace through this statement and discover what action is taken when **a** is assigned 20, 15, 0, and -30, respectively. For **a = 20**, the expression **a > 0** is **TRUE**, hence

```
a % 2 == 0
```

is evaluated. This is **TRUE** so

```
sum1 = sum1 + a;
```

is executed and control is transferred to

```
cout << setw(17) << "All done" << endl;
```

For **a = 15, a > 0** is **TRUE** and

```
a % 2 == 0
```

is evaluated. This is **FALSE**, so

```
sum2 = sum2 + a;
```

is executed and control is again transferred out of the nested statement to

```
cout << setw(17) << "All done" << endl;
```

For **a = 0, a > 0** is **FALSE**, thus

```
a == 0
```

is evaluated. Since this is **TRUE**, the statement

```
cout << setw(18) << "a is zero" << endl;
```

is executed and control is transferred to

```
cout << setw(17) << "All done" << endl;
```

Finally, for **a = -30, a > 0** is **FALSE**, thus

```
a == 0
```

is evaluated. This is **FALSE**, so

```
neg_sum = neg_sum + a;
```

is executed and control is transferred to

```
cout << setw(17) << "All done" << endl;
```

Note that this example traces through all possibilities involved in the nested statement. This is essential to guarantee your statement is properly constructed.

Designing solutions to problems that require multiway selection can be difficult. A few guidelines can help. If a decision has two courses of action and one is complex and the other is fairly simple, nest the complex part in the **`if`** option and the simple part in the **`else`** option. This method is frequently used to check for bad data. An example of the program design for this could be:

```
            .
            . (get the data)
            .

if (data_ok)
            .
            . (complex action here)
            .
else (message about bad data)
```

This method could also be used to guard against dividing by zero in computation. For instance, we could have

```
divisor = <value>;
if (divisor != 0)
            .
            . (proceed with action)
            .
else
      cout << "division by zero" << endl;
```

When there are several courses of action that can be considered sequentially, an extended **`if . . . else`** should be used. To illustrate, consider the program fragment of Example 5.10.

EXAMPLE 5.10

Let us write a program fragment that allows you to assign letter grades based on students' semester averages. Grades are to be assigned according to the following scale:

Average	Grade
100 >= X >= 90	A
90 > X >= 80	B
80 > X >= 70	C
70 > X >= 55	D
55 > X	E

Extended **`if`** statements can be used to accomplish this as follows:

```
if (average >= 90)
      grade = 'A';
else if (average >= 80)
      grade = 'B';
else if (average >= 70)
      grade = 'C';
else if (average >= 55)
      grade = 'D';
else
      grade = 'F';
```

Because any average of more than 100 or less than zero would be a sign of some data or program error, this example could be protected with a statement as follows:

```
if ((average <= 100) && (average >= 0))
         .
         . (compute letter grade)
         .
else
         cout << setw(38) << "There is an error. Average "
              << "is" << setw(8) << average << endl;
```

Protecting parts of a program in this manner will help you avoid unexpected results or program crashes. It also allows you to identify the source of an error.

Form and Syntax

The rule for matching **else** in nested selection statements is:

> *When an* **else** *is encountered, it is matched with the most recent* **if** *that has not yet been matched.*

The matching of **if**s with **else**s is a common source of errors. When designing programs, you should be very careful to match them correctly. For example, consider the following situation, which can lead to an error:

```
if (<condition 1>)
         .
         . (action 1)
         .
else
         .
         . (action 2)
         .
```

where action 1 consists of an **if** statement. Specifically, suppose you want a fragment of code to read a list of positive integers and print those that are perfect squares. A method of protecting against negative integers and zero could be:

```
cin >> num;
if (num > 0)
         .
         . (action 1 here)
         .
else
         cout << num << " is not positive." << endl;
```

If we now develop action 1 so that it prints only those positive integers that are perfect squares, it is

```
if (sqrt(num) == int(sqrt(num)))
     cout << num << endl;
```

Nesting this selection statement in our design, we have

```
cin >> num;
if (num > 0)
      if (sqrt(num) == int(sqrt(num))
            cout << num << endl;
      else
            cout << num << " is not positive." << endl;
```

If you now use this segment with input of 20 for **num**, the output is

```
20 is not positive.
```

Thus, this fragment is not correct to solve the problem. The indenting is consistent with our intent, but the actual execution of the fragment treated the code as

```
cin >> num;
if (num > 0)
      if (sqrt(num) == int(sqrt(num)))
            cout << num << endl;
      else
            cout << num << " is not positive." << endl;
```

because the **else** is matched with the most recent **if**. This problem can be resolved by redesigning the fragment as follows:

```
cin >> num;
if (num <= 0)
      cout << num << " is not positive." << endl;
else if (sqrt(num) == int(sqrt(num)))
      cout << num << endl;
```

It is very important to use a consistent, readable writing style when using nested or extended **if** statements. The style used here for nested **if** statements is to indent each nested statement a single tab stop. Also, each **else** of an **if . . . else** statement is in the same column as the **if** of that statement. This allows you to see at a glance where the **else**s match with the **if**s. For example,

```
if
      if
      else
else
```

An extended **if** statement has all the **else**s on the same indenting level as the first **if**. This reinforces the concept of extended **if**. For example,

```
if
else if
else if
else
```

We conclude this section with an example that uses nested **if** statements.

EXAMPLE 5.11

Write a program that computes the gross pay for an employee of the Clean Products Corporation of America. The corporation produces three products: A, B, and C. Supervisors earn a commission of 7% of sales and representatives earn 5%. Bonuses of $100 are paid to supervisors whose commission exceeds $300 and to representatives whose commission exceeds $200. Input is in the form

```
S 18 15 10
```

where the first position contains an **S** or **R** for supervisor or representative, respectively. The next three integers include the number of units of each of the products sold. Because product prices may vary over time, the constant definition section will be used to indicate the current prices. The constants for this problem will be

```
const float SUPER_RATE = 0.07;
const float REP_RATE = 0.05;
const float A_PRICE = 13.95;
const float B_PRICE = 17.95;
const float C_PRICE = 29.95;
```

A first-level pseudocode development for this problem is

1. Get the data
2. Compute commission and bonus
3. Print heading
4. Print results

The structure chart for this is given in Figure 5.4. Module specifications for each of the main modules follow:

Module: Get the data
Task: Read input data from the keyboard.
Outputs: employee classification and sales of products A, B, and C

Module: Compute commission and bonus
Task: if a supervisor

```
            compute total commission
            compute bonus
      else
            compute total commission
            compute bonus
```

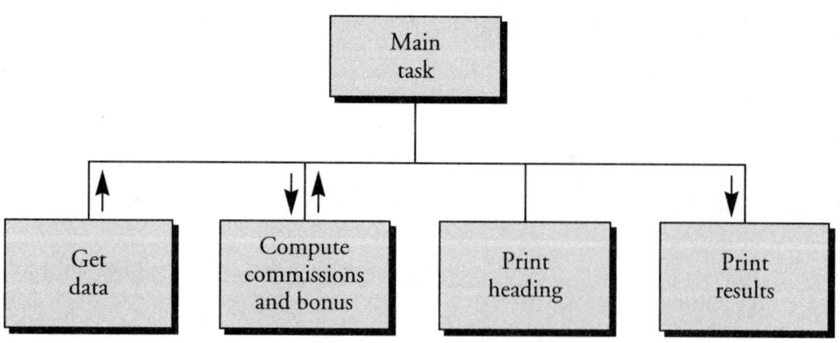

◆ FIGURE 5.4
Structure chart for Example 5.11

Inputs: classification, a_sales, b_sales, c_sales
Outputs: a_commission, b_commission, c_commission, total_commission, bonus

Module: Print heading
Task: Print a heading for the report.

Module: Print results
Task: Print the employee's report.
Inputs: classification
a_sales
b_sales
c_sales
a_commission
b_commission
c_commission
total_commission
bonus

Modules for Get data, Print heading, and Print results are similar to those previously developed. The module Compute the commission and bonus requires some development. Step 2 of the pseudocode becomes

```
2. Compute commission and bonus
   2.1 if employee is supervisor
           compute supervisor's earnings
       else
           compute representative's earnings
```

where "compute supervisor's earnings" is refined to

```
2.1.1 compute commission from sales of A
2.1.2 compute commission from sales of B
2.1.3 compute commission from sales of C
2.1.4 compute total commission
2.1.5 compute supervisor's bonus
      2.1.5.1 if total commission > 300
                  bonus is 100.00
              else
                  bonus is 0.00
```

A similar development follows for computing a representative's earnings. Step 3 will be an appropriate function to print a heading. Step 4 will contain whatever you feel is appropriate for output. It should include at least the number of sales, amount of sales, commissions, bonuses, and total compensation.

The main program for this problem is

```
int main()
{
      int a_sales, b_sales, c_sales;            // Sales of Products A, B, C
      float a_comm, b_comm, c_comm;             // Commission on sales of A, B, C
      float bonus;                              // Bonus, if earned
      float total_commission;                   // Commission on all products
      char classification;                      // S-Supervisor or R-Representative
```

```
      get_data(classification, a_sales, b_sales, c_sales);
      compute_commission_and_bonus(classification, a_sales,
            b_sales, c_sales, a_comm, b_comm,
            c_comm, total_commission, bonus);
      print_heading(classification);
      print_results(classification, a_sales, b_sales, c_sales, a_comm, b_comm,
            c_comm, total_commission, bonus);
      return 0;
}
```

A complete program for this is

```
// This program computes gross pay for an employee. Note the use of constants
// and selection.

// Program file: sales.cpp

#include <iostream.h>
#include <iomanip.h>

const float SUPER_RATE = 0.07;
const float REP_RATE = 0.05;
const float A_PRICE = 13.95;
const float B_PRICE = 17.95;
const float C_PRICE = 29.95;
const char SKIP = ' ';

// Function: get_data
// gets input data from the user
//
// Outputs: Outputs: employee classification and sales of products A, B, and C

void get_data(char &classification, int &a_sales, int &b_sales, int &c_sales);

// Function: compute_commission_and_bonus
// If a supervisor
//             compute total commission
//             compute bonus
//      else
//             compute total commission
//             compute bonus
// Inputs: classification, a_sales, b_sales, c_sales
// Outputs: a_commission, b_commission, c_commission,
// total_commission, bonus

void compute_commission_and_bonus(char classification, int a_sales,
       int b_sales, int c_sales, float &a_commission, float& b_commission,
       float &c_commission, float &total_commission, float &bonus);

void print_heading(char classification);
```

```
// Function: print_results
// Prints employee's report
//
// Inputs:     classification
//            a_sales
//            b_sales
//            c_sales
//            a_commission
//            b_commission
//            c_commission
//            total_commission
//            bonus

void print_results(char classification, int a_sales, int b_sales, int c_sales,
     float a_comm, float b_comm, float c_comm, float total_commission,
     float bonus);

// Function: print_heading
// Print heading for results
//
// Input: classification

void print_heading(char classification);

int main()
{
      int a_sales, b_sales, c_sales;            // Sales of Products A, B, C
      float a_comm, b_comm, c_comm;             // Commission on sales of A, B, C
      float bonus;                              // Bonus, if earned
      float total_commission;                   // Commission on all products
      char classification;                      // S-Supervisor or R-Representative

      get_data(classification, a_sales, b_sales, c_sales);
      compute_commission_and_bonus(classification, a_sales,
            b_sales, c_sales, a_comm, b_comm,
            c_comm, total_commission, bonus);
      print_heading(classification);
      print_results(classification, a_sales, b_sales, c_sales, a_comm, b_comm,
            c_comm, total_commission, bonus);
      return 0;
}

void get_data(char &classification, int &a_sales, int &b_sales, int &c_sales)
{
      cout << "Enter S or R for classification.";
      cin >> classification;                                                    1
      cout << "Enter a_sales, b_sales, c_sales.";
      cin >> a_sales >> b_sales >>c_sales;
}
```

```
void compute_commission_and_bonus(char classification, int a_sales,
      int b_sales, int c_sales, float &a_commission, float& b_commission,
      float &c_commission, float &total_commission, float &bonus)
{
      if (classification == 'S')            // Supervisor
      {
           a_commission = a_sales * A_PRICE * SUPER_RATE;
           b_commission = b_sales *
           B_PRICE * SUPER_RATE;
           c_commission = c_sales * C_PRICE * SUPER_RATE;
           total_commission = a_commission + b_commission + c_commission;
           if (total_commission > 300.0)
                  bonus = 100.0;
           else
                  bonus = 0.0 ;                                                  2
      }
      else                                  // Representative
      {
           a_commission = a_sales * A_PRICE * REP_RATE; b_commission = b_sales *
           B_PRICE * REP_RATE;
           c_commission = c_sales * C_PRICE * REP_RATE;
           total_commission = a_commission + b_commission + c_commission;
           if (total_commission > 200.0)
                bonus = 100.0;
           else
                bonus = 0.0;
      }
}

void print_heading(char classification)
{
      cout << endl;
      cout << setw(10) << SKIP << "Clean Products Corporation of America"
           << endl;
      cout <<  setw(10)  <<  SKIP <<  "------------------------------"
           << endl;
      cout << endl;
      cout << setw(10) << SKIP << "Sales Report for" << setw(10)
           << "June" << endl;
      cout << endl;                                                              3
      cout << setw(10) << SKIP << "classification"<< endl;
      if (classification == 'S')
           cout << setw(12) << SKIP << "Supervisor"<< endl;
      else
           cout << setw(12) << SKIP << "Representative"<< endl;
      cout << endl;
      cout << setw(12) << SKIP << "Product      Sales       Commission" << endl;
      cout << setw(12) << SKIP << "-----        ----        ---------" << endl;
      cout << endl;
}
```

```
void print_results(char classification, int a_sales, int b_sales, int c_sales,
      float a_comm, float b_comm, float c_comm, float total_commission,
      float bonus)

{
      cout << fixed << showpoint << setprecision(2);
      cout << setw(15) << SKIP << "A" << setw(13) << a_sales << setw(14)
           << a_comm << endl;
      cout << setw(15) << SKIP << "B" << setw(13) << b_sales << setw(14)
           << b_comm << endl;
      cout << setw(15) << SKIP << "C" << setw(13) << c_sales << setw(14)
           << c_comm << endl;                                                  4
      cout << endl;
      cout << setw(31) << "Subtotal"<< setw(3) << "$" << setw(9)
           << total_commission << endl;
      cout << endl;
      cout << setw(31) << "Your bonus is:" << setw(3) << "$" << setw(9)
           << bonus << endl;
      cout << setw(43) << "------" << endl;
      cout << endl;
      cout << setw(31) << "Total Due" << setw(3) << "$" << setw(9)
           << total_commission + bonus << endl;
}
```

A sample run produces the following output:

```
Enter R or S for classification. S
Enter a_sales, b_sales, c_sales 1100 990 510

            Clean Products Corporation of America

            Sales Report for        June

            classification          Supervisor

            Product      Sales      Commission
            -------      -----      ----------

            A            1100       1074.15

            B            990        1243.93

            C            510        1069.21

                  Subtotal         $3387.30

                  Your bonus is:    $100.00

                  Total Due        $3487.30
```

Program Testing

In actual practice, a great deal of time is spent testing programs in an attempt to make them run properly when they are installed for some specific purpose. Formal program verification is discussed in Section 5.6 and is developed more fully in subsequent course work. However, examining the issue of which data are minimally necessary for program testing is appropriate when working with selection statements.

As you might expect, test data should include information that tests every logical branch in a program. Whenever a program contains an **if . . . else** statement of the form

```
if (<condition>)
      (action 1 here)
else
      (action 2 here)
```

the test data should guarantee that both the **if** and the **else** options are executed.

Nesting and use of extended **if** statements require a bit more care when selecting test data. In general, a single **if . . . else** statement requires at least two data items for testing. If an **if . . . else** statement is nested within the **if** option, at least two more data items are required to test the nested selection statement.

For purposes of illustration, let us reexamine the module Compute Commission and Bonus from Example 5.11. This module contains the logic

```
if (classification == 'S')
          .
          .
          .
     if (total_commission  >  300.00)
               .
               .
               .
     else
               .
               .
               .
else
          .
          .
          .
if (total_commission  > 200.00)
          .
          .
          .
else
          .
          .
          .
```

To see what data should minimally be used to test this function, consider the following table:

Classification	Total Commission
S	400.00
S	250.00
R	250.00
R	150.00

It is a good idea to also include boundary conditions in the test data. Thus, the previous table could also have listed 300.00 as the total commission for **S** and 200.00 as the total commission for **R**.

In summary, you should always make sure every logical branch is executed when running the program with test data.

EXERCISES 5.4

1. Consider the program fragment

```
if (x >= 0.0)
      if x < 1000.00
      {
            y = 2 * x;
            if (x <= 500)
                  x = x / 10;
      }
      else
            y = 3 * x;
else
      y = abs(x);
```

Indicate the values of **x** and **y** after this fragment is executed for each of the following initial values of **x**.

a. `x = 381.5;`
b. `x = -21.0;`
c. `x = 600.0;`
d. `x = 3000.0;`

2. Write and run a test program that illustrates the checking of all branches of nested **if . . . else** statements.

3. Rewrite each of the following fragments using nested or extended **if** statements without compound conditions.

a.
```
if ((ch == 'M') && (sum > 1000))
     x = x + 1;
if ((ch == 'M') && (sum <= 1000))
     x = x + 2;
if ((ch == 'F') && (sum > 1000))
     x = x + 3;
if ((ch == 'F') && (sum <= 1000))
     x = x + 5;
```

b.
```
cin >> num;
if ((num > 0) && (num <= 10000))
{
     count = count + 1;
```

```
sum = sum + num;
}
else
     cout << setw(27) << "Value out of range" << endl;
```

c.
```
if ((a > 0) && (b > 0))
     cout << setw(22) << "Both positive" << endl;
else
     cout << setw(22) << "Some negative" << endl;
```

d.
```
if (((a > 0) && (b > 0)) || (c > 0))
     cout << setw(19) << "Option one" << endl;
else
     cout <<setw(19) << "Option two" << endl;
```

4. Consider each of the following program fragments.

a.
```
if (a < 0)
     if (b < 0)
             a = b;
     else
             a = b + 10;
cout << a << b << endl;
```

b.
```
  if (a < 0)
  {
       if (b < 0)
               a = b;
  }
else
       a = b + 10;
cout << a << b << endl;
```

c.
```
if (a == 0)
     a = b + 10;
else if (b < 0)
     a = b;
cout << a << b << endl;
```

d.
```
if (a >= 0)
     a = b + 10;
if (b < 0)
     a = b;
cout << a << b << endl;
```

Indicate the output of each fragment for each of the following assignment statements.

i.
```
a = -5;
b = 5;
```

ii.
```
a = -5;
b = -3;
```

iii.
```
a = 10;
b = 8;
```

iv.
```
a = 10;
b = -4;
```

5. Look back to Example 5.10, in which we assigned grades to students, and rewrite the grade assignment fragment using a different nesting. Could you rewrite it without using any nesting? Should you?

6. Many nationally based tests report scores and indicate in which quartile the score lies. Assuming the following quartile designation,

Score	Quartile
100–75	1
74–50	2
49–25	3
24–0	4

write a program to read a score from the keyboard and report in which quartile the score lies.

7. What are the values of **a**, **b**, and **c** after the following program fragment is executed?

```
a = -8; b = 21;
c = a + b;
if (a > b)
{
        a = b;
        c = a * b;
}
else if (a < 0)
{
        a = abs(a);
        b = b - a;
        c = a * b;
}
else
        c = 0;
```

8. Create minimal sets of test data for each part of Exercise 4 and for Exercise 7. Explain why each piece of test data has been included.
9. Discuss a technique that could be used as a debugging aid to guarantee that all possible logical paths of a program have been used.

5.5 switch Statements

OBJECTIVES

- to learn the syntax of the **switch** statement
- to understand how **switch** statements can be used as an alternate method for multiway selection
- to be able to use **switch** statements in designing programs

Thus far, this chapter has examined one-way selection, two-way selection, and multiway selection. Section 5.4 illustrated how multiple selection can be achieved using nested and extended **if** statements. Because multiple selection can sometimes be difficult to follow, C++ provides an alternative method of handling this concept, the **switch** statement.

Form and Syntax

C++ **switch** statements are often used when several options depend on the value of a single variable or expression. The general structure for a **switch** statement follows:

```
switch (<selector>)
{
        case <label 1> :        <statements 1>
                                break;
        case <label 2> :        <statements 2>
                                break;
                .
                .
                .
        case <label n > :       <statements n >
                                break;
        default:                <statements>
}
```

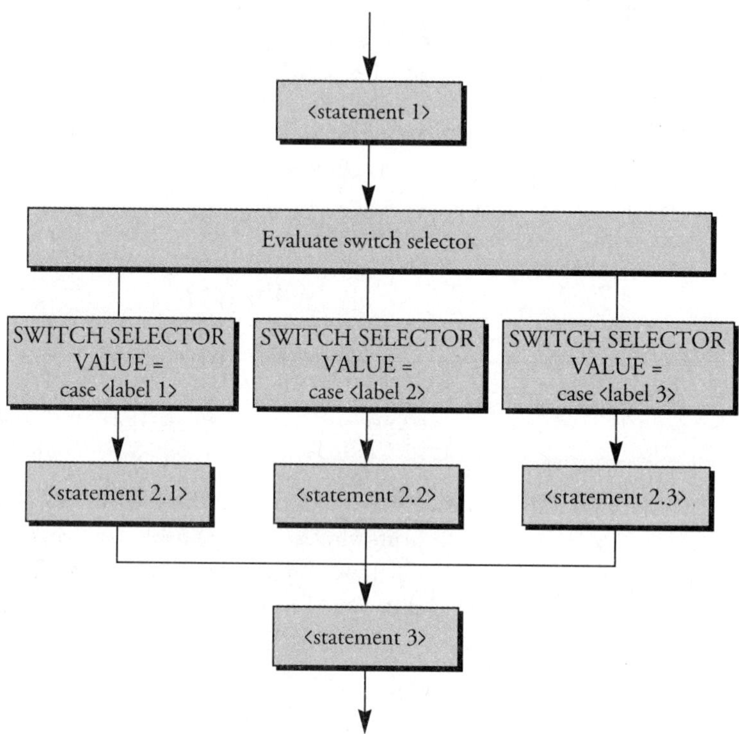

◆ **FIGURE 5.5**
The **switch** statement flow diagram

This structure is shown graphically in Figure 5.5. The words **switch, case, break**, and **default** are reserved. The selector can be any variable or expression whose value is any data type we have studied previously except for **float** (only ordinal data types can be used). Values of the selector constitute the labels. Thus, if **age** is an integer variable whose values might be 18, 19, and 20, we could have

```
switch (age)
{
        case 18 :       <statement 1>
                        break;
        case 19 :       <statement 2>
                        break;
```

```
        case 20 :       <statement 3>
                        break;
        default:        <default statement>
}
```

When this program statement is executed, the value of **age** will determine to which statement control is transferred. More specifically, the program fragment

```
age = 19;
switch (age)
{
    case 18 :       cout << "I just became a legal voter." << endl;
                    break;
    case 19 :       cout << "This is my second year to vote." << endl;
                    break;
    case 20 :       cout << "I am almost twenty-one." << endl;
                    break;
    default:        if (age > 20)
                         cout << "I have all of the privileges of adulthood."
                              << endl;
                    else
                         cout << "I have no privileges at all." << endl;
}
```

produces the output

```
This is my second year to vote.
```

Before considering more examples, several comments are in order. The flow of logic within a **switch** statement is as follows:

1. The value of the selector is determined.
2. The first instance of value is found among the labels.
3. The statements following this value are executed.
4. **break** statements are optional. If a **break** statement occurs within these statements, then control is transferred to the first program statement following the entire **switch** statement; otherwise, execution continues. In general, you should end every case with a **break** statement.

The selector can have a value of any type previously studied except **float**. Only ordinal data types may be used.

Several cases may be associated with an alternative action. For example, if **<statement 1>** should be run when **age** has the integer value of 10 or 100, the **switch** statement could appear as

```
switch (age)
{
        case 10:
        case 100 :      <statement 1>
                         break;
        case 19 :       <statement 2>
                         break;
        case 20 :       <statement 3>
                         break;
        default :       <default statement>
}
```

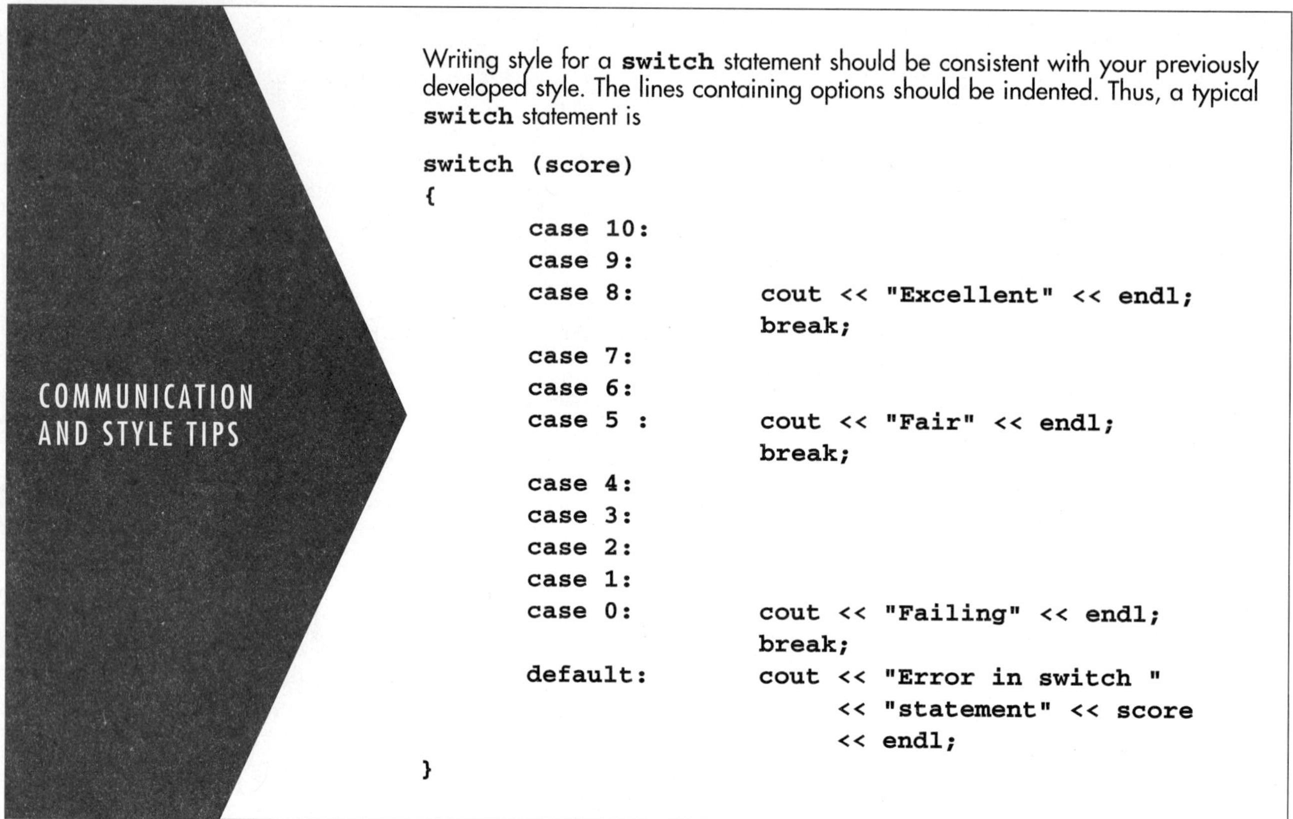

COMMUNICATION AND STYLE TIPS

Writing style for a **switch** statement should be consistent with your previously developed style. The lines containing options should be indented. Thus, a typical **switch** statement is

```
switch (score)
{
        case 10:
        case 9:
        case 8:          cout << "Excellent" << endl;
                         break;
        case 7:
        case 6:
        case 5 :         cout << "Fair" << endl;
                         break;
        case 4:
        case 3:
        case 2:
        case 1:
        case 0:          cout << "Failing" << endl;
                         break;
        default:         cout << "Error in switch "
                              << "statement" << score
                              << endl;
}
```

All possible values of the **switch** selector do not have to be listed. However, if a value that is not listed is used, subtle logic errors can occur. Consequently, it is preferable to use a *default option.* If certain values require no action, the program will finish executing the **switch** statement by running the default as the last option; for example,

```
switch (age)
{
        case 10:
        case 100 :     <statement 1>
                       break;
        case 19 :      <statement 2>
                       break;
        case 20 :      <statement 3>
                       break;
        default:       cout << "There is no case for " << age << endl;
}
```

Like the **break** statement, the **default** statement is optional.

At this stage, we will consider several examples that illustrate various uses of **switch** statements. Because our purpose is for illustration, the examples are somewhat contrived. Later examples will serve to illustrate how these statements are used in solving problems.

EXAMPLE 5.12

The selector can have a value of type **char**, and the ordinal of the character determines the option. Thus, the label list must contain the appropriate characters in single quotation marks. If **grade** has values **'A'**, **'B'**, **'C'**, **'D'**, or **'F'**, a **switch** statement could be

```
switch (grade)
{
        case 'A' :      points = 4.0;
                        break;
        case 'B' :      points = 3.0;
                        break;
        case 'C' :      points = 2.0;
                        break;
        case 'D' :      points = 1.0;
                        break;
        case 'F' :      points = 0.0;
}
```

EXAMPLE 5.13

Let us rewrite the following program fragment using a **switch** statement

```
if ((score == 10) || (score == 9))
      grade = 'A'
else if ((score == 8) || (score == 7))
      grade = 'B'
else if ((score == 6) || (score == 5))
      grade = 'C'
else
      grade = 'F';
```

If we assume **score** is an integer variable with values 0, 1, 2, . . . , 10, we could use a **switch** statement as follows:

```
switch (score)
{
        case 10:
        case 9:         grade = 'A';
                        break;
        case 8:
        case 7:         grade = 'B';
                        break;
        case 6:
        case 5:         grade = 'C';
                        break;
        case 4:
        case 3:
        case 2:
        case 1:
        case 0 : grade = 'F';
}
```

A NOTE OF INTEREST

A Software Glitch

The software glitch that disrupted AT&T's long-distance telephone service for nine hours in January 1990 dramatically demonstrates what can go wrong even in the most reliable and scrupulously tested systems. Of the roughly 100 million telephone calls placed with AT&T during that period, only about half got through. The breakdown cost the company more than $60 million in lost revenues and caused considerable inconvenience and irritation for telephone-dependent customers.

The trouble began at a "switch"—one of 114 interconnected, computer-operated electronic switching systems scattered across the United States. These sophisticated systems, each a maze of electronic equipment housed in a large room, form the backbone of the AT&T long-distance telephone network.

When a local exchange delivers a telephone call to the network, it arrives at one of these switching centers, which can handle up to 700,000 calls an hour. The switch immediately springs into action. It scans a list of 14 different routes it can use to complete the call, and at the same time hands off the telephone number to a parallel, signaling network, invisible to any caller. This private data network allows computers to scout the possible routes and to determine whether the switch at the other end can deliver the call to the local company it serves.

If the answer is no, the call is stopped at the original switch to keep it from tying up a line, and the caller gets a busy signal. If the answer is yes, a signaling-network computer makes a reservation at the destination switch and orders the original switch to pass along the waiting call—after that switch makes a final check to ensure that the chosen line is functioning properly. The whole process of passing a call down the network takes 4 to 6 seconds. Because the switches must keep in constant touch with the signaling network and its computers, each switch has a computer program that handles all the necessary communications between the switch and the signaling network.

AT&T's first indication that something might be amiss appeared on a giant video display at the company's network control center in Bedminster, New Jersey. At 2:25 p.m. on Monday, January 15, 1990, network managers saw an alarming increase in the number of red warning signals appearing on many of the 75 video screens showing the status of various parts of AT&T's worldwide network. The warnings signaled a serious collapse in the network's ability to complete calls within the United States.

To bring the network back up to speed, AT&T engineers first tried a number of standard procedures that had worked in the past. This time, the methods failed. The engineers realized they had a problem they'd never seen before. Nonetheless, within a few hours, they managed to stabilize the network by temporarily cutting back on the number of messages moving through the signaling network. They cleared the last defective link at 11:30 that night.

Meanwhile, a team of more than 100 telephone technicians tried frantically to track down the fault. Because the problem involved the signaling network and seemed to bounce from one switch to another, they zeroed in on the software that permitted each switch to communicate with the signaling-network computers.

The day after the slowdown, AT&T personnel removed the apparently faulty software from each switch, temporarily replacing it with an earlier version of the communications program. A close examination of the flawed software turned up a single error in one line of the program. Just one month earlier, network technicians had changed the software to speed the processing of certain messages, and the change had inadvertently introduced a flaw into the system. From that finding, AT&T could reconstruct what had happened.

Use in Problems

The **switch** statements should not be used for relational tests involving large ranges of values. For example, if one wanted to examine a range from 0 to 100 to determine test scores, nested selection would be better than a **switch** statement. We close this section with some examples that illustrate how **switch** statements can be used in solving problems.

EXAMPLE 5.14

Suppose you are writing a program for a gasoline station owner who sells four grades of gasoline: regular, premium, unleaded, and super unleaded. Your program reads a character (R, P, U, S) that designates which kind of gasoline was purchased and then takes subsequent action. The outline for this fragment is

```
cin >> gas_type);
switch (gas_type)
{
        case 'R' :      <action for regular>;
                        break;
        case 'P' :      <action for premium>;
                        break;
        case 'U' :      <action for unleaded>;
                        break;
        case 'S' :      <action for super unleaded>;
                        break;
}
```

Equivalent of Extended if statements

As previously indicated, **switch** statements can sometimes (ordinal data types) be used instead of extended **if** statements when multiple selection is required for solving a problem. The following example illustrates this use.

EXAMPLE 5.15

An alternative method of assigning letter grades based on integer scores between 0 and 100 inclusive is to divide the score by 10 and assign grades according to some scale. This idea could be used in conjunction with a **switch** statement as follows:

```
new_score = score / 10;
switch (new_score)
{
        case 10:
        case 9:         grade = 'A';
                        break;
        case 8:         grade = 'B';
                        break;
        case 7:         grade = 'C';
                        break;
        case 6:
        case 5:         grade = 'D';
                        break;
        case 4:
        case 3:
        case 2:
        case 1:
        case 0:         grade = 'F';
}
```

EXERCISES 5.5

1. Discuss the need for program protection when using a **switch** statement.
2. Show how the following **switch** statement could be protected against unexpected values.

```
switch (age / 10)
{
        case 10:
        case 9:
        case 8:
        case 7:      cout << setw(40) << "These are retirement years" << endl;
                     break;
        case 6:
        case 5:
        case 4:      cout << setw(40) << "These are middle age years" << endl;
                     break;
        case 3:
        case 2:      cout << setw(40) << "These are mobile years" << endl;
                     break;
        case 1:      cout << setw(40) << "These are school years" << endl;
}
```

3. Find all errors in the following statements.

a.
```
switch (a)
  case 1       :
                        break;
  case 2       :        a = 2 * a
                        break;
  case 3       ;        a = 3 * a;
                        break;
  case 4; 5; 6 :        a = 4 * a;
  }
```

b.
```
switch (num)
{
      case 5       num = num + 5;
                   break;
      case 6:
      case 7:      ; num = num + 6;
                   break;
      case 7, 8, 9, 10 : num = num + 10;
}
```

c.
```
switch (age)
{
      15, 16, 17 : y_count = y_count + 1;
                   cout << age << y_count << endl;
      case 18:
      case 19:
      case 20:     m_count = m_count + 1;
      case 21:     cout << age endl;
}
```

d.
```
switch (ch)
{
      a :     points =     4.0;
              break;
      b :     points =     3.0;
              break;
      c :     points =     2.0;
              break;
      d :     points =     1.0;
              break;
      e :     points =     0.0
}
```

e.
```
switch (score)
{
      case 5 :     grade = 'A';
                   break;
      case 4 :     grade = 'B';
                   break;
      case 3 :     grade = 'C';
                   break;
      case 2 :
      case 1:,
      case 0:     grade = 'E';
}
```

f.
```
switch (num / 10)
{
      case 1 :     num = num + 1;
                   break;
      case 2 :     num = num + 2;
                   break;
      case 3 :     num = num + 3;
}
```

4. What is the output from each of the following program fragments?

a.
```
a = 5;
power = 3;
switch (power)
{
      case 0:      b = 1;
                   break;
      case 1:      b = a;
                   break;
      case 2:      b = a * a;
                   break;
      case 3:      b = a * a * a;
}
cout << a << power << b << endl;
```

b.
```
gas_type = 'S';
cout << "You have purchased ";
switch (gas_type)
{
    case 'R':       cout << "Regular";
                    break;
    case 'P':       cout << "Premium";
                    break;
    case 'U':       cout << "Unleaded";
                    break;
    case 'S':       cout << "Super Unleaded";
}
cout << "gasoline" << endl;
```

c.
```
a = 6;
b = -3;
switch (a)
{
    case 10:
    case 9:
    case 8:         switch b
                    {
                        case -3:
                        case -4:
                        case -5:        a = a * b;
                                        break;
                        case 0:
                        case -1:
                        case -2:        a = a + b;
                    }
                    break;
    case 7:
    case 6:
    case 5:         switch (b)
                    {
                        case -5:
                        case -4:        a = a * b;
                                        break;
                        case -3:
                        case -2:        a = a + b;
                                        break;
                        case -1:
                        case 0:         a = a - b;
                    }
}
cout << a << b << endl;
```

d.
```
symbol = '-';
a = 5;
b = 10;
switch (symbol)
{
    case '+' :      num = a + b;
    case '-' :      num = a - b;
```

```
        case '*' :      num = a * b;
    }
    cout << a << b << num << endl;
```

5. Rewrite each of the following program fragments using a **switch** statement.

   a.
```
if (power = 1)
num = a;
if (power = 2)
     num = a * a;
if (power = 3)
num = a * a * a;
```

   b. Assume **score** is an integer between 0 and 10.

```
if (score > 9)
     grade = 'A'
else if (score > 8)
     grade = 'B'
else if (score > 7)
     grade = 'C'
else if (score > 5)
     grade = 'D'
else
     grade = 'E';
```

   c. Assume measurement is either **'M'** or **'N'**.

```
if (measurement == 'M')
{
     cout << setw(37) << "This is a metric measurement." << endl;
     cout << setw(42) << "It will be converted to nonmetric." << endl;
     length = num * CM_TO_INCHES;
}
else
{
     cout << setw(40) << " This is a nonmetric measurement. << endl;
     cout << setw(39) << "It will be converted to metric." << endl;
     length = num * INCHES_TO_CM;
}
```

6. Show how a **switch** statement can be used in a program to compute college tuition fees. Assume there are different fee rates for each of undergraduates (U), graduates (G), non-U.S. students (F), and special students (S).
7. Use nested **switch** statements to design a program fragment to compute postage for domestic (noninternational) mail. The design should provide for four weight categories for both letters and packages. Each can be sent first, second, third, or fourth class.

5.6 Assertions

OBJECTIVES

- to know how to use assertions as preconditions
- to know how to use assertions as postconditions

An *assertion* is a statement about what we expect to be true at the point in the program where the assertion is placed. For example, if you wish to compute a test average by dividing the **sum_of_scores** by **number_of_students**, you could state your intent that **number_of_students** is not equal to zero with a comment:

```
// assert that (number_of_students != 0)
class_average = sum_of_scores/ number_of_students;
```

Assertions are usually Boolean-valued expressions and typically concern program action. In the preceding example, the assertion that appears in a comment would remind the programmer that a certain condition must be true before an action is taken. Modern programming languages such as C++ provide a way of executing an assertion at run time. The computer verifies that the assertion is true, and if it is false, the computer halts program execution with an error message. To use this kind of feature in C++, you must include the **assert.h** library file:

```
#include <assert.h>
```

Then you can state your assertion by calling the function **assert** with the Boolean expression as a parameter. The previous example might now look like this:

```
assert(number_of_students != 0);
class_average = sum_of_scores / number_of_students;
```

At execution time, this program would halt with an error message before an attempt to divide by zero.

Assertions frequently come in pairs: one preceding program action and one following the action. In this format, the first assertion is a precondition and the second is a postcondition. To illustrate preconditions and postconditions, consider the following segment of code:

```
if (num1 < num2)
{
      temp = num1;
      num1 = num2;
      num2 = temp;
}
```

The intent of this code is to have **num1** be greater than or equal to **num2**. If we intend for both **num1** and **num2** to be positive, we can write

```
assert((num1 >= 0) && (num2 >= 0));          // Precondition
if (num1 < num2)
{
      temp = num1;
      num1 = num2;
      num2 = temp;
}
assert((num1 >= num2) && (num2 >= 0));       // Postcondition
```

As a second example, consider a **switch** statement used to assign grades based on quiz scores.

```
switch (score)
{
      case 10:      grade = 'A';
                    break;
      case 9:
      case 8:       grade = 'B';
                    break;
```

```
        case 7:
        case 6:        grade = 'C';
                       break;
        case 5:
        case 4:        grade = 'D';
                       break;
        case 3:
        case 2:
        case 1:
        case 0:        grade = 'E';
    }
```

Assertions can be used as preconditions and postconditions in the following manner.

```
assert((score >= 0) && (score <= 10));                    // Precondition
switch (score)
{
     case 10:      grade = 'A';
                   break;
     case 9:
     case 8:       grade = 'B';
                   break;
     case 7:
     case 6:       grade = 'C';
                   break;
     case 5:
     case 4:       grade = 'D';
                   break;
     case 3:
     case 2:
     case 1:
     case 0:       grade = 'E';
}
assert(((score = 10) && (grade = 'A')) ||                 // Postcondition
          ((score = 9) && (grade = 'B')) ||
          ((score = 8) && (grade = 'B')) ||
          ((score = 7) && (grade = 'C')) ||
          ((score = 6) && (grade = 'C')) ||
          ((score = 5) && (grade = 'D')) ||
          ((score = 4) && (grade = 'D')) ||
          (((score >= 0) && (score <= 3)) && (grade = 'E')));
```

Assertions can be used in *program proofs*. Simply put, a program proof is an analysis of a program that attempts to verify the correctness of program results. A detailed study of program proofs is beyond the scope of this text. If, however, you use assertions as preconditions and postconditions now, you will better understand them in subsequent courses. They are especially useful for making a program safer, even if you cannot be sure that their use will guarantee that the program is correct. If you do choose to use assertions in this manner, be aware that the postcondition of one action is the precondition of the next action.

FOCUS ON PROGRAM DESIGN

The Gas-N-Clean Service Station sells gasoline and has a car wash. Fees for the car wash are $1.25 with a gasoline purchase of $10.00 or more and $3.00 otherwise. Three kinds of gasoline are available: regular at $1.149, unleaded at $1.199, and super unleaded at $ 1.289 per gallon. Write a program that prints a statement for a customer. Input consists of number of gallons purchased, kind of gasoline purchased (R, U, S, or, for no purchase, N), and car wash desired (Y or N). Use the constant definition section for gasoline prices. Your output should include appropriate messages. Sample output for these data is

```
Enter number of gallons and press <Enter>. 9.7
Enter gas type (R, U, S, or N) and press <Enter>. R
Enter Y or N for car wash and press <Enter>. Y

               ***********************************
               *                                 *
               *     Gas-N-Clean Service Station  *
               *                                 *
               *           July 25, 1995          *
               *                                 *
               ***********************************

               Amount of gasoline purchased         9.700 Gallons

               Price per gallon               $     1.149

               Total gasoline cost            $    11.15

               Car wash cost                  $     1.25

               Total due                      $    12.40

                          Thank you for stopping

                          Please come again

                    Remember to buckle up and drive safely
```

A first-level pseudocode development is

1. Get data
2. Compute charges
3. Print results

A structure chart for this problem is given in Figure 5.6. Module specifications for the main modules follow:

Module: Get the data
Task: Get information interactively from the keyboard.
Outputs: number of gallons purchased, type of gasoline, a choice as to whether or not a car wash is desired

Module: Compute the charges
Task: Compute the gas cost, wash cost, and total cost.
Inputs: number of gallons, gas type, wash option
Outputs: gas cost, wash cost, total cost

FIGURE 5.6
Structure chart for the Gas-N-Clean Service Station problem

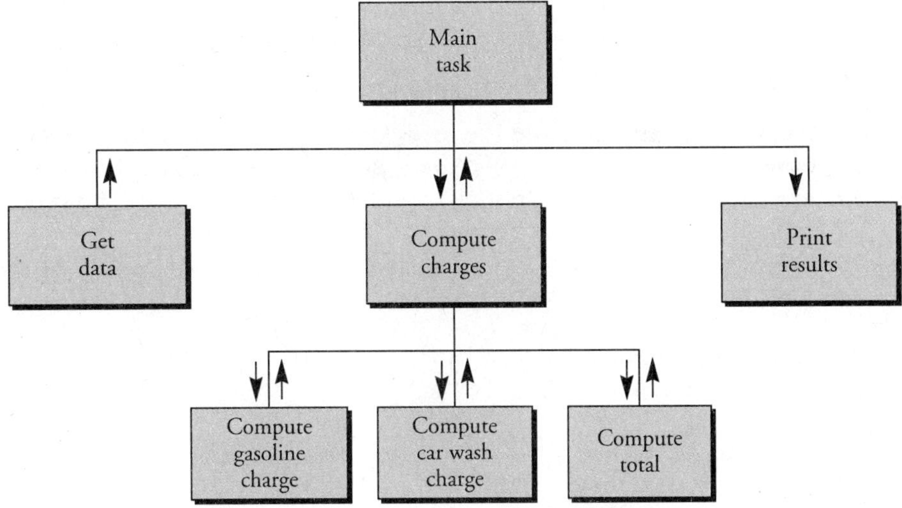

Module: Print the results
Task: Print the results.
Inputs: number of gallons purchased, type of gasoline, gas cost, wash cost, total cost

Further refinement of the pseudocode produces

```
1. Get data
   1.1 read number of gallons
   1.2 read kind of gas purchased
   1.3 read car wash option
2. Compute charges
   2.1 compute gasoline charge
   2.2 compute car wash charge
   2.3 compute total
3. Print results
   3.1 print heading
   3.2 print information in transaction
   3.3 print closing message
```

Module 2 consists of three subtasks. A refined pseudocode development of this step is

```
2. Compute charges
   2.1 compute gasoline charge
       2.1.1 switch gas_type
                 'R'
                 'U'
                 'S'
                 'N'
2.2 compute car wash charge
    2.2.1 if wash_option is yes
                 compute charge
          else
                 charge is 0.0
```

2.3 compute total
    2.3.1 Total is gas_cost plus wash_cost

A C++ program for this problem follows.

```
// This program is used to compute the amount due from a
// customer of the Gas-N-Clean Service Station. Constants
// are used for gasoline prices. Note the use of nested
// selection to compute cost of the car wash.

//Program file: gas.cpp

#include <iostream.h>
#include <iomanip.h>

const char SKIP = ' ';
const float REGULAR_PRICE = 1.149;
const float UNLEADED_PRICE = 1.199;
const float SUPER_UNLEADED_PRICE = 1.289;

// Function: print_heading
// Prints a signon message for program

void print_heading();

// Function: get_data
// Get information interactively from the keyboard.
// Outputs: number of gallons purchased, type of gasoline,
// a choice as to whether or not a car wash is desired

void get_data(float &num_gallons, char &gas_type, char &wash_option);

// Function : compute_charges
// Computes the gas cost, wash cost, and total cost
// Inputs: number of gallons, gas type, wash option
// Outputs: gas cost, wash cost, total cost

void compute_charges(int num_gallons, char gas_type, char wash_option,
       float &gas_cost, float &wash_cost, float &total_cost);

// Function: print_message
// Prints a signoff message for program

void print_message();

// Function: print_results
// Print the results
//
// Inputs: number of gallons purchased, type of gasoline, gas cost, wash option,
// wash cost, total cost

void print_results (float num_gallons, char gas_type, char wash_option,
     float gas_cost, float wash_cost, float total_cost);
```

```
int main()
{
      char gas_type;                // Type of gasoline purchased (R,U,S,N)
      char wash_option;             // Character designating option (Y,N)
      float num_gallons;            // Number of gallons purchased
      float gas_cost;               // Computed cost for gasoline
      float wash_cost;              // Car wash cost
      float total_cost;             // Total amount due

      get_data(num_gallons, gas_type, wash_option);
      compute_charges(num_gallons, gas_type, wash_option, gas_cost, wash_cost,
           total_cost);
      print_results (num_gallons, gas_type, wash_option, gas_cost, wash_cost,
           total_cost);
      return 0;
}

void print_heading()
{
     cout << endl;
     cout << setw(20) << SKIP << "****************************************"
          << endl;
     cout << setw(20) << SKIP << "*                                      *"
          << endl;
     cout << setw(20) << SKIP << "*    Gas-N-Clean Service Station       *"
          << endl;
     cout << setw(20) << SKIP << "*                                      *"
          << endl;
     cout << setw(20) << SKIP << "*" << setw(12) << SKIP << "July 25, 1992"
          << setw(12) << SKIP << " *" << endl;
     cout << setw(20) << SKIP << "*                                      *"
          << endl;
     cout << setw(20) << SKIP << "****************************************"
          << endl;
     cout << endl;
}

void get_data(float &num_gallons, char &gas_type, char &wash_option)
{
     cout << "Enter number of gallons and press <Enter>. ";
     cin >> num_gallons;
     cout << "Enter gas type (R, U, S, or N) and press <Enter>. ";
     cin >> gas_type;
     cout << "Enter Y or N for car wash and press <Enter>. ";
     cin >> wash_option;
}

void compute_charges(int num_gallons, char gas_type, char wash_option,
     float &gas_cost, float &wash_cost, float &total_cost)
{
     switch (gas_type)
```

```
    {
        case 'R':       gas_cost = num_gallons * REGULAR_PRICE;
                        break;
        case 'U':       gas_cost = num_gallons * UNLEADED_PRICE;
                        break;
        case 'S':       gas_cost = num_gallons * SUPER_UNLEADED_PRICE;
                        break;
        case 'N':       gas_cost = 0.0;
    }
    // Compute car wash cost
    if (wash_option == 'Y')
        if (gas_cost >= 10.0)
            wash_cost = 1.25;
        else
            wash_cost = 3.0;
    else
        wash_cost = 0.0;
    total_cost = gas_cost + wash_cost;
}

void print_message()
{
    cout << endl;
    cout << setw(28) << SKIP << "Thank you for stopping" << endl;
    cout << endl;
    cout << setw(30) << SKIP << "Please come again" << endl;
    cout << endl;
    cout << setw(20) << SKIP << "Remember to buckle up and drive safely"
        << endl;
    cout << endl;
}

void print_results (float num_gallons, char gas_type, char wash_option,
float gas_cost, float wash_cost, float total_cost)
{
    print_heading();
    cout << fixed << showpoint;
    cout << setw(10) << SKIP << "Amount of gasoline purchased"
        << setw(12) << SKIP << setw(6) << setprecision(3) << num_gallons
        << " Gallons" << endl;
    cout << setw(10) << SKIP << "Price per gallon" << setw(22)
        << SKIP << "$";
    switch (gas_type)
    {
        case 'R':   cout << setw(7) << REGULAR_PRICE << endl;
                    break;
        case 'U':   cout << setw(7) << UNLEADED_PRICE << endl;
                    break;
        case 'S':   cout << setw(7) << SUPER_UNLEADED_PRICE << endl;
                    break;
        case 'N':   cout << setw(7) << 0.0 << endl;
    }
```

```
        cout << setw(10) << SKIP << "Total gasoline cost"
             << setw(19) << SKIP << "$"
             << setw(6) << setprecision(2) << gas_cost << endl;
        if (wash_cost > 0)
             cout << setw(10) << SKIP << "Car wash cost"
                  << setw(25) << SKIP << "$" << setw(6) << wash_cost << endl;
        cout << setw(48) << SKIP << "-------" << endl;
        cout << setw(25) << SKIP << "Total due"
             << setw(14) << SKIP << "$" << setw(6) << total_cost << endl;
        print_message();
}
```

RUNNING, DEBUGGING AND TESTING HINTS

1. **if . . . else** is a single statement in C++.
2. A misplaced semicolon used with an **if** statement can be a problem. For example,

   Incorrect

   ```
   if (a > 0) ;
       cout << a << endl;
   ```

   Correct

   ```
   if (a > 0)
       cout << a << endl;
   ```

3. Be careful with compound statements as options in an **if . . . else** statement. They must be in a **{ . . . }** block, and a trailing **}** must not be followed by a semicolon.

   Incorrect

   ```
   if (a >= 0)
         cout << a << endl;
         a = a + 10;
   else
         cout << a << " is negative" << endl;
   ```

   Correct

   ```
   if (a >= 0)
   {
         cout << a << endl;
         a = a + 10;
   }
   else
         cout << a << " is negative" << endl;
   ```

4. Your test data should include values that will check both options of an **if . . . else** statement.

(continued)

RUNNING, DEBUGGING AND TESTING HINTS (CONTINUED)

5. The **if . . . else** statement can be used to check for other program errors. In particular,

   a. Check for bad data by

```
cin >> <data>;
if (<bad data>)
        .
        . (error message)
        .
else
        .
        . (proceed with program)
        .
```

   b. Check for reasonable computed values by

```
if (<unreasonable values>)
        .
        . (error message)
        .
else
        .
        . (proceed with program)
        .
```

   For example, if you were computing a student's test average, you could have

```
if (test_average > 100) || (test_average < 0)
        .
        . (error message)
        .
else
        .
        . (proceed with program)
        .
```

6. Be careful with Boolean expressions. You should always keep expressions reasonably simple, use parentheses, and minimize use of **!**.
7. Be careful to properly match **else**s with **if**s in nested **if . . . else** statements. Indenting levels for writing code are very helpful.

```
if (<condition 1>)
    if (<condition 2>)
        .
        . (action here)
        .
```

(continued)

RUNNING, DEBUGGING AND TESTING HINTS (CONTINUED)

```
        else
            .
            . (action here)
            .
    else
            .
            . (action here)
            .
```

8. The form for using extended **if** statements is

```
if (<condition 1>)
        .
        . (action 1 here)
        .
else if (<condition 2>)
        .
        . (action 2 here)
        .
else
        .
        . (final option here)
        .
```

9. Be sure to include **break** statements and a **default** option where necessary in a **switch** statement.

SUMMARY

Key Terms

{ . . . } block
compound Boolean expression
compound statement
control structure
extended **if** statement
logical operators: **&&**, **||**, **!**
negation
nested **if** statement
short-circuit evaluation
relational operator
robust
selection statement
simple Boolean expression
type definition

Key Terms (optional)

assertion
program proof

Keywords

break
case
default
if
else
switch
typedef

Key Concepts

- Boolean constants have the values **1 = TRUE** and **0 = FALSE**. To make these values obvious in programs, one can define them as symbolic constants. Because some C++ compilers use the symbols **TRUE** and **FALSE** for other purposes, one can "undefine" them with the preprocessor directive **#undef** before reusing them, as follows:

```
#undef TRUE
#undef FALSE
const int TRUE = 1;
const int FALSE = 0;
```

- Data types can be given more descriptive names by using a **typedef**. For example, a data type for Boolean variables can be defined with

```
typedef int boolean;
```

  and variables can then be declared with

```
boolean done = FALSE;
```

- Frequently used data definitions, such as those for the **boolean** type, can be placed in a program library and included in application programs. For example, the library file **boolean.h** can be included with

```
#include "boolean.h"
```

- Relational operators are **==, >, <, >=, <=, !=**.
- Logical operators **&&, ||**, and **!** are used as operators on Boolean expressions.
- Boolean expressions will be interpreted during execution as having the values 1 (meaning true) or 0 (meaning false).
- A complete priority listing of arithmetic operators, relational operators, and logical operators is

Expression or Operation	Priority
( )	Evaluate from inside out
!	Evaluate from left to right
*, /, %	Evaluate from left to right
+, -	Evaluate from left to right
<, <=, >, >=, ==, !=	Evaluate from left to right
&&	Evaluate from left to right
||	Evaluate from left to right

- The values of compound Boolean expressions connected by **||** or **&&** are computed by using short-circuit evaluation.
- A selection statement is a program statement that transfers control to various branches of the program.
- A compound statement is sometimes referred to as a **{ . . . }** block; when it is executed, the entire segment of code between the **{** and **}** is treated like a single statement.
- **if ... else** is a two-way selection statement.
- If the Boolean expression in an **if . . . else** statement is **TRUE**, the command following **if** is executed; if the expression is **FALSE**, the command following **else** is executed.

- Multiple selections can be achieved by using decision statements within decision statements; this is termed multiway selection.
- An extended **if** statement is a statement of the form

```
if (<condition 1>)
        .
        . (action 1 here)
        .
else if (<condition 2>)
        .
        . (action 2 here)
        .
else if (<condition 3>)
        .
        . (action 3 here)
        .
else
        .
        . (action 4 here)
        .
```

- Program protection can be achieved by using selection statements to guard against unexpected results.
- The **switch** statements can sometimes be used as alternatives to multiple selection.
- **default**, a reserved word in C++, can be used to handle values not listed in the **switch** statement.

PROGRAMMING PROBLEMS AND PROJECTS

The first 13 problems listed here are relatively short, but to complete them you must use concepts presented in this chapter.

Some of the remaining programming problems are used as the basis for writing programs for subsequent chapters as well as for this chapter. In this chapter, each program is run on a very limited set of data. Material in later chapters permits us to run the programs on larger databases. The problems marked by a color square are referred to and used repeatedly, so carefully choose which ones you work on and then develop them completely.

1. A three-minute telephone call to Scio, New York, costs $1.15. Each additional minute costs $0.26. Given the total length of a call in minutes and print the cost.
2. When you first learned to divide, you expressed answers using a quotient and a remainder rather than a fraction or decimal quotient. For example, if you divided 7 by 2, your answer would have been given as 3 r. 1. Given two integers, divide the larger by the smaller and print the answer in this form. Do not assume that the numbers are entered in any order.

3. Revise Problem 2 so that, if there is no remainder, you print only the quotient without a remainder or the letter r.
4. Given the coordinates of two points on a graph, find and print the slope of a line passing through them. Remember that the slope of a line can be undefined.
5. Dr. Lae Z. Programmer wishes to computerize his grading system. He gives five tests, then averages only the four highest scores. An average of 90 or better earns a grade of A; 80—89, a grade of B; and so on. Write a program that accepts five test scores and prints the average and grade according to this method.
6. Given the lengths of three sides of a triangle, print whether the triangle is scalene, isosceles, or equilateral.
7. Given the lengths of three sides of a triangle, determine whether or not the triangle is a right triangle using the Pythagorean theorem. Do not assume that the sides are entered in any order.
8. Given three integers, print only the largest.
9. The island nation of Babbage charges its citizens an income tax each year. The tax rate is based on the following table:

Income Tax	Tax Rate
$ 0–5,000	0
5,001–10,000	3%
10,001–20,000	5.5%
20,001–40,000	10.8%
Over $40,000	23.7%

   Write a program that, when given a person's income, prints the tax owed rounded to the nearest dollar.
10. Many states base the cost of car registration on the weight of the vehicle. Suppose the fees are as follows:

Weight	Cost
Up to 1500 pounds	$23.75
1500 to 2500 pounds	27.95
2500 to 3000 pounds	30.25
Over 3000 pounds	37.00

   Given the weight of a car, find and print the cost of registration.
11. The Mapes Railroad Corporation pays an annual bonus as a part of its profit sharing plan. This year all employees who have been with the company for 10 years or more will receive a bonus of 12% of their annual salary, and those who have worked at Mapes from 5 through 9 years receive a bonus of 5.75%. Those who have been with the company for less than 5 years receive no bonus.

   Given the initials of an employee, the employee's annual salary, and the number of years employed with the company, find and print the bonus. All bonuses are rounded to the nearest dollar. Output should be in the following form.

```
          MAPES RAILROAD CORP.

Employee xxx
Years of service nn
Bonus earned: $ yyyy
```

12. A substance floats in water if its density (mass/volume) is less than 1 g/cm^3. It sinks if it is 1 or more. Given the mass and volume of an object and print whether it will sink or float.

13. Mr. Arthur Einstein, your high school physics teacher, wants a program for English-to-metric conversions. You are given a letter indicating whether the measurement is in pounds (P), feet (F), or miles (M). Such measures are to be converted to newtons, meters, and kilometers, respectively. (There are 4.9 newtons in a pound, 3.28 feet in a meter, and 1.61 kilometers in a mile.) Given an appropriate identifying letter and the size of the measurement, convert it to metric units. Print the answer in the following form:

```
3.0 miles = 4.83 kilometers.
```

14. The Caswell Catering and Convention Service (Chapter 4, Problem 12) has decided to revise its billing practices and is in need of a new program to prepare bills. The changes Caswell wishes to make follow.

a. For adults, the deluxe meals will cost $15.80 per person and the standard meals will cost $11.75 per person, dessert included. Children's meals will cost 60 percent of adult meals. Everyone within a given party must be served the same meal type.

b. There are five banquet halls. Room A rents for $55.00, room B rents for $75.00, room C rents for $85.00, room D rents for $100.00 , and room E rents for $130.00. The Caswells are considering increasing the room fees in about six months and this should be taken into account.

c. A surcharge, currently 7%, is added to the total bill if the catering is to be done on a weekend (Friday, Saturday, or Sunday).

d. All customers will be charged the same rate for tip and tax, currently 18%. It is applied only to the cost of food.

e. To induce customers to pay promptly, a discount is offered if payment is made within 10 days. This discount depends on the amount of the total bill. If the bill is less than $100.00, the discount is 0.5%; if the bill is at least $100.00 but less than $200.00, the discount is 1.5%; if the bill is at least $200.00 but less than $400.00, the discount is 3%; if the bill is at least $400.00 but less than $800.00, the discount is 4%; and, if the bill is at least $800.00, the discount is 5%.

Test your program on each of the following three customers.

Customer A: This customer is using room C on Tuesday night. The party includes 80 adults and 6 children. The standard meal is being served. The customer paid a $60.00 deposit. *Customer B:* This customer is using room A on Saturday night. Deluxe meals are being served to 15 adults. A deposit of $50.00 was paid. *Customer C:* This customer is using room D on Sunday afternoon. The party includes 30 children and 2 adults, all of whom are served the standard meal.

Output should be in the same form as that for Problem 12, Chapter 4.

15. State University charges $90.00 for each semester hour of credit, $200.00 per semester for a regular room, $250.00 per semester for an air-conditioned room, and $400.00 per semester for food. All students are charged a $30.00 matriculation fee. Graduating students must also pay a $35.00 diploma fee. Write a program to compute the fees that must be paid by a student. Your program should include an appropriate warning message if a student is taking more than 21 credit hours or fewer than 12 credit hours. A typical line of data for one student would include room type (R or A), student number (in four digits), credit hours, and graduation status (T or F).

16. Write a program to determine the day of the week a person was born given his or her birth date. Following are the steps you should use to find the day of the week corresponding to any date in this century.
    a. Divide the last two digits of the birth year by 4. Put the quotient (ignoring the remainder) in **`total`**. For example, if the person was born in 1983, divide 83 by 4 and store 20 in **`total`**.
    b. Add the last two digits of the birth year to **`total`**.
    c. Add the last two digits of the birth date to **`total`**.
    d. Using the following table, find the "month number" and add it to **`total`**.

       January = 1
       February = 4
       March = 4
       April = 0
       May = 2
       June = 5
       July = 0
       August = 3
       September = 6
       October = 1
       November = 4
       December = 6
    e. If the year is a leap year and if the month you are working with is either January or February, then subtract 1 from the **`total`**.
    f. Find the remainder when **`total`** is divided by 7. Look up the remainder in the following table to determine the day of the week the person was born. Note that you should not use this procedure if the person's year of birth is earlier than 1900.

       1 = Sunday
       2 = Monday
       3 = Tuesday
       4 = Wednesday
       5 = Thursday
       6 = Friday
       0 = Saturday

       Typical input is

       ```
       5-15 78
       ```

    where the first entry (5-15) represents the birth date (May 15) and the second entry (78) represents the birth year. An appropriate error message should be printed if a person's year of birth is before 1900.

17. Community Hospital needs a program to compute and print a statement for each patient. Charges for each day are as follows:
    a. room charges: private room, $125.00; semiprivate room, $95.00; or ward, $75.00
    b. telephone charge: $1.75
    c. television charge: $3.50

    Write a program to get a line of data from the keyboard, compute the patient's bill, and print an appropriate statement. Typical input is

    ```
    5PNY
    ```

where **5** indicates the number of days spent in the hospital, **P** represents the room type (**P**, **S**, or **W**), **N** represents the telephone option (**Y** or **N**), and **Y** represents the television option (**Y** or **N**). A statement for the data given follows.

```
          Community Hospital

       Patient Billing Statement

Number of days in hospital: 5 Type of room: Private

Room charge                   $ 625.00

Telephone charge              $   0.00

Television charge             $  17.50

      TOTAL DUE            $642.50
```

18. Write a program that converts degrees Fahrenheit to degrees Celsius and degrees Celsius to degrees Fahrenheit. In the input the temperature is followed by a designator (F or C) indicating whether the given temperature is Fahrenheit or Celsius.

19. The city of Mt. Pleasant bills its residents for sewage, water, and sanitation every three months. The sewer and water charge is figured according to how much water is used by the resident. The scale is

Amount (gallons)	Rate (per gallon)
Less than 1000	\$0.03
1000 to 2000	\$30 + \$0.02 for each gallon over 1000
2000 or more	\$50 + \$0.015 for each gallon over 2000

The sanitation charge is \$7.50 per month.

Write a program to read the number of months for which a resident is being billed (1, 2, or 3) and how much water was used; then print a statement with appropriate charges and messages. Use the constant definition section for all rates and include an error check for incorrect number of months. Typical input is

```
3 2175
```

20. Al Derrick, owner of the Lucky Wildcat Well Corporation, wants a program to help him decide whether or not a well is making money. Data for a well will consist of one or two lines. The first line contains a single character (D for a dry well, O for oil found, and G for gas found) followed by a real number for the cost of the well. If an "O" or "G" is detected, the cost will be followed by an integer indicating the volume of oil or gas found. In this case, there will also be a second line containing an "N" or "S" indicating whether or not sulfur is present. If there is sulfur, the "S" will be followed by the percentage of sulfur present in the oil or gas. Unit prices are \$5.50 for oil and \$2.20 for gas. These should be defined as constants. Your program should compute the total revenue for a well (reduce output for sulfur present) and print all pertinent information with an appropriate message to Mr. Derrick. A gusher is defined as a well with profit in excess of \$50,000. Typical input is

```
G 8000.00 20000 S 0.15
```

21. The Mathematical Association of America hosts an annual summer meeting. Each state sends one official delegate to the section officer's meeting at this summer session. The national organization reimburses the official state delegates according to the following scale:

Round-trip Mileage	Rate
Up to 500 miles	15 cents per mile
501 to 1000 miles	$75.00 plus 12 cents for each mile over 500
1001 to 1500 miles	$135.00 plus 10 cents for each mile over 1000
1501 to 2000 miles	$185.00 plus 8 cents for each mile over 1500
2001 to 3000 miles	$225.00 plus 6 cents for each mile over
3001 or more miles	$285.00 plus 5 cents for each mile over 3000

Write a program that will accept as input the number of round-trip miles for a delegate and compute the amount of reimbursement.

22. Dr. Lae Z. Programmer (Problem 5) wants you to write a program to compute and print the grade for a student in his class. The grade is based on three examinations (worth a possible 100 points each), five quizzes (10 points each), and a 200-point final examination. Your output should include all scores, the percentage grade, and the letter grade. The grading
scale is

90 <= average	<= 100	A
80 <= average	< 90	B
70 <= average	< 80	C
60 <= average	< 70	D
0 <= average	< 60	E
Typical input is		

```
80 93 85 (examination scores)
9 10 8 7 10 (quiz scores)
175 (final examination)
```

23. Dr. Lae Z. Programmer now wants you to modify Problem 22 by adding a check for bad data. Any time an unexpected score occurs, you are to print an appropriate error message and terminate the program.

24. A quadratic equation is one of the form

$$ax^2 + bx + c = 0$$

where $a \neq 0$. Solutions to this equation are given by

$$x = \frac{-b \pm \sqrt{b^2 - 4ac}}{2a}$$

where the quantity (b^2 - $4ac$) is referred to as the discriminant of the equation. Write a program to read three integers as the respective coefficients (*a, b,* and *c*), compute the discriminant, and print the solutions. Use the following rules:

a. discriminant = 0 -> single root.

b. discriminant < 0 -> no real number solution.

c. discriminant > 0 -> two distinct real solutions.

25. Write a program that gets as input the lengths of three sides of a triangle. Output should first identify the triangle as scalene, isosceles, or equilateral. The program should use the Pythagorean theorem to determine whether or not scalene or isosceles triangles are right triangles. An appropriate message should be part of the output.

26. The sign on the attendant's booth at the Pentagon parking lot is

PENTAGON VISITOR PARKING	
Cars:	
First 2 hours	Free
Next 3 hours	0.50/hour
Next 10 hours	0.25/hour
Trucks:	
First 1 hour	Free
Next 2 hours	1.00/hour
Next 12 hours	0.75/hour
Senior Citizens:	No charge

Write a program that will accept as input a one-character designator (C, T, or S) followed by the number of minutes a vehicle has been in the lot. The program should then compute the appropriate charge and print a ticket for the customer. Any part of an hour is to be counted as a full hour.

27. Milt Walker, the chief of advertising for the Isabella Potato Industry, wants you to write a program to compute an itemized bill and total cost of his "This Spud's for You!" ad campaign. The standard black-and-white full-page ads have base prices as follows:

Drillers' News (code N)	\$ 400
Playperson (code P)	\$2000
Outdoors (code O)	\$ 900
Independent News (code I)	\$1200

Each ad is allowed 15 lines of print with a rate of \$20.00 for each line in excess of 15 lines. Each ad is either black and white (code B) and subject to the base prices, or is in color (code C) and subject to the following rates: Three color (code T), 40% increase over base; full color (code F), 60% increase over base.

Write a program to input Milt's choice of magazine (N, P, O, or I), the number of lines of print (integer), and either black and white (B) or color (C) with a choice of three colors (T) or full color (F). Output should include an appropriate title, all the information and costs used to compute the price of an ad, the total price of the ad, and finally the total price of all ads.

28. Write a program that will add, subtract, multiply, and divide fractions. Input will consist of a single line representing a fraction arithmetic problem as follows: integer/integer operation integer/integer. For example, a line of input might be

```
2/3 + 1/2
```

Your program should do the following:

a. Check for division by zero.

b. Check for proper operation symbols.

c. Print the problem in its original form.

d. Print the answer.

e. Print all fractions in horizontal form.

Your answer need not be in lowest terms. For the sample input

```
2/3 + 1/2
```

sample output is

```
2     1     7
-- + -- = --
3     2     6
```

29. Write an interactive program that permits the user to print various recipes. Write a procedure for each recipe. After the user enters a one-letter identifier for the desired recipe, a **switch** statement should be used to call the appropriate procedure. Part of the code could be

```
cin >> selection;
switch (selection)
{
        case 'J':       jambalaya;
                        break;
        case 'S':       spaghetti;
                        break;
        case 'T': tacos;
}
```

30. The force of gravity is different for each of the nine planets in our solar system. For example, on Mercury it is only 0.38 times as strong as on Earth. Thus, if you weigh 100 pounds (on Earth), you would weigh only 38 pounds on Mercury. Write an interactive program that allows you to enter your Earth weight and your choice of planet to which you would like your weight converted. Output should be your weight on the desired planet together with the planet name. The screen message for input should include a menu for planet choice. Use a **switch** statement in the program for computation and output. The relative forces of gravity are

Earth 1.00
Jupiter 2.65
Mars 0.39
Mercury 0.38
Neptune 1.23
Pluto 0.05
Saturn 1.17
Uranus 1.05
Venus 0.78

31. Cramer's Rule is a method for solving a system of linear equations. If you have two equations with variables x and y written as

$$ax + by = c$$
$$dx + ey = f$$

then the solution for x and y can be given as

$$x = \frac{\begin{vmatrix} cb \\ fe \end{vmatrix}}{\begin{vmatrix} ab \\ de \end{vmatrix}}$$

$$y = \frac{\begin{vmatrix} ac \\ df \end{vmatrix}}{\begin{vmatrix} ab \\ de \end{vmatrix}}$$

Using this notation,

$$\begin{vmatrix} ab \\ de \end{vmatrix}$$

is the determinant of the matrix

$$\begin{bmatrix} ab \\ de \end{bmatrix}$$

and is equal to *ae - bd.*

Write a complete program that will solve a system of two equations using Cramer's rule. Input will be all coefficients and constants in the system. Output will be the solution to the system. Typical output is

For the system of equations

$x + 2y = 5$

$2x - y = 0$

we have the solution

$x = 1$

$y = 2$

Use an **`if . . . else`** statement to guard against division by zero.

32. Contact a programmer and discuss the concept of robustness in a program. Prepare a report of your conversation for class. Your report should include a list of specific instances of how programmers make programs robust.

33. Conduct an unscientific survey of at least two people from each of the following groups: students in upper-level computer science courses, instructors of computer science, and programmers working in industry. Your survey should attempt to ascertain the importance of and use of robustness at each level. Discuss the similarities and differences of your findings with those of other class members.

34. Selecting appropriate test data for a program that uses nested selection is a nontrivial task. Create diagrams that allow you to trace the flow of logic when nested selection is used. Use your diagrams to draw conclusions about minimal test data required to test all branches of a program that uses nested selection to various levels.

CHAPTER

6 Repetition Statements

CHAPTER OUTLINE

The previous chapter on selection introduced you to a control structure that takes advantage of a computer's ability to make choices. A second major control structure takes advantage of a computer's ability to repeat the same task many times. The control structures for selection and repetition allow us to specify any algorithm we need to solve a problem with a computer.

This chapter examines the different methods C++ permits for performing a process repeatedly. For example, as yet we cannot conveniently write a program that solves the simple problem of adding the integers from 1 to 100 or processing the grades of 30 students in a class. By the end of this chapter, you will be able to solve these problems three different ways. The three forms of repetition (loops) are

1. **for <a definite number of times> <do an action>**
2. **while <condition is true> <do an action>**
3. **do <action> while <condition is true>**

Each of these three loops contains the basic constructs necessary for repetition: a variable is assigned some value, the variable value changes at some point in the loop, and repetition continues until the value reaches some predetermined value. When the predetermined value (or **boolean** condition) is reached, repetition is terminated and program control moves to the next executable statement.

6.1 Classifying Loops

OBJECTIVES

- to understand the difference between a pretest loop and a post-test loop
- to understand what a fixed repetition loop is
- to understand when to use a fixed repetition loop
- to understand what a variable condition loop is

Pretest and Post-test Loops

A loop that uses a condition to control whether or not the body of the loop is executed before going through the loop is a *pretest* or *entrance-controlled loop.* The testing condition is the *pretest condition.* If the condition is **TRUE**, the body of the loop is executed. If the condition is **FALSE**, the program skips to the first line of code following the loop. The **for** loop and the **while** loop are pretest loops.

A loop that examines a Boolean expression after the loop body is executed is a *post-test* or *exit-controlled loop.* This is the **do . . . while** loop.

Fixed Repetition Versus Variable Condition Loops

Fixed repetition (iterated) loops are used when it can be determined in advance how often a segment of code needs to be repeated. For instance, you might know that you need a predetermined number of repetitions of a segment of code for a program that adds the integers from 1 to 100 or for a program that uses a fixed number of data lines, for example, game statistics for a team of 12 basketball players. The number of repetitions need not be constant. For example, a user might enter information during execution of a program that would determine how often a segment should be repeated. In this chapter, we will introduce a class of **for** loops that are fixed repetition loops.

Variable condition loops are needed to solve problems for which conditions change within the body of the loop. These conditions involve sentinel values, Boolean flags, arithmetic expressions or end-of-line and end-of-file markers (see Chapter 9). A variable condition loop provides more power than a fixed repetition loop. The **while** and **do . . . while** loops are variable condition loops.

6.2 The for Loop

OBJECTIVES

- to understand how the loop control variable is used in a loop
- to understand the flow of control when using a fixed repetition loop in a program
- to be able to use a **for** loop in a program
- to be able to use a **for** loop that counts down in a program

The **for** loop is a pretest loop. Although one can write variable condition **for** loops in C++, we will discuss only fixed repetition **for** loops. The typical form of a **for** loop is

```
for ( <initialization expression>; <termination condition>; <update expression> )
        <statement>
```

In the following example, a **for** loop displays all of the numbers between 1 and 10:

```
for (i = 1; i <= 10; i = i + 1)
        cout << i << endl;
```

A **for** loop is considered to be a single executable statement. The information contained within the parentheses is referred to as the heading of the loop. The actions performed in the loop are referred to as the body of the loop.
The heading of a **for** loop consists of three parts:

1. *Initialization expression:* In fixed repetition **for** loops, this part sets a *control variable* to an initial value. This variable will control the number of times that the body of the loop is executed.
2. *Termination condition:* This part normally consists of a comparison of the control variable to a value. The body of the loop will execute while this condition is **TRUE**.
3. *Update expression:* This part normally consists of a statement that makes the value of the control variable approach the value specified in the termination condition. In **for** loops that count up, this part increments the control variable by some value; in **for** loops that count down, this part decrements the control variable by some value.

The internal logic of a **for** loop that counts up is as follows:

1. The *control variable* is assigned an initial value in the initialization expression.
2. The termination condition is evaluated.
3. If the termination condition is **TRUE** then
   (a) the body of the loop is executed and
   (b) the update expression is evaluated.
4. If the termination condition is **FALSE** then
   control of the program is transferred to the first statement following the loop.

As you can see, a **for** loop proceeds by *counting up* from a *lower bound* to an *upper bound.* A flow diagram for this example is given in Figure 6.1.

◆ FIGURE 6.1

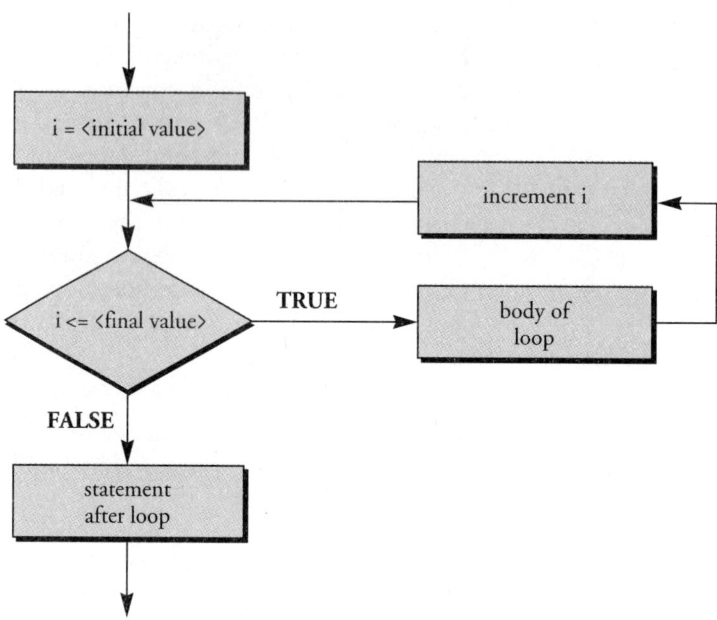

We have discussed only a typical form of the **for** loop, one that counts up. We will see variations on this form, such as **for** loops that count from an upper bound down to a lower bound, or count by some factor other than one, in later sections of this chapter.

The Increment and Decrement Operators

C++ has a pair of operators that increment or decrement variables. These operators are very concise and handy to use in loops. The increment operator, **++**, precedes a variable in a complete C++ statement. For example, the statement

```
++x;
```

would increment (add one to) the variable **x**. It has the same effect as the assignment statement

```
x = x + 1;
```

Thus, the example **for** statement could be rewritten more concisely as

```
for (i = 1; i <= 10; ++i)
        cout << i << endl;
```

The decrement operator, **--**, precedes a variable in a complete C++ statement. The operator has the effect of subtracting one from the variable and storing the result in it.

Accumulators

The problem of adding the integers from 1 to 100 needs only one statement in the body of the loop. This problem can be solved by code that constructs an *accumulator*. An accumulator merely sums values of some variable. In the following code, the loop control variable, **lcv**, successively assumes the values 1, 2, 3, . . . , 100.

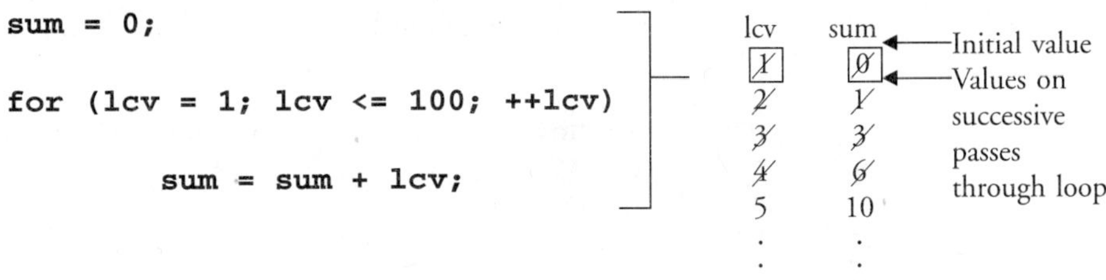

This program segment contains an example of graphic documentation. Throughout the text, these insets will be used to help illustrate what the code is actually doing. The insets are not part of the program; they merely show what some specific code is trying to accomplish.

To see how **sum** accumulates these values, let us trace through the code for several values of **lcv**. Initially, **sum** is set to zero by

```
sum = 0;
```

When **lcv** is assigned the value 1,

```
sum = sum + lcv;
```

produces

1	~~0~~ 1
lcv	**sum**

For **lcv = 2**, we get

2	~~1~~ 3
lcv	**sum**

lcv = 3 yields

3	~~3~~ 6
lcv	**sum**

Note that **sum** has been assigned a value equal to 1 + 2 + 3. The final value for **lcv** is 100. Once this value has been added to **sum**, the value of **sum** will be 5050, which is the sum of 1 + 2 + 3 + . . . + 100. Accumulators are frequently used in loops. The general form for this use is

```
accumulator = 0;
for (lcv = <initial value>; lcv <= <final value>; ++lcv)
      accumulator = accumulator + lcv;
```

Scope of a Loop Control Variable

In general, the loop control variable of a **for** loop must be declared before it is used in the loop. In accordance with the scope rules of C++, the scope of this variable will be the program block within which it is declared. However, on many occasions, a loop control variable will only be used within a loop. In these cases, using a variable whose scope extends beyond a loop opens the program to serious side effects. To minimize these, the loop control variable can be declared when it is initialized within the loop. The visibility of the variable will be restricted to the body of the loop and to the area of the program text below the loop but within the block where the loop appears. For example, the following loop performs the equivalent task of our first example, but its loop control variable cannot be accessed above the body of the loop:

```
// References to i are not allowed here
// (i has not been declared yet).

for (int i = 1; i <= 10; ++i)
        cout << i << endl;

// References to i are allowed here.
// Its value will be 11 when the loop is done.
```

In general, it is safe programming practice to restrict the scope of variables to only those areas of a program in which it is necessary to access them.

Some comments concerning the syntax and form of **for** loops are now necessary:

1. The loop control variable must be declared as a variable. We will usually declare this variable as part of the loop heading.
2. The loop control variable can be any valid identifier.
3. The loop control variable can be used within the loop just as any other variable except that the value of the variable should not be changed by the statements in the body of the loop.
4. The initial and final values can be constants or variable expressions with appropriate values.
5. The loop will be repeated for each value of the loop control variable in the range indicated by the initial and final values.

At this point you might try writing some test programs to see what happens if you do not follow these rules. Then consider the following examples, which illustrate the features of **for** loops.

EXAMPLE 6.1

Write a segment of code to list the integers from 1 to 10 together with their squares and cubes. This can be done by

```
for (int j = 1; j <= 10; ++j)
    cout << j << setw(10) << j * j << setw(8) << j * j * j << endl;
```

This segment produces

```
 1         1       1
 2         4       8
 3         9      27
 4        16      64
 5        25     125
 6        36     216
 7        49     343
 8        64     512
 9        81     729
10       100    1000
```

EXAMPLE 6.2

Write a **for** loop to produce the following design:

Assuming the first asterisk is in column 20, the following loop will produce the desired result. Note carefully how the output is formatted.

```
for (int j = 1; j <= 5; ++j)
    cout << setw(21 - j) << '*' << setw(2 * j - 1) << '*' << endl;
```

EXAMPLE 6.3

When computing compound interest, it is necessary to evaluate the quantity $(1 + r)^n$ where r is the interest rate for one time period and n is the number of time periods. A **for** loop can be used to perform this computation. If we declare a variable **base,** this can be solved by

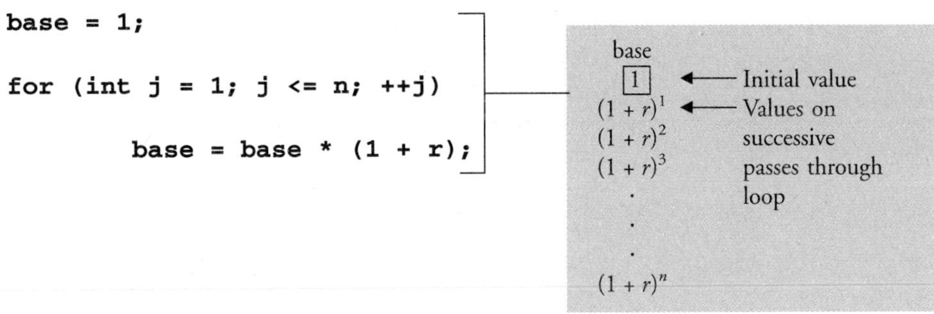

for Loops that Count Down

A second kind of pretest, fixed repetition loop is a **for** loop that counts down. This loop does exactly what you expect; it is identical to a **for** loop that counts up, except the loop control variable is decreased by one instead of increased by one each time through the loop. This is referred to as a *decrement.* The test is loop control value >= final value. The loop terminates when the loop control value is less than the final value. The decrement operator is used to adjust the loop control variable on each pass through the loop. Proper form and syntax for a loop of this type are the same as that of **for** loops that count up; however, the contents of the statements within the loop heading will be the opposite of those for loops that count up:

1. The initialization part sets the control variable to an upper bound rather than a lower bound.
2. The termination part consists of a comparison to see whether the control variable is greater than or equal to a value that is the lower bound of the loop.
3. The update part decrements rather than increments the control variable by some value.

We will now consider an example of a **for** loop that counts down.

EXAMPLE 6.4

Illustrate the control values of a **for** loop that counts down by writing the control value during each pass through the loop. The segment of code for this could be

```
for (int k = 20; k >= 15; --k)
        cout << "K =" << setw(4) << k << endl;
```

and the output is

```
K =   20
K =   19
K =   18
K =   17
K =   16
K =   15
```

Loops that Count by Factors Other than One

Thus far, we have examined **for** loops that count up or count down. They do this by incrementing or decrementing a loop control variable by one. There are some occasions when we would like to count by a factor of two or more. One example is the problem of adding all of the even numbers between a lower and an upper bound. For this problem, the loop should count up or down by twos. The following example solves this problem for the numbers 2 through 10 by incrementing the loop control variable by two in an assignment expression:

```
sum = 0;
for (int j = 2; j <= 10; j = j + 2)
        sum = sum + j;
cout << sum << endl;
```

Writing Style for Loops

As you can see, writing style is an important consideration when writing code using loops. There are three features to consider. First, the body of the loop should be indented. Compare the following two pieces of code:

```
for (int j = 1; j <= 10; ++j)
{
        cin >> num >> amt;
        total1 = total1 + amt;
        total2 = total2 + num;
        cout << "The number is" << setw(6) << num << endl;
}
cout << "The total amount is" << fixed << showpoint << setw(8) << setprecision(2)
     << total1 << endl;
average = total2 / 10.0;
```

```
for (int j = 1; j <= 10; ++j)
{
cin >> num >> amt;
total1 = total1 + amt;
total2 = total2 + num;
cout << "The number is" << setw(6) << num << endl;
}
cout << "The total amount is" << fixed << showpoint << setw(8) << setprecision(2)
     << total1 << endl;
average = total2 / 10.0;
```

The indenting in the first segment makes it easier to determine what is contained in the body of the loop than it is in the second segment, without any indenting.

Second, blank lines can be used before and after a loop for better readability. Compare the following:

```
cin >> x >> y;
cout << fixed << showpoint;
cout << setw(6) << setprecision(2) << x << setw(6) << y << endl;
cout << endl;

for  (int j = -3; j <= 5; ++j)
        cout << setw(3) << j << setw(5) << '*' << endl;

sum = sum + x;
cout << setw(10) << setprecision(2) << sum << endl;
```

```
cin >> x >> y;
cout << fixed << showpoint;
cout << setw(6) << setprecision(2) << x << setw(6) << y << endl;
cout << endl;
for  (int j = -3; j <= 5; ++j)
        cout << setw(3) << j << setw(5) << '*' << endl;
sum = sum + x;
cout << setw(10) << setprecision(2) << sum << endl;
```

Again, the first segment is a bit more clear because it emphasizes that the entire loop is a single executable statement and makes it easy to locate the loop.

Third, comments used within loops make them more readable. In particular, a comment could accompany the end of a compound statement that is the body of a loop. The general form for this is

```
// Get a test score
for (int j = 1; j <= 50; ++j)
{
        .
        . (body of the loop)
        .
} // end of for loop
```

We close this section with an example that uses a **for** loop to solve a problem.

There are three features you may wish to incorporate as you work with **for** loops. First, loop limits can be defined as constants or declared as variables and then have assigned values. Thus, you could have

```
const int LOOP_LIMIT = 50;
```

Second, the loop control variable could be declared as

```
int lcv;
```

The loop could then be written as

```
for (lcv = 1; lcv <= LOOP_LIMIT; ++lcv)

        .
        . (body of the loop here)
        .
```

Third, a loop limit could be declared as a variable and then the user would enter a value during execution.

```
int loop_limit;
        .
        .
        .
cout << "How many entries? ";
cin >> loop_limit;
for (lcv = 1; lcv <= loop_limit; ++lcv)
```

EXAMPLE 6.5

Suppose you have been asked to write a segment of code to compute the test average for each of 30 students in a class and the overall class average. Data for each student consist of the student's initials and four test scores.

A first-level pseudocode development is

1. Print a heading
2. Initialize total
3. Process data for each of 30 students
4. Compute class average
5. Print a summary

A **for** loop could be used to implement step 3. The step could first be refined to

3. Process data for each of 30 students
    - 3.1 get data for a student
    - 3.2 compute average
    - 3.3 add to total
    - 3.4 print student data

The code for this step is

```
for (int lcv = 1; lcv <= CLASS_SIZE; ++lcv)
{
      cout << "Enter three initials and press <Enter>. ";
      cin >> init1 >> init2 >> init3;
      cout << "Enter four test scores and press <Enter>. ";
```

```
        cin >> score1 >> score2 >> score3 >> score4;
        average = (score1 + score2 + score3 + score4) / 4.0;
        total = total + average;
        cout << endl;
        cout << setw(4) << init1 << init2 << init3;
        cout << setw(6) <<score1 << setw(6) << score2
             << setw(6) << score3 << setw(6) <<score4;
        cout << setprecision(2) << setw(10) << average
             << endl;
}
```

EXERCISES 6.2

1. What is the output from each of the following segments of code?

   a.
   ```
   for (k = 3; k <= 8; ++k)
        cout << setw(k) << '*' << endl;
   ```
   b.
   ```
   for (j = 1; j <= 10; ++j)
        cout << stew(4) << j << ":" << setw(5)
             << (10-J) << endl;
   ```
   c.
   ```
        a = 2;
   for (j = (3 * 2 - 4); j <= 10 * a; ++j)
        cout << stew(4) << j << endl;
   ```
   d.
   ```
   for (j = 50; j >= 30; --j)
        cout << setw(5) << (51 - j) << endl;
   ```

2. Write a test program for each of the following.

   a. Illustrate what happens when the loop control variable is assigned a value inside the loop.

   b. Demonstrate how an accumulator works. For this test program, sum the integers from 1 to 10. Your output should show each partial sum as it is assigned to the accumulator.

3. Write segments of code using a loop that counts up and a loop that counts down to produce the following designs. Start each design in column 2.

   a.
   ```
    *
    *
    *
    *
   ```
   b.
   ```
    ***
     ***
      ***
       ***
        ***
         ***
          ***
           ***
   ```
   c.
   ```
        *
       * *
      *   *
     *     *
    ***   ***
      *   *
      *   *
      *****
   ```

d.
```
*********
 *******
  *****
   ***
    *
```

4. Which of the following segments of code do you think accomplishes its intended task? For those that do not, what changes would you suggest?

a.
```
for (k = 1; k <= 5; ++k);
    cout << k << endl;
```

b.
```
sum = 0;
for (j = 1; j <= 10; ++j)
      cin >>a;
sum = sum + a;
cout << setw(15) << sum << endl;
```

c.
```
      sum = 0;
for (j = -3; j <= 3; ++j)
      sum = sum + j;
```

d.
```
a = 0;
for (k = 1; k <= 10; ++k)
{
      a = a + k;
      cout << setw(5) << k << setw(5) << a << setw(5)
           << (a + k) << endl;
}
cout << setw(5) << k << setw(5) << a << setw(5)
      << (a + k) << endl;
```

5. Produce each of the following outputs using a loop that counts up and a loop that counts down.

a. 1 2 3 4 5

b.
```
*
  *
    *
      *
        *
```

6. Rewrite the following segment of code using a loop that counts down to produce the same result.

```
sum = 0;
for (k = 1; k <= 4; ++k)
{
        cout << setw(21 + k) << endl;
        sum = sum + k;
}
```

7. Rewrite the following segment of code using a loop that counts up to produce the same result.

```
for (j = 10; j >= 2; --j)
        cout << setw(j) << j << endl;
```

A NOTE OF INTEREST

Charles Babbage

The first person to propose the concept of the modern computer was Charles Babbage (1791–1871), a man truly ahead of his time. Babbage was a professor of mathematics at Cambridge University, as well as an inventor. As a mathematician, he realized the time-consuming and boring nature of constructing mathematical tables (squares, logarithms, sines, cosines, and so on). Because the calculators developed by Pascal and Leibniz could not provide the calculations required for these more complex tables, Babbage proposed the idea of building a machine that could compute the various properties of numbers, accurate to 20 digits.

With a grant from the British government, he designed and partially built a simple model of the difference engine. However, the lack of technology in the 1800s prevented him from making a working model. Discouraged by his inability to materialize his ideas, Babbage imagined a better version, which would be a general-purpose, problem-solving machine—the analytical engine.

The similarities between the analytical engine and the modern computer are amazing. Babbage's analytical engine, which was intended to be a steam-powered device, had four components:

1. A "mill" that manipulated and computed the data
2. A "store" that held the data
3. An "operator" of the system that carried out instructions
4. A separate device that entered data and received processed information via punched cards.

After spending many years sketching variations and improvements for this new model, Babbage received some assistance in 1842 from Ada Augusta Byron (see the next Note of Interest).

8. Write a complete program that produces a table showing the temperature equivalents in degrees Fahrenheit and degrees Celsius. Let the user enter the starting and ending values. Use the formula

```
cels_temp = 5.0/9.0 (faren_temp - 32.0)
```

9. Write a complete program to produce a chart consisting of the multiples of 5 from -50 to 50 together with the squares and cubes of these numbers. Use a function to print a suitable heading and user-defined functions for square and cube.

10. The formula $A = P(1 + R)^N$ can be used to compute the amount due (A) when a principal (P) has been borrowed at a monthly rate (R) for a period of N months. Write a complete program that will read in the principal, annual interest rate (divide by 12 for monthly rate), and number of months and then produce a chart that shows how much will be due at the end of each month.

6.3 while Loops

OBJECTIVES

- to understand when variable repetition should be used in a program
- to understand why **while** is a variable repetition loop
- to understand the flow of control when using a **while** loop
- to be able to use a counter in a **while** loop
- to be able to use a **while** loop in a program

In Section 6.2, we studied **for** loops in which the body of the loop is repeated a fixed number of times. For some problems, this kind of loop is inappropriate, because a segment of code may need to be repeated an unknown number of times. The condition controlling the loop must be variable rather than constant. C++ provides two repetition statements that are especially well suited to handle variable control conditions, one with a pretest condition and one with a post-test condition.

A useful pretest loop with variable conditions in C++ is the **while** loop. The condition controlling the loop is a Boolean expression written between parentheses. Correct form and syntax for such a loop are

```
while ( <Boolean expression> )
        <statement>
```

Note that the parentheses enclosing the Boolean expression are required. The flow diagram for a **while** loop is given in Figure 6.2. Program control, when using a **while** loop, is in order as follows:

1. The loop condition is examined.
2. If the loop condition is **TRUE**, the entire body of the loop is executed before another check is made.
3. If the loop condition is **FALSE**, control is transferred to the first statement following the loop. For example,

   ```
   a = 1;
   while (a < 0)
   {
           num = 5;
           cout << num << endl;
           a = a + 10
   }
   cout << a << endl;
   ```

   produces the single line of output

   ```
   1
   ```

Before analyzing the components of the **while** statement, we should consider a short example.

◆ FIGURE 6.2

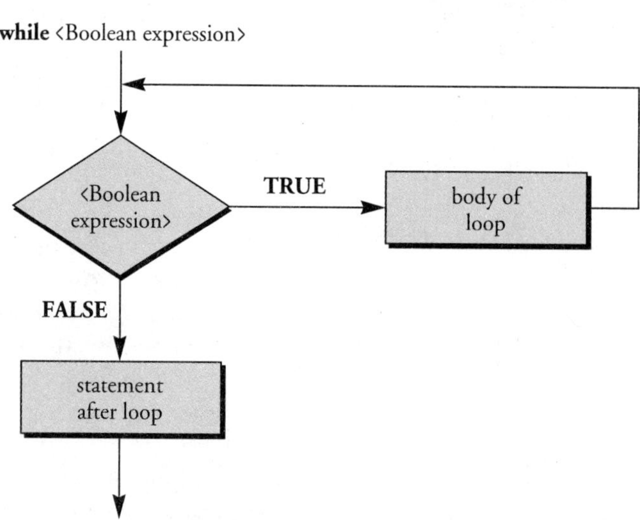

EXAMPLE 6.6 This example prints some powers of two.

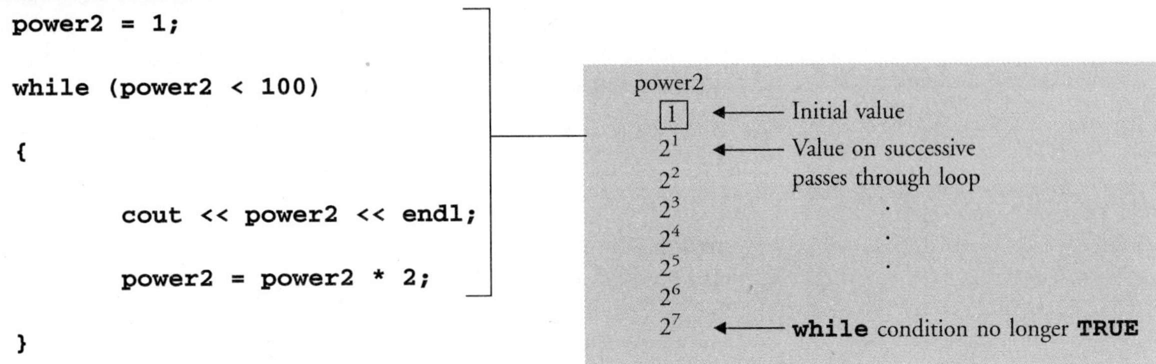

The output from this segment of code is

```
1
2
4
8
16
32
64
```

With this example in mind, let us examine the general form for using a **while** loop.

1. The condition can be any expression that has a Boolean value. Standard examples include relational operators and Boolean variables; thus, each of the following would be appropriate.

```
while (j < 10)
while (a < b)
while (! done)
```

2. The Boolean expression must have a value prior to entering the loop.
3. The body of the loop can be a simple statement or a compound statement.
4. Provision must be made for appropriately changing the loop control condition in the body of the loop. If no such changes are made, the following could happen:
   a. If the loop condition is **TRUE** and no changes are made, a condition called an *infinite loop* is caused. For example,

```
a = 1;
while (a > 0)
{
        num = 5;
        cout<< num << endl;
}
cout << a << endl;
```

The condition **a > 0** is **TRUE**, the body is executed, and the condition is retested. However, because the condition is not changed within the loop body, it will always be **TRUE** and will cause an infinite loop. It will not produce a compilation error but, when you run the program, the output will be a column of fives.

b. If the loop condition is **TRUE** and changes are made, but the condition never becomes **FALSE**, you again have an infinite loop. An example of this is

```
power3 = 1;
while (power3 != 100)
{
        cout << power3 << endl;
        power3 = power3 * 3
}
```

Since the variable **power3** never is assigned the value 100, the condition **power3 < 100** is always **TRUE**. At run time, the computer will continue to multiply **power3** by 3 until an integer overflow error occurs.

Sentinel Values

The Boolean expression of a variable control loop is frequently controlled by a *sentinel value.* For example, a program might require the user to enter numeric data. When there are no more data, the user will be instructed to enter a special (sentinel) value. This then signifies the end of the process. Example 6.7 illustrates the use of such a sentinel.

EXAMPLE 6.7

Here we write a segment of code that allows the user to enter a set of test scores and then print the average score.

```
num_scores = 0;
sum = 0;
cout << "Enter a score and press <Enter>, -999 to quit. ";
cin >> score;
while (score != -999)
{
        num_scores = num_scores + 1;
        sum = sum + score;
        cout << "Enter a score and press <Enter>, -999 to quit. ";
        cin >> score;
}
if (num_scores > 0)
{
        average = sum / float(num_scores);
        cout << endl;
        cout << "The average of" << setw(4) << num_scores << " scores is"
             << fixed << showpoint << setw(6) setprecision(2) << average << endl;
}
else
        cout << "No scores were entered" << endl;
```

Writing Style

Writing style for **while** loops should be similar to that adopted for **for** loops; that is, indenting, skipped lines, and comments should all be used to enhance readability.

Using Counters

Because **while** loops can be repeated a variable number of times, it is a common practice to count the number of times the loop body is executed. This is accomplished by declaring an appropriately named integer variable, initializing it to zero before the loop, and then incrementing it by one each time through the loop. For example, if you use **count** for your variable name, Example 6.6 (in which we printed some powers of two) could be modified to

```
count = 0;
power2 = 1;

while (power2 < 100)
{
        cout << power2 << endl;
        power2 = power2 * 2;
        count = count + 1;
}

cout << "There are" << setw(4) << count << " powers of 2 less than 100." << endl;
```

The output from this segment of code is

```
 1
 2
 4
 8
16
32
64

There are 7 powers of 2 less than 100.
```

Although the process is tedious, it is instructive to trace the values of variables through a loop where a *counter* is used. Therefore, let us consider the segment of code we have just seen. Before the loop is entered, we have

0	1
count	**power2**

The loop control is **power2 < 100 (1 < 100)**. Since this is **TRUE**, the loop body is executed and the new values become

1	2
count	**power2**

Prior to each successive time through the loop, the condition **power2 < 100** is checked. Thus, the loop produces the following sequence of values:

count	power2
1	2
2	4
3	8
4	16
5	32
6	64
7	128

Although **power2** is 128, the remainder of the loop is executed before checking the loop condition. Once a loop is entered, it is executed completely before the loop control condition is reexamined. Because **128 < 100** is **FALSE**, control is transferred to the statement following the loop.

Compound Conditions

All previous examples and illustrations of **while** loops have used simple Boolean expressions. However, because any Boolean expression can be used as a loop control condition, compound Boolean expressions can also be used. For example,

```
cin >> a >> b;
while ((a > 0) && (b > 0))
{
        cout << a << b << endl;
        a = a - 5;
        b = b - 3;
}
```

will go through the body of the loop only when the boolean expression **(a > 0) && (b > 0)** is **TRUE**. Thus, if the values of **a** and **b** obtained from the keyboard are

```
17  8
```

the output from this segment of code is

```
17          8

12          5

 7          2
```

Compound Boolean expressions can be as complex as you wish to make them. However, if several conditions are involved, the program can become difficult to read and debug; therefore, you may wish to redesign your solution to avoid this problem.

EXERCISES 6.3

1. Compare and contrast **for** loops with **while** loops.
2. Write a test program that illustrates what happens when you have an infinite loop.
3. What is the output from each of the following segments of code?

a.
```
k = 1;
while (k <= 10)
{
      cout << k << endl;
      k = k + 1;
}
```
b.
```
a = 1;
while (17 % a < 5)
{
      cout << a << 17 % a << endl;
      a = a + 1;
}
```
c.
```
a = 2;
b = 50;
while (a < b)
      a = a * 3;
cout << a << b << endl;
```
d.
```
count = 0;
sum = 0;
while (count < 5)
{
      count = count + 1;
      sum = sum + count;
      cout << "The partial sum is" << setw(4) << sum
            << endl;
}
cout << "The count is" << setw(4) << count << endl;
```
e.
```
x = 3.0;
y = 2.0;
while (x * y < 100)
      x = x * y;
cout << setprecision(2) << setw(10) << x setw(10)
      << y < endl;
```

4. Indicate which of the following are infinite loops and explain why they are infinite.

a.
```
j = 1;
while (j < 10)
      cout << j;
      j = j + 1;
```
b.
```
a = 2;
while (a < 20)
{
      cout << a << endl;
      a = a * 2;
}
```
c.
```
a = 2;
while (a < 20)
{
      cout << a << endl;
      a = a * 2;
}
```

A NOTE OF INTEREST

Ada Augusta Byron

Ada Augusta Byron, Countess of Lovelace (1815–1852), became interested in Charles Babbage's efforts when she was translating a paper on the analytical engine from French to English. Upon meeting Babbage, she began the task of writing an original paper. Through the process, she documented Babbage's ideas and made it possible to understand Babbage's original intentions. Over time, she became a full collaborator on the project, correcting some errors and suggesting the use of the binary system of storage rather than the decimal.

Lady Lovelace's most important contribution was her concept of a loop. She observed that a repetition of a sequence of instructions often was necessary to perform a single calculation. Thus, she discovered that by using a single set of cards and a conditional jump facility, the calculation could be performed with a fraction of the effort. This idea has earned her the distinction of being the first programmer. In honor of her role as the first computer programmer, the U.S. Department of Defense named its computer language Ada.

d.
```
b = 15;
while (b / 3 == 5)
{
      cout << b << b / 5 << endl;
      b = b - 1;
}
```

5. Write a **while** loop for each of the following tasks.

a. Print a positive real number, **num**, and then print successive values where each value is 0.5 less than the previous value. The list should continue as long as values to be printed are positive.

b. Print a list of squares of positive integers as long as the difference between consecutive squares is less than 50.

6. Write a segment of code that reads a positive integer and prints a list of powers of the integer that are less than 10,000.

6.4 do . . . while Loops

OBJECTIVES

- to understand that a **do...while** loop is a post-test loop
- to understand the flow of control using a **do...while** loop
- to be able to use a **do...while** loop in a program
- to be able to use **do...while** loops with multiple conditions

The previous two sections discussed two kinds of repetition. We looked at fixed repetition using **for** loops and variable repetition using **while** loops. C++ provides a second form of variable repetition, a **do . . . while** loop, which is a *post-test* or *exit-controlled loop.* The basic form and syntax for a **do . . . while** loop are

```
do
{
      <statement>
} while (<Boolean expression>);
```

A flow diagram for a **do . . . while** loop is given in Figure 6.3. Prior to examining this form, let us consider the following fragment of code:

◆ FIGURE 6.3

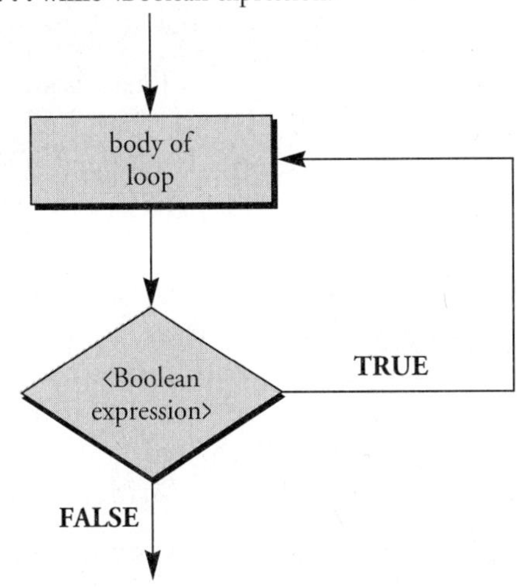


```
count = 0;
do
{
        count = count + 1;
        cout << count << endl;
} while (count < 5);
cout << setw(10) << "All done" << endl;
```

The output for this fragment is

```
1
2
3
4
5
All done
```

With this example in mind, the following comments concerning the use of a **do . . . while** loop are in order.

1. The Boolean expression must have a value before it is used at the end of the loop.
2. The loop must be entered at least once because the Boolean expression is not evaluated until after the loop body has been executed.
3. When the Boolean expression is evaluated, if it is **TRUE**, control is transferred back to the top of the loop; if it is **FALSE**, control is transferred to the next program statement.
4. Provision must be made for changing values inside the loop so that the Boolean expression used to control the loop will eventually be **FALSE**. If this is not done, you will have an infinite loop, as shown here:

```
j = 0;
do
{
   j = j + 2;
   cout << j << endl;
} while (j != 5);
```

5. Writing style for using **do . . . while** loops should be consistent with your style for other loop structures.

There is one important difference between **while** and **do . . . while** loops. A **do . . . while** loop must be executed at least once, but a **while** loop can be skipped if the initial value of the Boolean expression is **FALSE**. Because of this, **do . . . while** loops are generally used less frequently than **while** loops.

EXAMPLE 6.8

An early method of approximating square roots was the Newton-Raphson method. This method consisted of starting with an approximation and then getting successively better approximations until the desired degree of accuracy was achieved.

Writing code for this method, each **new_guess** is defined to be

```
new_guess = 1.0/2.0 * (old_guess + number / old_guess)
```

Thus, if the number entered was 34 and the first approximation was 5, the second approximation would be

```
1/2 * (5 + 34 / 5)  (5.9)
```

and the third approximation would be

```
1/2 * (5.9 + 34 / 5.9)  (5.83135593)
```

Let's see how a **do . . . while** loop can be used to obtain successively better approximations until a desired degree of accuracy is reached. Assume **number** contains the number whose square root we wish to approximate, **old_guess** contains a first approximation, and **DESIRED_ACCURACY** is a defined constant. A loop used in the solution of this problem is

```
cout << setprecision(8) << setw(12) << new_guess << endl;
do
{
     old_guess = new_guess;
     new_guess = 1/2 * (old_guess + number / old_guess);
     cout << setw(12) << new_guess << endl;
} while (abs(new_guess - old_guess) >= DESIRED_ACCURACY);
```

If **DESIRED_ACCURACY** is 0.0001, **number is 34**, and **new_guess** is originally 5, the output from this segment is

```
5.00000000

5.90000000

5.83135593

5.83095191

5.83095189
```

EXAMPLE 6.9

Interactive programming frequently requires the use of a menu to give the user a choice of options. For example, suppose you want a menu like this one:

```
Which of the following recipes do you wish to see?

   (T)acos
   (J)ambalaya
   (G)umbo
   (Q)uit

Enter the first letter and press <Enter>.
```

This screen message could be written as a function **menu** and the main program could use a **do . . . while** loop as follows:

```
do
{
        menu();
        cin >> selection;
        switch (selection)
        {
               case 'T' :     tacos();
                              break;
               case 'J' :     jambalaya();
                              break;
               case 'G' :     gumbo();
                              break;
               case 'Q' :     goodbye_message();
        }
} while (selection != 'Q');
```

where **tacos**, **jambalaya**, **gumbo**, and **goodbye_message** are each separate functions with appropriate messages.

Compound Conditions

The Boolean expression used with a **do . . . while** loop can be as complex as you choose to make it. However, as with **while** loops, if the expression gets too complicated, you might enhance program readability and design by redesigning the algorithm to use simpler expressions.

Choosing the Correct Loop

"Which type of loop should I use?" is a question often faced by programmers. A partial answer is easy. If a loop is to be repeated a predetermined number of times during execution, a **for** loop is preferable. If the number of repetitions is not known, one of the variable control loops is preferable.

The more difficult part of the answer is deciding which variable control loop is appropriate. Simply stated, if a control check is needed before the loop is executed, use a **while** loop. If the check is needed at the end of the loop, use a **do . . . while** loop. Remember, however, that a **do . . . while** loop must always be executed at least once. Therefore, if there is a possibility that the loop will never be executed, a **while** loop must be used. For example, when reading data (especially from files, see Chapter 9), if there is a possibility of no data, a **while** loop must be used with a prompting input statement or other control check prior to the loop. Thus, you could have

```
cout << "Enter a score, -999 to quit. ";
cin << score;
while (score != -999)
{
      .
      . (process data)
      .
      cout << "Enter a score, -999 to quit. ";
      cin << score;
}
```

In the event either variable control loop can be used, the problem itself might help with the decision. Does the process need to be repeated until something happens, or does the process continue as long as (while) some condition is true? If either of these is apparent, use the code that most accurately reflects the solution to the problem.

Data Validation

Variable condition loops can be used to make programs more robust. In particular, suppose you are writing an interactive program that expects positive integers to be entered from the keyboard, with a sentinel value of -999 to be entered when you wish to quit. You can guard against bad data by using the following:

```
do
{
      cout << "Enter a positive integer; <-999> to quit. ";
      cin >> num;
} while ((num > 0) && (num != -999));
```

This process of examining data prior to its use in a program is referred to as *data validation*, and loops are useful for such validation. A second example of using a loop for this purpose follows.

EXAMPLE 6.10

One problem associated with interactive programs is guarding against typing errors. This example illustrates how a **do . . . while** loop can be used to avoid having something entered other than the anticipated responses. Specifically, suppose users of an interactive program are asked to indicate whether or not they wish to continue by entering either a **Y** or **N**. The screen message could be

```
Do you wish to continue? <Y or N>
```

You wish to allow any of **Y**, **y**, **N**, or **n** to be used as an appropriate response. Any other entry is considered an error. This can be accomplished by the following:

```
do
{
     cout << "Do you wish to continue? <Y or N> ";
     cin >> response;
     good_response = (response == 'Y') || (response == 'y') ||
     (response == 'N') || (response == 'n');
} while (! good_response);
```

Any response other than those permitted as good data (**Y, y, N, n**) results in **good_response** being **FALSE** and the loop being executed again.

EXERCISES 6.4

1. Explain the difference between a pretest loop and a post-test loop.
2. Indicate what the output will be from each of the following code fragments.

a.
```
a = 0;
b = 10;
do
{
      a = a + 1;
      b = b - 1;
      cout << a << b << endl;
} while (a <= b);
```

b.
```
power = 1;
do
{
      power = power * 2;
      cout << power << endl;
} while (power <= 100);
```

c.
```
j = 1;
do
{
      cout << j << endl;
      j = j + 1;
} while (j <= 10);
```

d.
```
a = 1;
do
{
      cout << a << 17 % a << endl;
      a = a + 1;
} while (17 % a != 5);
```

3. Indicate which of the following are infinite loops and explain why.

a.
```
j = 1;
do
{
      cout << j << endl;
} while (j <= 10);
j = j + 1;
```

b.
```
a = 2;
do
{
      cout << a << endl;
      a = a * 2;
} while (a <= 20);
```

c.
```
a = 2;
do
{
      cout << a << endl;
      a = a * 2;
} while (a != 20);
```

d.
```
b = 15;
do
{
      cout << b << b / 5 << endl;
      b = b - 1;
} while (b / 3 >= 5);
```

4. Write a **do . . . while** loop for each of the following tasks.
   a. Print a positive real number, **num**, and then print successive values where each value is 0.5 less than the previous value. The list should continue as long as values to be printed are positive.
   b. Print a list of squares of positive integers as long as the difference between consecutive squares is less than 50.
5. Discuss whether or not a priming read is needed before a **do . . . while** loop that is used to get data.
6. Give an example of a situation that would require a predetermined number of repetitions.
7. In mathematics and science, many applications require a certain level or degree of accuracy obtained by successive approximations. Explain how the process of reaching the desired level of accuracy would relate to loops in C++.
8. Write a program that utilizes the algorithm for approximating a square root as shown in Example 6.8. Let the defined accuracy be 0.0001. Input should consist of a number whose square root is desired. Your program should guard against bad data entries (negatives and zero). Output should include a list of approximations and a check of your final approximation.
9. Compare and contrast the three repetition structures previously discussed in this chapter.

6.5 Loop Verification

OBJECTIVES

- to understand how input assertions and output assertions can be used to verify loops
- to understand how loop invariants and loop variants can be used to verify loops

Loop verification is the process of guaranteeing that a loop performs its intended task. Such verification is part of program testing and correctness to which we referred in Chapter 5.

Some work has been done on constructing formal proofs to determine if loops are "correct." We now examine a modified version of loop verification; a complete treatment of the issue will be the topic of subsequent course work.

Preconditions and Postconditions with Loops

Preconditions and postconditions can be used with loops. Loop preconditions are referred to as *input assertions.* They state what can be expected to be true before the loop is entered. Loop postconditions are referred to as *output assertions.* They state what can be expected to be true when the loop is exited.

To illustrate input and output assertions, we consider the mathematical problem of summing the proper divisors of a positive integer. For example, we have these integers:

Integer	Proper Divisors	Sum
6	1, 2, 3	6
9	1, 3	4
12	1, 2, 3, 4, 6	16

As part of a program that will have a positive integer as input, and as output, will have a determination of whether the integer is perfect (sum = integer), abundant (sum > integer), or deficient (sum < integer), it is necessary to sum the divisors. The following loop performs this task:

```
divisor_sum = 0;
for (trial_divisor = 1; trial_divisor <= num / 2; ++trial_divisor)
     if (num % trial_divisor == 0)
         divisor_sum = divisor_sum + trial_divisor;
```

An input assertion for this loop is

```
Precondition:        1. num is a positive integer.
                     2. divisor_sum = 0.
```

An output assertion is

```
Postcondition: divisor_sum is the sum of all proper divisors of num.
```

When these are placed with the previous code, we have

```
divisor_sum = 0;
assert((num > 0) && (divisor_sum > 0));
for (trial_divisor = 1; trial_divisor <= num / 2; ++trial_divisor)
        if (num % trial_divisor == 0) then
               divisor_sum = divisor_sum + trial_divisor;
// Postcondition: divisor_sum is the sum of all proper divisors of num.
```

Note that we pass the precondition to the **assert** function of C++, so that the run-time system actually establishes the truth of that assertion. However, we cannot do this with the postcondition, because the sum of all the proper divisors of a number is just what we are computing in the **for** loop!

Invariant and Variant Assertions

A *loop invariant* is an assertion that expresses a relationship between variables that remains constant throughout all iterations of the loop. In other words, it is a statement that is true both before the loop is entered and after each pass through the loop. An invariant assertion for the preceding code segment could be

```
divisor_sum is the sum of proper divisors of num that are less than or equal to
trial_divisor.
```

A *loop variant* is an assertion whose truth changes between the first and final execution of the loop. The loop variant expression should be stated in such a way that it guarantees the loop is exited. Thus, it contains some statement about the loop variable being incremented (or decremented) during execution of the loop. In the preceding code, we could have

```
trial_divisor is incremented by 1 each time through the loop. It eventually exceeds
the value num / 2, at which point the loop is exited.
```

Variant and invariant assertions usually occur in pairs.

We now use four kinds of assertions—input, output, variant, and invariant—to produce the formally verified loop that follows:

```
divisor_sum = 0;

// Precondition:     1. Num is a positive integer.          (input assertion)
//                   2. divisor_sum = 0.
```

```
assert((num > 0) && (divisor_sum == 0));

for (trial_divisor = 1; trial_divisor <= num / 2; ++trial_divisor)

// trial_divisor is incremented by 1 each time              (variant assertion)
// through the loop. It eventually exceeds the
// value (num / 2), at which point the loop is exited.

     if (num % trial_divisor == 0)
          divisor_sum = divisor_sum + trial_divisor;

// divisor_sum is the sum of proper divisors of              (invariant assertion)
// num that are less than or equal to trial_divisor.

// Postcondition: divisor_sum is the sum of                  (output assertion)
// all proper divisors of num.
```

In general, code that is presented in this text does not include formal verification of the loops. This issue is similar to that of robustness. In an introductory course, a decision must be made on the trade-off between learning new concepts and writing robust programs with formal verification of loops. We encourage the practice, but space and time considerations make it inconvenient to include such documentation at this level. We close this discussion with another example illustrating loop verification.

EXAMPLE 6.11

Consider the problem of finding the greatest common divisor (**gcd**) of two positive integers. To illustrate, we have this information:

num1	num2	gcd(num 1, num2)
8	12	4
20	10	10
15	32	1
70	40	10

A segment of code to produce the **gcd** of two positive integers after they have been ordered as **small**, **large**, is

```
trial_gcd = small;
gcd_found = FALSE;
while (! gcd_found)
     if ((large % trial_gcd == 0) && (small % trial_gcd == 0))
     {
          gcd = trial_gcd;
          gcd_found = TRUE;
     }
     else
          trial_gcd = trial_gcd - 1;
```

Using assertions as previously indicated, this code would appear as

```
trial_gcd = small;
gcd_found = FALSE;

// Precondition:      1. small <= large
//                    2. trial_gcd (small) is the first candidate for gcd
//                    3. gcd_found is FALSE

assert((small <= large) && (small == trial_gcd) && ! gcd_found);

while (! gcd_found)

// trial_gcd assumes integer values ranging from small
// to 1. It is decremented by 1 each time through the
// loop. When trial_gcd divides both small and large,
// the loop is exited. Exit is guaranteed since 1
// divides both small and large.

       if ((large % trial_gcd == 0) && (small % trial_gcd == 0))

// When trial_gcd divides both large and small, then gcd is assigned that value.

       {

              assert((large % trial_gcd == 0) && (small % trial_gcd == 0));

              gcd = trial_gcd;
              gcd_found = TRUE;
       }
       else
              trial_gcd = trial_gcd - 1;

// Postcondition: gcd is the greatest common divisor of small and large.
```

EXERCISES 6.5

1. Write appropriate input assertions and output assertions for each of the following loops.

   a.
   ```
   cin >> score;
   while (score != -999)
   {
         num_scores = num_scores + 1;
         sum = sum + score;
   cout << "Enter a score; -999 to quit. ";
   cin >> score;
   }
   ```

   b.
   ```
   count = 0;
   power2 = 1;
   while (power2 < 100)
   {
         cout << power2 << endl;
         power2 = power2 * 2;
         count = count + 1;
   }
   ```

c. (From Example 6.8)

```
do
{
      old_guess = new_guess;
      new_guess = 1/2 * (old_guess + number / old_guess);
      cout << setprecision(8) << setw(10) << new_guess << endl;
} while (abs(new_guess - old_guess) < DESIRED_ACCURACY);
```

2. Write appropriate loop invariant and loop variant assertions for each of the loops in Exercise 1.
3. Consider the following loop. The user enters a number, **guess**, and the computer then displays a message indicating whether the guess is correct, too high, or too low. Add appropriate input assertions, output assertions, loop invariant assertions, and loop variant assertions to the following code.

```
correct = FALSE;
count = 0;
while ((count < MAX_TRIES) && (! correct))
{
          count = count + 1;
          cout << "Enter choice number " << count << endl;
          cin >> guess;
          if (guess == choice)
          {
                    correct = TRUE;
                    cout << "Congratulations!" << endl;
          }
          else if (guess < choice)
                    cout << "Your guess is too low" << end;
          else
                    cout << "Your guess is too high" << endl;
}
```

6.6 Nested Loops

OBJECTIVES

- to be able to use nested loops
- to understand the flow of control when using nested loops
- to be able to employ a consistent writing style when using nested loops

In this chapter, we have examined three loop structures. Each of them has been discussed with respect to syntax, semantics, form, writing style, and use in programs. But remember that each loop is treated as a single C++ statement. In this sense, it is possible to have a loop as one of the statements in the body of another loop. When this happens, the loops are said to be *nested.*

Loops can be nested to any depth; that is; a loop can be within a loop within a loop, and so on. Also, any of the three types of loops can be nested within any loop. However, a programmer should be careful not to design a program with nesting that is too complex. If program logic becomes too difficult to follow, you might be better off redesigning the program, perhaps by splitting off the inner logic into a separate subprogram.

Flow of Control

As a first example of using a loop within a loop, consider

```
for (k = 1; k <= 5; ++k)
      for (j = 1; j <= 3; ++j)
            cout << (k + j) << endl;
```

When this fragment is executed, the following happens:

1. Variable **k** is assigned a value.
2. For each value of **k**, the following loop is executed.

```
for (j = 1; j <= 3; ++j)
     cout << (k + j) << endl;
```

Thus, for **k = 1**, the "inside" or nested loop produces the output

```
2
3
4
```

At this point, **k = 2** and the next portion of the output produced by the nested loop is

```
3
4
5
```

The complete output from these nested loops is

```
2
3 from k = 1
4

3
4 from k = 2
5

4
5 from k = 3
6

5
6 from k = 4
7

6
7 from k = 5
8
```

As you can see, for each value assigned to the index of the outside loop, the inside loop is executed completely. Suppose you want the output to be printed in the form of a chart as follows:

```
2    3    4

3    4    5

4    5    6

5    6    7

6    7    8
```

The pseudocode design to produce this output is

1. for (k = 1; k <= 5; ++k)
        produce a line

A refinement of this is

1. for (k = 1; k <= 5; ++k)
    1.1 print on one line
    1.2 advance the printer

The C++ code for this development becomes

```
for (k = 1; k <= 5; ++k)
{
        for (j = 1; j <= 3; ++j)            // print on one line
                cout << setw(4) << (k + j);
        cout << endl;                       // advance the printer
}
```

Our next example shows how nested loops can be used to produce a design.

EXAMPLE 6.12

Use nested **for** loops to produce the following output:

```
*
**
***
****
*****
```

The left asterisks are in column 10. The first-level pseudocode to solve this problem could be

1. for (k = 1; k <= 5; ++k)
        produce a line

A refinement of this could be

1. for (k = 1; k <= 5; ++k)
    1.1 print on one line
    1.2 advance the printer

Step 1.1 is not yet sufficiently refined, so our next level could be

1. for (k = 1; k <= 5; ++k)
    1.1 print on one line
        1.1.1 put a blank in column 9
        1.1.2 print k asterisks
    1.2 advance the printer

We can now write a program fragment to produce the desired output as follows:

```
for (k = 1; k <= 5; ++k)
{
        cout << setw(9) << ' ';
        for (j = 1; j <= k; ++j)
                cout << *';
        cout << endl;
}
```

A significant feature has been added to this program fragment. Note that the upper bound for the inner loop is the loop control variable of the outer loop.

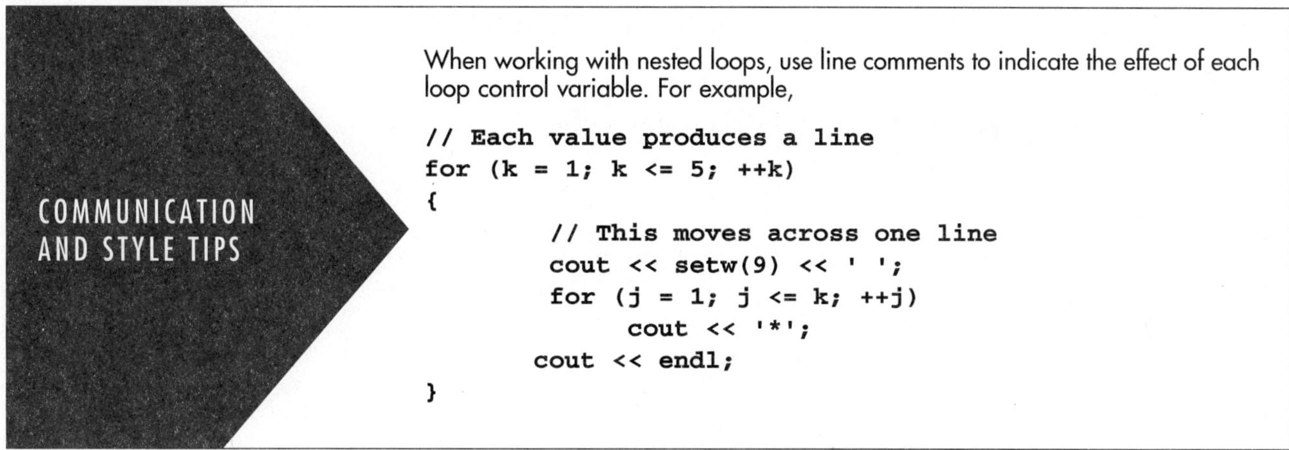

COMMUNICATION AND STYLE TIPS

When working with nested loops, use line comments to indicate the effect of each loop control variable. For example,

```
// Each value produces a line
for (k = 1; k <= 5; ++k)
{
        // This moves across one line
        cout << setw(9) << ' ';
        for (j = 1; j <= k; ++j)
             cout << '*';
       cout << endl;
}
```

Thus far, nested loops have been used only with **for** loops, but any of the loop structures can be used in nesting. Our next example illustrates a **do . . . while** loop nested within a **while** loop.

EXAMPLE 6.13

Trace the flow of control and indicate the output for the following program fragment:

```
a = 10;
b = 0;
while (a > b)
{
       cout << setw(5) << a << endl;
       do
       {
            cout << setw(5) << a << setw(5) << b << setw(5) << (a + b) << endl;
            a = a - 2;
       } while (a > 6);
       b = b + 2;
}
cout << endl;
cout << setw(20) << "All done" << endl;
```

The assignment statements produce

10	0
a	**b**

and **a > b** is **TRUE**; thus, the **while** loop is entered. The first time through this loop the **do . . . while** loop is used. Output for the first pass is

```
10
10   0   10
```

and the values for **a** and **b** are

8	0
a	**b**

The Boolean expression **a > 6** is **TRUE** and the **do . . . while** loop is executed again to produce the next line of output:

```
8     0     8
```

and the values for **a** and **b** become

6	0
a	**b**

At this point, **a > 6** is **FALSE** and control transfers to the line of code

```
b = b + 2;
```

Thus, the variable values are

6	2
a	**b**

and the Boolean expression **a > b** is **TRUE**. This means the **while** loop will be repeated. The output for the second time through this loop is

```
6
6     2     8
```

and the values for the variables are

4	4
a	**b**

Now **a > b** is **FALSE** and control is transferred to the line following the **while** loop. Output for the complete fragment is

```
10
10    0     10
8     0      8
6
6     2      8

            All done
```

This example is a bit contrived and tracing the flow of control somewhat tedious. However, it is important for you to be able to follow the logic involved in using nested loops.

Writing Style

As usual, you should be aware of the significance of using a consistent, readable style of writing when using nested loops. There are at least three features you should consider.

1. *Indenting:* Each loop should have its own level of indenting. This makes it easier to identify the body of the loop. If the loop body consists of a com-

pound statement, the **{** and **}** should start in the same column. Using our previous indenting style, a typical nesting might be

```
for (k= 1; k <= 10; ++k)
{
        while (a > 0)
        {
                do
                {
                         .
                         .
                         .
                } while (<condition>);     // end of do . . . while loop
                <statement>
        }                                  // end of while loop
        <statement>
}                                          // end of for loop
```

If the body of a loop becomes very long, it is sometimes difficult to match the **{** with the proper **}**. In this case, you should either redesign the program (for example, write a separate subprogram) or be especially careful.

2. *Using comments:* Comments can precede a loop and explain what the loop will do, or they can be used with statements inside the loop to explain what the statement does. They should be used to indicate the end of a loop where the loop body is a compound statement.
3. *Skipping lines:* This is an effective way of isolating loops within a program and making nested loops easier to identify.

A note of caution is in order with respect to writing style. Program documentation is important; however, excessive use of comments and skipped lines can detract from readability. You should develop a happy medium.

Statement Execution in Nested Loops

Using nested loops can significantly increase the number of times statements get executed in a program. To illustrate, suppose a program contains a **do . . . while** loop that gets executed six times before it is exited, as illustrated here:

```
          ┌ do
          │ .
6 times   │ . (action here)
          │ .
          └ while (<condition 1);
```

If one of the statements inside this loop is another loop, the inner loop will be executed six times. Suppose this inner loop is repeated five times whenever it is entered. This means each statement within the inner loop will be executed 6 × 5 = 30 times when the program is run. This is illustrated by

```
          do
        ┌ {
        │         .
        │         . (action here)
        │         .
6 times │
        │         while (<condition 2>)                    ┐
        │         {                                        │
        │               <statement>       // 30 times      │
        │         }                       // end of while  │ 5 times
        │         .                                        │
        │         .                                        │
        │         .                                        │
        └ } while (<condition 1>);                         ┘
```

When a third level of nesting is used, the number of times a statement is executed can be determined by the product of three factors, $n_1 * n_2 * n_3$, where n_1 represents the number of repetitions of the outside loop, n_2 represents the number of repetitions for the first level of nesting, and n_3 represents the number of repetitions for the innermost loop.

We close this section with an example of a program that uses nested loops to print a multiplication table.

EXAMPLE 6.14

This example presents a complete program whose output is the multiplication table from 1 × 1 to 10 × 10. A suitable heading is part of the output.

```
// Program file: multab.cpp

#include <iostream.h>
#include <iomanip.h>

const char INDENT = ' ';

// Function: print_heading
// Print a heading for multiplication table

void print_heading();

// Function: print_table
// Print multiplication table

void print_table();

int main()
{
      print_heading();
      print_table();
      return 0;
}
```

```
void print_heading()
{
      cout << endl;
      cout <<  setw(17) << INDENT << "Multiplication Table" << endl;
      cout <<  setw(17) << INDENT << "--------------------" << endl;
      cout <<  setw(10) << INDENT << "(  Generated by nested for loops   )"
               << endl;
      cout << endl;
}

void print_table()
{
      int row, column;

      //Print the column heads
      cout  << setw(10) << INDENT << "        1  2  3  4  5  6  7  8  9 10"
            << endl;
      cout  << setw(10) << INDENT << "---!------------------------------"
            << endl;
      // Now start the loop
      for (row = 1; row <= 10; ++row)
      {
            // print one row
            cout << setw(12) << row << " !";
            for (column = 1; column <= 10; ++column)
                  cout << setw(3) << (row * column);
            cout << endl;
      } // end of each row
      cout << endl;
}
```

The output from this program is

```
             Multiplication Table
             --------------------
        ( Generated by nested for loops )

              1    2    3    4    5    6    7    8    9   10
    ---!-------------------------------------------------------
      1 !     1    2    3    4    5    6    7    8    9   10
      2 !     2    4    6    8   10   12   14   16   18   20
      3 !     3    6    9   12   15   18   21   24   27   30
      4 !     4    8   12   16   20   24   28   32   36   40
      5 !     5   10   15   20   25   30   35   40   45   50
      6 !     6   12   18   24   30   36   42   48   54   60
      7 !     7   14   21   28   35   42   49   56   63   70
      8 !     8   16   24   32   40   48   56   64   72   80
      9 !     9   18   27   36   45   54   63   72   81   90
     10 !    10   20   30   40   50   60   70   80   90  100
```

A NOTE OF INTEREST

A Digital Matter of Life and Death

The radiation-therapy machine, a Therac 25 linear accelerator, was designed to send a penetrating X ray or electron beam deep into a cancer patient's body to destroy embedded tumors without injuring skin tissue. But in three separate instances in 1985 and 1986, the machine failed. Instead of delivering a safe level of radiation, the Therac 25 administered a dose that was more than 100 times larger than the typical treatment dose. Two patients died and a third was severely burned.

The malfunction was caused by an error in the computer program controlling the machine. It was a subtle error that no one had picked up during the extensive testing the machine had undergone. The error surfaced only when a technician happened to use a specific, unusual combination of keystrokes to instruct the machine.

The Therac incidents and other cases of medical device failures caused by computer errors have focused attention on the increasingly important role played by computers in medical applications. Computers or machines with built-in microprocessors perform functions that range from keeping track of patients to diagnosing ailments and providing treatments.

"The impact of computers on medical care and the medical community is the most significant factor that we have to face," says Frank E. Samuel Jr., president of the Health Industry Manufacturers Association (HIMA), based in Washington, D.C. "Health care will change more dramatically in the next 10 years because of software-driven products than for any other single cause." Samuel made his remarks at a recent HIMA-sponsored conference on the regulation of medical software.

At the same time, reports of medical devices with computer-related problems are appearing more and more frequently. In 1985, the Food and Drug Administration (FDA) reported that recalls of medical devices because of computer faults had roughly doubled over the previous five years. Since then, the number of such complaints has risen further.

The FDA, in its mandated role as guardian of public health and safety, is now preparing to regulate the software component of medical devices. The agency's effort has already raised questions about what kinds of products, software, and information systems should be regulated.

EXERCISES 6.6

1. Write a program fragment that uses nested loops to produce each of the following designs.

a.
```
*****
 ****
  ***
   **
    *
```

b.
```
   *
  ***
 *****
*******
 *****
  ***
   *
```

c.
```
***
***
***
***
******
******
******
```

2. What is the output from each of the following code fragments?

a.
```
for (k = 2; k <= 6; ++k)
{
          for (j = 5; j <= 10; ++j)
                   cout << (k + j);
          cout << endl;
}
```

b.
```
for k = 2; k <= 6; ++k)
{
          for (j = 5; j <= 10; ++j)
                   cout << (k + j);
          cout << endl;
}
```

c.
```
sum = 0;
a = 7;
while (a < 10)
{
        for (k = a; k <= 10; ++k)
                sum = sum + k;
        a = a + 1;
}
cout << sum << endl;
```

d.
```
   sum = 0;
for (k = 1; k <= 10; ++k)
        for (j = (10 * k - 9); j <= (10 * k); ++j)
                sum = sum + J;
cout << sum << endl;
```

3. What output is produced from the following segment of code?

```
a = 4;
b = 7;
do
{
        num = a;
        while (num <= b)
        {
                for (k = a; k <= b; ++k)
                        cout << setw(4) << num;
                cout << endl;
                num = num + 1
        } // end of while
        cout << endl;
        a = a + 1;
}
while (a != b); // end of do...while loop
```

4. Write a program fragment that uses nested loops to produce the following output.

```
2    4    6    8   10

3    6    9   12   15

4    8   12   16   20

5   10   15   20   25
```

6.7 Repetition and Selection

OBJECTIVES

- to be able to use a selection statement within the body of a loop
- to be able to use a loop within an option of a selection statement

Selection Within Repetition (Loops)

In Chapter 5 we discussed the use of selection statements. In this chapter we have discussed the use of three different types of loops. It is now time to see how they are used together. We will first examine selection statements contained within the body of a loop.

EXAMPLE 6.15

Write a program fragment that computes gross wages for employees of the Florida OJ Canning Company. The data consist of three initials, the total hours worked, and the hourly rate; for example,

```
JHA 44.5 12.75
```

Overtime (more than 40 hours) is computed as time-and-a-half. The output should include all input data and a column of gross wages.

A first-level pseudocode development for this program is

```
1. while more_employees
       1.1 process one employee
       1.2 print results
```

This could be refined to

```
1. while more_employees
       1.1 process one employee
           1.1.1 get data
           1.1.2 compute wage
       1.2 print results
```

Step 1.1.2 can be refined to

```
1.1.2 compute wage
      1.1.2.1 if hours <= 40.0
                   compute regular time
                 else
                   compute time-and-a-half
```

and the final algorithm for the fragment is

```
1. while more_employees
   1.1 process one employee
       1.1.1 get data
       1.1.2 compute wage
             1.1.2.1 if hours <= 40.0
                          compute regular time
                        else
                          compute time-and-a-half
   1.2 print results
```

The code for this fragment follows:

```
cout << fixed << showpoint;
cout << "Any employees? <Y> or <N> ";
cin >> choice;
more_employees = (choice == 'Y') || (choice == 'y');
while (more_employees)
{
        cout << endl;
        cout << "Enter initials, hours, and payrate. ";
        cin >> init1 << init2 << init3 << hours << pay_rate;
        if (hours <= 40.0)
                total_wage = hours * pay_rate;
        else
```

```
        {
              overtime = 1.5 * (hours - 40.0) * pay_rate;
              total_wage = 40 * pay_rate + overtime;
        }
        cout << endl;
        cout << setw(5) << init1 << init2 << init3;
        cout << setprecision(2) << setw(10) << hours << setw(10) << pay_rate;
        cout << setw(10) << '$' << setw(7) << total_wage;
        cout << endl;
        cout << "Any more employees? <Y> or <N> ";
        cin >> choice;
        more_employees = (choice == 'Y') || (choice == 'y');
}
```

Repetition (Loops) Within Selection

The next example illustrates the use of a loop within an **if** statement.

EXAMPLE 6.16

Write a program fragment that allows you to read an integer from the keyboard. If the integer is between 0 and 50, you are to print a chart containing all positive integers less than the integer, their squares, and their cubes. Thus, if 4 is read, the chart is

```
1    1    1

2    4    8

3    9   27
```

The design for this problem has a first-level pseudocode development of

1. cin num
2. if (num > 0) && (num < 50)
    2.1 print the chart

Step 2.1 can be refined to

2.1 print the chart
    2.1.1 for (k = 1; k <= (num - 1); ++k)
        2.1.1.1 print each line

We can now write the code for this fragment as follows:

```
cin >> num;
if ((num > 0) && (num < 50))
        for (k = 1; k <= num - 1; ++k)
            cout << k << (k * k) << (k * k * k << endl;
```

EXERCISES 6.7

1. Find and explain the errors in each of the following program fragments. Assume all variables have been suitably declared.

a.
```
a = 25;
flag = TRUE;
```

```
while (flag == TRUE)
     if (a >= 100)
     {
             cout << a << endl;
             flag = FALSE;
     }
```

b.
```
for (k = 1; k <= 10; ++k)
     cout << k << (k * k) << endl;
if (k % 3 == 0)
{
     cout << k;
     cout << " is a multiple of three" << endl;
}
```

2. What is the output from each of the following program fragments? Assume all variables have been suitably declared.

a.
```
for (k = 1; k <= 100; ++k)
     if (k % 5 == 0)
             cout << k << endl;
```

b.
```
j = 20;
if (j % 5 == 0)
        for (k = 1: k <= 100; ++k)
                cout << k << endl;
```

c.
```
a = 5;
b = 90;
do
{
     b = b / a - 5;
     if (b > a)
             b = a + 30;
} while (b >= 0);
cout << a << b << endl;
```

d.
```
count = 0;
for (k = -5; k <= 5; ++k)
     if (k % 3 == 0)
     {
             cout << "k = " << setw(4) << k<< " output ";
             while (count < 10)
             {
                     count = count + 1;
                     cout << setw(4) << count << endl;
             }
             count = 0;
             cout << endl;
     }
```

e.
```
a = 5;
b = 2;
if (a < b)
     for (k = a; k <= b; ++k)
             cout << k << endl;
else
     for (k = a; k >= b; --k)
             cout << k << endl;
```

f.
```
for (k = -5; k <= 5; ++k)
{
     cout << "k = " << setw(4) << k " output ";
     a = k;
     if (k < 0)
            // k = -5, -4, -3, -2, -1
            do
            {
                  cout << setw(5) << (-2 * a) <<
endl;
                  a = a + 1;
            } while (a > 0);
     else // K = 0, 1, 2, 3, 4, 5
            while (a % 2 == 0)
            {
                  cout << a << endl;
                  a = a + 1;
            }
     cout << endl;
}
```

3. Write a program fragment that reads reals from the keyboard, counts the number of positive reals, and accumulates their sum.
4. Given two integers, **a** and **b**, **a** is a divisor of **b** if **b % a = 0**. Write a complete program that reads a positive integer **b** and then prints all the positive divisors of **b**.

FOCUS ON PROGRAM DESIGN

This program illustrates the combined use of repetition and selection statements. This is the problem statement: Write a program that allows positive integers to be entered from the keyboard and, for each such entry, list all primes less than or equal to the number. The program should include a check for bad data and use of a sentinel value to terminate the process. Typical output for the integer 17 is

```
Enter a positive integer; <-999> to quit. 17

          The number is 17. The prime numbers less than or equal
          to 17 are:

                              2
                              3
                              5
                              7
                             11
                             13
                             17

Enter a positive integer; <-999> to quit. -999
```

For purposes of this program, note the mathematical property that a number **k** is prime if it has no divisors (other than 1) less than its square root. For example, because 37 is not divisible by 2, 3, or 5, it is prime. Thus, when we check for divisors, it is only necessary to check up to **sqrt(k)**. Also note that 1 is not prime by definition.

A first-level pseudocode development for this problem is

1. Get a number
   while more_data
2. Examine the number
3. Get a number

A structure chart for this problem is shown in Figure 6.4. The module specifications for the main modules are

Module: Get a number
Task: Get an entry from the keyboard.
Output: a number

Module: Examine the number
Task:
if the number is 1
    Print a message
else
    Print a heading.
    Print list of all primes less than or equal to the integer read
Input: The integer read

◆ FIGURE 6.4

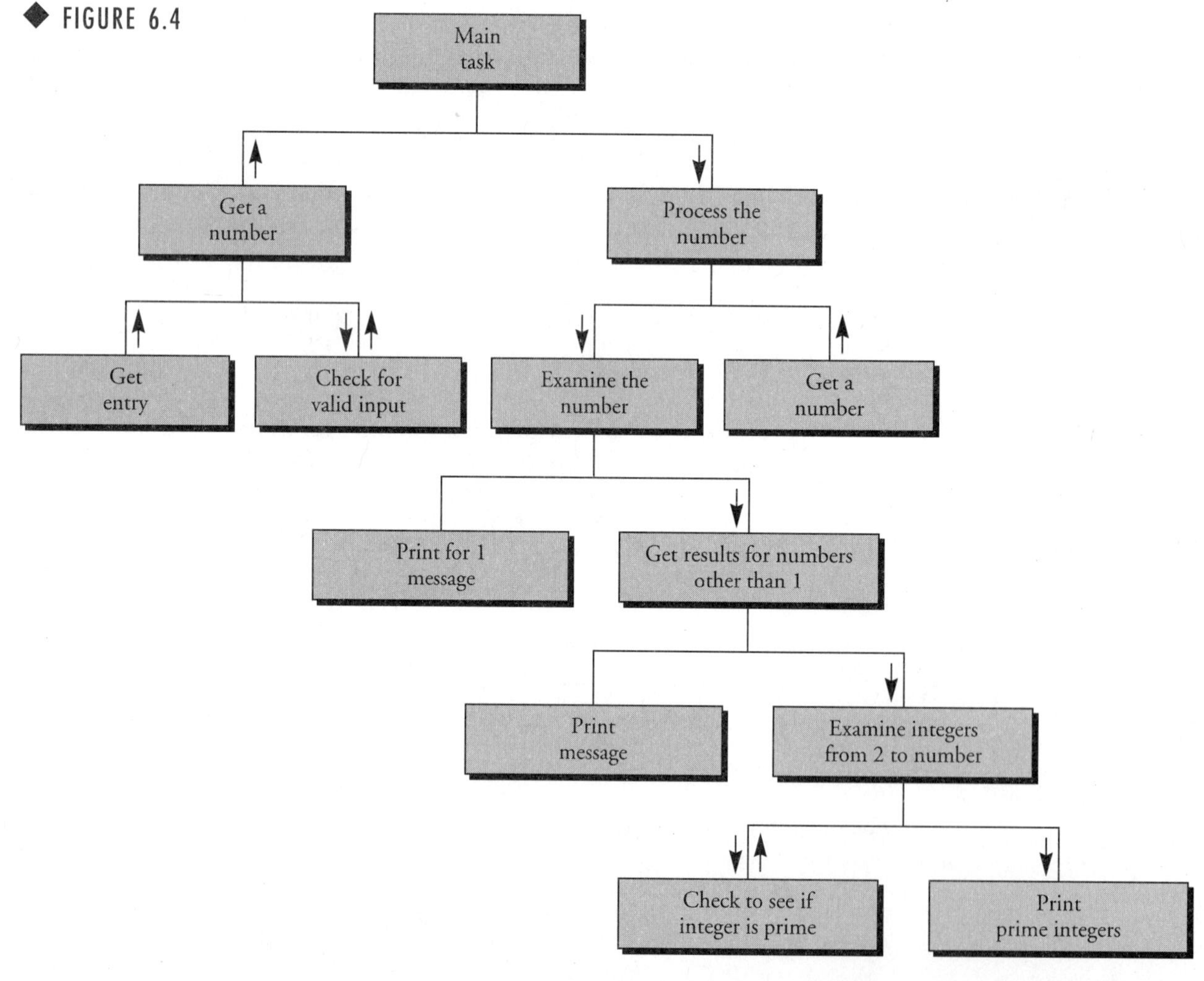

A second-level development is

```
1. Get a number
   1.1 Get entry from the keyboard
   while more_data
   2. Examine the number
   if number is 1
      2.1 print a message for 1
   else
      list the primes
      2.2 print a message
      2.3 check for primes less than or equal to number
   3. Get a number
      3.1 Get entry from the keyboard
      3.2 Check for valid entry
```

Step 2.3 can be refined to

```
2.3 check for primes less than or equal to number
for (k = 2; k <= number; ++k)
    2.3.1 check to see if k is prime
    2.3.2 if k is prime
          print k in list of primes
```

Instead of maintaining **more_data** as a simple Boolean flag, we will write a function that takes the number as a parameter, determines whether or not the number is the sentinel value, and returns **TRUE** or **FALSE** depending on what it finds. The pseudocode for this function is

```
Make sure it is a valid entry or the sentinel value for terminating the process.
If it is the sentinel value, return FALSE; otherwise, return TRUE.
```

Thus, the complete pseudocode development is

```
1. Get a number
   1.1 Get entry from the keyboard

while more_data

2. Examine the number
if number is 1
   2.1 print a message for 1
else
   list the primes
   2.2 print a message
   2.3 check for primes less than or equal to number
   for (k = 2; k <= number; ++k)
       2.3.1 check to see if k is prime
       2.3.2 if k is prime
             print k in list of primes
3. Get a number
   3.1 Get entry from the keyboard
   3.2 Check for valid entry
```

With this pseudocode development, the main program would be

```
num = get_a_number();
while (more_data(num))
{
     examine_the_number(num);
     num = get_a_number(num);
}
```

The complete program for this problem follows:

```
// Program file: primes.cpp

#include <iostream.h>
#include <iomanip.h>
#include <math.h>
#include "boolean.h"

const char SKIP = ' ';

int get_a_number();

// Function: print_one_message
// Print a message for 1

void print_one_message();

// Function: print_message
// Print a heading for the output
//
// Input: the integer read

void print_message(int number);

// Function: list_all_primes
// Print list of all primes less than or equal to the integer read
//
// Input: the integer read

void list_all_primes(int number);

// Function: list_all_primes
// If integer read is one,
// then print a message for one
// else
// Print list of all primes less than or equal to the integer read
/ /
// Input: the integer read

void examine_the_number(int number);

// Function: more_data
// Determines whether number = -999 (the sentinel for end of input)
// Input: the integer read
// Output: TRUE, if the input is not the sentinel, FALSE otherwise
```

```
boolean more_data(int number);

int main()
{
      int number;

      number = get_a_number ();
      while (more_data(number))
      {
             examine_the_number (number);
             number = get_a_number ();
      }
       return 0;
}

int get_a_number()
{
       int number;
       boolean done;

       do
       {
               cout << endl;                                                          1
               cout << "Enter a positive integer; <-999> to quit.";
               cin >> number;
               done = (number == -999) || (number >= 0);
       } while (! done);     // assumes valid data
       return number;
}

void print_one_message()
{
       cout << endl;
       cout << setw(10) << SKIP << "------------------------------" << endl;
       cout << endl;
       cout << setw(20) << SKIP << "1 is not prime by definition." << endl;
}

void print_message(int number)
{
       cout << endl;
       cout << setw(10) << SKIP << "------------------------------" << endl;
       cout << endl;
       cout << setw(20) << SKIP << "The number is " << number
             << " The prime numbers" << endl;
       cout << setw(20) << SKIP << "less than or equal to "<< number
            << " are:" << endl;
       cout << endl;
}

void list_all_primes(int number)
{
```

```
        boolean prime;
        int candidate, divisor;
        float limit_for_check;

        for (candidate = 2; candidate <= number; ++candidate)
        {
                prime = TRUE;
                divisor = 2;
                limit_for_check = sqrt(candidate);
                while ((divisor <= limit_for_check) && prime)
                        if (candidate % divisor == 0)
                                prime = FALSE;          // Candidate has a divisor
                        else
                                divisor = divisor + 1;
                if (prime)                              //Print list of primes
                        cout << setw(35) << candidate << endl;
        }
}

void examine_the_number(int number)
{
        if (number == 1)
                print_one_message();
        else
        {
                print_message(number);
                list_all_primes (number);
        }
}

boolean more_data(int number)
{
        return number != -999;
}
```

Sample runs of this program produce this output:

```
    Enter a positive integer; <-999> to quit. 10

                                    ------------------------------------------
                                    The number is 10. The prime numbers
                                    less than or equal to 10 are:

                                          2
                                          3
                                          5
                                          7

    Enter a positive integer; <-999> to quit. 17

                                    ------------------------------------------
```

```
                    The number is 17. The prime numbers less than or equal
                    to 17 are:

                                 2
                                 3
                                 5
                                 7
                                11
                                13
                                17

Enter a positive integer; <-999> to quit. 1

                    1 is not prime by definition.

Enter a positive integer; <-999> to quit. 25

                          --------------------------------------------
                    The number is 25. The prime numbers less than or equal
                    to 25 are:

                                 2
                                 3
                                 5
                                 7
                                11
                                13
                                17
                                19
                                23

Enter a positive integer; <-999> to quit. -3
Enter a positive integer; <-999> to quit. 2

                          --------------------------------------------
                    The number is 2. The prime numbers less than or equal
                    to 2 are:

                                 2

Enter a positive integer; <-999> to quit. -999
```

More efficient algorithms than what we used here do exist. However, the purpose of this program was to see how loops can be used to solve a problem.

RUNNING, DEBUGGING AND TESTING HINTS

1. Most errors involving loops are not compilation errors. Thus, you will not be able to detect most errors until you try to run the program.
2. A syntax error that will not be detected by the compiler is a semicolon after a **while** statement. The fragment

```
while more_data;
{
        cin >> a;
        cout << a << endl;
}
```

   is incorrect and will not get past **while more_data;**. Note that this is an infinite loop.
3. Carefully check entry conditions for each loop.
4. Carefully check exit conditions for each loop. Make sure the loop is exited (not infinite) and that you have the correct number of repetitions.
5. Loop entry, execution, and exit can be checked by
   a. pencil and paper check on initial and final values
   b. count of the number of repetitions
   c. use of debugging output statements:
      i. Boolean condition prior to loop,
      ii. variables inside loop,
      iii. values of the counter in loop,
      iv. Boolean values inside the loop, and
      v. values after loop is exited.

SUMMARY

Key Terms

accumulator
counter
data validation
decrement
fixed repetition (iterated) loop
infinite loop
input assertion
loop invariant
loop variant
loop verification
nested loop
output assertion
post-test (exit-controlled) loop
pretest condition
pretest (entrance-controlled) loop
sentinel value
variable condition loop

Keywords

do **for** **while**

Key Concepts

◆ The following table provides a comparison summary of the three repetition structures discussed in this chapter.

Traits of Loops	**for** Loop	**while** Loop	**do . . . while** Loop
Pretest loop	Yes	Yes	No
Post-test loop	No	No	Yes
{ . . . } for compound statements	Required	Required	Required
Repetition	Fixed/variable	Variable	Variable

◆ A fixed repetition loop is to be used when you know exactly how many times something is to be repeated.

- The basic form of a **for** loop is

```
for (j = 1; j <= 5; ++j)
     <statement>
```

- A **while** loop is a pretest loop that can have a variable loop control; a typical loop is

```
score = 0;
sum = 0;
more_data = TRUE;
while (more_data)
{
   sum = sum + score;
   cout << "Enter a score; -999 to quit. ";
   cin >> score;
   more_data = (score != -999);
}
```

- A counter is a variable whose purpose is to indicate how often the body of a loop is executed.
- An accumulator is a variable whose purpose is to sum values.
- An infinite **while** loop is caused by having a **TRUE** loop control condition that is never changed to **FALSE**.
- A post-test loop has a Boolean condition checked after the loop body has been completed.
- A **do . . . while** loop is a post-test loop; a typical loop is

```
do
{
   cout << "Enter a positive integer; <-999> to quit . ";
   cin >> num;
} while ((num > 0) && (num != -999));
```

- **do . . . while** and **while** are variable control loops; **for** is usually a fixed control loop.
- **while** and **for** are pretest loops; **do . . . while** is a post-test loop.
- Any one of these loops can be nested within any other of the loops.
- Indenting each loop is important for program readability.
- Several levels of nesting make the logic of a program difficult to follow.
- Loops and conditionals are frequently used together. Careful program design will facilitate writing code in which these concepts are integrated; typical forms are

```
while (<condition1>) do
{
     .
     .
     .

    if (<condition2>)
         .
         .
         .
```

```
        else
          .
          .
          .
    } // end of while
```

◆ and

```
    if <condition>
    {
        .
        .
        .
        for (j = <value1>; j <= <valueN>; ++j)
        {
              .
              .
              .
        } // end of for loop . . .
    } // end of if...else
            .
            .
            .
```

PROGRAMMING PROBLEMS AND PROJECTS

1. The Caswell Catering and Convention Service (Problem 12, Chapter 4, and Problem 14, Chapter 5) wants you to upgrade their program so they can use it for all of their customers.
2. Modify your program for a service station owner (Focus on Program Design, Chapter 5) so that it can be used for an unknown number of customers. Your output should include the number of customers and all other pertinent items in a daily summary.
3. Modify the Community Hospital program (Problem 17, Chapter 5) so that it can be run for all patients leaving the hospital in one day. Include appropriate bad data checks and daily summary items.
4. The greatest common divisor (gcd) of two integers *a* and *b* is a positive integer *c* such that *c* divides *a*, *c* divides *b*, and for any other common divisor *d* of *a* and *b*, *d* is less than or equal to *c*. (For example, the gcd of 18 and 45 is 9.) One method of finding the gcd of two positive integers (*a*, *b*) is to begin with the smaller (*a*) and see if it is a divisor of the larger (*b*). If it is, then the smaller is the gcd. If not, find the next largest divisor of *a* and see if it is a divisor of *b*. Continue this process until you find a divisor of both *a* and *b*. This is the gcd of *a* and *b*.

Write an interactive program that will accept two positive integers as input and then print out their gcd. Enhance your output by printing all divisors of *a* that do not divide *b*. A sample run could produce

```
Enter two positive integers. 42 72

The divisors of 42 that do not divide 72 are:

        42
        21
        14
         7

The gcd of 42 and 72 is 6.
```

5. The least common multiple (LCM) of two positive integers *a* and *b* is a positive integer *c* such that *c* is a multiple of both *a* and *b* and for any other multiple *m* of *a* and *b, c* is a divisor of *m*. (For example, the LCM of 12 and 8 is 24.) Write a program that allows the user to enter two positive integers and then print the LCM. The program should guard against bad data and should allow the user the option of "trying another pair" or quitting.

6. A perfect number is a positive integer such that the sum of the proper divisors equals the number. Thus, 28 = 1 + 2 + 4 + 7 + 14 is a perfect number. If the sum of the divisors is less than the number, it is deficient. If the sum exceeds the number, it is abundant.

a. Write a program that allows the user to enter a positive integer and then displays the result indicating whether the number entered is perfect, deficient, or abundant.

b. Write another program that allows the user to enter a positive integer *N* and then displays all perfect numbers less than or equal to *N*.

Your programs should guard against bad data and should allow the user the option of entering another integer or quitting.

7. In these days of increased awareness of automobile mileage, more motorists are computing their miles per gallon (mpg) than ever before. Write a program that will perform these computations for a traveler. Data for the program will be entered as indicated by the following table:

Odometer Reading	Gallons of Fuel Purchased
18828 (start)	—
19240	9.7
19616	10.2
19944	8.8
20329	10.1
20769 (finish)	10.3

The program should compute the mpg for each tank and the cumulative mpg each time the tank is filled. Your output should produce a chart with the following headings:

```
Odometer   Odometer   Fuel     Miles    Fuel     Miles    Mpg      Mpg
(begin)    (end)      (tank)   (tank)   (trip)   (trip)   (tank)   (trip)
```

8. Parkside's Other Triangle is generated from two positive integers, one for the size and one for the seed. For example,

Size 6, Seed 1	Size 5, Seed 3
1 2 4 7 2 7	3 4 6 9 4
3 5 8 3 8	5 7 1 5
6 9 4 9	8 2 6
1 5 1	3 7
6 2	8
3	

The size gives the number of columns. Seed specifies the starting value for column 1. Column *n* contains *n* values. The successive values are obtained by adding 1 to the previous value. When 9 is reached, the next value becomes 1.

Write a program that reads pairs of positive integers and produces Parkside's Other Triangle for each pair. The check for bad data should include checking for seeds between 1 and 9 inclusive.

9. Modify the sewage, water, and sanitation problem (Problem 19, Chapter 5) so that it can be used with data containing appropriate information for all residents of the community.

10. Modify the program for the Lucky Wildcat Well Corporation (Problem 20, Chapter 5) so that it can be run with data containing information about all of Al Derrick's wells.

11. Modify the program concerning the Mathematical Association of America (Problem 21, Chapter 5). There will be 50 official state delegates attending the next summer national meeting. The new data file will contain the two-letter state abbreviation for each delegate. Output should include one column with the state abbreviation and another with the amount reimbursed.

12. In Fibonacci's sequence, *0, 1, 1, 2, 3, 5, 8, 13, . . .* the first two terms are 0 and 1 and each successive term is formed by adding the previous two terms. Write a program that will read positive integers and then print the number of terms indicated by each integer read. Be sure to test your program with data that includes the integers 1 and 2.

13. Dr. Lae Z. Programmer is at it again. Now that you have written a program to compute the grade for one student in his class (Problems 5, 22, and 23, Chapter 5), he wants you to modify this program so it can be used for the entire class. He will help you by making the first entry be a positive integer representing the number of students in the class. Your new version should compute an overall class average and the number of students receiving each letter grade.

14. Modify the Pentagon parking lot problem (Problem 26, Chapter 5) so that it can be used for all customers in one day. In the new program, time should be entered in military style as a four-digit integer. The lot opens at 0600 (6:00 a.m.) and closes at 2200 (10:00 p.m.). Your program should include appropriate summary information.

15. The Natural Pine Furniture Company (Problem 7, Chapter 4) now wants you to refine your program so that it will print a one-week pay report for each employee. You do not know how many employees there are, but you do know that all information for each employee is on a separate line. Each line of input will contain the employee's initials, the number of hours worked, and the hourly rate. You are to use the constant definition section for the following:

Federal withholding tax rate	18%
State withholding tax rate	4.5%
Hospitalization	$25.65
Union dues	$ 7.85

Your output should include a report for each employee and a summary report for the company files.

16. Orlando Tree Service, Incorporated, offers the following services and rates to its customers:

a. Tree removal $500 per tree
b. Tree trimming $80 per hour
c. Stump grinding $25 plus $2 per inch for each stump whose diameter exceeds ten inches. The $2 charge is only for the diameter inches in excess of ten.

Write a complete program to allow the manager, Mr. Sorwind, to provide an estimate when he bids on a job. Your output should include a listing of each separate charge and a total. A 10% discount is given for any job whose total exceeds $1000. Typical data for one customer are

```
R 7
T 6.5
G 8    8    10    12    14    15    15    20    25
```

where **R**, **T**, and **G** are codes for removal, trimming, and grinding, respectively. The integer following **G** represents the number of stumps to be ground. The next line of integers represents the diameters of stumps to be ground.

17. A standard science experiment is to drop a ball and see how high it bounces. Once the "bounciness" of the ball has been determined, the ratio gives a bounciness index. For example, if a ball dropped from a height of 10 feet bounces 6 feet high, the index is 0.6 and the total distance traveled by the ball is 16 feet after one bounce. If the ball were to continue bouncing, the distance after two bounces would be 10 ft + 6 ft + 6 ft + 3.6 ft = 25.6 ft. Note that distance traveled for each successive bounce is the distance to the floor plus 0.6 of that distance as the ball comes back up.

Write a program that lets the user enter the initial height of the ball and the number of times the ball is allowed to continue bouncing. Output should be the total distance traveled by the ball. At some point in this process, the distance traveled by the ball becomes negligible. Use the constant section to define a "negligible" distance (for example, 0.00001 inches). Terminate the computing when the distance becomes negligible. When this stage is reached, include the number of bounces as part of the output.

18. Write a program that prints a calendar for one month. Input consists of an integer specifying the first day of the month (1 = Sunday) and an integer specifying how many days are in a month.

19. An amortization table shows the rate at which a loan is paid off. It contains monthly entries showing the interest paid that month, the principal paid, and the remaining balance. Given the amount of money borrowed (the principal), the annual interest rate, and the amount the person wishes to repay each month, print an amortization table. (Be certain that the payment desired is larger than the first month's interest.) Your table should stop when the loan is paid off, and should be printed with the following heads.

```
MONTH NUMBER      INTEREST PAID      PRINCIPAL PAID      BALANCE
```

20. Computers work in the binary system, which is based on powers of 2. Write a program that prints out the first 15 powers of 2 beginning with 2 to the zero power. Print your output in headed columns.

21. Print a list of the positive integers less than 500 that are divisible by either 5 or 7. When the list is complete, print a count of the number of integers found.

22. Write a program that reads in 20 real numbers, then prints the average of the positive numbers and the average of the negative numbers.

23. In 1626, the Dutch settlers purchased Manhattan Island from the Indians. According to legend, the purchase price was $24. Suppose that the Indians had invested this amount at 3% annual interest compounded quarterly. If the money had earned interest from the start of 1626 to the end of last year, how much money would the Indians have in the bank today? (*Hint:* Use nested loops for the compounding.)

24. Write a program to print the sum of the odd integers from 1 to 99.

25. The theory of relativity holds that as an object moves, it gets smaller. The new length of the object can be determined from the formula:

$$\text{NewLength} = \text{Original Length} * \sqrt{(1 - B^2)}$$

where B^2 is the percentage of the speed of light at which the object is moving, entered in decimal form. Given the length of an object, print its new length for speeds ranging from 0 to 99% of the speed of light. Print the output in the following columns:

```
Percent of Light          Speed          Length
----------------          -----          ------
```

26. Mr. Christian uses a 90%, 80%, 70%, 60% grading scale on his tests. Given a list of test scores, print out the number of A's, B's, C's, D's, and F's on the test. Terminate the list of scores with a sentinel value.

27. The mathematician Gottfried Leibniz determined a formula for estimating the value of pi (π):

$$\pi/4 = 1 - 1/3 + 1/5 - 1/7 + 1/9 - 1/11 + \ldots$$

Evaluate the first 200 terms of this formula and print its approximation of π.

28. In a biology experiment, Carey finds that a sample of an organism doubles in population every 12 hours. If she starts with 1000 organisms, in how many hours will she have 1 million?

29. C++ does has a function that permits raising a number to a power. We can easily write a program to perform this function, however. Given an integer to represent the base number and a positive integer to represent the power desired, write a program that prints the number raised to that power.

30. Mr. Thomas has negotiated a salary schedule for his new job. He will be paid one cent ($0.01) the first day, with the daily rate doubling each day. Write a program that will find his total earnings for 30 days. Print your results in a table set up as follows:

```
Day Number    Daily Salary          Total Earned
     1             .01                   .01

     2             .02                   .03

     3              .                     .

     .              .                     .

     .              .                     .

    30
```

31. Write a program to print the perimeter and area of rectangles using all combinations of lengths and widths running from 1 foot to 10 feet in increments of 1 foot. Print the output in headed columns.

32. Teachers in most school districts are paid on a salary schedule that provides a salary based on their number of years of teaching experience. Suppose that a beginning teacher in the Babbage School District is paid $19,000 the first year. For each year of experience after this up to 12 years, a 4% increase over the preceding value is received. Write a program that prints a salary schedule for teachers in this district. The output should appear as follows:

```
Years Experience                     Salary

       0                            $19,000

       1                            $19,760

       2                            $20,550

       3                            $21,372

       .                               .

       .                               .

       .                               .

      12
```

(Actually, most teacher's salary schedules are more complex than this. As an additional problem, you might like to find out how the salary schedule is determined in your school district and write a program to print the salary schedule.)

33. The Euclidean algorithm can be used to find the greatest common divisor (gcd) of two positive integers (n_1, n_2). For example, suppose $n_1 = 72$ and $n_2 = 42$; you can use this algorithm in the following manner:

(1) Divide the larger by the smaller:

72 = 42 * 1 + 30

(2) Divide the divisor (42) by the remainder (30):

42 = 30 * 1 + 12

(3) Repeat this process until you get a remainder of zero:

30 = 12 * 2 + 612 = 6 * 2 + 0

The last nonzero remainder is the gcd of n_1 and n_2.

Write a program that lets the user enter two integers and then prints each step in the process of using the Euclidean Algorithm to find their gcd.

34. Cramer's Rule for solving a system of equations was given in Problem 31, Chapter 5. Add an enhancement to your program by using a loop to guarantee that the coefficients and constants entered by the user are precisely those that were intended.

35. Gaussian Elimination is another method used to solve systems of equations. To illustrate, if the system is

$$x - 2y = 1$$
$$2x + y = 7$$

Gaussian Elimination would start with the augmented matrix

$$\begin{bmatrix} 1 & -2 & 1 \\ 2 & 1 & 7 \end{bmatrix}$$

and proceed to produce the identity matrix on the left side

$$\begin{bmatrix} 1 & 0 & 3 \\ 0 & 1 & 1 \end{bmatrix}$$

At this stage, the solution to the system is seen to be $x = 3$ and $y = 1$.

Write a program in which the user enters coefficients for a system of two equations containing two variables. The program should then solve the system and display the answer. Your program should include the following:

a. A check for bad data

b. A solvable system check

c. A display of partial results as the matrix operations are performed.

36. A Pythagorean triple consists of three integers *A*, *B*, and *C* such that $A^2 + B^2 = C^2$. For example, 3 , 4, 5 is such a triple because $3^2 + 4^2 = 5^2$. These triples can be generated by positive integers *m*, *n*, ($m > n$) where $a = m^2 - n^2$, $b = 2mn$, and $c = m^2 + n^2$. These triples will be primitive (no common factors) if *m* and *n* have no common factors and are not both odd. Write a program that allows the user to enter a value for *m* and then prints all possible primitive Pythagorean triples such that $m > n$. Use one function to find the greatest common factor of *m* and *n*, another to see if *m* and *n* are both odd, and another to guard against overflow. For the input value of $m = 5$, typical output would be

```
m   n   a   b   c   a²   b²   c²

2   1   3   4   5    9   16   25

3   2   5  12  13   25  144  169

4   1  15   8  17  225   64  289

4   3   7  24  25   49  576  625

5   2  21  20  29  441  400  841

5   4   9  40  41   81 1600 1681
```

37. This chapter's Focus on Program Design problem determined whether or not an integer was prime by checking for divisors less than or equal to the square root of the number. The check started with 2 and incremented trial divisors by 1 each time as seen by the code

```
prime = TRUE;
divisor = 2;
limit_for_check = sqrt(candidate);
while ((divisor <= limit_for_check) && prime)
     if (candidate % Divisor == 0)
         prime = FALSE;
     else
         divisor = divisor + 1;
```

Other methods can be used to determine whether or not an integer *N* is prime. For example, you may

a. check divisors from 2 to *N* - 1 incrementing by 1.

b. check divisors from 2 to (*N* - 1)/2 incrementing by 1.

c. check divisor 2, 3, 5, . . . (*N* - 1)/2 incrementing by 2.

d. check divisor 2, 3, 5, . . . sqrt(*N*) incrementing by 2.

Write a program that allows the user to choose between these options in order to compare relative efficiency of different algorithms. Use a function for each option.

38. The prime factorization of a positive integer is the positive integer written as the product of primes. For example, the prime factorization of 72 is

72 = 2 * 3 * 3 * 4

Write a program that allows the user to enter a positive integer and then displays the prime factorization of the integer. A minimal main program could be

```
num = get_a_number ();
if (number_is_prime(num))
     cout << num<< " is prime" << endl;
else
     print_factorization(num);
```

Enhancements to this program could include an error trap for bad dta and a loop for repeated trials.

39. As you might expect, instructors of computer science do not agree on whether a **do . . . while** loop or a **while** loop is the preferred variable control loop in C++. Interview several computer science instructors at your institution to determine what preference (if any) they have regarding these two forms of repetition. Prepare a class report based on your interviews. Include advantages and disadvantages of each form of repetition.

40. Examine the repetition constructs of at least five other programming languages. Prepare a report that compares and contrasts repetition in each of the languages. Be sure to include information such as which languages provide for both fixed and variable repetition and which languages have more than one kind of variable repetition. Which language appears to have the most desirable form of repetition? Include your rationale for this decision in your report.

41. Examine some old computer science texts and talk to some computer science instructors who worked with the early languages to see how repetition was achieved in the "early days." Prepare a brief chronological chart for class display that depicts the various stages in developing repetition.

CHAPTER 7 Strings

CHAPTER OUTLINE

Thus far in this text, you have been designing algorithms to solve problems, and coding your solutions in C++ using the major control structures of sequencing, selection, iteration, and functional abstraction. In this chapter, we begin a shift in focus that will guide us through the rest of the text. We consider how to solve problems by structuring the data of a program appropriately, using strings as our first example.

We have been using strings in C++ programs for the purpose of displaying messages to the user. However, many problems require that we be able to take strings as input from the user and analyze them. For example, names, words, phrases, and sentences are frequently used as part of some information that must be analyzed. Word processing programs would be very difficult to design and implement without high-level algorithms and data structures for string processing.

We began this chapter by examining how to represent a string as a data type. We will show how to declare string variables that can be input and output with the standard operators. Then we will study some standard C++ library functions for processing string variables, and write some functions of our own for analyzing them. Finally, we will use strings to explore the design and implementation of new data types with C++ *classes.*

7.1 Thinking of Strings as an Abstract Data Type

Data Abstraction

When designing the solution to a problem initially we are not concerned about the specifics of how data will be manipulated. These are implementation details that can (and should) be dealt with at a fairly low level in a modular development. The properties of a data structure, however, are part of the design at a fairly high level.

The separation between the conceptual definition of a data structure and its eventual implementation is called *data abstraction.* This process of deferring details to the lowest possible level parallels the method of designing algorithms; that is, design first and do implementation details last.

Abstract Data Types

Two abstraction concepts have been previously discussed: functional or procedural abstraction and data abstraction. A third form of abstraction arises from the use of data types. In Chapter 4, we mentioned that one kind of module in a program consists of a set of operations and related data. We referred to a module of this kind as an *abstract data type,* and pointed out that such modules already exist in

OBJECTIVES

- to understand the need for data abstraction and abstract data types in a program
- to understand how to define a string type and declare string variables
- to understand how to initialize string variables with input or assignment
- to understand how to output string variables
- to understand how to represent and access the component parts of a string represented as an array
- to understand how to use standard string library functions to perform such operations as comparisons

programming languages for standard data types such as **int, float**, and **char**. We now provide a more formal definition of an abstract data type:

> An abstract data type (ADT) consists of a set of values, a defined set of properties of these values, and a set of operations for processing the values.

Note that the definition of an ADT makes no mention of how it is implemented, or even of the uses to which it may be put in a program. We have not been overly concerned about the implementation details of any of the standard abstract data types in C++. Indeed, we have barely been aware of them at all. In this and the following chapters, you will learn how to construct new data types that both solve interesting problems and behave in a similar way—so as not to distract users with detail. Your growth as a computer scientist will be enhanced if you develop a perspective of abstract data types and use this perspective in the design of problem solutions.

The String ADT

Strings are used to represent textual information. Strings themselves have an internal structure consisting of a sequence of character values. To keep our discussion of strings simple for the moment, we will ignore how strings are represented in the memory of computers and how their component parts are manipulated. We will focus only on the operations it would be useful to have on whole strings, and defer the details of their implementation until later sections. Some of the most useful operations on strings follow:

1. The input of string data from the keyboard into a string variable
2. The output of string data from a string variable to the terminal screen
3. Copying of data from one string variable to another
4. Testing two strings for the relationships less than, greater than, or equality.

Programmers who use these operations are called *clients* of the string type. Clients would like to view the string operations abstractly. That is, the only information about these operations available to clients should be the declarations of C++ functions and their supporting comments. If the required functions are already available in a standard C++ library, clients can simply use these. If they are not available, other programmers, called *servers,* will have to write them and make them available to clients as a new library. The main point here is that clients who use strings should know as little about their internal representation as clients who use standard data types such as **int** and **char**. For example, a client of strings should be able to write the following code, which displays the numerically greater of two integer values and the alphabetically greater of two string values:

```
int x, y;
string name1, name2;

cout << "Enter two integers, separated by a space: ";
cin >> x >> y;
if (x > y)
        cout << x << endl;
else
        cout << y << endl;
cout << "Enter two names, separated by a space: ";
```

```
cin >> name1 >> name2;
if (string_greater(name1, name2))
        cout << name1 << endl;
else
        cout << name2 << endl;
```

Note that the client declares string variables in the same way as integer variables, simply by using a type name and a list of variable names. Note also that the use of the operations does not reveal how they are implemented or how the data are represented. In the following sections, we will play the roles of clients who use the abstract string data type and servers who implement it, though in large software projects, clients and servers are seldom the same individuals.

Before we can play the role of clients who declare and use string variables, we must play the role of servers who define a data type to represent strings. We begin by presenting a fairly formal specification of the operations provided by the string ADT. The inputs, outputs, and any other assumptions about the data or the effects of the operations are described in terms of preconditions and postconditions, as introduced in Chapter 5:

Input operation
Preconditions: The parameter is a string variable in an unpredictable state.
Postconditions: String variable contains a string value input from the keyboard.

Output operation
Preconditions: The parameter is a string variable, appropriately initialized.
Postconditions: The value of the variable is displayed on the screen.

Copy operation
Preconditions: The first parameter is a string variable in an unpredictable state. The second parameter is a string literal, or a string variable appropriately initialized. The number of characters stored in the second parameter does not exceed the maximum physical size of the first parameter.
Postconditions: The value of the second parameter is copied into the first parameter.

Length operation
Preconditions: The parameter is a string variable, appropriately initialized.
Postconditions: The number of characters currently in the string is returned.

Equality operation
Preconditions: The two parameters are string variables appropriately initialized.
Postconditions: The Boolean value TRUE is returned if the strings are equal, and FALSE is returned otherwise.

Less than operation
Preconditions: The two parameters are string variables appropriately initialized.
Postconditions: The Boolean value TRUE is returned if the first string is less than the second string, and FALSE is returned otherwise.

Greater than operation
Preconditions: The two parameters are string variables appropriately initialized.
Postconditions: The Boolean value TRUE is returned if the first string is greater than the second string, and false is returned otherwise.

Implementing the String ADT

Perhaps the quickest and easiest way to implement a string ADT is to do so in a way that is compatible with the way that strings are implemented and used by two important C++ libraries, the **string.h** library and the **iostream.h** library. This strategy, called *software reuse,* gives clients immediate access to many high-level operations for string processing, including input and output operations.

We represent a string as an *array of characters.* This representation is compatible with the one used in the standard libraries. For now, the only thing we need to know is that an array of characters is a sequence of memory locations capable of storing many characters. The size or number of memory locations available in any array is specified by an integer constant in the type definition. Here is an example of code that uses an integer constant and an array type to define a new string type name:

```
const int MAX_STRING_SIZE = 11;
typedef char string[MAX_STRING_SIZE];
```

The form of the type definition that uses an array is

typedef <element type> <new type name>[integer constant];

You have already seen **typedef** used to create a synonym, **boolean**, for a predefined type, **int**, in Chapter 5. The present example specifies that **char** is the type of data stored in each memory location in an array, **string** is the name of the type, and **MAX_STRING_SIZE** is the number of memory locations available in any string variable for storing characters.

Declaring String Variables

When a string type name is available, we can play the role of clients by using the type name to declare string variables. Our example of code can be extended with the declaration of two variables:

```
const int MAX_STRING_SIZE = 11;
typedef char string[MAX_STRING_SIZE];
string first_name, last_name;
```

Several comments are in order at this point:

1. When the computer encounters the variable declarations, it reserves memory for two arrays that can store 11 characters each.
2. The computer places a special character called the *null character,* represented by '\0' in C++, in the first memory cell in each array. The rest of the data in the two arrays is unpredictable.
3. The null character is used by several standard C++ string library functions as a sentinel value to detect the end of the character data actually in a string variable at any given time. Library functions that insert characters into string variables will move the null character to the appropriate position to indicate the new end of the string. The null character is not counted as part of the string data, and programmers normally need not concern themselves with processing it. However, its presence in all strings implies that the size of the

◆ FIGURE 7.1
Memory allocated for two new string variables

first_name	\0										
	0	1	2	3	4	5	6	7	8	9	10
last_name	\0										

arrays used to represent the strings must always be one greater than the maximum number of characters stored in the arrays. Thus, in our example, **MAX_STRING_SIZE** is 11, but the array will represent strings of up to 10 characters in length.

The state of the two string variables in this example is illustrated in Figure 7.1. Note that each memory cell in the arrays is labeled with a number, ranging from 0 to 10, and that the null character is stored at position 0. We will demonstrate shortly how to use these numbers to access individual characters within strings.

Input and Output of String Variables

If we use the standard input and output streams, **cin** and **cout**, the input and output of string variables become very easy. To input a string from the keyboard into a string variable, we use the name of the string variable in an input statement. For example, assuming that string variables are declared as above, the statements

```
cout << "Enter the first name: ";
cin >> first_name;
cout << "Enter the last name: ";
cin >> last_name
```

will prompt the user to enter two names at the keyboard. The computer handles string input at the keyboard in the same way it handles numeric input. Leading and trailing whitespace characters are ignored. The string data are entered into a string variable when a carriage return is encountered or the next string data appear on a line.

The following statement would input two strings separated by whitespace characters, without prompting the user:

```
cin >> first_name >> last_name;
```

Suppose the user entered the names "Mary" and "Lopez" at the keyboard. The state of the two string variables would be as shown in Figure 7.2. Note that the computer has moved the null character to the right of the input data in each string.

◆ FIGURE 7.2
String variables after input of string values

first_name	M	a	r	y	\0						
	0	1	2	3	4	5	6	7	8	9	10
last_name	L	o	p	e	z	\0					

Once string variables have been modified with input statements, their contents can be displayed on the terminal screen with output statements. For example, the following statement displays the full name just entered:

```
cout << "The full name is " << first_name << " "
     << last_name << endl;
```

The computer displays all of the characters in the arrays, up to but not including the null character. The format of string data for output is handled in the same way as numeric data. A string can be aligned in a desired column by using **setw** to specify a field width:

```
cout << setw(40) << first_name << " " << last_name
     << endl;
```

EXAMPLE 7.1

This example is a C++ program that prompts for the user's name and age and responds with a message.

```
// Program file: strio.cpp

#include <iostream.h>

const int MAX_STRING_SIZE = 11;
typedef char string[MAX_STRING_SIZE]
string first_name, last_name;

int main()
{
      string first_name, last_name;
      int age;

      cout << "Enter your first name: ";
      cin >> first_name;
      cout << "Enter your last name: ";
      cin >> last_name;
      cout << "Enter your age: ";
      cin >> age;
      cout << first_name << " " << last_name << ", you're only " << age
            << " years old?" << endl;
      return 0;
}
```

A run of this program with sample input produces

```
Enter your first name: John
Enter your last name: Barleycorn
Enter your age: 43
John Barleycorn, you're only 43 years old?
```

Assignment to String Variables

One common way to initialize a string variable is to assign a value to it when it is declared. The form for this declaration is

<string type name> <variable name> = <string value>;

where **<string value>** is a *string literal* or sequence of characters enclosed in double quotes. For example, the declarations

```
const int MAX_STRING_SIZE = 11;
typedef char string[MAX_STRING_SIZE];
string first_name = "John";
string last_name = "Barleycorn";
```

would not only reserve memory for two strings, but initialize them with string values as well. The state of the two string variables is shown in Figure 7.3.

Two comments are in order at this point.

◆ FIGURE 7.3
String variables after initialization

first_name	J	o	h	n	\0						
	0	1	2	3	4	5	6	7	8	9	10
last_name	B	a	r	l	e	y	c	o	r	n	\0

1. Because C++ does no *range bound error* checking with arrays, you should be careful to use string literals whose lengths are less than the size of the target string variables. *The length of a string literal should be at most one character less than the size of the target string variable.*
2. *A declaration is the only place where you can assign a string variable a value.* All other attempts to assign values to string variables will cause errors in most C++ implementations. You might think that this restriction would prohibit common operations such as copying a string value from one variable into another, but we will demonstrate an easy way to do this in a moment.

Using Standard String Library Functions

Once we have initialized string variables, it would be useful to be able to copy their contents to other string variables or to compare two strings for their lexicographic order. The use of the built-in assignment and comparison operations with string variables is not supported in most C++ implementations. However, there are several functions in the standard **string.h** library that cover our needs for assignment and comparison fairly well.

The first of these functions, **strcpy**, has the form

strcpy(<destination string variable>, <source string>)

This function will copy the source string, including its null character, into the destination string variable. In effect, the function performs the assignment

<destination string variable> = <source string>

which is normally disallowed in many implementations of C++. The source string or second parameter to **strcpy** can be either a string variable or a string literal. The first parameter or destination string variable is modified as a result of the operation. Once again, care should be taken that the length of the source string is less than the maximum size of the destination string variable.

EXAMPLE 7.2

This example is a C++ program that uses a temporary string variable to exchange the values of two other string variables. Note the use of the assignment operator to initialize the string variables in the declaration, and the use of **strcpy** to perform the same operation in the statements.

```
// Program file: strswap.cpp

#include <iostream.h>
#include <string.h>

const int MAX_STRING_SIZE = 21;
typedef char string[MAX_STRING_SIZE];

int main()
{
      string first_name = "John";
      string last_name = "Doe";
      string temp;

      cout << first_name << " " << last_name << endl;
      strcpy(temp, first_name);
      strcpy(first_name, last_name);
      strcpy(last_name, temp);
      cout << first_name << " " << last_name << endl;
      return 0;
}
```

The output of this program would be

```
John Doe
Doe John
```

Another operation that is frequently used with strings is comparison. Each string has some lexicographic relationship to any other string, as defined by the collating sequence of characters within the strings. For example, the strings "hi", "there", and "Jane" are in the lexicographic relationship "Jane" < "hi"< "there" (note that 'J' precedes 'h' as an ASCII value). However, we cannot use the operator < in a program to demonstrate this relationship. Instead, we can use the standard string library function **strcmp**. This function has the form

strcmp(<left string>, <right string>)

where the left string is a variable or literal that would appear to the left of a comparison operator, and the right string is a variable or literal that would appear to the right of a comparison operator. Neither the left string nor the right string is modified. The function has the following behavior:

1. It returns an integer less than 0 if the left string is less than the right string.
2. It returns 0 if the left string is equal to the right string.
3. It returns an integer greater than 0 if the left string is greater than the right string.
4. It returns an integer less than 0 if the left string is a substring of the right string, beginning with the first character in each string.

EXAMPLE 7.3

The following C++ program compares two input strings and displays a message about their lexicographic relationship:

```
// Program file: strcomp.cpp

#include <iostream.h>
#include <string.h>

const int MAX_STRING_SIZE = 21;
typedef char string[MAX_STRING_SIZE];

int main()
{
      string name1, name2;
      int order;
      char sign;

      cout << "Enter the first name: ";
      cin >> name1;
      cout << "Enter the second name: ";
      cin >> name2;
      order = strcmp(name1, name2);
      if (order < 0)
              sign = '<';
      else if (order > 0)
              sign = '>';
      else
              sign = '=';
      cout << name1 << " " << sign << " " << name2 << endl;
      return 0;
}
```

Here are several sample runs of this program:

```
Enter the first name: Mary
Enter the second name: Mary
Mary = Mary

Enter the first name: Jane
Enter the second name: Bill
Jane > Bill

Enter the first name: Jane
Enter the second name: Marks
Jane < Marks

Enter the first name: William
Enter the second name: Williams
William < Williams
```

Another useful string library function, **strcat**, *concatenates* one string to the end of another string. This function is used to build larger strings out of smaller ones. Its form is

strcat(<first string>, <second string>);

where the first string is a string variable and the second string is either a variable or a literal. **strcat** places the characters in the second string at the end of the characters in the first string, and returns the result in the first string. Note that the first string is modified, but the second string is not.

The last string library function that we will introduce is **strlen**. Its form is

strlen(<string>)

This function takes a string variable or literal as a parameter, and returns the number of characters currently in the string. Recall that a declaration of a string variable merely reserves space in computer memory for holding string data. Until the string is initialized with data, its length is actually zero. After the string is initialized, its length can range up to one less than the size of the array that represents the string. The following piece of C++ code will output zero immediately after the string variable is declared, and then output its new length after the user initializes it:

```
const int MAX_STRING_SIZE = 21;
typedef char string[MAX_STRING_SIZE];
string name;

cout << strlen(name) << endl;
cout << "Enter your name: ";
cin >> name;
cout << strlen(name) << endl;
```

A sample run of this code would produce

```
0
Enter your name: Beatrice
8
```

EXAMPLE 7.4

This example is a C++ program that checks for a possible range bound error before it concatenates one string to another one.

```
// Program file: strcheck.cpp

#include <iostream.h>
#include <string.h>

const int MAX_STRING_SIZE = 21;
typedef char string[MAX_STRING_SIZE];

int main()
{
      string first_name1, last_name

      cout << "Enter the first name: ";
      cin >> first_name
      cout << "Enter the second name: ";
```

```
        cin >> last_name2;
        if (strlen(first_name1) + strlen(last_name) >= MAX_STRING_SIZE)
                cout << "ERROR: not enough memory to concatenate names.";
        else
        {
                strcat(first_name, last_name);
                cout << first_name;
        }
        cout << endl;
        return 0;
}
```

Note that the test for the error computes the sum of the lengths of the two input strings. This will be the length of the string that results from the concatenation. The length of this new string must be at most one less than the size of the array representing it.

Accessing Characters Within String Variables

Because we represent string variables as arrays of characters, we can access individual characters at different positions in a string by using an operation called *array indexing.* An *index* is an integer value used to specify a memory location in an array. In C++, the index of the first memory location in an array is 0, the index of the second is 1, and so on, until the index of the last memory location in the array, which is always the size of the array minus 1. Array indexing is used both to get the value of data stored in a memory location and to store data there as well. For example, the following code stores the character 'a' in the first position in a string, and then outputs the value at that position:

```
const int MAX_STRING_SIZE = 21;
typedef char string[MAX_STRING_SIZE];
string name;

name[0] = 'a';
cout << name[0] << endl;
```

The general form of an array indexing operation is

<array variable>[<integer value>]

The integer value can be an integer literal, an integer variable, a symbolic integer constant, or any other expression that returns an integer value. There are two important points to make about array indexing with strings:

1. If MAX_STRING_SIZE is the size of the array, then a reference of the form

   ```
   <string variable>[MAX_STRING_SIZE]
   ```

   is a range bound error and could cause the program to behave mysteriously at run time. With array indexing, `<string variable>[MAX_STRING_SIZE - 1]` indicates the position of the last data location in the array, and `<string variable>[0]` indicates the first data location.

2. The null character normally will be found one index position beyond the last character of the string currently stored in an array. Thus, if **strlen(<string variable>)** is the number of characters in the string, the reference

```
<string variable>[strlen(<string variable>)]
```

will be to the array cell containing the null character.

Much string processing at the character level consists of traversing the array of characters with a loop. The general form of a loop that visits every character in a string should be

```
int length = strlen(string_variable);

for (int index = 0; index < length; ++index)
        do something with string_variable[index];
```

Note that the first character visited in the array is at position 0, whereas the last character visited is at position **length - 1**. If the string's length is 0, then the body of the loop is not entered and no characters are visited at all. Note also that we compute the length of the string before the loop is started. If we computed the string's length in the heading of the loop, the program might be very inefficient.

EXAMPLE 7.5

Suppose a user wishes to count the number of instances of a given character in a string. The user enters the string and the character at the keyboard, and the program displays a count of the number of instances of the character in the string. The following C++ program would solve this problem:

```
// Program file: charcnt.cpp

#include <iostream.h>
#include <string.h>

const int MAX_STRING_SIZE = 21;
typedef char string[MAX_STRING_SIZE];

int main()
{
      string word;
      char ch;
      int count, length;

      cout << "Enter the word: ";
      cin >> word;
      cout << "Enter the character to be counted: ";
      cin >> ch;
      length = strlen(word);
      count = 0;
      for (int j = 0; j < length; ++j)
              if (word[j] == ch)
                      ++count;
```

```
    cout << "There are " << count << " " << ch << "s in "
         << word << endl;
    return 0;
}
```

A sample run of this program would produce

```
Enter the word: macadamia
Enter the character to be counted: a
There are 4 a's in macadamia
```

EXERCISES 7.1

1. Indicate which of the following string comparisons are TRUE or FALSE using the full ASCII character set.
   a. "Mathematics" less than "CompScience"
   b. "Jefferson" less than "Jeffersonian"
   c. "Smith Karen" less than "Smithsonian"
   d. "Tom" greater than "apple"
   e. "#45" less than or equal to "$45"
   f. "Hoof in mouth" less than "Foot in door"
   g. "453012" greater than "200000"
2. Write a test program that allows you to examine the following Boolean expressions.
   a. "William Joe" < "Williams Bo"
   b. "James" > "Jameson"
3. Assume the following declarations.

```
typedef char string20[20];
typedef char string10[10];
string20 a = "There are 19 chars.";
string20 b = "Only 14 chars.";
string10 c = "8 chars.";
```

   a. Indicate whether the following are valid or invalid.

```
  i. a = b;
 ii. c = a + b;
iii. strcpy(b, a);
 iv. strcpy(c, b);
  v. strcat(b, c);
 vi. for (int j = 0; j < 20; ++j)
       c[j] = a[j] + b[j];
vii. for (int j = 0; j < 20; ++j)
       if (j <= 10)
           a[j] = c[j];
       else
           b[j] = c[j];
```

   b. Write a segment of code that will make the string **c** consist of the strings **a** and **b** where the lesser (alphabetically) of **a** and **b** is the first part of **c**.
4. Assume string variable **word** of size 100 has been declared and data have been read into it from the keyboard. Write a segment of the code to count the number of occurrences of the letter 'M' in the string **word**.

Defining String Functions

OBJECTIVES

- to learn how to write functions that process an array implementation of strings
- to learn how to pass strings as parameters to functions
- to learn about some useful string processing functions
- to learn how to place the code for an abstract data type in a program library

Now that we are armed with a high-level representation of string variables and some high-level standard C++ operations, we can focus on building some useful string processing functions of our own. First of all, it would be useful to create string comparison functions that correspond more closely to the standard C++ comparison operators <, =, and >. The string library function **strcmp** returns one of three possible integer values, depending on which of these relationships is true. For example, we would like a function with a more specific name, **string_equal**, that returns a Boolean value and can be used in the context of Boolean expressions in **if** statements and loops. We will design and implement **string_equal**, and leave the development of other string comparison functions as exercises.

The declaration of **string_equal** is

```
// Function: string_equal
// Tests two strings to see if they are equal
//
// Inputs: two strings
// Output: Boolean value TRUE, if the strings are equal,
// FALSE otherwise

boolean string_equal(string str1, string str2);
```

The implementation simply checks the result of calling the **strcmp** function with the two parameters:

```
boolean string_equal(string str1, string str2)
{
      return strcmp(str1, str2) == 0;
}
```

Many string processing operations test individual characters for certain properties or modify the characters in some way. For example, it would be useful to determine whether a string contains only digits, or to convert the letters in a string to uppercase. For this reason, C++ provides a standard library of character processing functions, **ctype.h**. The forms of two typical character functions, **isdigit** and **toupper**, are

isdigit(<character value>)

toupper(<character value>)

isdigit tests the character parameter to determine whether it is a digit. If it is, the function returns a nonzero value. If it is not, the function returns zero. Several other functions exist that perform tests of this sort in the **ctype.h** library. All of them are prefixed with **is**. **toupper** tests the character parameter to determine whether it is a lowercase letter. If it is, the function returns the corresponding uppercase letter. If it is not, the function returns the original character parameter. None of the functions in the **ctype.h** library modifies its parameters.

Functions for processing strings as input parameters are defined like any other functions in C++. You decide on an appropriate name to describe the task, and then specify the input for the function. Let's write a function that tests a string to see whether it can represent an integer. This function would be useful for detecting errors in numeric input from the keyboard. The function takes a string as a parameter, and returns a Boolean value. This value will be TRUE if all of the characters in the string are digits, or FALSE otherwise. The declaration of the function is:

```
// Function: is_integer
// Tests for a valid decimal representation of an integer
//
// Input: a string
// Output: a Boolean value (TRUE if valid, FALSE otherwise)

boolean is_integer(string str);
```

The implementation examines each character in the string, until a character is not a digit or the last character is reached. We use a **while** loop to terminate execution when the first nondigit is found:

```
boolean is_integer(string str)
{
        boolean no_bad_digits = TRUE;
        int i, length;

        i = 0;
        length = strlen(str);
        while (no_bad_digits && (i < length))
                if (! isdigit(str[i]))
                        no_bad_digits = FALSE;
                else
                        ++i;
        return no_bad_digits;
}
```

EXAMPLE 7.6

This example is a C++ program that checks an input string to see whether it is a valid representation of an integer:

```
// Program file: intcheck.cpp

#include <iostream.h>
#include <string.h>
#include <ctype.h>

#include "boolean.h"

const int MAX_STRING_SIZE = 21;
typedef char string[MAX_STRING_SIZE];

// Function: is_integer
// Tests for a valid representation of an integer
//
// Input: a string
// Output: a Boolean value (TRUE if valid, FALSE otherwise)

boolean is_integer(string str);
```

```
int main()
{
      string number;

      cout << "Enter an integer: ";
      cin >> number;
      if (is_integer(number))
            cout << "A valid representation";
      else
            cout << "Not a valid representation";
      cout << endl;
      return 0;
}

boolean is_integer(string str)
{
      boolean no_bad_digits = TRUE;
      int i, length;

      i = 0;
      length = strlen(str);
      while (no_bad_digits && (i < length))
            if (! isdigit(str[i]))
                  no_bad_digits = FALSE;
            else
                  ++i;
      return no_bad_digits;
}
```

Here are several sample runs of this program:

```
Enter an integer: 3214
A valid representation

Enter an integer: 3,214
Not a valid representation

Enter an integer: 3.214
Not a valid representation
```

Now that we have a function to check that a string is a valid representation of an integer, it is useful to write a function that converts a valid representation to the corresponding integer value. The declaration of this function, which will accept a string representation of an integer as a parameter and return the corresponding integer, is

```
// Function: to_integer
// Converts a string representation to an integer
//
// Input: a string representing an integer in digits
// Output: the corresponding integer value

int to_integer(string str);
```

The implementation of the function assumes that the string parameter represents an integer. Therefore, it uses a **for** loop to visit each character in the string. The algorithm for converting a string of digits to an integer value is not difficult. Each digit in the string represents a power of ten. As the loop visits each digit from left to right in the string, it multiplies a running total by 10 and adds the integer value represented by the digit to the total. The running total is initially zero. Here is the algorithm:

```
Set total to 0
For each digit from the leftmost to the rightmost do
       Set total to 10 * total
       + the integer value represented by the digit
```

As you saw in Chapter 3, the integer value represented by a digit is obtained by subtracting '0' from the digit. The implementation of **to_integer** is

```
int to_integer(string str)
{
       int length, total;

       length = strlen(str);
       total = 0;
       for (int j = 0; j < length; ++j)
               total = 10 * total + str[j] - '0';
       return total;
}
```

EXAMPLE 7.7

This example is a C++ program that accepts only valid integer input from the keyboard before using it in computation.

```
// Program file: toint.cpp

#include <iostream.h>
#include <string.h>
#include <ctype.h>

#include "boolean.h"

const int MAX_STRING_SIZE = 21;
typedef char string[MAX_STRING_SIZE];

// Function: is_integer
// Tests for a valid decimal representation of an integer
//
// Input: a string
// Output: a Boolean value (TRUE if valid, FALSE otherwise)

boolean is_integer(string str);

// Function: to_integer
// Converts a string representation to an integer
//
// Input: a string representing an integer in digits
// Output: the corresponding integer value
```

```
int to_integer(string str);

int main()
{
      string number;

      cout << "Enter an integer: ";
      cin >> number;
      if (is_integer(number))
            cout << "The integer is " << to_integer(number);
      else
            cout << "Not a valid representation";
      cout << endl;
      return 0;
}

boolean is_integer(string str)
{
      boolean no_bad_digits = TRUE;
      int i, length;

      i = 0;
      length = strlen(str);
      while (no_bad_digits && (i < length))
            if (! isdigit(str[i]))
                  no_bad_digits = FALSE;
            else
                  ++i;
      return no_bad_digits;
}

int to_integer(string str)
{
      int length, total;

      length = strlen(str);
      total = 0;
      for (int j = 0; j < length; ++j)
             total = 10 * total + str[j] - '0';
      return total;
}
```

Here are several sample runs of this program:

```
Enter an integer: 3214
3214

Enter an integer: 3,214
Not a valid representation

Enter an integer: 3.214
Not a valid representation
```

Our final example of a programmer-defined string function is one that modifies its parameter. This function converts the letters in its string parameter to uppercase. This function will be useful for handling case sensitivity in searching and sorting problems in Chapter 10. In C++, the contents of array parameters can be modified even though they are not declared as reference parameters. The reason for this is that the address of the actual array parameter is passed to the function, even when the & symbol is not included in the declaration. In fact, you should be careful to omit the & symbol from a declaration in any case of array parameters. The declaration of our **make_uppercase** function for strings is

```
// Function: make_uppercase
// Converts the letters in a string to uppercase
//
// Input: a string
// Output: the input string with the letters converted to uppercase

void make_uppercase(string str);
```

The implementation uses a **for** loop to visit every character in the string. It passes each character to the **toupper** function mentioned previously. The result is stored back into the string:

```
void make_uppercase(string str)
{
        int length = strlen(str);

        for (int j = 0; j < length; ++j)
                str[j] = toupper(str[j]);
}
```

Building a Library of String Functions

As we begin to write more programs that use string variables, it becomes tedious to type out or even copy the associated data type definitions and function implementations for each new program. It would be convenient to package all of this code in a separate file and have the system bring it into any application that uses it automatically. We can accomplish this by building our own library to be included by any program that needs to use strings. Put another way, we would like to separate the roles of clients and server for the string type by confining the server to the task of writing the string library, and clients to the task of using the library. We introduced the concept of a programmer-defined library in Chapter 5, where we placed the definitions of Boolean constants and a type name in such a file.

Our new library will contain the constant and type definitions for the string type. It will also contain the string processing functions developed so far in this chapter. The code is written in two files that are separate from the client program files. We will call these files **strlib.h** and **strlib.cpp. strlib.h** is called a *header file.* A header file contains the definitions of constants and types and the function declarations that are available to clients. The contents of our header file will have the form

```
#ifndef <file identifier>
<constant and type definitions>
<function declarations>
#define <file identifier>
#endif
```

Note the use of the preprocessor directives **#ifndef, #define**, and **#endif**. These directives are used to prevent the preprocessor from including a library file more than once in an application at compile time. Thus far in this text, we have not had to worry about this possibility, because only one client, the main program application, has been including files. However, the string library file will now include the **boolean.h** file, and a main program application may do so as well. The new directives work to prevent multiple inclusions from occurring as follows:

1. The first directive, **#ifndef**, asks if a file identifier has been defined. If it has, that means that the library file has already been preprocessed, so the preprocessor skips the current inclusion by jumping to **#endif** at the end of the file.
2. If the file identifier has not been defined, the preprocessor will reach the **#define** directive after preprocessing the library file. This directive then makes visible a global file identifier, so that the next inclusion after this one will behave as in step 1.

For example, the **boolean.h** header file should be rewritten so that multiple inclusions will be avoided:

```
// Library header file: boolean.h

#ifndef BOOLEAN_H

const int TRUE = 1;
const int FALSE = 0;

typedef int boolean;

#define BOOLEAN_H
#endif
```

Note that the file identifier, **BOOLEAN_H**, is not likely to be used by an application or another library file.

An example header file for the library with the functions we have developed so far in this chapter is

```
// Library header file: strlib.h

#ifndef STRINGLIB_H

#include "boolean.h"

const int MAX_STRING_SIZE = 21;
typedef char string[MAX_STRING_SIZE];

// Function: string_equal
// Tests two strings to see if they are equal
//
```

```
// Inputs: two strings
// Output: Boolean value TRUE, if the strings are equal, FALSE otherwise

boolean string_equal(string str1, string str2);

// Function: is_integer
// Tests for a valid representation of an integer
//
// Input: a string
// Output: a Boolean value (TRUE if valid, FALSE otherwise)

boolean is_integer(string str);

// Function: to_integer
// Converts a string representation to an integer
//
// Input: a string representing an integer in digits
// Output: the corresponding integer value

int to_integer(string str);

// Function: make_uppercase
// Converts the letters in a string to uppercase
//
// Input: a string
// Output: the input string with the letters converted to uppercase

void make_uppercase(string str);

#define STRINGLIB_H
#endif
```

The other library file for the string type, **strlib.cpp**, is called an *implementation file.* This file contains the implementations of the functions for the library, as well as preprocessor directives to include any other libraries required for the implementation:

```
// Library implementation file: strlib.cpp

#include <string.h>
#include <ctype.h>
#include "strlib.h"

// Function implementations

boolean string_equal(string str1, string str2)
{
      return strcmp(str1, str2) == 0;
}

boolean is_integer(string str)
{
```

```
        boolean no_bad_digits = TRUE;
        int i, length;

        i = 0;
        length = strlen(str);
        while (no_bad_digits && (i < length))
                if (! isdigit(str[i]))
                        no_bad_digits = FALSE;
                else
                        ++i;
        return no_bad_digits;
}

int to_integer(string str)
{
        int length, total;

        length = strlen(str);
        total = 0;
        for (int j = 0; j < length; ++j)
                total = 10 * total + str[j] - '0';
        return total;
}

void make_uppercase(string str)
{
        int length = strlen(str);

        for (int j = 0; j < length; ++j)
                str[j] = toupper(str[j]);
}
```

Note that the new library includes the two standard C++ library header files **string.h** and **ctype.h**. The header file for our own library, **strlib.h**, is also included, so that the implementation has access to the data and function declarations.

The code in the library can now be tested. All we need is a small main program to serve as a driver for our library. For example, the following program might test the library we have written thus far:

```
// Program file: testib.cpp

#include <iostream.h>

#include "boolean.h"
#include "strlib.h"

int main()
{
        string word1, word2, number;

        cout << "Testing strlib functions." << endl << endl;
        cout << "Testing string_equal." << endl;
```

```
    cout << "Enter two different words several times, "
         << "and then two identical words." << endl << endl;
    do
    {
          cout << "Enter the first word: ";
          cin >> word1;
          cout << "Enter the second word: ";
          cin >> word2;
    } while (! string_equal(word1, word2));
    cout << "Testing make_uppercase." << endl;
    make_uppercase(word1);
    cout << word1 << endl;
    cout << "Testing is_integer." << endl;
    cout << "Enter several bad representations of integers," << endl;
    cout << "and then a good one." << endl << endl;
    do
    {
            cout << "Enter an integer: ";
            cin >> number;
            cout << "The integer is " << number << endl;
    } while (! is_integer(number));
    cout << "Testing to_integer." << endl;
    cout << "Enter several good representations of integers," << endl;
    cout << "and then a bad one." << endl << endl;
    cout << "Enter an integer: ";
    cin >> number;
    while (is_integer(number))
    {
            cout << "The integer is " << to_integer(number) << endl;
            cout << "Enter an integer: ";
            cin >> number;
    }
    cout << "Testing completed." << endl;
    return 0;
}
```

A sample run of this program would be

```
Testing strlib functions.

Testing string_equal.
Enter two different words several times,
and then two identical words.

Enter the first word: Mark
Enter the second word: Mary
Enter the first word: Janice
Enter the second word: Mary
Enter the first word: Mary
Enter the second word: Mary
Testing make_uppercase.
MARY
Testing is_integer.
Enter several bad representations of integers, and then a good one.
```

```
Enter an integer: 34.5
The integer is 34.5
Enter an integer: 67.4
The integer is 67.4
Enter an integer: 21
The integer is 21
Testing to_integer.
Enter several good representations of integers, and then a bad one.
Enter an integer: 16
The integer is 16
Enter an integer: 1034
The integer is 1034
Enter an integer: 4.6
Testing completed.
```

This little driver program tests the tools provided by our library. If there are syntax errors in the library file, the preprocessor will detect them before the file is included. The library file can be easily built and tested incrementally. A more complete version of our library is left as an exercise. Another library implementation, using a C++ class definition, is developed in Section 7.3.

EXERCISES 7.2

1. Add the other two string comparison functions, **string_less** and **string_greater**, to the library **strlib.cpp**.
2. Write separate string comparison functions for equal to, less than, and greater than that are not case sensitive.
3. Write a function **make_lowercase** that changes the uppercase letters in its string parameter to lowercase letters.
4. Write a character processing function, **isvowel**, that tests a character to determine whether or not it is a vowel. Use the function in a program to count the number of vowels in an input string.
5. Write a function **remove_punctuation** with one string parameter. The function should modify its parameter by removing the punctuation mark ('.', ',', '?', '!', ':', or ';') at the end of the string, if there is one.
6. Write a function **capitalize** with one string parameter. The function should modify its parameter by capitalizing its first letter and making all of the other letters lowercase.
7. Write a function **string_swap** that exchanges the values of two string variables.
8. Clients of our abstract string type would like to examine individual characters in strings, without having to perform array indexing. Write a function **nth_char** that takes two parameters, a string and the position of a desired character, and returns the character at the specified position in the string. Specify in the declaration that the position parameter must range from one to the length of the string, inclusive.
9. Write a function **append_char**. This function takes a string and a character as parameters. If there is room for the character in the string, the function places it after the last character (be sure to move the null character over, as well). If there is no room for the character in the string, the function does nothing.
10. The constant definition for the maximum length of all strings is located in the **strlib.h** file. This means that all applications that include this file will be restricted to the use of strings of this maximum size. Explain how you could place this definition in some other part of the system so that different applications could specify their own maximum sizes of strings.

A NOTE OF INTEREST

Why Computer Scientists Number Things from Zero to *N* – 1

In Chapter 1, we mentioned that C++ incorporates features of high-level programming languages that make programs easy to read, modify, and maintain, and features of low-level programming languages that give programmers control over the structure and behavior of real computers. The numbering of array indices from zero rather than one is one of the low-level features of the language that calls for further comment.

An array index is numbered from zero in C++ because of the way in which the individual array cells are represented and accessed in the computer's memory. You can think of the computer's memory as a huge stack of cells or little boxes. Each cell has an address, which allows the computer to locate it and either fetch data from it or store data in it. Now, suppose that five of these cells have to be allocated for a new array variable in a program. The computer locates the next available contiguous block of five cells, and copies the address of the first cell into a sixth cell. This address will be the *base address* of the entire array. Suppose this base address is 276 in our example, and a programmer wishes to store data in the second cell of the array. The address of the second cell, or 277, can be computed by taking the base address of the array, or 276, from the sixth cell and adding 1 to it. The address of the third cell can be obtained by adding 2 to the base address, the address of the fourth cell by adding 3, and so on. In general, the address of the *N*th cell in an array can be computed by adding *N* – 1 to the base address. The value *N* – 1 is called the *offset* of the *N*th cell from the base address. The offset of the first cell in any array is zero, and the offset of the last cell is *N* – 1, where *N* is the total number of cells in the array.

There is also a more important reason why an array index is numbered from zero. The address of the first cell in the entire memory of a computer typically is zero. The address of the last cell in memory is then *N* – 1, where *N* is the total number of cells in memory. You might think that computer scientists are a weird bunch, having set up computer systems so that their internal components are numbered in a way that is consistently off by one from the way that ordinary folks would number them. However, there is a very good reason to number things from zero to *N* – 1 in computers. Each address must itself be capable of being stored in a memory cell in the computer. As you know, a memory cell can store a number of finite size. The size of the number represented depends on the number of bits available in the memory cell. In general, numbers ranging from zero to $2^N - 1$ can be stored in a memory cell containing *N* bits. For example, numbers ranging from zero to 255 and representing the ASCII character set can be stored in eight-bit memory cells.

Most computer scientists agree that it would be better to number an array index from one to *N* in a high-level programming language. This notation would be more intuitive and agree with common sense. Some languages, like Pascal, allow the programmer to specify the lowest and highest index values when an array type is defined, and a Pascal programmer typically will define an index from one to *N*. The compiler then takes care of translating a reference like **`a[1]`** to the underlying machine address **`a[0]`**.

You might then ask why the designers of C++ still made array indexing a low-level feature of the language. The reason is that programmers can then manipulate arrays not just with standard indexing, but with *pointer arithmetic*. Assume the reference **`a[1]`** in C++ adds 1 to the base address of the array **`a`**. Then the reference **`a`** by itself is to the base address of the array. Therefore, the reference **`*(a + 1)`** locates the same array cell in memory as the reference **`a[1]`**. Needless to say, pointer arithmetic is an even lower level feature of C++ than regular indexing, and is not recommended for novices!

7.3 Recasting the String Type as a Class

Abstract Data Types and Data Security

Viewed as an abstract data type, the string type developed in the preceding sections consists of a set of high-level operations, such as copying, input, output, comparisons, and concatenation. Viewed as a C++ implementation, the string type consists of a **`typedef`** and several C++ function definitions. Some of these definitions are provided in the C++ library **`string.h`**, while we have created the others in a library **`strlib.h`**. Though this implementation of the string ADT is quite useful, it is not ideal. The primary problem is that the data in the implementation are not secure. There are too many ways in which client modules

OBJECTIVES

- to understand problems with data security that arise during the development of abstract data types
- to learn about implementing abstract data types as classes that guarantee data security
- to examine the implementation and use of the string ADT as a class
- to learn the advantages of using classes rather than **typedef** in C++

can access the data and cause side effects. For example, the length of a given string should change only as a result of running string processing functions with it, typically with code like

```
string greeting;                         // Length of the
                                         // string is 0 here.

strcpy(greeting, "Hi");                  // Length of the
                                         // string is 2 here.

strcat(greeting, " There!");             // Length of the
                                         // string is 9 here.
```

Given the scope rules of C++, nothing prevents the user of this module from removing the null character, **'\0'**, which marks the end of the data in the string, from its current position in the array. The following line of code does just that:

```
greeting[strlen(greeting)] = ' ';       // Substitute ' ' for
                                         // '\0' in string.
```

Because the null character has been overwritten in the array, the length of the string is now undefined. Many of the string processing functions will no longer operate as expected with this string.

Errors due to side effects in large software systems are usually more subtle than this one. But the problem is quite general. What we would like to do is to develop a way of writing a software module that restricts the access that users have to the module's data to just those operations or functions provided by the module. Program comments, warnings, and self-imposed restraint are not enough: These restrictions must be imposed by the compiler of the programming language. In other words, statements such as the last one should be prohibited outside of the module that implements the data structure.

Data Encapsulation and Classes

An ADT should give clients just a *logical view* of the data, in terms of the operations on it, so that clients need not be concerned with the details of how the data are *represented.* For example, a string ADT might have operations for assignment, output, input, and comparisons. Ideally, the user of a string should not be able to access its component parts except by invoking these operations. If this is the case, the data are said to be *encapsulated.* Clearly, if we can encapsulate the data within modules, then we can control the kind of communication among modules that causes errors in large software systems, and we will be less likely to disturb other modules during the maintenance of a given module.

C++ allows programmers to define ADTs as *classes.* By defining an ADT as a class, we can restrict the access that clients have to the data of any objects or *instances* of that class. An instance of a class or an object is like an intelligent agent that takes a request for a service from a client and processes its own internal data to carry out the request.

We now show how to define and implement strings as a class. Since this is your first opportunity to define and implement a C++ class, do not expect to master all of the details right away. We will develop other ADTs as classes in later chapters, and we will use the string class developed here in the rest of the text.

Declaring a String Class

At a minimum, the string class should provide clients with the following operations:

1. Create string objects and name them with variables.
2. Input data into a string object.
3. Output a string object.
4. Copy the contents of a string object to another string object.
5. Compare two string objects for the standard relationships of equality, etc.
6. Examine the current length of a string object.
7. Examine the character at a given position in a string object.
8. Append a character to the end of a string object.

As in Section 1, these operations should be specified more formally, in terms of their preconditions and postconditions. For example, the **append** operation should assume that the current length of the string is less than the maximum number of characters that can be stored in a string. The ADT can enforce conditions, where necessary, by invoking the C++ **assert** function introduced in Chapter 5. The development of these specifications is left as an exercise.

A description of an individual class in C++ consists of two parts, a *declaration section* and an *implementation section,* which are usually placed in separate files. This arrangement resembles the one we used in Section 7.2 for constructing a new library. The first file for our string class, called **strlib.h**, contains the declaration section of the class. Its text appears as follows:

```
// Class declaration file: strlib.h

#ifndef STRLIB_H

#include <iostream.h>

#include "boolean.h"

// Declaration section

const int MAX_STRING_SIZE = 21;

class string
{

      public:

      // Class constructors

      string();
      string(const char str[MAX_STRING_SIZE]);
      string(const string &str);

      // Member functions

      int length();
      char nth_char(int n);
```

```
        void append_char(char ch);
        boolean operator == (const string &str);
        boolean operator < (const string &str);
        boolean operator > (const string &str);
        boolean operator <= (const string &str);
        boolean operator >= (const string &str);
        boolean operator != (const string &str);
        string& operator = (const char str[MAX_STRING_SIZE]);
        string& operator = (const string &str);
        friend istream& operator >> (istream &is, string &str);
        friend ostream& operator << (ostream &os, const string &str);

        private:

        // Data members

        char data[MAX_STRING_SIZE];

};

#define STRLIB_H
#endif
```

The general form for writing a simple class declaration section in C++ is

```
<preprocessor directives>
<constant definitions>
class <class name>
{
        public:
        <public data declarations>
        <public function declarations>
        private:
        <private data declarations>
        <private function declarations>
};
```

Several items call for further comment:

1. The data and the functions belonging to a class are called its *members.* The data are sometimes called *data members,* and the functions are sometimes called *member functions.*
2. *Public* members can be used directly by the client of the class. They should be restricted to the minimum necessary to serve a client.
3. *Private* members cannot be used directly by a client. Private member functions may be invoked indirectly by invoking public member functions, and private member data may be accessed indirectly by invoking public member functions.
4. The declarations of the member functions look exactly like the declarations of other functions in C++.
5. A semicolon must follow the right curly brace at the end of the declaration part of the class.

6. Note that the single data member declared in the string class declaration, **data**, is an array of characters. This is just the representation that we used in Section 7.1, but now the array and its components will not be directly accessible to clients.

Implementing a String Class

For the implementation of the string class, we will borrow some ideas about representing the character data in a string from the array implementation in Section 7.1. By doing this, our new implementation can continue to draw on and benefit from the string operations provided by the C++ library **string.h**.

The string class implementation section will have the form

```
// Class implementation file: strlib.cpp
// Implementation section
#include <string.h>
#include <ctype.h>
#include <assert.h>
#include "strlib.h"
<function implementation 1>
.
.
<function implementation n>
```

The headings of the function implementations must have the form

```
<return type> <class name>::<function name> (<optional parameter list>)
```

This form enables the compiler to resolve conflicts with the names of other, globally defined functions. Otherwise, data declarations and function implementations have the same syntax as those you have already seen in C++.

Creating Instances of a String Class with Class Constructors

Instances of a class, or objects, can be created in C++ in several ways. We can declare one or more instances as variables. If no *class constructors* are provided in the class declaration, the computer creates the named instances and leaves their data members in an unpredictable state, just as with ordinary C++ variable declarations. To guarantee that new instances of a class always have their data members initialized, you should specify class constructors for that purpose.

Default Class Constructors

Our string class declaration specifies three class constructors. The first constructor, **string()**, is run when a program declares string variables as in the following code:

```
string first_name, last_name;
```

This kind of class constructor is called a *default class constructor*. It should provide a reasonable initial value for an object when the client does not specify one. In this case, clients want the two strings that are to be initialized to be empty. Thus, the implementation of the default constructor function should set the first character in the array data member to the null character:

```
string::string()
{
        data[0] = '\0';
}
```

Note that the implementer references the array data member, **data**, for the string object even though it is not visible as a parameter. The use of the prefix **string**:: in a function heading allows the data and other member functions of the string class to be visible in the function implementation. Note also that the class constructor has no return type.

Class Constructors for Specifying Initial Values

The second constructor, **string(const char str[MAX_STRING_SIZE])**, is run when clients wish to declare a string variable with an initial string value, as in the code

```
string name("John Doe");
```

In this example, the client appears to pass a string literal as a parameter to the variable **name**. What really happens is that the computer runs the second constructor function. This function expects a *constant parameter,* which represents the parameter passing mode of string literals in C++. The implementation of this constructor invokes the **strcpy** function to copy the string literal into the data member for the new string object:

```
string::string(const char str[MAX_STRING_SIZE])
{
        strcpy(data, str);
}
```

Copy Constructors

The third constructor is called the *copy constructor* for the string class. The computer runs this function automatically whenever a string object is passed by value as a parameter to a function. Recall that when C++ passes data by value in a parameter, the data value is copied to a temporary memory location for the use of the function. If a class does not specify its own copy constructor, the computer performs what is known as a *shallow copy* of the object when it is passed by value. In a shallow copy, not all of the object's data members are necessarily copied into temporary memory locations.

To guarantee a complete copy in all situations, we define a copy constructor that takes another string object as a parameter:

```
string::string(const string &str)
{
        strcpy(data, str.data);
}
```

The parameter, a string object, is passed by *constant reference.* This mode of passing parameters combines the efficiency of pass by reference with the safety of pass by value. Though the address of the actual parameter will be passed when the function is called, the compiler will not permit the data in the parameter to be modified. The data member of the new string object, called the *receiver object,* is the first parameter to **strcpy**. The data member of the string object to be copied, called the *parameter object,* is accessed by the expression **str.data**. In general, any of the data members of a parameter like this one can be accessed within a member function in the class implementation by using the form

<parameter name>.<data member name>

Processing Instances of a String Class

Once a string object has been created and initialized, clients can process it by using any public member function. For example, the following code appends the character 's' to a string initialized as "rose":

```
string flower("rose");

flower.append_char('s');
```

Note that the dot notation is used again with an object. In this case, we run a member function by prefixing the object's name and a dot to it. The general form for this operation, called *sending a message to an object,* is

<object name>.<public member function name>(<parameter list>);

The **append_char** member function first uses **assert** to verify that its preconditions are TRUE. Then it adds the character parameter and the null character to the end of the object receiving the message:

```
void string::append_char(char ch)
{
        int length = strlen(data);

        assert(length < MAX_STRING_SIZE - 1);
        data[length] = ch;
        data[length + 1] = '\0';
}
```

Note that unlike the constructor functions, the **append_char** function specifies a return type, **void**, in its implementation. In general, the headings of the function implementations must match up with the declarations in the class declaration module. The implementation of the **length** and **nth_char** member functions is left as an exercise.

String Operators, Polymorphism, and Overloading

Many of the built-in operators in C++ are *polymorphic.* The term *polymorphic* means "many structures." For example, +, ==, and >> are polymorphic for integers and real numbers. This means that the same operators designate the same general operations (arithmetic, comparions, input/output), even though the actual operations performed may vary with the type or structure of the operands (think of the difference between scanning input characters and converting them to an integer and doing the same thing for a real number, even though the symbol >> is used for both).

C++ allows a programmer to reuse any built-in operator (or function name, also) to designate an operation on new data types. This process is called *overloading an operation.* For example, rather than use the named function

```
string_equal(str1, str2)
```

clients can use

```
str1 == str2
```

We begin by specifying the declaration of the member function to be overloaded:

```
boolean operator == (const string &str);
```

Note that **operator** is a reserved word in C++. The receiver object will be the left operand of the comparison, and the parameter object will serve as the right operand. The general form for specifying operators is

<return type> operator <standard operator symbol> (<parameter list>);

The implementation is written by placing a similar form in the function heading:

```
boolean string::operator == (const string &str)
{
        return strcmp(data, str.data) == 0;
}
```

Note that the implementation makes use of the **strcmp** function introduced in Section 7.1.

The operators <=, >=, <, >, and != can all be used to designate and implement the other comparison functions specified in the class declaration module. These functions will have roughly the same form as the one we have developed here, and the implementations are left as exercises.

The string class declaration module specifies two different member functions for assignment:

```
string& operator = (const string &str);
string& operator = (const char str[MAX_STRING_SIZE]);
```

The first one allows assignments of one string variable to another, whereas the second one allows assignments of string literals to string variables. The assignment operator in C++ should normally return an *l-value.* An l-value is an object that can be the target of an assignment operation in C++. In the case of simple assignment statements such as **a = b**;, the l-value returned by the operation is not used. However, in the case of a *cascade* of assignments, such as **(a = b) = c**;, the expression **(a = b)** must return an l-value that can serve as the target of the value **c**. In this case, the l-value returned should be **a**.

For this mechanism to work correctly, the return type of an assignment operator should be a reference to the class of the target object. The return type for our assignment operator for strings is therefore specified as **string&**. The implementations of each assignment operation are similar, but not exactly the same:

```
string& string::operator = (const string &str)
{
       strcpy(data, str.data);
       return *this;
}

string& string::operator = (const char str[MAX_STRING_SIZE])
{
       strcpy(data, str);
       return *this;
}
```

The effect of the first line of code in each implementation should be obvious to you by now. In the first case, we access the parameter object's data member to copy the source string to the receiver string. In the second case, we copy the parameter, a string literal, directly. The effect of the second line of code is to return the receiver object. The reserved word **this** always refers to the address of the receiver object. To gain access within the return statement to the object itself, we apply the *dereference operator* (*) to **this**. The receiver object will be returned as an l-value because the return type is specified as a reference to a class.

Friends of a Class

The other operators that we wish to reuse for the string class are <<, the inserter for output streams, and >>, the extractor for input streams. Instead of code like

```
word.input();
word.output();
cout << endl;
```

we would like to see code like this:

```
cin >> word;
cout << word << endl;
```

Reusing these operators will cause us to extend the definitions in the built-in stream classes in C++. First, we must locate the classes where the operators are already defined. The inserter belongs to the **ostream** class, and the extractor belongs to the **istream** class. These two classes define, respectively, the abstract behavior of all output streams and all input streams in C++. The class **ofstream** (for output files) inherits behavior from **ostream**, the class **ifstream** (for input files) inherits behavior from **istream**, and the class **iostream** (for keyboard and screen) inherits behavior from both **ostream** and **istream**. The class hierarchy diagram in Figure 7.4 depicts the relationships among the stream classes. Some careful changes will allow us to use these operators for both interactive and file

◆ FIGURE 7.4
Class hierarchy diagram of some stream classes

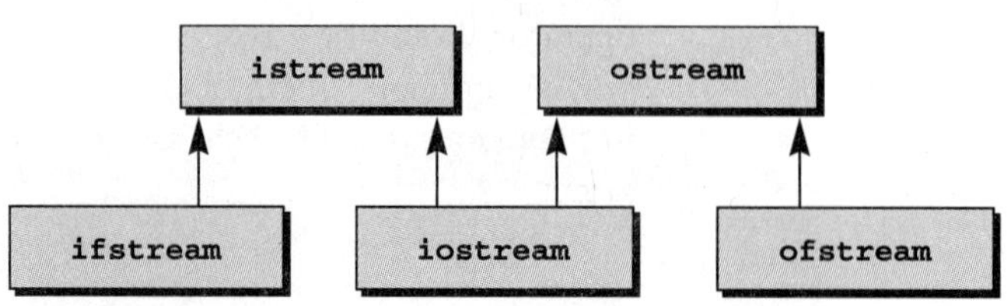

input and output of our string objects. Operations on file streams are discussed in detail in Chapter 9.

There should be files for the **ostream** and **istream** classes somewhere in your C++ implementation. We could add our new definitions of the operators to these files, but that would not be a good design tactic. Modifying a standard C++ library file reduces the portability of a software system, in that these modifications will also have to be made to the corresponding library on any other computer system. Instead, C++ provides a means of overloading an operator from a client class (the stream class, in this case) from within a server's (the string class's) module. This is known as *becoming a friend of a class.* To accomplish this, we prefix the declaration of a member function in the server class with the reserved word **friend**. For example, to reuse the inserter operator of the **ostream** class we write the following declaration:

```
friend ostream& operator << (ostream &os, const string &str);
```

The are two things to note about this declaration.

1. The expression **ostream&** means "address of a stream." This is the type of object returned by the stream operators. Its purpose is to serve as a receiver or l-value for the next message sent in a cascade of messages in a statement, such as

   ```
   cout << "Hi" << " there!" << endl;.
   ```

2. An output stream and a string are passed as parameters to the operator.

The implementation of our extractor accesses the data in the string parameter's array representation and sends it to the output stream parameter:

```
ostream& operator << (ostream &os, const string &str)
{
        os << str.data;
        return os;
}
```

Note that the built-in function designated by the inserter (output an array of characters) is used to implement a new function designated by the inserter (output a string object). One benefit of using << in our implementation is that we do not need to learn anything new about output streams in order to add a new class of objects to those that can be output. Moreover, the use of << allows this behavior to be valid for either output file streams (see Chapter 9) or the standard output stream (the screen).

The extractor operator receives similar treatment. We first declare an extractor that is a friend for the **istream** class:

```
friend istream& operator >> (istream &is, string &str);
```

The implementation of our extractor uses >> to read characters from the stream into the string parameter's array representation.

```
istream& operator >> (istream &is, string &str)
{
        is >> str.data;
        return is;
}
```

In general, when a particular member function of a server class (like our string class) is qualified as a **friend** for a client class (the stream classes in our example), the data and member functions of the server class become accessible to the client class within the implementation of the member function in question.

EXAMPLE 7.8

The following program uses the string class that we have just developed to place two input strings in alphabetical order and output them.

```
// Program file: alphabet.cpp

#include <iostream.h>

#include "boolean.h"

#include "strlib.h"

int main()
{
      string word1, word2, temp;

      cout << "Enter the first word: ";
      cin >> word1;
      cout << "Enter the second word: ";
      cin >> word2;
      if (word1 > word2)
      {
             temp = word1;
             word1 = word2;
             word2 = temp;
      }
      cout << word1 << " " << word2 << endl;
      return 0;
}
```

Classes Versus typedefs

We are now in a position to assess the alternatives of representing a string type with a **typedef** or as a class. First, we summarize the benefits of using **typedef**:

1. We can define a new string type and the associated high-level operations quickly, using techniques we already understand well.
2. Because the representation of a string type as an array is compatible with the representation used in standard C++ stream and string libraries, many high-level operations are already available for our new type.

There is only one apparent cost of using **typedef** to define a string type. The representation of a string is globally defined. Therefore, the representation is unprotected from indiscriminate use by clients.

The most apparent benefit of defining a string type as a class is that the representation is protected. The access of clients to data is limited to operations specified by the string class. The cost of using classes is having to learn some new syntax.

A NOTE OF INTEREST

Pure and Hybrid Object-Oriented Languages

It is possible to classify programming languages in terms of the degree to which they possess object-oriented features. Older languages like FORTRAN, C, and standard Pascal have no object-oriented features at all. None of them supports classes, user-defined polymorphic operators, data encapsulation, or message passing.

Smalltalk and Eiffel purport to be object-oriented languages in a "pure" sense. In these languages, every data type is a class. All data values, including classes themselves, are objects. All subprograms and operators can be overloaded. Data can be fully encapsulated. Every operation on data comes about as a result of a message being sent to an object.

A third class of languages is a hybrid of object-oriented languages and older languages. Many of these are the older languages themselves, with object-oriented features grafted on. For example, C++ is an extension of C. Most current implementations of Pascal have object-oriented extensions. CLOS, or Common LISP Object System, is an object-oriented extension that comes with almost every Common LISP package.

The difference between hybrid languages and the pure object-oriented languages is that it is possible to write programs in a hybrid language that omit the object-oriented features entirely. For example, one could write a large program, or even a large software system consisting of many library modules, in C++ that would be indistinguishable from a C program. This possibility has led to a debate in the computer science community concerning the desirability of hybrid languages.

Proponents of the pure object-oriented languages argue that the object-oriented approach has superceded more traditional styles of programming. Therefore, one should use a language that enforces the superior approach, rather than a language that allows drift or slippage into inferior approaches. Moreover, proponents claim that the pure languages are better vehicles for training new computer scientists, because they enforce object-oriented thinking from the very beginning.

Proponents of the hybrid languages offer several counters to these points. First, it is not clear that object orientation is the best or most natural way to approach all problems. For example, problems in numerical analysis may find more natural solutions in terms of systems of functions, calling for a function-oriented approach. The notion of sending a message to a number to add one to itself seems somewhat silly from this perspective. A hybrid language offers object orientation as one possible approach, among others, that can be chosen when it is the most natural alternative.

Second, although object orientation might be the best possible approach to the design and maintenance of large software systems, smaller programs might be more easily designed and written using traditional techniques of structured programming.

Finally, a pure object-oriented language may not be the best vehicle for teaching programming. Beginning programmers start with simple problems, but pure object-oriented languages do not rest on a simple model of computation. Beginning programmers need to learn about the structure and behavior of real computers, about concepts such as memory, the distinction between an address and a data value, branching, and subprogram calls. Pure object-oriented languages tend to insulate a programmer from these features of real machines.

We suggest that you study and try out several of these languages, if they are available, and make your own judgments about the relative virtues of pure object-oriented and hybrid programming languages.

This assessment applies to the choice of **`typedef`** or class for representing any abstract data type. In general, the benefit of security achieved with encapsulation in classes far outweighs the cost of learning the new syntax. A hidden benefit, which does not appear in our discussion of the string class, is that once a class has been developed, it can be very quickly specialized to create new abstract data types. We will see examples of this power in later chapters.

EXERCISES 7.3

1. Write complete formal specifications for the string class operations listed at the beginning of this section.
2. Implement all the string operations specified by the class declaration, and test the string class with the program from Example 7.8.
3. Describe the difference between the references to **`data`** and **`str.data`** in operations like **`strcpy(data, str.data)`** in the string class implementation.

4. Try to access the data member **data** of a string object in a C++ program, and explain what happens.
5. One could reimplement the auxiliary string processing functions discussed in Section 7.2 either as top-level C++ functions [for example, **is_integer(<string object>)**] or as string member functions [for example, **<string object>.is_integer()**]. Try each of these alternatives in a C++ program, and discuss the advantages and disadvantages of each version.

FOCUS ON PROGRAM DESIGN

Good writing style traditionally has emphasized short to medium-length words and sentences. An important part of text evaluation is obtaining statistics on word and sentence length. This kind of computation is now a standard tool provided with word processing packages. Let us design a small text analysis system that works on individual sentences entered at the keyboard. The program will proceed interactively as follows:

1. The user is prompted for a sentence, which is a series of words ending with a word that is terminated by a period ('.').
2. The system computes and displays statistics about the number of words in the sentence and the average length of a word. It also displays the longest word in the sentence.
3. The user is asked whether another input is desired with a yes/no prompt. If the answer is 'Y', the program repeats steps 1 and 2, and if 'N', the program terminates.

The top-level module runs a simple query driver loop:

Module: Main program
Do
    Prompt for a sentence
    Analyze a sentence
    Query for further input
While query does not equal 'N'

Here is a C++ main program that represents this main program module:

```
void main()
{
      char query;
      do
      {
            cout << "Enter a sentence [terminating with a period ('.')]: ";
            analyze_sentence();
            cout << "Run once more? [Y/N]: ";
            cin >> query;
      } while ((query == 'Y') || (query == 'y'));
      return 0;
}
```

The module to analyze a sentence is responsible for taking input from the keyboard computing the statistics, and displaying them. This process can be described by a loop that reads individual words from the keyboard, until a word terminated by a period is entered:

Module: Analyze a sentence
Task: Read words from keyboard and update statistics, until word ending with '.' is reached

Initialize the data
Do
Input a word
Update the statistics
While the word does not end with '.'
Display the statistics

The statistics will consist of the number of words, the total number of characters in the words, the average length of a word, and the longest word in the sentence. Therefore, this module will need two integer variables and two string variables to maintain the data. The integer data are locally declared, initialized to 0, and simply passed to the other modules for further processing:

```
void analyze_sentence()
{
        string word, longest_word;
        int word_count, char_count;

        word_count = 0;
        char_count = 0;
        do
        {
                cin >> word;
                update_statistics(word, longest_word, word_count, char_count);
        } while (word.nth_char(word, word.length()) != '.');
        display_statistics(longest_word, word_count, char_count);
}
```

The module for updating the statistics is responsible for increasing the count of characters and words, and changing the value of the longest word if necessary.

Module: Update statistics
Task: Adjust character count and word count and adjust longest word if necessary
Inputs: The current input word, the longest word so far, word count, character count

If the length of current input word > length of longest word so far then
    Set longest word so far to current input word
Increment the word count by one
Increment the character count by the length of the input word

Updating statistics compares the length of the current input word to the length of the longest word seen so far. If the new word is longer, it becomes the longest word.

```
void update_statistics(string word, string &longest_word, int &word_count,
        int &char_count)
{
        int length = word.length();

        if (length > longest_word.length())
                longest_word = word;
        ++word_count;
        char_count = char_count + length;
}
```

The display of statistics module computes the average length of a word as a function of the word count and the character count. Then it displays the labeled statistics on the terminal screen:

```
void display_statistics(string longest_word, int word_count, int char_count)
{
        cout << endl << "Number of words: " << word_count << endl;
        cout << "Number of characters: " << char_count << endl;
        cout << "Average length of a word: " << char_count / word_count << endl;
        cout << "Longest word: " << longest_word << endl << endl;
}
```

Our program will use the string class library developed in this chapter. The main C++ program is

```
// Program file: stats.cpp

#include <iostream.h>

#include "boolean.h"

#include "strlib.h"

// <function declarations>

void main()
{
        char query;
        do
        {
                cout << "Enter a sentence [terminating with a period ('.')]: ";
                analyze_sentence();
                cout << "Run once more? [Y/N]: ";
                cin >> query;
        } while ((query == 'Y') || (query == 'y'));
}

// <function implementations>
```

RUNNING, DEBUGGING AND TESTING HINTS

1. When defining a string type as an array of characters, always leave room for the null character in the array. The maximum size of an array should therefore be one greater than the number of characters allowed in a string.
2. Make sure that there is room in a string variable for storing character data. For example, the lengths of the two string parameters should be examined before they are passed to the **`strcat`** function. If the sum of their lengths is less than the maximum size of the string type, then the function can be run safely.
3. When using array indexing to access characters in a string, be careful to avoid range bound errors. In general, a safe array index value is an integer ranging from 0 to one less than the size of the array.
4. Do not use the & symbol when defining string parameters (implemented as arrays) for a function. Array parameters are automatically passed by reference anyway.
5. Be sure to account for case sensitivity when designing string processing programs. For example, the string "Jane" is not the same as the string "jane". Use a case conversion function if case sensitivity should be disabled.
6. Try to run potentially expensive functions, like **`strlen`**, outside of loops.

SUMMARY

Key Terms

array indexing
array of characters
cascade
class
class constructor
class declaration section
class implementation section
client
concatenate
constant parameter
constant reference
copy constructor
data member
encapsulation
friend of a class
header file
implementation file
index
instance
l-value
member function
null character
overloading
polymorphism
range bound error
receiver object
server
software reuse
stream class hierarchy
string literal

Key Words

class
friend
private
public
this

Key Concepts

- Data abstraction is the process of separating a conceptual definition of a data structure from its implementation details.
- An abstract data type (ADT) consists of a class of objects, a defined set of properties for the objects, and a set of operations for processing the objects.
- Strings can be treated as abstract data by defining a string type with **`typedef`**, as follows:

```
const int MAX_STRING_SIZE = 21;
typedef char string[MAX_STRING_SIZE];
```

- Variables and function parameters can then be declared by using the string type, as follows:

```
string last_name, first_name;

boolean string_equal(string str1, string str2);
```

- A number of high-level operations on strings are already available in the C++ libraries **string.h** and **iostream.h**. Software should be reused in this way wherever possible.
- The standard input and output operators, << and >>, can be used for interactive input and output of strings. Where **word** is a string variable, the statements

```
cin >> word;
cout << word << endl;
```

would take input of a string from the keyboard and echo it on the terminal screen.
- The library function **strcpy** can be used to assign or copy the contents of a string to a string variable. The library function **strlen** returns the number of characters currently in a string variable. Where **word** is a string variable, the statements

```
strcpy(word, "Hello");
cout << strlen(word) << endl;
```

would display 5 on the terminal screen.
- The null character (**'\0'**) normally marks the end of the characters currently stored in a string variable. The standard library functions make use of this sentinel character.
- If strings are represented as arrays of characters, we can use array indexing to access individual characters at selected positions in the strings. Where **str1** and **str2** are strings defined in this way, the assignment

```
str2[0] = str1[0]
```

copies the character at the first position in **str1** to the first position in **str2**.
- The loop

```
for (int index = 0; index <= strlen(str1); ++index)
    str2[index] = str1[index];
```

would copy all of the characters, including the null character, in **str1** to **str2**.
- Where **word** is a string variable, the loop

```
for (int index = 0; index <strlen(word); ++index)
    cout << word[index];
```

would display all of the characters in the string variable before the null
- Libraries for abstract data types can be created by specifying a header file and an implementation file.
- Multiple inclusions of a library file can be avoided by using the **#ifndef**, **#define**, and **#endif** preprocessor directives in the library header file, as follows:

```
#ifndef <file identifier>

<constant and type definitions>

<function declarations>

#define <file identifier>
#endif
```

- A class declaration specifies the public and private data and function members for a class of objects.
- A class implementation provides the implementations of the member functions for a class of objects.
- Polymorphic operators have the same general meaning, but can be used with data of different types or classes.
- A polymorphic operator can be reused by declaring a member function as an **operator**.
- A polymorphic operator an also be reused by declaring a function member to be a **friend** of the class in which the operator is defined.

PROGRAMMING PROBLEMS AND PROJECTS

1. Write and test a function, **robust_read_int**, that handles the problem of bad digits in integer input from the keyboard. The function should read the data as a string and test it for bad digits. If all of the digits are valid, the function converts the string representation to an integer value and returns it. Otherwise, the function displays an error message, prompts for new input, and repeats the process until a valid integer is successfully entered. The function should use string library functions wherever possible.
2. Add a parameter to **robust_read_int** from Problem 1 that serves as the prompt to the user for new input. Test the function with prompts from several different applications, such as "Enter the person's age:" or "Enter the number of computers sold:".
3. Write and test a function, **robust_read_float**, that performs the same kind of error handling as **robust_read_int** (Problems 1 and 2), but detects bad digits in real numbers. The function should return a **float** value (remember that C++ allows integers to be assigned to **float** variables).
4. Write and test a program that determines whether or not input strings are palindromes. A palindrome is a string that reads the same forward or backward. Run the program on palidromes such as "TOT" and "MADAMIMADAM", and on strings that are not palindromes, such as "STRING".
5. Write a program that counts the number of times a given word appears in a sentence. The inputs from the keyboard are a given word, and then a sentence, which is a series of words ending in a word that ends with a period ('.'). The program should not be case sensitive.
6. Write a Boolean function, **proper_name**, that tests a string to see whether or not it is a proper name. A proper name begins with an uppercase letter.
7. Write a function, **make_adverb**, that takes a string variable as a parameter. The function assumes that the string represents an adjective. The function should change the string to an adverb by concatenating the string "ly" with it.
8. Write a function, **make_plural**, that takes a string as a parameter. The function assumes that the string represents a noun. If the string ends in 's', the function

changes it to the plural form by adding 'es' to it; otherwise, the function constructs the plural form by simply adding 's'.

9. Write a function, **`strip_punctuation`**, that removes a trailing punctuation mark from a string if one exists.
10. Write a function, **`our_copy`**, that performs the same operation as **`strcpy`** (but does not use **`strcpy!`**).
11. Write a function, **`search_char`**, that takes a string variable and a character value as parameters. The function returns an integer value. This value should be -1 if the character parameter does not occur anywhere in the string. Otherwise, this value should be the position (counting from 0) of the first instance of the character in the string.
12. Write a function, **`position_copy`**, that takes a string variable and two integer values, **`low`** and **`high`**, as input parameters. The function returns a string variable as an output parameter. This output string parameter should contain the portion of the input string that lies between the two integer inputs. You can assume that the user of the function will pass two integer values that are in the relationship

    `0 <= low <= high < length of string.`

13. Write a function, **`substring`**, that takes two string variables as input parameters. If the second string parameter is a substring within the first string parameter, the function returns as its value an integer denoting the starting position of the first occurrence of the substring in the other string. Otherwise, the function returns -1, to indicate that there were no occurrences of the substring in the other string.

CHAPTER

8 Building Structured Data with Classes and Objects

CHAPTER OUTLINE

The first seven chapters of this text have acquainted you with a wide range of tools and techniques for programming and problem solving in C++. The first set of tools is the fundamental operations of arithmetic, assignment, input, and output. The second set of tools consists of the control structures of selection and looping. The third set of tools represents the abstraction mechanisms of functions and data structures and the techniques of structured programming and modular design. You now have the means to design, implement, and test correct, efficient, readable, and maintainable programs that solve interesting problems.

Nevertheless, through the study and development of large and complex software systems over the years, computer scientists have come to the conclusion that the techniques and tools that we have discussed are far from adequate for dealing with the challenges of building these systems. In this chapter, we will discuss how a relatively new method of software development, called *object-oriented programming,* can be added to our arsenal of tools and techniques for problem solving. We begin with a discussion of the basic ideas of this philosophy. Then we introduce some simple examples in C++ that illustrate some of these ideas. Finally, we develop some typical data structures using object-oriented methods.

8.1 The Philosophy of Object-Oriented Programming

OBJECTIVES

- to understand the problems associated with software maintenance
- to understand the way in which reuse of software enhances software maintenance
- to become familiar with some basic terms of object-oriented programming

The Problem of Software Maintenance

Perhaps the most serious problem posed by a large software system is that of *maintaining* it over a period of years. After the initial release of a commercial system, users send complaints about errors and requests for additional features or functions to the developers almost immediately. Before a new version with corrections and additional features or functions can be released, the developers must search through the system to fix the errors and add or remove features or functions. They must do so in such a way as not to disturb other parts of the system that are already working correctly. Moreover, the developers must divide up the maintenance tasks so that they can work independently and efficiently. Finally, some of the developers who maintain the software may not have been on the original development team. All of these factors add time and cost to the maintenance of large software systems.

The tools and techniques of structured programming and modular design go part of the way toward easing the software maintenance task. For example, if an error occurs in a particular function of a system, a programmer might locate the error in a C++ function within a particular library file and be able to fix the problem by changing a single line of code within the function. If an error occurs while the system is using a particular data structure such as a linked list, a programmer might find and correct the problem in the C++ library file where the list processing functions are implemented.

In Chapter 7, we saw that another kind of error, a side effect, is more difficult to track down. Many side effects are caused by allowing clients too much access to the implementation of a module. We also saw that implementing a module as a class in C++ helps to control this kind of side effect by encapsulating or denying clients direct access to the data.

Reuse of Software

Another major factor that adds to the cost of software maintenance is the need to rewrite entire modules to add features or functions to a system. For example, suppose that a module already exists in a bank management system for processing checking accounts. Savings accounts resemble checking accounts to a certain extent, as do the functions for processing each kind of account. However, using conventional structured programming techniques, developers must add a completely new module with a different set of data type definitions and functions for savings accounts. Much of this code will not only be redundant, but may also contain errors.

Developers should be able to *reuse* existing software modules to build new ones. In the example of savings and checking accounts, a developer could write a module for handling the structure and behavior that all accounts have in common. Other developers could then *specialize* this module, with extra data or functions, for more specific kinds of accounts. By reusing software, developers can eliminate the redundancy and many of the errors that occur with more conventional methods. As we will see shortly, object-oriented programming provides a way of reusing software in this manner.

Basic Ideas and Terminology of Object-Oriented Programming

We need to become acquainted with some of the basic ideas and terminology of object-oriented programming before we look at some examples. According to this perspective, an *object* is a collection of *attributes* and *behavior.* The attributes of an object are defined by the data values that are stored in it. For example, the attributes of a student object might be a name ("John Doe"), a class (SOPHOMORE), and a grade point average (3.56). The behavior of an object is defined by the set of *messages* to which it responds. For example, we might send a message to a list object requesting its current length. It would respond by returning its length as a value. Or we might send a message to a list to remove its first element. It would respond by deleting its first element, decrementing its own length, and returning the deleted element as a value. One or more parameters may also be sent with a message to an object. For example, a new element might be sent with a message to insert it into a list object. The list would respond by inserting the element into its proper place and incrementing its own length. If an object does not respond to a message sent to it, the system will halt with an error, preferably at compile time.

We can think of an object as a *server,* to which a user makes requests as a *client.* None of the data belonging to a server is accessible to a client, unless the client invokes a server-defined request to use or modify that data. In other words, the data belonging to an object is fully encapsulated. Figure 8.1 illustrates these concepts.

Each object is an instance of a class that defines its data and behavior. The user of an object obtains its services by creating an instance of its class and then

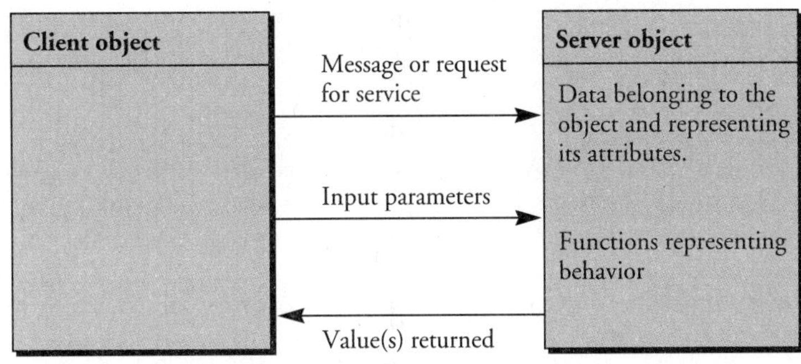

FIGURE 8.1
Anatomy of objects as clients and servers

sending messages to this instance. The implementer of an object defines its services or behavior by defining the class to which the object belongs. An object that passes a message to another object is called the *sender* of the message; the object that receives the message is called the *receiver.*

The common behavior of several classes may be generalized by defining a *base class.* Each of the original, more specific classes can retain its own distinctive behavior as a *derived class.* Behavior can be added to a derived class to specialize it further, even if this behavior redefines the behavior already defined in the base class. The process of adding derived classes therefore allows developers to reuse existing software very easily.

As we saw in Chapter 7, the common behavior of several classes is also expressed by means of overloading the operations that define similar behavior. The operators that designate these operations are said to be *polymorphic,* or to have many forms. A polymorphic operator, such as <, really has one general meaning when used by clients: determine whether two objects are related by less than. But it can have more than one specific meaning when implemented by different server classes, such as integers and strings, which carry out different operations on different data representations to determine the relation.

The following sections illustrate the use of these ideas to develop reusable software modules in C++.

8.2 A Bank Account Class

OBJECTIVES

- to be able to follow the basic steps in the design of a class to solve a problem
- to be able to specify a class abstractly in terms of its attributes and behavior
- to be able to convert an abstract specification of a class to a C++ class declaration module
- to be able to write a C++ implementation module that corresponds to a class declaration

Our first example of the design of a class comes from the domain of finance and data processing.

User Requirements

Consider the problem of managing bank accounts. Banks offer several different kinds of accounts, such as checking, checking with interest, passbook savings, and CD accounts, among others. Security is absolutely essential. We do not want Smith's deposit going into Jones's account, unless it is a joint account. Therefore, we would like to represent different but related classes of bank accounts, and do so in a way that protects the data belonging to each instance of an account.

We can start by thinking of an abstract class called **`account`**. This class will define the data that belong to any account object, and the behavior that any account object should exhibit. The data might be just a balance, represented by a **`float`**. The behavior might be expressed by messages to

1. Deposit an amount.
2. Withdraw an amount.
3. Look up the balance.

A NOTE OF INTEREST

The Origins of the Object-Oriented Philosophy

We saw in an earlier note of interest that a philosophy can serve as the underpinning of a new approach to problem solving and software design. Such was the case with function-oriented programming. This approach was the direct result of efforts of two computer scientists, John McCarthy and John Backus, to bring a certain formal theory of computation, the recursive lambda calculus, to bear on the design of complex software systems. The object-oriented approach to problem solving and software design has a different kind of origin. In this case, there is no single theory of computation we can point to as the model for the approach. Object orientation in languages, programming style, and thinking has evolved over time and is the result of diverse sources and trends that eventually converged on a single body of ideas. However, there is one computer scientist in whose vision these sources and trends have been brought together. This scientist, Alan Kay, recounts the history of the development of the object-oriented philosophy in "The Early History of Smalltalk," *ACM SIGPLAN Notices,* Volume 28, No. 3, March, 1993. Some of the important sources in the development of the object-oriented approach were

Ivan Sutherland's work on an interactive graphical programming environment called *Sketchpad.*
The development of Simula, a language for representing classes of objects.
Kay's work on Smalltalk, the first complete environment for object-oriented software development.
The work of Douglas Engelbart, Daniel Ingalls, Kay, and others at Xerox on WIMP (window, icon, mouse, pull-down menu) user interfaces.

The first two messages would each take one **float** parameter representing the amount, and the object would return a **float** representing the updated balance. The third message would take no parameters, and the object would return a **float** representing the current balance of the account.

In addition to this behavior, clients should be able to create new account objects, either by specifying an initial value for the balance or by assuming that the object will initialize its own balance to 0.00. Clients should also be able to assign a bank account object to a bank account variable, and to pass a bank account parameter by value to a C++ function.

Specifying the Operations

A formal specification of the bank account operations follows:

Create operation (default value)
Preconditions: The account object is in an unpredictable state.
Postconditions: **balance** is set 0.00 in the account object.
Create operation (initial value specified)
Preconditions: The account object is in an unpredictable state, and the parameter **new_balance** is a real number representing the initial amount to be deposited into the account.
Postconditions: **balance** is set to **new_balance** in the account object.
Deposit operation
Preconditions: The receiver object is appropriately initialized, and **amount** is the amount (a real number) to be deposited.
Postconditions: **balance** is increased by **amount**, and its value is returned to the sender.
Withdraw operation
Preconditions: The receiver object is appropriately initialized, and **amount** is the amount (a real number) to be withdrawn.

Postconditions:	If there are sufficient funds, **balance** is decreased by **amount**, and its value is returned to the sender; otherwise, -1 is returned to the sender.
Get balance operation	
Preconditions:	The receiver object is appropriately initialized.
Postconditions:	**balance** is returned to the sender.
Assignment operation	
Preconditions:	The receiver and parameter objects are appropriately initialized.
Postconditions:	The attributes of the parameter object have been copied into the receiver object, and a reference to the receiver is returned.

Declaring the Class

Now that we are aware of the requirements and specifications of an abstract account class, we can implement it in C++. As we saw in Chapter 7, a description of an individual class in C++ usually consists of two parts, a declaration section and an implementation section, that are placed in separate files. The first file for our account class, named **account.h**, contains the declaration section of the class. Its text appears as follows:

```
// Class declaration file: account.h

#ifndef ACCOUNT_H

// Declaration section

class account
{

        public:

        // Class constructors

        account();
        account(float initial_balance);
        account(const account &a);

        // Member functions

        float deposit(float amount);
        float withdraw(float amount);
        float get_balance();
        account& operator = (const account &a);

        private:

        // Data members

        float balance;

};

#define ACCOUNT_H
#endif
```

Note that the copy constructor, which is the third class constructor declared here, was not included in the formal specifications. For every new class introduced in this text, we will assume that clients desire to have a copy constructor, and one will appear in each class declaration.

Implementing the Class

The second file, containing the implementation section of the class, is named **account.cpp**:

```
// Class implementation file: account.cpp

#include "account.h"

// Implementation section

account::account()
{
      balance = 0.00;
}

account::account(float initial_balance)
{
      balance = initial_balance;
}

account::account(const account &a)
{
      balance = a.balance;
}

float account::deposit(float amount)
{
      balance = balance + amount;
      return balance;
}

float account::withdraw(float amount)
{
      if (amount > balance)
            return -1;
      else
      {
            balance = balance - amount;
            return balance;
      }
}

float account::get_balance()
{
        return balance;
}
```

```
account& account::operator = (const account &a)
{
      balance = a.balance;
      return *this;
}
```

EXAMPLE 8.1 The following program illustrates the use of the account class that we have just defined.

```
// Program file: bankdriv.cpp

#include <iostream.h>
#include <iomanip.h>

#include "account.h"

int main()
{
      account judy(50.00);                    // Set up two accounts and a dummy target
      account jim(100.00);
      account target;

      cout << fixed << showpoint << setprecision(2);
      cout << "Judy's balance = $"
           << judy.get_balance() << endl;              // Look up balances
      cout << "Jim's balance = $" << jim.get_balance() << endl;
      cout << "Depositing $20.00 to Jim, new balance = $" // A deposit
           << jim.deposit(20.00) << endl;
      cout << "Result of overdraft from Judy ($51.00) = " // An attempted overdraft
           << judy.withdraw(51.00) << endl;
      target = judy;                                   // Copy to dummy target
      cout << "Target's balance = $" << target.get_balance() << endl;
      return 0;
}
```

The output that this program produces is

```
Judy's balance = $50.00
Jim's balance = $100.00
Depositing $20.00 to Jim, new balance = $70.00
Result of overdraft from Judy ($51.00) = -1.00
Target's balance = $50.00
```

Using the Class with Functions

There are many occasions for which we might want to include a class in a program and process its instances by means of functions. For example, consider the problem of interacting with the user for the input of the amount to withdraw from a bank account. We may already have an application that contains a set of user interface functions created for this purpose. Suppose that this program has represented accounts as real numbers, and we now wish to use our account class. The function for interacting with a user for a withdrawal might have looked like this:

```
typedef float account;
.
.
.
void make_withdrawal(account &this_account)
{
        float amount;

        cout << "Enter the amount to withdraw: ";
        cin << amount;
        if ((amount > this_account) || (amount < 0))
                cout << "Sorry, insufficient funds." << endl;
        else
        {
                this_account = this_account - amount;
                cout << "Thank you. Your new balance is " << this_account << endl;
        }
}
```

Our new version can reuse this function by passing an account object as the parameter, and using member functions to perform the appropriate tasks:

```
void make_withdrawal(account &this_account)
{
        float amount;

        cout << "Enter the amount to withdraw: ";
        cin << amount;
        if ((amount > this_account.get_balance()) || (amount < 0))
                cout << "Sorry, insufficient funds." << endl;
        else
        {
                this_account.withdraw(amount);
                cout << "Thank you. Your new balance is "
                     << this_account.get_balance() << endl;
        }
}
```

An alternative to this approach is to make this function a member of the account class. Then it could be invoked as

```
this_account.make_withdrawal();
```

There are two problems with this second approach:

1. It makes more work for the developer, who must write new code for the account class rather than reuse existing code in the user interface module.
2. It makes application-specific components, such as the messages to the user in a particular context, part of a general class definition. This makes the account class less general and application independent than it should be.

As you can see, the processing of classes and their instances integrates very easily with the more conventional style of programming in C++. This feature enables developers to introduce objects and the object-oriented style into an existing software system without redesigning and rewriting the entire system.

EXERCISES 8.2

Each of these exercises asks you to add attributes or behavior to the bank account class we have just discussed.

1. Add a data member for representing an account user's name, using the string class developed in Chapter 7. Add behavior so that each account is given a user's name when it is created.
2. Add a data member for representing a password, using the string class developed in Chapter 7. Add behavior so that each account is given a password when it is created.
3. Update the member function **get_balance**, **deposit**, and **withdraw** so that each takes a user name and password as parameters. Perform the expected operations only if the name and password sent by the client match the name and password data members of the account. Otherwise, do nothing.
4. Add a data member to maintain a record of the number of times a user has failed to enter the correct name and password. It should be set to zero when the account is created and whenever the user successfully makes a deposit, withdrawal, or balance check. It should be incremented whenever these operations are unsuccessful.
5. Add a **private** member function that is run when the number of failed transactions becomes greater than 3. It should print a message that the user's ATM card is being confiscated.

8.3 A Rational Number Class

OBJECTIVES

- to be able to design a numeric class whose use and behavior are compatible with the use and behavior of built-in numeric data types
- to understand the use of overoaded operations in designing a numeric class with conventional behavior
- to be able to use overloaded operations to implement mixed-mode operations on new classes and built-in data types

Our next example of the design of a class comes from pure mathematics, a different domain than that of finance and data processing. C++ has standard data types for representing real numbers and integers, but not rational numbers. In this section, we develop a new class, called **rational**, that allows applications to use rational numbers in much the same way as the other kinds of numbers are used.

User Requirements

A rational number has two atributes, a numerator and a denominator, both of which are integer values. One constructor operation for rational numbers should therefore take two integer parameters representing these attributes. For example, one might create the rational numbers 1/2 and 5/6 as follows:

```
rational one_half(1, 2);
rational five_sixths(5, 6);
```

The state of the objects representing these two numbers is depicted in Figure 8.2.

Because rational numbers are expressed in the form

$$\frac{numerator}{denominator}$$

definitions of the form

```
rational <name>(<integer>, 0);
```

should not be allowed. Therefore, a precondition of the class constructor is that the denominator can be any integer other than zero.

Clients should be able to perform some standard arithmetic operations on rational numbers and output the resulting values. For example, the following statement would output the sum of the two example numbers just defined to the screen:

```
cout << one_half + five_sixths << endl;
```

The output of this statement would be

```
4/3
```

Note that the sum of the two numbers is expressed in lowest terms.

◆ FIGURE 8.2
The state of two rational number objects

	one_half		five_sixths
numerator	1	numerator	5
denominator	2	denominator	6

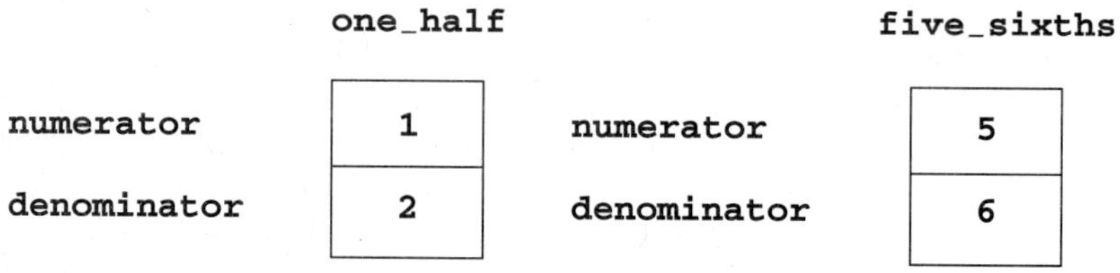

Keyboard input of rational numbers would allow users to work with rational numbers interactively. To make the scanning of the input simple, we might require a definite format, such as

<integer>/<integer><enter key>

Assignment of one rational number to another should also be provided, in the form

<rational number variable> = <rational number object>

where **<rational number object>** is the value returned by an expression.

Finally, users of rational numbers would like to compare them for the standard relationships of equality, less than, and greater than. The following code is an example of the use of the equality operator with two rational numbers:

```
rational one_half(1, 2);
rational number;

cout << "Enter a rational number: ";
cin >> number;
if (number == one_half)
.
.
.
```

Note that we have provided a second class constructor that takes no initial values for the numerator and the denominator. This constructor is used to create rational number objects that will be targets of subsequent input or assignment operations. These numbers can be given a default initial value of 1/1.

Specifying the Operations

Now that the clients' requirements have been discussed, we can present a formal specification of the desired operations for rational numbers:

Create operation (default value)
Preconditions: The rational number is in an unpredictable state.
Postconditions: **numerator** is set to 1, and **denominator** is set to 1.

Create operation (initial value specified)

Preconditions: The rational number is in an unpredictable state, **new_numer** is an integer value, and **new_denom** is an integer value other than zero.

Postconditions: **new_numer/new_denom** is first reduced to lowest terms. Then **numerator** is set to **new_numer**, and **denominator** is set to **new_denom**.

Addition operation

Preconditions: Receiver and parameter objects are rational numbers appropriately initialized.

Postconditions: A rational number representing the sum of the two rational numbers is returned.

Subtraction operation

Preconditions: Receiver and parameter objects are rational numbers appropriately initialized.

Postconditions: A rational number representing the difference of the two rational numbers is returned.

Multiplication operation

Preconditions: Receiver and parameter objects are rational numbers appropriately initialized.

Postconditions: A rational number representing the product of the two rational numbers is returned.

Division operation

Preconditions: Receiver and parameter objects are rational numbers appropriately initialized, and the denominator of the parameter object does not equal zero.

Postconditions: A rational number representing the division of the two rational numbers is returned.

Equality operation

Preconditions: Receiver and parameter objects are rational numbers appropriately initialized.

Postconditions: The Boolean value TRUE is returned if the two rational numbers are equal, and FALSE is returned otherwise.

Assignment operation

Preconditions: Receiver and parameter objects are rational numbers appropriately initialized.

Postconditions: **numerator** and **denominator** of the parameter object are copied into the receiver object.

Input operation

Preconditions: The receiver is an **istream** object appropriately initialized, and the parameters are a rational number object appropriately initialized and an **istream** object appropriately initialized. The form of input to the stream should be

<integer>/<integer> <enter key>

Postconditions: The numerator and the denominator in the rational number parameter are modified by the input values, and the istream object is returned.

Output operation

Preconditions: The receiver is an **ostream** object appropriately initialized, and the parameters are a rational number object appropriately initialized and an **ostream** object appropriately initialized.

Postconditions: The rational number parameter is written to the stream in the form **<numerator>/<denominator>**.

Note that the specifications state that a rational number will not be created if the denominator is a zero, and that any new rational number will be reduced to lowest terms when it is created.

The class declaration module for rational numbers can now be presented:

```
// Class declaration file: rational.h

#ifndef RATIONAL_H

// Declaration section

#include <iostream.h>

#include "boolean.h"

class rational
{

public:

// Class constructors

rational();
rational(int new_numer, int new_denom);
rational(const rational &r);

// Member functions

rational operator + (rational r);
rational operator - (rational r);
rational operator * (rational r);
rational operator / (rational r);
boolean operator == (rational r);
rational& operator = (rational r);
friend istream& operator >> (istream &is, rational &r);
friend ostream& operator << (ostream &os, rational r);

private:

// Data members

int numerator, denominator;

// Member function

void reduce();

};

#define RATIONAL_H
#endif
```

There are several things to note about this class declaration:

1. A third class constructor, the copy constructor, has been included so that rational numbers may be passed by value as parameters to functions.
2. Rational numbers are passed by value, rather than by constant reference, to the member functions. Recall that we used the constant reference mode for string parameters in Chapter 7, for reasons of efficiency. Because passing a rational number by value requires copying only two integer values, this mode can be used here.
3. The input and output operators of the stream classes are specified as friends, as they were in Chapter 7.
4. The class declaration declares **reduce** as a **private** member function. This function will be run by the class implementation whenever a rational number object must be reduced to lowest terms.

Implementing the Class

The class implementation for rational numbers appears in the **rational.cpp** file. We present the portion of the file that defines the three class constructors below:

```
// Class implementation file: rational.cpp

#include <assert.h>

#include "rational.h"
#include "gcd.h"

// Implementation section

rational::rational()
{
        numerator = 1;
        denominator = 1;
}

rational::rational(int new_numer, int new_denom)
{
        assert(new_denom != 0);
        numerator = new_numer;
        denominator = new_denom;
        reduce();
}

rational::rational(const rational &r)
{
        numerator = r.numerator;
        denominator = r.denominator;
}
```

Only the second constructor calls for comment. A precondition of the operation is that the **new_denom** parameter must not be a zero. Therefore, the implementation verifies this condition with the C++ **assert** function. A postcondition of the operation is that the new rational number has been reduced to lowest terms. To achieve this result, we compute the greatest common divisor of the two parameters, and then reduce them by dividing by this factor. Here is the implementation of the **reduce** function:

```
void rational::reduce()
{
        int common_divisor = gcd(numerator, denominator);
        numerator = numerator / common_divisor;
        denominator = denominator / common_divisor;
}
```

The implementation of the **gcd** function, which was used in an example in Section 6.5, appears in the library file **gcd.cpp**, and is left as an exercise.

The development of the arithmetic operations for rational numbers depends on our knowledge of the rules of rational number arithmetic. These rules are specified by the following relations:

$$\frac{n_1}{d_1} + \frac{n_2}{d_2} = \frac{n_1 d_2 + n_2 d_1}{d_1 d_2}$$

$$\frac{n_1}{d_1} - \frac{n_2}{d_2} = \frac{n_1 d_2 - n_2 d_1}{d_1 d_2}$$

$$\frac{n_1}{d_1} \times \frac{n_2}{d_2} = \frac{n_1 n_2}{d_1 d_2}$$

$$\frac{n_1 / d_1}{n_2 / d_2} = \frac{n_1 d_2}{d_1 n_2}$$

We present the implementation of the addition operation, and leave the others as exercises:

```
rational rational::operator + (rational r)
{
        int numer = numerator * r.denominator + r.numerator * denominator;
        int denom = denominator * r.denominator;
        rational sum(numer, denom);
        return sum;
}
```

The first two lines of code in this implementation use the rule for addition to compute the numerator and the denominator of the sum. The third line uses these values to construct a new rational number expressed in lowest terms. The last line returns the new rational number to the caller of the function.

The output operation writes a rational number to an output stream in the form **<numerator>/<denominator>**:

```
ostream& operator << (ostream &os, rational r)
{
        os << r.numerator << "/" << r.denominator;
        return os;
}
```

Note that we have been careful to write the data to the output stream in exactly the same form as it might appear for reading from an input stream. This technique will become important when we start processing file streams in Chapter 9.

The input operation expects data in the input stream to have the form **<integer>/<integer>**. Therefore, the implementation uses **assert** to enforce the use of this format:

```
istream& operator >> (istream &is, rational &r)
{
        char division_symbol;
        is >> r.numerator >> division_symbol >> r.denominator;
        assert(division_symbol == '/');
        assert(r.denominator != 0);
        r.reduce();
        return is;
}
```

Note that the implementation also verifies that the denominator from the input stream is not a zero, and reduces the rational number to lowest terms.

The implementations of the assignment and equality operations are left as exercises.

EXAMPLE 8.2

This example is a program that prompts the user for three rational numbers and outputs the result of an expression of the form **r1 + r2 * r3**.

```
// Program file: ratdriv.cpp

#include <iostream.h>

#include "rational.h"

int main()
{
      rational r1, r2, r3;
      cout << "Enter the first number (<integer>/<integer>): ";
      cin >> r1;
      cout << "Enter the second number (<integer>/<integer>): ";
      cin >> r2;
      cout << "Enter the third number (<integer>/<integer>): ";
      cin >> r3;
      cout << "The result of r1 + r2 * r3 is " << r1 + r2 * r3 << endl;
      return 0;
}
```

An example run of this program might produce the output

```
Enter the first number (<integer>/<integer>): 1/2
Enter the second number (<integer>/<integer>): 1/2
Enter the third number (<integer>/<integer>): 1/2
The result of r1 + r2 * r3 is 3/4
```

Note that the output is **3/4** rather than **3/2**. This means that the standard operator precedence of multiplication over addition is also enforced for rational numbers.

Mixed-Mode Operations

In Chapter 3, you were introduced to the notion of a mixed-mode operation. This kind of operation has two operands of different types, and performs a type conversion operation before computing a result value. For example, the addition operation promotes an integer operand to a real number before adding it to a real number operand. The result returned is then a real number.

When a rational number class is added to a software system, clients might be provided with a similar capability to perform mixed-mode operations on rational numbers and other kinds of numbers. For example, where the operands are an integer and a rational number, the integer would first be promoted to a rational number, and then rational number arithmetic would be performed. Where the operands are a real number and a rational number, the rational number would first be promoted to a real number, and then real number arithmetic would be performed. The following code and its output when executed illustrate some mixed-mode operations:

```
rational one_half(1, 2);
cout << fixed << showpoint;
cout << "Rational + integer =" << one_half + 2 << endl;
cout << "Rational + real =" << one_half + 3.4 << endl;

Rational + integer = 5/2
Rational + real = 3.9
```

Table 8.1 illustrates some operand and return types for addition.

We can provide mixed-mode operations for arithmetic with rational numbers by overloading. Let's consider just the case of addition, and leave the other operations for exercises. For the cases where the first operand is a rational number, we add public member functions to the class declaration module of the rational number class:

```
rational operator + (int operand);
float operator + (float operand);
```

Each of these operations adds a number (an **int** or a **float**) to the receiver object, a rational.

To add an **int** to a rational number, we must promote the **int** to a rational number. We use the **int** parameter to create a new rational number object, and then add it (using the rational number operation named '+') to the receiver:

```
rational rational::operator + (int operand)
{
        rational new_operand(operand, 1);
        return *this + new_operand;
}
```

◇ TABLE 8.1
Types of data for mixed-mode addition

Operand 1 Type	Operand 2 Type	Result Type
int	rational	rational
rational	int	rational
float	rational	float
rational	float	float

To add a **float** to a rational number, we must promote the rational number to a **float**. We cast the receiver's numerator as a float, divide the result by its denominator, and then add the result (using the real number operation '+') to the **float** parameter:

```
float rational::operator + (float operand)
{
        return float(numerator) / denominator + operand;
}
```

The other two addition operations expect a rational number as the second operand. In these cases, the rational number is not the receiver object. Therefore, they must be declared outside of the class declaration, at the global level:

```
rational operator + (int left_operand, rational right_operand);
float operator + (float left_operand, rational right_operand);
```

Note that both operands now appear as formal parameters within the parameter lists of the declarations. The implementation of the first operation is

```
rational operator + (int left_operand, rational right_operand)
{
        rational new_operand(left_operand, 1);
        return new_operand + right_operand;
}
```

The implementation of the last addition operation requires that the rational number parameter be promoted to a **float** before it is added to the **float** parameter. However, because the code is no longer within the scope of the class declaration (we can't use the prefix **rational::** in the function heading), we do not have access to the numerator and denominator of the rational number. To solve this problem and preserve information hiding, we declare a new member function, **make_float**, that promotes its object to a **float**. Its implementation is left as an exercise, but we use it here to implement the last addition operation:

```
float operator + (float left_operand, rational right_operand)
{
        return left_operand + right_operand.make_float();
}
```

EXERCISES 8.3

1. Complete the implementation of the rational number class, including the mixed-mode operations and the **make_float** type cast, and test it with a simple driver program. (*Hint:* Two rational numbers are equal if and only if $n_1d_2 = n_2d_1$.)
2. What is the total number of mixed-mode operations (+, –, *, /) for the three data types **int**, **float**, and **rational**?
3. State a general formula for the total number of mixed-mode operations, where M is the number of operators and N is the number of data types.
4. The implementation of rational numbers presented in this section always reduces a rational number to lowest terms when it is created. Another method would be to wait until an output operation to express a rational number in lowest terms. Assess the costs and benefits of these two strategies. (Be sure to take into account the speed of evaluating complex arithmetic operations and the possibility of integer overflow.)
5. Rational numbers such as 9/1 should be output as whole numbers, and used as whole numbers in arithmetic and comparison operations. Write a member function,

whole_number, that returns a Boolean value and a type cast, **make_int**, that can be used in conjunction to convert such numbers to integers.

8.4 Derived Classes and Inheritance

OBJECTIVES

- to understand how the behavior and attributes of a class can be reused by developing a derived class that inherits them
- to understand how to control access to data and behavior so that they are available to derived classes but protected from clients

One of the advantages of using classes and objects in a program is that they can be reused to develop new features. Consider the bank account example of Section 8.2. We defined a class to represent the kind of data and behavior that any account might possess, such as depositing into or withdrawing from a balance. Many more specialized kinds of bank accounts exist that have both this general sort of data and behavior and also other, more specific data and behavior. For example, a savings account will need data and operations to compute the interest on the balance. A timed savings account will not allow withdrawals before a certain date from the time of the deposit.

Instead of reinventing the wheel and defining a whole new class for each of these types of bank accounts, we can make each new kind of account a derived class of our abstract account class. Each class derived from **account** then *inherits* all of the common, more abstract data and behavior from the account class. To each derived class we need only add the data and behavior necessary to define it as a special class of account.

C++ provides support for defining derived classes. A derived class declaration is quite similar to a top-level class declaration. For example, here is a declaration of a **savings_account** class, with specific data and behavior for representing the computation of interest:

```
// Class declaration file: savings.h

#ifndef SAVINGS_H

#include "account.h"

// Declaration section

class savings_account : public account
{
        public:

        // Class constructors

        savings_account(float initial_balance);

        // Member functions

        float get_interest();
        void compute_interest(float rate);

        private:

        // Data members

        float interest;

};

#define SAVINGS_H
#endif
```

The only difference in form between a derived class declaration and a top-level class declaration lies in the text immediately following the reserved word **class**. As before, we have the name of the new class. Then we see a colon (":"), followed by an *access specifier,* followed by the name of the class from which the new class is being derived. The form for this is

class <new derived class name> : <access specifier> <parent class name>

The access specifier in this example is the reserved word **public**. This means that the public members of the base class are also public in the derived class. If this specifier were the reserved word **private**, then the public members of the base class would become private members in the derived class. Figure 8.3 is a class hierarchy diagram showing the relationship between the account class and the savings account class. Note that the member functions **deposit**, **withdraw**, and **get_balance** are not declared in the savings account class. They are declared in the base class, **account**, but are still considered public members of the savings account class by inheritance.

The implementation file of the savings account class is

```
// Class implementation file: savings.cpp

// Implementation section

#include "savings.h"

savings_account::savings_account(float initial_balance)
        : account(initial_balance)
{
        interest = 0.00;
}

float savings_account::get_interest()
{
        return interest;
}

void savings_account::compute_interest(float rate)
{
        interest = get_balance() * rate;
}
```

◆ FIGURE 8.3
The account and savings account classes

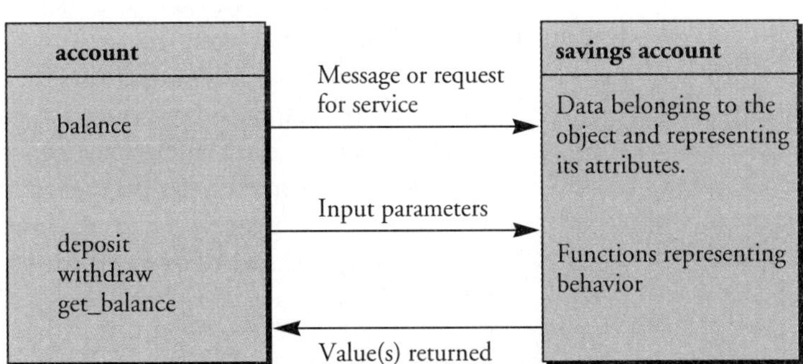

The class constructor for **savings_account** must first run the constructor for the base class, **account**, so that the data members belonging to the base class can be initialized. This is done by placing an expression of the form

: <base class constructor name> (<list of actual parameters>)

immediately after the heading of the constructor for the derived class. After this step, the data member **interest** belonging to the derived class is initialized.

Within the implementation of the member function **compute_interest**, we cannot refer directly to the savings account's balance. The reason for this is that access to private data members cannot be inherited from a base class. Therefore, we must access the savings account's balance indirectly, by invoking the base class public member function **get_balance**. As you might suppose, lack of direct access to the data members of a base class can make the use of derived classes and reuse inconvenient. We will see a way to remedy this problem shortly.

The following lines of code create and use a new instance of our savings account class:

```
savings_account my_account(50.00);
my_account.withdraw(20.00);
my_account.compute_interest(.025);
cout << fixed << showpoint << setprecision(2);
cout << "Balance = $" << my_account.get_balance() << endl;
cout << "Interest = $" << my_account.get_interest() << endl;
```

The first line declares a new savings account called **my_account**. The computer runs the class constructor for savings accounts. This in turn runs the class constructor in the base class, which gives **my_account** an initial balance of 50.00. The constructor in the derived class then sets the interest to a default value of 0.00.

The second line sends a message to **my_account** to withdraw 20.00. Since this member function is also not defined for savings accounts, the computer locates and runs the function as defined in the base class.

The third line sends a message to **my_account** to compute the interest, with a rate of .025. Since a member function is defined for this message directly in the **savings_account** class, this function is invoked.

The last two lines of code send messages to **my_account** for the values of the balance and interest so they can be displayed to the user. The request for the balance has the effect of invoking a member function of the base class, whereas the request for the interest has the effect of invoking a member function of the derived class.

The rule that the computer uses for deciding which member function to run when a message is sent to an object is fairly simple. If a member function corresponding to the message exists in the defining class, then it is run. Otherwise, the computer searches for a member function in the base class, if one exists. This search continues until a member function is found in the next most immediate ancestor class, if one exists. If no member function is found, a syntax error occurs. The same search process occurs for **public** data member references as well.

As you can see, derived classes and inheritance provide powerful techniques for reusing software and eliminating redundant code.

EXAMPLE 8.3

The following driver program tests the savings account class that we have just implemented:

```
// Program file: bankdriv.cpp

#include <iostream.h>
#include <iomanip.h>
#include "savings.h"

int main()
{
      savings_account smith(0.00), jones(45.00);

      cout << fixed << showpoint << setprecision(2);
      cout << "Smith's balance = $" << smith.get_balance() << endl;
      cout << "Jones's balance = $" << jones.get_balance() << endl;
      smith.deposit(50.00);
      cout << "Smith's balance = $" << smith.get_balance() << endl;
      cout << "Jones's balance = $" << jones.get_balance() << endl;
      smith.withdraw(20.00);
      cout << "Smith's balance = $" << smith.get_balance() << endl;
      cout << "Jones's balance = $" << jones.get_balance() << endl;
      smith.compute_interest(.025);
      cout << "Smith's interest = $" << smith.get_interest() << endl;
      return 0;
}
```

The program produces the output

```
Smith's balance = $0.00
Jones's balance = $45.00
Smith's balance = $50.00
Jones's balance = $45.00
Smith's balance = $30.00
Jones's balance = $45.00
Smith's interest = $0.75
```

Inheritance and Protected Members

In the previous section, we mentioned that **private** data members of a base class cannot be directly referenced from a derived class. For example, the savings account class must invoke a **public** member function of the account class, such as **get_balance()**, to access the value of the private data member **balance**. This kind of encapsulation is too restrictive. A derived class ought to be able to access frequently used and modified data members of a base class directly. A less restrictive type of encapsulation can be obtained by using the access specifier **protected** for certain data and member functions. A data or function member of a class is considered *protected* if it is visible to a derived class, but not visible to any other part of a program. Thus, **protected** members behave like **public** members for derived classes, but like **private** members for any other classes or modules in a software system.

The following code updates the account class by making the balance a **protected** data member rather than a **private** one:

```
// Class declaration file: account.h

#ifndef ACCOUNT_H

// Declaration section

class account
{

        public:

        // Class constructors

        account(float initial_balance);
        account(const account &a);

        // Member functions

        float deposit(float amount);
        float withdraw(float amount);
        float get_balance();

        protected:

        // Data members

        float balance;

};

#define ACCOUNT_H
#endif
```

We have replaced the reserved word **private** in the previous version with the reserved word **protected**. The implementation section of this module is the same as before.

Once we have made this change in the account class declaration, we can refer to the data member **balance** in the savings account class declaration. For example, the member function **compute_interest** can be changed so that the balance is referenced directly:

```
void savings_account::compute_interest(float rate)
       {
       interest = balance * rate;
       }
```

EXERCISES 8.4

1. Where would you define the data and behavior for representing passwords in savings accounts? Which access mode should a password have within the class hierarchy?
2. Add members to the savings account class given in this section for maintaining a current interest rate.

3. A checking account is a special version of an account that requires data and behavior for maintaining the number of checks written. Write a derived class of account called **checking_account** that captures this information.
4. Draw a diagram showing the hierarchy of classes used in a system that manages checking and savings accounts.
5. Some checking accounts bear interest. Propose a strategy for reusing the existing classes in a bank management system to support checking accounts with interest. Draw a diagram of the new class hierarchy.
6. Unlike the other kinds of accounts, timed savings accounts may not permit access via a password. Explain how you would fit timed savings accounts into a bank management system as a new class, in such a way that the use of a password for these accounts would be disallowed. Draw a diagram of the new class hierarchy.

COMMUNICATION AND STYLE TIPS

1. Data and function members that must be used by the entire system should be declared **public**. In general, there should be very few public data members of a class.
2. Data and function members that must be used by derived classes should be declared **protected**.
3. Data and function members that should be used only by the defining class should be declared **private**.

FOCUS ON PROGRAM DESIGN

Thus far in this text, the end-of-chapter focus section has stated a problem, written out the top-level design of a solution as an algorithm, refined the design if necessary, and presented a complete program to solve the problem. In more recent chapters, we have had to focus more on the design of the appropriate data structures for solving a problem as well. Now that we are using object-oriented techniques, our focus must shift somewhat further away from top-down design and refinement of algorithms. In this section, we present part of a complete program, and leave the rest for the programming problems and projects. In fact, it would be in the object-oriented spirit if this project and those to follow were divided up among students who form a team of programmers.

We begin as usual with a problem statement. But now we immediately consider how the behavior of certain classes of objects can help to solve the problem. If these classes have already been written, we can use them right away. If they do not quite fit the problem at hand, perhaps we can reuse them by creating a derived class for the desired behavior. Some algorithm and data structure design will still be necessary at the level of implementing a new class, but in general, there will be less work to do because there is less code to write. Rather than thinking in terms of data structures and algorithms, we can think in terms of clients and servers, many of which already exist and simply need to be hooked together in the appropriate way.

Consider the problem of simulating an automated teller machine (ATM). An ATM is a server that allows users to enter a name (on the card) and password to gain access to different kinds of bank accounts. The user can then select among various functions, each of which may request other inputs. A successful transaction results in output to the user, and may result in a change to an account. An unsuccessful transaction (using a bad password, for example) may lead to other outputs.

The ATM relies on other servers for support. Three of these are an **iostream** class, a string class, and an account class. The role of the ATM is to serve as an interface handler that controls the communication between a user and his or her account. Put another way, you can think of an ATM class as both a model for an ATM machine and as an "application class" that drives the simulation.

To design an object-oriented system to solve this problem, we first take an inventory of existing classes to see how they can capture the desired behavior. Let's assume that we have an account class at our disposal. The account class has been extended to support user names and passwords.

Now that we know what we have, we can think about what we have to develop. The ATM can be represented as a new class. It will use, as servers, the **iostream** class, the string class, and the account class. It will maintain the following data members:

1. Master name and password (used to start up or shut down the system)
2. Current account (the account currently being processed).

The ATM will serve users in two different modes:

1. *Master user mode:* This mode allows an authorized bank employee to start up the machine in customer mode, to perform service functions such as entering a new account, and to shut the machine down.
2. *Customer mode:* This mode allows an authorized customer to access an account to perform transactions.

Let's look at the abstract behavior that the ATM provides for each mode.

1. Master mode
    1.1 enter a new account
    1.2 start customer mode
    1.3 shut machine down
2. Customer mode
    2.1 get name and password
    2.2 if they belong to master mode then
    2.3 run master mode
    2.4 else if they belong to an account then
    2.5 perform a transaction on the account
    2.6 else handle user error

Many of the numbered items in both modes describe messages to which an ATM object can respond. Master mode really is a menu-driven command interpreter. Let's develop code for the algorithm. First, when the message **master_mode** is sent to an ATM object, a member function should enter a command loop. The loop should display the master mode menu and wait for the user to enter the number of a command. When this occurs, the ATM runs the corresponding member function. After the function returns, the loop is entered once more. The following code might be an implementation of the **master_mode** member function:

```
void ATM::master_mode()
{
      int command;

      do
```

```
        {
                print_master_menu();
                command = get_command(1, 3);
                switch (command)
                {
                        case 1:     enter_account();
                                    break;
                        case 2:     customer_mode();
                                    break;
                        case 3:     shut_down();
                }
        } while (command != 3);
}
```

Note that the manager launches customer mode by entering command 2, and shuts the machine down by entering command 3.

The member function **customer_mode** is

```
void ATM::customer_mode()
{
       string name, password;
       boolean master_on = FALSE;

       do
       {
               cout << "Enter your name: ";
               cin >> name;
               cout << "Enter your password: ";
               cin >> password;
               if (master_account(name, password))
                       master_on = TRUE;
               else if (customer_account(name, password))
                       perform_transaction();
               else
                       cout << "Sorry, you entered an incorrect name or password."
                            << endl;
       } while (! master_on);
}
```

master_account is a member function that returns TRUE if the name and password match those of an authorized employee, and FALSE otherwise. The loop terminates when an authorized employee enters a name and password for master mode.

perform_transaction displays a menu of transaction options to the user, takes a command number, and performs the corresponding command:

```
void ATM::perform_transaction()
{
       int command;

       print_transaction_menu();
       command = get_command(1, 3);
       switch (command)
```

```
        {
                case 1:        get_balance();
                               break;
                case 2:        make_deposit();
                               break;
                case 3:        make_withdrawal();
        }
}
```

As you can see, the ATM class that we have developed thus far is a large body of code, broken down into many small member functions (the use of classes does not free developers entirely from top-down design and algorithm development!). Most of these can be declared **private**, for the internal use of the ATM class only. A single member function, **master_mode**, can be declared **public**. This function can be invoked from a main program in C++, right after an ATM instance is declared. It would run master mode and wait for commands. The main program would be

```
// Program file: atmdriv.cpp

#include <iostream.h>

#include "atm.h"

int main()
{
        string name, password;

        cout << "Enter your name: ";
        cin >> name;
        cout << "Enter your password: ";
        cin >> password;
        ATM teller(name, password);
        teller.master_mode();
        return 0;
}
```

Here is the header file for the ATM class:

```
// Class declaration file: atm.h

#ifndef ATM_H

#include "boolean.h"
#include "account.h"

// Declaration section

class ATM
{

        public:

        // Class constructors
```

```
        ATM(string n, string p);

        // Member functions

        void master_mode();

        private:

        // Data members
        // Used to start up or shut
        // down the system

        string master_name, master_password;

        // The account currently being processed

        account current_account;

        // Member functions

        void customer_mode();
        boolean master_account(string n, string p);
        boolean customer_account(string n, string p);
        void perform_transaction();
        void get_balance();
        void make_deposit();
        void make_withdrawal();
        int get_command(int low, int high);
        void enter_account();
        void shut_down();
        void print_transaction_menu();
        void print_master_menu();

};

#define ATM_H
#endif
```

The complete implementation file is left as an exercise.

RUNNING, DEBUGGING AND TESTING HINTS

1. Before you write a definition of a new class, write out a description of the data members and abstract behavior that the class should exhibit.
2. Write a simple driver program to test each member function of a class.

SUMMARY

Key Terms

access specifier
attribute
base class
behavior
class hierarchy
derived class
inheritance
protected member
receiver
sender

Keywords

protected

Key Concepts

- A class defines the abstract behavior and attributes belonging to an object.
- Objects provide services by responding to the messages sent by clients.
- Objects can be used to model or simulate objects in the real world, such as bank accounts, or computational objects, such as rational numbers.
- Classes can reuse data and behavior by inheriting them from a base class.
- Derived classes can specialize inherited behavior by extending it or overriding it.
- Data and behavior can be hidden from all users by declaring them **`private`** within a class.
- Data and behavior can be made available to all users by declaring them **`public`** within a class.
- Data and behavior can be made available to derived classes but hidden from all other users by declaring them **`protected`** within a class.

SUGGESTION FOR FURTHER READING

Booch, Grady, *Object-Oriented Analysis and Design,* 2nd ed., Redwood City, CA: Benjamin/Cummings, 1994.

Coad, Peter, and Yourdon, Edward, *Object-Oriented Analysis,* 2nd ed., Englewood Cliffs, NJ: Yourdon Press, 1991.

Jacobson, I., Christerson, M., Jonsoon, P., and Overgaard, G., *Object-Oriented Software Engineering,* Reading, MA: Addison-Wesley, 1992.

Rumbaugh, J., *et al., Object-Oriented Modeling and Design,* Englewood Cliffs, NJ: Prentice Hall, 1991.

Wirfs-Brock, R., Wilkerson, B., and Wiener, L. *Designing Object-Oriented Software,* Englewood Cliffs, NJ: Prentice Hall, 1990.

PROGRAMMING PROBLEMS AND PROJECTS

1. Implement and extend the ATM class to handle user errors by confiscating a card after three unsuccessful attempts to gain access to an account.
2. Write a program to be used by the registrar of a university. The program should get information from the keyboard and the data for each student should include student name, student number, classification (1 for freshman, 2 for sophomore, 3 for junior, 4 for senior, or 7 for special student), hours completed, hours taking, and grade-point average. You should design a class to represent a student as an abstract data type. This class should use the string class developed in Chapter 7.
3. Robert Day, basketball coach at Indiana College, wants you to write a program to help him analyze information about his basketball team. He wants a data structure for each player containing the player's name, position played, high school graduated from, height, scoring average, rebounding average, grade-point average, and seasons

of eligibility remaining. You should design a class to represent a player as an abstract data type.

4. Complex numbers are numbers of the form $a + bi$ where a and b are real and i represents **`sqrt(-1)`**. Complex number arithmetic is defined by

Sum	$(a + bi) + (c + di) = (a + c) + (b + d)i$
Difference	$(a + bi) - (c + di) = (a - c) + (b - d)i$
Product	$(a + bi)(c + di) = (ac - bd) + (ad + bc)i$
Quotient	$(a + bi)/(c + di) = \frac{ac + bd}{c^2 + d^2} + \frac{(bc - ad)i}{c^2 + d^2}$

Write a program that will perform these calculations on two complex numbers. Each line of data consists of a single character designator (S, D, P, or Q) followed by four reals representing two complex numbers. For example, $(2 + 3i) + (5 - 2i)$ is represented by

```
S2 3 5 - 2
```

An instance of a class should be used for each complex number. The arithmetic operators should be overloaded to carry out the operations. Input and output should be in the form $a + bi$ (overload the input and output operators as well).

5. The Readmore Public Library wants a program to keep track of the books checked out. Information for each book should be kept in an object and the data members should include the author's name, a nonfiction designator (Boolean), the title, the library catalog number, and the copyright date. Each customer can check out at most ten books. Develop an abstract data type for representing a book as a C++ class. There should be public member functions for returning each attribute of a book, and input and output operations for initializing and printing them as well.

6. Modify Problem 5 so that a daily printout is available that contains a summary of the day's transactions at the Readmore Public Library. You will need an object for each customer containing the customer's name and library card number. Be sure to make provision for books that are returned.

7. Write a program that uses objects to analyze poker hands. Each hand consists of five objects (cards). Each object should have one data member for the suit and one for the value. Rankings for the hands from high to low are

straight flush
four of a kind
full house
flush
straight
three of a kind
two pair
one pair
none of the above

Your program should read data for five cards from the keyboard, evaluate the hand, and print out the hand together with a message indicating its value.

8. Problem 7 can be modified in several ways. A first modification is to compare two different hands using only the ranking indicated. A second (more difficult) modification is to also compare hands that have the same ranking. For example, a pair of 8s is better than a pair of 7s. Extend Problem 7 to incorporate some of these modifications.

9. The University Biology Department has a Conservation Club that works with the state Department of Natural Resources. Their project for the semester is to help capture and tag migratory birds. You have been asked to write a computer program to help them store information. In general, the program must have information for each bird tagged entered interactively in an object for subsequent use. For each bird tagged, you need a data member for the tag number, tagging site, sex, bird type, date, and name of the DNR officer doing the tagging. After all data have been entered, the program should print the contents of the object.

10. Mrs. Crown, your computer science instructor, wants to keep track of the maintenance record of her computers and has turned to you for help. She wants to keep track of the type of machine, its serial number (up to ten characters), the year of purchase, and a Boolean variable indicating whether the machine is under service contract. Write a program that permits the entry of this information and prints a record for a machine.

11. Write a program to read data containing the name, address, telephone number, and class of friends into an object and print its contents.

12. The Falcon Manufacturing Company wishes to keep computerized structures of its telephone-order customers. They want the name, street address, city, state, and zip code for each customer. They include either a "T" if the customer is a business, or an "F" if the customer is an individual. A 30-character description of each business is also included. An individual's credit limit is in the structure.

    Write a program to read the information for the customer from the keyboard and print the information on the screen.

13. Visit your local registrar and discuss how structures of students are processed. Discover what data are kept for each student, how the data are entered, and what the data members for each student are. Have the registrar explain what operations are used with a student's data. Specifically, how is information added to or deleted from a student's record? What kinds of lists must the registrar produce for those within the system who need information about students?

    Prepare a written report of your visit for the class. Be sure to include a graphic that shows how a student's record can be envisioned.

14. Select an unworked problem from the previously listed programming problems for this chapter. Construct a structure chart and write all documentary information necessary for this problem. Do not write code. When finished, have a classmate read your documentation to see if precisely what is to be done is clear.

CHAPTER 9 Files

CHAPTER OUTLINE

Having now completed eight chapters, you've made significant steps in the process of learning to use a programming language for the purpose of solving problems. Thus far, however, it has been impossible to work with large amounts of data. To write programs that solve problems using large databases, it is necessary to be able to store, retrieve, and manage the data. Consider the relatively simple problem of using a computer to compute and print water bills for a community of 30,000 customers. If the data needed consist of a customer name, address, and amount of water used, you can imagine that entering this information interactively every billing period would involve an enormous amount of time. In addition to saving that time, it is often desirable to save information between runs of a program for later use. For example, in large software systems, the information output by one program might be the input of another program.

To avoid these problems, we can store data in some secondary storage device, usually magnetic tapes or disks. Data can be created by one program, stored on these devices, and then accessed by other programs when necessary. It is also possible to modify and save this information for other runs of the same program or for running another program using these same data. In this chapter, we look at storage and retrieval of data in another data structure called a *file.*

9.1 Streams and Stream Processing

OBJECTIVES

- to understand the use of streams in obtaining input and output data
- to understand how streams are used to access data in files
- to be able to use loops with file streams

Before you can work with files, you need to become acquainted with the notion of a *stream.* You can think of a stream as a channel or conduit on which data are passed from senders to receivers. Data can be sent out on a stream; in which case, we are using an *output stream.* Or data can be received from a stream; in which case, we are using an *input stream.* Streams are connected to *devices.* For example, at program startup, the standard input stream, named by **`cin`**, is connected to the keyboard device, and the standard output stream, named by **`cout`**, is connected to the terminal screen. Thus, you can think of the keyboard as the *source* from which data are received from an input stream, and of the terminal screen as the *destination* to which data are sent on an output stream.

The essential characteristic of stream processing is that data elements must be sent to or received from a stream one at a time or in *serial* fashion. For example, if we have a collection of data elements to be printed on the terminal screen, they must be written one after the other, not all at once. When you think about the use of streams for interactive input and output, this restriction makes sense. For output, each character sent to the output stream must wait its turn to be displayed on a terminal screen. For input, the receiver in the program must wait for each character typed at the keyboard.

We can think of a stream as an abstract data type. Stream processing requires at least five abstract operations. First, the stream must be *opened* for use. If the stream has been opened for input, an operation is needed to *get* the next data item from the stream. In addition, an operation is needed to detect the *end of an input stream,* or the condition that there are no more data to be received from the stream. If the stream has been opened for output, an operation is needed to *put* the next data item into the stream. Finally, when the program is finished using a stream, an operation is necessary to *close* it.

The Standard Input and Output Streams

You are already familiar with the use of the standard input and output streams in C++. Let's take a look at how they work in more detail. These streams and the operations we perform on them become available to a program by including the **iostream.h** library. In the case of the standard input stream, a programmer obtains access to the variable **cin**, which names the stream, and the operator **>>**, which is used to receive or get the next data item from the stream. In the case of the standard output stream, a programmer obtains access to the variable **cout**, which names the stream, and the operator **<<**, which is used to send or put the next data item to the stream. The operations that open and close these streams are run automatically by the system when the program begins and finishes execution. Opening the streams simply connects each stream to its respective device, the keyboard or the terminal screen. Closing the streams disconnects them. The standard input and output streams and the devices to which they are connected are depicted in Figure 9.1.

File Streams

Files are data structures that are stored on a *disk device.* To work with a file, you must connect a stream to the file on a disk. The kind of stream used to receive input from a file is called an *input file stream.* The kind of stream used to send output to a file is called an *output file stream.* Input and output file streams and the devices to which they are connected are depicted in Figure 9.2. To create a file stream, you must first include the C++ library file **fstream.h.** After doing so, two new classes, **ofstream** (output file stream) and **ifstream** (input file stream), become available to a program.

◆ FIGURE 9.1
The standard input and output streams and their devices

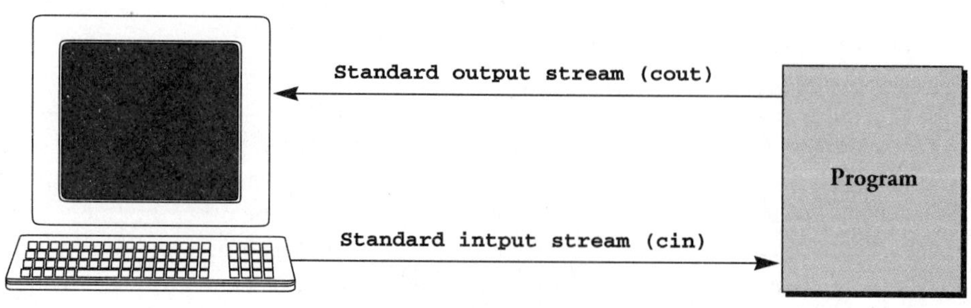

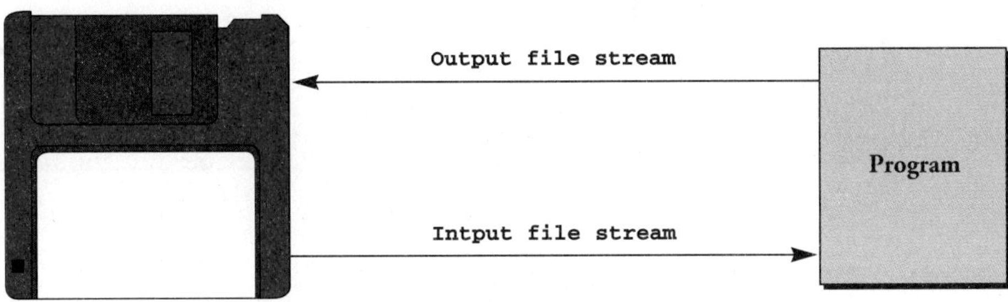

◆ FIGURE 9.2
Input and output file streams and a disk device

Output File Streams

You can declare and open an output file stream as in the following example:

```
#include <fstream.h>
.
.
.
ofstream out_file;
.
.
.
out_file.open("myfile");
```

Syntactically, the second line of code is a C++ variable declaration. The class name, **ofstream**, appears on the left, followed by the variable name, **out_file**. The third line of code tells the system to connect the output file stream to a file on disk named **"myfile"**. The syntax of this statement is that used for expressing calls of member functions with objects introduced in Chapters 7 and 8. It consists of the name of the file stream, followed by a period ("."), followed by a call to the **open** function with a string parameter. When this statement is executed, the following steps take place:

1. If a file named **"myfile"** exists on disk, it is opened for output and connected to the output stream **out_file**. If any data are in the file when it is opened, the data are erased from the file.
2. Otherwise, a file named **"myfile"** does not exist on disk. A new file with that name is created, opened for output, and connected to the output stream **out_file**.

The general form for creating an output file stream is

```
ofstream <stream variable name>;
<stream variable name>.open(<file name>);
```

The stream variable name can be any legitimate C++ identifier. The file name must be a string that is consistent with the way files can be named on your particular implementation. You should consult your local system manual for the rules governing the naming of files.

When a program is finished using a file stream, it should be closed. Most computer systems close any data files when a program terminates execution. However, the **close** function can be run with the file stream to do this under program control. If **out_file** is an output file stream, the following statement will close the stream:

```
out_file.close();
```

Note that the name of the file does not appear as a parameter to this function, as it does with **open**.

Detecting Errors Opening and Closing Files

Occasionally, an error occurs when a program attempts to open or close a stream on a file. For example, a disk may be full and no more room exists for new data when a new file is requested. To detect these errors, C++ provides a fail function, **fail()**, for use with streams. The following code shows how to detect and respond to these errors in opening and closing an output file stream:

```
#include <fstream.h>
#include <assert.h>
.
.
.
ofstream out_file;
.
.
.
out_file.open("myfile");
assert(! out_file.fail());
       <send data to file>
out_file.close();
assert(! out_file.fail());
```

Using Output File Streams

Once a file stream has been opened for output, all of the operations for terminal screen output that you are familiar with can be used for file output. For example, assuming that the variable **out_file** names an output file stream, the following statement will write a line of text to the file:

```
out_file << "This is a test." << endl;
```

Note that this statement has exactly the same format as a statement to write the same data to the terminal screen using the standard output stream:

```
cout << "This is a test." << endl;
```

The output of integers and real numbers works the same way:

```
out_file << "The number ten is " << 10 << " or " << 10.0
         << endl;
```

If the C++ library for formatting output, **iomanip.h**, is included, you will be able to use familiar formatting commands with file output:

```
#include <iomanip.h>
.
.
.
out_file << setprecision(4);
out_file << setw(10) << 3.1416 << endl;
```

There are two important points to note here about output streams.

1. The operations on output streams are *abstract.* It does not matter whether the destination of the output is a file on disk or the terminal screen. All we need to know is the name of the stream and the form of the statement to send data to the stream. Moreover, the results of sending data to output streams are similar, even when the destinations are different devices. The data saved in a disk file should "look the same" as the data displayed on a terminal screen. You can verify that this is the case by running our sample statements, and then examining the contents of your test file with a local text editor.
2. Programs that use output stream processing are *portable.* They can be written on one hardware system, transported to another hardware system, and then recompiled and run on the latter system without changes to the code. This will be true even though the representation of files on a disk and data on a terminal screen tend to vary greatly from system to system. If we had to make changes to a program every time we wanted to move it to a new hardware system, we would have an enormous maintenance headache. The use of conventional output streams insulates a program from these machine dependencies in areas where they are most likely to occur.

Loops with Output File Streams

Most of the examples of sending data to an output file stream that we have seen thus far are unrealistic, in that only one or two data values are written. Programs typically output large amounts of data to files. One typical form of data processing with files takes input data from the user at the keyboard, processes the data, and writes the results to a file. A pseudocode algorithm for this process is

```
Open the output file
Read data from the keyboard
While data do not equal a sentinel value do
        Process the data
        Write the result to the file, followed by a carriage return
        Read data from the keyboard
Close the output file
```

Note that each data value will be followed by a carriage return in the file. It is essential that a carriage return or a space character be used to separate the data values in the file. This will allow the data values to be recognized and read from the file subsequently.

EXAMPLE 9.1

The following program uses a **while** loop to read integers from the keyboard and write them to a file until a sentinel is encountered.

```
// Program file: kbdfile.cpp

#include <iostream.h>
#include <fstream.h>

const int SENTINEL = -999;
```

```
int main()
{
      int data;
      ofstream out_file;

      out_file.open("myfile");
      cout << "Enter an integer (-999 to end input): ";
      cin >> data;
      while (data != SENTINEL)
      {
            out_file << data << " ";
            cout << "Enter an integer (-999 to end input): ";
            cin >> data;
      }
      out_file.close();
      return 0;
}
```

Input File Streams

You can create an input file stream as in the following example:

```
#include <fstream.h>
.
.
.
ifstream in_file;
.
.
.
in_file.open("myfile");
```

Syntactically, the first line of code is a C++ variable declaration. The class name, **ifstream**, appears on the left, followed by the variable name, **in_file**. The third line of code tells the system to connect the input file stream to a file on disk named **"myfile"**. The syntax of this statement is the same as that for output streams. When this statement is executed, the following steps take place:

1. If a file named **"myfile"** exists on disk, it is opened for input and connected to the input stream **in_file**.
2. Otherwise, a file named **"myfile"** does not exist on disk. On some implementations of C++, a new file with that name is created, opened for input, and connected to the input stream **in_file**.

The general form for creating an input file stream is

> ifstream <stream variable name>;
> <stream variable name>.open(<file name>);

The stream variable name can be any legitimate C++ identifier. The file name must be a string that is consistent with the way files can be named on your particular system.

Using Input File Streams

We have seen that programs can use the standard operator **<<**, called an *inserter,* to send data to the terminal screen or to an output file. Programs can also use the standard operator **>>**, called an *extractor,* to receive data from the keyboard or from an input file.

Let us review what happens when a program gets data from the keyboard or standard input stream.

1. The user types one or more characters at the keyboard, followed by a blank space or by a carriage return.
2. The computer converts the characters to the data value that the characters represent. What the characters represent depends on the type of variable used for input. For example, the characters '1', '0', and '4' will be converted to the integer value 104 if the program's input statement is receiving the input data for an integer variable. Or the same characters will be placed into a string value "104" if the input statement is using a string variable.
3. The computer stores the data value from step 2 in the variable following the **>>** operator.

The success of an input operation from the keyboard thus depends on two things: the format of the data typed by the user, and the data type of the variable appearing in the input statement. For example, the code

```
int int_var;
float float_var;
string string_var;

cin >> int_var >> float_var >> string_var;
```

will run successfully, if the user types a string of digits, followed by one or more whitespace characters, followed by a string of digits that may or may not contain a decimal point, followed by one or more whitespace characters, followed by a string of characters, followed by optional whitespace characters, and ending with a carriage return.

There are two important things to note about the standard input stream. First, at the source or keyboard, the data are individual characters. At the receiving end, however, these data are implicitly converted to a type that the program can use, such as integers, real numbers, or strings.

Once we are aware of these two conditions, we can proceed to use an input file stream in the same way as we use the keyboard. For example, assuming that the file **"myfile"** contains a line of characters representing an integer, a real number, and a string, the following program will successfully read these data from the file and display it on the terminal screen:

```
// Program file: filescr.cpp

#include <iostream.h>
#include <fstream.h>
#include <assert.h>
#include "strlib.h"
```

```
int main()
{
        int int_var;
        float float_var;
        string string_var;
        ifstream in_file;
        in_file.open("myfile");
        assert(! in_file.fail());
        in_file >> int_var >> float_var >> string_var;
        cout << int_var << float_var << string_var << endl;
        in_file.close();
        assert(! in_file.fail());
        return 0;
}
```

COMMUNICATION AND STYLE TIPS

The use of the **<<** and **>>** operators in programs that process files enhances program maintenance. Because these operators work with integers, real numbers, and strings, client programmers do not have to change the code of the input and output operations when the data type of the elements in the file is changed. In general, servers should use the standard operators to define input and output operations for new classes, as was illustrated with strings in Chapter 7 and rational numbers in Chapter 8.

Loops with Input File Streams

The contents of an input file are almost never as precisely determined as those you just saw in the last example. Usually, all we know is the general format of a file and the type of data used to receive the input. The number of these data values that are stored in the file is *indefinite.* There may be 2, 20, or 20,000 of them. Processing input file data will consist of reading each data value from the file stream, processing it, and halting when there are no more data to be read from the stream.

C++ provides a special function, **eof()**, that returns nonzero (meaning TRUE) when there are no more data to be read from an input file stream, and zero (meaning FALSE) otherwise. The general form for using this function is

<input file stream>.eof()

If we assume that **data** is the variable into which each data element of a file will be read, **in_file** is the input file stream, and **process_data(data)** is the specification of a function that processes the data, then the following code can serve as a model of input file processing in many C++ programs:

```
in_file >> data;
while (! in_file.eof())
{
        process(data);
        in_file >> data;
}
```

There are several important points to make about this model:

1. An attempt to read an initial datum from the file stream must be made *before* the **eof** function is executed. If the file contains no data initially, then **eof** will return TRUE after this initial input operation. This operation is sometimes called a *priming input statement.*
2. Placing the **eof** condition at the beginning of a **while** loop guards against processing data after the program has reached the end of the file stream.
3. Placing the next extraction operation at the bottom of the loop allows the loop to advance through the file to the end of the input data.
4. When this model is used, remember that **eof** is TRUE when an attempt to read a value is made and there are no remaining values in the file.

EXAMPLE 9.2

The following program reads integers from an input file and displays them in a column on the terminal screen. The program assumes that the integers in the file are separated by one or more whitespace characters.

```
// Program file: intfile.cpp

#include <iostream.h>
#include <fstream.h>

int main()
{
	int data;
	ifstream in_file;
	in_file.open("myfile");
	in_file >> data;
	while (! in_file.eof())
	{
		cout << data << endl;
		in_file >> data;
	}
	in_file.close();
	return 0;
}
```

COMMUNICATION AND STYLE TIPS

1. Always test for the end-of-file condition before processing data read from an input file stream. This means:
   a. Use a priming input statement before the loop.
   b. Use an input statement at the bottom of the loop.
2. Use a **while** loop for getting data from an input file stream. (A **for** loop is desirable only when you know the exact number of data items in the file.)

A NOTE OF INTEREST

Career Opportunities in Computer Science

The list "Fastest Growing Occupations, 1990–2005," published by the Bureau of Labor Statistics, includes computer programmers and computer system analysts. During this time period, the number of these jobs is expected to increase by 78.9%. If this job grouping is broadened to include all computer and data processing professionals, 24,000 workers joined the employment rolls between December 1991 and December 1992. Employment grew 4% in this area, compared to 0.5.% for total nonagricultural employment (*Forecasts: Cahners Economics*). Employment of computer professionals is expected to grow much faster than the average of all occupations through the year 2005 (*Occupational Outlook Handbook*).

In 1992, a total of 751 employers were surveyed to determine which academic disciplines were of greatest interest to employers. Of these, 60% mentioned computer science. The relative ranking of the disciplines has remained very stable since 1980 when they were first compiled. The same three disciplines—computer science, electrical engineering, and mechanical engineering—have been on the top of the list, sought after by about two-thirds of the responding companies. (Peterson, *Job Opportunities*).

Unemployment among computer specialists is traditionally exceptionally low, and almost all who enter the workforce find jobs. In 1990, the median annual income was about $38,700 for a systems analyst and about $34,000 for a computer programmer (*Occupational Outlook Handbook*).

All able students—particularly women and minorities, who have been traditionally underrepresented in the sciences—are encouraged to consider computer science as a career.

EXERCISES 9.1

1. Assume that an input file stream, **in_file**, has been opened on a file containing two integers, and that **number** is an integer variable. Describe what happens when each of the following pieces of code is run:

a.
```
in_file >> number;
cout << number << endl;
in_file >> number;
cout << number << endl;
in_file >> number;
cout << number << endl;
```
b.
```
in_file >> number;
while (! in_file.eof())
{
     cout << number << endl;
     in_file >> number;
}
```
c.
```
while (! in_file.eof())
{
     in_file >> number;
     cout << number << endl;
}
```

2. Write and test a program that allows you to input your name, address, and age from the keyboard (define a string type and variables for the first two inputs). Then save this information in an output file. Be sure to place separators, either spaces or carriage returns, between the data values in the file. Examine the file with a text editor to make sure that the data have been saved.

3. Write and test a program to input the data from the output file of Exercise 2 and display it on the terminal screen.

4. Extend the program of Exercise 1 so that you can input many names, addresses, and ages from the keyboard and then save them in a file (halt keyboard input when name is "done").
5. Extend the program of Exercise 2 so that it reads all of the names, addresses, and ages from a file and displays them on the terminal screen.
6. Write a program that copies integers from an input file to an output file. You should assume that the data in the input file are separated by spaces or carriage returns. Test the program with files containing zero, one, and ten data values. You can create test files with a text editor.
7. Extend the program of Exercise 6 so that it echoes the input data to the terminal screen as they are processed.

9.2 Using Functions with Files

OBJECTIVES

- to be able to design functions for use with file streams
- to be able to use file streams in conjunction with strings
- to understand the use of buffered input of data from file streams into strings

Now that you know how to create and use file streams, we will examine how to write functions that package some useful file handling operations. Consider the problem of opening a file. This process is seldom as simple as we have seen in our examples so far, where we have assumed that the only file being processed is named **"myfile"**. In many cases, the user will be asked for the name of the desired file to be opened for input or output. This task involves prompting the user for the file name, reading the name into a string variable (as defined in Chapter 7), and passing the variable on to the **open** operation for the file stream. In addition, we might also check for a successful opening of the stream. We can hide these details in a pair of functions, **open_input_file** and **open_output_file**, that can be called in any application as follows:

```
open_input_file(in_file);
open_output_file(out_file);
```

in_file and **out_file** have been declared as input and output file streams, respectively.

Each function opens a stream on the file whose name the user specifies. The file stream is returned as a reference parameter. The declaration of **open_input_file** is

```
// Function: open_input_file
// Prompts user for a file name and opens
// input stream on the file
//
// Outputs: an input file stream

void open_input_file(ifstream &in_file);
```

The implementation of **open_input_file** is

```
void open_input_file(ifstream &in_file)
{
      char in_file_name[80];

      cout << "Enter the input file name: ";
      cin >> in_file_name;
      in_file.open(in_file_name);
      assert(! in_file.fail());
}
```

Note that the file stream is passed as a *reference parameter.* You should never try to pass a stream as a value parameter. This may be a syntax error in some implementations of C++. **open_output_file** has a similar declaration and implementation.

Another useful function copies the contents of a file of integers to another file. The function assumes that the two files have been successfully opened, one for input and one for output. Its declaration declares just the file stream parameters:

```
// Function: copy_integers
// Copies integers from one file to another
//
// Inputs: an opened input file wherein integers are separated by spaces
// and an opened output file
// Output: an output file containing the contents of the input file

void copy_integers(ifstream &in_file, ofstream & outfile);
```

The implementation uses our standard **while** loop structure for input file processing:

```
void copy_integers(ifstream &in_file, ofstream & outfile)
{
	int data;

	in_file >> data;
	while (! in_file.eof())
	{
		out_file << data << " ";
		in_file >> data;
	}
}
```

EXAMPLE 9.3

The following program uses the functions developed above to copy integers from an input file to an output file.

```
// Program file: intfile.cpp

#include <iostream.h>
#include <fstream.h>
#include <assert.h>

int main()
{
	int data;
	ifstream in_file;
	ofstream out_file;

	open_input_file(in_file);
	open_output_file(out_file);
	copy_integers(in_file, out_file);
	in_file.close();
	out_file.close();
	return 0;
}
```

Note that the **copy_integers** function assumes that the application will be opening and closing its files. File processing functions can be more general if they are not responsible for these details.

Files and Strings

File and string processing form the backbone of many word processing and database applications. In the following examples, we will use the string class developed in Section 7.3. Consider the problem of searching for a given word in a file. The user inputs the desired word and file name from the keyboard. The program searches for the first instance of the word in the file. If the word is found, the program displays the position of the word in the file and asks the user whether a search for the next instance is desired. If the word is not found, the program terminates with a message. An algorithm describing the top-level process is

```
Set position to 0
Open input file
Get word from user
Do
        Search file for next instance of word
        If word is found then
                Display position of word in file
                Ask user whether another search is desired
        Else
                Display message that word was not found
While word was found and another search is desired
Close input file
```

The main loop can be controlled by two Boolean flags, **word_found** and **another_search**. The process of searching a file for the next instance of a given word can be handled by a function, **search_for_word**. The function has four parameters: an opened input file stream, the desired word, the **word_found** flag, and the position of the word in the file. We can use the **open_input_file** function developed earlier in the chapter to open the file and detect an error. We can now translate the main algorithm to a main program in C++:

```
int main()
{
        string desired_word;
        boolean word_found, another_search;
        char query;
        ifstream in_file;
        int position = 0;

        open_input_file(in_file);
        cout << "Enter the word you would like to find: ";
        cin >> desired_word;
        do
        {
                search_for_word(in_file, desired_word, position, word_found);
                if (word_found)
                {
```

```
                        cout << "The word is at position " << position << endl;
                        cout << "Search for the next instance?[Y/N] ";
                        cin >> query;
                        another_search = (query == 'Y') || (query == 'y');
                }
                else
                        cout << "The word was not found." << endl;
        } while (word_found && another_search);
        in_file.close();
        return 0;
}
```

The declaration of the function that performs the search is

```
// Function: search_for_word
// Searches for the next instance of a given word in a file
//
// Inputs: an opened input file stream, a word, and a position
// Outputs: the file stream and a Boolean flag that will be TRUE
// if the next instance of the word was found, or FALSE otherwise.
// If the word was found, its position in the file will be returned.
// If the word was not found, the file stream will be at its end

void search_for_word(ifstream &in_file, string desired_word,
     int &position, boolean &word_found);
```

On each call, the function advances through the file stream, until the next instance of the desired word is found or the end-of-file condition is reached. The function increments the position parameter after reading each word. If the function finds the word in the file, it sets the flag to TRUE and returns the word's position; otherwise, it sets the flag to FALSE. An algorithm describing the search process is

```
Read a word from the file
Increment the position
While not end of file and the input word does not equal the desired word do
        Read a word from the file
        Increment the position
Set word_found to not end of file
```

Note that the loop stops when we hit the end of file (there are no more words to consider) or when we have found the next instance of the desired word. The loop describes a standard process called *sequential search.* In a sequential search, we begin at the first available data item, examine it, and continue until a match is found or we run out of items to consider. If the search terminates with no more items to consider, then we have not found a match, as the assignment to the flag at the end of the algorithm indicates. The translation of the algorithm into the C++ function is

```
void search_for_word(ifstream &in_file, string desired_word,
     int &position, boolean &word_found)
{
        string input_word;

        in_file >> input_word;
        ++position;
        while (! in_file.eof() && (input_word != desired_word))
```

```
        {
                in_file >> input_word;
                ++position;
        }
        word_found = ! in_file.eof();
}
```

Note that the end-of-file condition is tested before the strings are compared in the **while** loop condition. The order of these two subexpressions within the Boolean expression is critical. If the end-of-file condition is TRUE, the next subexpression will be skipped over, and the Boolean expression will return FALSE. This kind of process, known as short-circuit evaluation, was introduced in Chapter 5 and guards against errors such as comparing two strings when the data for one are not defined. In our example, if the two strings were compared before the end of file was tested and end of file happened to be TRUE, the program might produce mysterious and erroneous results.

The complete C++ program for searching for a word in a file is left as an exercise.

Buffered File Input

We frequently wish to take account of the line-by-line format of text in file processing. For example, we might want to count the number of lines in a file or copy the contents of one file to another with the same format. Unfortunately, the techniques we have seen thus far are inadequate for this purpose. The standard **>>** operator for file input treats the end-of-line character in a file as a separator between words, not lines.

C++ provides an **istream** function, **getline**, that will allow us to input lines of text from files. The form of a call to **getline** for reading a line of text is

<input stream>.getline(<character array variable>, <maximum length>);

getline reads characters from the input stream and stores them in the character array variable, until the number of characters read is one less than the maximum length specified or the end-of-line character is reached in the stream. The end-of-line character is not stored in the variable. However, the null character is stored in the variable. Therefore, the client must be careful to pass to **getline** a character array whose size is greater than or equal to the **<maximum length>** parameter.

For example, suppose we declared a character array variable called **line**, whose maximum possible size is 81, and we wished to read a line of text from a file stream called **in_file** into the variable. The following code declares the variable, inputs the text, and places the null character in the appropriate position in the character array:

```
char line[81];
in_file.getline(line, 81);
```

The maximum number of characters that can be read is one less than the size of the array. This will allow room for the null character to be placed at the end of the array if the line of text is 80 characters.

getline supports a process called *buffered file input.* This process utilizes a block of computer memory called a *buffer,* into which the data from a file are placed for transmission to a program. The main advantage of buffered file input is efficiency: because the system reserves a block of memory of definite size for input data, the process can run very quickly. The main disadvantage is that some data may not be read, if the data extend beyond the size of the buffer. Therefore, when we use **getline** for file processing, we must be careful to assume that the length of a line in a text file does not exceed the maximum size of a variable that we use to receive the input.

EXAMPLE 9.4

In this example, we copy the contents of one text file to another, maintaining the line-by-line format. We assume that the maximum length of a line of text in the source file is 100 characters, or **MAX_STRING_SIZE - 1**.

```
// Program file: buffcopy.cpp

#include <iostream.h>
#include <fstream.h>
#include <assert.h>

const int MAX_STRING_SIZE = 101;

// Function: open_input_file
// Prompts user for a file name and opens input stream on the file
//
// Outputs: an input file stream

void open_input_file(ifstream &in_file);

// Function: open_output_file
// Prompts user for a file name and opens output stream on the file
//

// Outputs: an output file stream

void open_output_file(ofstream &out_file);

// Function: copy_file
// Copies contents of one text file to another
//
// Inputs: opened input and output file streams

void copy_file(ifstream &in_file, ofstream &out_file);

int main()
{
      ifstream in_file;
      ofstream out_file;

      open_input_file(in_file, in_file);
      open_output_file(out_file);
      copy_file(in_file, out_file);
      in_file.close();
      out_file.close();
      return 0;
}
```

```
void open_input_file(ifstream &in_file)
{
	char in_file_name[MAX_STRING_SIZE];
	cout << "Enter the input file name: ";
	cin >> in_file_name;
	in_file.open(in_file_name);
	assert(! in_file.fail());
}

void open_output_file(ofstream &out_file)
{
	char out_file_name[MAX_STRING_SIZE];

	cout << "Enter the output file name: ";
	cin >> out_file_name;
	out_file.open(out_file_name);
	assert(! out_file.fail());
}

void copy_file(ifstream &in_file, ofstream &out_file)
{
	char line[MAX_STRING_SIZE];

	in_file.getline(line, MAX_STRING_SIZE);
	while (! in_file.eof())
	{
		out_file << line << endl;
		in_file.getline(line, MAX_STRING_SIZE);
	}
}
```

EXERCISES 9.2

1. Write a function that counts and displays on the screen the number of words in an input file. The program assumes that words in the file are separated by blank spaces or carriage returns. Test the program with files containing no words, one word, and several words.
2. Write a function that determines what the longest word in a file is. The function should display the longest word and its length on the terminal screen.
3. Write a function that finds and displays the average length of the words in a file.
4. Write a function that prompts the user for a word from the keyboard. Write a second function that counts the number of times that this word appears in a file. The program that uses this function should display the word count on the terminal screen.
5. The **getline** function works with the standard input stream, **cin**, as well as with input file streams. Write a program that takes string input from the keyboard with **getline**.
6. The **getline** function expects a string parameter that has been defined as a character array. Show how you can overload the **getline** function so that clients can use it with an instance of the string class developed in Chapter 7.
7. The use of the **open** function with a character array parameter causes the same problem as the **getline** function (Exercise 6). Show how you can overload this function, for both input file streams and output file streams, so that clients can pass an instance of the string class to it instead.

A NOTE OF INTEREST

Computer Ethics: Viruses

Tiny programs that deliberately cause mischief are epidemic among computers and are causing nervousness among those who monitor them.

Written by misguided or immature programmers, the "computer viruses" are placed on computer systems by piggybacking them on legitimate programs and messages. There, they may be passed along or instructed to wait until a prearranged moment to burst forth and destroy data.

At NASA Headquarters in Washington, several hundred computers had to be resuscitated after being infected. NASA officials have taken extra precautions and reminded their machines' users to follow routine computer hygiene: Don't trust foreign data or strange machines.

Viruses have the eerie ability to perch disguised among legitimate data just as biological viruses hide among genes in human cells, then spring out unexpectedly, multiplying and causing damage. Experts say that even when they try to study viruses in controlled conditions, the programs can get out of control and erase everything in a computer. The viruses can be virtually impossible to stop if their creators are determined enough.

"The only way to protect everybody against them is to do something much worse than the viruses: Stop talking to one another with computers," says William H. Murray, an information-security specialist at Ernst and Whinney financial consultants in Hartford, Connecticut.

Hundreds of programs and files have been destroyed by the viruses, and thousands of hours of repair or prevention time have been logged. Programmers have quickly produced antidote programs with such titles as Vaccine, Flu Shot, Data Physician, and Syringe.

Experts say known damage is minimal compared with the huge, destructive potential. They express the hope that the attacks will persuade computer users to minimize access to programming and data.

Viruses are the newest of evolving methods of computer mayhem. One type of virus is the Trojan Horse: It looks and acts like a normal program but contains hidden commands that eventually take effect, ordering mischief. The "time bomb" explodes at a set time; the "logic bomb" goes off when the computer arrives at a certain result during normal computation. The "salami attack" executes barely noticeable small acts, such as shaving a penny from thousands of accounts.

A virus typically is written as perhaps only a few hundred characters in a program containing tens of thousands of characters. When the computer reads legitimate instructions, it encounters the virus, which instructs the computer to suspend normal operations for a fraction of a second. During that time, the virus instructs the computer to check for other copies of itself and, if none is found, to make and hide copies. Instruction to commit damage may be included.

Is Your Machine at Risk?

1. Computer viruses are actually miniature computer programs. Most were written by immature programmers intent on destroying information in computers for fun.
2. Those who write virus programs often conceal them on floppy disks that are inserted in the computer.
3. An immature programmer makes the disk available to others, saying it contains a useful program or game. These programs can be lent to others or put onto computerized "bulletin boards" where anyone can copy them for personal use.
4. A computer receiving the programs will "read" the disk and the tiny virus program at the same time. The virus may then order the computer to do a number of things:

- Tell it to read the virus and follow instructions.
- Tell it to make a copy of the virus and place it on any disk inserted in the machine today.
- Tell it to check the computer's clock, and on a certain date destroy all information that tells where data are stored on any disk: If an operator has no way of retrieving information, it is destroyed.
- Tell it not to list the virus programs when the computer is asked for an index of programs.

5. In this way, the computer will copy the virus onto many disks—perhaps all or nearly all the disks used in the infected machine. The virus may also be passed over the telephone, when one computer sends or receives data from another.
6. Ultimately hundreds or thousands of people may have infected disks and potential time bombs in their systems.

9.3 Character Input and Output

OBJECTIVES

- to be able to obtain character data from input and output file streams
- to be able to distinguish character-level input and output from the input and output of other data types

Many problems call for the input and output of individual characters with file streams. Consider the problems of counting the total number of characters in a file and counting the total number of lines of text in a file. If these data include individual space or carriage return characters, we cannot rely on formatting conventions and the use of the **>>** operator for input. Recall that the **>>** operator treats space or carriage return characters as separators between data values in an input stream. Therefore, the **>>** operator cannot be used to input whitespace characters as data values in their own right. C++ provides two lower level operators, **get** and **put**, for handling character-level operations on streams.

Character Output with put

Character output with **put** is not much different than character output with **<<**. Assuming that **name** is a character array and **out_file** is an output file stream, the following two loops will have exactly the same effect on the file:

```
for (int j = 0; j < strlen(name); j ++)
       out_file << name[j];

for (int j = 0; j < strlen(name); j ++)
       out_file.put(name[j]);
```

The form of a statement that uses **put** is

<output file stream>.put(<character value>);

put is called as a function with a character value as its parameter. The function call is associated with the output stream by placing a period (".") between the name of the stream and the name of the function.

In general, **put** is defined such that it can work with any output stream. The loop

```
for (int j = 0; j < strlen(name); j ++)
      cout.put(name[j]);
```

will print the contents of the string on the terminal screen.

Character Input with get

Character input with **get** works in much the same way as character input with **>>**. One difference is that blank space and carriage return characters will be treated as character values in their own right. The form of a statement that uses **get** is

<input stream>.get(<character variable>);

The following statement would get the first character in a file and place it in the character variable **ch**:

```
in_file.get(ch);
```

Detecting the End of File at the Character Level

A special character value is reserved to mark the end of a file of characters. In the case of an empty file, this character is the only character present in the file. It is important to detect this character during input, so that further input is not attempted. It turns out that after the end-of-file character has been read with **get**, the **eof** function will return TRUE. Otherwise, it will return FALSE.

<file stream>.eof() can be used to control a **while** loop for processing an entire stream of characters. A standard form of a loop for processing character-level input from a file stream is

```
<input stream name>.get(<character variable>);
while (! <input stream name>.eof())
     process_data(<character variable>);
     <input stream name>.get(<character variable>);
```

Note the order of the operations in this process. We get a character first, since there will be at least one character in the file. Then the condition in the **while** loop protects the program from attempting to get or process any more characters when the end-of-file condition becomes TRUE. The first step in the body of the loop is to process the character just read (either the initial one or the one from the previous pass through the loop). The second step in the loop is to get the next character, which eventually will be the end-of-file character.

The next three examples illustrate algorithms for counting the number of characters in a file, counting the number of lines in a file, and copying the contents of one file to another file.

EXAMPLE 9.5

```
// This program counts and displays the number of characters in a file.
// We don't count the end-of-file character as one of these.

// Program file: charcnt.cpp

#include <iostream.h>
#include <fstream.h>

int main()
{
      ifstream in_file;
      char ch;
      int count;

      in_file.open("myfile");
      count = 0;
      in_file.get(ch);
      while (! in_file.eof())
      {
            ++count ;
            in_file.get(ch);
      }
      cout << "The total number of characters in myfile is " << count << endl;
      in_file.close();
      return 0;
}
```

EXAMPLE 9.6

To count the number of lines of text in a file, we can count the number of instances of the carriage return character denoted by `'\n'` in C++.

```
// This program counts and displays the number of lines in a file.

// Program file: linecnt.cpp

#include <iostream.h>
#include <fstream.h>

int main()
{
	ifstream in_file;
	char ch;
	int count;

	in_file.open("myfile");
	count = 0;
	in_file.get(ch);
	while (! in_file.eof())
	{
		if (ch == '\n')
			++count;
		in_file.get(ch);
	}
	in_file.close();
	cout << "The total number of lines in myfile is " << count << endl;
	return 0;
}
```

EXAMPLE 9.7

```
// This program copies the contents of one file to
another file.

// Program file: copyfile.cpp

#include <iostream.h>
#include <fstream.h>

int main()
{
	ifstream in_file;
	ofstream out_file;
	char ch;

	in_file.open("myfile");
	out_file.open("newfile");
	in_file.get(ch);
	while (! in_file.eof())
	{
		out_file.put(ch);
		in_file.get(ch);
```

```
        }
        in_file.close();
        out_file.close();
        return 0;
}
```

The last example calls for some comment. We copy every character from the input file to the output file, except for the input file's end-of-file character. This might lead you to think that the output file has no end-of-file character. However, the computer takes care of appending an end-of-file character to an output file whenever it is closed. Therefore, we were right to ignore the input file's end-of-file character. If we had copied it to the output file, this file would have contained two end-of-file characters, and would not have reflected the contents of the input file accurately.

EXERCISES 9.3

1. Assume that an input file stream, **in_file**, has been opened on a file, and that **ch** is a character variable. Describe what happens when each of the following pieces of code is run:

   a.
   ```
   in_file.get(ch);
   cout.put(ch);
   in_file.get(ch);
   cout.put(ch);
   in_file.get(ch);
   cout.put(ch);
   ```
   b.
   ```
   in_file.get(ch);
   while (! in_file.eof())
   {
        cout.put(ch);
        in_file.get(ch);
   }
   ```
   c.
   ```
   while (! in_file.eof())
   {
        in_file.get(ch);
        cout.put(ch);
   }
   ```
2. Write a program that deletes all blanks from a file. Your program should save the revised file for later use. (*Hint:* Copy the contents of the input file to another file, omitting the blanks.)
3. Write a program using a **switch** statement to scramble a file by replacing all blanks with an asterisk (*), and interchanging all A's with U's and E's with I's. Your program should print out the scrambled file and save it for subsequent use.
4. Write a program to update a file by numbering the lines consecutively as 1, 2, 3, ... The input file should not be modified.
5. Write a program to count the number of uppercase characters in a file.
6. Write a program to count the number of words in a text file. Assume that each word is followed by a blank or a period. The program should use **get** rather than **>>** to receive the input from the file.
7. Write a program to find the longest word in a file. Output should include the word and its length. The program should use **get** rather than **>>** to receive the input from the file.

8. Write a program to compute the average length of words in a file. The program should use **get** rather than **>>** to receive the input from the file.
9. Write a program that performs a search-and-replace operation on a file. The program will prompt the user for the word to search for and the word to use as a replacement. The program should replace all of the instances of the target word with the replacement word.

FOCUS ON PROGRAM DESIGN

The summary program for this chapter analyzes sentences in a file of text. It builds on the summary program in Chapter 7, in which we analyzed single sentences entered from the keyboard. That program displayed statistics about the number of characters and words in the sentence, and printed the longest word in the sentence as well. We used strings to represent words and string functions to handle the tasks of input, output, comparison, and determining word length.

The current program will prompt the user for a file name and open the file. If no error occurs, the program will compute and display statistics for

1. The total number of sentences in the file
2. The total number of words in the file
3. The average length of a sentence in the file
4. The length of the longest sentence in the file.

The program will recognize several kinds of sentences: those ending in a period ('.'), a question mark ('?'), and an exclamation point ('!'). Normally, a word ending with one of these characters will be treated as the last word in a sentence. As a special case, if one of these characters does not end the last word in the file, then that word is also treated as the last word in a sentence.

After the statistics are displayed, the program will ask the user if the analysis of another file is desired. If the answer is "Yes," the program will repeat the process; otherwise, the program will terminate execution.

A reasonable top-level module is

```
Do
        Open input file
        If there was no error opening the file then
                Initialize data
                Analyze sentences in file
                Close input file
                Display statistics
        Else
                Display error message
        Query user for another analysis
While answer to query = "Yes"
```

Before we can examine the submodules within this module, we must make explicit the data that are transmitted among them. The modules for opening and closing a file, and for analyzing sentences in the file, require a file stream. The modules for initializing data, analyzing sentences, and displaying statistics all require three integers, which represent the total number of sentences, the total number of words, and the length of the longest sentence. The average sentence length of a sentence can be computed locally in the display statistics module as a function of the other data. This data flow is shown in the structure chart in Figure 9.3.

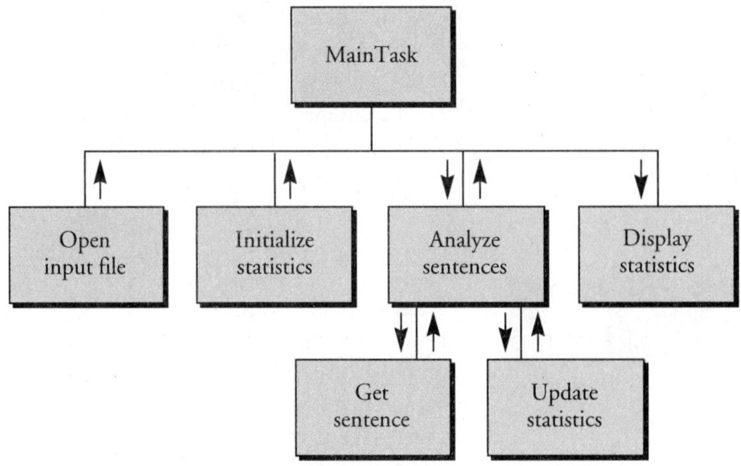

◆ FIGURE 9.3
A structure chart for analyzing sentences

The main module translates to the following C++ main program:

```
int main()
{
      char query;
      ifstream in_file;
      int word_count, sentence_count, longest_sentence_length;

      do
      {
            open_input_file(in_file);
            initialize_data(word_count, sentence_count, longest_sentence_length);
            analyze_sentences(in_file, word_count, sentence_count,
                  longest_sentence_length);
            in_file.close();
            display_statistics(word_count, sentence_count, longest_sentence_length);
            cout << "Analyze another file?[Y/N] ";
            cin >> query;
      } while ((query == 'Y') || (query == 'y'));
      return 0;
}
```

The module to initialize the data sets all of the integers to 0.

Module: Initialize data
Task: Sets all integers to 0
Outputs: integers representing the total number of sentences, the total number of words, and the length of the longest sentence

Set sentence count to 0
Set word count to 0
Set longest sentence length to 0

The C++ implementation is

```
void initialize_data(int &word_count, int &sentence_count,
      int &longest_sentence_length)
```

```
{
        word_count = 0;
        sentence_count = 0;
        longest_sentence_length = 0;
}
```

The module to analyze sentences must repeatedly invoke a process we developed in the program in Chapter 7 to analyze a single sentence. The difference here is that we read a sentence from a file and return just a word count. This value is then passed with the other data to a submodule that updates the statistics. The subprocesses are structured within a standard input file process.

Module: Analyze sentences
Task: Read sentences from a file and compute statistics
Inputs: a file stream and integers representing the total number of sentences, the total number of words, and the length of the longest sentence
Outputs: the integers updated

```
Do
        Get a word count on an input sentence
        If the word count > 0 then
                Update statistics
While not end of file
```

Note that a sentence may have a word count of zero. This occurs only in the special case where the input file is empty. The C++ implementation maintains the word count of the current input sentence as a local variable, **current_count**:

```
void analyze_sentences(ifstream &in_file, int &word_count, int &sentence_count,
      int &longest_sentence_length)
{
      int current_count;

      do
      {
            get_sentence(in_file, current_count);
            if (current_count > 0)
                  update_statistics(current_count, word_count, sentence_count,
                        longest_sentence_length);
      } while (! in_file.eof());

}
```

The module to display statistics computes the average length of a sentence and displays the four integer values with descriptive labels. Here is the C++ implementation:

```
void display_statistics(int word_count, int sentence_count,
      int longest_sentence_length)
{
      cout << endl << "Statistics for the current file. " << endl << endl;
      cout << "The number of words is " << word_count << "." << endl;
      cout << "The number of sentences is " << sentence_count << "." << endl;
      cout << "The average length of a sentence is "
           << word_count / sentence_count << "." << endl;
      cout << "The longest sentence had " << longest_sentence_length
           << " words." << endl << endl;
}
```

The get sentence module reads words from the file and maintains a count of them. This is an iterative process with two possible termination conditions: either the end of file has been reached, or the last input word contains a sentence termination character ('.', '?', or '!') at the end.

Module: Get sentence
Task: Reads words from a sentence and maintains a count of words
Input: an input file stream
Output: the count of words in the sentence; 0 words means no sentence at all

```
Set count to 0
Read a word from the file
If not end of file then
        Increment count by one
        While not end of file and word not at end of sentence do
                Read a word from the file
                Increment count by one
```

The initial test for an end of file guards against the case where the file is empty. The C++ implementation is

```
void get_sentence(ifstream &in_file, int &count)
{
        string word;

        count = 0;
        in_file >> word;
        if (! in_file.eof())
        {
                ++count;
                while (! in_file.eof() && ! end_of_sentence(word))
                {
                        in_file >> word;
                        ++count;
                }
        }
}
```

The update statistics module increments the word count and the sentence count and adjusts the length of the longest sentence if necessary.

Module: Update statistics
Task: Increments word and sentence counts and adjusts length of longest sentence if necessary
Inputs: integers representing the number of words in the current sentence, the total number of sentences, the total number of words, and the length of the longest sentence
Outputs: the last three input integers updated

```
Increment the word count by the number of words in the current
sentence
Increment the sentence count by one
If number of words in the current sentence > length of the longest
sentence then
```

Set length of the longest sentence to number of words in the current sentence

The C++ implementation is

```
void update_statistics(int current_count, int &word_count,
      int &sentence_count,
      int &longest_sentence_length)
{
      word_count = word_count + current_count;
      ++sentence_count;
      if (current_count > longest_sentence_length)
            longest_sentence_length = current_count;
}
```

At the lowest level of our design, the end-of-sentence module tests a word to see whether it marks the end of a sentence.

Module: End of sentence
Task: Determine whether a word marks the end of a sentence
Input: a word
Output: TRUE, if the word ends with '.', '?', or '!'; FALSE otherwise

Here is the C++ implementation of the module:

```
boolean end_of_sentence(string word)
{
      char last_ch = word.nth_char(word.length());

      return(last_ch == '.') || (last_ch == '?') || (last_ch == '!');
}
```

RUNNING, DEBUGGING AND TESTING HINTS

1. >> treats an end-of-line marker and a blank space as input separators.
2. **get** treats an end-of-line marker and a blank space as character data.
3. Always test for the end-of-file condition after getting a character from an input file. If the condition is TRUE, do not attempt to process the most recently read character or to read more characters from the file.

SUMMARY

Key Terms

buffer	input file stream	source device
destination device	output file stream	stream
end of input stream	serial processing	

Key Concepts

- Files can be used to store data between runs of a program.
- Access to file stream operations can be obtained by

  #include <fstream.h>.

- An input file stream can be declared by

  ifstream <stream name>;.

- An output file stream can be declared by

```
ofstream <stream name>;.
```

- File streams must be opened before they can be written to or read from.
- A file stream can be opened by

```
<stream name>.open(<file name>);.
```

- A file stream can be closed by

```
<stream name>.close();.
```

- An error in connecting a stream to a file can be detected by

```
<stream name>.fail();.
```

- For input data of most types, reading from a file stream can be accomplished by

```
<input file stream name> >> <variable name> . . .
                         >> <variable name>;.
```

- For output data of most types, writing to a file stream can be accomplished by

```
<output file stream name> << <expression> . . .
                          << <expression>;.
```

- When reading data from a file stream with `>>`, the absence of more data in an input stream can be detected by reading a datum and then running

```
<input stream name>.eof().
```

  This condition will be TRUE if there is no more data to be read, and FALSE otherwise.
- When reading character-level input, the absence of more data in an input stream can be detected by reading a character and then running

```
<input stream name>.eof().
```

- A line of text can be read from an input stream by using the buffered input function getline, as follows:

```
<input stream name>.getline(<character array variable>,
<maximum length>);.
```

- Character data can be read from an input stream by

```
<input stream name>.get(<character variable>);.
```

- Character data can be written to an output stream by

```
<output stream name>.put(<character value>);.
```

- A file exists outside the program block in secondary storage.

PROGRAMMING PROBLEMS AND PROJECTS

1. Write a program to print the contents of a text file omitting any occurrences of the letter "e" from the output.
2. A text file contains a list of integers in order from lowest to highest. Write a program to read and print the text file with all duplications eliminated.
3. Mr. John Napier, professor at Lancaster Community College, wants a program to compute grade-point averages. Each line of a text file contains three initials followed

by an unknown number of letter grades. These grades are A, B, C, D, or E. Write a program that reads the file and prints a list of the students' initials and their grade-point averages. (Assume an A is 4 points, a B is 3 points, and so on.) Print an asterisk next to any grade-point average that is greater than 3.75.

4. An amortization table (Problem 19, Chapter 6) shows the rate at which a loan is paid off. It contains monthly entries showing the interest paid that month, the principal paid, and the remaining balance. Given the amount of money borrowed (the principal), the annual interest rate, and the amount the person wishes to repay each month, print an amortization table. (The payment desired must be larger than the first month's interest.) Your table should stop when the loan is paid off, and should be printed with the following heads:

```
MONTH NUMBER   INTEREST PAID   PRINCIPAL PAID   BALANCE
```

Create an enumerated data type for the month number. Limit this to require that the loan be paid back within 60 months.

5. Mr. Christian (Problem 26, Chapter 6) uses a 90%, 80%, 70%, 60% grading scale on his tests. Given a list of test scores, print the number of A's, B's, C's, D's, and E's on the test. Terminate the list of scores with a sentinel value.

6. Write a program to print the perimeter and area of rectangles using all combinations of lengths and widths running from 1 foot to 10 feet in increments of 1 foot. Print the output in headed columns.

7. Using a team of three or four students, contact businesses and offices that use computers for data storage. Find exactly how they enter, store, and retrieve data. Discuss with them methods by which they use their databases and how large the databases are. Discuss what they like and dislike about data entry and retrieval. Ask if they have suggestions for modifying any aspect of working with their databases. Prepare a report for class that summarizes your team's findings.

8. Write a program that can be used as a text analyzer. Your program should be capable of reading an input file and keeping track of the frequency of occurrence of each letter of the alphabet. There should also be a count of all characters (including blanks) encountered that are not in the alphabet. Your output should be the data file printed line-by-line followed by a histogram reflecting the frequency of occurrence of each letter in the alphabet. For example, the following histogram indicates five occurrences of a, two of b, and three of c.

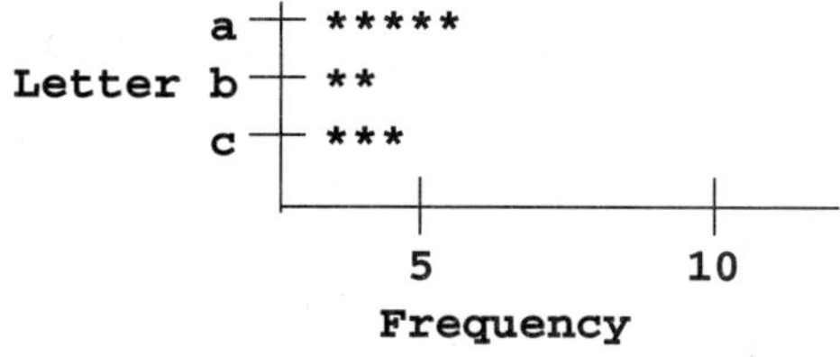

9. The Third Interdenominational Church has on file a list of all of its benefactors (a maximum of 20 names, each up to 30 characters) along with an unknown number of amounts that each has donated to the church. You have been asked to write a program that does the following:

  a. Print the name of each donor and the amount (in descending order) of any donations given by each.

  b. Print the total amounts in ascending order.

  c. Print the grand total of all donations.

  d. Print the largest single amount donated and the name of the benefactor who made this donation.

10. Read in a list of 50 integers from the data file **numberlist**. Place the even numbers into an output file called **even**, the odd numbers into an output file called **odd**, and the negatives into an output file called **negative**. Print all three files after all numbers have been read.

11. Ms. Alicia Citizen, your school's student government advisor, has come to you for help. She wants a program to total votes for the next student government election. Fifteen candidates will be in the election with five positions to be filled. Each person can vote for up to five candidates. The five highest vote getters will be the winners.

A data file called **votelist** contains a list of candidates (by candidate number) voted for by each student. Any line of the file may contain up to five numbers, but if it contains more than five numbers, it is discarded as a void ballot. Write a program to read the file and print a list of the total votes received by each candidate. Also, print the five highest vote getters in order from highest to lowest vote totals.

12. The data file **instructorlist** contains a list of the instructors in your school along with the room number to which each is assigned. Write a program that, given the name of the instructor, does a linear search to find and print the room to which the instructor is assigned.

13. Update the ATM management program from Chapter 8 to store new bank accounts in a file. The **<<** and **>>** operations should be used to define output and input operations for an account, and each new account entered from the keyboard in master mode should be stored at the end of the output file.

14. Add a member function to the ATM class of Problem 13 that displays the contents of a file of bank accounts on the screen. The function should be added to the master mode menu.

CHAPTER 10 Arrays

CHAPTER OUTLINE

Thus far in this text, we have been able to store large amounts of data in files, but we have been unable to manipulate it in a convenient way. For example, we can write a program that allows the user to enter a long list of bank accounts interactively and save the list in a file. However, the file structure does not efficiently support functions to process the accounts in the list, such as searching for an account, updating information in it, or computing statistics on all of the accounts in the list. Other objects are difficult to represent at all with the data structures at our disposal. Consider the example of representing a student whose attributes are a name and a list of ten quiz grades. Representing these attributes as eleven separate named data members in a class definition is unwieldy.

Fortunately, C++ provides a structured data type called an *array* to facilitate solving problems that require working with large amounts of data. The use of arrays permits us to set aside a group of memory locations that we can then manipulate as a single entity or that gives us direct access to any component. We already used arrays in Chapter 7 to develop strings. Other standard applications for arrays include creating tabular output (tables), alphabetizing a list of names, analyzing a list of test scores, and keeping an inventory.

In this chapter, we discuss the use of the array as a general data structuring mechanism. Then we develop two classes, the ordered collection and the sorted collection, that make array processing safe and convenient.

10.1 Arrays

Basic Idea and Notation

As previously mentioned, many instances arise in which several variables of the same data type are required. Let us at this point work with a list of five integers: 18, 17, 21, 18, and 19. Prior to this chapter, we would have declared five variables—**A**, **B**, **C**, **D**, and **E**—and assigned them appropriate values, or read them from the keyboard. This would have produced five values in memory, each accessed by a separate identifier.

18	17	21	18	19
A	B	C	D	E

OBJECTIVES

- to understand the basic concept of an array
- to use correct notation for arrays
- to be able to declare arrays with variable declarations and with type definitions
- to be able to use array components with appropriate arithmetic operations
- to be able to use array components with appropriate input and output statements

If the list was very long, this would be an inefficient way to work with these data; an alternative is to use an array. In C++, we declare a variable as an array variable using either of the following methods:

```
1. int list[5];
2. typedef int list_type[5];
   list_type list;
```

With either of these declarations, we now have five integer variables with which to work. They are denoted by

list[0]	list[1]	list[2]	list[3]	list[4]

and each is referred to as a *component* (or *element*) *of the array.* A good way to visualize these variables is to assume that memory locations are aligned in a column on top of each other and the name of the column is **list**. If we then assign the five values of our list to these five variables, we have the following in memory:

list	
18	list [0]
17	list [1]
21	list [2]
18	list [3]
19	list [4]

The components of an array are referred to by their relative position in the array. This relative position is called the *index* or *subscript* of the component. In the array of our five values, the component **list[2]** has an index of 2 and a value of 21. Note that an array index is always numbered from zero rather than one. The index of the last component in an array is always $N - 1$, where N is the number of elements in the array.

For the sake of convenience, you may choose to depict an array by listing only the index beside its appropriate component. Thus, **list** could be shown as

list	
	0
	1
	2
	3
	4

If you choose this method, remember that the array elements are referenced by the array name and the index, for example, **list[2]** for the third component. Whichever method you use, it is important to remember that each array component is a variable and can be treated exactly like any other declared variable of that base type in the program.

Declaring an Array

An earlier declaration of an array was

```
int list[5];
```

Let us now examine this declaration more closely. Several comments are in order.

1. The key word **int** indicates the data type for the components. This can, of course, be another data type such as **char**, as we have seen in our definition of a string type.
2. **[5]** is the syntax that indicates the array consists of five memory locations accessed by specifying each of the numbers, 0, 1, 2, 3, and 4. We frequently say the array is of length five. The information inside the brackets must be an integer constant or an expression whose value can be computed at compile time. This value must lie in the range from 1 to an upper bound defined for the particular system on which you are running your programs. (You can look this value up in the manual for your system.) The integer constant can be expressed either literally (**[5]**) or as a named constant (**[MAX_LIST_SIZE]**). The latter form is preferred for better program maintenance.
3. **list**, the name of the variable, can be any valid identifier. As always, it is good practice to use descriptive names to enhance readability.

The form for declaring an array variable is

```
<component type> <variable name> [ <integer value> ] ;
```

where **<component type>** is any predefined or user-defined data type and **<variable name>** is any valid identifier.

The following example illustrates another declaration of an array variable.

EXAMPLE 10.1

Suppose you want to create a list of 10 integer variables for the hours worked by 10 employees as follows:

Employee Number	Hours Worked
0	35
1	40
2	20
3	38
4	25
5	40
6	25
7	40
8	20
9	45

Declare an array that has 10 components of type **int** and show how it can be visualized. A descriptive name for the variable could be **hours**. There are 10 items, so we will define a constant, **MAX_LIST_SIZE = 10**, and use **[MAX_LIST_SIZE]** in the array variable declaration. Because the data consist of integers, the component type will be **int**. An appropriate definition and subsequent declaration could be

```
const int MAX_LIST_SIZE = 10;
int hours[MAX_LIST_SIZE];
```

At this stage, the components can be visualized as

hours	
	hours[0]
	hours[1]
	hours[2]
	hours[3]
	hours[4]
	hours[5]
	hours[6]
	hours[7]
	hours[8]
	hours[9]

After making appropriate assignment statements, **hours** can be visualized as

hours	
35	hours[0]
40	hours[1]
20	hours[2]
38	hours[3]
25	hours[4]
40	hours[5]
25	hours[6]
40	hours[7]
20	hours[8]
45	hours[9]

Other Element Types

The previous two arrays used element types that were integers. The following examples illustrate some array definitions with other element types.

EXAMPLE 10.2

Declare an array that allows you to store the hourly price for a share of IBM stock. A descriptive name could be **stock_prices**. A price is quoted at each hour from 9:00 A.M. to 3:00 P.M., so we will use **MAX_LIST_SIZE = 7** in the declaration section. Because the data consist of real numbers, the data type must be **float**. A possible declaration could be

```
const int MAX_LIST_SIZE = 7;
float stock_prices[MAX_LIST_SIZE];
```

This would then allow us to store the 9:00 A.M. price in **stock_prices[0]**, the 1:00 P.M. price in **stock_prices[4]**, and so on.

EXAMPLE 10.3

The declaration

```
const int MAX_LIST_SIZE = 6;
char alphas[MAX_LIST_SIZE];
```

will reserve six character components.

EXAMPLE 10.4

The declaration

```
#include "boolean.h"
const int MAX_LIST_SIZE = 4;
boolean flags[MAX_LIST_SIZE];
```

will produce an array whose components are Boolean values.

It is important to note that in each example, the array components will have no predictable values assigned until the program specifically makes some kind of assignment. Declaring an array does not assign values to any of the components.

COMMUNICATION AND STYLE TIPS

The use of descriptive constants is not essential for creating arrays. However, programs that use this method are much easier to maintain than those that use declarations such as **`int list[20];`**. You will appreciate the use of symbolic constants and array type names better when you learn how to process arrays with loops and functions in the following sections of this chapter.

Assignment Statements

Suppose we have declared an array

```
constant int MAX = 5;
int a[MAX];
```

and we want to put the values 1, 4, 9, 16, and 25 into the respective components. We can accomplish this with the assignment statements

```
a[0] = 1;
a[1] = 4;
a[2] = 9;
a[3] = 16;
a[4] = 25;
```

If variables **`b`** and **`c`** of type **`int`** are declared in the program, then the following are also appropriate assignment statements.

```
a[3] = b;
c = a[2];
a[2] = a[4];
```

If you want to interchange values of two components (for example, exchange **`a[2]`** with **`a[3]`**), you could use a third integer variable:

```
b = a[2];
a[2] = a[3];
a[3] = b;
```

This exchange is frequently used in sorting algorithms, so let us examine it more closely. Assume **`b`** contains no previously assigned value, and **`a[2]`** and **`a[3]`** contain 4 and 9, respectively.

[ ]	4	a[2]
b	9	a[3]

The assignment statement **b = a[2];** produces

4	4	a[2]
b	9	a[3]

The assignment statement **a[2] = a[3];** produces

4	9	a[2]
b	9	a[3]

and finally the assignment statement **a[3] = b;** produces

4	9	a[2]
b	4	a[3]

in which the original values of **a[2]** and **a[3]** have been interchanged.

Arithmetic

Components of an array can also be used in any appropriate arithmetic operation. For example, suppose **a** is the following array of integers

a	
1	a[0]
4	a[1]
9	a[2]
16	a[3]
25	a[4]

and that the values of the components of the array are to be added. This could be accomplished by the statement

```
sum = a[0] + a[1] + a[2] + a[3] + a[4];
```

Each of the following would also be a valid use of an array component:

```
b = 3 * a[1];
c = a[4] % 3;
d = a[1] * a[4];
```

For the array **a** given earlier, these assignment statements produce

55	12	1	100
sum	b	c	d

Some invalid assignment statements and the reasons they are invalid follow:

```
a[6] = 7;
```

This statement will compile and run. However, because 6 is not a valid subscript for the array, the program may behave strangely.

```
a[2.0] = 3;
```

The statement will not compile, because a subscript of type **float** is not allowed.

Reading and Writing

Because array components are names for variables, they can be used in input and output statements. For example, if **scores** is an array of five integers and you want to input the scores 65, 43, 98, 75, and 83 from the keyboard, you could use the code

```
cin >> scores[0] >> scores[1] >> scores[2] >> scores[3]
    >> scores[4];
```

This would produce the array

scores	
65	scores[0]
43	scores[1]
98	scores[2]
75	scores[3]
83	scores[4]

If you want to print the scores above 80, you could use the code

```
cout << setw(10) << scores[2] << setw(10) << scores[4] << endl;
```

to produce

```
98          83
```

It is important to note that you cannot input or output values into or from an entire array by a reference to the array name. Statements such as **cout << a;** are legitimate, but will display the address of the array rather than its contents.

Out-of-Range Array References

You have seen that an array in C++ has index values in the range 0 . . . $N - 1$, where N is the number of cells for storing data in the array. For example, the data declarations

```
const MAX_LIST_SIZE = 5;
int week_days[MAX_LIST_SIZE];
```

cause the system to allocate five cells of memory for an array whose index ranges from 0 to 4. The index values used in array references should also range from 0 to 4. If a programmer uses an index value outside of this range, a *range bound error* is said to occur. If the offending index is a variable, as in

```
int i = 5;
week_days[i] = 10;
```

the error will occur at run time, though the computer will not halt program execution with an error message that this error has occurred.

Even if the offending index is a constant, as in

```
week_days[5] = 10;
```

the error will not be caught at compile time. *C++ does not do range bound error checking.* This means that the program will compile and execute, and the reference will be to some other area of memory than the cells allocated for the array. In the case of an assignment to that location, a serious side effect will occur and may cause the program to behave in very mysterious ways.

Range bound errors in C++ programs are most often caused by failure to remember that the upper bound on the array index is *N* – 1, where *N* is the number of cells in the array. One way to avoid range bound errors with arrays is to be careful always to use an index that satisfies the condition 0 <= index < *N*, where *N* is the integer constant used to define the array type. You may wish to use the C++ assertion facility to place this precondition on array references in spots in a program where range bound errors are likely to occur.

In Section 10.5, we will develop an array class that supports range bound checking.

EXERCISES 10.1

1. Using descriptive names, define an array type and declare subsequent variables for each of the following:
   a. A list of 35 test scores
   b. The prices of 20 automobiles
   c. The answers to 50 true or false questions
   d. A list of letter grades for the classes you are taking this semester
2. Write a test program in which you declare an array of three components, read values into each component, sum the components, and print the sum and value of each component.
3. Assume the array **list** is declared as

   ```
   int list[100];
   ```

   and that all other variables have been appropriately declared. Label the following as valid or invalid. Include an explanation for any that are invalid.
   a. `cin >> list[3];`
   b. `a = list[3] + list[4];`
   c. `cout << list;`
   d. `list[10] = 3.2;`
   e. `max = list[50];`
   f. `average = (list[0] + list[8]) / 2;`
   g. `cout << list[25, 50, 75];`
   h. `cout << list[10] + list[25];`
   i. ```
      for (j = 0; j < 100; ++j)
          cin >> list;
      ```
   j. `list[36] = list[100];`
   k. `list_type[47] = 92;`
   l. `list[40] = list[41] / 2;`
4. Change each of the following so that a **typedef** is used to define the array type.
   a. `char letter_list[26];`
   b. `char company_name[30];`
   c. `float score_list[30];`
5. Consider the array declared by

   ```
   int waist_sizes[5]
   ```

   a. Sketch how the array should be envisioned in memory.
   b. After assignments
   ```

```
waist_sizes[0] = 34;
waist_sizes[1] = 36;
waist_sizes[2] = 32;
waist_sizes[3] = 2 * 15;
waist_sizes[4] = (waist_sizes[0] + waist_sizes[2]) / 2;
```

have been made, sketch the array and indicate the contents of each component.

6. Let the array money be declared by

```
float money[3];
```

Let **temp, x**, and **y** be **float** variables and assume **money** has the following values:

money	
19.26	money[0]
10.04	money[1]
17.32	money[2]

Assuming **money** contains the values indicated before each segment is executed, indicate what the array would contain after each section of code.

a.
```
temp = 173.21;
x = temp + money[1];
money[0] = x;
```

b.
```
if (money[1] < money[0])
{
      temp = money[2];
      money[1] = money[1];
      money[0] = temp;
}
```

c.
```
money[2] = 20.0 - money[2];
```

7. Let the array **list** be declared by

```
float list[10];
```

Write a program segment to initialize all components of **list** to 0.0.

A NOTE OF INTEREST

Monolithic Idea: Invention of the Integrated Circuit

One of the most significant breakthroughs in the history of technology occurred in the late 1950s. Prior to 1958, computer circuitry was limited because transistors, diodes, resistors, and capacitors were separate units that had to be wired together and soldered by hand. Although designers could design intricate computer supercircuits using 500,000 transistors, they were almost impossible to build because of the extensive handwork involved. For example, a circuit with 100,000 components could require more than 1,000,000 soldered connections. It was virtually impossible to assemble that many components without human error. Thus, the electronics industry was faced with an apparently insurmountable limit.

About this time, Jack St. Clair Kilby developed what has come to be known as the Monolithic Idea. He decided you could put the components of an entire circuit in a monolithic block of silicon. The idea, together with Robert Noyce's work on interconnecting circuits, allowed electronics engineers to overcome the obstacle presented by separate components. Kilby and Noyce's work resulted in the integrated circuit, the most important new product in the history of electronics. For their efforts, both men were awarded the National Medal of Science.

10.2 Using Arrays

OBJECTIVES

- to be able to use loops to input data into an array
- to be able to use loops to output data from an array
- to be able to assign array values by component assignment

Loops for Input and Output

One advantage of using arrays is the small amount of code needed when **for** loops are used to manipulate array components. For example, suppose a list of 100 scores is to be used in a program. If an array is declared by

```
const int MAX_LIST_SIZE = 100;
int scores[MAX_LIST_SIZE ];
```

the values can be read into the array using a **for** loop as follows:

```
for (j = 0; j < MAX_LIST_SIZE ; ++j)
{
     cout << "Enter a score: ";
     cin >> scores[j];
}
```

Note that the control variable is initialized to zero, and that the comparison in the termination condition is a simple less than operator (<). The reason for this is that the index positions in the array have been defined to range from 0 to 99, inclusive. Note also that the size of the array, **MAX_LIST_SIZE**, is used both in the array variable declaration and in the **for** loop. If we want to change the size of the array, we need only change the value 100 in the constant definition, and not in the array variable declaration or in the loop. As always, the use of symbolic constants greatly enhances program maintenance. Note finally that a statement such as **cin >> score** will not have the desired effect. You may only read data elements into individual components of the array.

Loops can be similarly used to produce output of array components. For example, if the array of test scores just given is to be printed in a column,

```
for (j = 0; j < MAX_LIST_SIZE; ++j)
     cout << scores[j] << endl;
```

will accomplish this. If the components of **scores** contain the values

scores	
78	scores[0]
93	scores[1]
.	.
.	.
82	scores[99]

the loop for writing produces

```
78
93
.
.
.
82
```

Note that you cannot cause the array components to be printed by a statement such as **cout << scores**. You must refer to the individual components.

Loops for output are seldom this simple. Usually we are required to format the output in some manner. For example, suppose the array **scores** is as declared earlier and we wish to print 10 scores to a line, each with a field width of five spaces. The following segment of code would accomplish this.

```
for (j = 0; j < MAX_LIST_SIZE; ++j)
{
     cout << setw(5) << scores[j];
     if (j % 10 == 0)
          cout << endl;
}
```

Loops for Assigning

Loops can also be used to assign values to array components. In certain instances, you might wish to have an array contain values that are not read from the keyboard. The following examples show how loops can be used to solve such instances.

EXAMPLE 10.5

Recall array **a** in Section 10.1 in which we made the following assignments:

```
a[0] = 1;
a[1] = 4;
a[2] = 9;
a[3] = 16;
a[4] = 25;
```

These assignments could have been made with the loop

```
for (j = 0; j < 4; ++j)
     a[j] = (j + 1) * (j + 1);
```

EXAMPLE 10.6

Suppose an array is needed whose components contain the letters of the alphabet in order from A to Z. Assuming you are using the ASCII character set, the desired array could be declared by

```
const int MAX_LIST_SIZE = 26;
char alphabet[MAX_LIST_SIZE];
```

The array alphabet could then be assigned the desired characters by the statement

```
for (j = 0; j < MAX_LIST_SIZE; ++j)
     alphabet[j] = char(j + 'A');
```

If **j = 0;** we have

```
alphabet[0] = char('A');
```

Thus,

```
alphabet[0] = 'A';
```

Similarly, for **j = 1;** we have

```
alphabet[1] = char(1 + 'A');
```

Eventually we obtain

alphabet	
'A'	alphabet[0]
'B'	alphabet[1]
'C'	alphabet[2]
.	.
.	.
.	.
'Z'	alphabet[25]

Assignment of values from components of one array to corresponding components of another array is a frequently encountered problem. For example, suppose the arrays **a** and **b** are declared as

```
const int MAX_LIST_SIZE = 50;
float a[MAX_LIST_SIZE];
float b[MAX_LIST_SIZE];
```

If **b** has been assigned values and you want to put the contents of **b** into **a** component by component, you must use the loop

```
for (j = 0; j < MAX_LIST_SIZE; ++j)
     a[j] = b[j];
```

Now suppose you tried a shortcut, by assigning one whole array variable to another:

```
a = b;
```

This assignment does *not* cause 50 assignments to be made at the component level. In some implementations of C++, the assignment will cause the name **a** to be an alias for the array **b**. The reason for this is that references to array variables are really references to the addresses of the arrays. In other implementations of C++, the assignment is a syntax error. It would be a good practice to write a function that copies components from one array to another and use it in your various programs.

Processing with Loops

Loops are especially suitable for reading, writing, and assigning array components, and they can be used in conjunction with arrays to process data. The following examples illustrate additional uses of loops for processing data contained in array variables.

EXAMPLE 10.7

Recall the problem earlier in this section in which we read 100 test scores into an array. Assume the scores have been read and you now wish to find the average score and the largest score. Assume variables **sum, max**, and **average** have been appropriately declared. The following segment will compute the average.

```
sum = 0;
for (j = 0; j < MAX_LIST_SIZE; ++j)
     sum = sum + scores[j];
average = sum / MAX_LIST_SIZE;
```

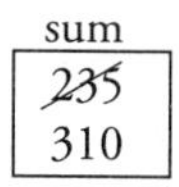

sum: ~~235~~ 310

	scores
0	80
1	65
2	90
j = 3	75
.	.
.	.
97	93
98	86
99	79

For example, on the fourth time through the **for** loop, **sum** would accumulate from 235 to 310.

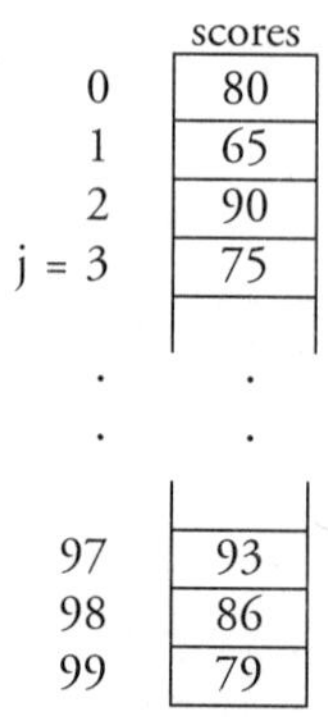

The maximum score can be found by using the following segment of code:

```
max = scores[0];
for (j = 1; j < MAX_LIST_SIZE; ++ j)
     if (scores[j] > max)
          max = scores [j];
```

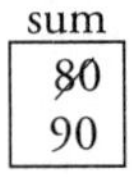

sum: ~~80~~ 90

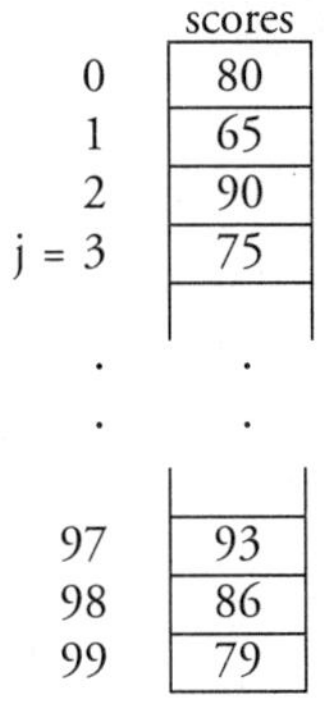

	scores
0	80
1	65
2	90
j = 3	75
.	.
.	.
97	93
98	86
99	79

For example, when **j** is 2, **max** would be updated from 80 to 90.

EXAMPLE 10.8

Write a segment of code to find the smallest value of array **a** and the index of the smallest value. Assume the variables have been declared as

```
const int MAX_LIST_SIZE = 100;
float a[MAX_LIST_SIZE];
float min;
int index;
```

and the values have been read into components of **a**. The following code will solve the problem:

```
index = 0;
for (j = 1; j < MAX_LIST_SIZE; ++ j)
     if (a[j] < a [index])
          index = j;
```

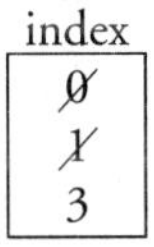

index: ~~0~~ ~~1~~ 3

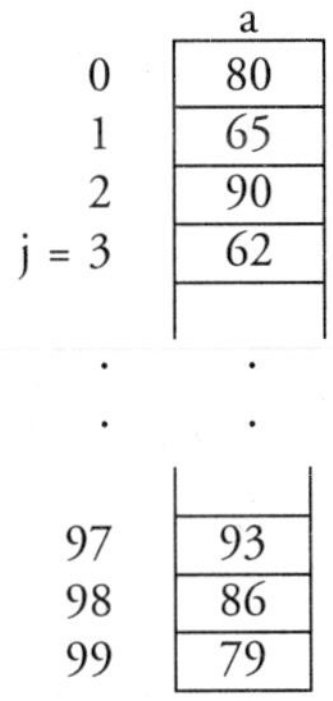

	a
0	80
1	65
2	90
j = 3	62
.	.
.	.
97	93
98	86
99	79

For this data, when **j** is 3, **index** would be updated from 1 to 3.

A standard problem encountered when working with arrays is that of not knowing exactly how many components of an array will be needed. In C++, the standard array data type has a fixed size. Thus, you must decide some upper limit for the length of the array. A standard procedure is to declare a reasonable limit, keeping two points in mind.

1. The length must be sufficient to store all the data.
2. The amount of storage space must not be excessive; do not set aside excessive amounts of space that will not be used.

EXERCISES 10.2

1. Assume the following array declarations:

```
typedef int num_list_type[5];
typedef boolean answer_list_type[10];
typedef char name_list_type[20];

num_list_type list, scores;
answer_list_type answers;
name_list_type initials;
```

Indicate the contents of the arrays after each segment of code.

a.
```
for (j = 0; j < 5; ++j)
    list[j] = j / 3;
```

b.
```
for (j = 1; j < 6; ++j)
{
    list[j - 1] = j + 3;
    scores[j - 1] = list[j - 1] / 3;
}
```

c.
```
for (j = 0; j < 10; ++j)
    if (j % 2 == 0)
        answers[j] = TRUE;
    else
        answers[j] = FALSE;
```

d.
```
for (j = 0; j < 20; ++j)
    initials[j] = char(j + 64);
```

2. Write a test program to illustrate what happens when you try to use an index that is not in the defined range for an array; for example, try to use the loop

```
for (j = 0; j < 10; ++j)
     cin >> a[j];
```

when **a** has been declared as **int a[5];**

3. Let the array **best** be declared by

```
int best[30];
```

and assume that test scores have been read into **best**. What does the following section of code do?

```
count = 0;
for (j = 0; j < 30; ++j);
     if (best[j] > 90)
          ++count;
```

4. Declare an array and write a segment of code to do the following:
   a. Read 20 integer test scores into the array.
   b. Count the number of scores greater than or equal to 55.
5. Declare an array using a **typedef** and write a section of code to read a name of 20 characters from a line of input.
6. Let the array **list** be declared by **int list[7];** and assume the components have values of

list	
-2	list[0]
3	list[1]
0	list[2]
-8	list[3]
20	list[4]
14	list[5]
-121	list[6]

Show what the array components would be after the following program segment is executed:

```
for (j = 0; j < 7; ++j)
       if (list[j] < 0)
                 list[j] = 0;
```

7. Assume array **a** is declared as

```
float a[100];
```

Write a segment of code that uses a loop to initialize all components to zero.

8. Let the array **n** be declared as **char n[21];** and assume the array components have been assigned the values

J	O	H	N		S	M	I	T	H
n[0]	n[1]	n[2]	n[3]	n[4]	n[5]	n[6]	n[7]	n[8]	n[9]

What output is produced by the following?

a.
```
for (j= 0; j < 10; ++j)
    cout << n[j];
cout << endl;
```

b.
```
for (j= 0; j < 5; ++j)
    cout << n[j];
cout << ", ";
for (j= 0; j < 4; ++j)
    cout << n[j];
cout << endl;
```

c.
```
for (j = 9; j >= 0; --j)
    cout << n[j];
```

9. Assume an array has been declared as

```
int test_scores[50];
```

Write a segment of code to print a suitable heading (assume this is a list of test scores) and then output a numbered list of the array components.

10.3 Array Parameters and Functions

OBJECTIVES

- to be able to use functions to process arrays
- to be able to pass arrays as parameters to functions
- to understand the difference between array parameters and parameters of other data types

Functions can be used with array parameters to maintain a structured design. Consider the problem of computing the mean of a list of test scores. We can represent the list of scores as an array that can be passed to several functions for processing. A first-level pseudocode development of a solution to this problem is as follows:

1. Get the scores **(function get_data)**
2. Compute the average **(function calc_mean)**
3. Print a header **(function print_header)**
4. Print the results **(function print_results)**

The functions **get_data**, **calc_mean**, and **print_results** all take an array parameter and an integer parameter representing the number of data elements currently stored in the array. Here are the declarations of these functions:

```
// Function: get_data
// Gets list of scores from the user at the keyboard
// until a sentinel is entered
//
// Inputs: length, representing the maximum physical size
// of the list
// Outputs: an array of integers representing the list
// and length, representing
// its logical size
```

```
void get_data(int list[ ], int &length);

// Function: calc_mean
// Computes the mean of the scores in the list
//
// Inputs: an array of integers and its length
// Output: a real number representing the mean of the
// integers in the array

float calc_mean(int list[ ], int length);

// Function: print_results
// Displays the scores and the mean score
//
// Inputs: an array of integers and the mean on the
// screen

void print_results(int list[ ], int length, float ave);
```

There are several things to note about these declarations:

1. None of the arrays appears to be passed by reference to the functions, but they all are. Recall from our discussion of character arrays in Section 7.2 that the address of an actual parameter of an array is always passed to a function. In the case of actual parameters that are array variables, the corresponding formal parameters in the function will serve as aliases for the variables. Therefore, changes to the array cells referenced by a formal array parameter will also be changes to the array cells referenced by the actual parameter.
2. The maximum size of each array does not appear to be specified in the formal parameter declarations, where we see a pair of empty square brackets (**[ ]**). Because the arrays are all passed by reference, the computer does not have to know how large the actual array will be when a function is called. Leaving the physical size of the array unspecified in the formal parameter declaration will allow a function to be called with arrays of different physical sizes, as long as the element type (in this case, **int**), is the same.
3. The **length** parameter for **get_data** represents the *physical size* of the array parameter when the function is called, and it represents the *logical size,* or number of data elements input, when the function returns.
4. Though the form **<element type> <parameter name> [ ]** is most commonly used to declare array parameters, other forms may specify the physical size of the array or may precede the array parameter name with an array type name.

The implementation of **get_data** is

```
void get_data(int list[ ], int &length)
{
      int data, logical_length;

      logical_length = 0;
      cout << "Enter an integer (" << INPUT_SENTINEL
           << " to end input): ";
      cin >> data;
      while ((logical_length < length) && ! end_of_input(data))
```

```
    {
        list[logical_length] = data;
        ++logical_length;
        cout << "Enter an integer (" << INPUT_SENTINEL
             << " to end input): ";
        cin >> data;
    }
    length = logical_length;
}
```

Using two different lists and their lengths, **get_data** could be called by

```
const int MAX1 = 10;
const int MAX2 = 20;

int list1[MAX1];
int list2[MAX2];

int length1 = MAX1;
int length2 = MAX2;

get_data(list1, length1);
get_data(list2, length2);
```

The average score in a list could be computed by the function **calc_mean**:

```
float calc_mean (int list[ ], int length)
{
     int sum = 0;

     for (int j = 0; j < length; ++j)
          sum = sum + list[j];
     return float(sum) / length;
}
```

A function to print a heading would be written in a manner similar to that we have used previously. If we want the output to be

```
Test Scores
-----------
    99
    98
    97
    96
    95

The average score on this test was 97.00.
```

the function for the heading could be

```
void print_header()
{
      cout << endl;
      cout << "Test Scores" << endl;
      cout << "-----------" << endl;
      cout << endl;
}
```

A function to print the results could be

```
void print_results (int list[ ], int length, float ave)
{
      for (int j = 0; j < length; ++j)
           cout << setw(5) << list[j] << endl;
      cout << endl << fixed << showpoint << setprecision(2);
      cout << "The average score on this test was"
           << setw(6) << ave << endl;
}
```

This function could be called by

```
print_results(scores, length, ave);
```

where **ave** is found by

```
ave = calc_mean(scores, length);
```

The important thing to remember about array parameters is that they are treated very differently than parameters of other data types in C++. For reasons of efficiency, the address of a C++ array variable (which is actually identified by the array name and also is the address of the first data value in the array) is always passed to a function expecting an array parameter. The following rules of thumb will help in designing functions for processing arrays:

1. Never use the **&** symbol when specifying a formal array parameter in a function declaration or heading.
2. Specify a constant array formal parameter, of the form **const <element type> <parameter name> [ ]**, when you want to guarantee that no changes will be made to the array variable being passed to a function.

The special nature of array parameters in C++ can be a source of confusion for beginning programmers. In Section 10.5, we develop a new array class that allows array parameters to be treated like parameters of other data types in C++.

EXERCISES 10.3

1. Assume the following declarations have been made in a program.

```
typedef int row_type[10];
typedef float column_type[30];
typedef char string20_type[21];

row_type list1, list2;
column_type aray;
string20_type name1, name2;
int a[10];
int b[10];
```

Indicate which of the following are valid function declarations. Write an appropriate line of code that will use each valid declaration. Include an explanation for those that are invalid.

a. **void new_list (row_type x, column_type y);**
b. **void new_list (row_type &x, column_type &y);**
c. **void new_list (int x[ ]);**
d. **void new_list (row_type &x, row_type &y);**
e. **void new_list (row_type &row_type);**
f. **void word_week (int days[7]);**
g. **void surname (name x);**

h. `void surnames (string20_type x, string20_type y);`
i. `void get_data (int x, name &y);`
j. `void table (row_type &x, row_type &y);`

2. When possible, use the declarations of Exercise 1 to write function declarations so that each of the following statements in the main program is an appropriate call to a function. Explain any inappropriate calls.

   a. `old_list (list1, aray);`
   b. `change_list (list1, name1, b);`
   c. `scores (a, b);`
   d. `surname (string20_type);`

3. Write an appropriate function declaration and a line of code to call the function for each of the following.

   a. A function to input 20 test scores into an array.
   b. A function to count the number of occurrences of the letter 'A' in an array of 50 characters.
   c. A function to input integer test scores from the keyboard, count the number of scores, count the number of scores greater than or equal to 90, and save this information for later use.

4. Assume the following declarations have been made:

```
typedef int column_type[10];
column_type list1, list2;
```

   Indicate the contents of each array after the call to the corresponding function.

   a.

```
void sample (column_type &list1, column_type list2)
{
        for (int j = 0; j < 10; ++j)
        {
                list1[j] = j *j;
                list2[j] = list1[j] % 2;
        }
}

for (int k = 0; k < 10; ++k)
{
        list1[k] = 0;
        list2[k] = 0;
}
sample (list1, list2);
```

   b. Replace the function call with

```
sample (list2, list1);
```

   c. Replace the function call with consecutive calls

```
sample (list1, list2);
sample (list2, list1);
```

5. Write a function to examine an array of integers and then return the maximum value, minimum value, and number of negative values to the main program.

6. Discuss some of the implementation details you would need in order to read a list of names into an array.

Sorting and Searching an Array

OBJECTIVES

- to be able to sort an array using a selection sort
- to be able to search an array using a sequential search

Sorting an Array

Arrays often need to be sorted in either ascending or descending order. We will consider here one of the easier methods for doing this, the *selection sort,* and examine another method, the *quick sort,* in Chapter 12.

Suppose we have an array **a** of five integers that we wish to sort from smallest to largest. The values currently in **a** are as depicted on the left; we wish to end up with values as on the right.

a		a	
6	a[0]	1	a[0]
4	a[1]	4	a[1]
8	a[2]	6	a[2]
10	a[3]	8	a[3]
1	a[4]	10	a[4]

The basic idea of a selection sort is

For each index position *I*

1. Find the smallest data value in the array from positions *I* through length – 1, where length is the number of data values stored.
2. Exchange the smallest value with the value at position *I.*

The first pass through the loop produces

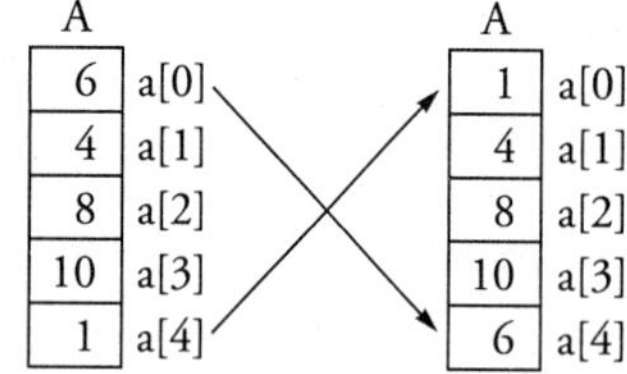

The second, third, and fourth passes produce

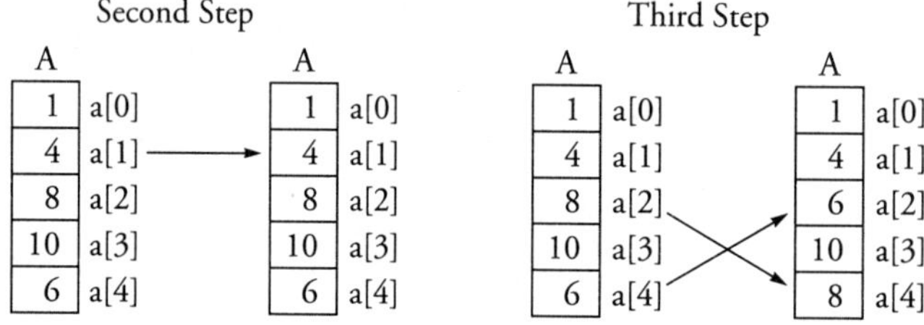

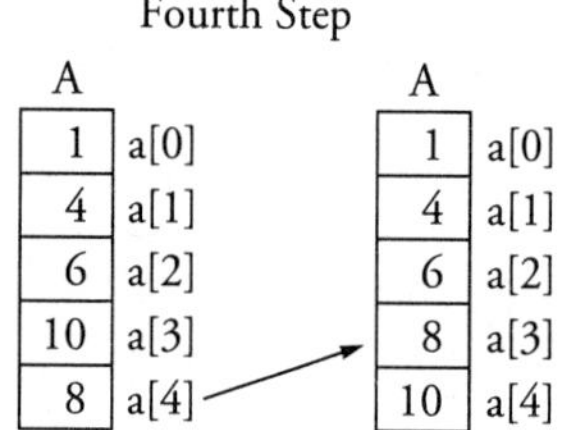

Notice that in the second pass, since the second smallest number was already in place, we need not exchange anything. Before writing the algorithm for this sorting procedure, note the following:

1. If the array is of length *n,* we need *n* – 1 steps.
2. We must be able to find the smallest number.
3. We need to exchange appropriate array components.

When the code is written for this sort, note that strict inequality (<) rather than weak inequality (<=) is used when looking for the smallest remaining value. The algorithm to sort by selection is

For each j from 0 to n - 1 do
    Find the smallest value among a[j], a[j + 1], . . . a[n - 1]
        and store the index of the smallest value in index
    Exchange the values of a[j] and a[index], if necessary

In Section 10.2, Example 10.8, we saw a segment of code required to find the smallest value of array **a**. With suitable changes, we will incorporate this in the segment of code as a function, **find_smallest**, for the selection sort. We will also develop a function, **swap**, that exchanges the elements in an array when necessary.

Using these two functions, the implementation of a **sort** function is

```
void sort(int a[ ], int length)
{
      int min_index = 0;

      for (int j = 0; j < length - 1; ++j)
      {
            min_index = find_minimum(a, j, length);
            if (min_index != j)
                  swap(a[j], a[min_index]);
      }
}
```

The function for finding the minimum value in an array takes three parameters: the array, the position to start the search, and the length or logical size of the array. The function returns the index position of the minimum element in the array. Its implementation uses a **for** loop:

```
int find_minimum(int a[ ], int first, int length)
{
      int min_index = first;

      for (int k = first + 1; k < length; ++k)
            if (a[k] < a[min_index])
                  min_index = k;
      return min_index;
}
```

The **swap** function exchanges the values of two integer variables:

```
void swap(int &x, int &y)
{
      int temp = x;
      x = y;
      y = temp;
}
```

Let us now trace this sort for the five integers in the array we sorted at the beginning of this section.

a	
6	a[0]
4	a[1]
8	a[2]
10	a[3]
1	a[4]

For **`j = 0, min_index = 0`** (in **`find_minimum`**), and this produces

0
min_index

For the loop (in **`find_minimum`**) **`for (k = 1; k < 5; ++k)`**, we get successive assignments

k	min_index
1	1
2	1
3	1
4	4

The statements (in **`swap`**)

```
temp = a[j];
a[j] = a[min_index];
a[min_index] = temp;
```

produce the partially sorted array:

a	
1	a[0]
4	a[1]
8	a[2]
10	a[3]
6	a[4]

EXAMPLE 10.9

This example accomplishes these tasks:

1. Inputs real numbers from the keyboard.
2. Prints the numbers in a column of width six with two places to the right of the decimal.
3. Sorts the array from low to high.
4. Prints the sorted array using the same output format.

An expanded pseudocode development for this is

1. Print greeting **`(function print_greeting)`**
2. Get data **`(function get_data)`**
3. Output list of data **`(function print_list)`**
4. Sort list **`(function sort_list)`**
5. Output sorted list **`(function print_list)`**

```
// Program file: sort.cpp

// This program illustrates the use of a sorting algorithm
// with an array of reals. Output includes data in both an
// unsorted and a sorted list. The data are formatted and
// numbered to enhance readability.

#include <iostream.h>
#include <iomanip.h>
#include "boolean.h"

const char SKIP = ' ';
const int MAX_LIST_SIZE = 5;
const float INPUT_SENTINEL = -999.0;

// Function: print_heading
// Displays sign-on message about purpose of the program

void print_greeting();

// Function: get_data
// Reads data from keyboard into list
//
// Inputs: length represents physical size of list
// Outputs: a list of real numbers and its length, representing logical size of
// list

void get_data(float list[ ], int &length);

// Function: print_list
// Prints contents of list to terminal screen
//
// Inputs: a list of real numbers and its length

void print_list(float list[ ], int length);

// Function: sort_list
// Sorts contents of list into ascending order
//
// Inputs: a list of real numbers and its length
// Output: a sorted list of real numbers

void sort_list(float list[ ], int length);

// Function: end_of_input
// Informs caller whether or not input data is end-of-input sentinel
//
// Input: a real number
// Output: TRUE, if number is end of input sentinel, FALSE otherwise

// Function: find_minimum
// Finds position of minimum element in list between first and length
//
```

```
// Inputs: a list, the first position, and the length
// Output: the index position of the minimum element in the list

int find_minimum(float list[ ], int first, int length);

// Function: swap
// Exchanges two real numbers
//
// Inputs: two real number variables
// Outputs: the two variables, with their values exchanged

void swap(float &x, float &y);

boolean end_of_input(float data);

int main()
{
       int length = MAX_LIST_SIZE;
       float list[MAX_LIST_SIZE];

       print_greeting();
       get_data(list, length);
       cout << setw(10) << SKIP << "The original list is as follows:'' << endl;
       cout << endl;
       print_list(list, length);
       sort_list(list, length);
       cout << setw(10) << SKIP << "The sorted list is as follows:" << endl;
       cout << endl;
       print_list(list, length);
       return 0;
}

void print_greeting()
{
cout << setprecision(2) << fixed << showpoint;
cout << endl;
cout << setw(10) << SKIP << "This sample program does the following:"
     << endl;
cout << endl;
cout << setw(12) << SKIP << "1 Gets reals from the keyboard." << endl;
cout << setw(12) << SKIP << "2 Prints the data." << endl;
cout << setw(12) << SKIP << "3 Sorts the data from low to high." << endl;
cout << setw(12) << SKIP << "4 Prints a sorted list of the data."
     << endl;
cout << endl;
}

void get_data(float list[ ], int &length)
{
        int logical_length = 0;
        float data;

        cout << "Enter a real number (-999 to stop input): ";
        cin >> data;
```

```
        while((logical_length < length) && ! end_of_input(data))
        {
             list[logical_length] = data;
             ++logical_length;
             cout << "Enter a real number (-999 to stop input): ";
             cin >> data;
        }
        if (! end_of_input(data) && (logical_length == length))
              cout << "There is more data." << endl;
        length = logical_length;
}

void print_list(float list[ ], int length)
{
        cout << endl;
        for (int j = 0; j < length; ++j)
              cout << setw(12) << SKIP << '<' << j + 1 << '>' << setw(6)
                   << list[j]
                   << endl;
}

void sort_list(float list[ ], int length)
{
        int min_index = 0;

        for (int j = 0; j < length - 1; ++j)
        {
              min_index = find_minimum(list, j, length);
              if (min_index != j)
                   swap(list[j], list[min_index]);
        }
}

int find_minimum(float list[ ], int first, int length)
{
        int min_index = first;

        for (int j = first + 1; j < length; ++ j)
              if (list[j] < list[min_index])
                      min_index = j;
        return min_index;
}

void swap(float &x, float &y)
{
        float temp = x;
        x = y;
        y = temp;
}

boolean end_of_input(float data)
{
        return data == INPUT_SENTINEL;
}
```

The output for this program is

```
This sample program does the following:

   1 Gets reals from the keyboard.
   2 Prints the data.
   3 Sorts the data from low to high.
   4 Prints a sorted list of the data.

The original data are as follows:

   <1>     34.56

   <2>     78.21

   <3>     23.30

   <4>     89.90

   <5>     45.00

The sorted list is as follows:

   <1>     23.30

   <2>     34.56

   <3>     45.00

   <4>     78.21

   <5>     89.90
```

Searching an Array

The need to search an array for a value is a common problem. For example, you might wish to replace a test score for a student, delete a name from a directory or mailing list, or upgrade the pay scale for certain employees. These and other problems require you to be able to examine elements in some list until the desired value is located. When it is found, some action is taken. In this section, we assume all lists are nonempty.

The searching algorithm we examine is the most common method, a *sequential (linear) search.* This process is accomplished by examining the first element in some list and then proceeding to examine the elements in the order they appear until a match is found. Variations of this basic process include searching a sorted list for the first occurrence of a value, searching a sorted list for all occurrences of a value, and searching an unsorted list for the first occurrence of a value. We will look at another method, the *binary search,* in Chapter 12.

To illustrate a sequential search, suppose you have an array **a** of integers and you want to find the first occurrence of some particular value (**num**). As you search the array, if the desired value is located, you want to print its position. If the value is not in the array, an appropriate message should be printed. The code for such a search follows:

```
index = 0;
while ((index < length) && (num != a[index]))
      ++index;
```

A reasonable message for output is

```
if (index == length)
      cout << num << " is not in the list." << endl;
else
      cout << num << " is in position" << setw(5)
           << index << endl;
```

Let's now consider some variations of this problem. Our code works for both a sorted and an unsorted list. However, if we are searching a sorted list, the algorithm can be improved. For example, if the array components are sorted from low to high, we need to continue the search only until the value in an array component exceeds the value of **num**. At that point, there is no need to examine the remaining components. The only change required in the loop for searching is to replace **num != a[index]** with **num > a[index]**. Thus, we have

```
index = 0;
while ((index < length) && (num > a[index]))
      ++index;
```

A relatively easy modification of the sequential search is to examine a list for all occurrences of some value. When searching an array, you would generally print the positions and values when a match is found. To illustrate, if **a** is an array of integers and **num** has an integer value, we can search **a** for the number of occurrences of **num** by

```
count = 0;
for (index = 0; index < length; ++index)
     if (num == a[index])
     {
          ++count;
          cout << num << " is in position" << setw(5)
               << index<< endl;
     }
```

This code works for an unsorted list. A modification of the code for working with a sorted list is included as an exercise.

EXERCISES 10.4

1. Assume the array **column** is to be sorted from low to high using the selection sort.

column
-20
10
0
10
8
30
-2

   a. Sketch the contents of the array after each of the first two passes.
   b. How many exchanges are made during the sort?
2. Write a test program that prints the partially sorted arrays after each pass during a selection sort.

A NOTE OF INTEREST

Too Few Women in the Computer Science Pipeline?

Studies show that women in computer science programs in U.S. universities terminate their training earlier than men do. Between 1983 and 1986 (the latest year for which we have such figures) the percentage of bachelor's degrees in computer science awarded to women was in the range of 36 to 37% and the percentage of master's degrees was in the range of 28 to 30%. During the same time span, the percentage of doctoral degrees awarded to women was in the range of only 10 to 12%, and it has remained at that level, with the exception of a slight increase in 1989. If we look at the people who are training the future computer scientists, we may find a clue as to why this discrepancy exists. Women currently hold only 6.5% of the faculty positions in the computer science and computer engineering departments in the 158 PhD-granting institutions included in the 1988–1989 Taulbee Survey. In fact, a third of these departments have no female faculty members at all. This pattern of decreasing representation is often described as pipeline shrinkage: as women move along the academic pipeline, their percentages continue to shrink.

The ACM Committee on the Status of Women has made a number of recommendations to promote change, including the following:

Ensure equal access to computers for young girls and boys and develop educational software appealing to both.

Establish programs (such as science fairs, scouting programs, and conferences in which women speak about their careers in science and engineering) to encourage high school girls to continue with math and science.

Develop programs to pair undergraduate women with women graduate students or faculty members who serve as role models, providing encouragement and advice.

Provide women with opportunities for successful professional experiences (such as involvement in research projects) beginning as early as the undergraduate years.

Establish programs that make women computer scientists visible to undergraduates and graduate students. Women can be invited to campuses to give talks or to serve as visiting faculty members (as, for example, in the National Science Foundation's Visiting Professorships for Women).

Encourage men and women to serve as mentors for young women in the field.

Maintain lists of qualified women computer scientists to increase the participation of women in influential positions such as program committees, editorial boards, and policy boards.

Establish more reentry programs that enable women who have stopped their scientific training prematurely to retrain as computer scientists.

Increase awareness of, and sensitivity to, subtle discrimination and its effects.

Develop and enforce safety procedures on campus. Provide safe access at all hours to public terminal areas, well-lit routes from offices to parking lots, and services to escort those walking on campus after dark.

Provide affordable, quality childcare.

3. Change the code for the selection sort so it sorts an array from high to low.
4. Write a complete program that does the following:
   a. Read 10 reals into an array from the keyboard.
   b. If the first real is positive, sort the array from high to low; if it is negative, sort the array from low to high.
   c. Print a numbered column containing the sorted reals with the format of 10 columns of field width and two decimal places of precision.
5. Modify the selection sort by including a counter that counts the number of assignments of array elements made during a sort.
6. Using the modification in Exercise 5, sort lists of differing lengths that contain randomly generated numbers. Display the results of how many assignments were made for each sort on a graph. Use lists whose lengths are multiples of 10.
7. Suppose you have an array of student names and an array of these students' test scores. How would the array of names be affected if you sorted the test scores from high to low?

10.5 A Safe Array Class

OBJECTIVES

- to understand why standard arrays are not safe
- to be able to design and implement a new array class that performs run-time range checking

User Requirements

The C++ array is a useful data structure, but some features can cause inconvenience for clients or, even worse, errors in clients' programs. Perhaps the most serious problem is the absence of built-in range checking, either at compile time or at run time. Recall that references to data locations within an array must be specified by an index value that is within the range from zero (the first location) to **MAX_ARRAY_SIZE - 1** (the last location), where **MAX_ARRAY_SIZE** is the number of locations specified by the array variable declaration. Because range errors go undetected, they may cause undesirable behavior such as logic errors (unexpected output) or system crashes (side effects on the underlying operating system). Clearly, an array would be safer if it detected range errors and halted program execution with a message, rather than cause logic errors or crashes.

Other features of arrays are inconvenient. For example, a client ought to be able to copy the contents of one whole array to another by means of a simple assignment statement (**a = b**), though this is prohibited in most implementations of C++. A client might also wish to compare two arrays for equality, which would mean the equality of the data elements at each position in the two arrays.

We can solve many of these problems by defining a new class in C++ to represent arrays. The class will assume that all arrays have the same maximum physical size, and they all contain the same type of data elements. Each of these attributes will be defined by client applications before the array class is defined. Clients are expected to define the constant **MAX_ARRAY_SIZE** and the type name **element** for these purposes, and to place them in the header file **element.h**. For example, a client might provide information for an array class capable of holding 50 integers as follows:

```
// Library header file: element.h

#ifndef ELEMENT_H

const int MAX_ARRAY_SIZE = 50;
typedef int element;

#define ELEMENT_H
#endif
```

The use of instances of the safe array class should be consistent with the use of standard C++ arrays. In particular, the use of the subscript notation for referencing data elements within an array should be supported. For example, the following code would declare and initialize an array of 50 integers to zero:

```
array a;

for (int j = 0; j < MAX_ARRAY_SIZE; ++j)
      a[j] = 0;
```

Specifying the Operations

A formal specification of the operations for the safe array class follows:

Create operation

Preconditions:	The array is in an unpredictable state.
Postconditions:	Memory is reserved for an array object capable of storing **MAX_ARRAY_SIZE** data elements.

Subscript operation

Preconditions:	The receiver is an array object, appropriately initialized. The index parameter is an integer value in the range `0 <= index < MAX_ARRAY_SIZE`.
Postconditions:	The location of the data element, which can be used either to reference or to store a value, is returned.

Assignment operation

Preconditions:	The receiver is an array object in an unpredictable state. The parameter is an array object, appropriately initialized.
Postconditions:	The contents of the parameter object are copied into the receiver object.

Equality operation

Preconditions:	The receiver is an array object, appropriately initialized. The parameter is an array object, appropriately initialized. Objects in the arrays can be compared using a standard equality operation.
Postconditions:	Returns TRUE if each pair of objects in the two arrays are equal, and FALSE otherwise.

Declaring the Class

The four operations specified for the safe array class are creation, subscripting, assignment, and testing for equality. To maintain consistency with the conventional uses of arrays, we will use the standard operators for subscripting, assignment, and equality in the class declaration, and provide overloaded operations for them in the class implementation.

```
// Class declaration file: array.h

#ifndef ARRAY_H

// Declaration section

// We assume that the type element and
// the constant MAX_ARRAY_SIZE have been defined by the
// application in element.h

#include "boolean.h"
#include "element.h"

class array
{

        public:

        // Class constructors

        array();
        array(const array &a);

        // Member functions
```

```
        element& operator [ ] (int index);
        array& operator = (const array &a);
        boolean operator == (const array &a);

        private:

        // Data members

        element data[MAX_ARRAY_SIZE];

};

#define ARRAY_H
#endif
```

Note that the data member for a safe array object is represented as an unsafe array. The implementation will detect any range errors that might occur before accessing data elements in this unsafe array.

Implementing the Class

The first member functions to be implemented are the creation operation and the the copy constructor. The creation operation initializes no data members, and therefore runs no statements of its own:

```
array::array()
{
}
```

The copy constructor iterates through the elements in the data member of the safe array parameter, copying the value of each into the corresponding location in the data member of the receiver object:

```
array::array(const array &a)
{
     for (int j = 0; j < MAX_ARRAY_SIZE; ++j)
          data[j] = a.data[j];
}
```

The assignment operation requires a similar process of copying data elements from the array parameter to the receiver object. In this case, a reference to the receiver is returned:

```
array& array::operator = (const array &a)
{
     for (int j = 0; j < MAX_ARRAY_SIZE; ++j)
          data[j] = a.data[j];
     return *this;
}
```

Note that both of these operations assume that an assignment operation exists for the element objects. Remember that complex objects (like bank accounts, strings, and safe arrays) should implement their own assignment operations, so that all of their data members are accurately copied.

The equality operation can be implemented as a simple search for two elements that are not equal. As soon as the search finds such a pair, the process stops and returns FALSE. Otherwise, if the search reaches the end of the arrays, it returns TRUE:

```
boolean array::operator == (const array &a)
{
     boolean equal = TRUE;
     int j = 0;

     while ((j < MAX_ARRAY_SIZE) && equal)
            if (data[j] != a.data[j])
                 equal = FALSE;
            else
                 ++j;
     return equal;
}
```

The subscript operation provides the primary benefit of a safe array class: run-time range checking. The implementation uses **assert** to enforce the preconditions governing the index value. If the value of the index parameter is out of range, the program will halt with an error message. Otherwise, the operation returns a reference to the data element at the specified index position in the data member:

```
element& array::operator [ ] (int index)
{
     assert((index >= 0) && (index < MAX_ARRAY_SIZE));
     return data[index];
}
```

EXAMPLE 10.10 The following program is a driver for testing most of the safe array class operations.

```
// Program file: araydriv.cpp

#include <iostream.h>

#include "array.h"

int main()
{
      array a, b;
      int i;

      for (i = 0; i < MAX_ARRAY_SIZE; ++i)           // Test subscripts
           a[i] = i;

      cout<< "Values in array a are: " << endl;
      for (i = 0; i < MAX_ARRAY_SIZE; ++i)
           cout << a[i] << " ";
      cout << endl;

      b = a;                                          // Test assignment
```

```
    cout<< "Values in array b are: " << endl;
    for (i = 0; i < MAX_ARRAY_SIZE; ++i)
         cout << b[i] << " ";
    cout << endl;

    if (b == a)                                   // Test comparison
          cout << "They're equal" << endl;
    else
          cout << "They're not equal" << endl;

    cout << a[MAX_ARRAY_SIZE] << endl;            // Test range error check
    return 0;
}
```

When run with **MAX_ARRAY_SIZE = 10**, the program produces the following output (the error message generated by **assert** may vary on different implementations):

```
Values in array a are:
0 1 2 3 4 5 6 7 8 9
Values in array b are:
0 1 2 3 4 5 6 7 8 9
They're equal
Assertion failed: (index >= 0) && (index < MAX_ARRAY_SIZE), file array.cpp,
line
 39
(press <return> to exit)
```

EXERCISES 10.5

1. Write and test a program that runs the following code with safe arrays and explain what happens:

   ```
   array a;
   for (int i = 0; i <= MAX_ARRAY_SIZE; ++i)
         a[i] = i;
   ```

2. Discuss the limitations imposed by the use of the **element** type to define the safe array class.
3. Discuss the limitations imposed by the use of the constant **MAX_ARRAY_SIZE** to define the safe array class.
4. Discuss the feasibility of using safe and unsafe arrays in the same application, in order to overcome the limitations of the safe array class.
5. The assignment and equality operations for safe arrays reference every memory location in the arrays. Discuss any problems that might arise from these references. For example, predict what happens when you run the following pieces of code:

   a.
   ```
   array a;
   for (int i = 0; i < MAX_ARRAY_SIZE; ++i)
         cout << a[i] << endl;
   ```
   b.
   ```
   array a, b;
   a = b;
   ```
   c.
   ```
   array a, b;
   for (int i = 0; i < MAX_ARRAY_SIZE; ++i)
         a[i] = i;
   ```

```
if (a == b)
      cout << "They're the same" << endl;
else
      cout << "They're not the same" << endl;
```

10.6 An Ordered Collection Class

OBJECTIVES

- to understand the difference between the physical size of an array and its logical size
- to be able to design and implement a new class that prohibits references to uninitialized data elements in an array

User Requirements

In almost any application that uses an array, the client must distinguish between the *physical size* of the array (the maximum number of memory locations available for data elements) and the *logical size* of the array (the number of data elements currently stored in the array). Failure to do this can cause errors when clients attempt to access data locations in an array where no data values have yet been stored. For example, an array **list** might be declared to have a maximum number of five integer elements, and three integers might be currently stored in positions 0 through 2. This situation is depicted in Figure 10.1. The data at index positions 3 and 4 are still be unpredictable, so the references **list[3]** and **list[4]** for these values may cause errors.

Clients can keep track of the logical array within a physical array in two ways:

1. The first method stores a special sentinel value at the index position immediately following the last data element currently in the array. As you saw in Chapter 7, this method is used by C++ to recognize the boundary of a string value (the null character) within an array of characters. The cost of this method is that one location in the array must be given up to store the sentinel value. Moreover, some data elements, such as bank account objects, might not be easily represented as sentinel values.
2. The second method omits a sentinel value, but maintains a separate integer variable as a counter of the number of data elements currently stored in the array. We have seen this method used in many examples in this chapter, where a variable **length** maintains this value. When a new array is declared or reinitialized, **length** is set to zero, to reflect the fact that there are no data elements stored in the array. **length** is then passed with the array variable to any function that processes the array. Any subscript reference to a data element in an array, either for looking up or for storing a value, should use an index that satisfies the condition **0 <= index < length**. The costs of this method are that a separate variable must be maintained for the length or logical size of the array, and extra operations must be provided for adding or removing data elements.

We can use the second method to develop a new class or ADT called an *ordered collection.* An ordered collection provides subscript access to just those data locations where elements have been stored. It does this by maintaining its own logical size as an attribute. A client can request the logical size of an ordered collection, determine whether subscripting is allowed, and, if so, what the legitimate range of an index should be. Finally, a set of operations for adding or

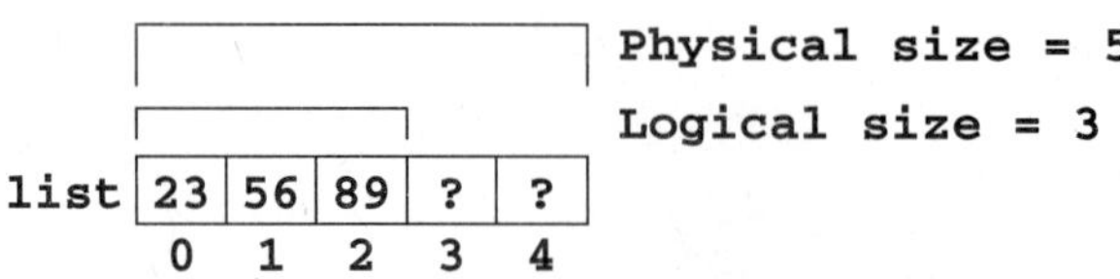

FIGURE 10.1
The logical size of an array may be different from its physical size

removing data elements is provided by the ordered collection class. A piece of code that illustrates the use of ordered collections of integers follows:

```
ordered_collection list1, list2;
int i, length;

// length should be 0
cout << "Length of list1 = " << list1.length() << end;

// Store data elements in
// 1/2 of the physical array
for (i = 0; i < MAX_ARRAY_SIZE / 2; ++i)
        list1.add_last(i);

// Print the logical array
for (i = 0; i < list1.length(); ++i)
        cout << i << " " << list[i] << endl;

// Copy one logical array to another
list2 = list1;

// Compare logical arrays
if (list1 == list2)
        cout << "They're equal" << endl;
else
        cout << "They're not equal" << endl;

// Remove and print each value
// and the length of the logical
// array after each removal
length = list1.length();
for (i = 0; i < length; ++i)
      cout << "Value = " << list1.remove_first()
           << "Length = " << list1.length() << endl;

// Halt with error: no data exists!
cout << list1[0] << endl;
```

As you can see, an ordered collection class allows clients to work with logical arrays in a manner that preserves the use of conventional array operations such as subscripting, assignment, and comparison. The difference is that the use of ordered collections is safer than the use of arrays, because references to unitialized data elements are not allowed.

Specifying the Operations

The formal specification of the operations for an ordered collection follows:

Create operation	
Preconditions:	The ordered collection is in an unpredictable state.
Postconditions:	Memory is reserved for an ordered collection object capable of storing **MAX_ARRAY_SIZE** data elements, and **length** is set to 0.

Length operation
Preconditions: The receiver is an ordered collection object, appropriately initialized.
Postconditions: The value of **`length`** is returned.

Subscript operation
Preconditions: The receiver is an ordered collection object, appropriately initialized, **`length`** must be greater than 0, and the **`index`** parameter is an integer value in the range **`0 <= index < length`**.
Postconditions: The location of the data element, which can be used either to reference or to store a value, is returned.

Assignment operation
Preconditions: The receiver is an ordered collection object in an unpredictable state. The parameter is an ordered collection object, appropriately initialized.
Postconditions: The contents of the parameter object, from position 0 to position **`length - 1`**, are copied into the receiver object, and the receiver's length is set to the parameter's length.

Equality operation
Preconditions: The receiver is an ordered collection object, appropriately initialized. The parameter is an ordered collection object, appropriately initialized. Objects in the ordered collection can be compared using a standard equality operation.
Postconditions: Returns TRUE if the two collections are the same length and each pair of objects in the two collections is equal, and FALSE otherwise.

Add last operation
Preconditions: The receiver is an ordered collection object, appropriately initialized. The parameter is an **`element`** object, and **`length < MAX_ARRAY_SIZE`**.
Postconditions: **`length`** is incremented by one, and the parameter element is placed in the last position in the ordered collection.

Remove last operation
Preconditions: The receiver is an ordered collection object, appropriately initialized, and **`length > 0`**.
Postconditions: **`length`** is decremented by one, and the last data element in the ordered collection is returned.

Add first operation
Preconditions: The receiver is an ordered collection object, appropriately initialized, the parameter is an **`element`** object, and **`length < MAX_ARRAY_SIZE`**.
Postconditions: **`length`** is incremented by one, the data elements in the ordered collection are shifted up by one index position, and the parameter element is placed in the first position in the ordered collection.

Remove first operation
Preconditions: The receiver is an ordered collection object, appropriately initialized, and **`length > 0`**.
Postconditions: **`length`** is decremented by one, the data elements in the ordered collection that come after the first element are shifted down by one index position, and the first element in the ordered collection is returned.

Remove operation	
Preconditions:	The receiver is an ordered collection object, appropriately initialized, the parameter is the data element to be removed, the parameter must equal an element currently in the list, and **`length`** is greater than zero.
Postconditions:	**`length`** is decremented by one, and the data elements in the ordered collection that come after the parameter element are shifted down by one index position.

Declaring the Class

The class declaration module for the ordered collection class is

```
// Class declaration file: ordercol.h

#ifndef ORDERCOL_H

// Declaration section

// We assume that the type element and
// the constant MAX_ARRAY_SIZE have been defined by the
// application in element.h

#include "boolean.h"
#include "element.h"

class ordered_collection
{

      public:

      // Class constructors

      ordered_collection();
      ordered_collection(const ordered_collection &oc);

      // Member functions

      int length();
      element& operator [ ] (int index);
      ordered_collection& operator = (const ordered_collection &oc);
      boolean operator == (const ordered_collection &oc);
      void add_last(element e);
      element remove_last();
      void add_first(element e);
      element remove_first();
      void remove(element e);

      protected:
```

```
        // Data members

        element data[MAX_ARRAY_SIZE];
        int c_length;

};

#define ORDERCOL_H
#endif
```

Note that the data member for storing the data elements is represented in the same way as the data member of a safe array. We name the data member for representing the length **c_length**, to avoid name conflicts with the member function **length.** We also declare the data members to be **protected,** so that any derived classes of **ordered_collection** will have direct access to them.

Implementing the Class

Many of the operations on an ordered collection resemble those on a safe array, except that the **c_length** data member is updated and used as a limit rather than **MAX_ARRAY_SIZE**. Instead of doing nothing, the first class constructor sets **c_length** to zero to indicate an ordered collection with no data elements:

```
ordered_collection::ordered_collection()
{
        c_length = 0;
}
```

The copy constructor iterates through the elements in the data members of the two ordered collections, but uses the length of the parameter collection as an upper bound:

```
ordered_collection::ordered_collection(const ordered_collection &oc)
{
        for (int j = 0; j < oc.c_length; ++j)
                data[j] = oc.data[j];
        c_length = oc.c_length;
}
```

The implementations of the assignment and equality operations are similar, and are left as exercises. The subscript operation enforces the precondition that the index parameter is greater than or equal to zero and less than **c_length :**

```
element& ordered_collection::operator [ ] (int index)
{
      assert((index >= 0) && (index < c_length));
      return data[index];
}
```

The **add_last** operation enforces the precondition that **c_length** is less than **MAX_ARRAY_SIZE**, so there will be room in the array to store the data element:

```
void ordered_collection::add_last(element e)
{
      assert(c_length < MAX_ARRAY_SIZE);
      data[c_length] = e;
      ++c_length;
}
```

Note the order of the statements in this implementation. The value of **c_length** will always be one greater than the index position of the last data element currently in the ordered collection. Therefore, the expression **data[c_length]** refers to the next available location for new data, where **c_length < MAX_ARRAY_SIZE**. We are careful to store the new data element there, and increment **c_length** afterwards.

The **remove_last** operation enforces the precondition that **c_length** is greater than zero. It then decrements **c_length** by one and returns the data element that was at the end of the ordered collection:

```
element ordered_collection::remove_last()
{
    assert(c_length > 0);
    --c_length;
    element removed_item = data[c_length];
    return removed_item;
}
```

Note that the order of the statements for modifying **c_length** and accessing the data element is the inverse of the order of the statements in the implementation of **add_last**. Whenever **c_length** is decremented, it can be used to access the data value that used to be at the end of the ordered collection.

The three remaining operations—**add_first, remove_first**, and **remove**—may involve substantial movement of data elements within the array representing the ordered collection. For example, when we remove the first data element, all of the data to the right of this position must be shifted one position to the left. Before this can be done, the data element in the first position must be saved in a temporary location. Starting with position zero, a **for** loop copies the data element in the next location into the position immediately to the left. This process continues until the element at position **c_length - 1** has been copied. Finally, **c_length** is decremented:

```
element ordered_collection::remove_first()
{
    assert(c_length > 0);
    element removed_item = data[0];
    for (int i = 0; i < c_length -1; ++i)
        data[i] = data[i + 1];
    --c_length;
    return removed_item;
}
```

The implementations of the **remove_first** and **remove** operations are left as exercises.

EXAMPLE 10.11

This example program inputs a series of bank account objects, as discussed in Chapter 8, from a file into an ordered collection. It then displays the contents of each account on the screen. The program assumes that the **element** type has been defined as **account**, that the standard stream operations have been overloaded for account objects, and that the file **myfile** contains the accounts. The program will display a message if there is not enough room in the ordered collection for all of the accounts in the file.

```
// Program file: bankfile.cpp

#include <iostream.h>
#include <fstream.h>
#include "account.h"
#include "ordercol.h"

int main()
{
      ifstream in_file;
      ordered_collection accounts;
      account new_account;

      in_file.open("myfile");
      in_file >> new_account;
      while (! in_file.eof() && (accounts.length() < MAX_ARRAY_SIZE))
      {
            accounts.add_last(new_account);
            in_file >> new_account;
      }
      if (! in_file.eof() && (accounts.length() == MAX_ARRAY_SIZE))
            cout << "Some accounts could not be input into the list. " << endl;
      in_file.close();
      for (int i = 0; i < accounts.length(); ++i)
           cout << accounts[i] << endl;
      return 0;
}
```

EXERCISES 10.6

1. Discuss the difference between the physical size of an array and its logical size.
2. Clients complain that halting the program with an error message is too severe a price to pay for attempting to remove a data element from an empty ordered collection. They argue that a Boolean flag could be returned, indicating the success or failure of the operation, instead. Discuss the relative merits of these two approaches.
3. Someone has proposed using an ordered collection rather than an array to implement a string class. She claims that the new implementation will not have to waste a storage location on the null character. Discuss the merits of this proposal.
4. Implement the remaining operations for the ordered collection class, and test it with the sample code presented earlier in this section.
5. Add an operation to the ordered collection class to search the collection for a given element. If the element is found, its index position in the ordered collection should be returned. Otherwise, -1 should be returned. You should use the sequential search algorithm developed in Section 10.4.
6. Add an operation to the ordered collection class to sort the data elements in the collection. You should use the selection sort algorithm developed in Section 10.4.
7. Add an operation to input data elements from an input stream into an ordered collection. You should use the **`friend`** designation with the **`>>`** operator of the **`istream`** class, as we did for strings in Chapter 7. Be sure that this operation has the same functionality as the process described in example 10.11.
8. Add an operation for output of ordered collections, similar to the one for input in Exercise 7.

10.7 A Sorted Collection Class

OBJECTIVES

- to understand the difference between an ordered collection and a sorted collection
- to be able to design and implement a sorted collection class

User Requirements

Many applications demand that data values be kept in sorted order. For example, dictionaries and telephone books are two kinds of collections of data values that must be maintained in alphabetical order. One could use the ordered collection class to represent these kinds of data, as long as a sort operation is provided to alphabetize the data after additions of data to the collection. However, the sort operation can be very expensive to use with large collections. Clearly, an ordered collection that could maintain its contents in sorted form without resorting to a sort operation would be very desirable for these applications.

We can design a new class, called a *sorted collection,* that fulfills these requirements. The new class has many of the characteristics of an ordered collection, such as a length and subscripting to look up a data element's value. However, to keep its data elements sorted, a sorted collection prohibits insertions at arbitrary positions in the collection. The sorted collection permits only one insertion operation, and that one operation always puts a data element in its proper place in the collection.

Specifying the Operations

Because a sorted collection has so many of the attributes and behaviors of an ordered collection, it will be convenient to specify it as a derived class of an ordered collection. The situation here is similar to that of the savings account class discussed in Chapter 8. We assume that all of the operations on ordered collections can be used on sorted collections, except for adding a data element to the beginning or the end of the collection, and for subscripting for the target of an assignment statement. We add an operation called **`add`** for insertions that enforces a sorted order in the collection:

Create operation
Preconditions: The sorted collection is in an unpredictable state.
Postconditions: Memory is reserved for a sorted collection object capable of storing **`MAX_ARRAY_SIZE`** data elements, and **`length`** is set to 0.

Length operation
Preconditions: The receiver is a sorted collection object, appropriately initialized.
Postconditions: The value of **`length`** is returned.

Subscript operation
Preconditions: The receiver is a sorted collection object, appropriately initialized, **`length`** must be greater than 0, and the **`index`** parameter is an integer value in the range **`0 <= index < length`**.
Postconditions: The data element is returned for use as a value only.

Assignment operation
Preconditions: The receiver is a sorted collection object in an unpredictable state. The parameter is a sorted collection object, appropriately initialized.
Postconditions: The contents of the parameter object, from position 0 to position **`length - 1`**, are copied into the receiver object, and the receiver's length is set to the parameter's length.

Equality operation

Preconditions: The receiver is a sorted collection object, appropriately initialized. The parameter is a sorted collection object, appropriately initialized. Objects in the sorted collection can be compared using a standard equality operation.

Postconditions: Returns TRUE if the two collections are the same length and each pair of objects in the two collections is equal, and FALSE otherwise.

Add operation

Preconditions: The receiver is a sorted collection object, appropriately initialized, the parameter is an **element** object, and **length < MAX_ARRAY_SIZE**.

Postconditions: **length** is incremented by one, and the parameter element is placed in its proper position in the sorted collection.

Remove last operation

Preconditions: The receiver is a sorted collection object, appropriately initialized, and **length > 0**.

Postconditions: **length** is decremented by one, and the last data element in the sorted collection is returned.

Remove first operation

Preconditions: The receiver is a sorted collection object, appropriately initialized, and **length > 0**.

Postconditions: **length** is decremented by one, the data elements in the sorted collection that come after the first element are shifted down by one index position, and the first element in the sorted collection is returned.

Remove operation

Preconditions: The receiver is an sorted collection object, appropriately initialized. The parameter is the data element to be removed, the parameter must equal an element currently in the list, and **length > 0**.

Postconditions: **length** is decremented by one, and the data elements in the ordered collection that come after the parameter element are shifted down by one index position.

Declaring the Class

The class declaration module for the sorted collection class is

```
// Class declaration file: sortcol.h

#ifndef SORTCOL_H

// Declaration section

// We assume that the type element and
// the constant MAX_ARRAY_SIZE have been defined by the
// application in element.h

#include "element.h"
#include "ordercol.h"

class sorted_collection : protected ordered_collection
{
```

```
        public:

        // Class constructors

        sorted_collection();
        sorted_collection(const sorted_collection &sc);

        // Member functions

        // These five are inherited from
        // the base class
        ordered_collection::length;
        ordered_collection::operator ==;
        ordered_collection::remove_first;
        ordered_collection::remove_last;
        ordered_collection::remove;

        // These three are
        // implemented here.
        sorted_collection& operator = (const sorted_collection &sc);
        const element& operator [ ] (int index);
        void add(element e);

        // Data members defined in base class

};

#define SORTCOL_H
#endif
```

There are several things to note about this class declaration:

1. The sorted collection class inherits attributes and behavior from the ordered collection class in **protected** mode. This means that **public** and **protected** data and member functions from the ordered collection or base class will be available for the implementation of the sorted collection class, unless they are redefined by the sorted collection class. If inheritance were specified in **public** mode, all of the **public** members of the ordered collection class, such as **add_first**, would also be available to other clients as well. A derived class should be declared in **protected** mode whenever we wish to deny other clients access to some of the public members of the base class.
2. Other clients are given access to five member functions of the base class by listing them in the following form in the **public** section:

<class name>::<member name>;

   This kind of declaration is called an *access adjustment.* In general, an access adjustment broadens the scope of access no wider than the mode of access specified by the base class.

3. The remaining three member function declarations specify operations to be implemented by the sorted collection class. Note that the assignment and the subscript operations are not inherited from the base class. In the case of the assignment, we must return the address of an object of a specific class (sorted collection, in this case). In the case of the subscript, we prohibit the use of the returned element as an l-value by specifiying the return type as a constant reference.

Implementing the Class

The class constructors for the sorted collection simply invoke the corresponding constructors in the base class:

```
sorted_collection::sorted_collection()
        : ordered_collection()
{
}

sorted_collection::sorted_collection(const sorted_collection &sc)
        : ordered_collection(sc)
{
}
```

The new operation to add a data element by putting it in its proper place calls for some development. The operation faces three possiblities:

1. The collection is empty. The new data element goes at the beginning.
2. The new data element is greater than the last element in the collection. The new data element goes at the end.
3. The new data element is less than or equal to some data element in the middle of the collection. We search for this place, shift the data elements over to the right from there, and put the new data element in that place.

The implementation reflects these alternatives as follows:

```
void sorted_collection::add(element e)
{
        int place = 0;

        assert(c_length < MAX_ARRAY_SIZE);
        if ((c_length == 0) || (e > data[c_length - 1]))
                data[c_length] = e;
        else
        {
                while (e > data[place])
                    ++place;
                for (int index = c_length; index > place ; --index)
                    data[index] = data[index - 1];
                data[place] = e;
        }
        ++c_length;
}
```

The implementations of the assignment and subscript operations are left as exercises.

EXERCISES 10.7

1. Implement the assignment and subscript operations for sorted collections.
2. Design and test a program that attempts to use the subscript operator to assign a value to a position in a sorted collection. Explain the error that occurs.
3. Explain why the subscript operator for ordered collections cannot be used for sorted collections. What effect will this have on clients of sorted collections?
4. Draw a class hierarchy diagram that describes the relationships among the array data type, the safe array class, the ordered collection class, and the sorted collection class.
5. Design and implement a class constructor for sorted collections that takes an ordered collection as a parameter. The constructor should add the data from the ordered collection to the sorted collection.
6. Design and implement a member function called **`merge`** for sorted collections. **`merge`** takes a sorted collection as a parameter. A precondition is that the sum of the lengths of the receiver and parameter collections must be less than or equal to **`MAX_ARRAY_SIZE`**. **`merge`** should add the data elements of the parameter collection to the receiver collection.

10.8 Multidimensional Arrays

OBJECTIVES

- to understand the need for representing the data for some problems as a two-dimensional grid
- to be able to represent this data structure as a two-dimensional array
- to be able to declare a two-dimensional array
- to be able to manipulate the components of a two-dimensional array
- to be able to use two-dimensional arrays with functions

The arrays that we have been using thus far are *one dimensional,* in that we locate each data element in the array by specifying a single index position. However, some data structures are more naturally modeled by representing the data in the form of a rectangular grid in which each element is located by specifying a row and column. For example, consider the problem of representing a *bitmap* for a monochrome computer screen. The bitmap consists of a set of Boolean values representing the state of the dots or pixels on the screen. TRUE means "on" or the pixel is white; FALSE means "off" or the pixel is black. Each pixel or bit also has a position, specified by counting down and to the right from the upper left corner of the screen, starting with position <0, 0>, where the first coordinate is the row position and the second coordinate is the column position, to the lower right corner, whose position represents the upper bounds (-1) of the rows and columns (see Figure 10.2).

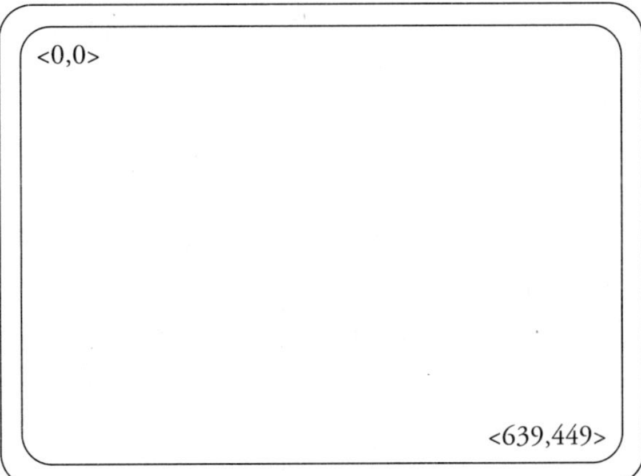

◆ FIGURE 10.2
Positions of pixels in upper left corner and lower right corner of screen

◆ FIGURE 10.3
A two-dimensional array representing a bitmap

	0	1	2	3	4	5
0	0	0	0	0	0	0
1	0	0	0	0	0	0
2	1	1	1	1	1	1
3	0	0	0	0	0	0
4	0	0	0	0	0	0

We can conveniently represent a bitmap as a two-dimensional array of Boolean values. You can think of the array as a rectangular grid of data cells, formatted into rows and columns. Figure 10.3 depicts a two-dimensional array of five rows and six columns (representing quite a small bitmap!). As you might expect with C++, the rows are numbered from zero to $R - 1$, where R is the number of rows, and the columns are numbered from zero to $C - 1$, where C is the number of columns. Note that the data elements in row 2 have been set to TRUE (1 in C++), while all of the other data elements have been set to FALSE (0 in C++). Thus, this would be a bitmap representation of a horizontal line displayed in the middle of a screen or window.

The type for a bitmap can be specified with a **typedef:**

```
const MAX_ROW_SIZE = 5;
const MAX_COL_SIZE = 6;

typedef boolean bitmap[MAX_ROW_SIZE] [MAX_COL_SIZE];
```

The form for defining a two-dimensional array type is

```
typedef <element type> <type name>[<integer constant>] [<integer constant>];
```

Note two things about this definition:

1. It resembles a definition of a one-dimensional array type, except that the sizes of the two dimensions are specified by the integer constants enclosed in the square brackets.
2. The first set of brackets always encloses the number of rows in an array, whereas the second set of brackets always encloses the number of columns in an array.

Alternatively, a two-dimensional array variable could be declared with the following form:

```
<element type> <variable name>[<integer constant>] [<integer constant>];
```

Two-dimensional array variables can be listed in declarations just like one-dimensional arrays:

```
bitmap screen1, screen2;
```

References to individual data elements within a two-dimensional array use two index values. For example, the following statement would assign the value TRUE to the cell in row 3, column 1, of the array **screen1:**

```
screen1[3][1] = TRUE;
```

Two-dimensional array indexing in C++ always has the form

<array variable>[<integer value of row>] [<integer value of column>]

Now suppose that we wish to initialize the bitmap **screen1** so that all of its bits are off (set to FALSE). In general, processing a two-dimensional array requires the use of nested loops. In this particular case, we wish to visit every cell in the array and set it to FALSE. Therefore, we use a nested **for** loop:

```
for (int row = 0; row < MAX_ROW_SIZE; ++row)          // move through each row
     for (int col = 0; col < MAX_COL_SIZE; ++col)     // move through each col
          screen1[row][col] = FALSE;
```

Note that the inner loop visits all of the columns in one row before the outer loop moves to the next row. This is called processing the array in *row-major order.* An alternative method, using *column-major order,* could be specified as

```
for (int col = 0; col < MAX_COL_SIZE; ++row)          // move through each col
     for (int row = 0; row < MAX_ROW_SIZE; ++col)     // move through each row
          screen1[row][col] = FALSE;
```

Searching a two-dimensional array for a given value requires the use of a nested **while** loop. This is left as an exercise.

Two-dimensional arrays are passed as parameters to functions in the same way as other arrays. For example, we could package the code for initializing a bitmap in a function **clear_bitmap**:

```
void clear_bitmap(bitmap map)
{
for (int row = 0; row < MAX_ROW_SIZE; ++row)
     for (int col = 0; col < MAX_COL_SIZE; ++col)
          map[row][col] = FALSE;
}
```

COMMUNICATION AND STYLE TIPS

1. Use descriptive identifiers when working with two-dimensional arrays. For example, **row** and **col** are appropriate identifiers for index variables, and **MAX_ROW_SIZE** and **MAX_COL_SIZE** are useful identifiers for specifying the upper bounds of an array type.
2. Remember that C++ does not report range bound errors with any arrays, so use care when indexing.

EXERCISES 10.8

1. Define a C++ type for representing bitmaps of 300 rows and 400 columns.
2. Define a C++ type for representing two-dimensional arrays of integers that have 20 rows and 10 columns.
3. Write a C++ function that searches the arrays defined in Exercise 2 for a given integer value. The function should return the row and column positions if the value is found, as well as the Boolean value TRUE. If the value is not found, the function should return FALSE.
4. Assume that a bitmap has the same number of rows and columns, and that **clear_bitmap** has been run to initialize all of the bits. Write a C++ function that

sets the bits to FALSE on a diagonal running from the upper left corner of the bitmap to the lower right corner.

5. Discuss the design of a safe bitmap class.

FOCUS ON PROGRAM DESIGN

As you saw in Chapter 7, much of word processing involves the use of strings to represent words or sentences. Many applications must maintain tables or dictionaries that are keyed by words that are associated with other information, like salaries or phone numbers. We will examine how to set up a table that allows an application to count the frequencies of all of the words in a file. The application will use the sorted collection class developed in Section 10.7.

The input to the program will be a text file. The output will be two columns of data. In the first column will be an alphabetical listing of the words in the file. In the second column will be integers representing the frequency of each word in the file.

To solve this problem, the program will need two classes of objects: one for representing a word and its frequency, and the other for representing a table of such objects. We can define a new class, called **entry**, to represent a word and its frequency. Because the words must appear in alphabetical order when displayed, the table of entries can be represented as a sorted collection.

An entry class will have two attributes: a string representing a word and an integer representing the word's frequency. The operation to create an entry will take a new word as a parameter, and set its frequency to 1. The class will support operations to increment the frequency and to return the values of the word and its frequency.

The sorted collection class is the same as that developed in Section 10.7, with the addition of a search function. You developed a search function for ordered collections in Exercise 5 of Section 10.6. That function should be modified so that its parameter is a string rather than a data element. The implementation of the function should compare the string with the data element. This means that the entry class should provide comparison operations that take strings as parameters as well as entries as parameters. Comparisons of entries are still needed for the **add** and **remove** operations.

The completion of these two classes is left as an exercise. We now describe the design of the program. The general idea is to enter a loop that reads words from a file. As each word is input, the program searches the collection for an entry for that word. If no entry is found, the program creates one with the word and adds it to the collection. If an entry is found, the program indexes into the collection with the value returned by the search function, and sends the increment message to the entry for the word. When this process is completed, the program loops through the collection, displaying the word and frequency of each entry in an appropriate format. Therefore, we have two top-level program modules:

1. Enter the data from the file into the table.
2. Display the data from the table to the screen.

The main program block would be

```
int main()
{
	sorted_collection table;

	get_data(table);
	print_results(table);
	return 0;
}
```

The **get_data** function prompts the user for a file name, opens it for input, runs the loop described earlier, and closes the file:

```
void get_data(sorted_collection &table)
{
        ifstream in_file;
        string word;
        char fname[10];
        int index;
        entry old_entry;

        cout << "Enter the file name: ";
        cin >> fname;
        in_file.open(fname);
        in_file >> word;
        while (! in_file.eof())
        {
               index = table.search(word);
               if (index == -1)
               {
                        entry new_entry(word);
                        table.add(new_entry);
               }
               else
               {
                       old_entry = table[index];
                       old_entry.increment();
                       table.remove(old_entry);
                       table.add(old_entry);
               }
               in_file >> word;
        }
        in_file.close();
}
```

The **print_results** function displays a header and then loops through the table, displaying the word and the frequency of each entry on a line:

```
void print_results(sorted_collection &table)
{
        entry next_entry;

        cout << setw(25) << "Word" << setw(5) << "Frequency" << endl;
        for (int i = 0; i < table.length(); ++i)
        {
             next_entry = table[i];
             cout << setw(25) << next_entry.word()
                   << setw(5) << next_entry.frequency() << endl;
        }
}
```

RUNNING, DEBUGGING AND TESTING HINTS

1. Do not attempt to use a subscript that is out of range. Suppose we have

   ```
   int list[6];
   ```

   An inadvertent reference such as

   ```
   for (int j = 0; j <= 6; ++j)
   cout << list[j];
   ```

   may produce mysterious results at run time.
2. Comparing array components to each other can lead to errors in using subscripts. Two common misuses are shown.
   a. Attempting to compare **a[j]** to **a[j + 1]**. If this does not stop at **a[length - 2]**, then **j + 1** will be out of range.
   b. Attempting to compare **a[j - 1]** to **a[j]**. This presents the same problem at the beginning of an array. Remember, **j - 1** should have a value that is not less than zero.
3. Using a safe array class that supports run-time range checking will help to catch the errors described in tips 1 and 2.
4. Make sure the array index is correctly initialized, and that the termination condition evaluates all of the relevant subconditions. For example,

   ```
   length = 0;
   in_file >> data;
   while ((length < MAX_ARRAY_SIZE) && ! in_file.eof())
   {
         a[length] = data;
         ++length;
         in_file >> data
   }
   ```

   The first value is stored in **a[0], a[length]** will not be referenced when **length == MAX_ARRAY_SIZE**, and **length** will indicate the number of data elements read when the loop is finished.
5. Make sure that all array elements that are referenced for their values have been initialized. Avoid using loops with **MAX_ARRAY_SIZE** as an upper bound, unless you are initializing an array. Use an integer variable to maintain the logical size of the array. Better still, use an ordered collection class to guarantee that references to unitialized data in an array will be caught at run time.

SUMMARY

Key Terms

access adjustment
bitmap
column-major order
component (element) of an array
index (subscript)
logical size
one-dimensional array
ordered collection
physical size
row-major order
selection sort
sequential (linear) search
sorted collection
two-dimensional array

Key Concepts

- An array is a structured variable; a declaration of a single variable reserves several memory locations for data elements.

- It is good practice to use a symbolic constant to declare the size of array variables; for example,

```
const int MAX_ARRAY_SIZE = 10;
int list1[MAX_ARRAY_SIZE];
float list2[MAX_ARRAY_SIZE];
```

- Arrays can be visualized as lists; thus, the preceding arrays could be envisioned as

list1		list2
	0	
	1	
	2	
	3	
	4	
	5	
	6	
	7	
	8	
	9	

- Each component of an array is a variable of the declared type and can be used in the same way as any other variable of that type.
- Loops can be used to read data into arrays; for example,

```
length = 0;
in_file >> data;
while ((length < MAX_ARRAY_SIZE) && ! in_file.eof())
{
        a[length] = data;
        ++length;
        in_file >> data
}
```

- Loops can be used to print data from arrays; for example, if **scores** is an array of 20 test scores, the scores can be printed by

```
for (int j = 0; j < 20; ++j)
        cout << scores[j] << endl;
```

- Manipulating components of an array is generally accomplished by using the index as a loop variable; for example, assuming the preceding **scores** array, to find the smallest value in the array we can use

```
small = scores[0];
for (int j = 1; j < 20; ++j)
        if (scores[j] < small)
                small = scores[j];
```

- A selection sort is one method of sorting elements in an array from high to low or low to high. This sort repeatedly finds the minimum element in the unsorted portion of the array and exchanges it with the first element in that portion.
- C++ array parameters are always passed by reference, and should not be declared as reference parameters.

- A sequential search of a list consists of examining the first item in a list and then proceeding through the list in sequence until the desired value is found or the end of the list is reached.
- The physical size of an array is the total number of memory locations available for storing data elements in it.
- The logical size of an array is the number of data elements currently stored in it; this size may differ from the array's physical size.
- An ordered collection enables clients to work with just the logical size of an array of data elements.
- A sorted collection enables clients to work with an array of data elements whose alphabetical ordering is maintained automatically.
- Two-dimensional arrays may be specified by declaring a variable that has upper bounds on two indices:

```
boolean bitmap[20] [10];
```

- References to cells in two-dimensional arrays specify the index of the row first and the index of the column second:

```
bitmap[row] [col] = FALSE;
```

PROGRAMMING PROBLEMS AND PROJECTS

1. Using the ordered collection class developed in Section 10.6 and the sorted collection class developed in Section 10.7, write a program to read an unknown number of integer test scores from the keyboard (assume at most 150 scores). Print the original list of scores, the scores sorted from low to high, the scores sorted from high to low, the highest score, the lowest score, and the average score.
2. Write a program to help you balance your checkbook. The input consists of the beginning balance and then a sequence of transactions, each followed by a transaction code. Deposits are followed by a "D" and withdrawals are followed by a "W." The output should consist of a list of transactions, a running balance, an ending balance, the number of withdrawals, and the number of deposits. Include an appropriate message for overdrawn accounts. Your program should represent the attributes and behavior of a transaction as a class.
3. One of the problems faced by designers of word processors is that of printing text without separating a word at the end of a line. Write a program to read several lines of text as input. Then print the message with each line starting in column 10 and no line exceeding column 70. No word should be separated at the end of a line.
4. Your local state university has to raise funds for an art center. As a first step, they are going to approach five previously identified donors and ask for additional donations. Because the donors wish to remain anonymous, only the respective totals of their previous donations are available for input. After they are contacted, the additional donations are listed at the end of input in the same order as the first 5 entries. Write a computer program to read the first 20 entries into one data structure and the second 5 entries into a second data structure. Compute the previous total donations and the new donations for the art center. Print the following:
   a. The list of previous donations
   b. The list of new donations
   c. An unsorted list of total donations
   d. A sorted list of total donations
   e. Total donations before the fund drive
   f. Total donations for the art center
   g. The maximum donation for the art center

Be sure to choose the appropriate data structures from the safe array class, the ordered collection class, or the sorted collection class, as developed in Sections 10.5, 10.6, and 10.7, respectively.

5. Read in a list of 10 integers from the keyboard. Place the even numbers into a collection called **`even`**, the odd numbers into a collection called **`odd`**, and the negatives into a collection called **`negative`**. Print all three collections after all numbers have been read.
6. Read in 10 real numbers. Print the average of the numbers followed by all the numbers that are greater than the average.
7. Read in the names of five candidates in a class election and the number of votes received by each. Print the list of candidates, the number of votes they received, and the percentage of the total votes they received sorted into order from the winner to the person with the fewest votes. You may assume that all names are 20 characters in length.
8. In many sports events, contestants are rated by judges with an average score being determined by discarding the highest and lowest scores and averaging the remaining scores. Write a program in which eight scores are entered, computing the average score for the contestant.
9. Given a list of 20 test scores (integers), print the score that is nearest to the average.
10. The Game of Nim is played with three piles of stones. There are three stones in the first pile, five stones in the second, and eight stones in the third. Two players alternate taking as many stones as they like from any one pile. Play continues until someone is forced to take the last stone. The person taking the last stone loses. Write a program that permits two people to play the game of Nim using an array to keep track of the number of stones in each pile.
11. There is an effective strategy that can virtually guarantee victory in the game of Nim. Devise a strategy and modify the program in Problem 10 so that the computer plays against a person. Your program should be virtually unbeatable if the proper strategy is developed.
12. The median of a set of numbers is the value in the middle of the set if the set is arranged in order. The mode is the number listed most often. Given a list of 21 numbers, print the median and mode of the list.
13. The standard deviation is a statistic frequently used in education measurement. Write a program that, given a list of test scores, will find and print the standard deviation of the numbers. The standard deviation formula can be found in most statistics books.
14. Revise Problem 13 so that after the standard deviation is printed, you can print a list of test scores that are more than one standard deviation below the average and a list of the scores more than one standard deviation above the average.
15. The z-score is defined as the mean score earned on a test divided by the standard deviation. Given input data containing an unknown number of test scores (maximum of 100), print a list showing each test score (from highest to lowest) and the corresponding z-score.
16. Salespeople for the Wellsville Wholesale Company earn a commission based on their sales. The commission rates are as follows:

Sales	Commission (%)
$0—1000	3
1001—5000	4.5
5001—10000	5.25
Over 10000	6

In addition, any salesperson who sells above the average of all salespeople receives a $50 bonus, and the top salesperson receives an additional $75 bonus.

Given the names and amounts sold by each of 10 salespeople, write a program that prints a table showing the salesperson's name, the amount sold, the commission rate, and the total amount earned. The average sales should also be printed.

17. Write a language translation program that permits the entry of a word in English, with the corresponding word of another language being printed. The dictionary words can be stored in parallel collections, with the English array being sorted into alphabetical order prior to the first entry of a word. Your program should first sort the dictionary words.

18. Elementary and middle school students are often given the task of converting numbers from one base to another. For example, 19 in base 10 is 103 in base 4 ($1 \times 4^2 + 0 \times 4^1 + 3 \times 4^0$). Conversely, 123 in base 4 is 27 in base 10. Write an interactive program that allows the user to choose from the following:

<1>	Convert from base 10 to base A
<2>	Convert from base A to base 10
<3>	Quit

If option 1 or 2 is chosen, the user should then enter the intended base and the number to be converted. A sample run of the program would produce this output:

```
This program allows you to convert between bases. Which
of the following would you like?

      <1>      Convert from base 10 to base A
      <2>      Convert from base A to base 10
      <3>      Quit

Enter your choice and press <Enter>. 1

Enter the number in base 10 and press <Enter>. 237

Enter the new base and press <Enter>. 4

The number 237 in base 4 is: 3231

Press <Enter> to continue

This program allows you to convert between bases. Which
of the following would you like?

      <1>      Convert from base 10 to base A
      <2>      Convert from base A to base 10
      <3>      Quit

Enter your choice and press <Enter>. 2

What number would you like to have converted? 2332

Converting to base 10, we get:
```

```
        2 * 1 = 2
        3 * 4 = 12
        3 * 16 = 48
        2 * 64 = 128

The base 10 value is 190

Press <Enter> to continue

This program allows you to convert between bases. Which
of the following would you like?
        <1>     Convert from base 10 to base A
        <2>     Convert from base A to base 10
        <3>     Quit

Enter your choice and press <Enter>. 3
```

19. One of the principles underlying the concept of data abstraction is that implementation details of data structures should be deferred to the lowest possible level. To illustrate, consider the high-level design to which we referred in a previous discussion of data abstraction. Our program required you to work with a list of names and an associated list of numbers (student names and test scores). The following first-level design was suggested:

1. GetNames (function here);
2. GetScores (function here);
3. SortByName (function here);
4. PrintNamesAndScores (function here);
5. SortByScore (function here);

Write complete documentation for each of these modules, including a description of all parameters and data structures required.

Present your documentation to the class. Ask if your classmates have questions about the number or type of parameters, the data structures required, and/or the main tasks to be performed by each module.

20. Contact programmers at your university and/or some businesses and discuss with them the use of lists as a data type. Ask what kinds of programming problems require the use of a list, how the programmers handle data entry (list length), and what operations they perform on the list (search, sort, and so on). Give an oral report of your findings to the class.

21. Select a programming problem from this chapter that you have not yet worked on. Construct a structure chart and write all documentary information necessary for the problem you have chosen. Do not write code. When you are finished, have a classmate read your documentation to see if precisely what is to be done is clear.

22. Consult your local implementation of C++ to see if it supports graphics operations, such as drawing and erasing points on the screen. If your system allows this, write a program that uses the data structure and functions developed in Section 10.8 to represent and draw a diagonal line on the screen.

CHAPTER 11 Pointers, Dynamic Memory, and Dynamic Data Structures

CHAPTER OUTLINE

Material in the previous ten chapters has focused on several considerations involving the memory allocated for variables:

1. Their size (array length, for example) is fixed at compilation time.
2. A certain amount of memory is reserved for each variable and this memory is retained for the declared variables as long as the program or block in which the variable is defined is active.
3. They are normally declared in a variable declaration section.
4. The structure or existence of a variable cannot be changed during a run of the program (an exception is the length of a file).

A disadvantage of relying entirely on this memory allocation scheme is that the number of variables needed in a program must be predetermined. Thus, if you are working with an array and you anticipate needing a thousand locations, you would define

```
base_type a[1000];
```

This creates two problems. You may overestimate the length of the array and use only part of it; therefore memory is wasted. Or you may underestimate the necessary array length and be unable to process all the data until the program is modified. Fortunately, C++ solves these problems with the use of *dynamic memory allocation:*

1. Dynamic data structures can be defined by the programmer.
2. Memory for dynamic data is allocated under program control as needed and returned when not needed during the execution of a program; therefore, unneeded memory is not wasted and you are limited only by the available memory.
3. In some instances, working with dynamic data structures can be slower than working with other kinds of data structures; in particular, direct access of an array element may not have an analogue.
4. A significantly different method of accessing values stored in dynamic data structures must be developed since memory locations may not be predetermined.

A complete development of dynamic data structures is left to other courses in computer science. However, when finished with this chapter, you should have a reasonable understanding of dynamic data structures and be able to use them in a program. We carefully develop one type of dynamic data structure, the linked list. Others, such as stacks, queues, and binary trees, are developed in later courses.

You may find this material somewhat difficult. If so, do not get discouraged. Two reasons for the increased level of difficulty are that some of the work is not intuitive, and the level of abstraction is different from that of previous material. Therefore, as you work through this chapter, you are encouraged to draw several diagrams and write several short programs to help you understand concepts. Also you may need to reread the chapter or particular sections to grasp the mechanics of working with dynamic data.

11.1 Pointer Variables

OBJECTIVES

- to understand the difference between the address of a memory location and the value of a memory location
- to be able to define a pointer type and declare a pointer variable
- to be able to create dynamic memory and use a pointer variable to reference the contents of the dynamic memory
- to be able to create a dynamic data structure that contains a pointer to another dynamic data structure
- to understand the difference between a pointer variable and the dynamic memory referenced by the pointer
- to be able to use NULL with pointer variables

Computer Memory

Computer memory can be envisioned as a sequence of memory locations depicted as in Figure 11.1(a). An area where a value can be stored is called a *memory location.* When a variable is declared in the variable declaration section of a program, a memory location is reserved during execution of that program block. This memory location can be accessed by a reference to the variable name, and only data of the declared type can be stored there. Thus, if the declaration section is **int sum**; you can envision it as shown in Figure 11.1(b). If the assignment **sum = 56**; is made, we have the arrangement shown in Figure 11.1(c).

Each memory location has an *address.* This is an integer value that the computer must use as a reference to the memory location. When ordinary variables (such as **sum**) are used, the address of a memory location is used indirectly by the underlying machine instruction. However, when variables that access dynamic memory are used, the address is used directly as a reference or pointer to the memory location.

The *value* that is the address of a memory location must be stored somewhere in memory. In C++, this is stored in a *pointer variable.* A pointer variable (frequently denoted as **ptr**) contains the address of a memory location. To illustrate, assume **ptr** has been declared as a pointer variable. If 56 is stored in a memory location whose address is 11640, we can envision it as shown in Figure 11.1(d).

Working with Pointer Types and Variables

If we focus on a variable declaration for a moment, we see that a pointer type is defined in terms of a *base type.* The base type is the type of value pointed to by the pointer value. A pointer variable to an integer could be defined as

```
int *int_ptr;
```

The general form for defining pointer variables is

```
<base type name> *<variable name>;
```

where **<base type name>** is the name of any C++ data type and **<variable name>** is any legitimate C++ identifier. Alternatively, one could name a pointer type with **typedef**, and then declare a pointer variable of that type:

```
typedef int *int_ptr_type;

int_ptr_type int_ptr;
```

◆ FIGURE 11.1
(a) Computer memory. (b) Variable location in memory. (c) Value in variable sum. (d) Relationship between pointer and memory location.

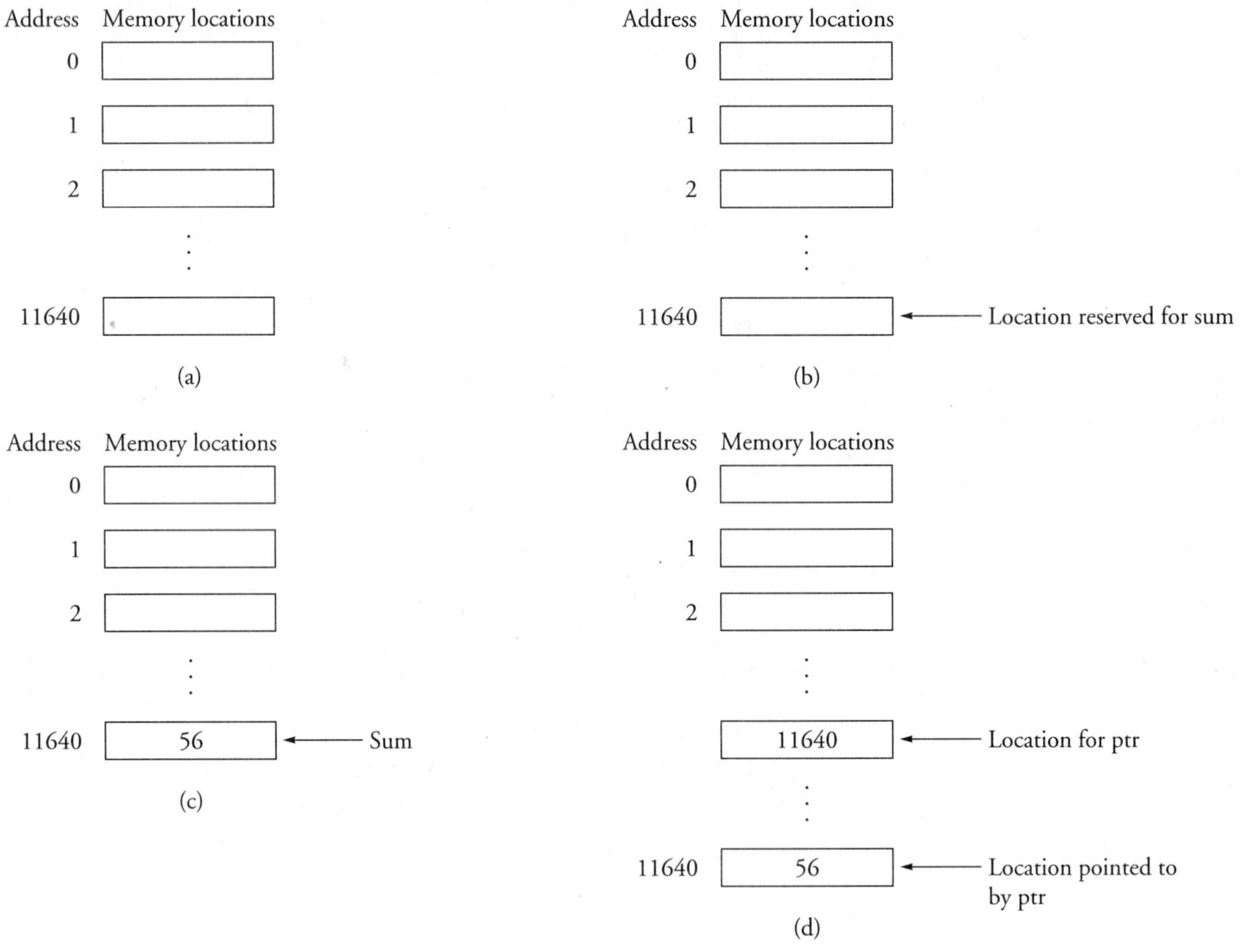

int_ptr cannot be assigned values of type **int; ptr** can only contain addresses of locations whose values are of type **int**. The code

```
float *float_ptr;
```

declares a pointer variable that can hold the address of a real number.

Initializing Pointer Variables

Before you can initialize a pointer variable, you need to include the C++ library **stdlib.h**:

```
#include <stdlib.h>
```

This library defines code for the pointer constant NULL. A pointer variable can be initialized in several ways.

1. Any pointer variable can be set to the NULL value. For example, **int_ptr = NULL**; will accomplish this. NULL is a special pointer value whose use we will discuss shortly.

2. Any pointer variable can be assigned the value of another pointer variable, as long as the two variables are of the same pointer type. Two pointer types are the same if they have the same base type. Thus, if **ptr** and **qtr** are variables of the same pointer type, the assignment **ptr = qtr**; will copy the pointer value stored in **qtr** into **ptr**.
3. Any pointer variable can be initialized to point to a value of its base type. This is accomplished by using the operator **new**. For example, **ptr = new int**; has the effect of storing a pointer to an integer value in **ptr**. Actually, **ptr** contains a pointer to a place where an integer value can be stored. This is illustrated as follows:

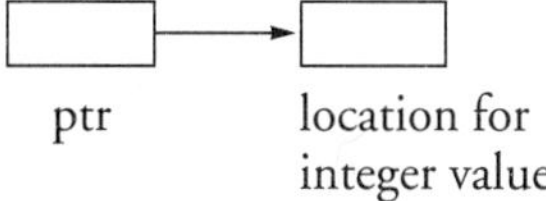

We will see how to store an integer value in this place shortly. The general form for using **new** to initialize a pointer variable is

<pointer variable> = new <base type>;

where the pointer variable's type has the same base type as **<base type>**. When we use **new**, we ask the computer to allocate memory for storing a value of the pointer's base type. This memory is *dynamic,* because it was not reserved when the pointer variable was declared.

Verifying Memory Allocation

When the computer processes a call to **new** from a program, it goes to an area of memory called a *heap* or *free store* to allocate an area of the appropriate size for storing a new data value. The heap might be a large area of memory in most systems, but its size is finite. Therefore, after repeated calls to **new**, the memory available for dynamic allocation will be used up. To avoid errors, a program can check to see whether this is the case and take the appropriate action. When heap memory is still available, **new** returns a pointer to a chunk of this memory. If there is no more heap memory, **new** returns the NULL value. In programs that use a large amount of dynamic memory, the following kind of code is recommended:

```
ptr = new base_type;
if (ptr != NULL)
      process(ptr);
else
      cout << "Error: no dynamic memory available." << endl;
```

where **process** indicates operations that access the area of memory pointed to by **ptr**. We will see shortly how to return unused dynamic memory from a program to the heap, so that this problem can be mitigated.

Accessing Data in Dynamic Memory

Suppose we declare a pointer variable and initialize it with **new**, as follows:

```
int *ptr;                // reserves memory for pointer value

ptr = new int;           // reserves memory for integer value
                         // and stores address as pointer value
```

The state of the computer's memory at this point can be illustrated by

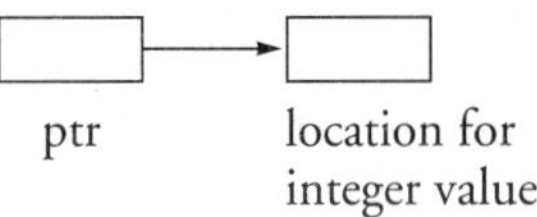

Note that a value is stored in **ptr**, but not in the area of memory denoted by this value. This second area of memory should be initialized with an integer value before it can be used. You do this by using the *dereference operator,* an asterisk (*). A *dereference* is an operation by which the system locates the area of memory pointed to by a pointer. Thus, the expression ***ptr** gives read/write access to the area of memory pointed to by **ptr**. For example, you could store the value 5 in this area by

```
*ptr = 5;
```

The state of the computer's memory can now be illustrated by

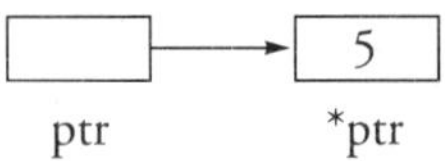

Once a value has been stored with a dereference operation, you can access it in the same way. For example, the statement **cout << *ptr << endl;** will display the number 5 on the terminal screen. Note that no parentheses are necessary to control the dereferencing. The general form of the dereference operation with * is

*<pointer variable>

where **<pointer variable>** is any variable of a pointer type. Dereferenced pointer variables can be used in any context used by ordinary variables of the same base type. To illustrate, assume that **ptr1** and **ptr2** are pointers to integers. If appropriate values (50 and 21) are in a data file, the segment

```
ptr1 = new int;
ptr2 = new int;
in_file >> *ptr1>> *ptr2;
cout << "The average of " << *ptr1 << " and" << *ptr2
     << " is " << (*ptr1 + *ptr2) / 2 << endl;
```

produces

```
The average of 50 and 21 is 35
```

Other Operations on Pointer Variables

When you use the function **new** to initialize a pointer variable, you are asking for dynamic memory to hold a value. This memory should be used as needed, and then returned to the heap for other use when not needed. To return a piece of dynamic memory to the heap, you use the operator **delete**. For example, if the pointer variable **ptr** points to a piece of dynamic memory, the statement **delete ptr;** will return the dynamic memory to the heap. The states of the computer memory before and after this statement can be depicted as follows:

COMMUNICATION AND STYLE TIPS

1. Like any variable, a pointer variable must be initialized before it is used. An attempt to use an uninitialized pointer variable may cause an error.
2. The dereference operator (*) should be used only after the pointer has been initialized with the address of a piece of dynamic memory. An attempt to dereference an uninitialized pointer variable or a pointer variable that contains the NULL pointer may cause an error.
3. In applications that use a large amount of dynamic memory, the success of a memory allocation operation with **`new`** should be checked by examining the pointer to see whether or not it is NULL.

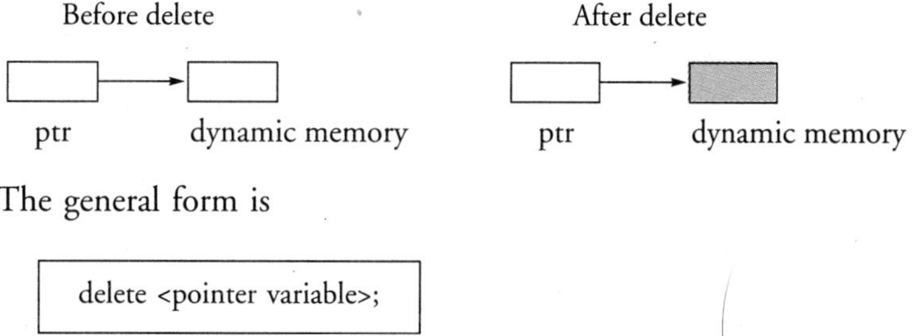

The general form is

```
delete <pointer variable>;
```

After you have returned a piece of dynamic memory to the system, you should not attempt to access a value in it with a pointer variable. It is possible to do so, but you will not be able to tell that you are now looking into deallocated space. Other parts of a program may now use this dynamic memory for their purposes. The pointer variable's value should be treated as unpredictable after a **`delete`**. The pointer should be reinitialized with either NULL or **`new`** before it can be used further.

Once they have been initialized, pointer variables can be compared for equality and inequality. For example, suppose pointer variables **`p`** and **`q`** have both been initialized to the NULL value. Then the comparison (**`p == q`**) will be TRUE, while the comparison (**`p != q`**) will be FALSE. The comparisons (**`p == NULL`**) and (**`q == NULL`**) will both be TRUE. Let's assume now that **`q`** is reinitialized to point to an area of dynamic memory, with **`q = new int`**. Then the comparison (**`p == q`**) will be FALSE.

In general, you should remember that pointer variables contain the addresses of other areas of memory. Though C++ supports arithmetic and output operations for pointer variables, for our purposes, the only useful operations will be assignment, comparison, dereference, and return of dynamic memory to the heap.

Pointers to Data Structures

The previous declarations of pointer variables are relatively uncomplicated; however, in actual practice, pointer types and variables are a bit more complex. For example, in the next section we will define a pointer to a data structure where one of the members in the data structure is a pointer to a data structure of the same type. These data structures are called *nodes,* and represent a very common use of pointers in programming. To define a node, we use a *structure definition.* An example is

```
struct node;                 // Empty definition of node type to introduce type name
typedef node *node_ptr;      // Definition of pointer type (pointer to a node)

struct node                  // Complete definition of node type
{
        string name;         // Data element to be stored in a node
        node_ptr next;       // Pointer to the next node
};

node_ptr list_of_names;      // Declaration of pointer variable
```

Notice that the type definition of **node_ptr** makes a reference to **node** before **node** is completely defined. The complete definition of **node** contains a member of type pointer to **node**. You will frequently want each structure to point to another structure. Using a structure definition with one member for a pointer permits this. The use of a structure definition with pointers is so common in programming that we will specify a conventional form for it:

```
struct <node type name>;
typedef <node type name>* <node pointer type name>;
struct <node type name>
{
            <member declaration 1 for data stored in node>
            .
            .
            .
            <member declaration N for data stored in node>
            <node pointer type name> next;
};
```

Several things call for comment:

1. **struct** is a reserved word.
2. An empty structure definition is needed to introduce the node type name before it is used. Its role is like that of a function declaration, which allows function names to be visible before they are implemented.
3. The components within the curly braces are called the *members* of the structure or node. They are similar to the data members of a class, except that they are all considered **public** here.
4. Several members of the node may contain the data stored there, such as names, phone numbers, and so forth.
5. There should be a member of the node that points to another node of the same type. Its name conventionally is **next**.
6. The structure definition ends with a semicolon (;) following the curly brace (}).

Alternatively, you could declare a pointer to a node without defining a **node_ptr** type:

```
struct node                    // Definition of a node type
{
      string name;             // Data element to be stored in a node
      node *next;              // Pointer to the next node
};

node *list_of_names;           // Declaration of pointer variable
```

After a pointer to a **node** structure has been declared, it can be initialized. First, we use **new** to allocate dynamic memory for the structure:

```
list_of_names = new node;
```

The state of the computer's memory can now be illustrated by

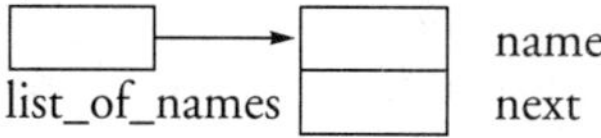

Then we have to initialize the **name** and **next** members within the node. It is convenient to use the *arrow operator,* ->, for this with a node. For example, we might input the name from the keyboard, and set the **next** pointer to NULL with an assignment:

```
cin >> list_of_names->name;
list_of_names->next = NULL;
```

These two lines of code are equivalent to the following two lines, which use the dereference operator:

```
cin >> *list_of_names.name;
*list_of_names.next = NULL;
```

The general form for using the -> operator is

<pointer to a node>-><member name>

You should be careful to assign NULL to the next member when initializing structures of this sort. If you are forming a sequence of dynamic data structures where each data structure contains a pointer variable for pointing to the next one, you can use NULL as a way to determine when you are at the end of a list. This idea is fully developed in the next section.

Enumerated Types

Some applications must represent objects such as colors, fruits, or days of the week. Rather than use strings for these representations, it is convenient and more efficient to define a set of *enumerated constants* and use them. Some examples are

```
enum fruit {APPLE, BANANA, PEAR};

enum color {RED, YELLOW, BLUE, GREEN};

enum day {MONDAY, TUESDAY, WEDNESDAY, THURSDAY, FRIDAY};
```

```
fruit my_fruit = BANANA;
color my_color = YELLOW;
day my_day = MONDAY;
```

Any value of an enumerated type can be assigned to or compared with a variable of that type. Enumerated values are more efficient to use than string values, because the computer represents them as simple integers. We will use enumerated types in some of the exercises and examples that follow.

EXERCISES 11.1

1. Discuss the difference between ordinary and dynamic variables.
2. Write a test program to declare a single pointer variable whose associated dynamic memory can have integer values.
   a. Ask for dynamic memory, assign it the value 25, and print the value.
   b. Ask for dynamic memory again, assign it the value 40, and print the value.

   At this stage of your program, where is the value 25 stored?
3. Illustrate the relationship between pointer variables and dynamic memory produced by

```
enum color {RED, YELLOW, BLUE, GREEN};

typedef color *color_ptr;

color_ptr ptr1, ptr2;

ptr1 = new color;
ptr2 = new color;
*ptr1 = BLUE;
*ptr2 = RED;
```

4. Assume the data declarations are given as in Exercise 3. Find all errors in the following.

```
a. *ptr1 = new color;
b. ptr2 = new color;
   ptr2 = YELLOW;
c. ptr1 = new color;
   ptr2 = new color;
   *ptr1 = RED;
   *ptr2 = *ptr1;
d. ptr1 = new color;
   ptr2 = new color;
   *ptr1 = RED;
   *ptr1 = *ptr2;
e. ptr1 = new color;
   ptr2 = new color;
   *ptr1 = RED;
   *ptr2 = ptr1;
f. ptr1 = NULL;
   *ptr1 = BLUE;
```

11.2 Linked Lists

OBJECTIVES

- to understand why a linked list is a dynamic data structure
- to be able to create a linked list
- to understand how pointers are used to form a linked list
- to be able to print data from a linked list

A *linked list* is the first dynamic data structure we will develop. It can be thought of as a list of data items where each item is linked to the next one by means of a pointer. Such a list can be envisioned as follows:

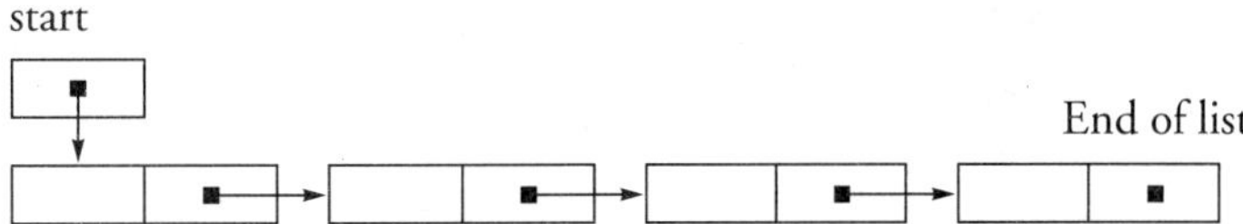

Items in a linked list are called *components* or *nodes*. These lists are used like arrays; that is, data of the same type can be stored in each node. As shown in the previous illustration, each node of a linked list can store certain data as well as point to the next node. Consequently, a structure is used for each node where one member of the structure is reserved for the pointer. If names are to be stored in such a list, we can use the structure definition from Section 11.1 as follows:

```
struct node
{
        string name;
        node *next;
};

node *list_of_names;
```

Thus, we can envision a list of names as

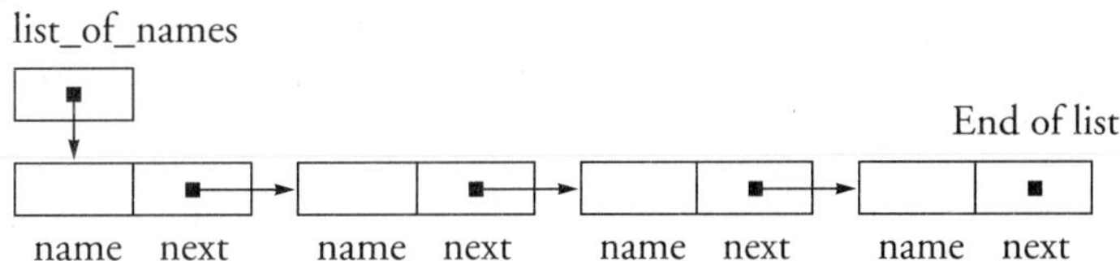

Creating a Linked List

One way to create a linked list is to add each new node to the end of the list. To do this, you need to identify the first node, the relationship (pointer) between successive nodes, and the last node. Pointers can be used to point to both the first node (**start**) and the last node (**last**). An auxiliary pointer is also used to point to the newest node (**current**). The pointer to the first node is not changed unless a new node is added to an empty list. The other pointers change as the linked list grows. When you have created such a list, the last node is usually designated by assigning NULL to the next pointer of that node. To illustrate, let's see how a linked list to hold five names can be formed. First, we define the type:

```
struct node;
typedef node *node_ptr;

struct node
{
        string name;
        node_ptr next;
};
```

and the variable declaration section

```
node_ptr start, last, current;       // Auxiliary pointers
```

To generate a linked list containing five nodes, we use the following code:

```
start = new node;
cout << "Enter a student's name: ";
cin >> start->name;
current = start;                          // Pointer to first node
for (int j = 1; j <= 4; ++j)
{
        last = new node;
        cout << "Enter a student's name: ";
        cin >> last->name;
        current->next = last;
        current = last;
}
current->next = NULL;
```

Let's now examine what happens when this segment of code is executed.

```
start = new node;
```

causes

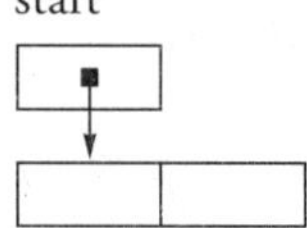


```
current = start;
```

produces

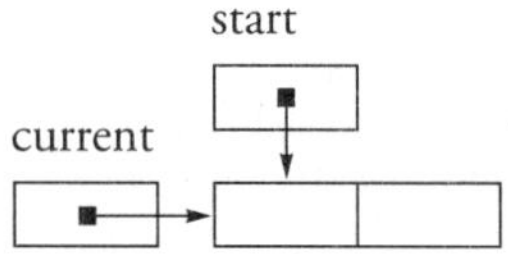

Now that we have started our list, the first pass through the **for** loop produces results as shown in Table 11.1. Each pass through the body of the **for** loop adds one element to the linked list and causes both **current** and **last** to point to the last node of the list. After the loop has been executed four times, we have the following list:

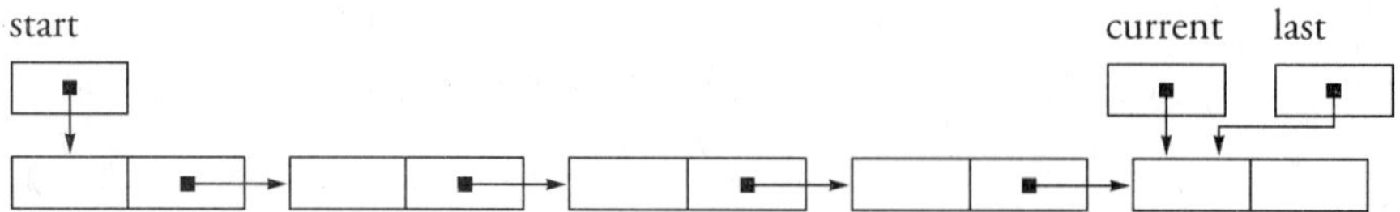

At this stage, the loop is exited and

```
current->next = NULL;
```

◇ TABLE 11.1
Adding a second node to a linked list

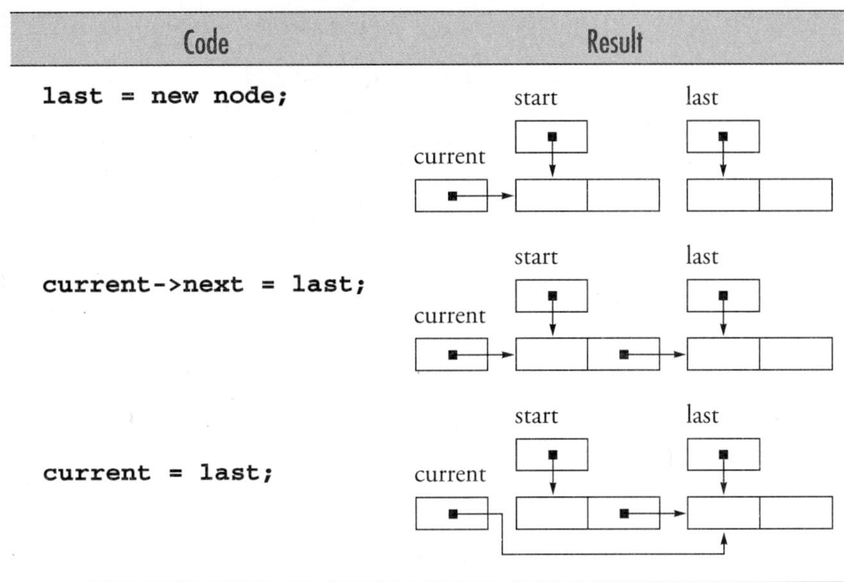

Code	Result
`last = new node;`	
`current->next = last;`	
`current = last;`	

produces

Now when we process the list, we can check the member name **next** to determine when the end of the list has been reached. In this sense, NULL is used in a manner similar to **eof()** with file streams.

EXAMPLE 11.1

Let's now create a linked list that can be used to simulate a deck of playing cards. We need 52 nodes, each of which is a structure with a member for the suit (club, diamond, heart, or spade); a member for the number (1 to 13); and a member for the next pointer. Such a structure can be defined as

```
enum suits {CLUB, DIAMOND, HEART, SPADE};

struct node;
typedef node *node_ptr;

struct node
{
        suits suit;
        int num;
        node_ptr next;
};
```

As before, we need three pointer variables; they can be declared as

```
node_ptr start, last, current;
```

If an ace is represented by the number 1, we can start our list by

```
start = new node;
start->suit = CLUB;
start->num = 1;
current = start;
last = start;
```

This beginning is illustrated by

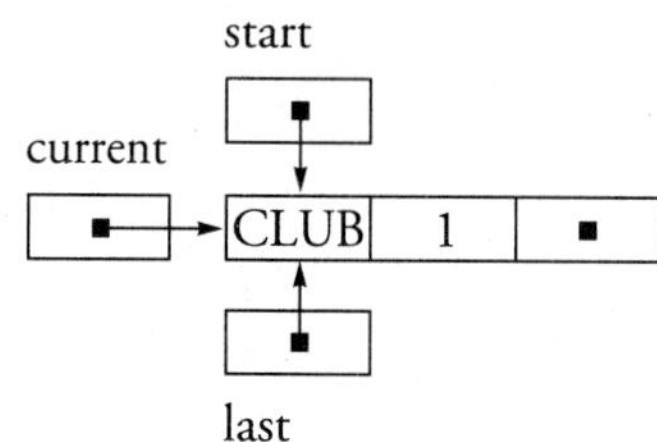

We can then generate the rest of the deck as follows:

```
for (int j = 2; j <= 52; ++j)
{
        last = new node;
        if (current->num = 13)                              // Start a new suit
        {
                last->suit = suits(int(current->suit) + 1);
                last->num = 1;
        }
        else                                                // Same suit, next number
        {
                last->suit = current->suit;
                last->num  = current->num + 1;
        }
        current->next = last;
        current = last;
}
current->.next = NULL;
```

The first time through this loop we have

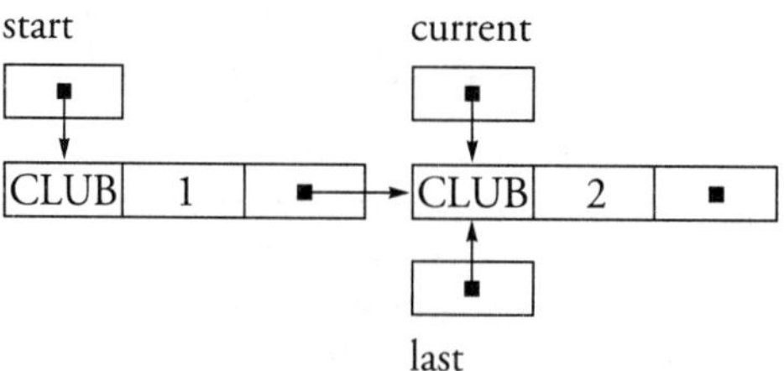

This loop is processed all 51 times and then exited so that when **current->next = NULL;** is executed, we have the list shown in Figure 11.2.

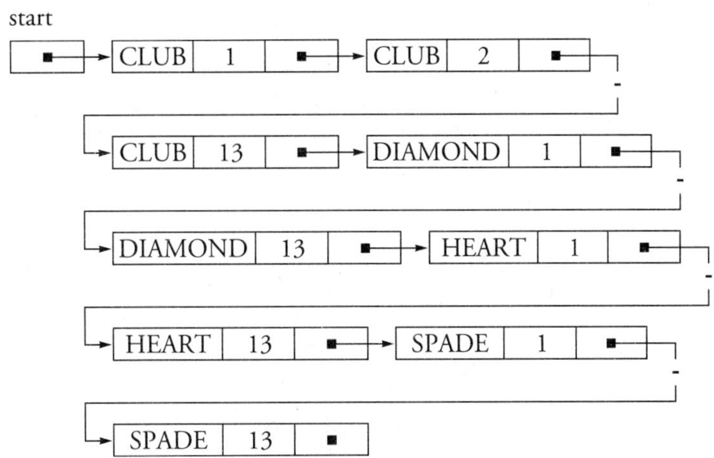

◆ FIGURE 11.2
A linked list simulating a deck of cards

`get_node`: A Useful Function

Because it is so important to initialize pointers properly and this is done so often in working with linked lists, we should design a function that makes this task simple and consistent. Whenever we need a new node for a linked list, we will call this function. The function takes as its parameter the data to be placed into the new node. It returns as its value a pointer to the new node. The caller of this function can count on two postconditions:

1. The data sent to the function will be stored in the data member of the node.
2. The next member of the node will be set to NULL.

Assuming that the node should contain data of type **`element`**, our function would be called as follows:

```
ptr = get_node(data);
```

Assuming that it returns a pointer of type **`node_ptr`**, the function's declaration would be

```
// Function: get_node
// Gets a new node containing data
//
// Input: data to be stored in the node
// Output: a pointer to the node containing the data

node_ptr get_node(element data);
```

The function's implementation would be

```
node_ptr get_node(element data)
{
        node_ptr temp = new node;

        temp->data = data;
        temp->next = NULL;
        return temp;
}
```

As you can see, the **get_node** function hides a fair amount of low-level code that would have to be written every time a programmer needs a new node for a list. This is a good example of a function that can make programs more readable and safe.

We can use **get_node** to set up our list of four names, assuming that **name** is a string:

```
cin >> name;
start = get_node(name);
current = start;                          // Pointer to first node
for (int j = 1; j <= 4; ++j)
{
        cin >> name;
        last = get_node(name);
        current->next = last;
        current = last;
}
```

For applications that use a large amount of dynamic memory, a safer **get_node** function would check the success of the **new** operation and halt program execution if no more memory is available in the heap:

```
node_ptr get_node(string data)
{
        node_ptr temp = new node;

        assert(temp != NULL);
        temp->data = data;
        temp->next = NULL;
        return temp;
}
```

We will illustrate the use of **get_node** with examples later in this chapter.

Printing from a Linked List

Thus far, we have seen how to create a dynamic data structure and assign data to components of such a structure. We conclude this section with a look at how to print data from a linked list.

The general idea is to start with the first component in the list, print the desired information, and then move sequentially through the list until the last component (NULL) is reached. There are two aspects of this algorithm that need to be examined. First, the loop control depends on examining the current structure for the value of NULL in the pointer member. If **p** is used to denote this member, we have

```
while (p != NULL)
{
        .
        .
        .
        process node pointed to by p
        .
        .
        .

}
```

Second, the loop increment is to assign the pointer (**p**) used as a loop control variable the value of the next member of the current structure. To illustrate, assume we have the definitions and declarations used previously to form a list of names. If we declare the variable **p** by

```
node_ptr p;
```

we can then print the names by

```
p = start;
while (p != NULL)
{
        cout << setw(40) << p->name << endl;
        p = p->next;
}
```

In general, printing from a linked list is done with a function. When a function is used, only the external pointer (**start** in our examples) needs to be used as a parameter. To illustrate, a function to print the previous list of names is

```
void print_names(node_ptr start)
{
        node_ptr p = start;

        while (p != NULL)
        {
                cout << setw(40) << p->name << endl;
                p = p->next;
        }
}
```

This would be called from the main program by

```
print_names(start);
```

COMMUNICATION AND STYLE TIPS

When processing a linked list, the pointer variable used to control the loop should always be checked to see whether or not it is NULL. If it is NULL, you should not attempt to dereference data with the -> operator and the pointer. Using a **while** loop whose first condition is a test of the form (**p != NULL**) will help to avoid these errors.

EXERCISES 11.2

1. Discuss the differences and similarities between arrays and linked lists.
2. Write a test program to transfer an unknown number of integers from a data file into a linked list and then print the integers from the linked list.
3. Write a function to be used with the test program in Exercise 2 to print the integers.
4. Explain why a linked list is preferable when you are getting an unknown number of data items from a data file.
5. Suppose you are going to create a linked list of structures where each structure in the list should contain the following information about a student: name, four test scores, 10 quiz scores, average, and letter grade.
   a. Define a structure to be used for this purpose.
   b. What pointer type(s) and pointer variable(s) are needed?

c. Assume the data for each student is on one line in the data file as

```
Smith Mary          97 98 85 90 9 8 7 10 6 9 10 8 9 7
```

i. Show how to get the data for the first student into the first component of a linked list.

ii. Show how to get the data for the second student into the second component.

6. Why are three pointers (**start, last, current**) used when creating a linked list?

7. Consider these definitions and declarations:

```
struct node;
typedef node *node_ptr;

struct node
{
        int num;
        node_ptr next;
};

node_ptr a, b, c;
```

a. Show how the schematic

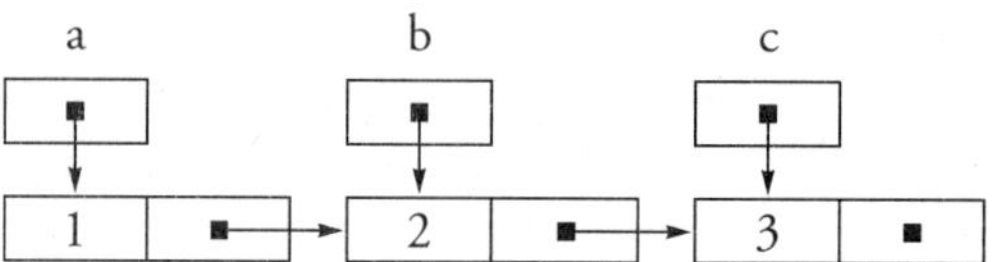

would be changed by each of the following:

i. `a = a->next;`
ii. `b = a;`
iii. `c = a->next;`
iv. `b->num = c->num;`
v. `a->num = b->next->num;`
vi. `c->next = a;`

b. Write one statement to change

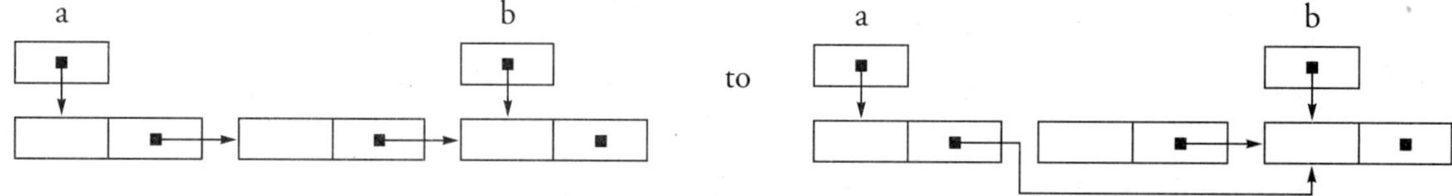

8. Assume the definitions and declarations in Exercise 7. Indicate the output for each of the following:

a.
```
a = new node;
b = new node;
a->num = 10;
b->num = 20;
b = a;
a->num = 5;
cout << a->num << b->num << endl;
```

b.
```
c = new node;
c->num = 100;
b = new node;
b->num = c->num % 8;
a = new node;
a->num = b->num + c->num;
cout << a->num << b->num << c->num << endl;
```
c.
```
a = new node;
b = new node;
a->num = 10;
a->next = b;
a->next->num = 100;
cout << a->num << b->num;
```
9. Write a function **sum** to sum the integers in a linked list of integers. Show how it is called from the main program.

11.3 Implementing the Ordered Collection Class as a Linked List

OBJECTIVES

- to understand the need for the use of dynamic memory in implementing a data structure
- to understand how pointers are manipulated in the process of inserting a node into a linked list
- to understand how pointers are manipulated in the process of removing a node from a linked list
- to understand how to search for a node at a given position in a linked list
- to understand how to search for a given data element in a linked list
- to understand the costs and benefits of different implementations of the same class or abstract data type

User Requirements Revisited

To explore how linked lists are processed, we will examine the use of a linked list to implement the ordered collection class introduced in Section 10.6. Recall that an ordered collection class allows clients to focus on the logical properties of a sequence or list of data elements, and to ignore the physical properties of the underlying data structure used to represent it. However, if this underlying data structure is an array, the physical size of the collection will often be different from its logical size. This difference will cause some clients to waste memory if the server uses a large array, or to obtain too little memory if the server uses a small array. Ideally, the server should provide only enough physical memory to represent the logical size of the ordered collection at any given time in the application. The use of a linked list with pointers will satisfy this requirement.

Another drawback to the array implementation of an ordered collection is the efficiency of certain operations. Adding or removing a data element at the end of the collection involves just an increment or decrement of the length attribute and the storage or retrieval of the data element with a subscript operation. However, the addition or removal of a data element from the beginning of the collection requires a shift of all of the other data elements in the array. The cost of this operation will be in direct proportion to the number of data elements and the size of each element to be copied. The use of a linked list with pointers will satisfy the requirement that all insertion and deletion operations be performed in a reasonable amount of time.

Specifying Operations

The formal specification of the operations for the ordered collection class was presented in Section 10.6. When we reimplement a class or abstract data type, it is a good idea to minimize the changes to the formal specification, so that the applications of clients will not be disturbed. The specifications of Section 10.6 will change only slightly. Because we are not using an array to implement the class, we can drop the references to **MAX_ARRAY_SIZE** from the specification. Thus, the create operation now makes no mention of the physical size of the memory allocated for a new ordered collection. The **add_first** and **add_last** operations also drop this reference from their preconditions. In its place, we assert as a precondition that memory must be available before the operation is performed:

Add first operation
Preconditions: The receiver is an ordered collection object, appropriately initialized, the parameter is an **element** object, and there is memory available for adding the element.
Postconditions: **length** is incremented by one, the data elements in the ordered collection are shifted up by one index position, and the parameter element is placed in the first position in the ordered collection.
Add last operation
Preconditions: The receiver is an ordered collection object, appropriately initialized, the parameter is an **element** object, and there is memory available for adding the element.
Postconditions: **length** is incremented by one, and the parameter element is placed in the last position in the ordered collection.

Declaring the Class

Because the specifications do not change, the declarations of the public member functions remain the same:

```
// Class declaration file: ordercol.h

#ifndef ORDERCOL_H

// Declaration section

// We assume that the type element has been defined by the application in element.h

#include "boolean.h"
#include "element.h"

class ordered_collection
{

        public:

        // Class constructors

        ordered_collection();
        ordered_collection(const ordered_collection &oc);

        // Class destructor

        ~ordered_collection();

        // Member functions

        int length();
        element& operator [ ] (int index);
        ordered_collection& operator = (const ordered_collection &oc);
        boolean operator == (const ordered_collection &oc);
        void add_last(element e);
```

```
        element remove_last();
        void add_first(element e);
        element remove_first();
        void remove(element e);

        protected:

        // Data members

        struct node;                    // Definition of a node type
        typedef node *node_ptr;         // Definition of a pointer to node type
        struct node                     // Completion of node type definition
        {
                element data;
                node_ptr next;
        };

        node_ptr start;                 // Pointer to the first node in the collection
        int c_length;

        // Member functions

        node_ptr get_node(element e);

};

#define ORDERCOL_H
#endif
```

There are three things to note about this class declaration:

1. A new **public** member function, a *class destructor,* has been added. This operation will be used by the computer to deallocate dynamic memory for parameters that are passed by value to functions, but will not be used directly by clients.
2. The linked list used to implement the ordered collection is specified by a set of type definitions as in Section 11.2. The two variable data members, **start** and **c_length**, will be used to maintain a pointer to the beginning of the linked list and the length of the list, respectively. The length of the list will always be the same as the length of the ordered collection.
3. A **protected** member function, **get_node**, which we developed in Section 11.2, will be used by the implementation to obtain new, initialized nodes to insert into the linked list.

The rest of this section develops the implementation of the ordered collection operations. Because we are implementing the collection as a linked list, our primary focus will be on linked list operations.

Initializing a Linked List

Before we can perform any operations on a linked list, it must be initialized. When a new ordered collection is created, the data member representing the linked list (**start**) should be in an *empty condition.* To make a list empty, we simply set the pointer to the beginning of the list to NULL. We then set **c_length** to 0, as in the array implementation. Thus, we have

```
ordered_collection::ordered_collection()
{
        start = NULL;
        c_length = 0;
}
```

Note that the linked list implementation of an empty ordered collection references no memory for storing data elements.

Another way to initialize a linked list is to copy the data from another linked list. This process occurs in the implementation of the copy constructor for the ordered collection. The basic idea is to iterate through the nodes in the parameter collection and add the data in each node to the end of the new collection:

```
ordered_collection::ordered_collection(const ordered_collection &oc)
{
        node_ptr probe = oc.start;

        start = NULL;
        c_length = 0;
        while (probe != NULL)
        {
                add_last(probe->data);
                probe = probe->next;
        }
}
```

Note that the precondition for **add_last**—that the new collection be appropriately initialized—must be satisfied by the assignment statements to **start** and **c_length** before the loop is entered. If **add_last** runs out of dynamic memory at any point during this operation, the program will halt with an error message.

Destroying a Linked List

The copy constructor is automatically invoked when an ordered collection is passed as a value parameter to a function. When this function returns, the memory allocated for the parameter must be deallocated. In the case of parameters that do not use dynamic memory (the array implementation in Section 10.6 is one such case), the computer deallocates memory automatically. In the case of a parameter that uses dynamic memory, the class is responsible for defining a *destructor operation* that the computer can invoke to deallocate memory. The class destructor is preceded by the tilde (~) character and appears in the **public** section of the class definition module. The implementation of the class destructor uses the **delete** operator to return any dynamic data to the heap. In the case of a linked list, the destructor iterates through the nodes and returns each one to the heap with **delete**:

```
ordered_collection::~ordered_collection( )
{
      node_ptr garbage;

      while (start != NULL)
      {
```

```
            garbage = start;
            start = start->next;
            delete garbage;
        }
}
```

Remember that the client will not have to invoke a class destructor, but that it must be defined by any server class that uses dynamic memory.

Adding an Element to the Beginning or End of a Linked List

The implementation of the **add_first** and **add_last** operations on ordered collections requires adding a new node to the beginning or end of a linked list. To insert a data element at the beginning of a linked list, we first get a new node for the data element, rearrange two pointers, and increment **c_length**:

```
void ordered_collection::add_first(element e)
{
        node_ptr new_node = get_node(e);

        new_node->next = start;
        start = new_node;
        ++c_length;
}
```

The effects of each of these statements on a linked list containing one node are depicted in Figure 11.3. Note that the order in which the pointers are reassigned is critical. Reversing their order would cause any nodes already in the list to be lost to the application. Note also that no copy operations are required to shift data elements in the linked list before the new node is added. This represents one of the advantages of a linked list implementation over an array implementation of collections.

◆ FIGURE 11.3
Inserting a new node at the beginning of a linked list

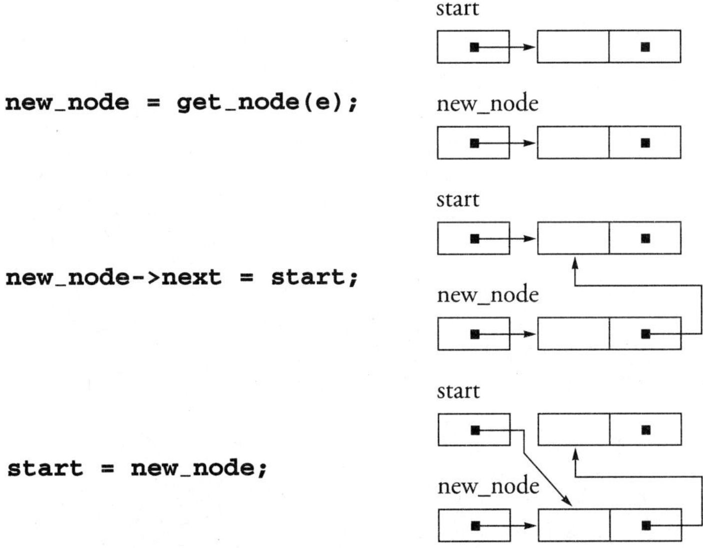

To insert a data element at the end of a linked list, we must consider two cases. First, the list might be empty. In that case, we can run **add_first** to perform the insertion. Otherwise, there is at least one node in the list. In that case, we search for the **next** pointer of the last node in the list. When this pointer is found, we get a new node with the data element, set the **next** pointer of the last node to the new node, and increment **c_length**:

```
void ordered_collection::add_last(element e)
{
        if (c_length == 0)
                add_first(e);
        else
        {
                node_ptr new_node = get_node(e);
                node_ptr probe = start;
                while (probe->next != NULL)
                        probe = probe->next;
                probe->next = new_node;
                ++c_length;
        }
}
```

The process of searching for the last node and inserting a new node at the end of a linked list is depicted in Figure 11.4.

◆ FIGURE 11.4
Inserting a new node at the end of a linked list

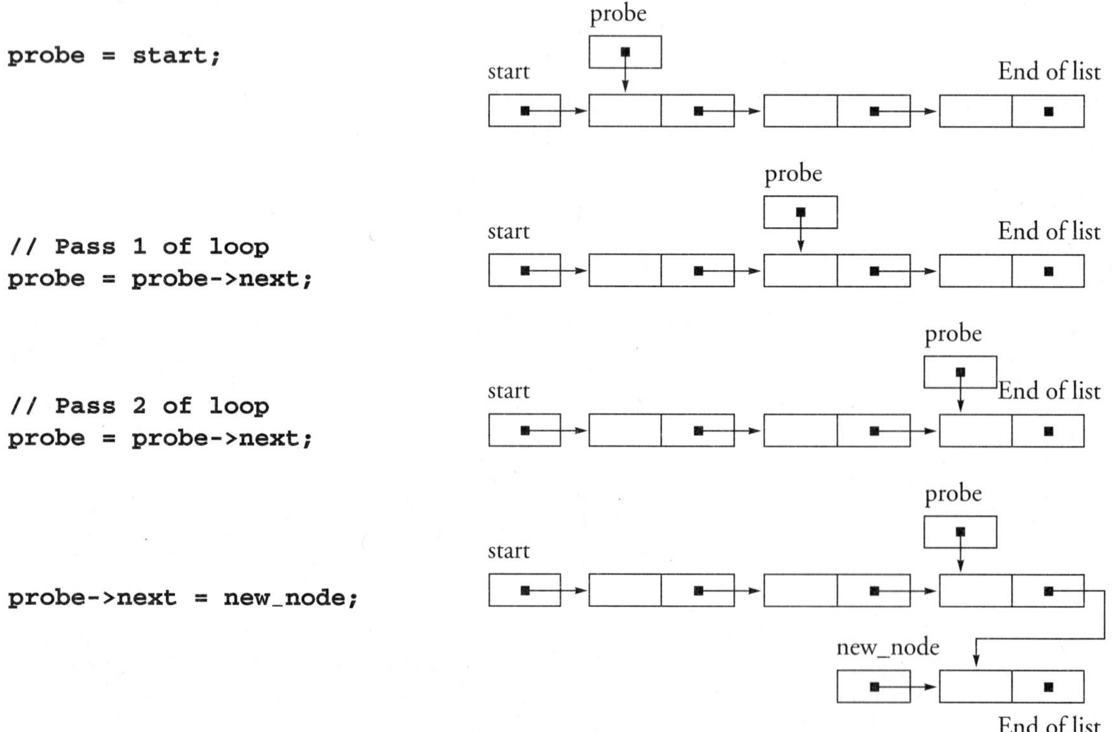

The implementation of the **get_node** operation resembles the one presented in Section 11.2, except for the function heading:

```
ordered_collection::node_ptr::ordered_collection::get_node(element e)
{
	node_ptr temp = new node;

	assert(temp != NULL);
	temp->data = e;
	temp->next = NULL;
	return temp;
}
```

Because the type name **node_ptr** is visible only within the scope of the **ordered_collection** class definition, the function heading requires an extra prefix (**ordered_collection::**) to resolve the scope of this identifier.

The Subscript Operation for Linked Lists

The subscript operation for ordered collections returns the address of the data element at an index position in the collection. This address can then be used as an l-value or an r-value, depending on whether the data element is being used as the target of an assignment or as a value. To implement the subscript operation with a linked list, we must search the list for the node containing the *i*th data element, where *i* is the **index** parameter. Then the address of the data element in the node can be returned. The implementation uses a count-controlled loop that runs from 1 to **index**, and advances a probe pointer through the list on each pass:

```
element& ordered_collection::operator [ ] (int index)
{
	node_ptr probe = start;

	assert((index >= 0) && (index < c_length));
	for (int i = 1; i <= index; ++i)
		probe = probe->next;
	return probe->data;
}
```

Note that the **for** loop uses the bounds **1** and **index**, rather than **0** and **index - 1**, as has been the case with loops that process arrays. The reason for this shift is that we are counting the number of times the **probe** must be advanced to reach the desired node. When **index == 0**, the loop is not entered at all and **probe == start**. A comparison of the linked list implementation of the subscript operation with the array implementation is left as an exercise.

Removing an Element from a Linked List

The ordered collection class has three data removal operations. Two of these—**remove_first** and **remove_last**—are positional. Their implementations resemble those of the corresponding insertion operations. **remove_first** aims a temporary pointer at the first node in the list, aims the **start** pointer at the second node or gives the start pointer the value of the **next** pointer of the first node, and invokes the **delete** operator to return the first node to the heap:

```
element ordered_collection::remove_first()
{
        element data;
        node_ptr garbage = start;

        assert(c_length > 0);
        data = start->data;
        start = start->next;
        delete garbage;
        --c_length;
        return data;
}
```

The effects of this sequence of statements are depicted in Figure 11.5.

◆ FIGURE 11.5
Removing a node from the beginning of a linked list

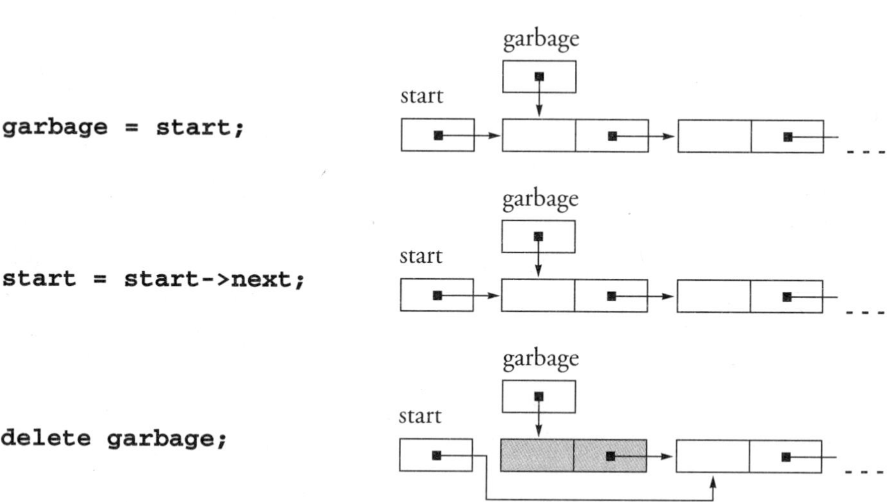
garbage = start;
start = start->next;
delete garbage;
garbage
start
garbage
start
garbage
start

remove_last has two cases two consider. The first case is that there is only one node in the list, so we run **remove_first**. The second case requires a search for the last node in the list, similar to the one we used for **add_last**. The only difference is that at the end of the search process, we must have a pointer to the node just before the one to be removed, so that we can set the **next** pointer of this node (the new last node of the list) to NULL. Therefore, we will maintain two temporary pointers—**probe** and **trailer**—during the search. **trailer** will always point to the node just in front of the node that **probe** points to in the list:

```
element ordered_collection::remove_last()
{
        assert(c_length > 0);
        if (c_length == 1)                  // Only one node in the list
                return remove_first();
        else
        {
                node_ptr probe = start;     // Search for last node in the list
                node_ptr trailer;
                while (probe->next != NULL)
```

```
                {
                        trailer = probe;
                        probe = probe->next;
                }
                element data = probe->data;    // Save data in temporary variable
                trailer->next = NULL;          // Set new last node
                delete probe;                  // Return old last node to heap
                --c_length;
                return data;
        }
}
```

The effects of this sequence of statements for a list containing two nodes are shown in Figure 11.6.

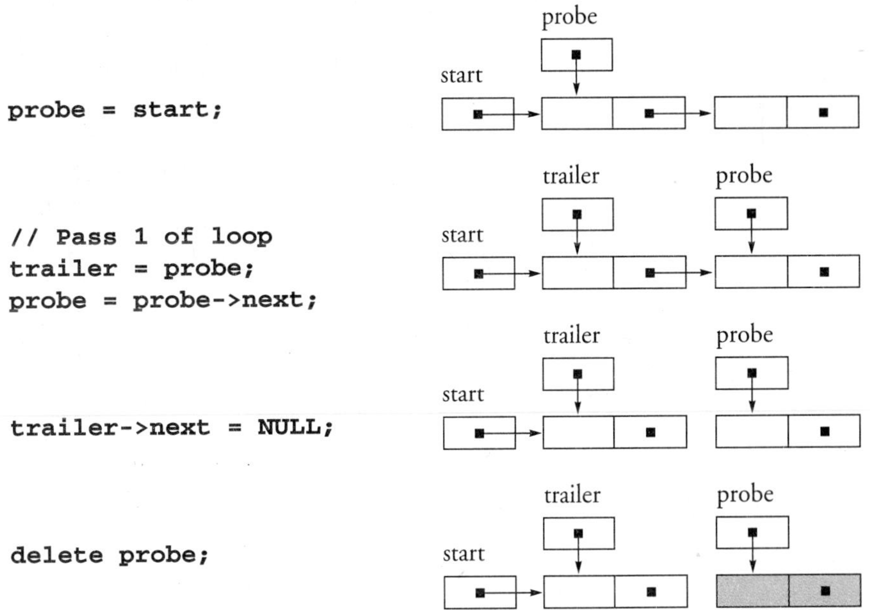
probe = start;
// Pass 1 of loop
trailer = probe;
probe = probe->next;
trailer->next = NULL;
delete probe;
start
probe
trailer

◆ FIGURE 11.6
Removing a node from the end of a linked list

The third removal operation, **remove**, takes a data element to be removed as a parameter. Once again, there are two cases to consider. In the first case, the element to be removed is in the only node in the list, so we invoke **remove-_first**. Otherwise, the function searches for the element in the list and removes it. As in **remove_last**, search uses a loop that advances **probe** and **trailer** pointers:

```
void ordered_collection::remove(element e)
{
        node_ptr probe = start;
        node_ptr trailer;
        boolean found = FALSE;

        assert(c_length > 0);
        if ((c_length == 1) && (probe->data == e))          // Only one node in list
                remove_first();
        else
```

```
        {
                while ((probe->next != NULL) && ! found)     // Search for element
                        if (probe->data == e)
                                found = TRUE;
                        else
                        {
                                trailer = probe;
                                probe = probe->next;
                        }
                assert(found);
                trailer->next = probe->next;                 // Remove node
                delete probe;
                --c_length;
        }
}
```

Note that we set the **next** pointer of the **trailer** node to the **next** pointer of the node to be deleted or aim the **next** pointer of the trailer node at the node following the node to be deleted, rather than just set the **next** pointer of the **trailer** node to NULL. This assignment will cover cases of removals from the middle of the list as well as at the end of the list. The effects of these statements for the removal of a given element that is in the middle of a linked list are depicted in Figure 11.7.

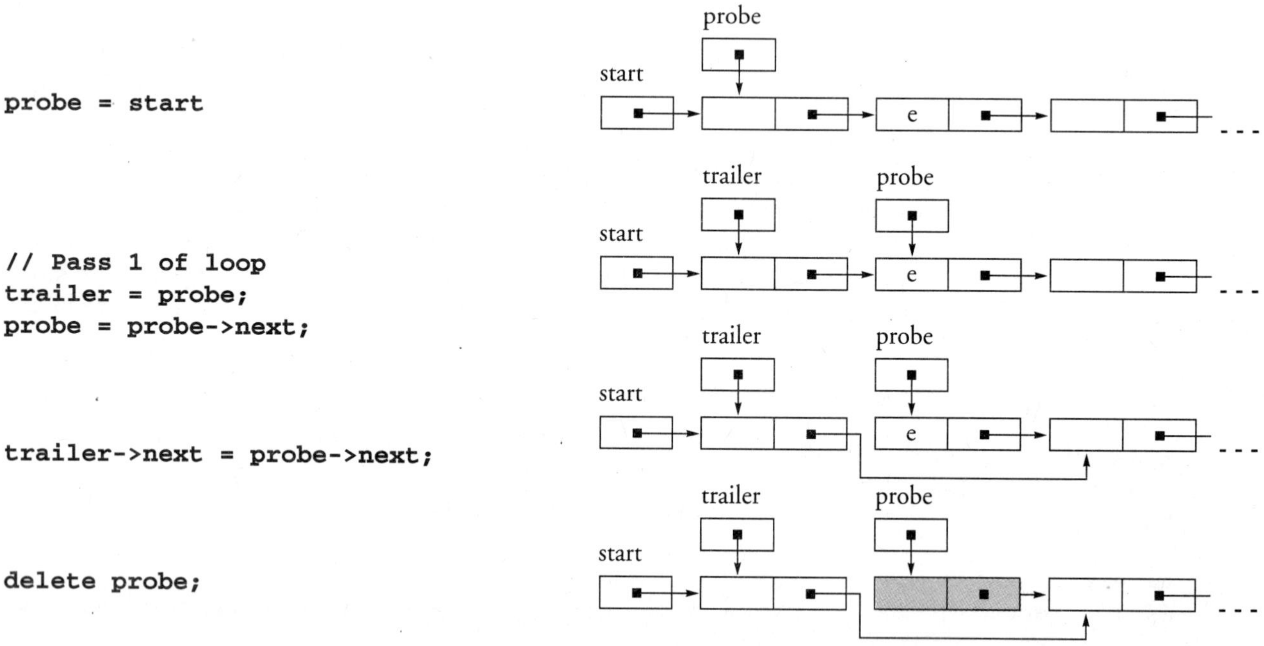

◆ FIGURE 11.7
Removing a given element from a linked list

```
probe = start

// Pass 1 of loop
trailer = probe;
probe = probe->next;

trailer->next = probe->next;

delete probe;
```

EXAMPLE 11.2

To illustrate how ordered collections implemented as linked lists can be used in conjunction with files, we present a simple program that inputs integers from a file into an ordered collection and then displays the contents of the collection on the screen.

```
// Program file: filtocol.cpp

#include <iostream.h>
#include <fstream.h>
#include "ordercol.h"

// Function: get_list
// Reads elements from file into ordered collection
//
// Inputs: an opened input file stream and an empty
ordered collection
// Outputs: the collection with data from the file

void get_list(ifstream &in_file, ordered_collection
     &list);

void print_list(ordered_collection list);

int main()
{
      ifstream in_file;
      ordered_collection list;

      in_file.open("myfile");
      get_list(in_file, list);
      in_file.close();
      print_list(list);
      return 0;
}

void get_list(ifstream &in_file, ordered_collection
     &list)
{
      int data;

      in_file >> data;
      while (! in_file.eof())
      {
            list.add_last(data);
            in_file >> data;
      }
}

void print_list(ordered_collection list)
{
      for (int i = 0; i < list.length(); ++i)
            cout << list[i] endl;
}
```

A NOTE OF INTEREST

Garbage Collection

Programs that make frequent use of dynamic memory can be error-prone. One kind of error that can occur is the failure to return pieces of dynamic memory to the heap when they are no longer needed. If this failure occurs often enough, the program will run out of memory, perhaps at a critical point in its task.

To avoid the problem of memory leakage, some programming languages have been designed so that the programmer does not have to worry about returning unused memory to the heap at all. The run-time system for these languages has a special module called a garbage collector that automatically recovers unused dynamic memory when it is needed.

Two such languages, Smalltalk and LISP, rely on dynamic memory for all of their data structures, so an automatic garbage collector is an essential part of their design. In Smalltalk, a pure object-oriented language, dynamic memory is used to create new objects. In LISP, which supports a linked list as a standard data structure, dynamic memory is used to add data elements to a list. When an application in either of these languages asks for a new piece of dynamic memory, the computer checks the heap to see whether the request can be satisfied. If not, the garbage collector is invoked, and all of the unused memory locations are returned to the heap. Then the request is granted, if enough dynamic memory is available.

The garbage collection mechanism works roughly as follows. Every memory location is marked as either referenced by the application or not. A memory location is referenced if it is named by a variable or is part of a linked structure pointed to by such a variable. When memory is allocated for variables, it is marked as referenced. When memory becomes completely unlinked from any variable references in a program, it is marked as unreferenced. Thus, only unreferenced memory locations will be candidates for being returned to the heap.

Garbage collection in early versions of LISP and Smalltalk sometimes degraded the performance of a program. During a collection, an application would appear to pause for a moment while the mechanism did its work. This is one reason why Smalltalk and LISP applications have not received much play in industry, where efficiency in time-critical tasks is a priority. However, much research and development have produced very efficient garbage collection algorithms, so that LISP and Smalltalk programs now perform as well as programs written in languages without any garbage collector.

Note that the only termination condition for the **while** loop in **get_list** is the **eof** condition. Because the ordered collection is implemented as a linked list using dynamic memory, the program does not have to check the length of the list against **MAX_ARRAY_SIZE**. This program will use only enough memory to represent the data in the file. If there is not enough memory for all of the data, the program will halt with an error message.

When this program is run on the data file

```
42 2 -10 0 45 100 52 78 91 99 86
```

the output is

```
42 2 -10 0 45 100 52 78 91 99 86
```

EXERCISES 11.3

1. Illustrate how the function **remove** works when the data element to be removed is at the end of a linked list.
2. Assess the costs and benefits of using a linked list implementation of an ordered collection rather than an array implementation.
3. Write implementations for the assignment and equality operations for the ordered collection class.
4. Remove the assertion from function **remove_first**, and run a program that calls **remove_first** with an empty ordered collection. Describe what happens.

5. Write a program to test for how many nodes can be allocated for an ordered collection of integers until the heap has no more memory. You can accomplish this by writing a count-controlled loop whose upper bound is an input integer and which adds a new data element to the beginning of the collection on each pass. Start with the input of a large integer, and if an error occurs, try another integer of half that size. If an error does not occur, repeat the input with an integer half again the size of the previous input. When your inputs can alternate between an integer that causes an error and an integer that is one less that does not cause an error, you will have determined how many nodes can be obtained for storing integers from the heap.
6. Write a member function to search an ordered collection for a given data element. The search function should return an integer value. If the element is found, the integer returned should be its position in the list (counting from 0). If the element is not found, the integer should be -1.
7. The copy constructor for the linked list implementation of ordered collections is costly. Describe why and propose a faster method.

11.4 Traversing a Linked List

OBJECTIVES

- to understand the cost of a linked list as a sequential access structure
- to be able to pass a function as a parameter to another function
- to understand how the development of a traversal function enhances the efficiency and maintainability of a software system that uses linked lists

One of the major drawbacks of using a linked list is that access to any node requires chaining through the pointers from the start of the list to the desired node. For large lists, this process can take an unreasonable amount of time. For example, the function that displays the data elements in a collection must use the subscript operation to access each element. This in turn requires a linear search for the position of the node in the linked list implementation. In applications where traversals of collections are frequent, performance may be quite poor.

Passing Functions as Parameters

One way to solve the traversal problem for a linked list implementation is to provide a member function that traverses the list and performs some operation on each data element. For example, the collection server could support a **print** function that prints all of the data elements in a single traversal of the linked list. The problem with this idea is that different applications will have different ways of formatting the output, requiring several different print functions. Moreover, other operations could be performed during a traversal, such as converting every name in a collection of names to uppercase format.

Clearly, we would like to provide a traversal function that does not tie the collection class too closely to the needs of an application (the kind of process applied to a data element), but that allows applications to apply any process that is desired to each data element in the collection. Ordered collections should support a general operation, **traverse**, to which a client could pass a parameter that performs a specialized operation on a data element. The client would be responsible for defining the operation on the element, while the server would be responsible for invoking it with each element in the list. C++ provides a special kind of data type, called *pointer to a function,* that enables servers to receive functions as parameters.

Let's first see how a client would pass a function as a parameter. Assuming that a client has defined a function, say, **print_data**, that takes a data element as a parameter and displays it on the screen, a client could print every element in a collection by invoking

```
collection.traverse(print_data);
```

In general, when functions are passed as actual parameters to other functions, the name of the function is passed. If the collection contains numbers and a function **add_one** has been written to increment its parameter by one, a client can increment all of the numbers in a collection by calling

```
collection.traverse(add_one);
```

Declaring and Implementing a Traversal Function

The declaration of the **traverse** function should have one formal parameter. This parameter is declared to be of type pointer to a function, as follows:

```
void traverse(void (* process ) (element &data));
```

This declaration of the formal function parameter has the following components:

1. The return type, **void**.
2. The formal parameter name, **process**, which has been declared using the * operator to indicate that it is a pointer. The parentheses are added to ensure that the * operation is evaluated first.
3. The list of formal parameters for the function. This should be a single parameter whose place will be taken by each data element in the collection as it is traversed. The formal parameter here is a reference parameter, indicating that the function being passed can modify the data element.

This declaration can be added to the list of public member function declarations in the class declaration module for the ordered collection class.

The implementation of the **traverse** function uses a standard heading for member functions. The body of the function consists of a **while** loop, which advances a **probe** pointer through the nodes in the linked list, and runs the function parameter with the data element stored in each node:

```
void ordered_collection::traverse(void (* process ) (element &data))
{
     node_ptr probe = start;

     while (probe != NULL)
     {
          process(probe->data);
          probe = probe->next;
     }
}
```

In a sense, function parameters are no different from parameters used to pass other kinds of data. You just think of the formal parameter, say, **process**, as a placeholder for any of a number of different specialized functions, like **print_data** or **add_one**. As long as the number and type of the parameters to these functions are consistent with the declaration of **traverse**, the strategy for implementing traversals that we have presented can make programs very efficient and maintainable.

EXERCISES 11.4

1. Add a **public** counter data member to the ordered collection class, and set it to zero when a new collection is created. The counter should be incremented in the subscript member function to keep track of the number of times that the probe pointer must advance from node to node in a linked list. Now write a test program that adds 10 integers to the beginning of an ordered collection and prints the integers using the subscript operator. Display the length of the list and the counter. Now

run the same program again and print 100 integers. What is the value of the counter? Can you make a prediction for the value of the counter for 1000 integers? Test your prediction with another run of the program.

2. Add the **traverse** function to the ordered collection class, and rewrite the program in Example 11.2 to take advantage of the **traverse** operation.
3. Write a function, **print_odd**, that will print only the odd numbers in a collection of numbers when passed as a parameter to **traverse**.

RUNNING, DEBUGGING AND TESTING HINTS

1. Be careful to distinguish between a pointer and its associated dynamic memory. Thus, if **ptr** is a pointer, the memory pointed to is ***ptr**.
2. When a piece of dynamic memory is no longer needed in a program, use **delete** so that the memory can be reallocated.
3. After using **delete** with a pointer, its referenced memory is no longer available. If you use **delete ptr**, then ***ptr** is unpredictable.
4. Be careful not to access the referenced variable of a pointer that is NULL. Thus, if the assignment

   ```
   ptr = NULL;
   ```

   is made, a reference to ***ptr** results in an error.
5. When using pointers with subprograms, be careful to pass the pointer, not the referenced memory, to the subprogram.
6. When creating dynamic data structures, be careful to initialize properly by assigning NULL where appropriate and keep track of pointers as your structures grow and shrink.
7. Operations with pointers require that they be of the same type. Thus, exercise caution when comparing or assigning them.
8. Values may be lost when pointers are inadvertently or prematurely reassigned. To avoid this, use as many auxiliary pointers as you wish. This is better than trying to use one pointer for two purposes.
9. Be sure to declare and implement a destructor operation for a class that uses dynamic memory.

SUMMARY

Key Terms

address (of a memory location)
class destructor
component (of a linked list)
dereference
dynamic data structure
free store
heap
linked list
node
pointer to a function
pointer variable
value (of a memory location)

Key Concepts

- Values are stored in memory locations; each memory location has an address.
- A pointer variable is one that contains the address of a memory location; pointer types can be declared by

  ```
  typedef int *int_ptr_type;
  ```

  where the asterisk (*) is used after the predefined data type.

- Dynamic memory is memory that is referenced through a pointer variable. Dynamic memory can be used in the same context as any variable of that type, and it is not declared in the variable declaration section. In the declaration **int *ptr;** the dynamic memory is available after **ptr = new int**; is executed.
- Dynamic variables are created by

```
ptr = new base_type;
```

  and destroyed (memory area made available for subsequent reuse) by

```
delete ptr;
```

- The success of dynamic memory allocation can be detected by examining the value returned by **new**. If it is NULL, then there is no more dynamic memory available.
- Assuming the definition

```
int *ptr;
```

  the relationship between a pointer and its associated dynamic variable is illustrated by the code

```
ptr = new int;
*ptr = 21;
```

  which can be envisioned as

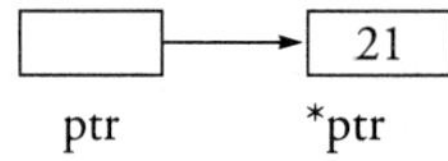

- NULL can be assigned to a pointer variable; this is used in a Boolean expression to detect the end of a list.
- Dynamic data structures differ from other data structures in that space for them is allocated under program control during the execution of the program.
- A linked list is a dynamic data structure formed by having each node contain a pointer that points to the next component; generally, each node is a structure with one member reserved for the pointer.
- A node is a component of a linked list.
- References to the components of a node structure use the arrow operator ->, as illustrated by

```
struct node
{
        int data;
        node *next;
};

node *ptr;

ptr = new node;
ptr->data = 45;
ptr->next = NULL;
```

- When creating a linked list, the final component should have NULL assigned to its pointer member.

- Printing from a linked list is accomplished by starting with the first component in the list and proceeding sequentially until the last component is reached.
- When a node is deleted from a linked list, it should be returned for subsequent use; this is done by using the standard operator **delete**.

Notes for Further Reading

Lambert, Kenneth A., and Naps, Thomas L., *Program Design and Data Structures with C++*, St. Paul, MN: West Publishing Company, 1996.

PROGRAMMING PROBLEMS AND PROJECTS

1. An index for a textbook can be created by a C++ program that uses dynamic data structures and works with a text file. Assume that input for a program is a list of words to be included in an index. Write a program that scans the text and produces a list of page numbers indicating where each word is used in the text.
2. One of the problems faced by businesses is how best to manage their lines of customers. One method is to have a separate line for each cashier or station. Another is to have one feeder line where all customers wait and the customer at the front of the line goes to the first open station. Write a program to help a manager decide which method to use by simulating both options. Your program should allow for customers arriving at various intervals. The manager wants to know the average wait in each system, average line length in each system (because of its psychological effect on customers), and the longest wait required.
3. Write a program to keep track of computer transactions on a mainframe computer. The computer can process only one job at a time. Each line of input contains a user's identification number, a starting time, and a sequence of integers representing the duration of each job. Assume all jobs are run on a first-come, first-served basis. Output should include a list of identification numbers, starting and finishing times for each job, and average waiting time for a transaction.
4. Several previous programming problems have involved keeping structures and computing grades for students in some class. If linked lists are used for the students' structures, such a program can be used for a class of 20 students or a class of 200 students. Write a record-keeping program that utilizes linked lists. Input is from an unsorted data file. Each student's information consists of the student's name, 10 quiz scores, six program scores, and three examination scores. Output should include the following:
   a. A list, alphabetized by student name, incorporating each student's quiz, program, and examination totals; total points; percentage grade; and letter grade
   b. Overall class average
   c. A histogram depicting class averages.
5. Design and implement the sorted collection class as a derived class of the ordered collection class as implemented in this chapter.
6. Mailing lists are frequently kept in a data file sorted alphabetically by customer name. However, when they are used to generate mailing labels for a bulk mailing, they must be sorted by zip code. Write a program to input an alphabetically sorted file and produce a list of labels sorted by zip code. The data for each customer follow:
   a. Name
   b. Address, including street (plus number), city, two-letter abbreviation for the state, and zip code
   c. Expiration information, including the month and year.

   Use a linked list to sort by zip code. Your labels should include some special symbol for all expiring subscriptions.

7. A stack is a kind of ordered collection, in which access to data items (for removal, addition, and look-up) is restricted to one end. Design and implement a stack class as a derived class of the ordered collection class.
8. A queue is a kind of ordered collection, in which items are added only at one end and are removed only from the other end. Design and implement a queue class as a derived class of the ordered collection class.
9. Linked lists can be presented by using either dynamic memory or arrays. Talk with a computer science instructor who prefers the dynamic memory approach and with one who prefers the array approach. List the advantages and disadvantages of each method. Give an oral report to your class summarizing your conversations with the instructors. Create a chart to use as part of your presentation.

CHAPTER 12

Advanced Topics: Recursion and Efficient Searching and Sorting

CHAPTER OUTLINE

The previous chapters presented techniques for developing programs to solve problems. Our choice of techniques has been guided by their usefulness in illustrating important introductory concepts in programming, such as the readability, maintainability, and correctness of programs. One other major criterion affecting the choice of problem-solving techniques in real-world programming is efficiency. Efficiency in computer science is a measure of the run-time and memory usage of computational processes. Frequently a solution that is clearest from a conceptual standpoint is not the most efficient one. Efficient solutions often require clever algorithmic design, and formal analysis is necessary to compare and predict how different solutions will behave with different data sets.

Although algorithm analysis is the subject of more advanced courses in computer science, we can give you a taste of the topic in this closing chapter. We will first discuss how recursive algorithms are run on real computers and examine the resources—processing time and memory—used by recursive processes. We will then introduce an improved algorithm for searching lists called *binary search,* and compare its efficiency to that of the sequential search algorithm introduced in Chapter 10. Next, we will introduce an improved algorithm for sorting lists called *quick sort,* and compare its efficiency to that of the selection sort algorithm discussed in Chapter 10. Finally, we will examine how linked lists lend themselves naturally to recursive processing.

12.1 Recursion

In the chapter on repetition, you saw how to control iterative processes by **`for`**, **`while`**, and **`do . . . while`** statements in C++. Let's now examine how recursive processing works and how it differs from iterative processing.

Recursive Processes

Many problems can be solved by having a subtask call itself recursively as part of the solution. Recursion is frequently used in mathematics. Consider, for example, the definition of $n!$ (n factorial) for a nonnegative integer n. This is defined by

OBJECTIVES

- to understand how recursion can be used to solve a problem
- to be able to use recursion to solve a problem
- to understand what happens in memory when recursion is used
- to understand how algorithms can be analyzed for run-time and memory usage
- to be able to weight the costs and benefits of using recursion

0! = 1

1! = 1

for $n > 1$, $n! = n * (n - 1)!$ Thus,

6! = 6 * 5! = 6 * 5 * 4! = 6 * 5 * 4 * 3! = 6 * 5 * 4 * 3 * 2! = 6 * 5 * 4 * 3 * 2 * 1

Another well-known mathematical example is the Fibonacci sequence. In this sequence, the first term is 1, the second term is 1, and each successive term is defined to be the sum of the previous two. More precisely, the Fibonacci sequence $a_1, a_2, a_3, \ldots, a_n$ is defined by

$a_1 = 1$

$a_2 = 1$

$a_n = a_{n-1} + a_{n-2}$ for $n > 2$

This generates the sequence

1, 1, 2, 3, 5, 8, 13, 21, . . .

In both examples, note that the general term was defined by using the previous term or terms.

What applications does recursion have for computing? In many instances, a function can be written to accomplish a recursive task. If the language allows a subprogram to call itself (C++ does, early versions of FORTRAN do not), it is sometimes easier to solve a problem by this process.

EXAMPLE 12.1

As an example of a recursive function, consider the sigma function—denoted by $\Sigma_{i=1}^{n}$—which is used to indicate the sum of integers from 1 to *n*. A C++ function that performs this task is as follows:

```
int sigma(int n)
{
      if (n <= 1)
            return n;
      else
            return n + sigma(n - 1);
}
```

To illustrate how this recursive function works, suppose it is called from the main program by a statement such as

```
sum = sigma(5);
```

In the **else** portion of the function, we first have

```
return 5 + sigma(4);
```

At this stage, note that **sigma(4)** must be computed. This call produces

```
return 4 + sigma(3);
```

If we envision these recursive calls as occurring on levels, we have

```
1. return 5 + sigma(4)
 2. return 4 + sigma(3)
  3. return 3 + sigma(2)
   4. return 2 + sigma(1)
    5. return 1
```

Now the end of the recursion has been reached and the steps are reversed for assigning values. Thus, we have

```
    5. return 1
   4. return (2 + 1) (= 3)
  3. return (3 + 3)  (= 6)
 2. return (4 + 6)   (= 10)
1. return (5 + 10)   (= 15)
```

Thus, **sigma(5)** computes the value 15.

Before analyzing what happens in memory when recursive subprograms are used, some comments about recursion are in order.

1. The recursive process must have a well-defined termination. This termination is referred to as a *stopping state.* In Example 12.1, the stopping state was

```
if (n <= 1)
     return n;
```

2. The recursive process must have well-defined steps that lead to the stopping state. These steps are usually called *recursive steps.* In Example 12.1, these steps were

```
return n + sigma(n - 1)
```

   Note that, in the recursive call, the parameter is simplified toward the stopping state.

What Really Happens?

What really happens when a subprogram calls itself? First, we need to examine the idea of a *stack.* Imagine a stack as a pile of cafeteria trays: The last one put on the stack is the first one taken off the stack. This is what occurs in memory when a recursive subprogram is used. Each call to the subprogram can be thought of as adding a tray to the stack. In the previous function, the first call creates a level of recursion that contains the partially complete return statement

```
return 5 + sigma(4)
```

This corresponds to the first tray in the stack. In reality, this is an area in memory waiting to receive a value for **5 + sigma(4)**. At this level, operation is temporarily suspended until a value is returned for **sigma(4)**. However, the call **sigma(4)** produces

```
return 4 + sigma(3)
```

This corresponds to the second tray on the stack. As before, operation is temporarily suspended until **sigma(3)** is computed. This process is repeated until finally the last call, **sigma(1)**, returns a value.

At this stage, the stack may be envisioned as illustrated in Figure 12.1. Since different areas of memory are used for each successive call to **sigma**, each variable **sigma** represents a different memory location. The levels of recursion that have been temporarily suspended can now be completed in reverse order. Thus, since the return

```
return sigma(1) = 1
```

has been made, then

```
return sigma(2) = 2 + sigma(1)
```

becomes

```
return sigma(2) = 2 + 1
```

This then permits

```
return sigma(3) = 3 + sigma(2)
```

to become

```
return sigma(3) = 3 + 3
```

Continuing until the first level of recursion has been reached, we obtain

```
sigma = 5 + 10
```

This "unstacking" is illustrated in Figure 12.2.

◆ FIGURE 12.1
Stack for the function **sigma**

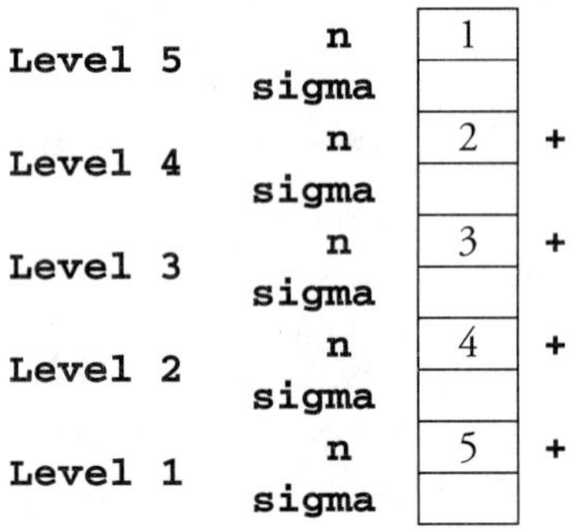

Level 5	**n**	1	
	sigma		
Level 4	**n**	2	+
	sigma		
Level 3	**n**	3	+
	sigma		
Level 2	**n**	4	+
	sigma		
Level 1	**n**	5	+
	sigma		

◆ FIGURE 12.2
"Unstacking" function sigma

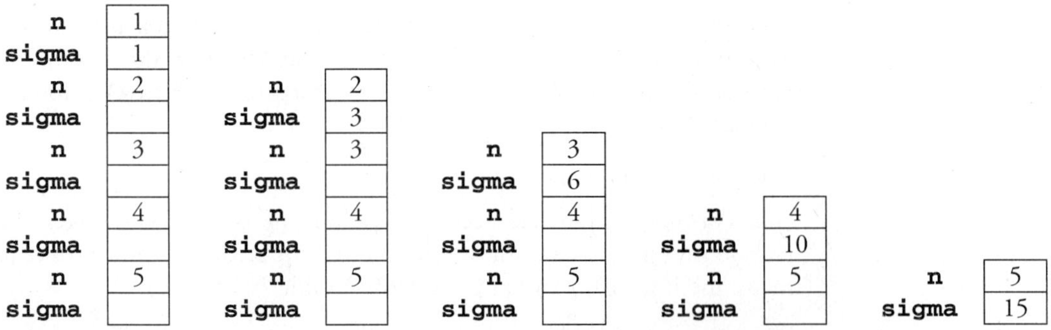

n	1								
sigma	1								
n	2	**n**	2						
sigma		**sigma**	3						
n	3	**n**	3	**n**	3				
sigma		**sigma**		**sigma**	6				
n	4	**n**	4	**n**	4	**n**	4		
sigma		**sigma**		**sigma**		**sigma**	10		
n	5	**n**	5	**n**	5	**n**	5	**n**	5
sigma		**sigma**		**sigma**		**sigma**		**sigma**	15

EXAMPLE 12.2

Let's now consider a second example of recursion. In this example, a function is used recursively to print a line of text in reverse order. Assume the line of text has only one period (and this is at the end of the line); the stopping state is when the character read is a period. Using the data line

```
This is a short sentence.
```

a complete program is

```
// This program uses a function recursively to print a
// line of text in reverse.

// Program file: revprint.cpp

#include <iostream.h>
#include <fstream.h>

// Function: stack_it_up
// Prints a series of input characters in reverse order,
// up until a '.'
//
// Input: an opened input file stream

void stack_it_up(ifstream &in_file);

int main()
{
      ifstream in_file;

      in_file.open("sentence");
      stack_it_up(in_file);
      in_file.close();
      return 0;
}

void stack_it_up(ifstream &in_file)
{
      char one_char;

      in_file.get(one_char);
      if (one_char != '.')
           stack_it_up(in_file);
      cout.put(one_char);
}
```

Output from this program is

```
.ecnetnes trohs a si sihT
```

In this program, as each character is read, it is placed on a stack until the period is encountered. At that time, the period is printed and then, as each level in the stack is passed through in reverse order, the character on that level is printed. The stack created while this program is running is illustrated in Figure 12.3.

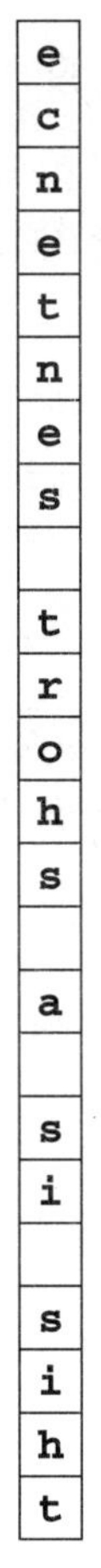

◆ FIGURE 12.3
Stack created by function **stack_it_up**

EXAMPLE 12.3

Let's now consider another example of a recursive function. Recall that the factorial of a nonnegative integer, *n*, is defined to be

$$1 * 2 * 3 \ldots * (n - 1) * n$$

and is denoted by *n*!. Thus,

```
4! = 1 * 2 * 3 * 4
```

For the sake of completing this definition, 1! = 1 and 0! = 1. A recursive function to compute *n*! is

```
int factorial(int n)
{
      if (n == 0)
            return 1;
      else
            return n * factorial(n - 1);
}
```

If this function is called from the main program by a statement such as

```
product = factorial(4);
```

we envision the levels of recursion as

```
1. return 4 * factorial(3)
 2. return 3 * factorial(2)
  3. return 2 * factorial(1)
   4. return 1 * factorial(0)
    5. factorial(0) = 1
```

Successive values would then be assigned in reverse order to produce the following:

```
    5. factorial(0)   = 1
   4. return (1 * 1) = 1
  3. return (2 * 1)  = 2
 2. return (3 * 2)   = 6
1. return (4 * 6)    = 24
```

Analyzing a Process for Running Time and Memory Usage

An efficient computational process solves a problem in a reasonable amount of time, using a reasonable amount of computer memory. An inefficient process solves a problem using an unreasonable amount of time and/or memory. What counts as reasonable or unreasonable may vary with user requirements and expectations. For example, a response time of one minute for searching a list of 10,000,000 names might be considered reasonable for some users but not others. Many times there is a trade-off between time and memory. Some users may be willing to pay more for extra memory if this allows data to be processed more quickly, while other users may have to settle for a slower processing time in order to economize on memory.

Computer scientists have discovered that some processes are inefficient no matter who the user is. Some processes would take billions of years on the fastest processor to solve some problems (usually involving large data sets), or would use so much memory that a physical computer to run them would be too expensive to build.

One way to measure the efficiency of a process is to examine how long it actually takes on different data sets and to examine how many memory cells are actually used. A faster and much easier method is to examine the algorithm and data structures that describe the process. One can tell directly from the text of the code how many times a given instruction will be executed with a given data set, and compare potential runs of the algorithm on different data sets. From this pencil and paper analysis, a formal measure of the efficiency of any algorithm can be derived.

To perform such an analysis, we usually pick an instruction in the algorithm that will run more times or fewer times, depending on whether the data or problem size is larger or smaller. As the data size becomes very large, the work that this instruction does will predominate over the work of the other instructions in the algorithm, so that the other instructions can be ignored. For example, a sorting algorithm might run a comparison on pairs of data elements in a list. The total number of comparisons performed for a complete run of the algorithm will vary with the size of the list and predominate as the size of the list becomes very large. From this analysis, we can derive a general formula that can be used to predict the behavior of the algorithm on lists of any size. Analyzing memory costs works the same way: We pick an instruction that demands some unit of memory, and analyze how that demand varies with the size of the data being processed.

Some standard relationships between processing time, memory use, and data or problem size have been discovered as a result of this kind of analysis. An

◇ TABLE 12.1
Some standard efficiency relationships

Amount of Work Done				
Data Size	Logarithmic	Linear	$N \log N$	Quadratic
1	1	1	1	1
10	4	10	40	100
100	7	100	700	10,000
1,000	10	1,000	10,000	1,000,000
10,000	14	10,000	140,000	100,000,000

algorithm has a *linear* behavior if the number of instructions executed or data units needed increases in direct proportion to the size of the problem. In other words, problems of size N require approximately N instructions to solve. An algorithm has *quadratic* behavior if the number of instructions executed or data units needed is proportional to the square of the size of the problem. In other words, problems of size N require approximately N^2 instructions executed. Other kinds of behavior that we will illustrate in our discussion in this chapter are called *logarithmic* ($\log_2 N$) and a combination of linear and logarithmic ($N \log_2 N$). As you can see from Table 12.1, logarithmic algorithms are the most efficient and quadratic algorithms are the least efficient of the algorithms we discuss. The numbers under the columns to the right of the data size column represent either the number of instructions that must be executed for a given data size, or the number of memory units needed for a given data size. We will refer to this table as we analyze algorithms in the following sections.

The Costs and Benefits of Recursion

You may have noticed that the previous recursive functions **sigma** and **factorial** could have been written using other iterative control structures. For example, we could rewrite the **sigma** function as follows:

```
int non_recursive_sigma(int n)
{
        int sum= 0;

        for (int j = 1; j < n; ++j)
             sum = sum + j;
        return sum;
}
```

It is not coincidental that the recursive function **sigma** can be rewritten using the function **non_recursive_sigma**. In principle, any recursive subprogram can be rewritten in a nonrecursive manner. Let's compare the time and memory resources required by each kind of process.

In general, a recursive process that requires N recursive calls requires $N + 1$ units of stack memory and processor time to manage the process. For example, in the cases of the **sigma** function or a function for traversing a linked list, the size of the recursive process grows in direct proportion to the size of the argument number or length of the list (see Section 12.4). These processes therefore require a linear growth of memory. The memory needed by some recursive processes, such as the one generated by a recursive Fibonacci function, grows even faster than the size of their arguments.

An equivalent iterative process always requires one unit of stack memory and processor time to manage the function call, regardless of the size of the problem. Thus, recursion generally requires more memory and processor time than the equivalent nonrecursive iteration.

What are the benefits of recursion? There are several. First, a recursive thought process may be the best way to think about solving the problem. If so, it naturally leads to using recursion in a program. Recursive algorithms form a subclass of simple and elegant solutions known as *divide and conquer algorithms* that are used throughout computer science. A classical example is the Towers of Hanoi problem, which requires a sequence of moving disks on pegs. This problem is fully developed as our next example.

Second, some recursive algorithms can be very short compared to other iterative solutions. Some nonrecursive solutions may require an explicit stack (a programmer-defined data structure that is distinct from the system stack used to run a recursive process) and unusual coding. In some instances, use of a recursive algorithm can be very simple, and some programmers consider recursive solutions elegant because of this simplicity. The Towers of Hanoi problem in Example 12.4 provides an example of such elegance.

Third and finally, subsequent work in C++ can be aided by recursion. For example, one of the fastest sorting algorithms available, the quick sort, uses recursion (see Section 12.3). Also, recursion is a valuable tool when working with dynamic data structures (see Section 12.4).

Having now seen several reasons why recursion should be used, let's consider when recursion should not be used. If a solution to a problem is easier to obtain using nonrecursive methods, it is usually preferable to use them because a nonrecursive solution will usually require less execution time and use memory more efficiently. Using the previous examples, the recursive function factorial should probably be written using iteration, but reversing a line of text would typically be done using recursion because a nonrecursive solution is difficult to write.

EXAMPLE 12.4

A classic problem called the Towers of Hanoi problem involves three pegs and disks as depicted in Figure 12.4. The object is to move the disks from peg A to peg C. The rules are that only one disk may be moved at a time and a larger disk can never be placed on a smaller disk. (Legend has it that this problem—but with 64 disks—was given to monks in an ancient monastery. The world was to come to an end when all 64 disks were in order on peg C.)

To see how this problem can be solved, let's start with a one-disk problem. In this case, merely move the disk from peg A to peg C. The two-disk problem is almost as easy. Move disk 1 to peg B, disk 2 to peg C, and use the solution to the

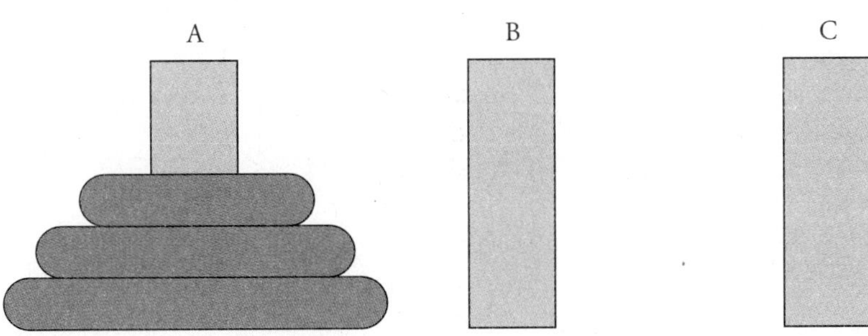

◆ **FIGURE 12.4**
The Towers of Hanoi problem

one-disk problem to move disk 1 to peg C. (Note the reference to the previous solution.)

Things get a little more interesting with a three-disk problem. First, use the two-disk solution to get the top two disks in order on peg B. Then move disk 3 to peg C. Finally, use a two-disk solution to move the two disks from peg B to peg C. Again, notice how a reference was made to the previous solution. By now you should begin to see the pattern for solving the problem. However, before generalizing, let's first look at the four-disk problem. As expected, the solution is as follows:

1. Use the three-disk solution to move three disks to peg B.
2. Move disk 4 to peg C.
3. Use the three-disk solution to move the three disks from peg B to peg C.

This process can be generalized as a solution to the problem for n disks.

1. Use the (n – 1)-disk solution to move (n - 1) disks to peg B.
2. Move disk n to peg C.
3. Use the (n – 1)-disk solution to move (n - 1) disks from peg B to peg C.

This general solution is recursive in nature because each particular solution depends on a solution for the previous number of disks. This process continues until there is only one disk to move. This corresponds to the stopping state when a recursive program is written to solve the problem. A complete interactive program that prints out each step in the solution to this problem follows:

```
// This program uses recursion to solve the classic Towers of Hanoi problem.

// Program file: hanoi.cpp

#include <iostream.h>

// Function: list_the_moves
// Move num disks from start peg to last peg, using spare peg
//
// Inputs: The number of disks to move, the initial peg, the working peg,
// the destination peg

void list_the_moves(int num_disks, char start_peg, char last_peg,
        char spare_peg);

int main()
{
      int num_disks;
      cout << "How many disks in this game? ";
      cin >> num_disks;
      cout << endl;
      cout << "Start with " << num_disks << " disks on Peg A" << endl;
      cout << endl;
      cout << "Then proceed as follows:" << endl;
      cout << endl;
      list_the_moves (num_disks, 'A', 'C', 'B');
      return 0;
}
```

```
void list_the_moves(int num_disks, char start_peg, char last_peg, char spare_peg)
{
      if (num_disks == 1)
           cout << "Move a disk from " << start_peg << " to " << last_peg
                << endl;
      else
      {
           list_the_moves (num_disks-1, start_peg, spare_peg, last_peg);
           cout << "Move a disk from " << start_peg << " to " << last_peg
                << endl;
           list_the_moves (num_disks-1, spare_peg, last_peg, start_peg);
      }
}
```

Sample runs for three-disk and four-disk problems produce the following:

```
How many disks in this game? 3

Start with 3 disks on Peg A

Then proceed as follows:

Move a disk from A to C
Move a disk from A to B
Move a disk from C to B
Move a disk from A to C
Move a disk from B to A
Move a disk from B to C
Move a disk from A to C

How many disks in this game? 4

Start with 4 disks on Peg A

Then proceed as follows:

Move a disk from A to B
Move a disk from A to C
Move a disk from B to C
Move a disk from A to B
Move a disk from C to A
Move a disk from C to B
Move a disk from A to B
Move a disk from A to C
Move a disk from B to C
Move a disk from B to A
Move a disk from C to A
Move a disk from B to C
Move a disk from A to B
Move a disk from A to C
Move a disk from B to C
```

A NOTE OF INTEREST

Recursion Need Not be Expensive

We have seen that the use of recursion has two costs: Extra time and extra memory are required to manage recursive function calls. These costs have led some to argue that recursion should never be used in programs. However, as Guy Steele has shown (in "Debunking the 'expensive procedure call' myth," *Proceedings of the National Conference of the ACM,* 1977), some systems can run recursive algorithms as if they were iterative ones, with no additional overhead. The key condition is to write a special kind of recursive function called a *tail-recursive* function. A function is tail-recursive if no work is done in the function after a recursive call. For example, according to this criterion, the factorial function that we presented earlier is not tail-recursive, because a multiplication is performed after each recursive call. We can convert this version of the factorial function to a tail-recursive version by performing the multiplication before each recursive call. To do this, we will need an additional parameter that passes the accumulated value of the factorial down on each recursive call. In the last call of the function, this value is returned as the result:

```
int fact_iter(int n, int result)
{
      if (n = 1)
            return result;
      else
            return fact_iter(n - 1,
                 n * result);
}
```

Note that the multiplication is performed before the recursive call of the function, when its parameters are evaluated. When the function is initially called, the value of **result** should be 1:

```
int factorial(int n)
{
      return fact_iter(n, 1);
}
```

Steele showed that a smart compiler can translate tail-recursive code in a high-level language to a loop in machine language. The machine code treats the function parameters as variables associated with a loop, and generates an iterative process rather than a recursive one. Thus, there is no linear growth of function calls and extra stack memory is not required to run tail-recursive functions on these systems.

The catch is that a programmer must be able to convert a recursive function to a tail-recursive function, and find a compiler that generates iterative machine code from tail-recursive functions. Unfortunately, some functions, like the one used to solve the Towers of Hanoi problem, are difficult or impossible to convert to tail-recursive versions, and the compiler optimizations are not part of the standard definitions of many languages, among them, C++. If you find that your C++ compiler supports this optimization, you should try converting some functions to tail-recursive versions and see if they run faster than the original versions.

EXERCISES 12.1

1. Explain what is wrong with the following recursive function:

```
float recur(float x)
{
      return recur(x / 2)
}
```

2. Write a recursive function that reverses the digits of a positive integer. If the integer used as input is 1234, output should be 4321.
3. Consider the following recursive function:

```
float a(float x, int n)
{
      if (n == 0)
            return 1.0;
      else
            return x * a(x, n - 1);
}
```

a. What would the value of **y** be for each of
   i. `y = a(3.0, 2);`
   ii. `y = a(2.0, 3);`
   iii. `y = a(4.0, 4);`
   iv. `y = a(1.0, 6);`
b. Explain what standard computation is performed by function **a**.
c. Rewrite function **a** using iteration rather than recursion.

4. Recall the Fibonacci sequence 1, 1, 2, 3, 5, 8, 13, 21, . . ., where for $n > 2$ the nth term is the sum of the previous two. Write a recursive function to compute the nth term in the Fibonacci sequence.
5. Write a function that uses iteration to compute $n!$.

Binary Search

OBJECTIVES

- to be able to use binary search to find a value in an array
- to be able to compare the costs and benefits of binary search and sequential search

Searching relatively small lists sequentially does not require much computer time. However, when the lists get longer (for example, telephone directories and lists of credit card customers), sequential searches are inefficient. In a sense, they correspond to looking up a word in the dictionary by starting at the first word and proceeding word-by-word until the desired word is found. Because extra computer time means considerably extra expense for most companies where large amounts of data must be frequently searched, a more efficient way of searching is needed.

If the list to be searched has been sorted, a particular value can be searched for by a method referred to as a *binary search*. Essentially, a binary search consists of examining a middle value of a list to see which half contains the desired value. The middle value of the appropriate half is then examined to see which half of the half contains the value in question. This halving process is continued until the value is located or it is determined that the value is not in the list.

We must make two assumptions in order to use a binary search:

1. The list must be represented as an array. This will allow us to find the middle data element in the list in constant time, by dividing the sum of the first index position and the last index position by two and using the subscript operation. If the list were represented as a linked structure, finding the position of the middle element would require a linear search in linear time.
2. The list must be sorted. Maintaining a sorted list may incur some overhead, which must also be evaluated.

The basic idea of binary search can be expressed recursively. If there are elements in the list remaining to be examined, we compare the target value to the element at the middle position in the list. If the target value equals this element, we return the position of the element. If the target value is greater than the element at the middle position, the target will be somewhere to the right of the middle position if it is in the list at all, so we recursively search the right half of the list. Otherwise, the target value will be to the left of the middle position if it is in the list at all, so we recursively search the left half of the list. If the target value is not in the list, we will run out of elements to consider at the end of some recursive process, so we return the value -1.

There are four input parameters to the problem: the target element, the list, the index value of the first position in the list, and the index value of the last position in the list. There is one value to be returned: -1 indicating that we have not found the target element in the list or an integer indicating its index position if we have found it. The initial value of the first position is zero. The initial value of the last index position is the number of data elements in the list minus one. A pseudocode algorithm for binary search is

```
If there are no more elements to consider then
        Return -1
Else
        Set midpoint to (last + first) / 2
        If the element at index midpoint = the target element then
             Return midpoint
        Else if the element at index midpoint > the target
             element then
             Search the left half of the array (from indices first to
             midpoint - 1)
        Else
             Search the right half of the array (from indices midpoint + 1 to last)
```

We assume that the program has defined a data type name, **list_type**, that specifies an array of elements that can be ordered. A C++ function representing the algorithm is thus

```
int binsearch(element target, list_type list, int first, int last)
{
        if (first > last)
                return -1;
        else
        {
                midpoint = (first + last) / 2;
                if (list[midpoint] == target)
                        return midpoint;
                else if (list[midpoint] > target)
                        return binsearch(target, list, first, midpoint - 1);
                else
                        return binsearch(target, list, midpoint + 1, last);
        }
}
```

We might provide a simpler interface to the search function for users, who should not have to worry about providing the extra parameter for **first**:

```
int search(element target, list_type list, int length)
{
        return binsearch(target, list, 0, length - 1);
}
```

Before continuing, let's walk through a binary search to better understand how it works. Assume **list** is the array

4	7	19	25	36	37	50	100	101	205	220	271	306	321

list[0] list[13]

with values as indicated. Furthermore, assume **target** contains the value 205. Then initially, **first, last**, and **target** have the values

0	13	205
first	last	target

A listing of values by each call of **binsearch** produces

	first	last	midpoint	list[midpoint]
After initial call	0	13	6	50
After second call	7	13	10	220
After third call	7	9	8	101
After fourth call	9	9	9	205

Note that we need only four comparisons to find the target at the ninth position in the list. To illustrate what happens when the value being looked for is not in the array, suppose **target** contains 210. The listing of values then produces

	first	last	midpoint	list[midpoint]
After initial call	0	13	6	50
After second call	7	13	10	220
After third call	7	9	8	101
After fourth call	9	9	9	205
After fifth call	10	9	9	205

At this stage, **first > last** and the recursive process terminates.

Let's now examine briefly the efficiency of a binary search compared to a sequential search. There are two worst cases for sequential search: When the target is at the last position in the list and when the target is not in the list at all. In each case, sequential search requires N equality comparisons for a list of N data elements. Therefore, sequential search is linear in the worst cases.

Binary search has a single worst case: When the target is not in the list at all. How many comparisons will it take to discover this for a list of length N? On the first call of the binary search function, we make one equality comparison. On the second call of the function, we have essentially thrown away half of the original list and are performing a comparison in the remaining half. This process of throwing away half of the data elements occurs on each call of the function. Therefore, the number of comparisons in the worst case will be equal to the number of times we can divide the original length of the list by two, or $\log_2 N + 1$. Binary search describes a logarithmic process.

Binary search is definitely more efficient than sequential search, as Table 12.1 illustrates. Binary search is also an excellent example of the benefits of using divide and conquer and recursive strategies in designing an algorithm. The only new cost of using this method is that we must assume that the array has been sorted. Maintaining a sorted array may take some extra time, so we must be careful to choose an efficient sorting algorithm. We will see another use of the divide and conquer strategy in designing an efficient sorting algorithm in the next section.

EXERCISES 12.2

1. Modify the sequential search function from Chapter 10 for sorted collections by putting a counter in the loop to count how many passes are made when searching a sorted array for a value. Write and run a program that uses this version on lists of length 15, 30, 60, 120, and 240. In each case, search for a value as follows and plot your results on a graph.
   a. A value in the first half
   b. A value in the second half
   c. A value that is not there

2. Repeat Exercise 1 for a binary search.
3. Suppose array **a** is

18	25	37	92	104
a[0]				a[4]

Trace the values using a binary search to look for

a. 18
b. 92
c. 76

4. Using a binary search on an array of length 35, what is the maximum number of passes through the loop that can be made when searching for a value?
5. Write a new version of binary search function using a C++ loop rather than a recursive function. Compare the two versions for efficiency, examining their memory requirements as well as their processing times.

12.3 Quick Sort

Several algorithms are available for sorting elements in lists. We worked with the selection sort in Chapter 10. This method works relatively well for sorting small lists of elements. However, when large databases need to be sorted, a direct application of an elementary sorting process usually requires a great deal of computer time. To demonstrate this point, let's do a brief analysis of the selection sort algorithm. Recall that the algorithm consists of a nested loop structure:

```
For each j from 0 to N - 2 do                    // Find the minimum n - 1 times
     Set index to j
     For each k from j + 1 to N - 1 do           // Find the index of the minimum
          If a[k] < a[index] then
               Set index to k
     If index does not equal j then             // Exchange values if necessary
          Swap(a[index], a[j])
```

OBJECTIVES

- to be able to use quick sort to sort the data elements in an array
- to be able to compare the costs and benefits of quick sort and selection sort

The instruction that will do the most work and vary with the data size the most is the comparison < in the **if** statement in the inner loop. On the first pass through the outer loop, the comparison will be performed $N - 1$ times in the inner loop. On the second pass through the outer loop, the comparison will be performed $N - 2$ times. On the last pass through the outer loop, the comparison will be performed once in the inner loop. Thus, the total number of comparisons will be

$$(N - 1) + (N - 2) + \ldots + 1$$

or

$$\frac{N^2 - N}{2}$$

Because the quadratic term predominates in this formula, we can ignore the other terms and conclude that selection sort exhibits quadratic behavior. As you can see from Table 12.1, this kind of behavior is very unreasonable for large data sets.

One of the fastest sorting techniques available is the *quick sort.* Like binary search, this method uses a recursive, divide and conquer strategy. The basic idea is to separate a list of elements into two parts, surrounding a distinguished element called the *pivot.* At the end of the process, one part will contain elements smaller than the pivot and the other part will contain elements larger than the pivot. Thus, if an unsorted list (represented as array **a**) originally contains

14	3	2	11	5	8	0	2	9	4	20
a[0]	a[1]				a[5]					a[10]

we might select the element in the middle position, **a[5]**, as the pivot, which is 8 in our illustration. Our process would then put all values less than 8 on the left side and all values greater than 8 on the right side. This first subdivision produces

pivot

4	3	2	2	5	0	8	11	9	14	20
a[0]	a[1]					a[6]				a[10]

Now, each sublist is subdivided in exactly the same manner. This process continues until all sublists are in order. The list is then sorted. This is a recursive process.

Before writing a function for this sort, let's examine how it works. First, why do we choose the value in the middle position? Ideally, we would like to pivot on the median of the entire list. However, searching a list for the median element is at best a linear process, whose cost would more than offset the benefit of the divide and conquer process of quick sort. Therefore, we choose the value in the middle as a compromise. As in binary search, the index of this value is found by **(first + last) / 2**, where **first** and **last** are the indices of the initial and final elements in the array representing the list. We then identify a **left_arrow** and **right_arrow** on the far left and far right, respectively. This can be envisioned as

pivot

14	3	2	11	5	8	0	2	9	4	20
left_arrow										right_arrow

where **left_arrow** and **right_arrow** initially represent the lowest and highest indices of the array components. Starting on the right, the **right_arrow** is moved left until a value less than or equal to the pivot is encountered. This produces

pivot

14	3	2	11	5	8	0	2	9	4	20
left_arrow									right_arrow	

In a similar manner, **left_arrow** is moved right until a value greater than or equal to the pivot is encountered. This is the situation just encountered. Now the contents of the two array components are swapped to produce

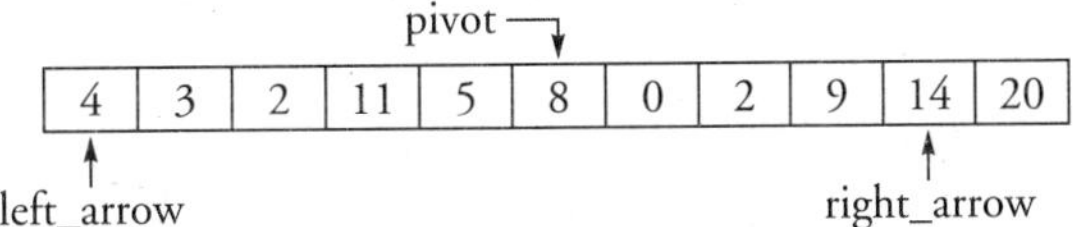

We continue by moving **right_arrow** left to produce

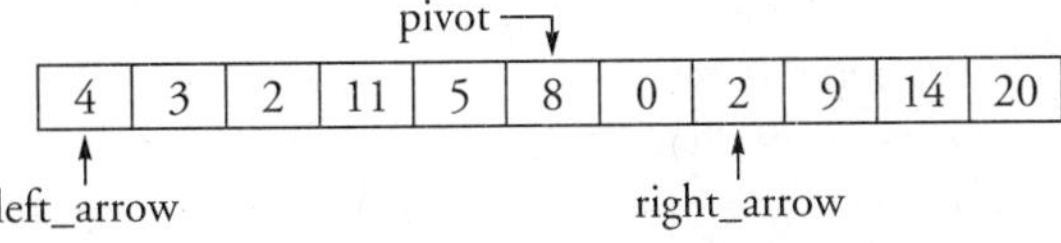

and moving **left_arrow** right yields

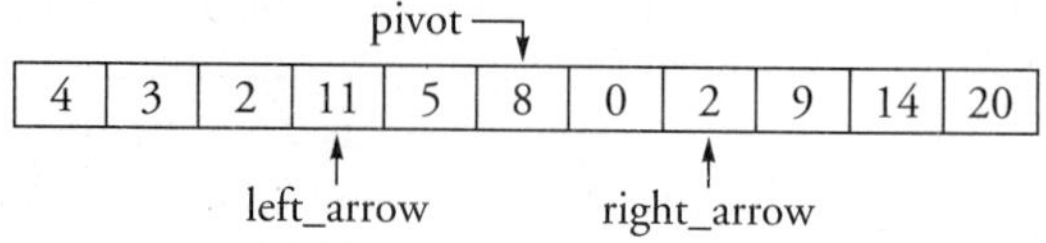

These values are exchanged to produce

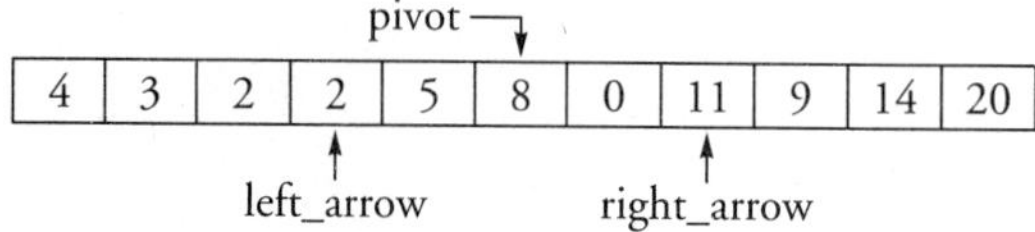

This process stops when **left_arrow > right_arrow** is TRUE. Since this is still FALSE at this point, the next **right_arrow** move produces

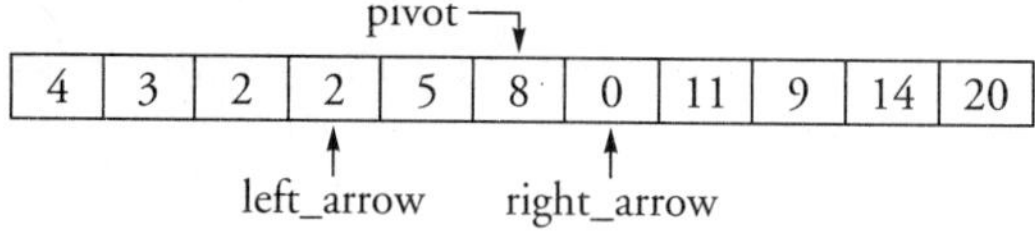

and the **left_arrow** move to the right yields

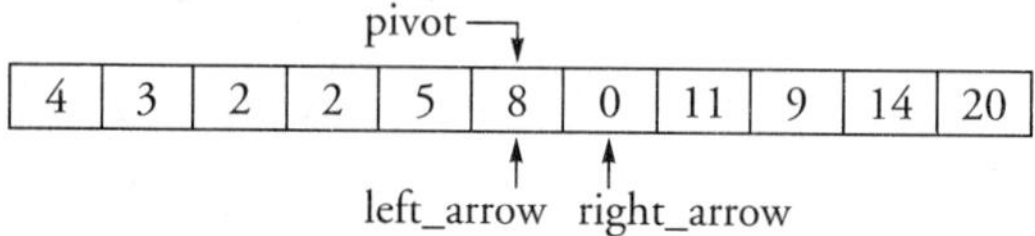

Because we are looking for a value greater than or equal to pivot when moving left, **left_arrow** stops moving and an exchange is made to produce

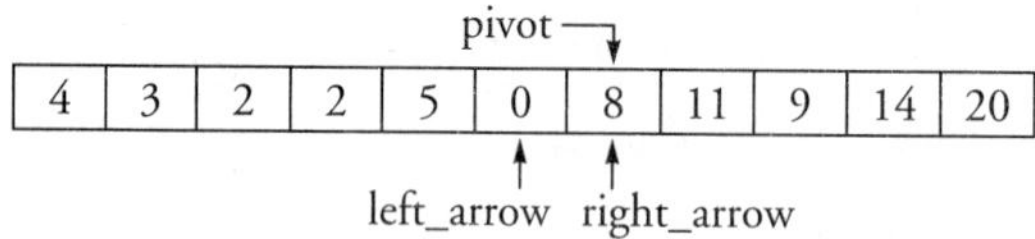

Notice that the pivot, 8, has been exchanged to occupy a new position. This is acceptable because pivot is the value of the component, not the index. As before, **right_arrow** is moved left and **left_arrow** is moved right to produce

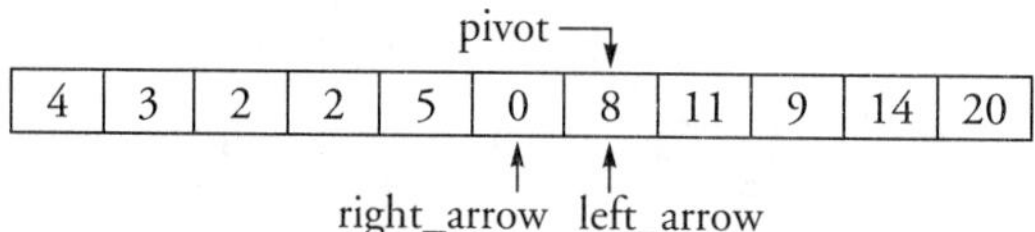

Since **right_arrow < left_arrow** is TRUE, the first subdivision is complete. At this stage, numbers smaller than **pivot** are on the left side and numbers larger than **pivot** are on the right side. This produces two sublists that can be envisioned as

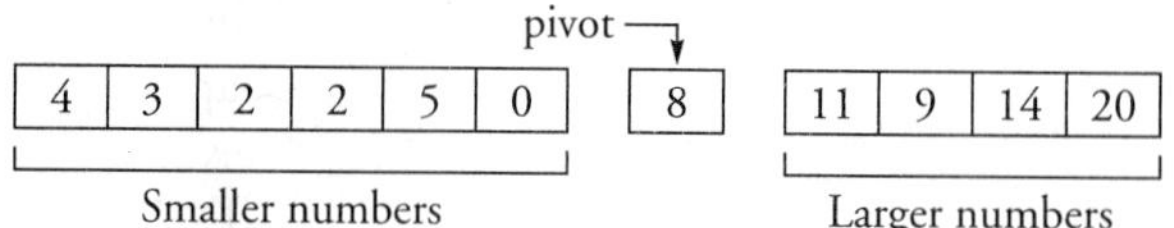

Each sublist can now be sorted by the same function. This would require a recursive call to the sorting function. In each case, the array is passed as a parameter together with the **right** and **left** indices for the appropriate sublist. We assume that the program has defined a data type name, **list_type**, that specifies an array of elements that can be ordered. A C++ function for this sort is

```
void quick_sort (list_type list, int left, int right)
{
      int pivot, left_arrow, right_arrow;

      left_arrow = left;
      right_arrow = right;
      pivot = list[(left + right) / 2];
      do
      {
             while (list[right_arrow] > pivot)
                   --right_arrow;
             while (list[left_arrow] < pivot)
                   ++left_arrow;
             if (left_arrow <= right_arrow)
             {
                     swap(list[left_arrow], list[right_arrow]);
                     ++left_arrow;
                     --right_arrow;
             }                           // switching elements and then moving
                                         // arrows
      }
       while (right_arrow >= left_arrow);
       if (left < right_arrow)
              quick_sort(list, left, right_arrow);
       if (left_arrow < right)
              quick_sort(list, left_arrow, right);
}
```

We might provide an interface function for users:

```
void sort(list_type list, int length)
{
       quick_sort(list, 0, length - 1);
}
```

Note that the two integer parameters specify the upper and lower bounds of the index values of elements actually in the array. Hence, the value 0 for the lower bound and **`length - 1`** for the upper bound are passed as actual parameters to **`quick_sort`**.

Now let's briefly analyze the quick sort algorithm for efficiency. We will assume the best case, in which the element at the middle of each sublist in the process happens to be the median of the sublist. This will cause the list to be split evenly around the pivot, so that each sublist will have close to $N/2$ elements. To carry out a partitioning of a list of N elements, each element other than the pivot must be compared with the pivot. Therefore, the first partitioning of an N element list into two sublists that each have approximately $N/2$ elements requires approximately N comparisons. Each of these sublists will also be partitioned, together requiring another N comparisons. Therefore, each recursive level of the process requires N comparisons. How many levels will there be? Recall from our discussion of binary search that the number of times we can subdivide a list of length N evenly is $\log_2 N$. Thus, in quick sort, the N comparisons at each level are performed approximately $\log_2 N$ times, so quick sort exhibits $N \log_2 N$ behavior in the best case.

A NOTE OF INTEREST

Gene Mapping: Computer Scientists Examine Problems of the Genome Project

Deciphering the human genome is much like trying to read the instructions on a computer disk filled with programs written in the zeros and ones of electronic code—without knowing the programming language.

That was the message from molecular biologists to computer scientists at a meeting sponsored by the National Research Council. The biologists hope to involve the computer scientists in the U.S. Human Genome Project, a 15-year, $3 billion effort to identify and locate the information contained in human chromosomes.

Computer scientists, with their experience in managing information and using arcane programming languages to store data and convey instructions, could be particularly valuable in helping to read and organize the three billion "letters" that make up the human genetic code, the biologists said.

"The entire program for making *me* is about 10 to the 10 bits," (about 10 trillion pieces of information) said Gerald J. Sussman, a professor of electrical engineering and computer science at the Massachusetts Institute of Technology. "It is no bigger than the U.S. Tax Code, or the design documents for the U.S. space shuttle." Figuring out what that program is, he said, is a computer science problem.

Biologists said they needed computer scientists to accomplish the following:

- Design easy-to-use databases that can handle the millions of pieces of information that need to be correlated to fully understand genetics—and life.
- Design computer networks that will allow biologists to share information conveniently.
- Create functions that will allow biologists to analyze information pulled from laboratory experiments.
- Write programs that will let biologists simulate the formation and development of proteins.

In cases where the middle element in a sublist is not also the median element, the sublists will not be evenly partitioned. The worst cases are where the middle element is also the largest or the smallest element. In these cases, one sublist will be almost the same size as the original list. This will cause more subdivisions to be made than in the ideal case. On the average, however, the middle element in a randomly ordered sublist should have a value that is somewhere within the range of values from the smallest to the median or from the median to the largest. On the average, then, the behavior of quick sort will be close to $N \log_2 N$. The analysis of the worst case behavior of quick sort is left as an exercise.

EXERCISES 12.3

1. Use the modified version of selection sort and quick sort to examine their relative efficiency; that is, run them on arrays of varying lengths, count the number of comparisons, and plot the results on a graph. What are your conclusions?
2. Explain how an array of objects with a key field, **`name`**, can be sorted using a quick sort.
3. Modify function **`quick_sort`** to use the median of the first three elements in an array as the pivot rather than the middle element.
4. The worst case behavior of the quick sort algorithm depends on the configuration of elements in the original list. Describe what this configuration would be, why it would cause quick sort to behave that way, and derive a formula that expresses the behavior.

12.4 Linked Lists and Recursion

OBJECTIVES

- to understand the natural fit of linked lists and recursive algorithms
- to understand the use of recursion to traverse a linked list in either direction
- to understand the use of recursion to accumulate a value while traversing a linked list

You may have noticed in Chapter 11 that a linked list is a *recursive data structure.* The structure of a linked list contains a component part that is either another list of the very same form or an empty list denoted by the NULL pointer. Recursive data structures lend themselves very naturally to processing by recursive functions. In this section, we examine some strategies and implementations of recursive list processing. For purposes of exposition, we define the following data structures for representing a linked list of numbers:

```
struct node;
typedef node *list_type;

struct node
{
    int data;
    list_type next;
};

list_type list;
```

Traversing a Linked List

Many operations on linked lists require us to visit each node sequentially. For example, we have seen that printing the contents of the nodes in a linked list involves this kind of process. We can describe a recursive algorithm for printing the contents of a linked list informally as

```
if the list is not empty then
    print the contents of the current node
    print the contents of the rest of the list
```

Note that the algorithm describes the two essential parts of a recursive process:

1. A termination of the process (when the list is empty)
2. A recursive step (where we run a process of the same form on a smaller data structure of the same form).

The termination condition in a recursive algorithm is usually handled by an **if** statement. The recursive step in the algorithm processes the data in the rest of the list. Therefore, it usually operates on the next pointer of the current node in the list.

A recursive function for printing the numbers in a linked list of the form defined in Section 11.3 is

```
void print_list(list_type list)
{
        if (! empty_list(list))
        {
                cout << list->data << endl;
                print_list(list->next);
        }
}
```

Searching for a target item in a linked list is a process that is similar to the process of printing all of the items, except that the search can stop when the target item is found. Moreover, this process should return a value to the caller, such as TRUE or FALSE. Assuming that the algorithm returns a Boolean value to the caller, a recursive search algorithm can be described informally as

```
if the list is empty then
      return FALSE
else if the item in the current node = the target item then
      return TRUE
else
      return the result of searching the rest of the list
```

There are two possible termination conditions of the recursive process, each of which returns a simple Boolean value. If the process ever hits the end of the list, the list will be empty and the target item will not be found. If the process finds the item somewhere in the list, it can halt the search and return TRUE. The recursive step, which searches the rest of the list, also returns a Boolean value. A recursive search function is

```
boolean search(int target, list_type list)
{
        if (empty_list(list))
              return FALSE;
        else if (list->data == target)
              return TRUE;
        else
              return search(target, list->next);
}
```

Accumulating a Value from a Linked List

Many problems call for processes that traverse a linked list to accumulate a value. Consider the problem of determining the length or number of nodes in a list. If we do not keep this value in a separate variable, we will need a process to count the number of nodes. A recursive algorithm for counting nodes would have two cases to consider:

1. The list is empty. In this case, the algorithm returns 0, the number of nodes in an empty list.
2. The list has at least one node. There may also be nodes in the rest of the linked list after this node. Therefore, in this case, the algorithm recursively counts the rest of the nodes in the list after this one, adds this count to 1, and returns the result.

The recursive algorithm can be described informally as

```
if the list is empty then
      return 0
else
      return the length of the rest of the list + 1
```

Note that this recursive process both moves ahead through the list and accumulates a value whenever it returns from a recursive call. A recursive length function is

```
int list_length(list_type list)
{
       if (empty_list(list))
              return 0;
       else
              return list_length(list->next) + 1;
}
```

The problem of finding the sum of all of the integers in a linked list can be solved by a very similar recursive process. Briefly, if the list is empty, the process returns 0. Otherwise, it returns the sum of the integer in the current node and the sum of the integers in the rest of the list. Informally, the recursive algorithm is

```
if the list is empty then
      return 0
else
      return the sum of the rest of the integers in the list
      + the integer in the current node
```

The function is

```
int sum_list(list_type list)
{
       if (empty_list(list))
              return 0;
       else
              return sum_list(list->next) + list->data;
}
```

Moving Backwards Through a Linked List

Consider the problem of printing all of the items in a linked list in reverse order. We need a way of beginning at the last node in the list and working our way back to the first node. Unfortunately, the next pointers in each node point in the wrong direction for implementing this process in terms of a simple loop that would move through the list from the last node to the first. If we think in terms of a recursive process, however, we can find an easy and elegant solution to this problem.

Recall from our discussion of recursion that as each recursive call of a function is made, the system keeps track of the state of the caller on a structure called a stack. As the overall recursive process ends and starts to unwind, each call returns to the state of its caller on the stack. We can use this information to design a recursive algorithm for moving backwards through a linked list.

First, we move forward recursively through the list until we reach the end (where the list is empty). As we go, the system is saving pointers to previous nodes on its run-time stack. *After* each recursive call, we visit a node to do our processing of the data there. This means that the first data to be processed will be the data in the last node in the list. The next data will be the data in the node *before* the last one, and so on. In effect, we traverse the list in reverse as the recursive process unwinds. Informally, the algorithm is

```
if the list is not empty then
      print the contents of the rest of the list in reverse
      print the data in the current node
```

A function for solving this problem is

```
void reverse_print_list(list_type list)
{
        if (! empty_list(list))
        {
                reverse_print_list(list->next);
                cout << list->data << endl;
        }
}
```

EXERCISES 12.4

1. Write a recursive function to return the product of the integers in a linked list.
2. Write recursive functions to insert an item into a linked list and to delete an item from a linked list.
3. Write a recursive function that searches a linked list for a given item. The function returns a pointer to the item's node if it is found, or the NULL pointer otherwise.
4. Rewrite the general traversal function from Section 11.4 as a recursive function.

A NOTE OF INTEREST

Fractal Geometry and Recursive Patterns

Fractal geometry as a serious mathematical endeavor began with the pioneering work of Benoit Mandelbrot, a Fellow of the Thomas J. Watson Research Center, IBM Corporation. Fractal geometry is a theory of geometric forms so complex that they defy analysis and classification by traditional Euclidean means. Yet fractal shapes occur universally in the natural world. Mandelbrot has recognized them not only in coastlines, landscapes, lungs, and turbulent water flow but also in the chaotic fluctuation of prices on the Chicago commodity exchange.

The c-curve that appears on the cover of this book is an instance of fractal shapes. It represents a series of recursive patterns of increasing levels of complexity. When the level is zero, the c-curve is a simple line, specified by the endpoints <x1, y1> and <x2, y2>. A level N c-curve is composed of two level $N - 1$ c-curves connected at right angles. Thus, a level 1 c-curve is composed of two perpendicular lines, and a level 2 c-curve is three quarters of a square, which begins to resemble the letter C.

Our level 12 c-curve was generated on a graphics workstation by running a recursive function written in C++:

```
void c_curve (int x1, int y1, int x2,
     int y2, int level)
{
     int xm, ym;

     if ( level == 0)
          draw_line(x1, y1, x2, y2);
     else
     {
          xm = (x1 + x2 + y1 - y2)/2;
          ym = (x2 + y1 + y2 - x1)/2;
          c_curve(x1, y1, xm, ym,
               level - 1);
          c_curve(xm, ym, x2, y2,
               level - 1);
     }
}
```

FOCUS ON PROGRAM DESIGN

A complete interactive program to illustrate the use of quick sort follows. The design for this program is

1. Fill the list
2. Sort the numbers
3. Print the list

The complete program is

```
// This program illustrates the quick sort as a sorting algorithm. The array
// elements
// are successively subdivided into "smaller" and "larger" elements in parts of the
// array. Recursive calls are made to the function quick_sort.

// Program file: qsort.cpp

#include <iostream.h>

const int LIST_MAX = 30;

typedef int list_type[LIST_MAX];

// Function: fill_list
// Reads numbers into list from keyboard
//
// Output: a list of numbers and its length

void fill_list(list_type list, int &length);

// Function: sort
// Sorts numbers in list into ascending order
//
// Inputs: a list of numbers in random order and its length
// Output: a sorted list

void sort(list_type, int length);

// Function: sort
// Sorts numbers in list into ascending order
//
// Inputs: a list of numbers in random order, 0, and list length - 1
// Output: a sorted list

void quick_sort(list_type list, int left, int right);

// Function: print_list
// Prints contents of list in a column on the screen
//
// Input: a list of numbers in random order and its length

void print_list(list_type list, int length);

// Function: swap
// Exchanges the values of two numbers
//
// Inputs: two integers
// Outputs: the two integers, exchanged in position
```

```
void swap(int &first, int &second);

int main()
{
      list_type list;
      int first, last, length;

      fill_list(list, length);
      cout << "The unsorted list is:" << endl;
      print_list(list, length);
      sort(list, length);
      cout << "The sorted list is:" << endl;
      print_list(list, length);
      return 0;
}

void fill_list(list_type list, int &length)

{
      int data;

      length = 0;
      cout << "Enter an integer, -999 to quit. ";
      cin >> data;
      while ((data != -999) && (length < LIST_MAX))
      {
            list[length] = data;
            ++length;
            cout << "Enter an integer, -999 to quit. ";
            cin >> data;
      }
}

void print_list(list_type list, int length)
{
      for (int index = 0; index < length; ++index)
            cout << list[index] << endl;
}

void sort(list_type list, int length)
{
      quick_sort(list, 0, length - 1);
}

void quick_sort (list_type list, int left, int right)
{
      int pivot, temp, left_arrow, right_arrow;

      left_arrow = left;
      right_arrow = right;
      pivot = list[(left + right) / 2];
      do
      {
      while (list[right_arrow] > pivot)
            --right_arrow;
```

```
      while (list[left_arrow] < pivot)
            ++left_arrow;
      if (left_arrow <= right_arrow)
{
            swap(list[left_arrow], list[right_arrow]);
            ++left_arrow;
            --right_arrow;
            }                              // switching elements and then moving
                                           // arrows
      }
      while (right_arrow >= left_arrow);
      if (left < right_arrow)
            quick_sort(list, left, right_arrow);
      if (left_arrow < right)
            quick_sort(list, left_arrow, right);
}

void swap(int &first, int &second)
{
      int temp;

      temp = first;
      first = second;
      second = temp;
}
```

A sample run of this program using the previous data produces

```
Enter an integer, -999 to quit. 14
Enter an integer, -999 to quit. 3
Enter an integer, -999 to quit. 2
Enter an integer, -999 to quit. 11
Enter an integer, -999 to quit. 5
Enter an integer, -999 to quit. 8
Enter an integer, -999 to quit. 0
Enter an integer, -999 to quit. 2
Enter an integer, -999 to quit. 9
Enter an integer, -999 to quit. 4
Enter an integer, -999 to quit. 20
Enter an integer, -999 to quit. -999

The sorted list is:

0
2
2
3
4
5
8
9
11
14
20
```

RUNNING, DEBUGGING AND TESTING HINTS

1. When using recursion, make sure the recursive process will reach the stopping state.
2. Sorting large files or long arrays can be very time consuming. Depending on the number of elements to be processed, use some form of divide and conquer; that is, divide the list, sort the elements, and then merge them. Very large databases may require several subdivisions and subsequent merges.

SUMMARY

Key Terms

binary search
divide and conquer algorithms
quick sort
recursive step
stack
stopping state
tail-recursive

Key Concepts

- Recursion is a process whereby a subprogram calls itself.
- A recursive subprogram must have a well-defined stopping state.
- Recursive functions in most programming languages require the use of a run-time stack to maintain the input parameters and return values of each recursive call.
- Recursive solutions are usually elegant and short, but generally require more memory than iterative solutions.
- Binary search is one of the fastest searching techinques available. It can use recursion and is based on the idea of separating a list into two parts.
- A quick sort is one of the fastest sorting techniques available. It uses recursion and is based on the idea of separating a list into two parts.
- Linked lists are recursive data structures; they lend themselves quite naturally to recursive processing.

SUGGESTIONS FOR FURTHER READING

Recursion and sorting are subjects of numerous articles and books. This chapter provided some samples of each. For variations and improvements on what is included here as well as other techniques, the interested reader is referred to the following books, which many consider to be classics in the field.

Baase, Sara, "Sorting," Chap. 2 in *Computer Algorithms: Introduction to Design and Analysis,* Reading, MA: Addison-Wesley, 1978.

Gear, William, *Applications and Algorithms in Engineering and Science,* Chicago: Science Research Associates, 1978.

Horowitz, Ellis, and Sartaz, Sahni, "Divide and Conquer," Chap. 3 in *Fundamentals of Computer Algorithms,* Potomac, MD: Computer Science Press, 1978.

Knuth, Donald, *The Art of Computer Programming,* Vol. 3, *Sorting and Searching,* Reading, MA: Addison-Wesley, 1975.

Roberts, Eric, *Thinking Recursively,* New York: John Wiley & Sons, 1986.

PROGRAMMING PROBLEMS AND PROJECTS

1. Write a program to update a mailing list. Assume you have a sorted master file of records in which each record contains a customer's name, address, and expiration code. Your program should input a file of new customers, sort the file, and merge the file with the master file to produce a new master.

2. The Bakerville Manufacturing Company has to lay off all employees who started working after a certain date. Write a program that does the following:
   a. Input a termination date.
   b. Search an alphabetical file of employee records to determine who will get a layoff notice.
   c. Create a file of employee records for those who are being laid off.
   d. Update the master file to contain only records of current employees.
   e. Produce two lists of those being laid off, one alphabetical and one by hiring date.
3. The Bakerville Manufacturing Company (Problem 2) has achieved new prosperity and can rehire 10 employees who were recently laid off. Write a program that does the following:
   a. Search the file of previously terminated employees to find the 10 with the most seniority.
   b. Delete those 10 records from the file of employees who were laid off.
   c. Insert the 10 records alphabetically into the file of current employees.
   d. Print four lists as follows:
      i. An alphabetical list of current employees
      ii. A seniority list of current employees
      iii. An alphabetical list of employees who were laid off
      iv. A seniority list of employees who were laid off.
4. The Shepherd Lions Club sponsors an annual cross-country race for area schools. Write a program that does the following:
   a. Create an array of records for the runners; each record should contain the runner's name, school, identification number, and time (in a seven-character string, such as 15:17:3).
   b. Print an alphabetical listing of all runners.
   c. Print a list of schools entered in the race.
   d. Print a list of runners in the race ordered by school name.
   e. Print the final finish order by sorting the records and printing a numbered list according to the order of finish.
5. The greatest common divisor of two positive integers *a* and *b*, GCD(*a*,*b*), is the largest positive integer that divides both *a* and *b*. Thus, GCD(102, 30) = 6. This can be found using the division algorithm as follows:

   102 = 30 * 3 + 12
   30 = 12 * 2 + 6
   12 = 6 * 2 + 0

   Note that

   $$\begin{aligned} GCD(102, 30) &= GCD(30, 12) \\ &= GCD(12, 6) \\ &= 6 \end{aligned}$$

   In each case, the remainder is used for the next step. The process terminates when a remainder of zero is obtained. Write a recursive function that returns the GCD of two positive integers.

6. A palindrome is a number or word that is the same when read either forwards or backwards. For example, "12321" and "mom" are palindromes. Write a recursive function that can be used to determine whether or not an integer is a palindrome.

Use this function in a complete program that reads a list of integers and then displays the list with an asterisk following each palindrome.

7. Recall the Fibonacci sequence discussed at the beginning of this chapter. Write a recursive function that returns the *n*th Fibonacci number. Input for a call to the function will be a positive integer.

8. Probability courses often contain problems that require students to compute the number of ways *r* items can be chosen from a set of *n* objects. It is shown that there are

$$C(n,r) = \frac{n!}{r!(n-r)!}$$

such choices. This is sometimes referred to as "*n* choose *r*." To illustrate, if you wish to select three items from a total of five possible objects, there are

$$C(5,3) = \frac{5!}{3!(5-3)!} = \frac{5*4*3*2*1}{(3*2*1)\ (2*1)} = 10$$

such possibilities. In mathematics, the number *C(n,r)* is a binomial coefficient because, for appropriate values of *n* and *r,* it produces coefficients in the expansion of $(x + y)^n$. Thus,

$$(x + y)^4 = C(4,0)x^4 + C(4,1)x^3y + C(4,2)xy^2 + C(4,3)xy^3 + C(4,4)y^4$$

   a. Write a function that returns the value *C(n,r).* Arguments for a function call will be integers *n* and *r* such that $n > r > 0$. (*Hint:* Simplify the expression $n!/[r!(n - r)!]$ before computing.)

   b. Write an interactive program that receives as input the power to which a binomial is to be raised. Output should be the expanded binomial.

9. Form a team of students (three or four) to identify some local business that has not yet computerized its customer records. The team should have a discussion with the owner or manager to determine how the customer records are used. After talking with the owner or manager, the team should design an information processing system for the business. The system should include complete specifications for the design. Particular attention should be paid to searching and sorting.

   The team should then give an oral presentation to the class and use appropriate charts and diagrams to illustrate their design.

Appendixes

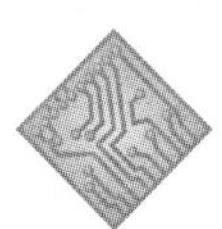

Appendix 1 Reserved Words

The following words have predefined meanings in C++ and cannot be changed. The words in bolface are discussed in the text. The other words are discussed in Stanley B. Lippman, *C++ Primer,* 2nd edition, Reading, MA: Addison-Wesley Publishing Company, 1993.

asm	continue	**float**	**new**	**signed**	try
auto	**default**	**for**	**operator**	sizeof	**typedef**
break	**delete**	**friend**	**private**	static	union
case	**do**	goto	**protected**	**struct**	**unsigned**
catch	**double**	**if**	**public**	**switch**	virtual
char	**else**	inline	register	template	**void**
class	**enum**	**int**	**return**	**this**	volatile
const	extern	**long**	**short**	throw	**while**

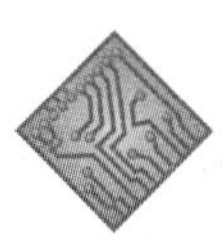

Appendix 2
Some Useful Library Functions

Some of the most commonly used library functions in the first course in computer science come from the libraries **math, ctype**, and **string**. Descriptions of the most important functions in each of these libraries is presented in the following five tables.

math

Function Declaration	Purpose
`double acos(double x);`	Returns arc cosine for *x* in range -1 to +1
`double asin(double x);`	Returns arc sine for *x* in range -1 to +1
`double atan(double x);`	Returns arc tangent of *x*
`double atan2(double y, double x);`	Returns arc tangent of *y/x*
`double ceil(double x);`	Rounds *x* up to next highest integer
`double cos(double x);`	Returns cosine of *x*
`double cosh(double x);`	Returns hyberbolic cosine of *x*
`double exp(double x);`	Returns *e* to the *x*th power
`double exp(double x);`	Returns absolute value of *x*
`double floor(double x);`	Rounds *x* down to next lowest integer
`double fmod(double x, double y);`	Returns remainder of *x/y*
`double ldexp(double x, double exp);`	Returns *x* times 2 to the power of exp
`double log(double x);`	Returns natural logarithm of *x*
`double log10(double x);`	Returns base 10 logarithm of *x*
`double pow(double x, double y);`	Returns *x* raised to power of *y*
`double sin(double x);`	Returns sine of *x*
`double sinh(double x);`	Returns hyberbolic sine of *x*
`double sqrt(double x);`	Returns square root of *x*
`double tan(double x);`	Returns tangent of *x*, in radians
`double tanh(double x);`	Returns hyperbolic tangent of *x*

ctype

Function Declaration	Purpose
`int isalnum(int ch);`	`ch is letter or digit`
`int isalpha(int ch);`	`ch is letter`
`int iscntrl(int ch);`	`ch is control character`
`int isdigit(int ch);`	`ch is digit (0-9)`
`int isgraph(int ch);`	`ch is printable but not ' '`
`int islower(int ch);`	`ch is lowercase letter`
`int isprint(int ch);`	`ch is printable`
`int ispunct(int ch);`	`ch is printable but not ' ' or alpha`
`int isspace(int ch);`	`ch is a whitespace character`
`int isupper(int ch);`	`ch is uppercase letter`
`int isxdigit(int ch);`	`ch is hexadecimal digit`
`int tolower(int ch);`	`Returns lowercase of ch`
`int toupper(int ch);`	`Returns uppercase of ch`

string

Function declaration	Purpose
`int *strcat(int *s1, const int *s2);`	Appends copy of s2 to end of s1
`int strcmp(const int *s1, const int *s2);`	Compares s1 and s2
`int *strcpy(int *s1, const int *s2);`	Copies s2 to s1, including '\0'
`int strlen(const int *s);`	Returns length of s, not including '\0'

Appendix 3 Syntax Diagrams

The following syntax diagrams correspond to the syntax forms used to describe the features of C++ discussed in the text. Two points of caution are in order. First, the diagrams in this appendix by no means represent an exhaustive description of C++. Second, many of the features discussed in this text have more than one syntactically correct construction (for example, **`main`** can be preceded by either **`int`** or **`void`**, but the C++ programming community prefers **`int`**). By confining your attention to preferred ways of using a small subset of features, we hope to place your focus on concepts rather than syntax. Students wanting to learn more features of C++ or other ways of expressing them are referred to Stanley B. Lippman, *C++ Primer,* 2nd edition, Reading, MA: Addison-Wesley Publishing Company, 1993.

The terms enclosed in ovals in the diagrams refer to program components that literally appear in programs, such as operator symbols and reserved words. The terms enclosed in boxes refer to program components that require further definition, either by another diagram or by reference to the text. The syntax of terms for which there are no diagrams, such as **`identifier, number, string,`** and **`character`**, should be familiar to anyone who has read this text.

Main program module

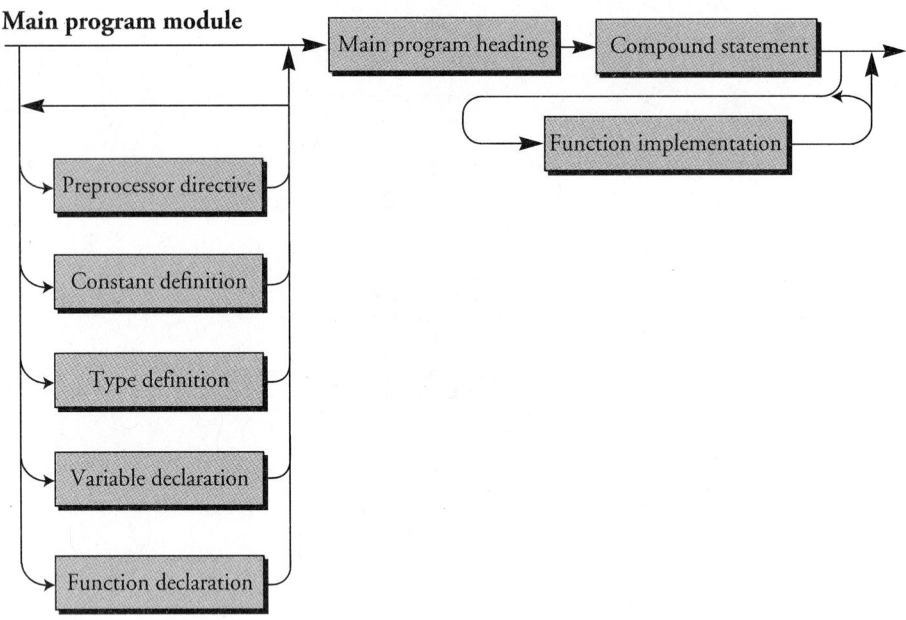

Preprocessor directive

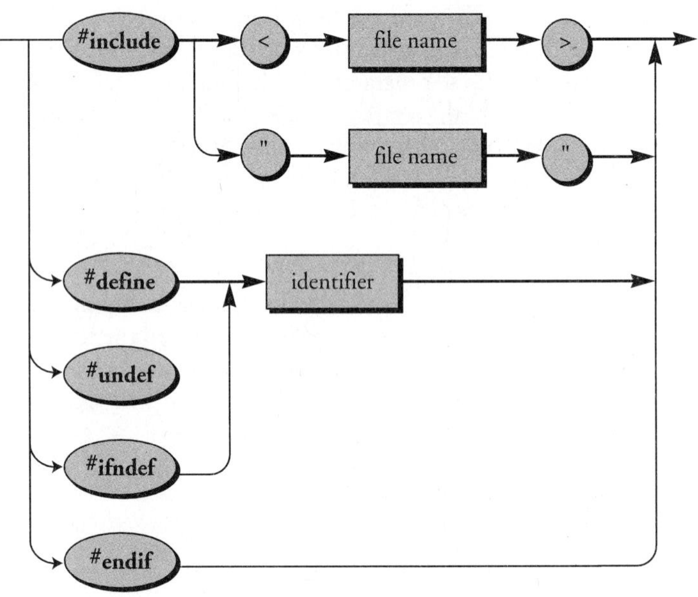

Constant definition

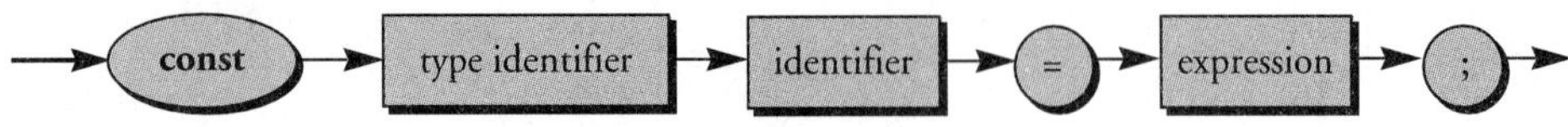

Type definition

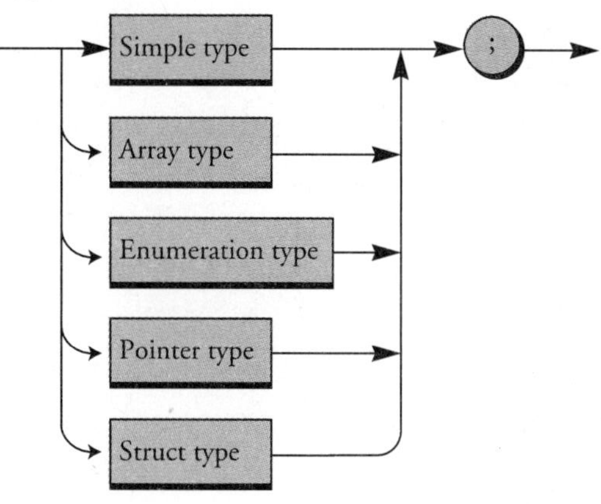

Simple type

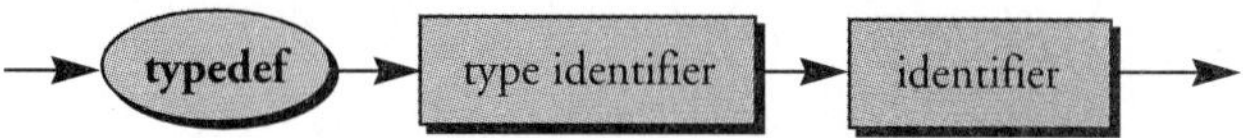

Array type

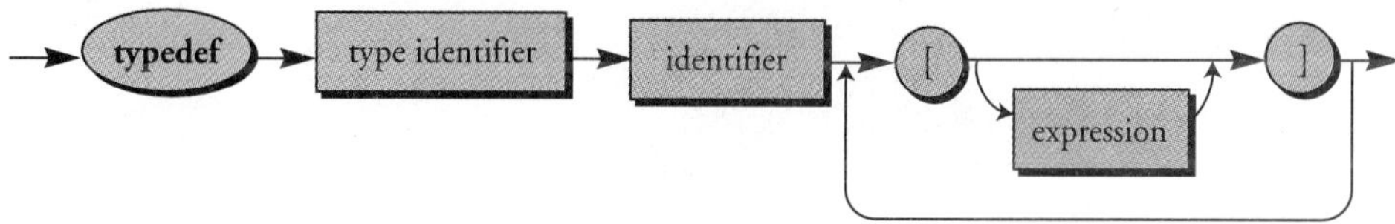

Enumeration type

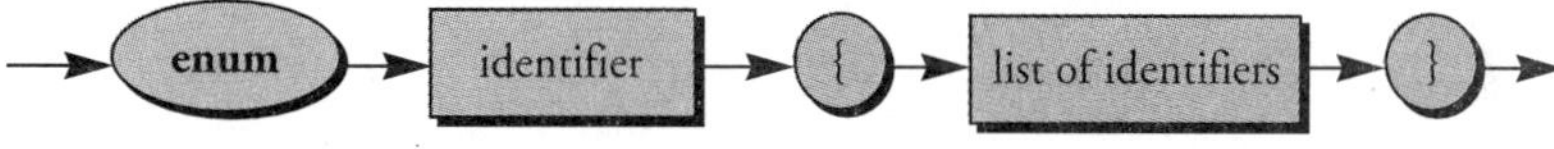

Pointer type

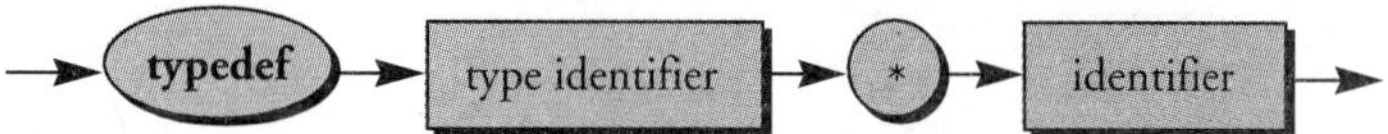

Struct type

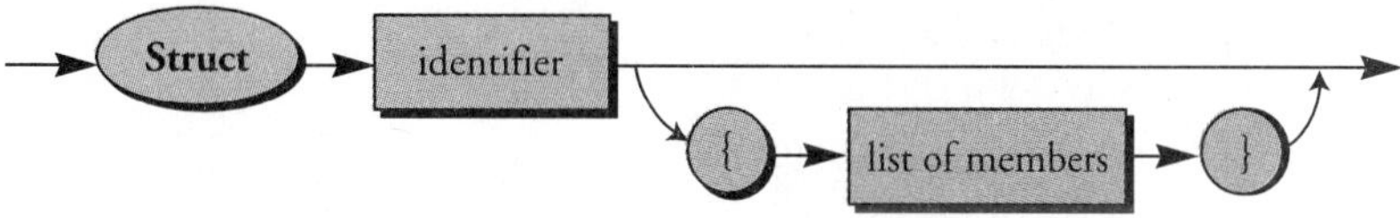

List of members

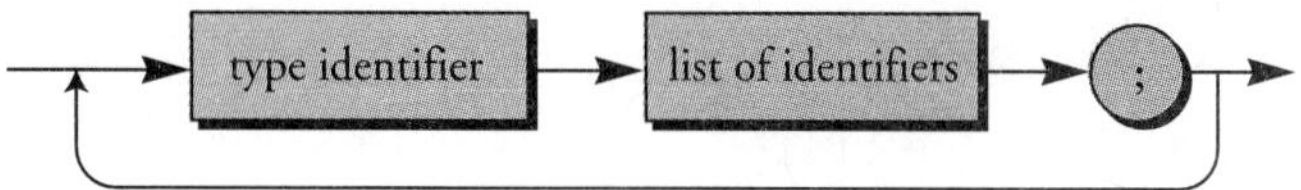

Variable declaration

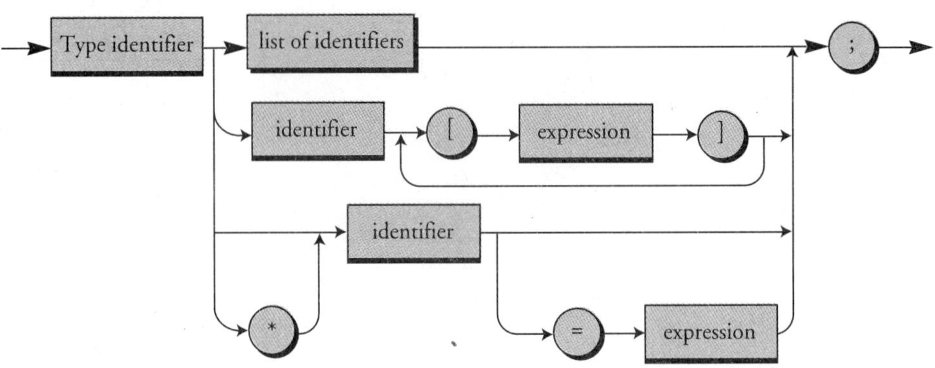

List of identifiers

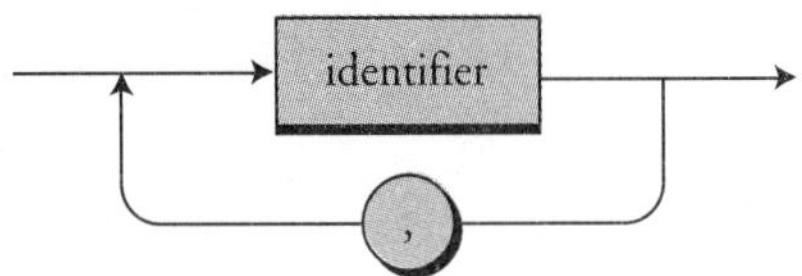

Function declaration

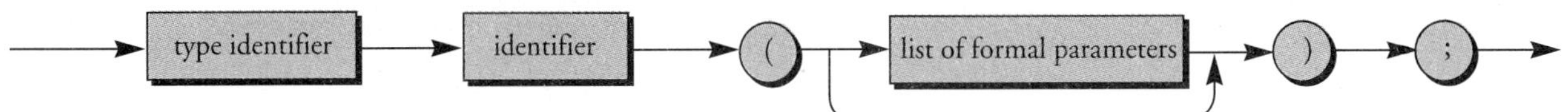

Main program heading

Compound statement

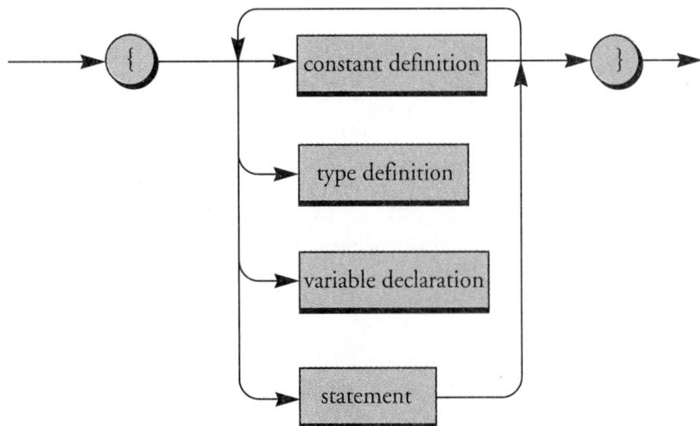

Statement

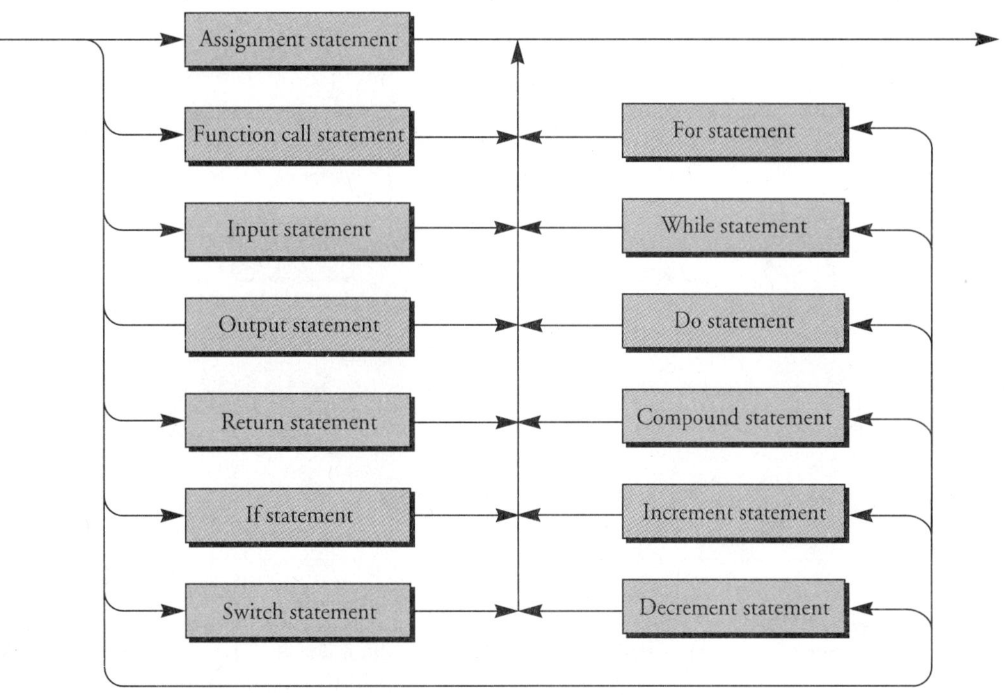

Assignment statement

Function call statement

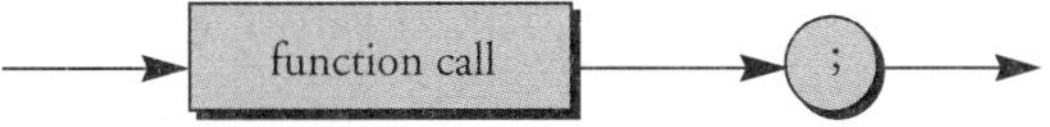

Input statement

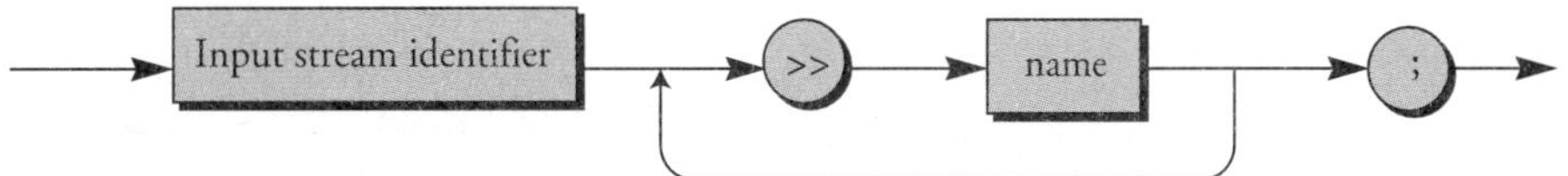

Output statement

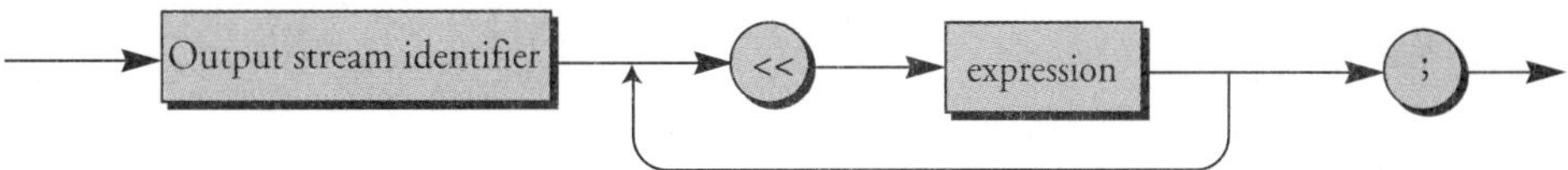

Return statement

If statement

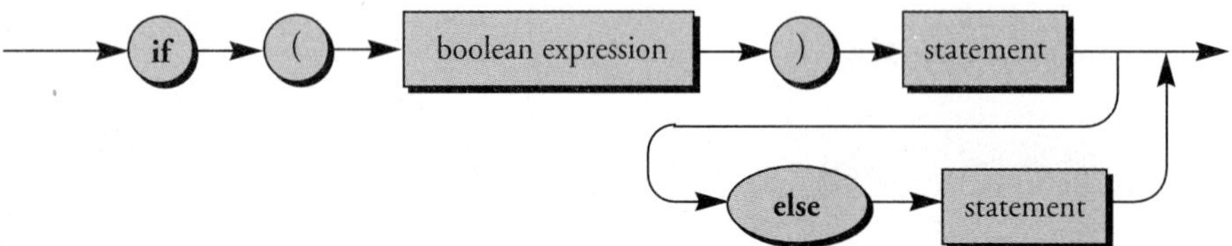

Switch statement

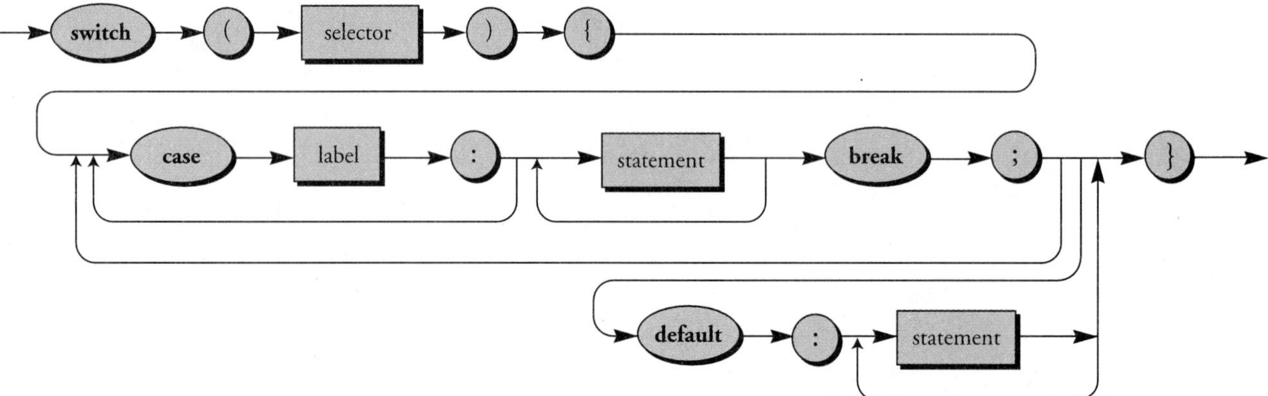

For statement

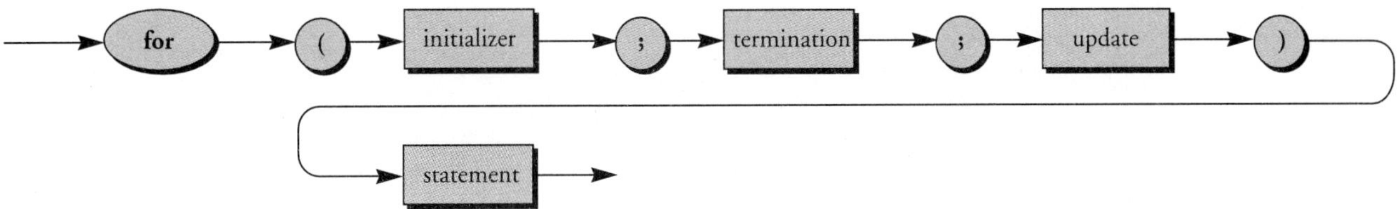

While statement

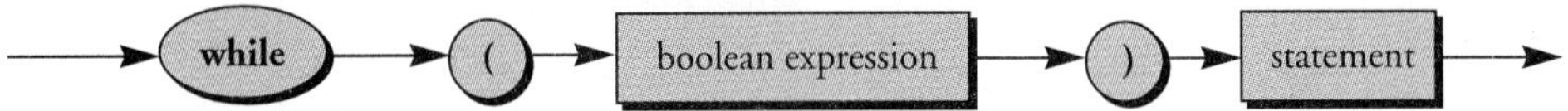

Do statement

Increment statement

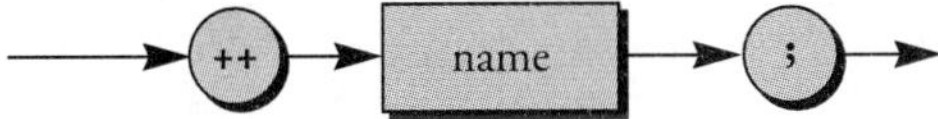

Decrement statement

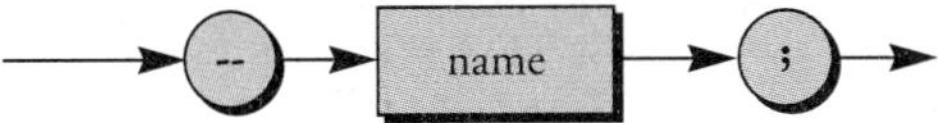

Function implementation

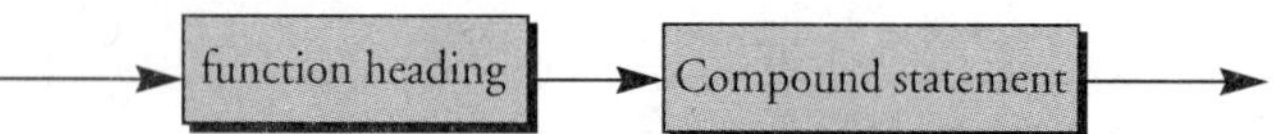

Function heading

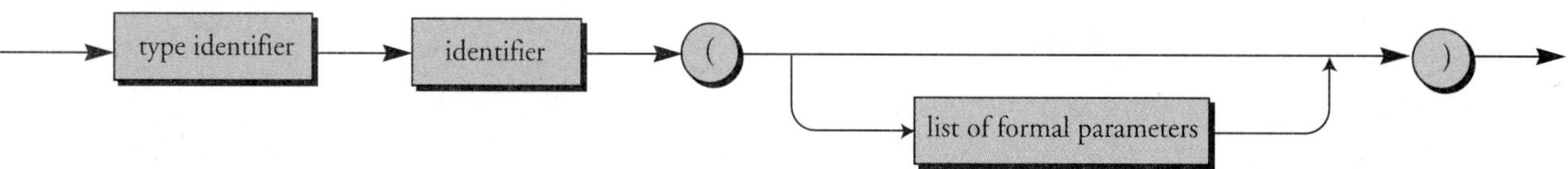

List of formal parameters

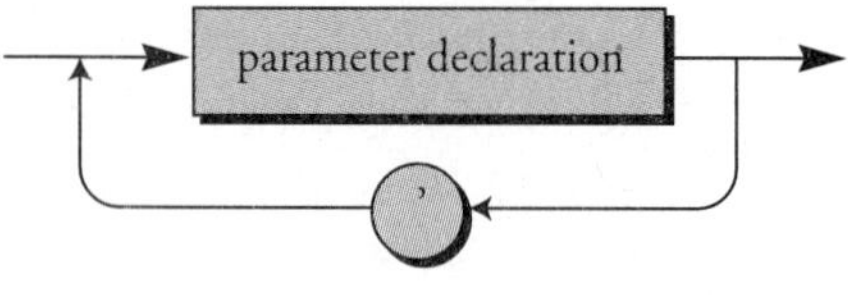

Parameter declaration

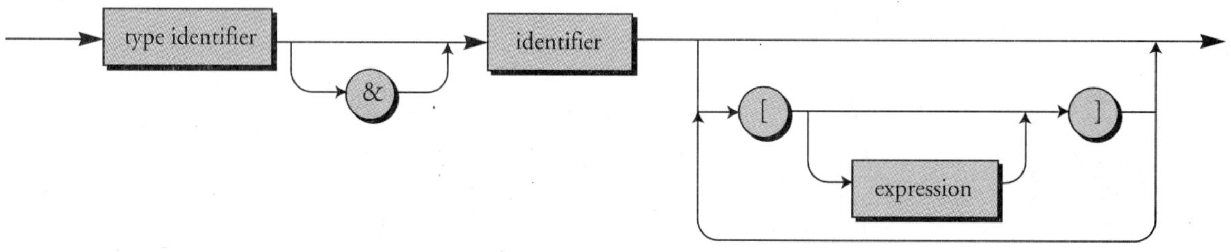

Expression

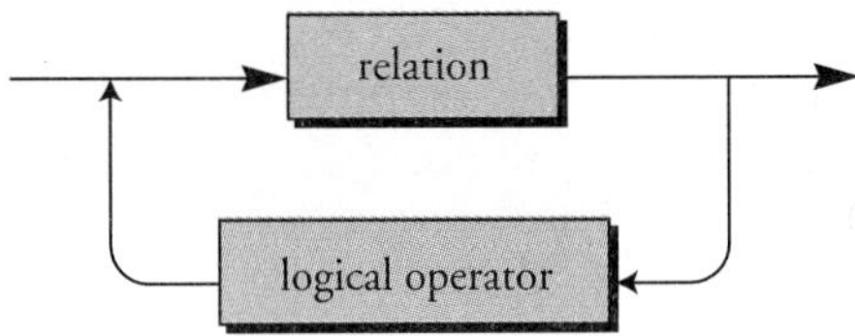

Relation

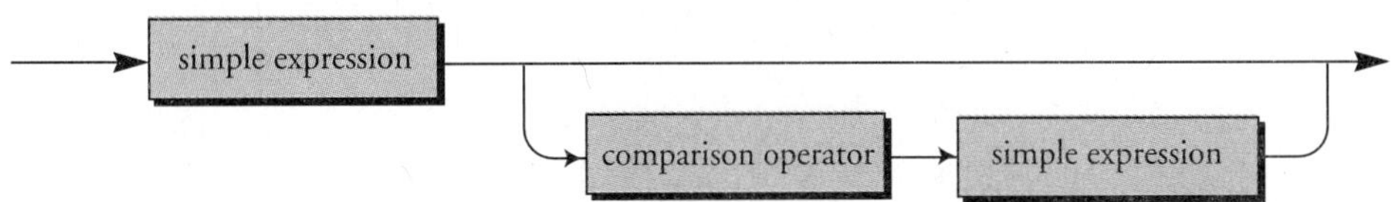

Simple expression

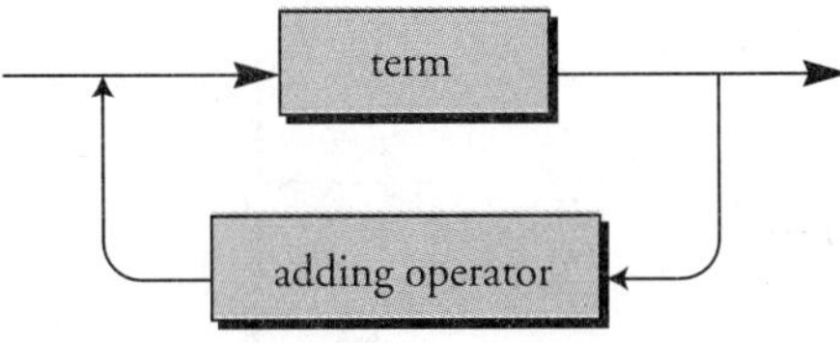

Term

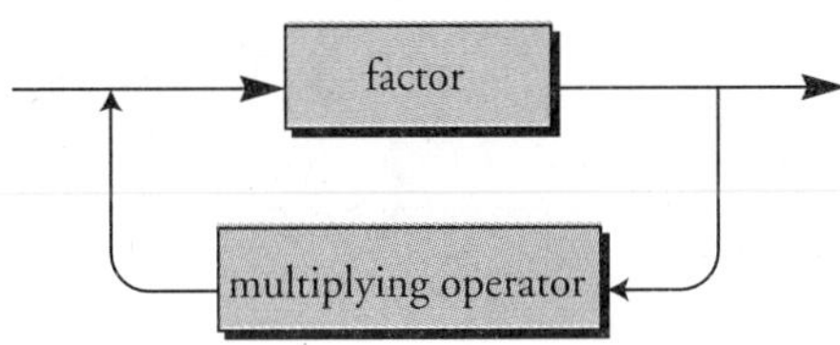

Factor

primary
-
!

Primary

number
string
character
name
function call
(
expression
)

Name

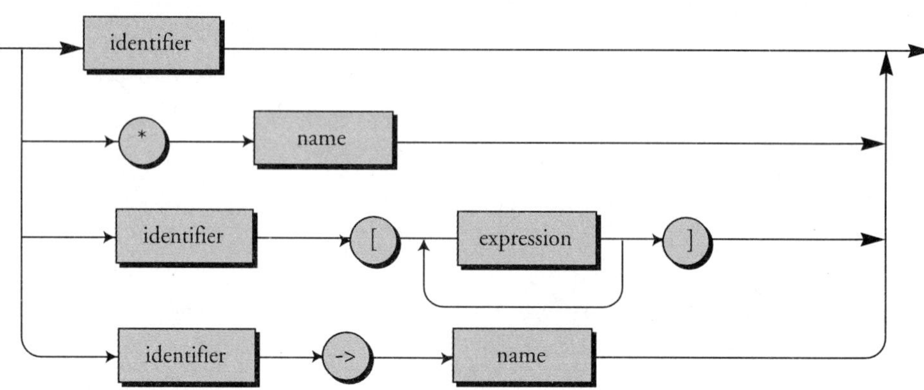

Function call

List of actual parameters

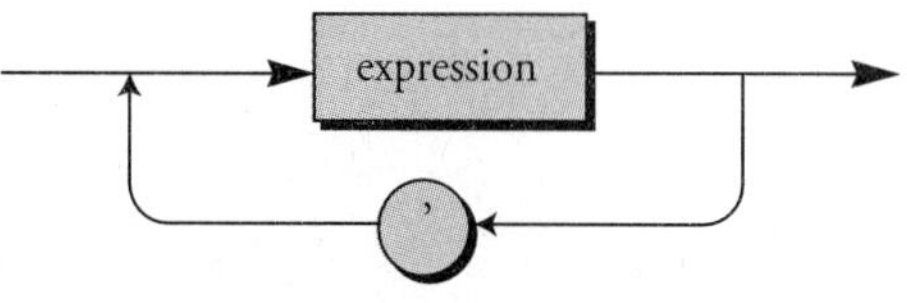

Logical operator

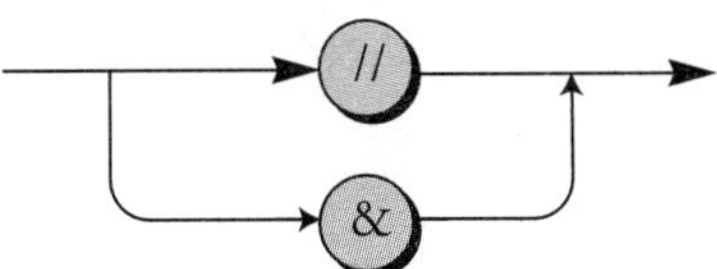

Adding operator

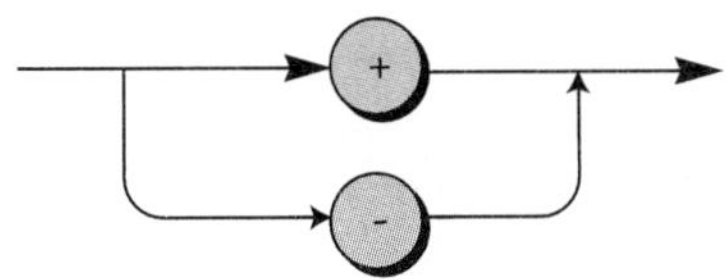

Comparison operator

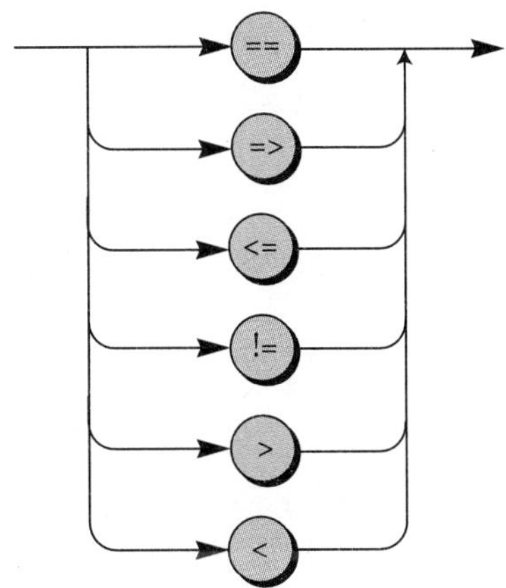

Multiplying operator

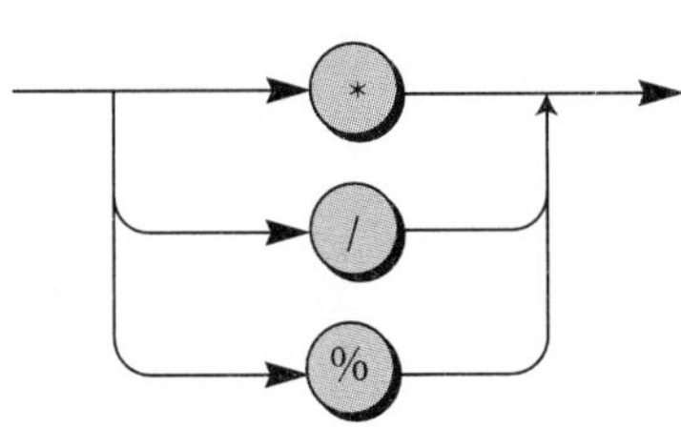

Class declaration module

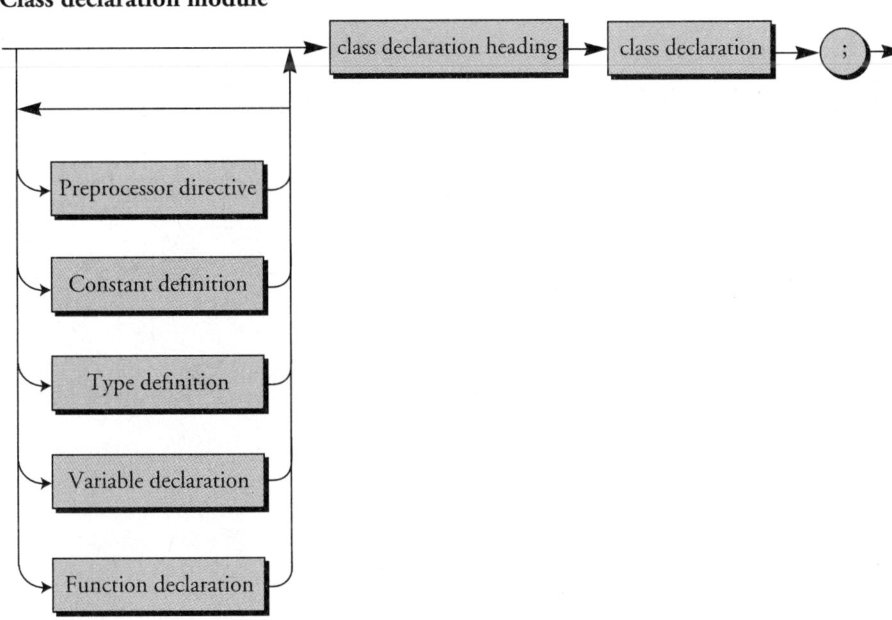

Class declaration heading

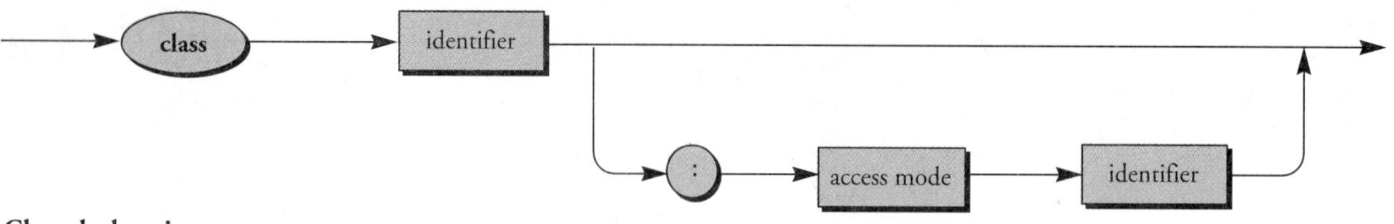

Class declaration

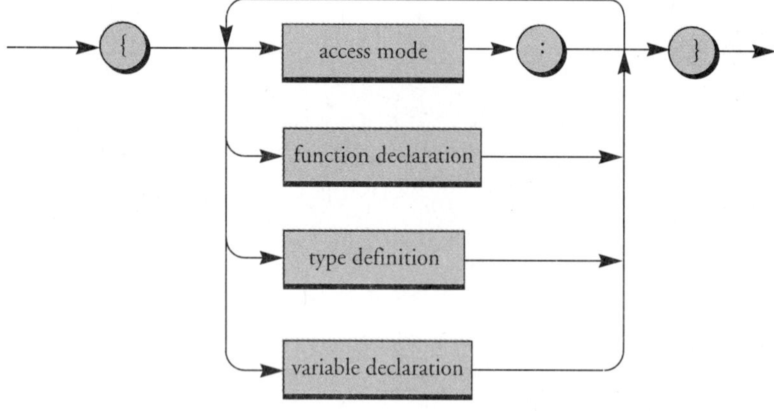

Access mode

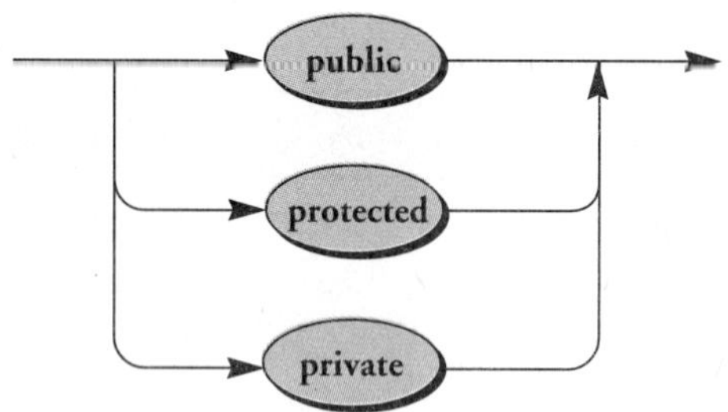

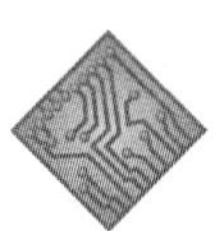

Appendix 4
The ASCII Character Set

The table included here shows the ordering of the ASCII character set. Note only printable characters are shown. Ordinals without character representations either do not have standard representation or are associated with unprintable control characters. The blank is denoted by " b̸ ".

The American Standard Code for Information Interchange (ASCII)

Left Digit(s)	Right Digit 0	1	2	3	4	5	6	7	8	9
3			b̸	!	"	#	$	%	&	'
4	(	)	*	+	,	−	.	/	0	1
5	2	3	4	5	6	7	8	9	:	;
6	<	=	>	?	@	A	B	C	D	E
7	F	G	H	I	J	K	L	M	N	O
8	P	Q	R	S	T	U	V	W	X	Y
9	Z	[	\	]	^	—	`	a	b	c
10	d	e	f	g	h	i	j	k	l	m
11	n	o	p	q	r	s	t	u	v	w
12	x	y	z	{	|	}	~			

*Codes < 32 or > 126 are nonprintable.

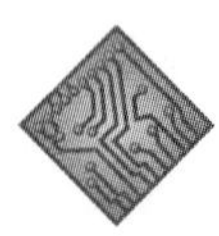

Appendix 5
Some Useful Format Flags

The use of the manipulators **setw, setprecision, fixed,** and **showpoint** to format output was introduced in Section 2.3. Because the use of **fixed** and **showpoint** in C++ has not been standardized, the statement

```
cout << fixed << showpoint;
```

may not have the desired effect of displaying real numbers in fixed point format with trailing zeros in some implementations of C++. However, the following way of specifying the same kind of format is standard, though not as simple:

```
cout << setiosflags (ios::fixed | ios::showpoint);
```

The **setiosflags** manipulator takes a list of flags as a parameter. The general form for using **setiosflags** is

setiosflags(<flag$_1$> | <flag$_2$> | ... | <flag$_n$>)

setiosflags also works with output file streams, as in the following statement:

```
output_file << setiosflags(ios::fixed | ios::showpoint);
```

Some useful flags are listed in the following table:

Flag Name	Meaning
ios::showpoint	Display decimal point with trailing zeros
ios::fixed	Display real numbers in fixed point notation
ios::scientific	Display real numbers in floating point notation
ios::right	Display values right justified

Glossary

abstract data type (ADT) A form of abstraction that arises from the use of defined types. An ADT consists of a class of objects, a defined set of properties of those objects, and a set of operations for processing the objects.

access adjustment A method of changing the access mode of an inherited member from within a derived class. For example, a derived class may inherit all members from a base class in protected mode, and then make some members public by means of access adjustments. *See also* **access mode, base class, derived class,** and **inheritance.**

access mode A symbol **(public, protected,** or **private)** that specifies the kind of access that clients have to a server's data members and member functions. *See also* **private member, protected member,** and **public member.**

accumulator A variable used for the purpose of summing successive values of some other variable.

actual parameter A variable or expression contained in a function call and passed to that function. *See also* **formal parameter.**

address Often called address of a memory location, this is an integer value that the computer can use to reference a location. See also **value.**

algorithm A finite sequence of effective statements that, when applied to the problem, will solve it.

alias A situation in which two or more identifiers in a program come to refer to the same memory location. An alias can become the cause of subtle side effects.

application software Programs designed for a specific use.

argument A value or expression passed in a function call.

arithmetic/logic unit (ALU) The part of the central processing unit (CPU) that performs arithmetic operations and evaluates expressions.

array A data structure whose elements are accessed by means of index positions.

array index The relative position of the components of an array.

ASCII collating sequence The American Standard Code for Information Interchange ordering for a character set.

assembly language A computer language that allows words and symbols to be used in an unsophisticated manner to accomplish simple tasks.

assertion Special comments used with selection and repetition that state what you expect to happen and when certain conditions will hold.

assignment statement A method of putting values into memory locations.

attribute A property that a computational object models, such as the balance in a bank account.

base class The class from which a derived class inherits attributes and behavior. *See also* **derived class** and **inheritance.**

behavior The set of actions that a class of objects supports.

binary digit A digit, either 0 or 1, in the binary number system. Program instructions are stored in memory using a sequence of binary digits. Binary digits are called *bits.*

binary search The process of examining a middle value of a sorted array to see which half contains the value in question and halving until the value is located.

bitmap A data structure used to represent the values and positions of points on a computer screen or image.

block The area of program text within a compound statement, containing statements and optional data declarations.

Boolean expression An expression whose value is either true or false. *See also* **compound Boolean expression** and **simple Boolean expression.**

bottom-up testing Independent testing of modules.

bus A group of wires imprinted on a circuit board to facilitate communication between components of a computer.

byte A sequence of bits used to encode a character in memory. *See also* **word.**

call Any reference to a subprogram by an executable statement. Also referred to as *invoke.*

central processing unit (CPU) A major hardware component that consists of the arithmetic/logic unit (ALU) and the control unit.

character set The list of characters available for data and program statements. *See also* **collating sequence.**

class A description of the attributes and behavior of a set of computational objects.

class constructor A member function used to create and initialize an instance of a class.

class declaration module An area of a program used to declare the data members and member functions of a class.

class destructor A member function defined by the programmer and automatically used by the computer to return dynamic memory used by an object to the heap when the program exits the scope of the object. *See also* **dynamic memory.**

class implementation module An area of a program used to implement the member functions of a class.

client A computational object that receives a service from another computational object.

code (writing) The process of writing executable statements that are part of a program to solve a problem.

cohesive subprogram A subprogram designed to accomplish a single task.

collating sequence The particular order sequence for a character set used by a machine. *See also* **ASCII collating sequence** and **EBCDIC collating sequence.**

column-major order A means of traversing a two-dimensional array whereby all of the data in one column are accessed before the data in the next column. *See also* **row-major order.**

comment A nonexecutable statement used to make a program more readable.

compatible type Expressions that have the same base type. A parameter and its argument must be of compatible type, and the operands of an assignment statement must be of compatible type.

compilation error An error detected when the program is being compiled. *See also* **design error, logic error, run-time error,** and **syntax error.**

compiler A computer program that automatically converts instructions in a high-level language to machine language.

compound Boolean expression Refers to the complete expression when logical connectives and negation are used to generate Boolean values. *See also* **Boolean expression** and **simple Boolean expression.**

compound statement Uses the symbols { and } to make several simple statements into a single compound statement.

conditional statement *See* **selection statement.**

constant A symbol whose value cannot be changed in the body of the program.

constant definition section The section where program constants are defined for subsequent use.

constant parameter A method of declaring a formal array parameter so that the value of an actual array parameter will not change in a function.

constant reference A method of declaring a formal parameter so that the actual parameter is passed by reference but will not change in a function.

control structure A structure that controls the flow of execution of program statements.

control unit The part of the central processing unit that controls the operation of the rest of the computer.

copy constructor A member function defined by the programmer and automatically used by the computer to copy the values of objects when they are passed by value to functions.

counter A variable used to count the number of times some process is completed.

data The particular characters that are used to represent information in a form suitable for storage, processing, and communication.

data abstraction The separation between the conceptual definition of a data structure and its eventual implementation.

data member A data object declared within a class declaration module.

data type A formal description of the set of values that a variable can have.

data validation The process of examining data prior to its use in a program.

debugging The process of eliminating errors or "bugs" from a program.

declaration sections The sections used to declare (name) symbolic constants, data types, variables, and subprograms that are necessary to the program.

decrement To decrease the value of a variable.

dereference The operation by which a program uses a pointer to access the contents of dynamic memory. *See also* **dynamic memory** and **pointer variable.**

derived class A class that inherits attributes and behavior from other classes. *See also* **base class** and **inheritance.**

design error An error such that a program runs, but unexpected results are produced. Also referred to as a *logic error. See also* **compilation error, run-time error,** and **syntax error.**

divide-and-conquer algorithms A class of algorithms that solves problems by repeatedly dividing them into simpler problems. *See also* **recursion.**

do . . . while loop A post-test loop examining a Boolean expression after causing a statement to be executed. *See also* **for loop, loops,** and **while loop.**

dynamic memory Memory allocated under program control from the heap and accessed by means of pointers. *See also* **heap** and **pointer variable.**

dynamic structure A data structure that may expand or contract during execution of a program. *See also* **dynamic memory.**

EBCDIC collating sequence The Extended Binary Coded Decimal Interchange Code ordering for a character set.

echo checking A debugging technique in which values of variables and input data are displayed during program execution.

effective statement A clear, unambiguous instruction that can be carried out.

empty statement A semicolon used to indicate that no action is to be taken. Also referred to as a *null statement.*

encapsulation The process of hiding implementation details of a data structure.

end-of-file marker A special marker inserted by the machine to indicate the end of the data file.

end-of-line character A special character ('\0') used to indicate the end of a line of characters in a string or a file stream.

entrance-controlled loop *See* **pretest loop.**

enumerated data type A set of symbolic constants defined by the programmer.

error *See* **compilation error, design error, logic error, run-time error,** and **syntax error.**

executable section Contains the statements that cause the computer to do something.

executable statement The basic unit of grammar in C++ consisting of valid identifiers, standard identifiers, reserved words, numbers, and/or characters, together with appropriate punctuation.

execute To carry out the instructions of a program.

exit-controlled loop *See* **post-test loop.**

exponential form *See* **floating point.**

extended if statement Nested selection where additional if . . . else statements are used in the else option. *See also* **nested if statement.**

field width The phrase used to describe the number of columns used for various output. *See also* **formatting.**

file stream A data structure that consists of a sequence of components that are accessed by input or output operations.

fixed-repetition loop A loop used when it is known in advance the number of times a segment of code needs to be repeated.

fixed point A method of writing decimal numbers where the decimal is placed where it belongs in the number. *See also* **floating point.**

floating point A method for writing numbers in scientific notation to accommodate numbers that may have very large or very small values. *See also* **fixed point.**

for loop A structured loop consisting of an initializer expression, a termination expression, an update expression, and a statement.

formal parameter A name, declared and used in a function declaration, that is replaced by an actual parameter when the function is called.

formatting Designating the desired field width when printing integers, reals, Boolean values, and character strings. *See also* **field width.**

free store *See* **heap.**

friend of a class The process of making the data members of one class available to another class.

function *See* **library function** and **user-defined function.**

functional abstraction The process of considering only what a function is to do rather than details of the function.

global identifier An identifier that can be used by the main program and all subprograms in a program.

global variable *See* **global identifier.**

hardware The actual computing machine and its support devices.

has-a relation The property of one class having an object of another class as a data member. *See also* **is-a relation.**

header file A C++ file that provides data and function declarations in a library to client modules.

heap An area of computer memory where storage for dynamic data is available.

high-level language Any programming language that uses words and symbols to make it relatively easy to read and write a program. *See also* **assembly language** and **machine language.**

identifiers Words that must be created according to a well-defined set of rules but can have any meaning subject to these rules. *See also* **library identifiers.**

implementation file A C++ file that provides the implementations of data and functions declared in a header file.

index *See* **array index** or **loop index.**

infinite loop A loop in which the controlling condition is not changed in such a manner to allow the loop to terminate.

information hiding The process of suppressing the implementation details of a function or data structure so as to simplify its use in programming.

inheritance The process by which a derived class can reuse attributes and behavior defined in a base class. *See also* **base class** and **derived class.**

input Data obtained by a program during its execution.

input assertion A precondition for a loop.

input device A device that provides information to the computer. Typical devices are keyboards, disk drives, card readers, and tape drives. *See also* **I/O device** and **output device.**

instance A computational object bearing the attributes and behavior specified by a class.

integer arithmetic operations Operations allowed on data of type `int`. This includes the operations of addition, subtraction, multiplication, division, and modulus to produce integer answers.

interface A formal statement of how communication occurs between subprograms, the main driver, and other subprograms.

invariant expression An assertion that is true before the loop and after each iteration of the loop.

invoke *See* **call.**

I/O device Any device that allows information to be transmitted to or from a computer. *See also* **input device** and **output device.**

is-a relation The property of one class being a derived class of another class. *See also* has-a relation, derived class, and base class.

iteration *See* **loops.**

keywords Either reserved words or library identifiers.

l-value A computational object capable of being the target of an assignment statement.

library constant A constant with a standard meaning, such as **`NULL`** or **`INT_MAX`**, available in most versions of C++.

library function A function available in most versions of C++. A list of useful C++ library functions is set forth in Appendix 2.

library identifiers Words defined in standard C++ libraries. *See also* identifiers.

linear search *See* **sequential search.**

linked list A list of data items where each item is linked to the next one by means of a pointer.

local identifier An identifier that is restricted to use within a subblock of a program.

local variable *See* **local identifier.**

logic error *See* **design error.**

logical operator Either logical connective (&, ||) or negation (!).

logical size The number of data items actually available in a data structure at a given time. *See also* **physical size.**

loop index Variable used for control values in a loop.

loop invariant An assertion that expresses a relationship between variables that remains constant throughout all iterations of the loop.

loop variant An assertion whose truth changes between the first and final execution of the loop.

loop verification The process of guaranteeing that a loop performs its intended task.

loops Program statements that cause a process to be repeated. *See also* **for loop, do . . . while loop,** and **while loop.**

low-level language *See* **assembly language.**

machine language The language used directly by the computer in all its calculations and processing.

main block The main part of a program.

main driver The main program when subprograms are used to accomplish specific tasks. *See also* **executable section.**

main (primary) memory Memory contained in the computer. *See also* **memory** and **secondary memory.**

main unit A computer's main unit contains the central processing unit (CPU) and the main (primary) memory; it is hooked to an input device and an output device.

mainframe Large computers typically used by major companies and universities. *See also* **microcomputer** and **minicomputer.**

manifest interface The property of a function such that, when the function is called, the reader of the code can tell clearly what information is being transmitted to it and what information is being returned from it.

member function A function declared within a class declaration module.

memory The ordered sequence of storage cells that can be accessed by address. Instructions and variables of an executing program are temporarily held here. *See also* **main memory** and **secondary memory.**

memory location A storage cell that can be accessed by address. *See also* **memory.**

merge The process of combining lists. Typically refers to files or arrays.

microcomputer A computer capable of fitting on a laptop or desktop, generally used by one person at a time. *See also* **mainframe** and **minicomputer.**

minicomputer A small version of a mainframe computer. It is usually used by several people at once. *See also* **mainframe** and **microcomputer.**

mixed-mode Expressions containing data of different types. The values of these expressions will be of either type, depending on the rules for evaluating them.

modular development The process of developing an algorithm using modules. *See also* **module.**

modularity The property possessed by a program that is written using modules.

module An independent unit that is part of a larger development. Can be a function or a class (set of functions and related data). *See also* **modular development.**

module specifications In the case of a function, a description of data received, information returned, and task performed by a module. In the case of a class, a description of the attributes and behavior.

negation The use of the logical operator ! to negate the Boolean value of an expression.

nested if statement A selection statement used within another selection statement. *See also* **extended if statement.**

nested loop A loop as one of the statements in the body of another loop.

nested selection Any combination of selection statements within selection statements. *See also* **selection statement.**

node One data item in a linked list.

null character The special character ('\0') used to mark the end of a string in C++.

null statement *See* **empty statement.**

object code *See* **object program.**

object program The machine code version of the source program.

opened for reading Positions an input stream pointer at the beginning of a file for the purpose of reading from the file.

opened for writing Positions an output stream pointer at the beginning of a file for the purpose of writing to the file.

opening a file Positions a pointer at the beginning of a file. *See also* **opened for reading and opened for writing.**

operating system A large program that allows the user to communicate with the hardware and performs various management tasks.

ordered collection A data structure that supports indexing for retrieval or change of data items, the detection of the logical size of the structure, and addition or removal of data items from the logical ends of the structure.

ordinal data type A data type ordered in some association with the integers; each integer is the ordinal of its associated character.

output Information that is produced by a program.

output assertion A postcondition for a loop.

output device A device that allows you to see the results of a program. Typically it is a monitor or printer. *See also* **input device** and **I/O device.**

overflow In arithmetic operations, a value may be too large for the computer's memory location. A meaningless value may be assigned or an error message may result. *See also* **underflow.**

overloading The process of using the same operator symbol or identifier to refer to many different functions. *See also* **polymorphism.**

parallel arrays Arrays of the same length but with different component data types.

parameter *See* **argument.**

parameter list A list of parameters. An actual parameter list is contained in the function call. A formal parameter list is contained in the function declaration and heading.

passed by reference When the address of the actual parameter is passed to a subprogram.

passed by value When a copy of the value of the actual parameter is passed to a subprogram.

peripheral memory *See* **secondary memory** and **memory.**

physical size The number of memory units available for storing data items in a data structure. *See also* **logical size.**

pointer variable Frequently designated as `ptr`, a pointer variable is a variable that contains the address of a memory location. *See also* **address** and **dynamic memory.**

polymorphism The property of one operator symbol or function identifier having many meanings. *See also* **overloading.**

postcondition An assertion written after a segment of code.

post-test loop A loop where the control condition is tested after the loop is executed. A do . . . while loop is a post-test loop. Also referred to as an *exit-controlled loop.*

precondition An assertion written before a particular statement.

pretest condition A condition that controls whether the body of the loop is executed before going through the loop.

pretest loop A loop where the control condition is tested before the loop is executed. A while loop is a pretest loop. Also referred to as an *entrance-controlled loop.*

primary memory *See* **main memory** and **memory.**

private member A data member or member function that is accessible only within the scope of a class declaration.

program A set of instructions that tells the machine (the hardware) what to do.

program heading The heading of the main block of any C++ program; it must contain the identifier main.

program proof An analysis of a program that attempts to verify the correctness of program results.

program protection A method of using selection statements to guard against unexpected results.

program walk-through The process of carefully following, using pencil and paper, steps the computer uses to solve the problem given in a program. Also referred to as a *trace.*

programming language Formal language that computer scientists use to give instructions to the computer.

prompt A message or marker on the terminal screen that requests input data.

protected member A data member or member function that is accessible only within the scope of a class declaration or within the class declaration of a derived class.

protection *See* **program protection.**

pseudocode A stylized half-English, half-code language written in English but suggesting C++ code.

public member A data member or member function that is accessible to any program component that uses the class.

quick sort A relatively fast sorting technique that uses recursion. *See also* **selection sort.**

r-value A computational object capable of being assigned to a variable.

range bound error The situation that occurs when at attempt is made to use an array index value that is less than 0 or greater than or equal to the size of the array.

reading from a file Retrieving data from a file.

real arithmetic operations Operations allowed on data of type `float`. This includes addition, subtraction, multiplication, and division.

receiver object A computational object to which a request is sent for a service.

recursion The process of a subprogram calling itself. A clearly defined stopping state must exist. Any recursive subprogram can be rewritten using iteration.

recursive step A step in recursive process that solves a similar problem of smaller size and eventually leads to a termination of the process.

recursive subprogram *See* **recursion.**

reference parameter A formal parameter that requires the address of the actual parameter to be passed to a subprogram. The value of the actual parameter can be changed within the subprogram.

relational operator An operator used for comparison of data items of the same type.

repetition *See* **loops.**

reserved words Words that have predefined meanings that cannot be changed. They are highlighted in text by capital boldface print; a list of C++ reserved words is given in Appendix 1.

return type The type of value returned by a function.

robust The state in which a program is protected against most possible crashes from bad data and unexpected values.

row-major order A means of traversing a two-dimensional array whereby all of the data in one row are accessed before the data in the next row. *See also* **column-major order.**

run-time error Error detected when, after compilation is completed, an error message results instead of the correct output. *See also* **compilation error, design error, logic error,** and **syntax error.**

scope of identifier The largest block in which the identifier is available.

secondary memory An auxiliary device for memory, usually a disk or magnetic tape. *See also* **main memory** and **memory.**

selection sort A sorting algorithm that sorts the components of an array in either ascending or descending order. This process puts the smallest or largest element in the top position and repeats the process on the remaining array components. *See also* **quick sort.**

selection statement A control statement that selects some particular logical path based on the value of an expression. Also referred to as a *conditional statement.*

self-documenting code Code that is written using descriptive identifiers.

sender A computational object that requests a service from another computational object.

sentinel value A special value that indicates the end of a set of data or of a process.

sequential algorithm *See* **straight-line algorithm.**

sequential search The process of searching a list by examining the first component and then examining successive components in the order in which they occur. Also referred to as *linear search.*

server A computational object that provides a service to another computational object.

short-circuit evaluation The process whereby a compound Boolean expression halts evaluation and returns the value of the first subexpression that evaluates to TRUE, in the case of ||, or FALSE, in the case of &&.

side effect A change in a variable, which is the result of some action taken in a program, usually from within a function.

simple Boolean expression An expression where two numbers or variable values are compared using a single relational operator. *See also* **Boolean expression** and **compound Boolean expression.**

software Programs that make the machine (the hardware) do something, such as word processing, database management, or games.

software engineering The process of developing and maintaining large software systems.

software reuse The process of building and maintaining software systems out of existing software components.

software system life cycle The process of development, maintenance, and demise of a software system. Phases include analysis, design, coding, testing/verification, maintenance, and obsolescence.

sorted collection A derived class of ordered collection, in which the data items are maintained in ascending or descending order. *See also* **ordered collection.**

source program A program written by a programmer. *See also* **system program.**

stack A dynamic data structure where access can be made from only one end. Referred to as a LIFO (last-in, first-out) structure.

standard simple types Predefined data types such as `int`, `float`, and `char`.

stepwise refinement The process of repeatedly subdividing tasks into subtasks until each subtask is easily accomplished. *See also* **structured programming** and **top-down design.**

stopping state The well-defined termination of a recursive process.

straight-line algorithm Also called *sequential algorithm,* this algorithm consists of a sequence of simple tasks.

string An abbreviated name for a string literal.

string literal One or more characters, enclosed in double quotes, used as a constant in a program.

string data type A data type that permits a sequence of characters. In C++, this can be implemented using an array of characters.

structure chart A graphic method of indicating the relationship between modules when designing the solution to a problem.

structured design A method of designing software by specifying modules and the flow of data among them.

structured programming Programming that parallels a solution to a problem achieved by top-down design. *See also* stepwise refinement and top-down design.

stub programming The process of using incomplete functions to test data transmission among them.

subblock A block structure for a subprogram. *See also* block.

subprogram A program within a program. Functions are subprograms.

subscript *See* array index or loop index.

syntax The formal rules governing construction of valid statements.

syntax diagramming A method to formally describe the legal syntax of language structures; syntax diagrams are set forth in Appendix 3.

syntax error An error in spelling, punctuation, or placement of certain key symbols in a program. *See also* compilation error, design error, logic error, and run-time error.

system software The programs that allow users to write and execute other programs, including operating systems such as DOS.

tail-recursive The property that a recursive algorithm has of performing no work after each recursive step. *See also* recursion.

test program A short program written to provide an answer to a specific question.

top-down design A design methodology for solving a problem whereby you first state the problem and then proceed to subdivide the main task into major subtasks. Each subtask is then subdivided into smaller subtasks. This process is repeated until each remaining subtask is easily solved. *See also* stepwise refinement and structured programming.

trace See program walk-through.

two-dimensional array An array in which each element is accessed by a reference to a pair of indices.

type *See* data type.

underflow If a value is too small to be represented by a computer, the value is automatically replaced by zero. *See also* overflow.

user-defined data type A new data type introduced and defined by the programmer.

user-defined function A new function introduced and defined by the programmer.

user-friendly A phrase used to describe an interactive program with clear, easy-to-follow messages for the user.

value Often called value of a memory location. Refers to the value of the contents of a memory location. *See also* address.

value parameter A formal parameter that is local to a subprogram. Values of these parameters are not returned to the calling program.

variable A memory location, referenced by an identifier, whose value can be changed during a program.

variable condition loop A repetition statement in which the loop control condition changes within the body of the loop.

variable declaration section The section of the declaration section where program variables are declared for subsequent use.

while loop A pretest loop examining a Boolean expression before causing a statement to be executed.

word A unit of memory consisting of one or more bytes. Words can be addressed.

writing to a file The process of entering data to a file.

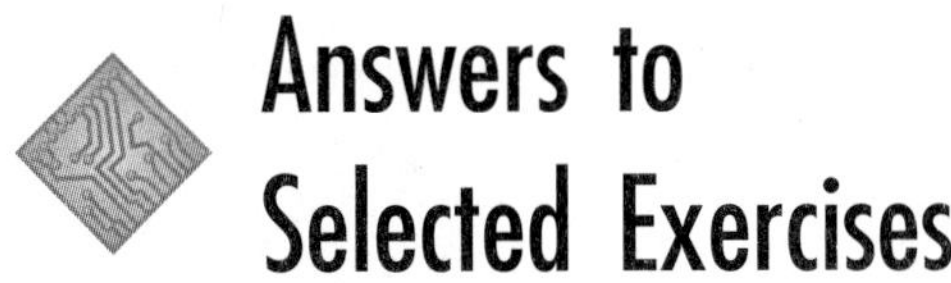

Answers to Selected Exercises

This section contains answers to selected exercises from the exercise sets at the end of each section. In general, answers to odd-numbered problems are given.

CHAPTER 2

Section 2.1

1. **a** and **c** are effective statements.
  b is not effective because you cannot determine when to perform the action.
  d is not effective because there is no smallest positive fraction.
  e is not effective because you cannot determine in advance which stocks will increase in value.

3. **a.** 1. Select a topic
  2. Research the topic
  3. Outline the paper
  4. Refine the outline
  5. Write the rough draft
  6. Read and revise the rough draft
  7. Write the final paper

  c. 1. Get a list of colleges
  2. Examine criteria (programs, distance, money, and so on)
  3. Screen to a manageable number
  4. Obtain further information
  5. Make a decision

5. **a.** First-level development:
  1. Get information for first employee
  2. Perform computations for first employee
  3. Print results for first employee
  4. 5. 6. } Repeat for second employee

  Second-level development:
  1. Get information for first employee
     1.1 get hourly wage
     1.2 get number of hours worked
  2. Perform computations for first employee
     2.1 compute gross pay
     2.2 compute deductions
     2.3 compute net pay
  3. Print results for first employee
     3.1 print input data
     3.2 print gross pay
     3.3 print deductions
     3.4 print net pay
  4. 5. 6. } Repeat for second employee

  Third-level development:
  1. Get information for first employee
     1.1 get hourly wage
     1.2 get number of hours worked
  2. Perform computations for first employee
     2.1 compute gross pay
     2.2 compute deductions
        2.2.1 federal withholding
        2.2.2 state withholding
        2.2.3 social security
        2.2.4 union dues
        2.2.5 compute total deductions
     2.3 compute net pay
        2.3.1 subtract total deductions from gross
  3. Print results for first employee
     3.1 print input data
        3.1.1 print hours worked
        3.1.2 print hourly wage
     3.2 print gross pay
     3.3 print deductions
        3.3.1 print federal withholding
        3.3.2 print state withholding
        3.3.3 print social security
        3.3.4 print union dues
        3.3.5 print total deductions
     3.4 print net pay
  4. 5. 6. } Repeat for second employee

7. There are several ways to solve this problem, one of which follows:
  1. Get the numbers as input
  2. Put them in order—small, large
  3. Check for a divisor
     3.1 if small is a divisor of large
        3.1.1 gcd is small
        else
        3.1.2 Decrease small until a common divisor is found

4. Print the results
   3.1.2 can be further refined as
   3.1.2 Decrease small until a common divisor is found
      3.1.2.2 do
         if **gcd_candidate** is a common divisor
            gcd is **gcd_candidate**
         else
            Decrease **gcd_candidate** by 1
         while a common divisor is not found

Section 2.2

3. **a** is valid.
   b is a Pascal program heading.
   c is missing a return type and should omit parameters.
   d is missing a return type and should use lowercase letters.

5. a. `const char GENDER = 'F';`
   b. `const char AGE = 18;`
   c. `const float PI = 3.1416;`

Section 2.3

1. **a**, **d**, **e**, and **g** are valid.
   b has a decimal.
   c has a comma.
   f is probably larger than `INT_MAX`.

3. **a.** 1.73E2
   b. 7.43927E11
   c. -2.3E-8
   d. 1.4768E1
   e. -5.2E0

5. **a** and **d** are integers.
   b, **c**, and g are reals.
   e and **f** are string literals.

7. a.
```
cout << setw(14) << "Score" <<
endl << endl;
cout << setw(13) << 86 << endl;
cout << setw(13) << 82 << endl;
cout << setw(13) << 79 << endl;
```

CHAPTER 3

Section 3.1

1. **a.** 11 **f.** 63
   b. -41 **g.** 48
   c. 3 **h.** 140
   d. 24 **i.** 1
   e. 126 **j.** 7

3. **a** and **b**, **c**, **f**, **g**, and **j** are valid, type integer.
   e, **h**, and **i** are valid, type float.
   d is invalid.

5. Output will vary according to local implementation.

Section 3.2

1. **a**, **b**, **e**, **f**, and **h** are valid assignment statements.
   c is invalid. A real cannot be assigned to an integer variable.
   d is invalid. An operand cannot be on the left of an assignment statement.
   g is invalid. IQ/3 is a float.

3.

	A	B
a.	3	-5
b.	26	31
c.	-3	-5
d.	9	9

5.
```
Gender        M
Age           23
Height        73 inches
Weight        186.5 lbs
```

7. column 11
```
*******************************
*                             *
*   Name      Age      Sex    *
*   ----      ---      ---    *
*   Jones      21        M    *
*                             *
*******************************
```

9.
```
        column 10

        This reviews string formatting.
When a letterAis used,
        Oops! I forgot to format.
        When a letter A is used,
        it is a string of length one.
```

Section 3.3

1. **cin** is the name of the standard input stream. This stream is connected to the keyboard and allows data to be input from the user. **cout** is the name of the standard output stream. This stream is connected to the terminal screen, and allows data to be output to the user.

Section 3.4

3. CPS 150 TEST #2 ----------------------------------
   Total points 100 My score 93 Class average 82.3

Section 3.6

7.
```
#include <iostream.h>

int main()
{
    for (int ascii_value = 'A'; ascii_value <= 'Z'; ++ascii_value)
            cout << char(ascii_value) << " " << ascii_value << endl;
    return 0;
}
```

CHAPTER 4

Section 4.2

1. c and d are valid.
   a has no types for the parameters.
   b has no return type.

Section 4.3

1. a. Both parameters should be declared as reference parameters rather than value parameters.
   b. **width** should be declared as a value parameter rather than a reference parameter.
   c. **radius** should be declared as a value parameter rather than a reference parameter.

Section 4.5

7. Identifiers for this program are represented schematically by the figure at right.

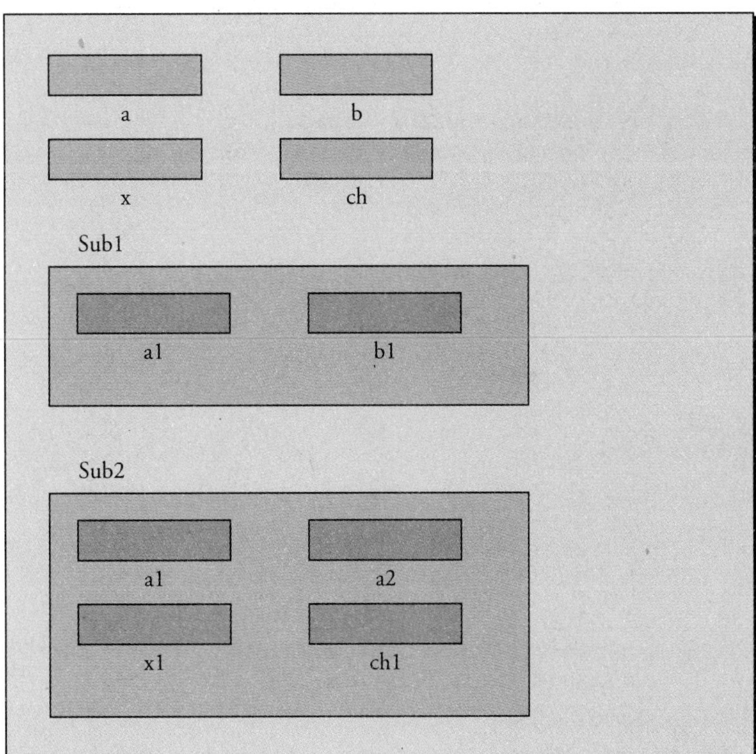

9. **10**
   20
   10
   30
   30
11. There are several syntax errors. **x1** is not visiblein the main program block. **x** cannot be used as an actual parameter for function **sub1**, because **x** is a **float** and **sub1** expects an **int** as a parameter. **x** and **y** are not visible inthe block of **sub1**.

CHAPTER 5

Section 5.1

1. 1 1 0
   0

3. a and b are TRUE
   c and d are FALSE

Section 5.2

1. a. 10 5
   b. No output
   c. 5 Since **b** has no value, the result will vary.
   d. 10 5
   e. 15 4
      15 4
   f. 10 5
3. a. has no error
   b. `3 < x < 10` cannot be evaluated. This should be `(3 < x) && (x < 10)`.
   c. The two statements following the condition should be enclosed in braces:

```
if (a > 0)
{
        count = count + 1;
        sum = sum + a;
}
```

5. Yes.
9.
```
{
    cin >> num1 >> num2 >> num3;
    total = total + num1 + num2 + num3;
    cout << num1 << " " << num2 << " " << num3 << endl;
    cout << total << endl;
}
```
11.
```
cin >> ch1 >> ch2 >>ch3;
if (ch1 <= ch2) && (ch2 <= ch3)
    cout << ch1 << ch2 << ch3 << endl;
```

Section 5.3

1. a. **-14**
   b. **5025**
      175
   c. **105**
      50

Section 5.4

1. a. 38.15 763.0
   b. -21.0 21.0
   c. 600.0 1200.0
   d. 3000.0 9000.0
3. a.
```
if (ch == 'M')
  if (sum > 1000)
        x = x + 1;
  else
        x = x + 2;
else if (ch == 'F')
  if (sum > 1000)
        x = x + 3;
  else
        x = x + 5;
```

b.
```
cin >> num;
if (num > 0)
      if (num <= 10000)
      {
              count = count + 1;
              sum = sum + num;
      }
      else
              cout << setw(27) << "Value out of range" << endl;
```
c.
```
if (a > 0)
      if (b > 0)
              cout << setw(22) << "Both positive" << endl;
      else
              cout << setw(22) << "Some negative" << endl;
```
d.
```
if (c < 0)
      if (a > 0)
             if (b > 0))
                     cout << setw(19) << "Option one" << endl;
             else
                     cout <<setw(19) << "Option two" << endl;
      else
              cout << setw(19) << "Option two" << endl;
else
      cout<<setw(19)<<"Option one"<< endl;
```
7. 8 13 104
a b c

Section 5.5

3. a has a semicolon rather than a colon after last label.
b has no colon after first label, no semicolon after first statement after first label, and has a list of values as last label.
c. Reserved word **case** is missing from first label, and no statements occur for some labels.
d. Reserved word **case** is missing from all labels.
e. Cases for 2 and 1 are missing statements.

CHAPTER 6

Section 6.2

1. a.
```
*
 *
  *
   *
    *
     *
```
b.
```
 1 :  9
 2 :  8
 3 :  7
 4 :  6
 5 :  5
 6 :  4
 7 :  3
 8 :  2
 9 :  1
10 :  0
```
c.
```
 2
 3
 4
 5
 6
 7
 8
 9
10
11
12
13
14
15
16
17
18
19
20
```
d.
```
 1
 2
 3
 4
 5
 6
 7
 8
 9
10
11
12
13
14
15
16
17
18
19
20
21
```

3. a.
```
for (int j = 1; j <= 4; ++j)
 cout << " *" << endl;
```
b.
```
for (int j = 1; j <= 4; ++j)
      cout << setw(j + 3) << "***" << endl;
```
c.
```
cout << setw(6) << "*" << endl;
for (int j = 1; j <= 3; ++j)
      cout << setw(6 - j) << "*" setw(2 * j) << "*" << endl;
cout << "**** ****" << endl;
for (int j = 1; j <= 2; ++j)
      cout << setw(7) << "* *" << endl;
cout << setw(7) << "***" << endl;
```
d. This is a "look ahead" problem that can be solved by a loop within a loop. This idea is developed in Section 5.6.

```
for (int j = 5; j >= 1; --j)
{
          cout << setw(6 - j) << " ";                  // Indent a line
          for (int k = 1; k <= 2 * j - 1; ++k)         // Print a line
                cout << "*";
          cout << endl;
}
```

5. a.
```
for (int j = 1; j <= 5; ++j)
 cout << setw(3) << j;
for (int j = 5; j >= 1; --j;
 cout << setw(3) << 6 - j;
```
b.
```
for (int j = 1; j <= 5; ++j)
      cout << setw(j) << '*' << endl
for (int j = 5; j >= 1; --j)
      cout << setw(6 - j) << '*' << endl;
```
7.
```
for (j = 2; j <= 10; ++j)
      cout << setw(j) <<j << endl;
```

Section 6.3

3. a.
```
 1
 2
 3
 4
 5
 6
 7
 8
 9
10
```
b.
```
1  0
2  1
3  2
4  1
5  2
```
c. 54 50

d.
```
The partial sum is  1
The partial sum is  3
The partial sum is  6
The partial sum is 10
The partial sum is 15
The count is 5
```
e. 96.00 2.00

5. a.
```
while (num > 0)
{
   cout << setw(10) << num << endl
   num = num - .5;
}
```

Section 6.4

1. A pretest loop tests the Boolean expression before executing the loop. A post-test loop tests the Boolean expression after the loop has been executed.

3. a.
```
1   9
2   8
3   7
4   6
5   5
6   4
```
b.
```
  2
  4
  8
 16
 32
 64
128
```
c.
```
 1
 2
 3
 4
 5
 6
 7
 8
 9
10
```
d.
```
1  0
2  1
3  2
4  1
5  2
```

Section 6.6

1. a.
```
for (int k = 1; k <= 5; ++k)
{
   cout << setw(k) << ' ';
   for (int j = k; j <= 5; ++j)
         cout << '*';
   cout << endl
}
```
c.
```
for (int k = 1; k <= 7; ++k)
      if (k < 5)
      {
            for (int j = 1; j <= 3; ++j)
                  cout << '*';
            cout << endl;
      }
      else
      {
            for (int j = 1; j <= 5; ++j
```

```
                        cout << '*';
                cout << endl;
        }
```

3.
```
4   5   6   7
4   5   6   7
4   5   6   7
4   5   6   7

5   6   7
5   6   7
5   6   7

6   7
6   7
```

Section 6.7

1. **a.** This is an infinite loop.
   b. The loop control variable, **k**, is unassigned once the **for** loop is exited. Thus, the attempt to use **k** in the expression **k % 3 = 0** may result in an error.

CHAPTER 7

Section 7.1

1. **a, b, c,** and **f** are FALSE.
3. **a.** i and ii are invalid on some implementation of C++.
   iii, v, vi, and vii are all invalid.
   b.
```
if (strcmp(a, b) < 0)
{
        strcat(c, a);
        strcat(c, b);
}
else
{
        strcat(c, b);
        strcat(c, a);
}
```

Section 7.2

1.
```
boolean string_less(string s1, string s2)
{
     return strcmp(s1, s2) < 0;
}

boolean string_greater(string s1, string s2)
}
     return strcmp(s1, s2) > 0;
}
```
3.
```
void make_lowercase(string s)
{
     int length = strlen(s);

     for (int i = 0; i < length; ++i)
             s[i] = tolower(s[i]);
}
```

5.
```
void remove_punctuation(string s)
{
    char ch = s[strlen(s) - 1];

    if ((ch == '.') || (ch == ',' || (ch == '?') || (ch == ':') || (ch == ';'))
            s[strlen(s) - 1] = '\0';
}
```

7.
```
void string_swap(string s1, string s2)
{
    string temp;

    strcpy(temp, s1);
    strcpy(s1, s2);
    strcpy(s2, temp);
}
```

9.
```
void append_char(string s, char ch)
{
    int length = strlen(s);

    if (length < MAX_STRING_SIZE)
    {
            s[length] =   ch;
            s[length + 1] = '\0';
    }
}
```

Section 7.3

3. The reference to **data** in the string class implementation picks out the data member of the receiver string. The reference to **str.data** in the string class implementation picks out the data member of the parameter string.

CHAPTER 8

Section 8.2

1. The **account** class declaration is modified by including the header file for the **strlib** library, by adding a string parameter to the first two class constructors, and by adding a private data member **name**:

```
#include "strlib.h"
.
.
.
     public:

     // Class constructors

     account(string initial_name);
     account(float initial_balance, string initial_name);
     account(const account &a);
.
.
.
     private:

     // Data members

     float balance;
     string name;
};
```

The three constructors and the assignment operator are then updated in the implementation:

```
account::account(string initial_name)
{
        balance = 0.00;
        name = initial_name;
}

account::account(float initial_balance, string initial_name)
{
        balance = initial_balance;
        name = initial_name;
}

account::account(const account &a)
{
        balance = a.balance;
        name = a.name;
}

account& account::operator = (const account &a)
{
        balance = a.balance;
        name = a.name;
        return  *this;
}
```

3. We assume that a private data member **password** has been added to the class declaration, and that appropriate modifications have been made to the declarations of member functions **deposit**, **withdraw**, and **get_balance**. The implementations are updated as follows:

```
float account::deposit(float amount, string your_name, string your_password)
{

        if ((your_name == name) && (your_password == password))
        {
                balance = balance + amount;
                return balance;
        }
        else
                return 0;
}

float account::withdraw(float amount, string your_name, string your_password)
{
        if ((your_name == name) && (your_password == password))
                if (amount > balance)
                        return -1;
                else
                {
                        balance = balance - amount;
                        return balance;
                }
        else
                return 0;
}
```

```
float account::get_balance(string your_name, string your_password)
{
        if ((your_name == name) && (your_password == password))
                return balance;
        else
                return 0;
}
```

Section 8.3

3. Total number of operations = *M* times *N*.
5. The following implementations cover all of the possibilities. If the rational number is already in lowest terms, then the implementations can be simplified and made more efficient.

```
boolean rational::whole_number()
{
       return (denominator == 1) || (numerator % denominator == 0);
}

int rational::make_int()
{
       if (denominator == 1)
               return numerator;
       else
               return numerator / denominator;
}
```

Section 8.4

1. Define a password in the base class. Its access mode should be **protected**.
5. A derived class of the checking account class, with attributes and behavior for maintaining interest, would allow much of the software to be reused.

CHAPTER 9

Section 9.1

1. a. The first two input statements read the two data values from the file, and they are displayed by the first two output statements. The third input statement also reads the second data value, because the end of file has been reached. Thus, the third output statement displays the second data value also.
   b. The first data value is read before the loop starts. It is output on the first pass through the loop, because the end-of-file condition is not yet true. Then the second data value is read at the bottom of the loop. The end-of-file condition is not yet true, so the loop is entered once more, where the second data value is output. At the bottom of the loop, the second data value is read once more, and the end-of-file condition becomes true, forcing an exit from the top of the loop.
   c. Because the **>>** operator must be run three times before the end-of-file condition becomes true, three outputs will occur. Thus, the second data value in the file is output twice to the screen.
3. We use the **strlib** library for strings. Note that all input can be received as strings.

```
// Program file: person.cpp

#include <iostream.h>
#include <fstream.h>
#include <assert.h>
#include "strlib.h"

int main()
```

```
{
        string  string_var;
        ifstream in_file;

        in_file.open("myfile");
        assert(!  in_file.fail());
        in_file >> string_var;
        cout << "Name:" << string_var << endl;
        in_file >> string_var;
        cout << "Address:" << string_var << endl;
        in_file >> string_var;
        cout << "Age:" << string_var << endl;
        in_file.close();
        assert(!  in_file.fail());
        return 0;
{
```

5. Note that the data for the person's name is received from a priming input, and also is received at the bottom of the loop.

```
// Program file: persons.cpp

#include <iostream.h>
#include <fstream.h>
#include <assert.h>
#include "strlib.h"

int main()
{
        string string_var;
        ifstream in_file;

        in_file.open("myfile");
        assert(!  in_file.fail());
        in_file >> string_var;
        while (! in_file.eof())
        {
                cout << "Name:" << string_var << endl;
                in_file >> string_var;
                cout << "Address:" << string_var << endl;
                in_file >> string_var;
                cout << "Age:" << string_var << endl;
                in_file >> string_var;
        {
        in_file.close();
        assert(!  in_file.fail());
        return 0;
}
```

CHAPTER 10

Section 10.1

1. a.
```
const int MAX_SCORES = 35;
typedef int score_list[MAX_SCORES];
score_list scores;
```
   b.
```
const int MAX_PRICES = 20;
typedef float price_list[MAX_PRICES];
price_list prices;
```
   c.
```
const int MAX_ANSWERS = 50;
typedef boolean answer_list[MAX_ANSWERS];
answer_list answers;
```
   d.
```
const int MAX_GRADES = 4;
typedef char grade_list[MAX_GRADES];
grade_list grades;
```
3. a, b, d, e, f, h, and l are valid.
   c will run, but display the address of the array.
   g uses three indexes, but the array expects one.
   i attempts to input a value into the address of the array.
   j `list[100]` is a range error.
   k Type names cannot be indexed.
5. `waist_sizes`

Value	Index
34	0
36	1
32	2
30	3
33	4

7.
```
for (int i = 0; i < 10; ++i)
     list[i] = 0.0;
```

Section 10.2

1. a. `list`

Value	Index
0	0
0	1
0	2
1	3
1	4

   b. `list`

Value	Index
4	0
5	1
6	2
7	3
8	4

   `scores`

Value	Index
1	0
1	1
2	2
2	3
2	4

   c. `answers`

Value	Index
TRUE	0
FALSE	1
TRUE	2
FALSE	3
TRUE	4
FALSE	5
TRUE	6
FALSE	7
TRUE	8
FALSE	9

   d. `initials`

Value	Index
A	0
B	1
C	2
D	3
E	4
.	
.	
S	20
T	19

3. The code counts the number of scores that are greater than 90.

5.
```
const int MAX_CHARS = 20;
typedef char name_type[MAX_CHARS];
name_type name;
int length = 0;
char ch;

cin >> ch;
while (ch != '\0')
{

     name[length] = ch;
     ++length;
     cin >> ch;

}
```

7.
```
for (int i = 0; i < 100; ++i)
    a[i] = 0;
```

9.
```
cout << "Test scores" << endl;
cout << "-----------" << endl;
for (int i = 0; i < 50; ++i)
     cout << setw(2) << i <<"." << setw(3) << test_scores[i] << endl;
```

Section 10.3

1. **a** is valid.
   b is invalid, because arrays are declared as reference parameters.
   c is valid.
   d is invalid, because arrays are declared as reference parameters.
   e is invalid, because a type name is ued to declare a parameter name.
   f is valid.
   g is invalid, because **name** has not been defined as a type.
   h is valid.
   i is invalid, because **name** has not been defined as a type.
   j is invalid, because arrays are declared as reference parameters.

3. a.
```
void input_scores(int scores[20]);
input_scores(scores);
```
   b.
```
int char_count(char name[50], char ch);
number = char_count(name, 'A');
```
   c.
```
void score_data(int scores[], int &length, int &count_90);
score_data(scores, length, count_90);
```

5.
```
void array_data(int data[MAX_ARRAY_SIZE], int &max, int &min, int &neg_values)
{
     max = INT_MIN;                           // Initial maximum value.
     min = INT_MAX;                           // Initial minimum value.
     neg_values = 0;                          // Initial count negative values.
     for (int i = 0; i < MAX_ARRAY_SIZE; ++i)
             if (data[i] > max)
                     max = data[i];
             if (data[i] < min)
                     min = data[i];
             if (data[i] < 0)
                     ++neg_values;
}
```

Section 10.4

1. **First pass** **Second pass**

First pass		Second pass	
-20	0	-20	0
10	1	-2	1
0	2	0	2
10	3	10	3
8	4	8	4
30	5	30	5
-2	6	10	6

3. We use a new function, **find_maximum**, that locates the largest value in the unsorted portion of the array. On each pass, the largest remaining value will be placed at the end of the sorted portion of the array. Thus, at the end of the process, the array will be sorted from high to low.

```
void sort(int a[ ], int length)
{
        int min_index = 0;

        for (int j = 0; j < length - 1; ++j)
        {
                min_index = find_maximum(a, j, length);
                if (min_index != j)
                        swap(a[j],  a[min_index]);
        }
}
```

5.
```
void sort(int a[ ], int length, int &count)
{
     int min_index = 0.
     count = 0;
     for (int j = 0; j < length - 1; ++j)
     {
              min_index = find_minimum(a, j, length);
              if (min_index != j)
              {
                      swap(a[j],  a[min_index]);
                      ++count;
              }
     }
}
```

7. The sort of the test scores will have no effect on the order of the names. If the test scores are all the same, then there will be no change in the meaning of the table. Otherwise, the names will no longer always be correlated with their test scores.

Section 10.5

1. When **i = MAX_ARRAY_SIZE**, the program encounters a reference to **a[MAX_ARRAY_SIZE]**. This violates the precondition of the subscript operation for the safe array class, and the program will halt with a run-time error.
3. There are two limitations. First, a client might not want to be responsible for defining this constant, but would rather rely on the array class to provide a default maximum size. Second, a client might want to declare arrays with different maximum sizes for different applications. However, this implementation restricts a client to one maximum size for all arrays.
5. In general, there is no way of telling which cells in a safe array actually contain data intended for use by a program at any given time. This is especially true right after a safe array is declared, where the contents of all of the cells are unpredictable. In each of the examples, the run-time system might allow the operations to be performed, because the arrays at least contain "garbage" values. However, the meanings of the programs are impossible to determine by inspection, because:
   a has not initialized any cells in the array **a**.
   b has not initialized any cells in array **a** or **b**.
   c has not initialized any cells in the array **b**.

Section 10.6

1. The physical size of an array is the number of cells of memory allocated for storing data in it. The logical size of the array is the number of data values currently stored in it that have meaning for a program.
3. This proposal has two problems. First, the ordered collection requires an integer data member to maintain the current logical size of the data structure. Thus, there is no memory savings when compared with the use of the null character as a sentinel in an array. Second, the new implementation must replicate much of the code for string operations already available in the standard **string** library that was used for the array implementation. It is hard to find any benefits that outweigh these two costs of the proposal.
5. The member function takes a target element as a parameter and returns the index position if the element is found or –1 if the element is not found.

```
int ordered_collection::search(element e)
{
        index = 0;
        while ((index < c_length) && (e != a[index]))
                ++index;
        if (index == c_length)
                return -1;
        else
                return index;
}
```

7. The member function assumes that the client has opened the input stream before the operation and will close it following the operation. The declaration of the member function is

```
friend istream& operator >> (istream &is, ordered_collection &oc);
```

The implementation of the member function is

```
istream& operator >> (istream &is, ordered_collection &oc)
{
      element e;

      oc.c_length = 0;
      is >> e;
      while (! is.eof() && (oc.c_length < MAX_ARRAY_SIZE))
      {
              oc.add_last(e);
              is >> e;
      }
      if (! is.eof() && (oc.c_length == MAX_ARRAY_SIZE))
              cout << "Some elements could not be input into the collection."
                   << endl;
      return is;
}
```

Section 10.7

1.
```
sorted_collection& sorted_collection::operator = (const sorted_collection &sc)
{
     for (int j = 0; j < sc.c_length; ++j)
             data[j] = sc.data[j];
     c_length = sc.c_length;
     return *this;
}
```

3. The subscript operator for ordered collections allows references to elements as l values or as r values. A sorted collection object should not allow references to elements as l values, because clients could then store elements that might violate the ordering of the elements in the collection.

5.
```
sorted_collection::sorted_collection(const ordered_collection &oc)
{
      c_length = oc.length();
      for (int i = 0; i < c_length; ++i)
            add(oc[i]);
}
```

Section 10.8

1.
```
const MAX_ROW_SIZE = 300;
const MAX_COL_SIZE = 400;

typedef boolean bitmap[MAX_ROW_SIZE] [MAX_COL_SIZE];
```

3.
```
boolean search(bitmap a, int target, int &row, int &col)
{
     boolean found = FALSE;

     row = 0;
     while (! found && (row < MAX_ROW_SIZE))       // Search rows.
     {
          col = 0;
          while (! found && (col < MAX_COL_SIZE)) // Search columns within a row.
                 if (a[row][col] == target)
                             found = TRUE;
                      else
                             ++col;
                 if (! found)
                      ++row;
     }
     return found;
}
```

5. A safe bitmap class would behave in the same way as a safe array class, except that range checks would be performed on both the row and the column indexes on all references to data in the bitmap.

CHAPTER 11

Section 11.1

1. Memory is allocated automatically for ordinary variables whenever their scope is entered in a program, and memory is deallocated automatically when that scope is exited. Memory for dynamic variables is allocated and deallocated only by means of instructions in a program.

3.

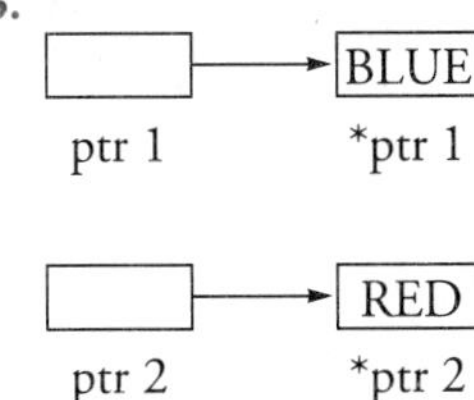

Section 11.2

1. Arrays and linked lists both represent linear sequences of data values. Arrays allow access to data elements in constant time. Linked lists allow access to data elements in linear time. Arrays require a contiguous block of storage with a fixed number of cells. Linked lists draw storage from any free cells in the heap, which may or may not be physically adjacent to each other.

3.
```
void print_list(list_type list)
{
     list_type probe = list;

     while (probe != NULL)
     {
           cout << probe->data;
           probe = probe->next;
     }
}
```

7. b. `a->next = a->next->next;`

9.
```
int sum(list_type list)
{
     list_type probe = list;
     int accum = 0;

     while (probe != NULL)
     {
           accum = accum + probe->data;
           probe = probe->next;
     }
     return accum;
}
```

Section 11.3

1. The function works in this case as in the others. The only difference is that **trailer->next** receives the value **NULL** to indicate that this is now the end of the list.

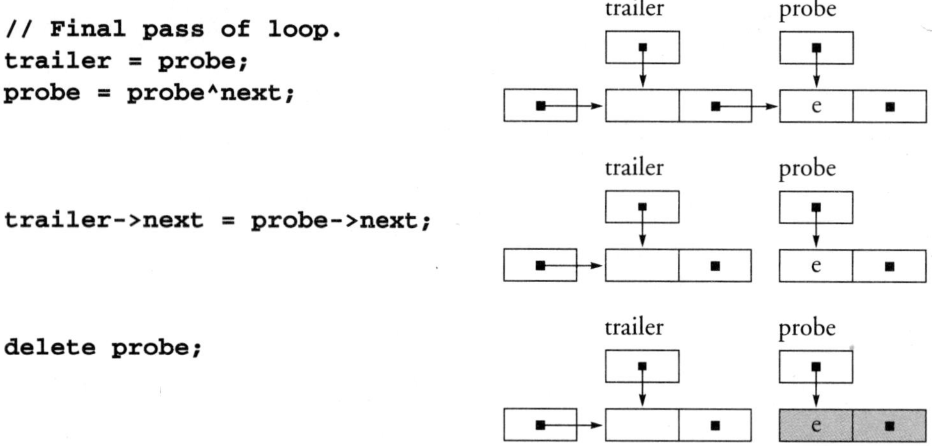
// Final pass of loop.
trailer = probe;
probe = probe^next;
trailer
probe
e
trailer->next = probe->next;
trailer
probe
e
delete probe;
trailer
probe
e

3. The assignment operation uses the same algorithm as the copy constructor:

```
ordered_collection& ordered_collection::operator =
      (const ordered_collection &oc)
{
        node_ptr probe = oc.start;

        start = NULL;
        c_length = 0;
        while (probe != NULL)
        {
              add_last(probe->data);
              probe = probe->next;
```

```
        }
        return *this;
}
```

The equality operation first checks the collections for unequal lengths. If the lengths are the same, the operation performs a pairwise comparison of the contents of the nodes in each linked list. This process stops at the first unequal pair of elements (returning FALSE) or at the end of the lists (returning TRUE):

```
boolean ordered_collection::operator == (const ordered_collection &oc)
{

        boolean equal = c_length == oc.c_length;
        int j = 0;
        node_ptr receiver = start;
        node_ptr parameter = oc.start;

        while ((receiver != NULL) && equal)
              if (receiver ->data != parameter->data)
                     equal = FALSE;
              else
              {
                     receiver = receiver->next;
                     parameter = parameter->next;
              }
        return equal;
}
```

7. The copy constructor currently copies each data value from the parameter object to the receiver object by running the **add_last** member function. Because this function must search for the end of the receiver list on each call, much time is wasted, especially in copying long lists. A faster method would not run **add_last**, but rather maintain a temporary pointer, **last**, to the last node inserted in the receiver. On each pass through the loop that traverses the parameter list, the parameter's data could be copied directly into a new node pointed to by **last->next**. This method forces the implementation to adjust the pointers during insertion.

Section 11.4

3.
```
void print_odd(int &number)
{
     if (number % 2 != 0)
            cout << number << endl;
{
```

CHAPTER 12

Section 12.1

1. There is no stopping state.
3. a. i. $y = 9.0$
   ii. $y = 8.0$
   iii. $y = 256.0$
   iv. $y = 1.0$
5.
```
int iter_factorial(int n)
{
     int partial_product = 1;

     for (int next_factor = 2; next_factor <= n; ++next_factor)
            partial_product = partial_product * next_factor;
     return partial_product;
}
```

Section 12.2

3. a. **num** = 18

	first	last	mid	a[mid]	found
Before loop	0	4	Undefined	Undefined	FALSE
After 1st pass	0	1	2	37	FALSE
After 2nd pass	0	1	0	18	TRUE

c. **num** = 76

	first	last	mid	a[mid]	found
Before loop	0	4	Undefined	Undefined	FALSE
After 1st pass	3	4	2	37	FALSE
After 2nd pass	3	2	3	92	

5.
```
int binsearch(element target, list_type list, int last
{
      int first = 0;

      boolean found = FALSE;
      while (! found && (first <= last))
      {
            midpoint = (first + last) / 2;
            if (list[midpoint] == target)
                  found = TRUE;
            else if (list[midpoint] > target)
                  last = midpoint - 1;
            else
                  first= midpoint + 1;
      }
      if (found)
          return midpoint;
      else
          return -1;
}
```

Section 12.4

1.
```
int product(list_type list)
{
     if (list == NULL)
              return 1;
     else
              return list->data * product(list->next);
}
```

3.
```
list_type search(list_type list, element e)
{
      if (list == NULL)
              return NULL;
      else if (list->data == e)
              return list;
      else
              return search (list->next);
}
```

Index

Credits

Photos

Page 10–11 Figures 1.4, 1.5a, 1.5b, 1.5c, and 1.6b: Courtesy of IBM Corporation

Page 10–11 Figures 1.5d and 1.6a: Courtesy of Apple Computer, Inc.

Page 12 Figure 1.8 L Robert Barclay

Notes Of Interest

Page 4: Ethics and Computer Science From the Minneapolis Star/Tribune, October 14, 1990, The Washington Post reprinted with permission.

Page 13: Why Learn C++
Richard P. Gabriel ("The end of history and the last programming language," Journal of Object-Oriented Programming, July-August, 1993).

Page 22: Software Verification
From Ivars Peterson, "Finding Fault: The Formidable Task of Eradicating Software Bugs," SCIENCE NEWS, February 16, 1991, Vol. 139. Reprinted with permission from SCIENCE NEWS, the weekly magazine of science. Copyright 1991 by Science Services, Inc.

Page 53: Herman Hollerith
Reprinted by permission from Introduction to Computers with BASIC, pp. 27-28, by Fred G. Harold. Copyright 1984 by West Publishing Company. All rights reserved. Photos courtesy of IBM Corporation.

Page 64: Communication Skills Needed
From P. Jackowitz, R. Plishka, J. Sidbury, J. Hartman, and C. White, ACM Press SIGCSE Bulletin 22, No. 1, (February, 1990). Copyright 1991, Association for Computing Machinery, Inc. Reprinted by permission of Association for Computing Machinery, Inc.

Page 67: Defined Constants and Space Shuttle Computing
Communications of the ACM 27, No. 9 (September, 1984); 880. Copyright 1984, Association for Computing Machinery, Inc. Reprinted by permission of Association for Computing Machinery, Inc.

Page 100: Computer Ethics: Hacking and Other Intrusions
Reprinted by permission from Computers Under Attack: Intruders, Worms, and Viruses, pp. 150-155, edited by Peter J. Denning, Article 7, "The West German Hacker Incident and Other Intrusions," by Mel Mandell. Copyright 1990, Association for Computing Machinery, Inc.

Page 142: George Boole
Adapted from William Dunham, Journey Through Genius: The Great Theorems of Mathematics, John Wiley & Sons, 1990. Photo: The Bettmann Archive.

Page 153: Artificial Intelligence
Reprinted by permission from The Mind Tool, Fifth ed., pp. 394-398, by Neill Graham. Copyright 1989 by West Publishing Company. All rights reserved.

Page 178: A Software Glitch
From Ivars Peterson, "Finding Fault: The Formidable Task of Eradicating Software Bugs," SCIENCE NEWS, February 16, 1991, Vol. 139. Reprinted with permission from SCIENCE NEWS, the weekly magazine of science. Copyright 1991 by Science Services, Inc.

Page 215: Charles Babbage
Reprinted by permission from Introduction to Computers with BASIC, pp. 24–26, by Fred G. Harold. Copyright 1984 by West Publishing Company. All rights reserved.

Page 222: Ada Augusta Byron
Reprinted by permission from Introduction to Computers with BASIC, pp. 26-27, by Fred G. Harold. Copyright 1984 by West Publishing Company. All rights reserved. Photo: The Bettmann Archive.

Page 240: A Digital Matter of Life and Death
From Ivars Peterson, "A Digital Matter of Life and Death," SCIENCE NEWS, March 12, 1988, Vol. 133. Reprinted with permission from SCIENCE NEWS, the weekly magazine of science. Copyright 1988 by Science Services, Inc. Photo courtesy of Ontario Hydro.

Page 344: Career Opportunities in Computer Science
From Carol Wilson, Western Kentucky University, Bowling Green, Kentucky, 1991.

Page 352: Computer Ethics: Viruses
From Philip J. Hilts, Science Lab, In the Washington Post National Weekly Edition, May 23-29, 1988. Reprinted by permission of The Washington Post.

Page 373: Monolithic Idea: Invention of the Integrated Circuit
Adapted from T. R. Reid, "The Chip," Science, February 1985, pp. 32-41.

Page 392: Too Few Women in the Computer Science Pipeline?
From Carol Wilson, Western Kentucky University, Bowling Green, Kentucky, 1991.

Page 474: Gene Mapping: Computer Scientists Examine Problems of Genome Project From The Chronicle of Higher Education, May 9, 1990. Reprinted by permission of The Chronicle of Higher Education.

IMPORTANT: PLEASE READ BEFORE OPENING THIS PACKAGE
THIS PACKAGE IS NOT RETURNABLE IF SEAL IS BROKEN.

lishing Corporation
erman Drive
ox 64779
ul, Minnesota 55164-0779

LIMITED USE LICENSE

ead the following terms and conditions carefully before opening this diskette package. Opening the diskette package ndicates your agreement to the license terms. If you do not agree, promptly return the entire product and related documentation unused.

By accepting this license, you have the right to use this Software and the accompanying documentation, but you do not become the owner of these materials.

This copy of the Software is licensed to you for use only under the following conditions:

1. PERMITTED USES

You are granted a non-exclusive limited license to use the Software under the terms and conditions stated in this license. You may:

a. Use the Software on a single computer.
b. Make a single copy of the Software in machine-readable form solely for backup purposes in support of your use of the Software on a single machine. You must reproduce and include the copyright notice on any copy you make.
c. Transfer this copy of the Software and the license to another user if the other user agrees to accept the terms and conditions of this license. If you transfer this copy of the Software, you must also transfer or destroy the backup copy you made. Transfer of this copy of the Software, and the license automatically terminates this license as to you.

2. PROHIBITED USES

You may not use, copy, modify, distribute or transfer the Software or any copy, in whole or in part, except as expressly permitted in this license.

3. TERM

This license is effective when you open the diskette package and remains in effect until terminated. You may terminate this license at any time by ceasing all use of the Software and destroying this copy and any copy you have made. It will also terminate automatically if you fail to comply with the terms of this license. Upon termination, you agree to cease all use of the Software and destroy all copies.

4. DISCLAIMER OF WARRANTY

Except as stated herein, the Software is licensed "as is" without warranty of any kind, express or implied, including warranties of merchantability or fitness for a particular purpose. You assume the entire risk as to the quality and performance of the Software. You are responsible for the selection of the Software to achieve your intended results and for the installation, use and results obtained from it. West Publishing Corporation does not warrant the performance of nor results that may be obtained with the Software. West Publishing Corporation does warrant that the diskette(s) upon which the Software is provided will be free from defects in materials and workmanship under normal use for a period of 30 days from the date of delivery to you as evidenced by a receipt.

Some states do not allow the exclusion of implied warranties so the above exclusion may not apply to you. This warranty gives you specific legal rights. You may also have other rights which vary from state to state.

5. LIMITATION OF LIABILITY

Your exclusive remedy for breach by West Publishing Corporation of its limited warranty shall be replacement of any defective diskette upon its return to West at the above address, together with a copy of the receipt, within the warranty period. If West Publishing Corporation is unable to provide you with a replacement diskette which is free of defects in material and workmanship, you may terminate this license by returning the Software, and the license fee paid hereunder will be refunded to you. In no event will West be liable for any lost profits or other damages including direct, indirect, incidental, special, consequential or any other type of damages arising out of the use or inability to use the Software even if West Publishing Corporation has been advised of the possibility of such damages.

6. GOVERNING LAW

This agreement will be governed by the laws of the State of Minnesota.

You acknowledge that you have read this license and agree to its terms and conditions. You also agree that this license is the entire and exclusive agreement between you and West and supersedes any prior understanding or agreement, oral or written, relating to the subject matter of this agreement.

West Publishing Corporation